Richmond Redeemed

RICHMOND REDEEMED

The Siege at Petersburg

RICHARD J. SOMMERS

Foreword by Frank E. Vandiver

DOUBLEDAY & COMPANY, INC.
Garden City, New York
1981

Library of Congress Cataloging in Publication Data

Sommers, Richard J.
Richmond Redeemed.

Bibliography: p. 591
Includes index.
1. Petersburg, Va.—Siege, 1864–1865.
I. Title.
E476.93.S65   973.7'37
ISBN: 0-385-15626-X
Library of Congress Catalog Card Number 79–7843

To
FRANK E. VANDIVER,
Scholar,
Teacher,
Friend

FOREWORD

In the abounding literature covering military operations of the Civil War, strangely little focuses on the siege of Petersburg. There are, of course, the standard sources—the *Official Records, Battles and Leaders of the Civil War,* and personal memoirs—but secondary studies stint the long story of Grant's battles around Richmond and Petersburg.

To the present the best modern scholarly works have been Douglas Freeman's *Lee* and *Lee's Lieutenants,* Bruce Catton's *Grant Takes Command,* and Shelby Foote's *The Civil War.* These, and all other sources, are now supplanted by Richard Sommers' book.

Sommers is a scholar who does prodigious research and writes refreshing, lucid prose. This book is more than a study of a siege, it is an analysis of battle command and a primer of humanity in war.

Sommers' research is matchless, and it elevates his fine book almost to the status of an original source. I have always considered John Bigelow's *The Campaign of Chancellorsville* the model campaign study of the Civil War. I think now that there are two model campaign accounts—Sommers ranks with Bigelow.

All students of the Civil War will read this book with profit and pleasure—so will students of war, of stress, of heroism, of humanity, for this is a book about courage. It is, I think, unique, a study to endure.

FRANK E. VANDIVER
North Texas State University
Denton

PREFACE

This book concerns the American Civil War. One of the most significant and influential events in the nation's history, the Civil War has always fascinated Americans. From the 1860s to the present, veterans, military men, buffs, and scholars have written on it. Their work has endowed the war with a great corpus of literature. Yet all their writing has not come close to exhausting the subject. There is no truth to the old canard that every aspect of the conflict has already been fully covered. To the contrary, the war is rich with scores of commanders, hundreds of units, thousands of operations that have never received full treatment. Nor are these untapped areas confined to obscure officers, inactive outfits, and inconsequential encounters. Many of the greatest campaigns of the war remain without modern scholarly study.

Petersburg is such an operation. It was the longest campaign of the Civil War. It was also one of the most important. And it was waged in the principal theater of the war between the foremost general on each side, R. E. Lee and U. S. Grant. When it began in mid-June 1864, the Confederate Army of Northern Virginia was still a formidable fighting force. When the siege ended nine and a half months later, that army had been vitiated and was only a week away from extinction. How was that once mighty army destroyed? And how did it manage to save itself, its capital, and its communications center for so long? To what extent was the course of operations affected by the opposing commanders, their principal subordinates, their combat units? What was the interrelationship of the campaign with simultaneous events elsewhere in the war? And what was the place of the siege in the evolving generalship of Grant and Lee and in the ongoing conduct of operations in the East since 1861?

Such questions suggest useful avenues of inquiry. Yet the campaign has received remarkably little attention from historians. Although several books have included it in recent decades, the foremost work remains Andrew A. Humphreys' *The Virginia Campaign of '64 and '65* in the old Scribner's *Campaigns of the Civil War* series. This pioneering study by a prominent Federal participant blazed a trail through the wilderness. Considerably researched in then unpublished reports in the War Department and judiciously written, it made a major contribution in its time. However, that time, 1883, has long passed. Thousands of sources, personal as well as official, written by other generals, junior officers, and enlisted men, have subsequently become available, either in print or in scores of manuscript repositories. These accounts provide the corpus of research material for a modern, scholarly study of Petersburg.

Yet present-day historians of the Civil War have not used this material. More than that, they have not adequately covered the siege. Whether students of the war as a whole, the war in the East, the Army of the Potomac, the Army of Northern Virginia, Grant, or Lee, they have not focused in detail on the campaign. Many have skimmed over the whole operation. Others have concentrated on only its opening and closing phases (June 12–18, 1864, and March 25–April 3, 1865, respectively) and have virtually ignored all that transpired between those terminal points. Only such unusual occurrences as the Battle of the Crater on July 30 or Hampton's Cattle Raid on September 14–17 have caught the attention of these writers.

There is, however, much more to Petersburg than a beginning, an ending, and two eye-catchers in between. Operations much more characteristic of the over-all conduct of the siege took place throughout the summer, fall, and winter. In those operations lies the answer to the questions previously posed. In those operations lies the history of the Siege of Petersburg.

This author hopes to recount that history. To begin with, this book will cover one part of the siege: Grant's Fifth Offensive of early autumn, with particular emphasis on its opening battles, Chaffin's Bluff and Poplar Spring Church. That phase was chosen primarily because it lacked coverage. Exploring it not only provides that coverage but also discloses that it was one of the most decisive portions of the campaign. It was highlighted by events and potentialities of far-reaching strategic and tactical significance. Yet through lack of previous study, these occurrences and opportunities have remained unknown until now. Studying the Fifth Offensive thus makes a contribution to knowledge and also suggests major reinterpretations of the course of the war in the East. It is just such discoveries that reward research into these and other vast untapped areas of the Civil War.

To present these results of research, a dual approach will be used. Because virtually all readers, professional and lay, will be unfamiliar with the operation, its course will be described in detail. Adding in this way to the sum total of knowledge about the Civil War is the book's major purpose. More than just relating information is projected, though. Throughout the narrative and in a final summary chapter of analysis, the strategy, tactics, and generalship of the operation will be assessed; the questions previously posed will be addressed; and the significant discoveries will be presented. Narrative and interpretation, based on extensive research, are thus the principal elements of this book. It is hoped that they will make a useful contribution to the history of the Civil War and to the larger field of military history.

The Civil War, after all, constitutes not only one period of America's history but also one segment of military history. That broader field is among the most honorable and instructive facets of Clio's discipline. It is the study of some of the most significant and influential events in the human experience. Wars bring some countries into being (the United States among them); wars terminate the existence of other countries (including the Confederacy); and wars produce a major and often epochal impact on the opposing sides. In affecting the fate of nations, wars also affect the lives of people. Such influential events are prime subjects for study. Military history is that study. It illumines the causes, course, and consequences of war; the role of armed forces in peacetime; and the multifaceted relationship of the military with its society. Like political, diplomatic, or any other kind of history, military history is amenable to rigorous canons of scholarship. Like them, it is capable of fulfilling the purpose of all historical study: contributing to knowledge and enhancing understanding of the human experience.

Military history has long attracted the general reading public and career military officers. Many wars, indeed, have generated huge followings of avid readers. Growing numbers of professional historians, too, have increasingly devoted attention to military subjects. Many of these scholars have rightly expanded the field to include such topics as civil-military relations, social composition of the armed forces, and so on. Their work represents an important increase of understanding of the military. Opening up new areas, however, should not lead to neglect of classical military history: wars, campaigns and battles, commanders, units, and common soldiers. Wars, after all, are central to the military experience. Campaigns and battles, conducted by commanders and fought by units of common soldiers, make up those wars. The study of such events and such men is, therefore, central to military history. Classical military history remains the heart of military history.

This book is within that realm of classical military history. As such, it

concentrates upon strategy, tactics, and generalship. Junior officers and
men in the ranks also receive considerable coverage. As a work of
scholarship, moreover, it is based upon research among thousands of
sources in over 100 manuscript repositories and libraries from Maine
to California and from Minnesota to Florida. Some 1,234 of these
sources, representing only material actually used, are entered in the
bibliography. Within that list, 71 per cent of the entries are unpublished sources. Such research and the resulting synthesis of sources
into a narrative will, it is hoped, make a contribution to the field that
will be appreciated by professionals. At the same time, the book is
written in a style intended to appeal to general readers as well. There is
no contradiction between scholarly writing and interesting writing. To
the contrary, an interesting style of writing is the best means for expressing the results of scholarly research.

In presenting these results in this style, the author uses certain terms
and certain forms of citation that should be explained beforehand.
Chief among them is the term "Autumn Offensive at Petersburg" itself.
Such a designation was not used by participants, nor is it current
among historians. Rather, the author has coined the term "Offensive"
to facilitate studying the prolonged operations on both sides of the
James River grouped under the generic heading "Siege of Petersburg."
The siege, of course, has a unity of its own that invites study in en-
tirety. Yet it did not consist of unbroken fighting but was marked by
long periods of quiescence, punctuated by outbreaks of major combat.
The siege may thus be resolved into its constituent phases. Each phase
opened with a Northern attack upon the Confederate cities or their
supply lines and lasted, many times for a week or more, until strategic
equilibrium was restored. Several discrete battles beyond the opening
onslaught were often fought before the strategic situation was stabilized. In many ways, each of these phases was thus a distinct campaign.
Yet because they formed part of the over-all campaign of Petersburg,
they are called "offensives" by this historian.

The First Offensive of the siege was the Kautz-Gillmore Fiasco of
the Ninth of June. Grant's First Offensive (the second of the siege) occurred in the middle of that month. He launched eight more such
offensives before finally capturing Petersburg and Richmond the following April. This book covers his Fifth Offensive of early autumn
(the sixth of the siege).

The other terminology to be explained is more widely, but not uni-
versally, known. It concerns designations of units. Southern corps were
numbered in respect to each army, whereas Federal corps were numbered in respect to the armed might of the United States. Both will be
denoted with roman numerals. Below the corps level on the Northern

side, divisions were numbered in regard to each corps, and brigades were numbered in regard to each division. (There were thus a "First Brigade, First Division, IX Corps"; a "First Brigade, Second Division, IX Corps"; a "First Brigade, First Division, X Corps"; etc.) The Graycoats, in contrast, rarely numbered their divisions and brigades. Each of those units was rather named after its official commander, whether or not he actually led it. By the fall of 1864, many such outfits were headed by other than official commanders. To differentiate between official titles and indications of actual commanders, the unit name will be capitalized in the former case but not in the latter. The defenders of Fort Johnson, for example, could be called "DuBose's *bri-gade*" (unofficial name) or "Benning's *Brigade*, Colonel DuBose commanding" (official title, with actual commander indicated). By the same token, the attackers of that fort may be termed "Fairchild's *bri-gade*" (unofficial title) or the "Third *Brigade*, Second *Division*, XVIII *Corps*" (official title).

Each side used the same system for designating troops smaller than brigades. Most such troops were regiments, particularly infantry regiments. Both terms are thus superfluous in unit names. Only if the outfit was an independent unit smaller than a regiment will its size be specified; only if it was other than infantry or was a special type of infantry will its branch be stated. In all such cases, its ordinal number and state will be given if they are part of its name. For instance, the 83rd Pennsylvania and the 4th Texas were infantry regiments; the 1st Michigan Sharpshooters and the 19th Virginia Militia were special types of infantry regiments; and the 5th North Carolina Cavalry and the 1st New York Mounted Rifles were regiments of horse. Examples of units smaller than regiments include: the 11th Georgia Light Artillery Battalion, the 18th South Carolina Heavy Artillery Battalion, the 4th Alabama Cavalry Battalion, the 1st New York Sharpshooter Battalion, the 2nd Maryland Battalion (note: an infantry battalion), the 3rd Vermont Light Battery, the 13th Massachusetts Heavy Artillery Company, the Andrew Sharpshooter Company, and the Oneida Cavalry Company.

Wherever the words "Battalion," "Battery," or "Company" are used, they refer to independent organic units raised by the states or the national governments. Other outfits of those sizes, however, were integral parts of larger units, usually regiments. These subunits are indicated by their own number or letter, followed by a slash and then their parent unit's name. Thus, "the 1/38th New Jersey" means "the First Battalion of the 38th New Jersey"; "F/1st Rhode Island Light Artillery" refers to "Battery F of the 1st Rhode Island Light Artillery"; "A/2nd Wisconsin Battalion" names "Company A of the 2nd Wisconsin Battalion"; and "B/1/17th U.S." signifies "Company B of the First Battalion of the 17th U.S." Note that, by themselves, these subordinate battalions are written out: "First Battalion" (of the 17th U.S.).

Beyond these terms in the text, certain expressions and forms are also used in the footnotes. Such footnotes are necessary to document historical writing, particularly when the subject matter is unfamiliar to most readers. To provide such references with precision, the author's dissertation (Rice University, 1970) contained at least one footnote for virtually every sentence. The resulting footnotes, 4,374 strong, filled 641 pages, single-spaced. Such lengthy citations and weighing of evidence are too extensive for this book. They have, accordingly, been telescoped into master footnotes: one per paragraph or even one per several closely related paragraphs. These master footnotes are long but do not take nearly as much space as thousands of individual notes would. To save more space, the lengthy assessment of the credibility of sources is deleted from the book; only the resulting conclusions are given. Each master note, however, indicates the corresponding passage of the dissertation. The interested reader may find in the latter work complete specificity of citations and also extensive weighing of evidence.

The footnotes are also full of short titles and abbreviations. Each publication is *initially* cited by its short title and thereafter by "op. cit." Fuller references may be found in the bibliography and need not be repeated in the notes. Manuscript repositories are comparably abbreviated throughout the notes. These abbreviations are identified at the beginning of the bibliography. This list of abbreviations will also prove helpful in identifying picture credits. As with the master footnotes, these shortcuts are taken in order that the references themselves may be preserved. If all the citations with all their appurtenances cannot be provided for each sentence, then it is better that the appurtenances go, that the particularity go, and that all the references remain in telescoped form. None of the sources themselves have been deleted. Through the considerate co-operation of the editor and the publisher, this acceptable accommodation has proved practicable.

ACKNOWLEDGMENTS

The author thanks his editor, Miss Jean Anne Vincent, and her staff, especially Miss Ann Sleeper, for the foregoing assistance and other acts of co-operation. Grateful acknowledgment is also given to the following private individuals and the staffs of the following libraries and manuscript repositories for making available pertinent source material: Mr. R. R. Adams (32nd Virginia) of Newport News, Virginia; Mrs. Dorothy Crump, Mrs. Virginia Jones, and Mrs. Alma Pate of the Alabama Department of Archives and History; Dr. Allen W. Jones of Auburn University; Mr. Harold Yoder of the Historical Society of Berks County, Pennsylvania; the staff of the Boston Athenaeum; the library staff of Boston University; the staff of the Boston Public Library; the library staff of the University of California at Santa Barbara; Dr. Gerald S. Brinton of New Cumberland, Pennsylvania; Mr. Dennis Casebier of Norco, California; the staff of the Charleston Library Society; Mr. Motley of the Chicago Historical Society; Mr. Teitelbaum of the Chicago Public Library; Mr. Gregory Coco of Gettysburg, Pennsylvania; Mr. Paul Palmer of Columbia University; Miss Eleanor Brockenbrough and Mr. Les Jensen of the Museum of the Confederacy; Mr. Robert Fowler, Mr. William C. Davis, and the staff of *Civil War Times Illustrated;* Miss Hoxie of the Connecticut Historical Society; Miss Jackie Rastigian of the Connecticut State Library; Mr. Willis J. Dance of Danville, Virginia; Miss Joanne Mattern of the Historical Society of Delaware; Miss Virginia Shaw of the Delaware Public Archives Commission; the staff of the Detroit Public Library; Dr. Mattie Russell and the late Mrs. Virginia Gray of Duke University; Mr. Donald R. Lennon of East Carolina University; Mrs. Mary Davis of Emory University; the staff of the Filson Club; Mr. J. Harmon Smith, Mr. Robert Williams, and Miss Gail Miller of the Georgia Department of Archives and History; Mrs. Hawes of the Georgia Historical Society; the library staff of the University of Georgia; Miss Caroline Jakeman of Harvard University; Colonel Harold B. Simpson of Hill Junior College; Dr. Ray Billington, Miss Mary Isabel Fry, and Mrs. Virginia Rust of the Huntington Library; Mr. Paul Spence and Miss Laurel Bowen of the Illinois State Historical Library; Mr. John Boroughs, Mr. Robert Costenbader, Mr. Peter Jones; Mr. William Ladd, Mr. Gerald Martin, and the late Mr. Lloyd Dunlap of the Library of Congress; Miss Marcelle Schertz and Mrs. Elsa Meier of Louisiana State University; Miss Ellen Barker, Mr. Walter Clayton, Mr. Henry Hahn, and Miss Arlene Palmer of the Maryland Historical Society; Dr. James Mohr of the University of Maryland/Baltimore County; Major William D. Matter of Harrisburg, Pennsylvania; Miss Geneva Kebler of the Michigan History Commission; Dr. Warren and Mr. Ewing of the University of Michigan; Mr. Russ Pritchard and Mrs. Stephanie Benko of the War Library of the National Commandery of the Military Order of the Loyal Legion of the United States; the staff of the Minnesota Historical Society; Miss Charlotte Capers, Mrs. W. D. Harrell, Mrs. T. E. Caldwell, and Mrs. Jane Melton of the Mississippi Department of Archives and History; Dr. Dallas Irvine, Mr. E. O. Parker, Mr. Robert Gruber, Mr. Dale Floyd, and Mr. Michael Musick of the National Archives; Mr. William K. Kay and Mr. Lee Wallace of the National Park Service; the staff of the Newberry Library; Mrs. Norbert Lacy of the New Hampshire Historical Society; Mr. Edwin Hunt of the New Hampshire Records Management and Archives Commission; Mr. Thaddeus Crom of the New Jersey Historical Society; Mr. Arthur Breton of the New-York Historical Society; the staff of the New York Public Library; Mr. C. F. W. Coker, Mrs. Mary Rogers, Mr. Roger C. Jones, and Mr. Weymouth T. Jordan of the North Carolina Department of Archives and History; Dr. J. Isaac Copeland, Dr. Carolyn Wallace, Miss Anna Brooke Allan, and Mr. Clyde Wilson of the University of North Carolina; Mr. Paul Eustace of the Historical Society of Pennsylvania; Mr. William Work, Mr. Charles Isett, Mrs. Mary Philpott, and Mrs. Martha Semmetti of the Pennsylvania Archives and History Commission; Mr. Ronald C. Filipelli of Pennsylvania State University; the historian and staff of the Petersburg National Battlefield Park; Mr. A. P. Clark of Princeton University; the library staff and especially Mr. Richard Perrine of Rice University; Mr. Charles Hinsdale and staff of the Richmond National Battlefield Park; Mr. Anthony Nicolosi of Rutgers University; Mrs. Granville Prior of the South Carolina Historical Society; Mr. Inabinett and Miss Jacobs of the University of South Carolina; the library staff of Stanford University; Dr. Paul Steiner of Philadelphia, Pennsylvania; the director of the Syms-Eaton Museum of Hampton, Virginia; Mr. Bryce Suderow of Penngrove, California; Mrs. Osburn and Mr. Haas of the Texas State Library; Mr. Chester Kielman and Mrs. Frances

Rodgers of the University of Texas; Mrs. Connie Griffith of Tulane University; Mr. Maxwell Whiteman of the Union League Club of Philadelphia; Colonel James Barron Agnew, Colonel Donald P. Shaw, and my colleagues on the staff of the U. S. Army Military History Institute; Mr. Robert Schnare and Mrs. Marie Capps of the U. S. Military Academy; Mr. Robert Mayo of the Valentine Museum; Mr. John Melville Jennings, Mr. William Rochal, Mr. Howson Cole, Mrs. J. A. V. Berry, and Mr. David Riggs of the Virginia Historical Society; Mrs. Ruth Watson of the Virginia Military Institute; Mr. VanSchreeven, Dr. Louis Manarin, Mr. Sella, and Mrs. Katherine Smith of the Virginia State Library; Mr. Augustus Hamblett of the University of Virginia; the staff of the Warren County Historical Society of Front Royal, Virginia; Mrs. Leora Wood Wells of Springfield, Virginia; Mr. Kermit Pike, Mrs. Alene White, and Mrs. Virginia Hawley of the Western Reserve Historical Society; Mrs. Gloria McGurk of the College of William and Mary; Dr. Josephine Harper of the State Historical Society of Wisconsin; the staff of the Wyoming Historical and Genealogical Society of Wilkes-Barre, Pennsylvania; and Mrs. Judith A. Schiff of Yale University.

No one who works in the Old Army Records Branch of the National Archives can fail to make special mention of the invaluable assistance provided by Mrs. Sara D. Jackson, long the trusted guide and friend of Civil Warriors who campaigned there and now the Archivist of the National Historical Publications and Records Commission. The author would also be remiss were he not to acknowledge with particular gratitude the courtesy and help shown him during his visits to Richmond by the late Mr. J. Ambler Johnston, Sr. Mr. Johnston's father, a soldier of the Salem Flying Artillery, helped save Fort Gregg—and Richmond—on September 29, 1864. The soldier's son ever cherished an interest in that battle and in those who study it.

Appreciation is also due to the many photo archivists who took the time to respond that they did not have the pictures requested. No picture has been located of several officers sought: Lieutenant Colonel Frederick Bass, 1st Texas; Major George Cook, 1st Connecticut Heavy Artillery; Colonel Joel R. Griffin, 3rd and 62nd Georgia (8th Georgia Cavalry); Colonel John M. Hughs, 25th Tennessee; Colonel Hilary P. Jones and Major Richard Cornelius Taylor, Confederate Artillery; Colonel Francis Pond, 62nd Ohio; and Commander Thomas R. Rootes, Confederate Navy. A photograph, painting, or drawing of any of these men would be of interest. Wartime views are preferable, but any picture from adult life is acceptable. Anyone knowing of the availability of such pictures would confer a boon upon the author by informing him of them.

Beyond locating sources, many individuals gave valued assistance in writing the history of the Fifth Offensive. Dr. S. W. Higginbotham of Rice University, Mr. E. B. Long of the University of Wyoming, and Dr. Russell F. Weigley of Temple University kindly tendered their wise and considered judgment of the work. Dr. William J. Galush of Loyola University/Chicago, Dr. Joseph L. Harsh of George Mason University, Dr. Minor Myers of Connecticut College, Dr. Thomas R. Stone of the U. S. Army, and especially Mr. William C. Davis of *Civil War Times Illustrated* provided friendship, understanding, and a willingness to listen, comment, and help over the years. My scores of friends in the Harrisburg Civil War Round Table offered a congenial atmosphere for pursuing my interest in the Civil War. Welcome financial support for research was generously granted by Rice University.

But, above all, special acknowledgment must be given to Dr. Frank E. Vandiver, long the Civil War professor at Rice University and since 1980 the President of North Texas State University. For two decades, I have known of him as a historian. From 1964 to 1970, I had the privilege of doing my graduate work under him. Since then, I have valued him as a friend. As a scholar of the first echelon, he makes a major contribution to the field of military history through the thoroughness of his research and the literary elegance of his writing. As a teacher in the true sense of the word, he creates the fundamental atmosphere in which students can learn. He stimulates them with learned counsel and tempers them with constructive guidance but never tampers with them with constrictive guidelines nor stunts them with warping prejudices of ideology and methodology. And as a friend, he provides advice, opportunity, and comradeship that are extremely welcome and valued. For all he had done, I can never repay him. But I can at least acknowledge my obligation to him and can, as a symbol of my appreciation, respectfully dedicate this book to him.

RICHARD J. SOMMERS
U. S. Army Military History Institute

CONTENTS

LIST OF PHOTOGRAPHS

Note: For photo credits, refer to List of
Abbreviations in the Bibliography.

LIST OF MAPS

Richmond Redeemed

CHAPTER I

"A Mere Question of Time"

The soldiers had never experienced a summer like the one just ended. Three years earlier, in 1861, conflict had been almost leisurely; the mere handful of battles then simply underscored the need to prepare massively for a Civil War that both North and South would go on to fight in earnest. The powerful armies that each side began forging those first months grappled more often and more bloodily the next two summers, yet even then frequent intervals between battles gave respite to the combatants.

In 1864, there would be no such respite. The new Federal General-in-Chief, Lieutenant General Ulysses S. Grant, regarded unrelenting pressure against the enemy as the means to take advantage of the North's numerical superiority. He, therefore, unleashed a simultaneous advance by all major Union forces from eastern Virginia to Georgia. Strategically and tactically, he constantly carried the war to the Army of Northern Virginia, the target of his personal efforts. Undaunted by repeated tactical reverses and staggering casualties, the Federal commander drove the Confederates from central Virginia almost to Richmond in the first month of operations, May 4–June 3. He thereby negated all that his opponent, General Robert E. Lee, had accomplished in two years of campaigning and once more imposed on Lee the constricting imperative of defending his capital.

Richmond was not just the seat of government; it was also a major center of arms and supplies and a key logistical interchange. Most of all, it was the symbol of Confederate independence. Defiantly placing their capital within 110 miles of Washington in 1861 flaunted Southern confidence. Saving the city from Major General George McClellan's grand army the following summer enshrined Richmond in Confederate hearts and minds. Rightly or wrongly, numerous legitimate military, political, economic, and psychological considerations compelled Lee to defend the city. He defended it best by carrying the war to the enemy and keeping them at a distance. But now the Union troops had forced him back to the city itself and severely restricted his strategic mobility by tying him down to its immediate defense. All too aware of what loss of initiative meant, he had declared:

> We must destroy this army of Grant's before he gets to James River. If he gets there, it will become a siege, and then it will be a mere question of time.[1]

In mid-June, however, Grant not merely reached but also crossed the James and nearly captured Petersburg, rail center of the capital. Lost opportunities, hesitant subordinate leadership, and a valorous Confederate defense cost him the city, though, so he settled down to besiege it. The siege ended six weeks of incessant battles, yet the pressure did not lessen. Grant kept his forces close up against the Graycoats to fix them in place strategically and tactically. Seven times during the ensuing summer he lashed out at the pinned-down foe, alternately attacking Petersburg frontally, striking from his right flank toward Richmond, extending his left flank toward Southern supply lines, and raiding deep into the Confederate rear. To maintain the pressure between these battles, shelling, sharpshooting, and picket forays flared daily between the lines east of town. There was no real respite from fighting. Never had the seasoned veterans in blue and gray experienced such a summer.

The weather only made matters worse. Tidewater Virginia was oppressively hot and dry that summer. Troops in the earthworks often suffered under the sun's beating rays, and men on the march stirred up choking clouds of dust. Relief from the sun, though not from the heat, could occasionally be found in the region's numerous forests, but the sand flies and mosquitoes teeming in the woods scourged anyone who sought shelter there. Nor did the infrequent rains do much good. They increased the humidity as often as they cooled, and the waters of the Peninsula, east of Richmond, became miasmatic swamps that added fever to the soldiers' afflictions.

Stagnant water and still air seemed to symbolize the course of the war itself. True, Grant had carried the war from the Rapidan River to the Appomattox River. True also, he had pinned down the Confederates and restricted their options. Yet he had failed to destroy them or capture Richmond. The Army of Northern Virginia, battered but defiant, still barred his path and blunted his every thrust. Heavy casualties, exhaustion, and the debilitating climate all helped transform the mobile war of spring into the grinding, monotonous attrition of summer. Should decisive victory remain elusive, Union politicians feared and Confederate soldiers hoped that the Northern electorate might— just might—repudiate the Lincoln administration and bring to office a peace candidate in the upcoming November election.

Such delays surprised but did not daunt Federal headquarters. Ever sanguine, Grant remained confident of ultimate success. As summer ended, chances for victory looked more promising. Autumn brought cooler weather, better suited for campaigning, and there would be an early frost that year. Fresh (though inexperienced) troops also became available as the first of the one-year regiments called for in late summer began reaching the front in mid-September. Most encouraging of all, the war started opening up again. In early August, the Federal navy had cut access to Mobile, principal Southern port on the eastern Gulf. On September 2, Major General William T. Sherman had broken his own deadlock in Georgia by taking Atlanta. And now from eastern Virginia came intelligence reports that, if pushed hard enough, Lee might abandon Petersburg, perhaps even Richmond itself.

The Northern commander prepared to push. Even before learning, on September 27, of the possible abandonment of the capital, he made plans to capture the rail center. He initially intended to detach an auxiliary force, 6,000 to 10,000 strong, to seal off Wilmington, North Carolina, the main entry point for blockade runners supplying the Virginia armies. In the meantime, his main body would strike west to cut the last railroad leading into Petersburg from the interior. It was the prospect of severing such arteries that had drawn Grant to Petersburg in the first place. The town was the rail center of Richmond, twenty-one miles to the north. From all directions rail lines converged on Petersburg: from City Point to the northeast, from Norfolk to the southeast, from Wilmington and points farther down the coast to the south, and from Lynchburg and the Great Valley to the west. The Richmond and Petersburg Railroad plus a good pike, in turn, linked the rail center to the capital. The Federal army immediately cut the two minor lines east of town in mid-June. Two months later, it finally managed to secure a foothold on the Weldon Railroad at Globe Tavern, three miles south of Petersburg. Confederates, however, continued to use that line as far north as Stony Creek Depot, whence they trans-shipped supplies by wagon into Petersburg. To interrupt these wagon trains and to break the Southside Railroad to Lynchburg became Grant's next objectives. Doing so would nullify the advantages of holding Petersburg and would ultimately imperil Richmond's only other practical long-term supply line, which ran southwest from the capital into the Carolina piedmont along the Danville Railroad and connecting lines. Were those two railroads cut, the Butternuts could not long sustain themselves along the remaining supply lines interior to the Old Dominion alone. Such a loss might be just the push needed to force Lee to abandon the line of the James. Grant set October 5 as the date for this grand onslaught.[2]

Events in the Shenandoah Valley hastened and altered this attack. Operations in the Valley had influenced the main armies in Virginia throughout the war. Confederate successes at First Manassas and the Seven Days in 1861 and 1862 were due largely to events in the Shenandoah country, and Southern victories there in June 1863 marked their greatest achievement in the Gettysburg Campaign. In 1864, Lee once more looked to the Valley to relieve the pressure on him in the Tidewater. He entrusted to Lieutenant General Jubal A. Early, commanding the II Corps, Army of Northern Virginia, prime responsibility for gaining the needed victory beyond the Blue Ridge. Since arriving in mid-June, Early managed to drive off local Union forces, threaten Washington, and tie down thirteen blue divisions, seven of which were diverted from Grant's main body. Weakening the force besieging Petersburg was a major accomplishment, but it was not enough for Lee. He demanded a decisive tactical victory, and when Early could not provide it, the senior officer, on September 17, ordered I Corps headquarters, Major General Joseph B. Kershaw's Infantry Division, and Lieutenant Colonel Wilfred E. Cutshaw's Artillery Battalion to return to the Tidewater in hopes these reinforcements would enable him to gain the needed victory directly over Grant. Barely had these troops reached the piedmont, however, when Major General Philip H. Sheridan, commanding the Federal Army of the Shenandoah, took advantage of their absence to defeat Early severely at Opequon Creek and Fisher's Hill on September 19 and 22, respectively. The victorious Bluecoats then pushed southward up the Valley and cut the Virginia Central Railroad, the artery that fed the Valley's rich foodstuffs to the capital.

Both commanders at Petersburg reacted promptly to these events. Lee returned Kershaw's and Cutshaw's combat forces in the piedmont to Early on September 23 and recalled only Lieutenant General Richard H. Anderson's I Corps headquarters to Richmond. Four days later, Lee detached Brigadier General Thomas L. Rosser's Laurel Brigade of Virginia Cavalry from his main army to reinforce Early. Lee had originally planned to exchange the horsemen for Kershaw's Division; now he lost them both. Far from gaining anything by this effort to bolster his command in the Tidewater, he thus ended up with a net loss of troops and two major defeats in the Valley. His old game of playing grand strategy along the Blue Ridge was no longer paying off.

The Southern chieftain might lose still more, for Grant, too, responded decisively to Sheridan's victories. The General-in-Chief initially feared that the battle of September 19 would lead the Secessionists to abandon the Valley, and he placed his troops on a vigilant defensive lest Early rejoin Lee to attack him. But when word of the second victory at Fisher's Hill dispelled these fears, Grant resumed the initiative to prevent Lee from reinforcing the Valley and to take advantage of any openings made by the detachment of aid to Early. Undeterred by perfectionists who grumbled that the army was unprepared to advance, Grant responded flexibly to the rapidly fluctuating strategic situation and got ready to take the offensive. He reached this decision around September 24, and over the next three days he issued his battle plans. Thursday, September 29, was fixed as the day of attack.

The massive drive projected for October 5 was thus moved forward one week. Moreover, although minor preparations for the amphibious expedition to North Carolina were allowed to continue, that operation was postponed in order to free more troops to attack Lee. Yet these were mere alterations in the original plan caused by events in the Valley, not a whole new plan. Grant remained convinced that he could push the Confederates out of the Tidewater that fall, and events beyond the Blue Ridge were but the catalysts that precipitated battle. He launched his autumn offensive—his Fifth Offensive of the siege—not just to tie down potential reinforcements to Early but also to defeat Lee. Richmond and Petersburg were the prizes Grant felt were at last within his grasp. His adversary had feared all along that, in a siege, "it will be a mere question of time." The Illinoisan was sure that the "time" for decisive Federal victory was now at hand.

The capital replaced Cape Fear as the secondary target of Grant's attack largely at the urging of his senior subordinate, Major General Benjamin F. Butler, commander of the Army of the James. Butler's sophisticated espionage system, supported by the testimony of deserters, disclosed the weakness of Confederate forces on the Peninsula. A massive strike there, the New Englander felt, would overrun these defenders and carry on to Richmond itself. On September 26, the two generals made a reconnaissance by boat up the James, which probably further suggested the desirability of attacking on the Northside. The lieutenant general, accordingly, decided to open his autumn offensive by sending Butler with eighteen brigades (26,600 men) across the James against Richmond. Grant hoped for the best but did not share his subordinate's optimistic view that the capital could be captured.

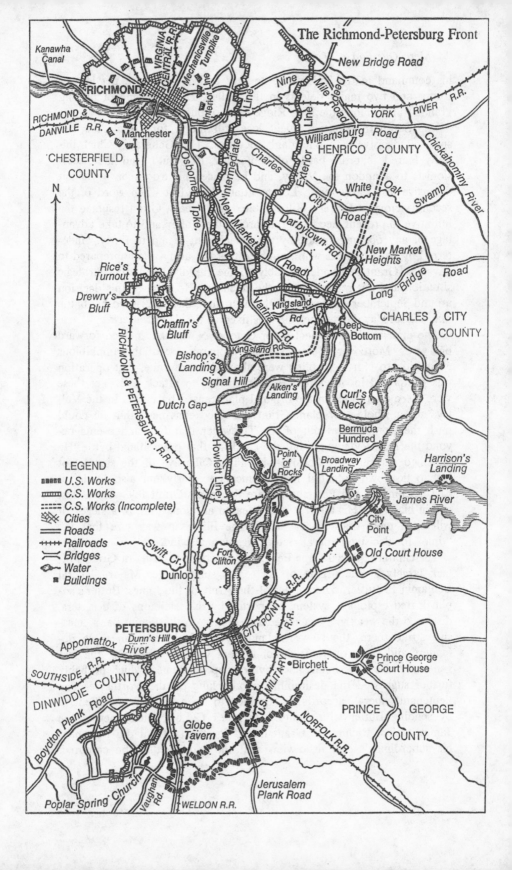

The Richmond-Petersburg Front

Kanawha Canal

VIRGINIA CENTRAL R.R.

Mechanicsville Turnpike

New Bridge Road

RICHMOND

Nine Mile Road

Deep Bottom Road

YORK RIVER R.R.

Chickahominy River

RICHMOND & DANVILLE R.R.

Manchester

Interior Line

Williamsburg Road

HENRICO COUNTY

Exterior Line

New Market

Charles City Road

White Oak Swamp

CHESTERFIELD COUNTY

N

Osborne Tpke.

New Intermediate

Darbytown Rd.

New Market Heights

Rice's Turnout

Road

Long Bridge Road

Drewry's Bluff

Chaffin's Bluff

Kingsland Rd.

Varina Rd.

Deep Bottom

CHARLES CITY COUNTY

Bishop's Landing

Kingsland Rd.

Aiken's Landing

Curl's Neck

Signal Hill

Dutch Gap

Howlett Line

Bermuda Hundred

LEGEND
U.S. Works
C.S. Works
C.S. Works (Incomplete)
Cities
Roads
Railroads
Bridges
Water
Buildings

Point of Rocks

Broadway Landing

Harrison's Landing

James River

City Point

RICHMOND & PETERSBURG R.R.

Swift Cr.

Fort Clifton

Old Court House

Dunlop

CITY POINT R.R.

PETERSBURG

Dunn's Hill

Appomattox River

CITY POINT R.R.

Prince George Court House

SOUTHSIDE R.R.

DINWIDDIE COUNTY

Birchett

U.S. MILITARY R.R.

PRINCE GEORGE COUNTY

Boydton Plank Road

NORFOLK R.R.

Globe Tavern

Poplar Spring Church

Vaughan Rd.

WELDON R.R.

Jerusalem Plank Road

The General-in-Chief was sure, though, that the onslaught would draw to the Peninsula many of the Confederate troops presently around Petersburg and thereby uncover the supply lines south of town. To take advantage of this opening, another 25,000 Bluecoats, fourteen brigades of the Army of the Potomac under Major General George G. Meade, stood ready to strike. Half of Grant's 102,000 men were to participate in this two-pronged attack; others could be called on if needed; and still others helped pin down Southerners in the works on both sides of the Appomattox. Only the four ironclads and approximately twenty-one other vessels of the powerful James River Naval Division of the North Atlantic Blockading Squadron, unable to pass the batteries on the Appomattox and the obstructions in the James, were to have little role in the Fifth Offensive.[3]

Assembling these two striking forces took some doing. Only 4,300 Unionists were already north of the James near Richmond—the garrison of the bridgehead at Deep Bottom and the labor force and guards digging the Dutch Gap Canal. Across from them on Bermuda Hundred, the peninsula between the right bank of the James and the left bank of the Appomattox, another 15,700 Northerners threatened the Richmond and Petersburg Railroad and protected the sensitive northwestern approach to City Point. That settlement—Grant's headquarters and main supply base, located on the right bank of the Appomattox where it entered the James—was secured by some 5,100 soldiers against troublesome guerrillas and bold cavalry raiders lurking in the woodlands east of Petersburg. A daring Confederate cavalry raid from Petersburg to a point just six miles down the James from City Point in mid-September underscored the need for such protection. Next time the horsemen might try to overrun the depot itself. Further to guard the supply lines, another 1,800 Yankees garrisoned three posts down the James below City Point. These scattered forces totaled 27,000 men. However, the bulk of Grant's troops—three corps and a cavalry division of the Army of the Potomac, the X Corps and the cavalry division of the Army of the James, 75,000 strong—were concentrated east and south of Petersburg. Grant would abandon none of these sectors, but he did authorize drawing off some troops from each to be massed in the area or transferred to other sectors. Such redistribution was clearly necessary if the right wing was to reach the desired strength of eighteen brigades.

Butler did some redistributing on his own. He used Colonel Joseph H. Potter's Provisional Brigade, XVIII Corps, consisting mostly of newly arrived, inexperienced one-year regiments, to replace veterans on garrison duty. Potter, accordingly, sent the 200th and 205th Pennsylvania to Old Court House, principal outpost of City Point, transferred

the 1/38th New Jersey and 2/184th New York to Brigadier General
Gilman Marston's First Separate Brigade down the James, and held his
other five new regiments and one experienced regiment ready to take
over the defenses at Bermuda Hundred. On being relieved, the 148th
New York, 55th Pennsylvania, 3/2nd Pennsylvania Heavy Artillery,
and 9th Vermont from the courthouse, plus the 89th New York from
downriver, massed on the Hundred, September 27–28. During those
same days, veterans already there got ready to turn over the trenches to
Potter on the night of September 28–29. In the meantime, the 1st and
37th U. S. Colored Troops ("USCT") from Marston's force, along with
the 4th, 6th, and 22nd USCT from the Dutch Gap area, rejoined their
divisional headquarters at Deep Bottom. Only a handful of experienced
troops now remained in garrison on the minor sectors: the 2nd New
Hampshire, E and H/16th New York Heavy Artillery, M/4th Massachusetts Cavalry, I/1st USCT Cavalry, and the 33rd New York Battery
with Marston; and C/1st Connecticut Heavy Artillery and a section of
the 7th New York Battery, together with 150 Negro recruits, all under
Major Thomas J. Strong, in Dutch Gap. Virtually all the other veterans
were preparing to join the attack. The XVIII Corps, which had almost
lost its identity in scattered garrison duty the past four weeks, was
being reconstituted as a mobile field force once more.

Yet Butler wanted his whole army together again, not just one corps.
His remaining troops had to come from Meade's sector south of the
lower Appomattox (that portion of the stream downriver from Camp-
bell's Bridge at Petersburg). First to arrive was Brigadier General August V. Kautz's Cavalry Division, which rode over to Bermuda Hundred, September 27, once Meade's own horsemen had relieved it on
patrol around Prince George Court House, the far left of the Union
rear line. The infantry, Major General David B. Birney's X Corps, was
slower coming. Although two reserve divisions of the II Corps took
over his trench line on the Federal right east of Petersburg on the night
of September 24–25, he simply massed his troops in the rear around
his corps headquarters at Friend's house. Butler expected Birney to
cross to the Hundred after dark on the twenty-seventh, but the junior
officer misunderstood and postponed his move one day. Except for
three batteries returned to the XVIII Corps on September 25, the X
Corps would not rejoin Butler until the eve of the onslaught. For the
next three days, Birney's troops simply rested—thankful that they had
escaped the ordeal of the trenches at last.[4]

Meanwhile, Meade, also, prepared his forces to move against the
Southern communications. Replacing Kautz and Birney, shifting the
weight of forces rightward to reduce attenuation of the II Corps, and
massing his reserves occupied the final week of September. As finally

arranged, Major General Winfield Scott Hancock's II Corps and four artillery brigades held the lines running south for two miles from the lower Appomattox to the Jerusalem Plank Road, closely confronting Petersburg from the east; the Negro division of the IX Corps and Major General Gouverneur K. Warren's V Corps extended the front west for three miles from the plank road to the foothold on the Weldon Railroad at Globe Tavern, facing north toward the Confederate works two miles away; the two white divisions of Major General John G. Parke's IX Corps were in reserve on both sides of the plank road; and Brigadier General David M. Gregg's Second Division of the Cavalry Corps of the Army of the Potomac patrolled the rear.

It was no accident that Hancock's corps assumed position east of town. These famous shock troops of the army's most skilled tactician had played a major role in every previous offensive that year. They had achieved a great deal in those five months, but they had also suffered a great deal—27,000 casualties, among them many of the ablest leaders and most experienced soldiers. Such losses had shredded the very fabric of the corps, and its most recent battle, Second Reams's Station on August 25, had ended in disaster. Now at last this unit would enjoy a brief respite as it sat out the offensive in the works east of Cockade City, as Petersburg was called. Although the men would be exposed to sniping and shelling and would render an important service by pinning down Secessionists near the town, they would at least be spared heavy fighting. The reserve divisions of the IX Corps, the more westerly brigades of the V Corps, and the cavalry—all of whom had suffered relatively fewer losses since May—would bear the brunt of the upcoming battle this time.

Redeploying the two Federal armies was only part of the preparation. As combat troops neared the front, they received extra ammunition, and the necessary complement of supply trains and ambulances joined them. At the same time, surplus wagons and hospitalized men vacated the forward positions and moved back to the inner lines around City Point. Every preparation was made as the forces stripped down to fighting trim.[5]

Enhancing Northern prospects was Confederate ignorance of the impending blow. Seventy per cent of Lee's 53,000 men remained around Petersburg: eighteen infantry brigades in the trenches immediately east and south of town, five more infantry brigades and the Cavalry Corps covering the communications and observing the Yankees' forward salient at Globe Tavern. Army headquarters itself was in this area at Dunn's Hill, just across the Appomattox from Petersburg. Another 7,500 Southerners stood guard north of that river in Chesterfield County, principally five brigades in the Howlett Line containing the

Army of the James at Bermuda Hundred plus various land and water
batteries between Petersburg and the Hundred and up the James as far
as Drewry's Bluff. Also patrolling the James between Howlett's and
Drewry's were the eight vessels of the James River Naval Squadron,
three of them ironclads. But north of the James there were only 8,700
soldiers including heavy artillerists and second-class units right around
Richmond. Of these, a mere 4,200 held the forward lines observing
Deep Bottom and Dutch Gap. Such dispositions were well suited to
covering the communications below Petersburg, but they would
scarcely block Butler's drive for the capital.[6]

Lee was conscious of his numerical weakness but perceived it as a
general handicap, not a pressing danger. Yankee incursions in the
Shenandoah Valley and far southwestern Virginia gave him more immediate concern and perhaps distracted him from the peril on his own
front. So little did he expect battle on the eve of the Fifth Offensive
that he gave his Chief-of-Artillery, Brigadier General William Nelson
Pendleton, leave of absence to bury his son, who had fallen at Fisher's
Hill. Confederate rank and file, by and large, no more suspected an immediate outbreak of fighting than did their commander. Recent defeats
in the Valley occupied their attention, as did the question of whether
the upcoming elections in the North would bring peace. But on their
own front, confidence in their general and themselves remained unshaken. Whenever Grant might strike, they would stop him as they had
done since May. Secure in such assurance, a few troops had already
begun building winter quarters.

Most soldiers meantime continued to endure the sniping, shelling,
and everlasting entrenching. The numbing danger and grinding drudg-
ery of trench warfare seemed greater perils than Yankee onslaughts.
How the men longed to get out of those trenches! Even if only to dig
new fortifications, a trip into the unravaged countryside could restore
their spirits wonderfully. And when they left the defenses to rest, it was
sheer bliss. Such pleasure came to some, then all, of Major General
Robert F. Hoke's Division the last two weeks of September in an arbo-
real paradise in Chesterfield County. What the respite meant was
eloquently recorded by a lieutenant of the 31st North Carolina:

> The most pleasant topic amongst us—I mean Hoke's Division—is
> that we are at last clear of the ditches, shells, & balls of every de-
> scription & are lying at ease on a beautiful hillside washing our
> faces at least once per day and [having] no work to do. You can't
> imagine how highly we appreciate such treatment. Since the 15 of
> June we have held a portion of the works in front of Petersburg &
> have never been relieved until now.

Unfortunately, such leisure could not continue for long. On September 26, a grand review before Lee himself climaxed the stay, and two days later the division returned to the most exposed sector of the trenches, the left flank east of Cockade City. It relieved Major General Bushrod R. Johnson's Division, which in turn fell back into reserve. Johnson did not cross to Chesterfield and continued to provide fatigue details, but at least he was out of the earthworks. Now perhaps his men, too, could get a little rest—assuming that nothing important occurred.[7]

Opportunities for rest around Petersburg were eagerly seized, for they were few and far between. The permanent artillery garrison of the capital, in contrast, had long enjoyed such luxuries as regular barracks and private vegetable gardens on their quiet sector. Combat veterans fortunate enough to serve on the seemingly quiescent Peninsula experienced comparable pleasures. The Salem Flying Artillery, for instance, received two thousand pounds of food and clothing from home and twenty-five new army shirts on September 28. A few miles south that same day, the seasoned veterans of the Texas Brigade enjoyed a dance sponsored by the bride of one of their colonels. For the heavy artillery, a permanent home; for the light artillery, a welcome contact with home; for the Texans, a pleasant diversion from the irretrievable separation from home—and all this on a quiet front: The war seemed far away from the Northside that September 28.

It also appeared far away to a soldier of the 4th Texas, who had to miss the dance in order to observe the Bluecoats at Deep Bottom. How seriously he regarded the danger is clear from his letter to "Charming Nellie":

> Just now we are on the north side of the James, about eight miles below Richmond, taking our ease something in the manner of the old planter's darkies down in Alabama. When they came from the field to dinner, he was accustomed to say to them, "Now, boys, while you are resting, suppose you hoe the garden." Thus General Lee said to us when we reached this place, "Now, gentlemen, while you are resting at the Phillips' House, suppose you watch Beast Butler's Negroes." At any rate, this is what we are doing, and not grumbling at the task either—the darkies, so far, appearing devoid of belligerent propensities, and picket duty consequently being very light. It breaks somewhat upon our *otium cum dignitate* and our *dolce far niente,* but it would not only be unmilitary and insubordination to refuse, but dangerous in the double sense of exposing us to courtmartial and to being suddenly and unexpectedly gobbled up by Mr. Butler and his Ethiopian cohorts.[8]

Only down on the James itself did war intrude upon the Peninsula. There heavy Union labor details, digging a canal across the narrow peninsula Dutch Gap to enable the navy to bypass obstructions and reach the James above Bermuda Hundred, drew constant shelling from Southern mortars on the opposite bank. But because batteries in Chesterfield did little damage, the Confederates sought better results by erecting a major new fortification on Signal Hill, a mile up the left bank from Dutch Gap. Federal lookouts and Confederate deserters soon reported the presence of the new works. Still, except for naval fire in their general direction, Butler left them alone. This fire from the big guns of the U.S.S. *Mackinaw* caused the Virginia reserves on the hill to break—an ominous indication of their shakiness—but it did not stop construction. Veteran Graycoats only laughed at the skittish reserves and kept on digging. Under the picks and shovels of large fatigue parties of soldiers, slaves, and even convicts, the ramparts steadily rose. By October 6, the Confederate generals estimated, the fort would be ready to reduce Dutch Gap.[9]

October 6 would be one week too late. For the confident generals, the dancing Texans, and the boastful pickets, time had already run out by September 28. That day the "Ethiopian cohorts" were preparing to display their "belligerent propensities" and "gobble up" the Butternuts. That day David Birney left his reserve position east of Petersburg and marched to rejoin Butler. On the morrow their devastating attack would shatter the serenity of the Northside.

CHAPTER II

◆

"The Object . . . Is to Surprise and Capture Richmond"

All roads led to Richmond. Seven major arteries fanned out across the Peninsula east of the capital. Farthest south was the Osborne Turnpike, which ran due south from the city for nine miles, past Chaffin's Bluff, to Graveyard Reach on the James. Near the northern end of the turnpike the New Market Road branched southeast, then east past New Market Heights, just north of Deep Bottom, and on down the Peninsula. The main highway on the Peninsula lay farther north: the Williamsburg Road running due east from the capital. From its southern side the Darbytown and the more northerly Charles City roads headed southeast basically parallel to the New Market Road. Next to the north was the Nine Mile Road, which ran east from Richmond and then turned south into the Williamsburg Road at Seven Pines; where the Nine Mile Road bent south, the New Bridge Road branched off northeast across the Chickahominy River. The principal avenue over that stream was still farther to the Confederate left: the Mechanicsville Turnpike, which ran northeast out of Richmond toward Fredericksburg.

Several crossroads linked these main arteries. The Kingsland Road ran tortuously northeast from the southern end of the Osborne Turnpike to the New Market Road just south of New Market Heights. Immediately east of the heights the Long Bridge Road headed northeast across the Darbytown and Charles City roads to the Williamsburg Road east of the Chickahominy. And west of the heights the Varina

Road cut south from the New Market Road and ran across the
Kingsland Road to the Varina house at Aiken's Landing on the James
opposite the northern part of Bermuda Hundred. In its upper portion
the Varina Road thus paralleled the more westerly Osborne Turnpike.
A few smaller roads also linked the main east–west highways.

This extensive network afforded the planters of the Peninsula ready
access to the capital. But because it equally afforded the Yankees
access to the city, securing the roads against them was essential to securing Richmond itself. To guard against such attack, formidable
works had been constructed, so that by September 1864, five lines
stood between the capital and the enemy. Completely encircling the
city, even south of the James, were the twenty-four detached forts and
batteries of the Interior Line. Farther out, the continuous ramparts of
the Intermediate Line curved around the city from the left bank above
to the left bank below town. An offshoot of the lower end of this line
ran south between the Osborne and New Market roads to Fort Gilmer
and then bent down to the northern face of the entrenched camp on
Chaffin's Bluff, seven and a half miles south of Richmond. The camp
not only anchored the right flank of the defenses but also covered the
water batteries on the bluff. Additional protection against naval attack
came from the works on the right bank just upstream at Drewry's
Bluff and downriver at Battery Semmes and Battery Dantzler (the latter being the left flank of the Howlett Line). To permit troops readily
to cross the river without passing through Richmond, four military
bridges spanned the James above Chaffin's Bluff. A further bulwark
against land attack on the Peninsula was the Exterior Line, which ran
northeast and then north from the northeastern corner of the entrenched camp past Seven Pines all the way across the Peninsula to the
heights of the Chickahominy, where it cut back west across and beyond
Mechanicsville Pike.

Virtually all these works, except Battery Semmes and the Howlett
Line, were erected during or immediately after McClellan's abortive
Peninsular Campaign of 1862. Two more lines were dug to guard
against Grant's more pressing threat in 1864. The New Market Line
left the Exterior Line just above the entrenched camp and ran east between the New Market and Kingsland roads to New Market Heights,
north of Deep Bottom. There it turned north and extended across the
Darbytown and Charles City roads toward the Chickahominy. A still
more advanced line was begun in September to run southwest from
New Market Heights along the ridge overlooking Aiken's Landing to
Signal Hill, a mile up the James from Dutch Gap. This line was intended to play a role in the projected attack on the canal on October 6.

This more southerly line, however, was far from complete, and the New Market Line itself was little more than a trench. Rain and lack of care, moreover, had caused the unoccupied Exterior Line to deteriorate. Only at Chaffin's Bluff and in the Intermediate and Interior lines did the fortifications have strong profiles.[1]

But whatever their condition, five lines did bar the roads of the Northside to the Union army, and powerful water batteries kept the Federal navy from Richmond. Ramparts alone, however, are mere impediments to enemy advance; to become actual barriers, they need garrisons. There lay the rub. Properly manning every mile of each line would have required Lee's entire army and more. Confederate leaders never projected such extensive garrisoning. Rather, they built unmanned works to meet every contingency and then counted on occupying them with mobile reserves, tactical or strategic, to meet specific threats. They were confident that the foe could no more attack the entire line simultaneously than they could defend it.

Such an assumption had worked well in mid-1862, when Lee's large army was readily available, and also for the next two years, when the Yankees were far away and required much time to approach. But by the autumn of 1864 these safeguards no longer existed. Now Lee was away, tied down defending another city, Petersburg, and the Bluecoats were close at hand: at Dutch Gap, at Deep Bottom, and over the James on Bermuda Hundred. With Lee, moreover, were most of the mobile reserves counted on to man the capital's defenses. As late as April 1864, he had grudgingly allowed the Department of Richmond two veteran infantry brigades. But the following month, he reclaimed them; a few weeks later he took the brigade that had replaced them, and in early July he called to Petersburg the last good regiment in the city. In their place, he sent the pitiable remnant of Bushrod Johnson's Tennessee Brigade. This once-proud combat unit from the Western Front had come to Virginia only in May to win new glory but also a shroud. During its first six weeks in the East, it incurred staggering casualties, and it was too far from home to find replacements. Losses had been qualitative as well. The promotion of Johnson and the deaths of his two able successors caused command to devolve on Colonel John M. Hughs of the 25th Tennessee, a brave guerrilla raider but a poor commander, whose negligence allowed discipline to disintegrate. Five regiments totaling less than 400 men, a force with little punch, less discipline, and no leadership, was all Lee could spare to defend the capital. Yet the brigade was the best in the Department of Richmond. It was, accordingly, entrusted with holding the key forward line at Signal Hill, just a mile from the enemy at Dutch Gap and only two miles from Aiken's Landing.

If Hughs's force seemed unimpressive, the other troops in the department were even worse. The Tennesseans at least had claim to a proud tradition and first-rate status. The remaining units lacked experience and were often second-class as well. By this period of the war, the dwindling manpower pool had forced the Confederacy to draft youths of seventeen and eighteen and middle-aged men of forty-five to fifty to serve in the reserves. By taking over draft and impressment duties, guarding supply lines, and garrisoning fortified cities, such reserves individually or collectively were intended to free more able-bodied men to join the field armies. No city needed a garrison more than Richmond, and several Virginia reserve battalions now helped defend her: the 1st at Chaffin's Bluff, the 2nd near New Market Heights, and the 3rd (Chrisman's) in Manchester, across the James from the capital. Numbers the reserves added, but experience, tactical cohesion, and even stamina they lacked.

Such infantry offered little support to the artillery garrison of the city. Even worse, the gunners seemed unable to take care of themselves. Although the five Virginia heavy artillery battalions on the Peninsula—Lieutenant Colonel John Minor Maury's at Chaffin's Bluff and the 10th–19th and 18th–20th in the Intermediate Line near Richmond—had been in service a long time, duty on an inactive front had bred neglect, indifference, and inexperience. Not enough guns were on hand, and many of those available were 6-pound smoothbores rejected by field armies. Shells were poorly distributed, and even sponges were sometimes unavailable. Drill was especially lacking since the men were forbidden to practice firing their pieces lest they waste precious gunpowder and damage civilian property in the field of fire. Moreover, actual combat experience was virtually nonexistent. And to top things off, the commander of the Artillery Defenses was Lieutenant Colonel (formerly Lieutenant General) John Clifford Pemberton, a conscientious and devoted officer but one so deeply mistrusted because he had lost Vicksburg that he could hardly inspire confidence.

Pemberton at least had more reliable light artillery. Both Major Alexander W. Stark's Battalion immediately north of Chaffin's and Lieutenant Colonel Charles E. Lightfoot's Battalion in the Intermediate Line had seen action. Yet even they had sunk below combat trim. The Louisiana Guard Artillery near Chaffin's, which joined Stark by September 29 if not before, was still recuperating from the debacle it had suffered at Rappahannock Bridge nearly eleven months earlier. Lightfoot's condition was even worse, since through mid-September his horses were too feeble to pull his guns, a severe handicap for field artillery.

Only in the most easterly line, outside the Department of Richmond, did any really effective troops serve. This New Market Line confronting the Union bridgehead at Deep Bottom required first-class defenders. Two months earlier the larger part of the Army of Northern Virginia had served there; as late as mid-August, Lee had placed twelve infantry brigades in that sector. But loss of the Weldon Railroad had caused him to draw most units on the Peninsula back to Petersburg. By late September, only two of his brigades, small ones at that, remained on the Northside: Benning's Georgia Brigade under Colonel Dudley DuBose of the 15th Georgia, and Gregg's Texas Brigade under Lieutenant Colonel Frederick Bass of the 1st Texas. Two inexperienced outfits from the Department of Richmond also helped hold the New Market Line: Lieutenant Colonel Wyatt M. Elliott's 25th (City of Richmond) Virginia Battalion and Lieutenant Colonel John Guy's 2nd Virginia Reserve Battalion. The veteran cavalry brigade from the city under Brigadier General Martin W. Gary also manned the trenches and patrolled east and north of the heights. Six guns of Lieutenant Colonel Robert Archelaus Hardaway's 1st Virginia Light Artillery Battalion of Lee's army lent weight to this line, and Hardaway's other ten pieces remained in reserve where the Exterior Line crossed the New Market Road. All of these units in the eastern line reported to the senior officer present, Brigadier General John Gregg of the Texas Brigade.

These front-line forces, on the New Market Line and at Chaffin's Bluff and Signal Hill, totaled approximately 4,400 men. Another 1,500 served in the Intermediate Line near the capital, and in an emergency some 2,700 reserves, militia, and local defense troops could be turned out in the city. Barely 6,000 men regularly on duty, all in units numerically weak, many in outfits qualitatively weak as well—such was the state of Richmond's defenders as autumn began.

To make matters worse, the few forces that were available were divided between two commands. The nearly 2,900 men on the New Market Line reported to Gregg, an officer of the Army of Northern Virginia. The balance served directly under Lieutenant General Richard S. Ewell, commanding the Department of Richmond. In an emergency the lieutenant general could, of course, issue orders to the Texan, but he normally did not command the junior officer. Feeble, one-legged Dick Ewell—"Old Bald Head," he was called—had served impressively as a division commander in 1862 but disappointingly as a corps commander in the next two years and had been politely shelved in the seemingly quiescent Department of Richmond for nearly the past four months. His poor health and poor record hardly commended him for over-all command on the Peninsula. Yet the considerate Lee would not deprive the old soldier of his own departmental sector by subordinating him to a brigadier. As a result, Ewell and Gregg operated independently of each other, each concerned primarily with defending his own front.

Lee recognized the folly of dividing the command. Partially for that reason, he recalled I Corps headquarters from the Valley to resume over-all command on the Northside. The corps commander, Anderson, though commissioned almost a year after Ewell, held sufficient rank to take charge east of the capital. On September 26, the South Carolinian reached Lee's army, and two days later he received his new assignment. He planned to assume his new command on Thursday. But by the time he reached Chaffin's Bluff at 11:00 A.M. that day, it was already seven hours too late.

Although the authorities belatedly undertook to correct the divided high command, they paid little heed to Ewell's other warnings about inadequate manpower, weapons, and supplies. Generals everywhere made such complaints, and the War Department evidently paid no special attention to Ewell's forebodings. His front was certainly weak, but the danger hardly seemed pressing. After all, only 4,300 Yankees served on the Northside, almost all of whom were despised Negroes. If the threat increased, Lee could presumably rush adequate reinforcements there from Petersburg to offset it as he had done twice before in the siege—provided the Bluecoats did not strike too hard and too fast. That chance Lee had to take. He marked Petersburg as being in greater danger, and there he kept most of his troops. Ewell and Gregg would have to get by with the limited resources at hand.[2]

The Southern high command thus ignored the weakness of Richmond's defenses. The Federal planners did not. Pickets, deserters, and highly sophisticated espionage systems accurately disclosed Confederate vulnerability on the Northside. Now that the General-in-Chief was resuming the offensive in the Tidewater, Butler persuaded him to take advantage of this weakness to seize Richmond itself. The senior officer hoped, yet doubted, that the capital would fall. He nonetheless felt sure that a major drive north of the James would draw enough defenders from Petersburg to expose the supply lines to Meade's attack. Butler, in contrast, was confident he could take Richmond. On the night of September 28–29, he summoned his principal officers to explain the operation.

It was an incongruous group that gathered at army headquarters at Point of Rocks late that night. The senior subordinate was Major General Edward Ord, commanding the XVIII Army Corps. A bluff, irascible, impetuous, willful old regular, he had held the equivalent of corps command since mid-1862, yet circumstance, wounds, and illness had given him little combat experience. This late in the war he had fought in only two battles. Lack of experience, however, was offset by the regard and friendship that Grant felt for him. The lieutenant general had repeatedly advanced Ord's career and the previous July had brought him to Petersburg to take over the XVIII Corps. Now in late September Ord would finally have a chance to lead an organized corps into battle. Even this late in the war, bold leadership by personal example remained Ord's idea of battlefield command. Indeed, he advocated—though did not practice—that officers should go into combat wearing scarlet capes to make their example more conspicuous. Whether these attributes of a captain or even a brigadier suited a corps commander remained to be seen.

Everything that Ord was, the other infantry commander was not. David Bell Birney was a citizen soldier, a Philadelphia lawyer by profession. He was also something of a political general, with strong ties to the Republican Party and immediate descent from the Liberty Party candidate for President in 1840 and 1844. Cold, aloof, frequently in trouble with professional officers above him, Birney contrasted diametrically with Ord in temperament and record. But there was another difference: Birney had experience, and that experience had tempered his natural ability to earn him a distinguished combat record in the famous Red Diamond Division of the Army of the Potomac. Politics had brought him into service, and it had probably saved him from the wrath of seniors on several occasions, but it did not elevate him from colonel to major general. He earned those two stars on the field of battle and won from Grant himself selection to the coveted command of the X Army Corps in July. Birney's service in the higher office, however, had not matched his divisional command. A tendency to use his forces piecemeal marred his direction. It was too early to tell whether he had exceeded his abilities or whether he would grow with experience. One thing, however, was certain: Birney was a fighter.

The record was equally clear on the third subordinate at the meeting, Brigadier General August V. Kautz of the Cavalry Division. Like Ord, he was an American regular officer. Although born in Baden, he had grown up in Ohio since infancy and was professionally trained in the American military tradition of West Point and the Old Army. Even so, his performance in the field suggested not so much U.S. regulars but those archetypal German immigrants, Franz Sigel and Carl Schurz, who had failed to lead successful revolutions in Germany in the 1840s, then came to America, only to fail to lead successful Union operations in the 1860s. Vanity, boastfulness, and disingenuousness marked him; tactical competence did not. Although he had shown administrative ability in the West in 1863, he had performed poorly since returning to the field in April 1864. In the succeeding five months his record included three ineffective raids, one of which ended disastrously; a severe defeat at the First Battle of Deep Bottom, loss of 2,500 cattle and most of one regiment to Confederate raiders far behind Union lines, and the dubious honor of immortalizing his name in the Kautz-Gillmore Fiasco of the Ninth of June (the first and worst of many failures to capture Petersburg). Such consistent ineptitude would have led to the relief of other officers but not Kautz. He was one of a handful of regulars who tied their fortunes to Butler. Perhaps because the army commander had so few professionals on his side, he protected those he did have. Kautz thus retained his command, and now army headquarters would try him once more.

Butler repaid loyalty from his subordinates, but woe to the junior officer, regular or volunteer, who crossed him in a matter great or petty. The general's vengeance, swift and terrible, had already cost two corps commanders their jobs. Such an officer, vindictive, trouble-making, frequently inept, would be easy to dismiss as the quintessential political general, utterly devoid of military ability and owing his high command solely to partisan considerations. Politics unquestionably dominated Butler's life. The quest for office, with visions of the presidency, would lead him across the political spectrum from conservative Democrat through Radical Republican to Greenbacker. Throughout, ambition was his guide; cunning and deceit his ready tools.

Military service, too, was a useful steppingstone for his career. He entered first the peacetime Massachusetts militia, then the wartime U.S. volunteers, both times as a general. Despite singular ineptitude as a battlefield commander, his high rank and political influence kept him on duty. Shifted from one command to another, he chanced to head the Department of Virginia and North Carolina when the great campaign of 1864 began. After insisting on taking field command of the department's Army of the James, he repeatedly proceeded to hamstring its operations. He also showed little regard for its internal cohesion and constantly disrupted it by shifting officers and regiments from one command to another. His disorganizing influence, indeed, left its impression upon the Army of the James quite as much as McClellan's organizing influence had set the tone for the Army of the Potomac. Still, Butler remained at its head, the ranking subordinate in Grant's army group.

Yet to adjudge Butler as nothing but the sum of these bad traits is to distort the historical record. He was a devoted husband and father and a loyal friend. He was also loyal to favored subordinates and to his soldiers, and his solicitude for the often despised Negro troops probably surpassed that of any major Union commander. Beyond these personal qualities he showed some military aptitude. He effectively cracked down on "occupied" Confederates and dissenting Northerners in his area of command who might undermine the war effort. He also demonstrated considerable administrative ability in governing territorial departments, as opposed to field armies. Then, too, he set up an effective intelligence system. Most significantly, he was developing a sense of strategic planning that would do credit to West Pointers. A master tactician he would never be; an accomplished strategist he had not always been; but his burgeoning strategic ability and his perceptive legal mind now marked him as an officer who could plan with some skill campaigns for his subordinates to execute. This ability was reflected in the directive he gave his executive officers the night of September 28.

His plan, a remarkable sixteen-page document, detailed the object, setting, and conduct of the operation. It made clear that Richmond was the goal and that drawing troops from Petersburg was a major secondary purpose. It also revealed how weak were the Southern defenses but underestimated by placing Confederate strength at 3,000, an error due primarily to dismissing and not counting artillery battalions as ineffectual. Still, Butler had a good assessment of the identity and location of Confederate units on the Northside, and he sought to take advantage of their weakness.

His left wing, two divisions of the XVIII Corps under Ord, was to make a surprise crossing of the James at Aiken's Landing, move up the Varina Road, storm the entrenched camp, turn west to the river to cut Confederate bridges at and above Chaffin's Bluff, and then head up the Osborne Turnpike for Richmond. At the same time, the right wing—the X Corps and the Negro division of the XVIII Corps under Birney—was to advance from Deep Bottom, carry New Market Heights, and strike northwest along the New Market Road toward the city. Once Birney cleared the barrier at the heights, Kautz was to move from Deep Bottom to the Darbytown Road and then gallop for the capital. No wagons were to cross the river without Butler's permission, and even artillery was not to encumber the vanguard. Nothing was to impede the three columns; they were to march light and strike fast. The operation would be a surprise attack at 4:30 A.M. by 26,600 men against a mere handful of defenders. It seemed certain to succeed, with Richmond the prize for the Union, extra pay and promotion the bounties for the first unit to reach the city—and perhaps the presidency the reward for Butler.

Not everyone shared the army commander's enthusiasm for the plan. When Grant asked his Chief Engineer, Brigadier General John G. Barnard, to critique it, the staff officer saw little gain and much danger from crossing at Aiken's. He recommended emphasizing the strike from Deep Bottom and then moving infantry as well as cavalry to the Darbytown Road to drive for Richmond. The General-in-Chief, how-

ever, rejected this suggestion. Butler's two-pronged attack looked good
to him, and he left it to the army commander to work out the details.
Now Butler, in turn, instructed Ord, Birney, and Kautz on what must
be done. The Massachusetts man made sure they understood, for this
was his plan, and he wanted no mistakes.[3]

By the time the ranking subordinates received their orders that night,
advance preparations had already been under way for several hours.
Throughout Wednesday, their soldiers drew ammunition, and the
reserve troops on Bermuda Hundred prepared for action. After dark
the strike columns themselves began gathering. Little was required of
Kautz. His division was already massed on Jones's Neck, the arm of
Bermuda Hundred leading to Deep Bottom, and he needed only order
it to be ready to move in the morning. Even then, he was not to cross
to the already congested bridgehead until the infantry began opening
the way for him.

The left wing of that infantry spent a busier evening. Only part of
Ord's force was already in reserve: four batteries, the two brigades that
had just rejoined him from detached service plus perhaps Colonel Harrison Fairchild's brigade, which may have been relieved from the Bermuda Hundred Line on Tuesday night. His remaining brigades and
batteries, however, still held that line, confronting Major General
George E. Pickett's Division and Brigadier General Edward L.
Thomas' Brigade in the Howlett Line. Ord could not vacate that sector lest the Butternuts swarm over the Peninsula and attack him while
he crossed the river. He accordingly left a strong artillery force in his
works: L/4th and A/5th U. S. Artillery, two sections of the 7th New
York Battery, E and two sections of M/3rd New York Light Artillery,
B-D-F-G-H and part of C/1st Connecticut Heavy Artillery, A and
H/13th New York Heavy Artillery, and M/3rd Pennsylvania Heavy
Artillery. To support the gunners, he left behind the 11th Connecticut,
5th Maryland, C/13th New Hampshire, and A/9th Vermont. To help
man the works and relieve the veteran infantry already there, he moved
the 40th Massachusetts and Potter's Provisional Brigade from reserve
into the trenches at about 9:00 P.M. The 40th and Potter's own 12th
New Hampshire were seasoned, but his other five regiments—the
206th, 207th, 208th, 209th, and 211th Pennsylvania—were big new
outfits that had been in the war zone less than a month. Such inexperienced "hayfeet" always provoked the derision of veterans, and even
on the eve of battle a combat-hardened soldier could not help scoffing:

> The troops moving in are fresh soldiers from Pennsylvania; some
> of whom are said to have received $1,500.00 in bounties to in-
> duce them to enlist. One of these freshmen in war college, while we

are halted, asks Andrew J. Robbins of [Company] G if the Thirteenth [New Hampshire] are now going to a battle, and the following colloquy ensues:

Robbins, in reply, "Oh, yes; we never move without going into a
battle."

Pennsylvania, "Do you suppose that we too will be ordered into
a battle?"

Robbins, "No, indeed. They won't put you in—you cost too
much to be risked in a battle; we didn't cost anything—so they
stick us in everywhere."

Pennsylvania thinks he sees the point, and the boys have a good
laugh with which to begin the day.

Soldiers could sneer, but it was for generals to think. Clearly they
decided wisely to leave their untrained troops on the secondary front
and concentrate their veterans for the attack. Of the roughly 7,000 men
left on Bermuda Hundred—including Brigadier General Charles K.
Graham's Naval Brigade, the pontonier company, and army headquarters guards—barely 800 were first-rate combat infantry. Most of
the available manpower of the XVIII Corps—two infantry divisions,
two battalions of the 1st New York Engineers, and six light batteries—
was allocated to the column of attack, 8,000 strong.

These veterans went through the routine of evening roll call and taps
to deceive Pickett. Then after Potter relieved them, they and the units
already in reserve began converging toward the James opposite Aiken's
Landing. The march was slow, with protracted periods of rest along the
way. During the delays some men napped; others boiled coffee; still
others prayed. Clearly something important was afoot, and each man,
in his own way, prepared himself for the morrow.

Some delay was inherent in concentrating so many troops at a single
crossing site, but much was due to unexpected complications at the
river. Unlike the X Corps, Ord did not have a bridge on which to
cross. His success, indeed, depended on building a bridge to Varina
and making a surprise crossing and attack. Only after dark could the
bridge be laid. A pontonier detail had gathered seventy-seven boats
during the day and at 7:30 P.M. began assembling the bridge. Work
proceeded well until the boats neared the left bank, where an unexpectedly low tide exposed a muddy shore. Dragging pontoons over the
remaining muck delayed completion by three hours. Still, by 2:00
A.M. the bridge of sixty-seven boats, 1,320 feet long, was in place. Fatigue details then spread dirt, hay, and perhaps manure on it to deaden
the sound of the crossing.

Word now went out to Ord's well-rested infantry to resume their

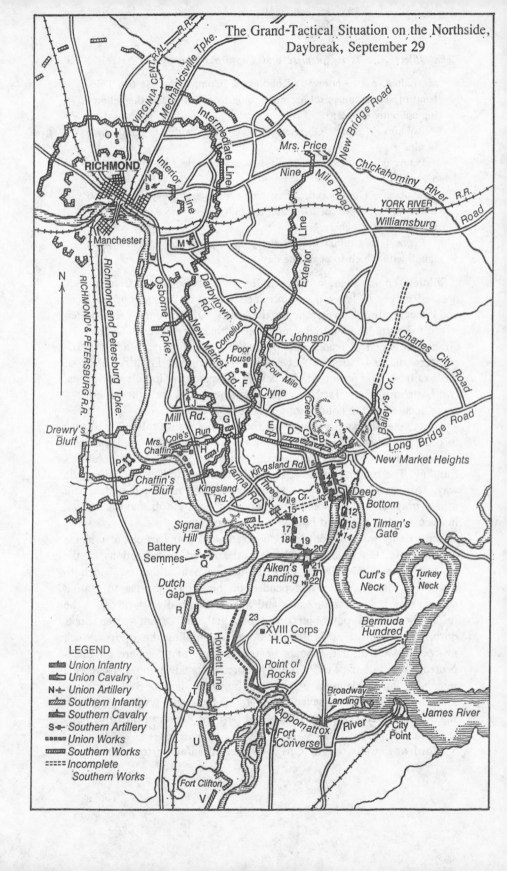

The Grand-Tactical Situation on the Northside,
Daybreak, September 29

Army of the James - BUTLER
Right Wing - BIRNEY

TERRY
1-Abbott
2-Pond
3-Plaisted

W. BIRNEY
4-W. Birney

PAINE
5-Duncan
6-Draper
7-Holman
11-Moore

FOSTER
8-Daggett
9-Pennypacker
10-Bell

Artillery
14-Jackson

Left Wing -ORD

STANNARD
15-Burnham
16-Stevens
17-Roberts

HECKMAN
18-Ripley
19-Jourdan
20-Fairchild

Engineers
21-Serrell

Artillery
22-Cook

Bermuda Hundred
23-Potter

Cavalry -KAUTZ
12-West
13-Spear

CONFEDERATE FORCES
GREGG
A - Gary
B - Bass
C - Elliott
D - DuBose
E - Guy
F - Hardaway

EWELL
K - Hughs
L - Snowden
G - Strange
H - Maury (Taylor)
J - Stark
M - Atkinson
N - Lightfoot
O - Howard

Miscellaneous

NAVAL BATTERIES
P - Terrett
Q - Goodwyn

PICKETT
R - Corse
S - Hunton
T - Steuart
U - Terry
V - Thomas

COMMENTARY

1. This map depicts the grand-tactical situation just prior to the outbreak of fighting. Birney is moving from Deep Bottom toward New Market Heights, and Ord is marching up the Varina Road toward the weak Confederate center.

2. The relative order of Terry's three brigades and of DuBose-Elliott is uncertain. The location of William Birney's brigade is also uncertain.

3. The relative order of Pickett's brigades is correct, but the length of their sectors is shown only symbolically.

march to the river. By about 3:00 A.M. his First Division began crossing. The 118th New York, soon followed by the 10th New Hampshire,
led the way. That evening both regiments had turned in their rifles for
Spencer repeaters. Now they spearheaded the advance, ready to
smother any resistance with heavy fire. But no shots contested their
progress. They reached the left bank unchallenged and fanned out
across the low ground in a skirmish line to cover the bridgehead. Now
the rest of the First Division, next the Second, and then the engineers
crossed to Aiken's. Still there was no resistance. Perhaps the dense fog
that hung over the river bottom concealed the crossing. Perhaps the
stringent security precautions, including requiring the men to hold bayonets and canteens to prevent their jangling, had been effective. Or perhaps the enemy pickets were negligent. Whatever the cause, as far as
the Northern generals could tell, the crossing was a complete surprise.
The riskiest part of the operation was now past, and prospects looked
excellent for Ord's wing to strike a telling blow.[4]

Meanwhile, downriver at Deep Bottom, Brigadier General Charles J.
Paine's Third Division of the XVIII Corps also prepared for action.
Seven of his Negro regiments were already at the post, and two more,
those Marston returned, arrived about midnight. To strengthen his
command further, he recalled extra-duty men, brigade provost guards,
even some prisoners to the ranks, although he left his divisional
provost troops behind to guard serious convicts. Some raw recruits,
too, may have joined him, while others definitely relieved veterans on
picket. Paine wanted as many men as possible on duty with their units.[5]

Paine's preparations were encouraging to Northern prospects, yet all
was not well at Deep Bottom. Midnight came and went, and still the X
Corps had not arrived from Petersburg. Butler had planned to move
the corps to Bermuda Hundred on Tuesday to give it a day's rest, but
Birney had postponed his departure until Wednesday afternoon. The
army commander was partly to blame for this delay. In his desire for
secrecy, he had originally told Birney that the move was preparatory to
the X Corps's sailing to another front on September 29. Not until the
Point of Rocks conference, Wednesday night, did the Pennsylvanian
learn that this was a ruse and that his troops were actually expected to
storm New Market Heights first thing in the morning. Why Birney misunderstood the original order to move to the Hundred and why Butler
permitted him to remain east of Petersburg are not clear. But it was
now all too apparent that the error would seriously hinder the attack.

Birney's men were already in motion by the time he learned their
true destination. His artillery and engineers left for Bermuda Hundred
by noon on September 28, but his seven infantry brigades did not start
until 3:00 P.M. He took pains to make sure the men were not encum-

bered with excess clothing or belongings, and he allowed only ammunition wagons to accompany the column. The main corps wagon trains were not to follow until 9:00 P.M. At first the march went well enough. The soldiers had greatly enjoyed their three-and-a-half-day respite from the trenches. Orders to march ended their breather, but the men did not mind, for rumors soon swept the ranks that they were marching to the James to sail to North Carolina. The X Corps, unlike Grant's other units, was not native to the Eastern Theater. Most of its service had been along the lower Atlantic coast, and only in the spring of that year had it come to Virginia. Its stay had not been pleasant; the dull, murderous monotony of trench warfare had been particularly trying. Now the prospect of leaving the Old Dominion, even if only to go fight in North Carolina, thrilled the men. Such expectations ended, seven miles into the march, as the troops turned from the City Point roads about dark to cross the pontoon bridge over the Appomattox at Broadway Landing, located about three miles west of the supply base. From the landing they wound their way for eight miles to and up Jones's Neck toward Deep Bottom. The soldiers now realized that they were marching to battle, all right, not around Wilmington but around forbidding New Market Heights, which had twice blunted their sorties out of the bridgehead.

More than dashed hopes beset the column that evening. As it reached Bermuda Hundred, darkness was falling. With sundown came all the problems of night marching, so taxing to soldiers: the need to go slowly to avoid wrong turns, fitful stops and starts, and long delays in the darkness. The men, moreover, were already tired from the long hike from Petersburg, and their heavy loads made matters worse. The ammunition wagons, even without the corps trains, also retarded movement. And to cap things off, the X Corps, especially its Second Division, was notorious for straggling. Against all these factors Birney's precautions and his subordinates' measures availed nothing. The X Corps virtually fell to pieces as it moved across Bermuda Hundred. Literally by the thousands, men fell from the ranks, proven soldiers as well as skulkers. One brigadier of the First Division later asserted that "my surgeons reported that they never saw so many men break down from sheer exhaustion as that night." One of his subordinates agreed: "Many who never fell out before dropped exhausted by the wayside." Matters were even worse in the Second Division, which lost about one third of its strength. Some men revived after a rest and were able to rejoin the colors. Unfortunately, the timetable for attacking had been cut so close that most did not get back before the corps moved into battle. Butler had expected the right wing to number over 16,000 men, including Paine's 3,800. But the X Corps was so weakened from its march that it could count only about 10,300 of a potential 12,400, including 1,200 artillerists. Even those who reached Deep Bottom, moreover, were debilitated by the ordeal. Nor did they have a day to rest as army headquarters had planned. The front of the column did not reach the *tête-de-pont* until near 2:00 A.M., and the rear straggled in ninety minutes later. Hardly had the exhausted soldiers bivouacked inside the bridgehead and in the field just to the north when orders came for them to stand to arms, ready to move by 4:00 A.M.[6]

Birney's fatigued units at Deep Bottom and Ord's much fresher forces at Aiken's Landing were not the only troops under arms in the predawn hours. Despite the lack of resistance, neither wing had crossed undetected. Both Gregg's and Hughs's outposts had discovered them and reported that the Yankees were north of the river. Hughs, accordingly, ordered his baggage to the rear and turned out his brigade on Signal Hill. The troops on New Market Heights were already eating breakfast and needed only to be alerted for action. Some Texans thought this exercise was just a false alarm or routine precaution, but their generals knew better. Gregg reportedly warned Ewell of the danger, and both officers definitely sent word to Lee. From the Howlett Line, Pickett dispatched similar tidings to Dunn's Hill. The army commander took the warnings seriously. At 6:30 A.M., before learning of the outbreak of fighting, he directed his Petersburg mobile reserve, three brigades of Major General Charles W. Field's Division, to move to the Peninsula. An hour later he ordered the Local Defense Troops in Richmond mobilized and sent to the front. And at 7:45 A.M., he requested Pickett to call on the navy to shell Unionists supposedly attacking Signal Hill. To brace Ewell for the imminent battle, Lee urged him to "take the field with all you have. Encourage the men to fight boldly."

Exhortations were fine, but Ewell needed soldiers. He had called for the Locals himself, but they required hours to turn out. Even worse, it would take all day for Field's entire command to reach the Northside. Ewell and Gregg would have to rely on the few troops originally at the front to meet the initial Federal attack. To compound the problem, they misused the meager forces at hand. The Confederates ran into difficulty Thursday morning not because they were surprised, not because they failed to take countermeasures, but because they took understandable but wrong ones. Despite limited co-operation, each general thought himself in greater danger and concentrated on defending only his own sector.

The department commander, from his field headquarters at Mrs. Chaffin's house inside the entrenched camp, evidently believed the Bluecoats were seeking to forestall his attack on Dutch Gap by capturing Signal Hill. He responded by leaving his one veteran brigade with his labor details on the hill and massing the bulk of the Chaffin's Bluff garrison on the right face of the entrenched camp astride the Osborne Turnpike. Few units were assigned farther to the left in the camp. Gregg, on the other hand, concluded that the Northerners were again attacking north from Deep Bottom, so he assembled his forces at New Market Heights. He may have ordered Hardaway's reserve artillery to reinforce the front, and he definitely turned out the troops already near the heights. Gary's cavalry left their horses behind the works and filed into the defenses, and to their right Bass's soldiers manned the works. Gregg, to be sure, may have initially dispatched the Georgians and perhaps the 2nd along the trench line toward Chaffin's, but tidings of the threat to his own sector apparently prompted him to send them back to reinforce the heights. The Texan thus massed on the far left, and the lieutenant general concentrated on the far right. With no over-all commander to co-ordinate operations, no one realized that the Varina Road, piercing their center, was left unguarded.[7]

Gregg at least managed to be in the proper place to meet the Union right wing. Just as he anticipated, it moved north from Deep Bottom straight for New Market Heights. The Yankees had arisen early. Barely had the X Corps bivouacked when word circulated shortly after 3:00 A.M. to prepare for action. No noisy drums beat the call to arms. Officers instead passed silently among the sleeping men to order them to wake up and fall in. The troops at last stripped down to fighting trim: arms, ammunition, a haversack, and one blanket. The heavy overcoats and knapsacks that had burdened their march to Deep Bottom were finally left behind. These tasks completed, some soldiers had time to boil coffee or gulp down a hasty breakfast, but those without time or provisions went hungry. To march virtually all night, to get only enough rest to feel sleepy, and then to have little or no breakfast were hardly the best preparations for battle, but there was no help for it. Birney had vowed his late departure from Petersburg would not delay the attack, and he remained determined to go into action at the scheduled time, 4:30. By about 4:00, his leading troops had formed ranks and were moving out. Within an hour, his reserve units were on the march, too.

The right wing advanced in three columns. Brevet Major General Alfred H. Terry's First Division, X Corps, marched northward up the main road from Deep Bottom. Farther west, Brigadier General William Birney's First Brigade, Third Division, X Corps (Negro troops), apparently moved north along a farm lane and then cut eastward to fall in behind Terry. On the left Paine, followed by Brigadier General Robert S. Foster's Second Division, X Corps, headed up the Grover House Road. The seven companies of the 4th Massachusetts Cavalry attached

to Birney and Paine accompanied the right wing, but neither Kautz's
horsemen nor most of Lieutenant Colonel Richard H. Jackson's X
Corps Artillery Brigade (possibly excepting M/1st U. S. Artillery) yet
crossed the river from Jones's Neck. The 17th New York Battery and
one section of M/3rd New York Light Artillery of Paine's command
also remained at Deep Bottom, along with most of Paine's recruits and
the 203rd Pennsylvania. This large but inexperienced regiment had
joined Foster only two days earlier and was not yet ready for the field.
New Market Heights was clearly no place for raw troops nor, for that
matter, for cavalry and artillery. Butler's orders made clear that infantry alone was to storm the position without awaiting artillery support.

These instructions specified the composition of Birney's attack. Terrain, in turn, governed its implementation. New Market Heights and
Four Mile Creek were the key features of the battlefield. The creek
rose on both sides of the Darbytown Road near the Exterior Line and
flowed south past the western end of the heights, across the New
Market Road, through Gregg's trenches, then through a difficult but
not impassable swamp to a point approximately five hundred yards
north of the upper portion of the Kingsland Road. There it turned east-
southeast through a wooded, overgrown ravine roughly parallel to the
two roads for the length of the battlefield. On the eastern edge of the
field it joined Bailey's Creek to form the wide, impenetrably swampy
creek mouth of Deep Bottom. From the east–west ravine the mostly
open ground sloped gently northward to the New Market Road. Immediately north of that highway loomed New Market Heights. From another Signal Hill, the western end of the heights where the creek
crossed the road on the southwest, to the southeastern corner opposite
the northern end of the Kingsland Road, the mile-long massif rose
forty to fifty feet in a steep but not unclimbable slope. From the road
junction an unassailably precipitous escarpment pulled away from the
highway to run a mile northeast to Camp Holly, overlooking a plain
extending east to Bailey's Creek and the southern end of the Long
Bridge Road.

Because this virtual cliff was so clearly invulnerable, previous Federal expeditions had moved farther north on the Darbytown Road to
try to flank its left. This time, however, army headquarters sought to
turn its right, west of the heights, thus not only bypassing the obstacle
but also cutting off Gregg's forces. Birney, therefore, ordered his right
to fix the Confederates in place while his left delivered the main blow.
To hold the right, Terry formed his entire division in line of battle on
reaching the Kingsland Road: Colonel Joseph C. Abbott's Second
Brigade, Colonel Francis B. Pond's First Brigade, and Colonel Harris M. Plaisted's Third Brigade, from left to right. Such a formation,
stretching as far east as the lower portion of Four Mile Creek, was

well suited to feinting along a broad front but clearly lacked the depth to storm fortifications. Even the subsequent arrival of William Birney, whose men deployed in brigade column of battalions southward from the Kingsland Road behind the First Division, did not appreciably enhance Terry's ability to attack. Rather, responsibility for taking the position rested with the heavy columns massed in depth farther left near the Grover House Road.

Surprisingly, the most inexperienced of all seventeen divisions in Grant's army group spearheaded those columns. Paine's command had never fought together as a unit, and his brigades separately had taken part in only three small battles and two big skirmishes. Nor were the Negroes' leaders exceptionally qualified. Although some of their briga-diers were potentially able combat commanders, Paine himself was me-diocre and relatively inexperienced. He had never commanded a divi-sion in battle and had not even led a brigade since the Second Teche Campaign. He was, admittedly, brave and conscientious. Despite debili-tating malaria, he dragged himself out to lead his troops this day. But beyond courage and a sense of duty, higher arts of command eluded him. He held high position not so much through merit as through But-ler's favoritism. Butler had put him in command, and now Butler gave him the key assignment. The major general selected this untried divi-sion not merely because it was fresh and, for the most part, well rested, but also because it was Negro. Unlike many Northern generals who viewed USCTs as uniformed ditchdiggers, Butler regarded them as combat soldiers and now gave them a chance to prove themselves in battle. Birney, who had seen his brother's black brigade fight well in August, readily adopted Butler's "suggestion" that Paine lead the at-tack.

The Negroes' debut was not auspicious. Although their skirmishers easily drove Confederate videttes across the Kingsland Road to Gregg's main picket line in the east–west ravine of Four Mile Creek, problems began once Paine's main body reached that road. Had he continued straight north, west of the creek, he would have encountered fewer ob-stacles and could have cut off the heights as intended. Instead, his lead brigade, Colonel Samuel Duncan's Third, deployed in two lines of bat-tle on the road (the 4th USCT in front, the 6th USCT echeloned to the left rear), then shifted east to narrow the gap between himself and Terry. Reducing the gap seemed desirable, but it hardly offset the resulting disadvantage of forcing Duncan to attack across the east–west portion of the creek and then move up the swampy left bank straight toward the heights.

Birney himself may have ordered this shift, but Paine must bear re-sponsibility for scattering his division. For one thing, he left his

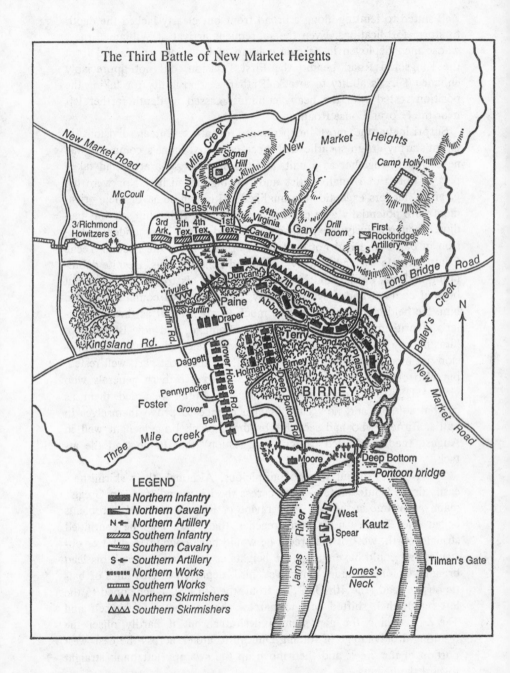

The Third Battle of New Market Heights

LEGEND
- Northern Infantry
- Northern Cavalry
- N← Northern Artillery
- Southern Infantry
- Southern Cavalry
- S← Southern Artillery
- Northern Works
- Southern Works
- ▲▲▲▲ Northern Skirmishers
- △△△△ Southern Skirmishers

skirmishers north of the upper end of the Grover House Road. Behind them, he massed Colonel Alonzo Draper's Second Brigade in column of companies just north of the Kingsland Road. Yet Draper's men were given so little to do that they lay down waiting for something to happen. Paine's rear brigade, Colonel John Holman's First, next moved eastward and massed in brigade column of divisions behind Duncan's center. This potential reserve, however, received no mission in the original attack. The only reinforcement Paine gave Duncan was the unbrigaded 2nd USCT Cavalry (dismounted) to skirmish beyond his right. The Second Division also did no more than mass in column of battalions along the Grover House Road south from the Kingsland Road. Thus six of Paine's regiments and all thirteen of Foster's remained in the rear. Only two regiments plus skirmishers mounted the attack. Echelon by echelon, the Federal striking force was falling apart. By army and wings, by columns and divisions, the Yankees had moved toward their targets. But at the actual point of attack, only one small brigade—roughly 1,100 men, nearly half of them skirmishers—was being committed against a position that had twice before defied two army corps.[8]

Those works, moreover, were no less formidable than they had been in July and August. Two lines of abatis—the first slashing, and behind it, to the north, chevaux-de-frise—obstructed the approach from the ravine. The shallow parapet itself ran along the crest of the slope just south of the New Market Road to afford sweeping fire over the entire field. The summit of the heights was reserved for artillery. There the First Rockbridge Artillery now took position in the redoubt at its

COMMENTARY

1. This map shows the tactical situation about 5:30 A.M., when Duncan launched the first attack. Skirmishers of the Third Division, XVIII Corps, are shown advancing on both of his flanks, and Draper is represented making his brief advance past Buffin's house. Draper subsequently moved eastward and attacked about where Duncan is shown. The 22nd USCT (the head of Holman's column) later skirmished west of Four Mile Creek and northeast of Buffin's house.

2. The positions of Pond and Holman are thought but not known to be correct.

3. Troops in the Confederate works are shown strung out in open order. The relative order but not necessarily the sectors of Bass's regiments seem correct, but the position of Gary's regiments is not certain. Elliott, too, was probably engaged, but his position is not known. DuBose's men, farther west, marched and countermarched but did not see action here.

4. Regimental deployment of Duncan's and Abbott's brigades is discussed in the text.

southeastern corner. Some of Gary's men supported the battery on the summit, but most of his three regiments manned the trenches facing Terry. To the troopers' right, the 1st Texas defended the sector where Four Mile Creek flowed through the works opposite Duncan, and Bass's remaining three regiments (the 4th and 5th Texas and 3rd Arkansas, left to right) plus Elliott's battalion prolonged the line westward confronting Draper. These were all the troops on hand. DuBose and Guy had not yet arrived; Hardaway, though on the march, never would reach the front; and the section of the Third Richmond Howitzers farther right along the trench at McCoull's House was too far west to affect the fighting. Gregg himself may have been at his headquarters behind his far right near the entrenched camp, in which case Gary presumably took charge at the heights. Their available forces numbered less than 1,800 men, strung out along the works more like a skirmish line than a line of battle. The right of the line could field only one man every fifteen feet; even on the threatened center, the 1st Texas could concentrate no more than one man every six feet. Such a weak command seemed incapable of withstanding a full-scale attack. Still, the infantry had always ranked among the best in the Army of Northern Virginia, and the cavalry had served well in the four months it had been brigaded together. Such forces were not about to yield their position without a fight.

The time for fighting was at hand. In the cool of the dying night, the Texans finished breakfast and awaited action. The Yankees came with the sun. The crackle of musketry south of the Kingsland Road near 5:00 A.M. heralded their advance. For a time skirmishing stabilized along the ravine, evidently as Birney took time to deploy. Then his voltigeurs cleared out the ravine, too. Behind them at least part of his line of battle became visible on the ridge overlooking the creek. About sunrise, 5:30, Duncan's line advanced down the slope from this array, as if to attack up the creek toward Bass's left. There was no doubt now: The Bluecoats were coming. The Texans closed their haversacks, picked up their rifles, and manned the parapets.[9]

Except for the retreating pickets, however, Bass's veterans held their fire until their targets, still indistinct in the lingering fog, came more squarely into range. The Negroes, too—their guns loaded but uncapped—did not break the momentum of their charge to open fire. For a few minutes an oppressive stillness hung over the field. Down to the creek came the Federals; still the Confederates reserved their fire. Over the stream the black soldiers splashed and dressed ranks on the other side—still no resistance. Then out of the ravine and up the sloping field they went, into the abatis. A few men followed picket paths through the slashing; others waited for pioneers to hack openings; and still others struggled over the obstructions. This was the moment the Graycoats had awaited. With the Northerners tangled in the abatis, the Texans in the trenches and the battery on the heights opened fire with devastating effect. Bass, unconcerned about the feeble demonstration by black skirmishers west of the creek, drew in his right to reinforce the 1st Texas facing Duncan. Gary, moreover, apparently advanced his most westerly regiment, the 24th Virginia Cavalry, to enfilade the Union right. These battle-tested Confederates were hard fighters under any circumstances, but their hatred of USCTs intensified their resistance. Their massed firing blasted the black brigade apart. Caught helplessly in the abatis, the Negroes suffered terrible casualties. White officers and black sergeants set courageous examples for their men, only to sacrifice themselves in vain. Duncan himself went down with four wounds. Of the handful who made it through the slashing, most were cut down before getting beyond the frise. The remnant who got through the palisade, in turn, bogged down in the marsh along the creek and came under enfilading fire from the west. Still, with incredible bravery, the vanguard pressed up the creek and penetrated the Southern works. Too many bleeding bodies lay upon the field, too few survivors remained, however, for this advance party to have any chance. From both flanks Bass's men swarmed upon them. Many of the Negroes were killed; others surrendered. Some were accepted as prisoners, but others, by the Southerners' own assertion, were then murdered.

While the vanguard was being wiped out, the rest of the Third Brigade, now under Colonel John Ames of the 6th USCT, crumbled and withdrew, a few companies in good order, more in total rout. Most men made it to the safety of the ravine, but some flung themselves on the ground seeking cover in the undulations of the earth, only to provide sport for Confederate marksmen. A few even opted for the uncertain fate of prisoner of war rather than risk further exposure. In just forty minutes the Negroes had been repulsed with staggering casualties. They had failed to storm the works and had, themselves, been destroyed as a tactical brigade for the rest of the day. Well might a survivor mourn, "It was a perfectly terrible encounter. . . . we were all cut to pieces."

To make matters worse, Duncan had been virtually abandoned to his fate. Paine had not committed the supporting First Brigade at all and had moved the Second Brigade too late to do any good. During the charge Draper had reformed ranks in brigade line of company columns and advanced toward a small east–west tributary emptying into the southwestern bend of the creek. Before he could reach the enemy pickets along the stream, let alone the Southern works, he had to shift east to the ravine to cover Ames's retreat. In Draper's former place west of the creek, Holman now threw out the 22nd USCT as voltigeurs. To the east, Terry, too, provided no more than skirmishing support. He had arrived later than the Negro division and had not intended to storm the heights anyway. Clearing out the ravine, posting his main body there under cover from the overshooting Virginia artillery, and sending skirmishers ahead to annoy Gary were all the First Division had to do. Its limited mission, however, allowed it to give Paine little support. For a time, Abbott even feared that his own left was threatened, although the advancing Butternuts were probably only Texans ranging over the field to gather arms and plunder the fallen in the wake of Duncan's defeat.[10]

One division repulsed, another deliberately waiting, two others in reserve, so little action that Confederates could roam the field looting —all this boded ill for the success of Butler's grand onslaught. The night before, he had confidently assured his corps commanders, that "if we are not mistaken in the force opposed to us, and if we are not we shall learn it very early, that force . . . need give us no alarm or trouble." Now it appeared that he was mistaken—and was learning it very early. Birney, however, would not abandon the offensive or even immobilize his column by committing his brother and Foster. The wing commander instead persisted in the original plan of taking the works with his leading divisions. Terry would press Gary more vigorously, and Paine would again deliver the main blow against Bass.

Again, too, Paine threw in his forces piecemeal. This time Draper was to charge, covered on his left by the 22nd USCT as skirmishers west of the creek but unsupported by Holman's other two regiments. Even without such help Draper gave himself greater depth than the Third Brigade. He deployed his three regiments—the 5th, 36th, and 38th USCT—in brigade line of regimental columns of division, six companies wide, ten ranks deep. Once his men were ready, he moved out of the ravine, up the left bank, over the field where Duncan had attacked. Southern artillery, which had played on him all along, now intensified its fire. To make matters worse, the fog had lifted by now, so Bass's men could see to fire on him right away. The USCTs braved this fire, broke into a charge, and pressed up the slope. But with their axis of advance too far west, they bogged down in the marshes along a rivulet of the creek. Hardly had they floundered through it when they ran into the abatis. Brought to a standstill under Bass's deadly shooting, the brigade disintegrated into an armed mob that could not resist the temptation to return a heavy but ineffectual fire. Draper realized that engaging in a firefight with entrenched opponents would be fatal, but in the din, delay, and death of battle, his efforts to resume the charge went unheard or unheeded. Once more the small strike force appeared left to its fate. Terry did little more than tie down Gary, and Holman's main body did nothing at all. Even the 22nd USCT could only cross the tributary and keep abreast of the Second Brigade, small gain now that much of DuBose's command had at last arrived behind Bass's right. It seemed that Draper would soon suffer Duncan's fate.

For what Draper himself called "half an hour of terrible suspense," his men bravely stood up to the telling fire. But as the sun rose higher into the sky, Confederate fire slackened. Battered and bloody as they were, the USCTs responded by resuming the charge. At last a few men heeded their officers' appeals to run forward yelling; others took up the battle cry, and then the whole brigade advanced. Through the abatis they went, then through the frise. At last they crowned the parapet itself and drove off the few remaining defenders. Most Confederates still in the area had withdrawn atop New Market Heights once the frise was penetrated. The enraged Negroes followed them there and seized the summit itself.

Farther west, the 22nd USCT consolidated into line of battle, pressed over the parapet, and reached the New Market Road. Part of the regiment then swept leftward along the trench line toward Mc-Coull's. The section of the Third Richmond Howitzers defended the position there for a time but soon withdrew. The First Rockbridge Artillery also abandoned the forward line as Terry's skirmishers, advancing simultaneously with Draper's renewed charge, swept over the trench. Then, to mask their weakness with boldness, the 3rd New Hampshire of Abbott and the 24th Massachusetts of Plaisted continued up the height toward the gunners. The battery escaped only minutes before the New Englanders poured over the crest. The Hampshiremen did not get the cannons, but they did capture a local civilian, Captain Luther Libby, whom they regarded as the owner of the building used for Libby Prison. In retaliation, the unfortunate fellow was soon incarcerated in Old Capitol Prison, from which, one wag concluded, he would not soon be "libbyrated." The time for vengeance would come later, though. Right now the Yankees had to look to their own security, lest they wind up in Libby themselves. For a time Terry's skirmishers and Draper's troops took up defensive positions to ward off any counterattack from the threatening Confederate horsemen nearby. But Gary soon rode off, and the Federals retained undisputed possession of the field. The barrier to Birney's wing, which had blocked the Union advance for over three months, was in Northern hands at last.[11]

The occupation of New Market Heights was an important tactical accomplishment and strategic breakthrough. Beyond that, the victory has come down to the present day as a great achievement of black soldiers proving themselves as fighting men. Ecstatic officers of the USCTs effused over their success; white Northern soldiers on the field acknowledged it; and even some of Bass's men begrudged the Negroes praise. Chief promoter of the legend was Ben Butler himself, who trumpeted the event for the rest of his life. Postwar historians of the black troops gladly picked up the theme, and modern writers have willingly and uncritically accepted it. Certainly nothing can detract from the heroism of Duncan's vanguard that reached the trench or from the valor of Draper's men who resumed the advance after suffering so severely. But to go beyond citing physical courage and allege that the blacks won a major tactical victory over the vaunted Texas Brigade belies the historical record. Bass clearly stopped them cold as long as he chose to contest the field, and their valor brought them only staggering casualties, not victory. By the time they overran the works, Bass's, Elliott's, and DuBose's main bodies were already gone, and only the artillery and Gary's weak rear guard of cavalry and infantry remained. The main body's withdrawal was what eased the resistance and permitted the advance to resume. Far from overwhelming a determined foe, Draper in effect charged into a virtually abandoned position and simply chased off a small rear guard from a position already conceded to him.

Why did the Southern infantry abandon a position they had initially held so successfully? The answer was simple. Gregg ordered them to rush back to Chaffin's farm as fast as possible. He needed them there because he had at last learned that Edward Ord was striking up the Varina Road against the Confederates' weak center.[12]

While Birney had battled at New Market Heights, the Federal left wing had also been busy. Ord's whole force had assembled in one long column of divisions around Aiken's Landing in the early morning. Just before daylight he launched his drive up the Varina Road. The 118th New York, the 10th New Hampshire, and the First Division sharpshooter battalion, all under the fiery Colonel Michael Donohoe of the 10th, still led the way as skirmishers. Cautiously the light infantry felt its way across the cornfield in the lingering darkness. As they neared the ridge a mile inland from the landing, pickets from the 17th–23rd Tennessee atop it at last challenged them. The Confederates' muzzleloaders, however, proved no match for the Yankees' repeaters. Donohoe's force now pressed up the slope and handily cleared the ridge.

Just as quickly, the Federals took advantage of their initial success. "Heave after them—double quick!" roared burly Brigadier General Hiram Burnham, corps officer of the day and commander of the leading Second Brigade. And heave after them Donohoe did. For two miles, he chased the Southerners up the Varina Road. Time and again they tried to rally; Hughs himself may have come to help steady them.

Time and again Donohoe drove them. Their outposts, their main line, their picket camp itself successively fell into his hands. A few New Yorkers dropped out at the camp to drink the coffee left steaming, but most Federals continued advancing. Only upon reaching the far edge of the woods northwest of Henry Cox's house did they finally halt to permit Ord's main body, 400 yards back, to catch up. Donohoe's rapid drive got the left wing off to a good start. It denied the Confederates time to deploy to meet it, and it outflanked and bade fair to isolate Hughs's main body on Signal Hill. But now more than skirmishers were needed. A mile away, on the far side of the open field that Donohoe had just reached, loomed the ramparts of Ewell's main line.[13]

The Varina Road continued northwest across the field for 1,300 yards, then bent sharply north and passed through the Exterior Line another 1,000 yards farther on. Four hundred yards southeast of the bend a lane, bordered on each side by a heavy rail fence, ran west 600 yards to Childrey's farmyard. Open, plowed fields surrounded the farmhouse. Farther north an inconsequential branch of the headwaters of Three Mile Creek flowed east across the road at the base of the ridge that the Exterior Line crowned. An abatis also protected this line, though not the entrenched camp, and a few chopped trees, left hanging to their stumps, cluttered the field farther south. Except for these minor barriers, the open field was unobstructed.

The woods where Donohoe took position and the forested marshes along the main course of Three Mile Creek farther north fringed the eastern border of the field. The Confederate works, in turn, defined the field's northern and western faces. In this area the far right of the Exterior Line bent sharply west from its main north–south axis and ran for half a mile along the northern end of the field to the entrenched camp. Battery No. 11 on the Varina Road and Battery No. 10 farther west lent weight to this line. Even stronger were the redoubts on the camp's eastern face along the field's western edge. About 200 yards south of the camp's northeastern corner, Battery No. 9, or Fort Harrison, jutted east from the camp wall, atop a hill. A small flèche enfiladed both curtain and fort wall where the two ramparts joined and helped cover the fort's sally port there. The fort's left flank, extending east from the gate, commanded all the ground northeastward to the Exterior Line. Harrison's face then bent back southwest along the hillcrest at a slightly acute angle from the left flank in order to rake the more southerly portion of the Varina Road emerging from the woods near Cox's. Where the face joined Battery No. 8, Harrison's right flank cut back rearward behind that redoubt and ran across the hilltop in two segments until it terminated at the upper end of the so-called Diagonal Line. No wall or palisade closed the fort's gorge; no frise strengthened its front; no glacis denied the enemy blind spots in the terrain below the hill. The strength of the fort lay only in a dry moat ringing the left flank and face and in its own sturdy uncrenelated ramparts that towered eighteen feet above the moat floor. No citadel existed within the fort, but the Great Traverse did divide it into smaller northern and larger southern portions. Immediately south of the fort's face and still atop the hill, Battery No. 8 protruded in the shape of a right-flanked demibastion. Just right of it, in turn, was little Battery No. 7. All three works atop the hill may justifiably be termed the Fort Harrison complex. To the Yankees gathering across the field, they appeared as one large, double-bastioned fort.

From No. 7 the curtain descended the hill and ran south nearly three quarters of a mile, past a bastion-shaped salient and Battery No. 6 to Battery No. 5 at Mountcastle's. There it turned perpendicularly westward for 1,000 yards through Batteries No. 4 and 3 to Battery No. 2, or Fort Maury, located on a hill immediately west of the Osborne Turnpike. The works north of Battery No. 5 thus enfiladed the left of the Varina Road, and those west of that redoubt commanded the right of the turnpike. Despite the advantages of such a position, the Butternuts apparently felt it vulnerable to breaching at its sharp southeastern salient. They, therefore, placed their main reliance on the interior Diagonal Line running almost straight southwest from Fort Harrison to Fort Maury. Three redoubts—Battery x, the double-bastioned White Battery, and Fort Hoke—strengthened this inner line, from northeast to southwest.

From the juncture of the two walls at Fort Maury, the curtain continued west about 333 yards to the so-called Jones's Salient and then another 100 yards to Chaffin's Bluff itself. Along the bluff for a mile upriver thirteen water batteries stood guard against naval attack. Then the upper camp wall, facing west and mostly north, ran north, northeast, and east through six batteries and eleven salients for nearly two miles back across the Osborne Turnpike to Fort Johnson. From Johnson the lower end of the Intermediate Line branched off north to Fort Gilmer, and the final sector of camp wall extended southeast half a mile through a little lunette to the northeast corner of the camp, where the Exterior Line abutted just above Fort Harrison. Within the vast cleared and wooded tracts of Chaffin's farm, which the camp enclosed, there was virtually no inner defense line, since the Diagonal Line was really the main line of resistance. The only available works were little detached Battery No. 1 on a hill behind Fort Maury plus an old, unrefused, largely useless four-battery trench running south half a mile from the northern wall and facing east toward the turnpike.[14]

The lack of interior defenses, of course, posed only a hypothetical problem to a large, resolute, well-deployed garrison manning the front line. Unfortunately for the Confederates, none of these qualities characterized the camp's defenders. Although some were brave, most so lacked combat experience that their reliability was questionable. Their lack of adequate numbers was even more obvious, and to make matters worse, such forces as were available were maldistributed. A large part of Maury's artillery battalion was already detached on fatigue duty on Signal Hill. Instead of recalling it, Ewell apparently reinforced it, Thursday morning, in the belief that the Yankees threatened the hill. Probably at his orders, moreover, many of the 200 artillerists remaining in camp concentrated on the right, covering the turnpike, rather than on the left near Fort Harrison. News of the enemy crossing caused the permanent garrison to assemble near the turnpike at 5:00 A.M. Major Richard Cornelius Taylor, commanding the battalion in Maury's temporary absence, then led it along the works, scattering weak detachments at key spots. Captain Andrew Judson Jones's Pamunkey Artillery held the far right in Jones's Salient; Lieutenant John E. Winder's Norfolk Howitzers and Captain Cornelius Tacitus Allen's Lunenburg Artillery respectively manned the White Battery and Battery x and presumably Forts Hoke and Maury; Lieutenant John Guerrant's Goochland Artillery entered the Fort Harrison complex; and finally Lieutenant Lemuel Davis' James City Artillery hurried on to Batteries No. 10 and 11 on the Exterior Line.

Taylor initially ordered his men to spread out along the ramparts and defend the camp with their muskets. However, what he beheld from Fort Harrison changed his mind. In Cox's woods across the way, hordes of Yankees could be seen massing. And nearer still, Childrey's field teemed with Federal voltigeurs, before whose relentless push Hughs's pickets, exhausted and nearly out of ammunition, were now retiring into the sally port. At last, the Confederate command realized that the upper part of the camp, not Signal Hill, was Ord's objective. This understanding came too late. Over half of Taylor's battalion was too far south to do any good, and Allen in Battery x and Davis on the Exterior Line could provide only minimal support. Guerrant's thirty-five men were the only artillerists available to defend Fort Harrison, and all Taylor could now do was to order them to man its guns.

Only then—again too late—did he discover the price of long months of neglect. Many of the big cannons originally at Chaffin's had been transferred to Petersburg during the summer; only belatedly had Lee begun replacing them. Many of the pieces then available were puny 6-pounders, discarded by the field armies. Fort Harrison fared better than most of Taylor's other works in that regard. Its six or seven pieces plus the two or three in adjacent Battery No. 8, a total of nine, numbered only two such little guns. The other seven cannons in the complex included two 8-inch columbiads, one 100-pounder Parrott, one 40-pounder, one or two 32-pounders, and one 30-pounder. The problem now facing the major was not the caliber but the usability of his guns. He discovered that most of their vents were clogged or even spiked. Not more than four of his pieces were operable. Such few as did work, though, the Goochlanders quickly loaded in a desperate effort to stop the XVIII Corps. Davis meantime was denied even that opportunity. His guns worked, all right; the problem was that his ammunition was too large to fit the bores of two of his four pieces.

As the cannoneers discovered these shortcomings, Gregg, who was near the western end of the Exterior Line, took steps to provide infantry support. Now that he at last perceived where the danger lay, he hastened couriers to recall his own troops from the New Market Line. Those forces, however, required much time to arrive; many, indeed, were already engaged with Birney. In the meanwhile, the Texan would have to make do with the few forces already at hand. He duly ordered the nearby 1st Virginia Reserve Battalion (apparently temporarily commanded by Major James Strange) to string out at ten-foot intervals along the upper camp wall and the Exterior Line between Batteries No. 9 and 11. Hughs's skirmishers and the 63rd Tennessee also took position in that sector, a few in Fort Harrison, most of them along the camp curtain north of the sally port. Meantime, five of the seven companies of Major James Moore's battalion of the 17th Georgia of DuBose's brigade, then in the camp to pick up a slave and convict-labor detail, disregarded Gregg's prebattle instructions to reinforce the heights now that they learned where the real threat was. On their own initiative, they entered Fort Harrison and operated a 32-pounder as well as provided infantry support. All these foot soldiers and gunners from Jones's Salient to Battery No. 11 totaled roughly 800 men; only one fourth of them were available in the threatened sector around Fort Harrison. Against this small force massed 8,000 Bluecoats. The consequences of divided Southern command misallocating the few available units to each flank and neglecting the center now became all too apparent.[15]

The Unionists, of course, remained unaware of these errors, but their intelligence reports had marked this sector as weak and vulnerable to attack. All they had to determine was how and where to strike. Ord, Brigadier General George J. Stannard commanding his First Division, and Stannard's three brigadiers now spent ten to fifteen minutes reconnoitering across Childrey's field while their main body massed in Cox's woods and Donohoe's skirmishers ranged ahead to drive Hughs into the entrenched camp. The officers readily marked Fort Harrison—with artillery fire already coming from its strongly profiled ramparts atop its commanding position—as the main Confederate stronghold. To the corps commander it was an obstacle to be masked, presumably while his force continued up the Varina Road toward Battery No. 11. Exercising the option army headquarters gave him the previous evening, he now sent Colonel Edward W. Serrell to bring up his two battalions of the 1st New York Engineers to entrench the corps's left flank. Waiting for Serrell's men to move from the rear to the head of the column would have seriously, perhaps fatally, delayed the attack. However, Ord, reportedly at Stannard's urging, soon changed his mind, dispensed with the engineers, and decided to assault Fort Harrison itself. Even so—this time, in disregard of Butler's direct orders—he determined to wait until his Second Division could take part. Again Stannard remonstrated. The ablest citizen soldier Vermont sent to the war, with an impressive combat record as a brigadier at Gettysburg and Petersburg, he felt little hesitancy about leading a division in battle for the first time. To him Fort Harrison was not a barrier but a key which, if quickly captured, would give control of the whole outer line. He urged attacking it right away with his own division, without wasting precious time awaiting the rear of the column. Finally, Ord consented.

The commanders returned from Childrey's field to find the First Division already deployed pursuant to Stannard's instructions, awaiting their orders. Donohoe's voltigeurs, now reinforced in the field by one company of the 188th Pennsylvania, two of the 8th Connecticut, and six or seven of the 21st Connecticut, continued skirmishing for the strike force. Behind them the rest of Burnham's Second Brigade formed the spearhead: the 96th New York in line of battle astride the Varina Road, the 8th Connecticut behind the 96th's center in column of divisions. To Burnham's left rear, just left of the road, the four regiments of Colonel Aaron F. Stevens's First Brigade ployed in brigade column of divisions: the 13th New Hampshire and 81st, 98th, and 139th New York, front to rear. Colonel Samuel H. Roberts' Third Brigade massed similarly to Stevens in Burnham's right rear, immediately right of the road. The 21st Connecticut originally led the brigade to Cox's, but now that most of it had taken position next to the 118th on Donohoe's left flank, Roberts replaced it in the van with the 58th Pennsylvania, which formed into line rather than column. The rest of the brigade was in column of divisions, though—probably the 188th, the 92nd New York, and the rest of the 21st, front to rear. Stannard thus forged a mighty bolt, rarely more than four companies wide and as much as fifty ranks deep, aimed straight for the face of Fort Harrison. Ord meantime directed Brigadier General Charles A. Heckman's Second Division, on nearing the front, to extend north through Cox's

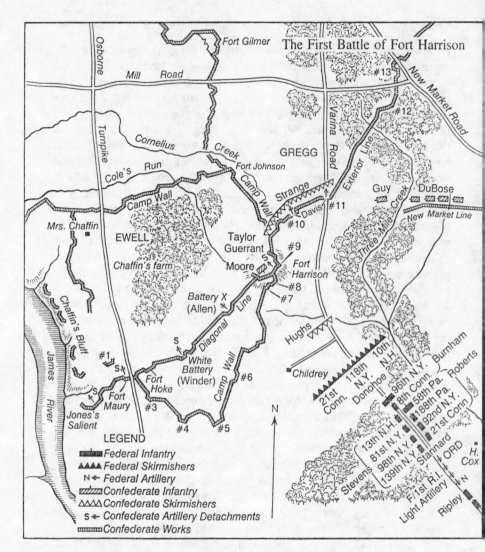

The First Battle of Fort Harrison

LEGEND

Federal Infantry
Federal Skirmishers
N Federal Artillery
Confederate Infantry
Confederate Skirmishers
S Confederate Artillery Detachments
Confederate Works

COMMENTARY

1. This diagram shows the tactical situation just before Stannard attacked. The First Division has formed column in the woods northwest of Cox's and is ready to advance. Donohoe's skirmishers are ranging over Childrey's field, and the Tennesseans are retiring into the works at and around Fort Harrison. Taylor has strung out his artillerists from Jones's Salient to Battery No. 11 and is now preparing to defend Fort Harrison. Gregg is rushing forward reinforcements from the New Market Line. Heckman's vanguard is just reaching Cox's farm.

2. In Roberts' brigade, the relative order of the 92nd New York and 188th Pennsylvania, as shown, is probable but not definite.

3. The relative position of two companies of the 8th Connecticut on Donohoe's skirmish line is not known.

woods and then advance in Stannard's right rear to attack Harrison's left flank. The First Division, however, no longer awaited Heckman's arrival. Shortly after 6:00, it moved off on its own.[16]

During the halt Stannard's men had fixed bayonets and had learned of the rewards army headquarters promised the first unit into Richmond. Now his orders to advance brought a sense of relief. Difficult as charging prepared defenses would be, waiting helplessly in the woods under enemy fire was worse, and the soldiers welcomed the opportunity to fight back. Donohoe still led the way, but since no enemy skirmishers remained outside the camp, he dropped off leftward at Childrey's lane to snipe and to cover Stannard's southern flank. The voltigeurs' departure unmasked the main body, which now pressed on toward the fort. Slowly, surely, with guns at the right shoulder shift as if on parade, the Bluecoats crossed the field. The fences along Childrey's lane proved no barrier and were easily thrown down. In the absence of real abatis, the few chopped trees in the field offered little obstacle, either. For that matter, Confederate shelling itself initially caused little delay. The inexperienced Goochlanders uniformly overshot the First Division back in the woods, and now their practice seemed no better. Twice the big 8-inch columbiad in the fort's left salient fired at the column; twice its shells flew harmlessly overhead. Such poor shooting brought only howls of scornful laughter from the Yankees. Laughing stopped with the third shot. It cut right through Roberts' brigade and struck down thirteen men. Now the Virginians had the range. Guerrant in the fort, Allen to the west, and Davis to the north blasted the column front and flank. The Federals were taking losses now—heavy losses, officers and men alike. Grim determination replaced earlier derision, and the division moved steadily on.

Its advance seemed too slow for Ord, Stannard, and Burnham viewing it from Cox's woods. Its pace, they felt, kept it exposed to enemy fire too long and also gave the Butternuts time to reinforce Fort Harrison. The generals sped staff officers to urge Stevens and Roberts, the ranking officers actually with the troops, to hurry the pace. The colonels refused to move faster. To double-quick, let alone run, the mile from the woods to the fort, they believed, would leave the men too exhausted to storm the stronghold. Those two brigadiers, accordingly, continued restraining the pace to conserve energy.

If their advance was too slow to please Northern generals, it looked disquietingly fast to Confederate commanders. Gregg was too far away to do much about it other than to urge his own troops to hasten toward the fort as they arrived. Taylor, though, was in a better position to resist. As he saw the Bluecoats leave the Varina Road at its sharp bend and continue northwest across the field, he ordered his cannoneers in

Harrison's left salient to change from shell to a double charge of grapeshot. By the time the Virginians could ram 160 pounds of iron into the ponderous 8-incher, the Northerners had left the road and were splashing across the rivulet of Three Mile Creek. Now the gunner jerked the lanyard; now Stannard's men neared the foot of the hill. The columbiad roared its mightiest blast—and when the smoke cleared, the big gun lay helplessly on the ground, jammed against its carriage, dismounted by its own recoil. Down in the field the First Division kept on coming.

The heavy shelling at least caused the Yankees to oblique to their right, and that move, in turn, exposed their left to the more southerly pieces in the Harrison complex plus Battery x. Such enfilading temporarily threw the First Brigade into confusion. When Stevens went to rally his men, he was cut down and left on the field with a severe hip wound that would end his army career. However, his successor, Lieutenant Colonel John B. Raulston of the 81st New York, soon restored order and led his troops forward. Virtually all the Unionists were now running to the shelter of the blind spot at the base of the hill. Even Donohoe and some of his skirmishers now rushed there, though other voltigeurs remained back in the field. At the foot of the hill, under the very walls of the fort, the Bluecoats found respite from the Confederate fire. Except for marksmen ranging up the hill slope to snipe at the gunners, the whole division was concealed from view. The folly of failing to build a glacis during long months of ease now became all too apparent.

This halt, however, made the Northern commanders back in Cox's woods fear that it would give Gregg time to beat the First Division to the fort. They could already see the vanguard of his troops from the New Market Line rushing along the Exterior Line toward Harrison. Again the generals hastened staff officers to speed the attack. Again Roberts preferred his own judgment to directives from the rear. He knew his tired men needed a break before storming the fort. Then, too, he could see that the Second Division was not coming up to help, though he could not know it had bogged down in the swamp along Three Mile Creek and was veering off on a tangent toward the Exterior Line. Such considerations were enough to make Roberts halt, no matter what the generals might say. The colonel was not a professional soldier like Ord. Nor was he a veteran of as much combat as Stannard and Burnham. Nor yet was he an inspiring leader of men; how could he be when he had just risen from his sickbed to lead his men into battle and even yet suffered the ravages of "bilious colic"? He was, nevertheless, an effective combat commander who could both halt and resume the attack in the immediate presence of the foe. Even before receiving his superiors' latest orders, he made his own decision that the brief respite had gone on long enough. Now he passed the word "in a slow, drawling, and an even, monotonous voice: 'Come, boys, we must capture that fort—now get up and start!'" He went on to make clear that the time for measured pace had passed. "Now, men," he continued, "just two minutes to take that fort! Just two minutes, men!"[17]

Regimental and brigade formation had long since been lost, and it was now a vast blue wave of hopelessly intermingled units that surged up the hill toward the fort. Winder and the gun crews farther south at last could bear on this tempting target, but they were ordered not to fire by a captain who mistook the charging Yankees for Hughs's retreating skirmishers. The Butternuts in Fort Harrison knew better and greeted the emerging Unionists with a final blast of infantry and artillery fire. Again, the Southerners succeeded only in dismounting one of their own guns, this time Moore's 32-pounder. Undaunted, the First Division replied with one volley of its own, then dashed into the moat. Most leaped into the fosse of the fort's face and then worked their way around to the fort's left flank. Others jumped directly into the left flank's moat. Once in the fosse, the Federals boosted, clawed, clambered, and—with ladders of bayoneted rifles rammed into the wall—climbed their way up the scarp and rampart for the decisive struggle.

The garrison was scarcely braced for this final contest. The cheering sight of Gregg's approaching reinforcements could not offset the defenders' many handicaps. The shock of rushing to a poorly maintained fort unexpectedly threatened on a supposedly quiescent front may have caused the Secessionists to enter the fight at a psychological disadvantage. Their problems increased as the climax neared. The ill-trained Virginia reserves, who had not stood up under the *Mackinaw*'s fire at Signal Hill, would hardly come to grips with the approaching foe. When their few premature volleys proved ineffectual, the right companies of reserves in the fort and along the immediately adjacent curtain to the north panicked and fled. The men of the 17th–23rd and 63rd Tennessee, who had earlier mocked the Virginians' skittishness, were not laughing now. Exhausted and low on ammunition from their running fight with Donohoe up the Varina Road, many of them, too, joined the 1st Battalion's flight. Some of the Goochlanders, also, broke for the rear.

This shameful conduct outraged Southern officers, yet the response of several senior commanders themselves left much to be desired. With his detachment disintegrating around him, John Hughs, the guerrilla, could only think to lower the drawbridge, ride out over the moat, coolly empty his pistol into the Yankees below, and then ride back, unharmed by the few shots from the dumfounded foe—a deed worthy of a mighty paladin but not of a brigade commander. Taylor, too, displayed more the bravery of despair than skillful command. When he dismounted the columbiad, he moved his gun crew to a nearby piece, discovered it inoperable, and then led most of his men south of the Great Traverse to work a 32-pounder there. En route he met Maury, who had just ridden up. The major briefed him with one gloomy sentence, "Col., the jig is up, we are surrounded," and then hurried on to his new station.[18] The battalion commander may have tried to rally the few soldiers remaining in the left salient, but he arrived too late to do much good. For all practical purposes, senior Confederate leaders ceased exercising command at the most vulnerable point.

Not all Southern officers and men, however, failed to meet their responsibilities. Most of Moore's men and some of Hughs's stayed in the fort. Guerrant's remaining gunners, unable to train their cannons on the moat, picked up rifle and pistol to join the infantry at the parapet firing at the Federal sharpshooters still sniping from the hill slope. Some artillerists even rained their tools down on the Bluecoats in the moat. More effective was the enfilading fire opened on the moat by riflemen who replaced the reserves along the camp wall north of the fort. Even this late, the Confederates continued displaying much individual bravery, but of cumulative bravery and of leadership there were too little to stop the First Division. The initial breakthrough understandably came near the left salient. There the commander of the 58th Pennsylvania, who had picked up the flag of the 188th Pennsylvania from its fallen color bearer, planted the first banner on the works. There, too, the first Federal infantry crowned the ramparts. The garrison took a heavy toll from the van of the Third Brigade but could not stop it. Indeed, the sight of the Northerners pouring over the parapets broke the resolve of the defenders, already badly shaken by the flight of most of their comrades. Orders for them to meet the Yankees with the bayonet now went unheeded; most of the artillerists simply ran away. Hughs may have joined them, but Maury, vainly trying to rally them, fell into Union hands, apparently at this time.

Now that the northeast salient was secure, the Federals swept over and around the Great Traverse to attack the defenders still holding out to the south. Few Confederates remained there, for Moore had already judged the situation hopeless and ordered his battalion to get away as best it could. Taylor, however, was so absorbed in successfully defending the fort's face against Donohoe that he did not realize the upper part of the fort had already fallen. Only Yankee fire into his left flank and rear alerted him to the true situation. Desperately he tried to rally his men to meet this new threat. However, he soon fell severely wounded, and his men were overwhelmed or driven off by the

Bluecoats pouring around the traverse and over the face. At about the same time one Northerner paused to lower the Confederate flag and plant the Union banner atop the Great Traverse.[19]

The capture of Taylor and the changing of the colors mark the end of resistance in Fort Harrison. The Federals had suffered staggering casualties, nearly five hundred men, in capturing this one redoubt, along with approximately fifty demoralized prisoners and about nine cannons, many of them useless. Not immediate gains but future prospects, however, are better measures of their success. They had broken through the outer defenses, rendered untenable the New Market Line, which Birney would at last proceed to occupy, and won great opportunities. Cutting off Gregg, destroying the bridges over the James, even taking the capital itself all seemed within their grasp. Two days earlier Grant had specified that "the object of this movement is to surprise and capture Richmond, if possible." Now such results appeared not only possible but also likely. And virtually the whole day remained to achieve them. It was still only 7:00 A.M.[20]

CHAPTER III

"Dah, Now! . . . Caw'pul Dick Done Dead!"

The fall of Fort Harrison posed the gravest clear and present danger of permanent capture Richmond ever faced to the day of her downfall. McClellan in 1862 and John Dix the following year had only been potential threats, and the *Galena,* Isaac Wistar, Judson Kilpatrick, and Philip Sheridan might each have entered the city but could not have retained it. Things were different on September 29. Now the Federal army in strength was not merely at the gates; it had also pierced the outer defenses and might well take Richmond itself. Capitalizing on this opportunity became the Northerners' main objective; forestalling it was the Confederates' primary mission.

Lee himself now took a larger role in defending the city. Ewell's report of the fort's capture made clear to him that more than Field's three brigades were needed on the Peninsula. The army commander, accordingly, ordered six more brigades and at least twelve batteries to set out for the Northside, and he placed another three brigades on standby to follow. He also directed Pickett to ascertain if a possible reduction of Union troops on Bermuda Hundred justified sending some of his men from the vital Howlett Line to Chaffin's. To guard the bridges over which these reinforcements would cross the river, Lee requested the assistance of Lieutenant Colonel George H. Terrett's garrison of marines and heavy artillery at Drewry's Bluff and Commander John K. Mitchell's James River Naval Squadron. Lee also counted on his earlier request of 7:45 to cause the ships to shell the Yankees' left, unaware that his message would not reach the Flag Officer until 2:00 P.M. And the army commander further called on General Braxton Bragg, the nominal General-in-Chief, to mobilize and throw forward the Local Defense Forces of Richmond.

So grave did Lee judge the crisis that he prepared to go to Chaffin's himself. Yet for some reason, presumably concern that Federal demonstrations on the Southside portended an attack there too, he postponed departing for several hours and relied on messages to keep in touch with Ewell. The Yankee threat against Petersburg and the logistical bottleneck along the single railroad through Chesterfield County, moreover, delayed transferring reinforcements to the Peninsula. Even the Locals in Richmond required time to mobilize and move to endangered sectors. Neither troops nor his personal direction could Lee provide to the critical sector in Henrico County that morning. All he could offer was his standard—and, in this case, clearly impracticable—exhortation to counterattack and recapture the lost ground.

Ewell, actually at the front, realized that retaking Fort Harrison immediately was out of the question. All his efforts would have to be devoted to preventing additional Northern gains. His paucity of manpower still handicapped him, and the divergent nature of his defensive requirements further complicated matters. He had to divide his weak force between his left, barring the direct approach to Richmond, and his far right, covering the Osborne Turnpike and the bridges over the James whence reinforcements would come. The upper bridges—one 1,400 feet above Drewry's Bluff, another 2 miles farther upriver, and a third 2 miles below the capital—were, admittedly, not in immediate peril, but the most important and useful bridge, the pontoons running to the entrenched camp's northwestern corner, was in dire danger. Fortunately, prepared works covered that bridge and Ewell's left, too. But then Fort Harrison had covered the entrenched camp, to no avail. What were needed were troops sufficiently numerous and steadfast to hold those works until reinforcements arrived. Some troops were already in place, the Pamunkey Artillery on the far right and Pemberton's heavies back near Richmond, and other units now rapidly moved into position. The Locals and other second-class troops sufficed to hold the Intermediate Line near the city, but more reliable veterans were needed along the lower end of that line near Fort Gilmer.

First to reach those works was half of the 1st Virginia Light Artillery Battalion. Hardaway's ten reserve guns had originally set out for New Market Heights, but all except the Howitzer section now countermarched toward Chaffin's farm. In their haste, the Virginians had to leave in camp, exposed to pillaging Unionists and local citizens, all the supplies that had arrived from home only the day before: "an unceasing source of regret to our men ever afterward," one later recalled. Little time remained for regrets that morning, though. By the time they lashed down the Mill Road into the Intermediate Line, Fort Harrison had already fallen, and the need to defend the more northwesterly works became apparent. These two companies, plus probably the crippled little four-gun Louisiana Guard Artillery, were the only organized troops in this sector, but they were seasoned veterans—with their sister companies of the battalion the sole representatives of the II Corps then in the Tidewater. Hardaway, himself judged by competent authority "one of the best officers in the army," did not hesitate to pit them against the foe. Captain Charles B. Griffin's Salem Flying Artillery swung into position in Fort Gregg, a small open redoubt immediately south of the Mill Road, to oppose the expected advance up the Varina Road. Captain Willis J. Dance's Powhatan Artillery continued south to Fort Johnson, where the Intermediate Line joined the camp wall, 3,200 feet northwest of Fort Harrison. From this small, unenclosed lunette whose gorge opened into the camp, now become Ewell's forward stronghold athwart the Yankees' path into the rear of his left wing, Dance's company began shelling the blue hordes milling in Fort Harrison.[1]

His fire provided the first check to the XVIII Corps. Victory inevitably disorganizes the triumphant almost as badly as the defeated, and so costly a success as capturing Fort Harrison temporarily wrecked the First Division. Roughly 18 per cent of its men lay bleeding on the field. The unregimented congregation of survivors lacked sufficient tactical cohesion, sufficient ammunition, even sufficient physical strength to undertake another full-scale charge against serious resistance. Dance's shelling plus musketry from part of the garrison who rallied in the wooden barracks just behind the fort provided the appearance of such resistance. Faced with it, the Yankees stopped and returned the fire. To support the riflemen, experienced gunners from the 92nd New York and presumably the 188th Pennsylvania as well as the 60 mounted artillerists turned the few operable captured cannons on the Butternuts.

Ord, Stannard, and Burnham, galloping up and entering the fort in the wake of the charge, at first encouraged such shooting back. The brigadier, indeed, became so carried away that he lent a hand in turning one of the captured guns on the Secessionists. But just before or just after sending a shell arching into their lines, he took a bullet in the bowels, spun around, fell to the ground in agony, and died almost immediately. He had not contributed as much to the victory as had others, yet his previous record suggests he would be missed in the close-in fighting to come. About the same time the Union high command suffered an even greater loss as Samuel Roberts, still debilitatingly ill, succumbed to the strain of the charge. No man had played a bigger role in taking Fort Harrison, but no man had suffered the exertion more, and now he collapsed and had to relinquish command. All three original brigadiers, at least four regimental commanders, and many other officers were thus incapacitated at the first onset. The need to find and assign their successors, Donohoe to the Second Brigade and Colonel Edgar M. Cullen of the 96th New York to the Third, further delayed the regrouping of forces that necessarily preceded resumption of the attack.

Yet Ord, Stannard, and Grant's liaison officer, Lieutenant Colonel Cyrus Comstock, knew that delay gave the enemy, too, time to regroup. No longer content to return Confederate fire, they now urged their men to roll up the penetrated camp walls and press on toward Fort Johnson. To their disgust and dismay, they found the armed mob at their disposal still too disorganized to have much punch. Even so, the First Division, virtually immobile as it was, could still overcome whoever stood within the path of its almost glacial outward expansion.

The Unionists resumed advancing around eight o'clock. The wooden barracks, closest at hand, fell first, yielding additional prepared breakfasts to tempt some victors to fall out. The northern curtain wall and the lower part of the Exterior Line were cleared next. Most of the 1st Virginia Reserve Battalion nearest the fort fled before its fall, but those farthest left remained to face the advancing Bluecoats. Guy reached the 1st's position just before Harrison fell. Soon afterward DuBose too arrived, the reinforcements that had so alarmed Ord and Stannard while Roberts paused in Childrey's field. Although these new troops got there too late to save the fort, the combative Gregg now ordered them to retake it. Most of them proved unworthy of their fighting general. Already demoralized by the flight of their comrades, the two Virginia battalions could not even withstand Stannard's renewed advance, let alone hurl him back. As he ate away at their right and as some of Heckman's division at last arrived to open a cross fire near Battery No. 10, the inexperienced reserves panicked and fled to the Intermediate Line in complete disorder. The only unit that did try to reach Fort Harrison, the 20th Georgia, was badly mauled, with a heavy loss of prisoners, by a large Federal force which burst on it by surprise around a bend in the works. The regiment abandoned the attack almost immediately and swung back east and north to rejoin DuBose. His main body meantime had moved straight on to support Hardaway without first making a stand in the Exterior Line.

As soon as the Georgia brigade interposed itself between the Yankees and Richmond, its van, Lieutenant Colonel William Shepherd's 2nd Georgia, sallied down the curtain from Fort Johnson to counterattack Stannard inside the camp. But again one isolated regiment proved

no match for the First Division and was easily repulsed. As the 2nd fell
back into the Intermediate Line, its brigadier assembled his whole
force there for defense. Dudley DuBose was a hard-driving, exacting
officer, ambitious to win a general's wreath around the three stars on
his collar. In the five months he had led Benning's Brigade, he had
sacrificed the love of his men for the respect of his superiors. His rigid
administration and tactical skill had earned that respect. Now his keen
eye discerned Fort Johnson as the key to blocking any effort to roll up
or outflank the Intermediate Line. There he made his stand with Shepherd's reassembling men plus the three companies of the 17th Georgia
not with Moore. Northward along the works from Johnson to Gilmer,
he strung out the 20th and then the 15th Georgia plus such few Virginia reserves as halted there in their flight to safety. The need to reinforce Dance against the prospective attack from Fort Harrison was obvious. But placing over half his command in the north–south works,
facing east, was equally imperative, for DuBose had probably seen—
and his rear guard surely reported—that large new Yankee units were
overrunning the Exterior Line on the Varina Road.[2]

These Bluecoats wore the white oakleaf of the Second Division,
XVIII Corps. They initially made good time double-quicking up the
Varina Road from Aiken's Landing to Cox's farm through the litter of
battle behind Stannard. As they neared Cox's, however, they encountered greater resistance from Fort Harrison's guns overshooting the
First Division. Although Taylor's fire inflicted few casualties on the
infantry, it delayed their advance by disabling a Napoleon of F/1st
Rhode Island Light Artillery, which somehow defied Butler's orders by
joining the column between the two divisions. Then, too, an exploding
shell unhorsed, stunned, and nearly killed Colonel Edward H. Ripley,
commanding Heckman's leading Second Brigade. The brigadier, however, recovered in minutes and rejoined his troops. The disabled gun,
too, was soon cleared out of the way, and the Second Division resumed
advancing.

While the First Division emerged from Cox's woods to attack Fort
Harrison, Heckman carried out Ord's directive to move northward
through the woods along Three Mile Creek and then strike west toward
the fort in conjunction with Stannard's charge farther left. These woods
proved the worst obstacle of all. The corps commander had apparently
not reconnoitered them before ordering in his troops. Only now did the
men discover that the terrain was not an open forest easily penetrable
by organized units but a typical Virginia swamp of marshy ground,
dense thickets, clinging undergrowth, and entangling brambles. To
make matters worse, Heckman sent part of Ripley's brigade and probably most of Colonel James Jourdan's First Brigade northward along

such an easterly axis that they entered the heart of the swamp near the creek itself. There the organized forces disintegrated from his control into individual soldiers picking, kicking, and tearing their way through the wilderness. Fairchild's Third Brigade, too, may have run afoul of the thickets but more likely remained idle back on Cox's farm. In either case, it also took no part in attacking Ewell's outer line.

Most of the Second Division thus bogged down during Stannard's attack on Fort Harrison. Only two of Heckman's seven regiments avoided or escaped the swamp in time to strike the forward works. Even they went off on tangents, both from their intended axis and from each other. Ripley, his two regiments deployed in brigade line of columns of division, apparently advanced farther west than the other units, so he partially avoided the swamp. His right element, the 8th Maine, to be sure, soon mired down and had to be left behind. However, he and his own 9th Vermont evidently encountered no serious obstacle and soon emerged from the woods into the open field north-northwest of Cox's. Allegedly on orders from division headquarters, the brigadier did not wheel west toward Fort Harrison but followed the course of the Varina Road toward the lower end of the Exterior Line. To avoid the abatis fringing those works, he shifted his column into the road itself. Confined in the sunken roadbed by the slashing on both sides, the massed regiment formed a tempting target for the two guns frowning down the highway from Battery No. 11. Every moment that they moved up the road and mounted the hill, the Bluecoats dreaded hearing a loud report that would send grape or canister cutting a bloody swath through their ranks.

But no such fire came. Even before Ripley approached, the Virginia reserves in that sector had crumbled away in the aftermath of Fort Harrison's fall. Seeing the reserves flee and the fort fall and discovering that No. 11 was ill prepared and low on ammunition, in turn, demoralized the James City Artillerists. Coming under attack themselves was more than they could stand, and they now fled to the Intermediate Line without even firing at the massed Vermonters. Ripley, like Draper farther east, thus entered a military vacuum rather than storming a defended line. Only as the 9th crossed the works did it first draw Confederate musketry, probably from DuBose's rear guard, who took time to deliver a parting volley as it hurried past. Only temporarily checked by this lethal blast, the 9th pressed on a short way and captured a few prisoners. Other Yankees remained in the redoubt to turn the one operable cannon on the fleeing foe. The regiment did not launch a full-scale pursuit, though, and its fire only hastened the Georgians' rush to the Intermediate Line.

At about the same time that the Second Brigade took Battery No.

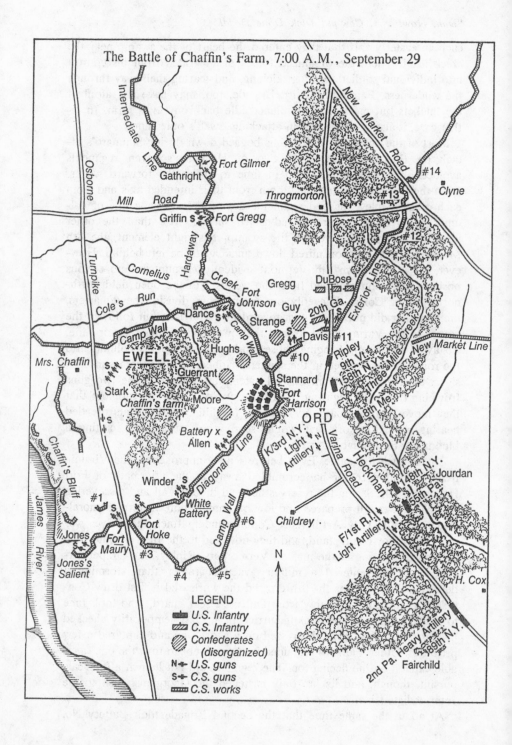

The Battle of Chaffin's Farm, 7:00 A.M., September 29

LEGEND

U.S. Infantry
C.S. Infantry
Confederates (disorganized)
N— U.S. guns
S— C.S. guns
C.S. works

11, Jourdan's own 158th New York cut across Ripley's rear to strike farther west. The New Yorkers, alone of Heckman's command, may actually have carried out his mission of attacking Fort Harrison, but they more likely charged Battery No. 10. After apparently first dropping to the ground to avoid one blast of grapeshot, they pressed on, overran the redoubt, and captured its two guns. The heavy fire the Federals delivered in the process likely contributed to the disintegration of the Virginia reserves Gregg was assembling there to counterattack Fort Harrison. Here too, Davis, Strange, and Guy put up little resistance before fleeing to the Intermediate Line. Here too, also, the Unionists contented themselves with holding the captured works and turning infantry and artillery fire on the retreating Southerners.[8]

The advance of the 9th and 158th hastened the collapse of the already shaken forces along the Exterior Line. It also alerted DuBose to the need to keep considerable troops north of Fort Johnson, facing east. And it made clear to Gregg how vulnerable were his troops from New Market Heights. Even though Davis, the Georgians, and the Virginia reserves had managed to reach the Intermediate Line, Gregg's other forces were now in danger of being cut off. The mounted troops were, of course, in little peril. Except for the weak rear guard that faced Birney's final charge and for some videttes that presumably continued keeping the Federal right wing under surveillance, Gary's horsemen simply remounted and rode safely west along the New Market Road. They may even have briefly taken position on Ewell's new center or left south of that highway. The two batteries, too, marched swiftly up that road to within the Exterior Line. In those works the reunited Howitzer company made a stand. The First Rockbridge Artillery

COMMENTARY

1. This map depicts the situation immediately following Stannard's capture of Fort Harrison. His division, though badly disorganized, is inside the camp: in position to move northwestward behind the Intermediate Line or southwestward down the Diagonal Line and to the James. Heckman, however, [all of his regiments but the 9th Vermont are represented symbolically] is moving northward too far east to follow through on the victory. Most of the original defenders meantime flee westward in disorder, and only the 20th Georgia tries to fight at the Exterior Line. DuBose's other regiments hurry toward the Intermediate Line, where Hardaway's two batteries take position. Stark, too, may already be moving into place. The Louisiana Guard Artillery, also, unlimbers somewhere on the Confederate left.

2. Southern guns are represented individually, not symbolically, except for those in Forts Hoke and Maury and the White Battery.

meantime continued on to take position in the Intermediate Line just west of the great Fort Gilmer salient.

However, the 25th Virginia Battalion and the Texas Brigade, as infantry, avoided this circuitous route simply by facing right and running west by the flank along the New Market Line. The foot soldiers' move made sense when the orders to withdraw were received, for it would bring them right where they were needed. By the time they actually began arriving, however, the situation had so changed that they were now in grave peril. Gregg, who had seen his right wing go to pieces after Fort Harrison fell, was keenly aware of the threat to his forces coming from New Market Heights. After sanctioning the retreat of the Georgians and the reserves to the Intermediate Line, he rode east to find his own brigade. He soon met it, still running but strung out in a long column that made clear that even these veterans suffered the strain of moving so rapidly after fighting so hard. The division commander wisely halted the column for fifteen minutes to let the van catch its breath while the rear caught up. Then he led it west to attempt rushing over the open ground, past the Unionists debouching from Fort Harrison, toward DuBose.

But when the Graycoats emerged from the woods, they encountered a danger far graver than Stannard posed. During Gregg's absence, the 9th and 158th had overrun Batteries No. 10 and 11, and more of Heckman's command now joined them there. The Second Division thus was directly athwart the Confederates' path. With his men in marching order, not battle order, the Texan had no intention of hurling them against the strong Yankee command. He instead doubled back into the woods, swung north, and tried to race around the Federals before they could cut him off. His quick thinking saved his force. The Unionists evidently did not grasp their opportunity. Still lacking leadership from division headquarters, they failed to search him out once he disappeared from their front. Except for enduring a light fire when he first burst on the Northerners, he was able to escape unscathed to the Intermediate Line.

Once there, he led his five battalions into the camp to try again to retake Fort Harrison, this time by charging directly into its open gorge. Mounting pressure on the Georgia brigade, however, caused him to cancel this attack. He left at least some of Elliott's companies in the camp and led Bass and perhaps the rest of the 25th back to aid DuBose. The general then assumed immediate command of all forces on the Fort Johnson–Fort Gilmer line. He brought to that sector not only a veteran brigade but also sound tactical sense and inspirational example that would do much to forge his conglomerate command into an effective fighting force.

Heckman's failure to intercept the Texans before they reached the Intermediate Line deprived the Federals of the one potential advantage of his erratic attacks. Despite the great achievements he and some of his men later attributed to his advance, it is the soldiers in gray, not those in blue, who should exult over what he did. His seizure of a forward line of works and its four guns amounts to little. The disintegration of the 1st and 2nd Virginia Reserve Battalions following the First Division's breakthrough convincingly suggests that the Exterior Line would have been abandoned anyway and could have been occupied at leisure. Nor did he take advantage of his position on the Varina Road to cut off Gregg. In the final analysis, what Heckman did was to throw his division in a false tactical direction so that it once more faced strong, defended Confederate works instead of following up Stannard's victory to take those fortifications from the right flank and rear.[4]

Heckman's error disturbed and probably infuriated Ord, who had counted on having both divisions well in hand at Fort Harrison. When the First penetrated the camp wall, the corps commander expected the Second to move in after it and immediately strike north behind the Intermediate Line with Ripley and south toward the pontoon bridge with Jourdan, while Fairchild provided a fresh reserve. Instead, the Second Division was nowhere to be seen, and the troops already inside the camp were too disorganized to reap any more than the most limited fruits of their victory. Still, the First Division was the only force at his disposal, and he tried to get it to launch another major attack, with the minimal results already described. While so occupied, he caught sight of infantry rushing west into the works northwest of Fort Harrison. For a moment he dared hope they were the lost Second Division storming those fortifications. As they broke ranks and manned the ramparts, however, he realized that the enemy had beaten him to the coveted objective. The Georgians' arrival complicated but hardly ruined prospects for attacking past Fort Johnson into their right rear. Yet the sight of them apparently made Ord fear that all hope of decisive victory turned upon what would be done in the next few minutes. He personally took it upon himself to tip the scales in favor of the Army of the James.

The dispassionate historian might argue that Ord could best have done this by meeting the responsibilities of his office and bringing up the Second Division for a belated but nonetheless promising strike around Shepherd's right. But dispassionate historians are rarely found amid the confusion of battle in a just-stormed fort, where the responsible commander must strive against the chaos of his surroundings to make decisions on the basis of limited information. In such circumstances, temperament and training subconsciously influence the general's response far more than study of either the past or the most im-

mediate present. Not only the prudent Meade or the thorough George
H. Thomas but even the combative Hancock, his aggressiveness tempered by long experience, would likely have chosen the more conservative approach of attempting to co-ordinate all forces under their control. Ord, however, had seen too little action the past three years to
restrain his natural tendency to get into the thick of the fray. In the
heat of battle, with the crisis of the attack apparently upon him, he
chose to become a small-unit combat commander who would literally
lead his men to victory. Even this decision could not lightly have been
criticized by that hypothetical historian seeking shelter behind the trav-
erses of embattled Fort Harrison. Albert Sidney Johnston at Shiloh,
Edwin V. Sumner at Antietam, and Ambrose E. Burnside (in unfulfilled intention) at Fredericksburg have, indeed, been scored for
becoming too involved in front-line fighting at the expense of over-all
control of their troops. But Napoleon at Arcola, Sheridan at Five
Forks, and Bedford Forrest on a host of battlefields are praised for setting personal examples that inspired their men to victory. History, in
sum, offers no sure guide to the propriety of such ventures and instead
contents itself with inferring justification from results. Actors in history
determine those results, and Edward Ord now elected to act boldly in
hopes that his personal leadership would spark a renewed advance.

The corps commander, seeing that the Confederate left was reinforced, decided to strike in the opposite direction to cut the bridges
across the James before they, too, could be adequately protected. Because no organized troops were available, he gathered a small party,
mostly company officers and skirmishers, and personally led them south
along the Diagonal Line. As soon as Stannard could get at least some
troops into shape, he brought the nucleus of Donohoe's and Cullen's
brigades (left to right) down the Diagonal Line immediately in Ord's
wake. Raulston and the remaining stragglers meantime stayed behind
to hold the fort and skirmish toward the camp's center and Fort Johnson.

The Bluecoats' advance outflanked Allen in Battery x, who had
gamely kept firing as long as they remained in Fort Harrison. Once
they struck southward, he abandoned his guns and hastily retreated to
Fort Maury. Detachments all along the line joined him en route;
Winder even braved Federal fire to wheel two little howitzers from the
White Battery to Fort Hoke. In Fort Maury and its strong outpost,
Fort Hoke, Allen, now commanding Maury's Battalion, made his stand.
His own Lunenburgers armed themselves with muskets stored in the
more southerly redoubt and lined the parapets as infantry, and the
Norfolk men served the few cannons (three, four, or six) in the two
lunettes. Farther down the curtain Jones trained his two pieces leftward
toward the real threat, and in the rear one of Stark's Virginia light bat-

teries (likely the four-gun McComas Artillery) perhaps already entered the camp and unlimbered in No. 1. Ewell looked for more troops to come down the Osborne Turnpike from Richmond, and he counted on Lieutenant Colonel R. Bogardus Snowden of the 25th Tennessee to lead the rest of Johnson's Brigade plus the work details north to the camp from their isolated and outflanked position on Signal Hill. None of these foot soldiers had yet arrived, however, so upon Allen's three or four artillery companies alone, no more than 125 to 200 men (even including Stark's battery), depended the safety of the bridge to Drewry's Bluff.

Against a well-organized Union division or even brigade, the Virginians would have had little chance. But fresh, tactically cohesive troops did not face them. Ord's little raiding party had occupied Battery x and the White Battery by default but was too weak or too poorly organized to overcome the first show of resistance. Checking Ord gave the Graycoats confidence to take on bigger odds when Stannard's main body soon came up. No fleeing supports and no defective cannon demoralized these heavy artillerists; no "blind spot" sheltered the enemy in their front—and, it must be admitted, no fresh troops challenged them. Spared the handicaps Guerrant had faced in Fort Harrison, these companies, in the supreme test, proved that even the inexperienced men of Maury's Battalion could give a good account of themselves. Both artillerists and musketeers poured forth fire brisk enough to halt Stannard. Even as Dance's shelling had first given pause to a potential Union advance, Allen's repulse of the drive to the James marked the first actual check of a deliberate, large-scale Northern effort to exploit the initial breakthrough. This success, along with the arrival of DuBose and Gregg on the Intermediate Line, considerably brightened Confederate prospects from the dark minutes immediately following the loss of Fort Harrison. On both right and left flanks the works had been manned and the Yankees' advance blunted.[5]

Equally reassuring, the Northerners still did not challenge the weak, unfortified line running through the center of the camp to link those two wings. Perhaps the very absence of works there provided no conspicuous target such as Forts Johnson and Maury. Then, too, the dense forest in the camp's center concealed the gaping hole between those two redoubts. Neither woods nor Yankee preoccupation elsewhere permanently guaranteed the security of the center, though. Accordingly, Ewell prudently assembled there his few available forces: many of Guerrant's and Hughs's men from Fort Harrison, Moore for a short time before he moved north to reinforce Shepherd, Elliott after he arrived from the New Market Line, and some of Stark's guns (probably the Mathews Artillery) on the far right in the old unrefused trench

west of the turnpike. Gary's cavalry, too, may have come there if they
did not serve between Forts Gilmer and Johnson.

Creating and maintaining such a battle line were far more difficult
tasks than simply redeploying Gregg's veterans on a different sector.
Most of the troops in the center, lacking much if any combat experience, gave little promise of withstanding in the open field Federals who
had stormed so strong a work as Fort Harrison. Ewell realized what a
doubtful factor they were and substituted for earthworks the force of
his own personality to rally them. Like Ord, the lieutenant general assumed personal command at a vital point and with promises of succor,
appeals, and threats revitalized his motley aggregation into a fighting
line. His leadership that day left a lasting impression on one of his
men:

> General Ewell was with the skirmish line, constantly encouraging
> them by his presence and coolness. I remember very distinctly how
> he looked, mounted on an old gray horse, as mad as he could be,
> shouting to the men and seeming to be everywhere at once. . . .
> [By] his cool courage and presence wherever the fight was hot-
> test [he] contributed as much . . . as any one man could have
> done.

More important, his leadership created a line through the camp connecting Gregg and Allen. It was, to be sure, almost as attenuated as a
skirmish line, but it was still a line. Ewell now boldly risked throwing it
forward to the edge of the woods to create a show of force. The sight
of these men, the roar of Stark's guns, and the pugnacity of Elliott's
covering voltigeurs evidently created the desired effect. The only available Bluecoats, Raulston's, made no serious effort to call the Southerners' bluff. Such few Union skirmishers as did venture west of Fort
Harrison were easily checked.

The department commander's decision to take personal charge of
one portion of his firing line and use it daringly thus paid off. At the
same time he avoided the danger of overly concerning himself with one
sector and remained alert to his other responsibilities. Affairs farther
north and in Richmond he justifiably left to local commanders and
Bragg, but he kept them posted on developments. He also kept himself
informed on the entire threat posed by the Army of the James. When
cavalry videttes reported the Yankees moving west along the New
Market Road from the heights, he retained sufficient perspective to
realize that his own immediate front would have to be weakened so
Gary could return to confront this new danger.[6]

Anticipating potential threats, meeting real ones, rallying his men,
and forming a new line made old, one-legged Dick Ewell a general and

a leader once more. The emergency of the moment, with its requirement for prompt action, overrode the lack of initiative that had plagued him for more than a year. At the same time, the purely tactical nature of his immediate problem drew forth his best qualities as a soldier. Such qualities had shown before, in those halcyon days ere the II Corps had ever heard of Cemetery Hill: at First and Second Winchester, at First Stephenson's Depot, at Cedar Mountain, at Strasburg, and above all at Cross Keys. Yet great as were his accomplishments then, they do not equal his achievement this day. Acting in the face of imminent disaster to forge and sustain a continuous line from Fort Gilmer to the James that bade fair to contain the Federal breakthrough and save Richmond was the greatest contribution Ewell ever rendered to the Confederate cause.

What he achieved is not diminished by occurrences within Union lines. Military history is replete with examples of skillful operations by one side complementing inept maneuvers by the opposition to produce decisive results. Not only Jackson but also Howard, after all, dictated the course of events at Chancellorsville, May 2, and one must study Pemberton as well as Grant to understand the Vicksburg Campaign. This duality of deciding factors also marked the Battle of Chaffin's Bluff. The Confederates, it is true, threw together and maintained a new line in the face of tremendous disadvantages, but it is equally true that developments in the Army of the James prevented the Yankees from mounting the most effective challenge to this line. The erratic moves of the Second Division, the disorganization and resulting impotence of the First Division, and the failure to attack the Confederate center in force all handicapped Union efforts to capitalize on the initial success. One result was the repulse of the feeble thrust toward the James. The first move against Fort Johnson proved no more successful. This probe against Shepherd and Dance was likely only the final phase of the outward expansion of the skirmishers of Raulston's disorganized command from Fort Harrison. Its defeat, nonetheless, made the defenders more sure of the tenability of their position, less fearful of the prowess of the formerly victorious foe.

The worst blow to Federal efforts, however, came not at the Intermediate Line but south of the White Battery, where Ord was personally leading his men. His counterpart in gray, Ewell, became a personal leader to try to change the course of events, succeeded, and won the plaudits of history. Now the Northern general made the same gamble, lost, and has come down in disfavor with those who speculate on what might have been. The principle criticism of Ord is not that he failed to reach the river but that he recklessly exposed himself to danger. With the fate of Burnham and Stevens and with his own battle-scarred body as reminders, he could have been under no illusion but that he risked his life by leading the vanguard. He took that chance in quest of victory—and could show for his efforts only tactical failure and a bullet wound in the right thigh. The wound was more painful than serious since no bones were broken, so he simply stanched the flow of blood with a tourniquet and attempted to retain command. The first surgeon to reach him, however, insisted that he go to the rear to receive proper attention. Such treatment required weeks, not minutes. Ord had no recourse but to relinquish command to his ranking subordinate, Heckman.

Assessing the impact of the Marylander's departure is difficult. His initial hesitation in Childrey's field and his failure to force his way across the Osborne Turnpike hardly provide convincing indices that he would have fulfilled army headquarters' intentions had he remained in command. Yet he was thoroughly familiar with those goals and at least used the right line of approach (though with inadequate force) to try to achieve them. The intriguing possibility, therefore, remains that, given more time, he would have mounted a bigger strike into the Butternuts' rear. His successor, in contrast, abandoned the effort to penetrate the breach at Fort Harrison and roll up the enemy's lines and instead launched direct frontal attacks on Ewell's strongest works. This derivative change of tactics singles out the wounding of Ord as the turning point of the Battle of Chaffin's Bluff.

Little in Heckman's record suggested he was fit for the new responsibilities thrust upon him. An ex-sergeant from the Mexican War and a former railroad conductor, he had seen little combat prior to 1864 during basically garrison duty in eastern Virginia and North Carolina. Only that spring did he finally come face to face with large-scale fighting. He then displayed great bravery but little tactical skill and less initiative. Promising opportunities repeatedly escaped him, and on May 16 he met disaster as his Star Brigade was outflanked, overwhelmed, and routed. He himself fell into Confederate hands and was held as a hostage under Union fire at Charleston. Only exchanged in mid-September, he chanced to receive a division command that fell open in the Army of the James. Now another vacancy elevated him again. In his first battle in 4½ months this soldier who could not lead even a brigade well was called on to direct a whole corps.

How much he should be blamed for what ensued partially depends on how familiar he was with the plans and objectives of the left wing. Butler later alleged that Ord kept Heckman completely in the dark, whereas Ripley asserted that the new corps commander was thoroughly familiar with the plans. Testimonies more contemporaneous, more objective, and more credible come from Ord and Comstock. Taken together, they suggest that Ord had not briefed him beforehand on the full scope of the plan but just prior to charging Fort Harrison and again on turning over command did indicate that he wanted the Second Division to penetrate the camp. On the later occasion the Marylander specified that the First Division should continue driving toward the James and that the other troops should "push on, attacking the works toward Richmond in succession." None of these sources, however, proves that Ord specified that Heckman was to take those works from the rear.

Even so, the Jerseyman may justifiably be criticized for failing to discern for himself the desirability of attacking prepared defenses from behind instead of from the front. He may allegedly be further rebuked for mentally collapsing under the burden of his new responsibilities. Some men, charged with duties greater than their talents, are paralyzed into inaction; in contrast, Heckman, according to his enemy Ripley, gave way to frantic, almost "crazed" activity, like a drowning man flailing the waves that engulf him. He must, moreover, be held to account for squandering his own brigades in piecemeal attacks rather than uniting them into an effective striking force against whatever goal he chose. Whether or not the Second Division nominally preserved its identity, presumably under Fairchild's command, is not known, but in effect it ceased functioning as a unit.[7]

Heckman set the pattern for his operations almost immediately after assuming corps command. He dashed his brigades, one by one, along their original deviant axis up the Varina Road, then against the front of the Intermediate Line. Only the First Brigade temporarily escaped this fate, perhaps because most of it had not yet emerged from the swamp. The Second Brigade, conspicuously available around Battery No. 11, was not so fortunate. The corps commander detected it there, hastily told Ripley to attack toward Forts Gilmer and Gregg, and then frantically galloped off on some other mission. Although few soldiers of the 8th Maine had yet rejoined him, the colonel promptly moved the available troops toward the frowning ramparts. The few Maine men on hand led the way as skirmishers; after them came the 9th Vermont in line of battle. They immediately drew heavy fire from Griffin's Salem men in Fort Gregg and Thomas Gathright's detail of ten Goochlanders in Fort Gilmer. Such shelling made the brigadier doubt his prospects for success. The farther his men advanced into this telling fire, the more his apprehension grew. Soon he sent a staff officer to ask Heckman to come examine this sector to see whether braving such shelling was justified. Before corps headquarters could respond, the colonel took it on himself to call off the charge. He ordered his men to retreat a short way and lie down in the shelter of a sunken roadbed, presumably the Varina Road, until the general's answer was received. That answer never came, and the Second Brigade remained isolated but relatively safe in its forward position for the rest of the morning.[8]

Ripley's charge never came near the Confederate works; it ranks as the feeblest thrust by a fresh, organized unit all day. His own inexperience as a brigadier may explain his limited effort, but so may his good sense. His small loss, despite the heavy fire, is no dishonor. The resolve to press ahead despite heavy casualties, which is the glory of a large force like Stannard's division, is but foolhardiness for a small, unsupported unit little bigger than a regiment. Many commanders of such small outfits, lacking Ripley's judgment, could total up much larger losses at the end of the day, but none could boast greater achievements. The first of those to try could be seen demonstrating the point while the New England brigade safely rested farther northeast.

Those troops were the Third Brigade of the Second Division. The rear of Ord's original column, they finally reached Childrey's field only as the First Division was storming Fort Harrison. Despite some fatigue and straggling from their rapid advance, they remained a fresh, available force to follow Stannard into the camp and spearhead the second attack. But the confusion of initial victory, Heckman's entanglement in the swamp, and the preoccupation of Ord with the vanguard caused both corps and division headquarters to overlook using Fairchild that way. They instead allowed the colonel to continue up Varina Road to Battery No. 11, where he halted and waited idly, bothered by Confederate shelling from the Intermediate Line and unaware of the opportunity to cut off the Texans arriving from New Market Heights.

Only after Heckman took over the left wing did the Third Brigade receive a mission. By then Dance's heavy fire and Shepherd's determined stand alerted the general to their "annoying fort" as the key to the Intermediate Line. He called on his senior brigadier to take it. The first full-scale attack on this crucial position invited careful planning, yet the corps commander again recklessly hurled his men against its strongest point. Instead of bringing them into the camp to penetrate the Confederate right rear, he ordered them to continue west from the Exterior Line against the abatis, moat, and rampart of the redoubt's front. To carry out this dangerous assignment, Fairchild formed the brigade into a flying wedge of three lines. The 1/2nd Pennsylvania Heavy Artillery spearheaded the advance; the other two battalions of that regiment were echeloned to its right rear and left rear; and the 89th New York made up a third line supporting the heavies. When preparations were complete, the troops hurried forward at the double-quick. But they moved alone. Ripley, already checked, remained idle farther right, and Jourdan stayed back at the Exterior Line. Again, a Northern unit advanced, unsupported, against an area sure to be defended in force.

DuBose, even more conscious than the Yankees of the crucial importance of Fort Johnson, took personal charge of its defense. His assets were meager: about 200 men in the redoubt itself, two regiments and a battery in the line north from there. Yet he was not without advantages. Virtually all his men were veterans, unlike the troops who had failed to hold the outer line. Shepherd, Dance, and Hardaway, moreover, were subordinates exceptionally qualified to get the most from their men in combat, and the brigadier also had great confidence in his own ability. Best of all, his troops could take advantage of their fortifications to meet this frontal attack from the east instead of having to fight in the open against an envelopment from the south. All morning his Georgians had run hither and thither to little purpose. Now they could stand and fight.

The Powhatan Artillery offered first challenge to the Union thrust. Initially its shelling did little damage to the still-distant foe. Even so, the Third Brigade's own tactical incohesiveness soon caused it to go to pieces. Double-quicking for over a mile exhausted the men. More and more fell out, and the 2nd was too short of officers to keep them in line. Indeed, the big, clumsy artillery regiment, larger than many brigades, had such a shortage of command personnel that its whole Third Battalion fell out of the left of the second line and drifted northward out of the attack. The New Yorkers, in turn, fell behind in crossing a little branch of Cornelius Creek that rose east of the fort and flowed north across the line of attack before turning west to run just north of the fort.

Thus only two battalions initially advanced into the cornfield, which stretched from the branch to the moat. By now Confederate shelling was taking its toll. Under no illusions, the heavies sent their colors to the rear and then doggedly clambered into the slashing. Dance now changed to canister, and the Georgia riflemen added their fire. Casualties increased rapidly. The Pennsylvanians' commander, Major James L. Anderson, soon fell, decapitated by a cannon shot, and many of his men were stretched out with him. Silencing the fort now assumed equal importance with storming it. The new regimental commander, Major David Sadler, allocated his strength accordingly. He left his own Second Battalion behind to provide covering fire while he led the First Battalion in a final rush for the ramparts. It was a bold gamble, but by then the brigade had broken into too many pieces to succeed. The covering troops failed to silence the fort, which continued cutting down the vanguard. The Bluecoats bravely pressed on across the field into the moat itself. The few who tried to crown the ramparts, however, were easily shot or captured. Most of Sadler's battalion remained trapped there between the lines. Only after his repulse did the 89th at last come up. Seeing his fate probably made it attack much less spiritedly, and it was easily checked. Both it and 2/2nd and such of Sadler's men as did not make it to the fosse then took cover behind the contours of the field and in brush along its borders and kept firing at the fort. Farther north, the 3/2nd set out for Fort Gregg but, like Ripley, was handily halted by artillery alone and fell back to the shelter of the sunken road.

DuBose thus stopped Fairchild cold. Yet the Georgians' victory was by no means assured. During the attack, supporting artillery fire had grievously wounded Shepherd, who was no longer able to exercise the command he refused to relinquish. Such fire apparently also disabled one of Dance's guns and may even have cut down the valiant captain himself, who was definitely wounded severely sometime during the day. The garrison, moreover, had dangerously depleted its ammunition simply in halting the Third Brigade. Both leadership and firepower might thus be lacking if Fairchild—supported, say, by Jourdan—renewed the attack. Heckman's continuing failure to co-ordinate and support his thrusts, however, left the Graycoats time to strengthen their position. Shepherd's appeal for more men and munitions brought troops from both flanks hurrying to his relief. Part of the 15th Georgia from Fort Gregg did not get there in time. However, during the interlude, Moore's battalion arrived with some badly needed ammunition recovered under fire from a wagon lying abandoned in the camp. As the bolstered defenders eagerly replenished their supply of bullets, the major assumed operational control of the fort.

He concluded that the best way to forestall another attack was to counterattack. The Third Brigade's exposed flanks invited such a blow. Sallying out the Mill Road against the Federals' right could be costly, though, even dangerous. On the other hand, conditions for surprising the opposite flank were perfect. There the camp wall to Fort Harrison masked the detachments of the 2nd and 17th Georgia which Moore sent stealthily ranging through the upper part of the camp to a point opposite the unsuspecting Yankees' left. Only the piercing sound of the Rebel Yell and the sight of this skirmish line sweeping across the curtain with a deadly volley alerted Fairchild's men, too late, to their danger. Fort Johnson simultaneously opened a crossfire from the west. Already shaken by its repulse, the Third Brigade went to pieces under this flank attack and crossfire and fled in disorder all the way to Battery No. 11. The victorious flankers roamed the cornfield in its wake to reap the fruits of success: abandoned arms and ammunition, booty from the fallen—and Sadler's doomed battalion of 150 men in the moat, who now surrendered en masse. On being pulled into the redoubt, the prisoners—already depressed by their capture—were utterly mortified to discover how few Southerners had vanquished them.

The most serious effort to breach the second Confederate line thus produced the most serious Northern defeat of the morning. The rout of the last available fresh Union brigade epitomized Heckman's misuse of his resources. Three hours before, prospects for decisive Federal victory looked bright and promising. By 10:00 A.M. they seemed faint and illusory. By the same token, the successful defense of the Intermediate Line buoyed Gregg's men. They were still too few in numbers to feel assured that the day was won, but at least they could see that they had thrown a barrier across the path of the previously unstoppable foe.[9]

Their chiefs inferred more than that from their victory. The prisoners Moore captured gave first evidence that white troops of the XVIII Corps were participating in the attack. Gregg promptly forwarded this valuable intelligence to army headquarters, which had long-awaited such confirmation. Until then, 5,700 Confederate infantry had remained idle in Chesterfield County: Thomas's Brigade of the Light Division on the far right, downriver from Petersburg, and Brigadier Generals William R. Terry's, George H. Steuart's, Eppa Hunton's, and Montgomery D. Corse's Brigades prolonging Pickett's line leftward along the Howlett Line in that order. The foot soldiers and the accompanying artillerists knew that something important was afoot. Although a strange sound occlusion prevented them from hearing the firing on the Northside, telltale clouds of cannon smoke over Chaffin's farm alerted them that fighting was under way. Anxiously they waited for news of the battle and for orders to respond. Potter's clumsy shows of force did little to divert their attention or to keep them in place. Butler, worried that deserters had alerted the Southerners to the weakness of Bermuda Hundred, sent word to the brigadier at 9:00 A.M. to counter the threat by displaying his force in the defenses. But instead of demonstrating or manning his works in strength, the Hampshireman simply placed his men atop his parapets. There they formed tempting targets until Confederate artillery and infantry fire drove them under cover. The Union guns then opened counterfire, but for once they came off worse; Battery E/3rd New York Light Artillery took heavy casualties. Neither side, however, sought a battle on that sector, so fighting soon subsided.

Even so, Lee could not be sure that this curious affair was not a ruse: that the XVIII Corps did not lie concealed behind Potter, waiting to strike the Richmond and Petersburg Railroad—the customary second prong of Grant's onslaught. Only on learning from Gregg that Ord had, indeed, left the Hundred did Dunn's Hill feel safe in ordering Pickett to ready troops for Chaffin's. Army headquarters' initial reaction to the intelligence was to direct the major general to pull a brigade into reserve pending further orders. Instead of withdrawing an organic brigade, Pickett grouped one regiment from each of his own brigades—

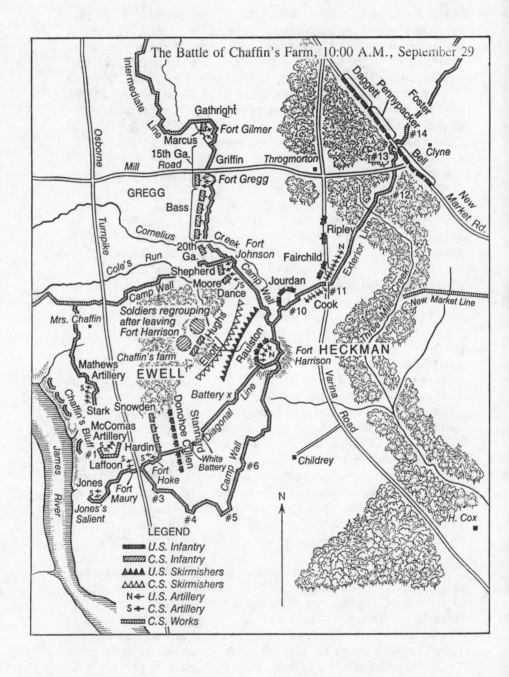

The Battle of Chaffin's Farm, 10:00 A.M., September 29

LEGEND

▭	U.S. Infantry
▱	C.S. Infantry
▲▲▲▲	U.S. Skirmishers
△△△△	C.S. Skirmishers
N ←	U.S. Artillery
S ←	C.S. Artillery
▥▥▥▥	C.S. Works

N

the 24th, 32nd, 53rd, and 56th Virginia—into a provisional brigade under hard-hitting Colonel Edgar B. Montague of the 32nd. The colonel soon received marching orders. He apparently took the train north, then marched across the James just above Drewry's Bluff. At about 1:00 P.M. he reported to Ewell—the first of the reinforcements from the Southside.

Strong local forces already defended the Osborne Turnpike by the time the Virginia brigade arrived, thanks to Allen's tenacity and Heckman's ineptitude. Squandering the Second Division in frontal attacks on Gregg's works not only ruled out turning those defenses but also deprived Stannard of the fresh troops necessary to penetrate Ewell's weak center and outflank Forts Maury and Hoke. The Vermonter, moreover, displayed little initiative. Instead of flanking westward, he continued butting his battered command in futile frontal probes against the heavies' main works. In holding the forts, Allen himself fell severely wounded at about 10:00 A.M. However, his immediate successor, Lieutenant Jugurtha Laffoon, kept his handful of men to their posts for a few more minutes until Snowden at last arrived from Signal Hill to throw a respectable line of battle across the First Division's path. With Snowden may have come Major Mark B. Hardin of the 18th Virginia Heavy Artillery Battalion, who may well have led Pemberton's fatigue details from Signal Hill. In any case, the major soon arrived to take charge of Maury's Battalion. Although wounded in the arm right away, he retained command and provided senior, field-grade leadership to the unit once more.

More senior leadership reached the front in late morning: Richard H. Anderson. He and his staff set out for Chaffin's early Thursday morning pursuant to prebattle orders to take command of the forward position on the Northside. En route they met Ewell's courier, who re-

COMMENTARY

1. This map represents the tactical situation following Heckman's failure to exploit initial Federal advantages. Laffoon has stopped Stannard's drive long enough for Snowden to arrive from Signal Hill and for the James River Naval Squadron to go into action downriver from the bluff. Ripley and Fairchild, too, have been repulsed and are regrouping on the Varina Road. Jourdan is thought to have remained inactive near Battery No. 10. Foster, however, has reached the field of action, has driven Gary's pickets from the Exterior Line, and is now cautiously moving toward Laurel Hill Church, located northwest of the juncture of the Varina and New Market roads.

2. The location of Bass, the 20th Georgia, Hughs, and Stark is only approximate. The position of the Louisiana Guard Artillery is not known.

3. Guns are shown symbolically.

ported that fighting raged at the bluff. They then galloped to the threatened sector. On arriving at about 11:00 A.M., they were briefed by
Ewell. The South Carolinian then presumably took charge of some
portion of the embattled line, perhaps the left.

Still more powerful help reached the bluff soon after Snowden and
before Anderson, as the most formidable Southern force in the area,
the James River Naval Squadron, finally came into action. Securing
naval support was not easy. First word of Fort Harrison's fall led Ewell
to call on Mitchell for assistance. The absent Flag Officer, however,
could not be found, and the only available vessels upriver, Lieutenant
Frank Shepperd's redoubtable ironclad flagship *Virginia II* and Lieutenant John Murdaugh's gunboat *Hampton,* were temporarily out of
service while changing the ironclad's armament. Fortunately, Battery
Semmes, downriver at Bishop's Landing, had spotted the Yankees attacking across Childrey's field and notified Commander Thomas R.
Rootes, temporarily commanding in Mitchell's absence, that something
was wrong. The acting Flag Officer promptly dispatched his two
wooden gunboats, Lieutenant William Wall's *Drewry* and Lieutenant
Charles Hays's *Nansemond,* upriver from the landing to Chaffin's Bluff
to see if Minor Maury needed help. As a further precaution, he put an
observer ashore to ascertain the state of affairs. This observer soon met
Ewell's messenger coming to ask the Navy's assistance in checking the
drive toward the James.

At last Rootes had definite information on which to act. He started
his two remaining vessels, his own *Fredericksburg* and Lieutenant John
S. Maury's *Richmond,* both powerful ironclads, north at about 9:00
A.M. Half an hour later, they took position in Graveyard Reach, a mile
below Fort Maury, far enough downriver to bear on the Osborne Turnpike as well as Fort Harrison. Meanwhile, Wall and Hays, their mission to Chaffin's proving unnecessary, took it on themselves to drop
back down to positions between the bluff and the ironclads. Rootes
was thus in position around 9:30. However, for some unknown reason,
perhaps due to the almost inevitable malfunctions of the Confederate
Navy, he did not start firing for roughly fifty minutes.

When he did open about 10:20, moreover, difficulty in elevating the
pieces, lack of sufficiently powerful charges, and poor shells and
powder caused his initial shots to fall short. So great was the emergency, however, that he decided to use more than normal allotments of
that precious commodity, gunpowder. The increased charges soon sent
shells soaring the proper elevation to burst within Union lines. Only
the *Nansemond* could not surmount its handicaps of poor shells and
limited range; it was almost immediately sent upriver to join the *Hampton* and Terrett's marines in carrying out Lee's request to cover the

pontoon bridge between Drewry's and Chaffin's Bluffs. Hays's place on the firing line was soon filled by Acting Master W. Frank Shippey's gunboat *Roanoke*. After filling out its skeleton crew with fifteen naval cadets from Lieutenant William Parker's school ship *Patrick Henry,* the *Roanoke* alternated stations between the bridge and the reach. An hour after the ships opened fire, Lieutenant William Mason's gunboat *Beaufort* sped Mitchell to the front and itself entered the fray. The torrent of shells that the nine or ten guns of these five vessels now poured into Chaffin's farm hardly did the severe damage that Southern naval leaders expected and claimed. The fire did, however, provide a psychological and a potential physical deterrent to the Bluecoats' push toward the Osborne Turnpike. Coming as it did after Allen's defense of Forts Hoke and Maury, Snowden's arrival, and Heckman's blunders, the shelling sealed the doom of Stannard's drive toward the James.[10]

Indeed, the arrival of Confederate reinforcements, the valorous stand of Southern troops initially on the Peninsula, and major tactical errors by the Yankees thwarted the further advance of the whole XVIII Corps. On both flanks Heckman now ceased attacking and contented himself with fire fights. On the left Stannard fell back slightly and did no more than skirmish with Snowden. The Second Division, too, engaged only in long-distance firing at the Intermediate Line.

Most of the fighting on the Union right and center was now done by Major George Cook's Artillery Brigade of the XVIII Corps. The brigade had taken no part in the capture of Fort Harrison, and even afterward Ord had not felt authorized to order it to cross to the Northside. He, accordingly, asked Butler to allow it to start moving. Either the army commander did so, or else Heckman, unaware of the prohibition against artillery on the Peninsula, simply called it forward himself. In either case, it started crossing soon after Harrison fell and began reaching the front prior to Fairchild's charge. One section of K/3rd New York Light Artillery entered the fort right away but found itself outgunned and withdrew after a brief fight. Battery H of that regiment may have soon replaced it there as Heckman determined to convert the stronghold into a light-artillery work. Fourteen more guns meantime massed farther right near Battery No. 11 to shell Fort Johnson: the Rhode Islanders, apparently A/1st Pennsylvania Light Artillery, and presumably six New York pieces. In contrast, at least F/5th U. S. Artillery and perhaps the remaining New York outfits stayed in reserve near the front. Evidently neither those reserve sections nor any other cannons were sent south to aid Stannard against Laffoon and the lowest pontoon bridge. The customarily trustworthy Northern artillery succeeded in battering its opponents, particularly Dance and Griffin, but failed to silence them. As the guns exchanged shots over the now largely quiescent infantry, the battle seemed to degenerate into the very artillery duel against which Butler's master battle plan had expressly warned.[11]

This dying down of heavy fighting must have pleased Ewell. All too conscious of the weakness of his position, he continued ignoring renewed urging from Dunn's Hill that he recapture Fort Harrison. For that matter, since the only unit to yet reach him from the Southside was I Corps headquarters, he knew that even his defensive line was vulnerable to a new Yankee onslaught. The respite in fighting was thus a godsend to the general and his men.[12]

The lull was regarded much differently by Edward Ord, who had remained on the field after relinquishing command. What troubled him was not the corps artillery going into action but the Unionists' inability to achieve greater gains. Initial delays in bringing Cook forward, word that Heckman was frittering away opportunities, successful Confederate stands at Forts Johnson and Hoke, and Rootes's entry into the fray made the major general progressively more frustrated and "anxious." He could, however, no longer control events at the front. Even his two messages to Butler and two more to Grant to send more cannon, infantry ammunition, and a new corps commander to the left wing seemed to produce no results. Finally, at about 10:00 A.M., the Marylander got into an ambulance and went via the Varina and Kingsland roads to Deep Bottom to search for the General-in-Chief. Yet by the time he reached the bridgehead, Grant was no longer there and could not be located. The subordinate then abandoned the quest and crossed to Bermuda Hundred to secure proper treatment.

Back at his base, he began telegraphing City Point of shortages at the front. It would be surprising if all his efforts did not secure the needed ammunition for the First Division. What he was unable to do, though, was to convey to the lieutenant general himself his own accurate assessment of the tactical situation. Ironically, this inability to establish contact derived from the same personal involvement in a low-level task that had cost him command of the corps in the first place. If Ord had not descended to being a courier, he could have seen Grant, who arrived at Fort Harrison from the northeast only minutes after the junior officer set out for Deep Bottom.[13]

Grant did not ride in the forefront of the attack the way his departing friend did. Never a personal leader by temperament, the General-in-Chief further acknowledged the restrictions of his office throughout his Virginia campaign by not unduly meddling in the prerogatives of his subordinates. Yet he did like to visit the combat zone, not to conduct tactical operations but to observe how the battle progressed and to obtain firsthand knowledge on which to base broad recommendations.

His behavior, September 29, was typical. Since conducting the attack on the Northside was the responsibility of his senior subordinate, the Illinoisan at first remained back at City Point to oversee operations on both sides of the James. But even before receiving the army commander's message of 8:30 A.M. that New Market Heights had definitely fallen and Fort Harrison reportedly as well, the lieutenant general turned over headquarters to Colonel Ely S. Parker of his staff and sailed to Deep Bottom with part of his staff to see how things were going. He disembarked about 9:30 and rode north to the New Market Road.

Because he was too little a personal leader to inspire intense devotion from his men, he was accustomed to ride through the ranks without arousing the cheers that always greeted, say, the magnetic McClellan. Now, too, Grant initially encountered only silence. But it was the silence of deepest respect as the Negro brigade of the X Corps stood in awe before their chieftain. "As soon as Grant was known to be approaching," wrote an officer of the 29th Connecticut, "every man was on his feet & quiet, breathless quiet, prevailed. A cheer could never express what we felt."[14] As he moved farther north, the mood changed. The white troops hardly revered him, nor did they love him, but their capture of works that had twice before checked them put them in the mood to cheer, and they loudly greeted his arrival among them.

Militarily, the situation seemed as encouraging as the welcome. A strong enemy position was now firmly in the control of Paine and Terry. Further to secure it, M/1st U. S. Artillery and either C/3rd Rhode Island Heavy Artillery or D/4th U. S. Artillery of Jackson's X Corps Artillery Brigade had advanced from Jones's Neck to just west of the heights. The third of those companies also moved to the front during the day. About 11:00 A.M., moreover, the 4th New Jersey Battery crossed to Deep Bottom and parked. Better yet, the second phase of the advance was already under way. Kautz, who had started crossing from Bermuda Hundred at six-thirty, had already passed through the infantry and was dashing for the Darbytown Road—and Richmond. Birney, moreover, had already set out west along New Market Road with his Second Division.

Then, too, Butler likely contributed to the over-all impression of success. The army commander had not witnessed the right wing's battle but did cross with the Cavalry Division and arrived on the field soon after fighting ended. Carefully picking his way through the bleeding USCTs strewn over the ground to where the cheering survivors thronged him on the New Market Line left Butler overcome with emotion. On reaching the works, he swore a "sacred oath" ever to uphold the race that had proved its manhood on that field. This outburst of

militarily irrelevant Negrophilia blinded him to the true situation.
Word that the left wing, with which the 4th Massachusetts Cavalry had
at last established contact, was also faring well further contributed to
the misimpression. He definitely assured Potter that "all goes as intended thus far" and likely told Grant the same thing during their brief
meeting.[15] Hence, everything the General-in-Chief could see and hear
during his short stay at the heights, doffing his hat to cheering soldiers
and listening to optimistic Butler, suggested that the operation was proceeding satisfactorily.

Appearances, however, were deceiving. Ord's repeated messages that
the left wing had run into difficulty were not reaching Butler or Grant.
The Massachusetts man, moreover, had virtually no means of his own
to ascertain the XVIII Corps's condition. The sole liaison officer he attached to the left wing soon rejoined him to report the capture of Fort
Harrison; thereafter, no one from army headquarters remained to report occurrences at Chaffin's. Nor did the top commanders grasp that
the apparently victorious right wing had problems, too. Its supposed
success virtually destroyed one of Paine's brigades and badly mauled
another; considerable time would be required to get them moving
again. Yet their position on the left meant that they were to follow Foster westward. Until they started, neither William Birney (himself de-
tained by Kautz's passing horsemen) nor Terry on the far right could
join the pursuit along the New Market Road. Then, too, Birney's absence with the Second Division left no one at the heights to expedite
movement of his other seven brigades. This potentially serious logistical
bottleneck, however, evidently escaped the notice of Grant, who soon
rode off westward to overtake Birney.

What the lieutenant general saw in the Second Division's wake could
hardly have pleased him. Long notorious for straggling and now
exhausted as well from the ordeal of the previous night's march, the
men of that unit were falling out by the score. The farther Foster went,
the weaker he grew. Still, the absence of any Confederate resistance enabled him to make fairly good time in covering the two and a half
miles of good road to the Exterior Line in a little over an hour. The
reunited Third Richmond Howitzers fell back from that position before
he arrived, but a scrappy detail of Gary's pickets remained to contest
those works. When the covering skirmishers of the 142nd New York
sent back word that the defense line was manned, Foster halted his entire column and deployed the rest of Colonel Rufus Daggett's leading
First Brigade to support them. Here Grant overtook the Second Division. Briefly he came under fire as Southern bullets overshot the New
Yorkers and fell among his retinue. Accustomed for years to facing
danger unflinchingly, he watched the fight unconcerned until he per-

ceived that his six-year-old son, Jesse, then visiting him, was also exposed. For a moment the grim commander who had sent thousands to their deaths became the devoted father who ordered an aide to take the child to safety. Then Grant returned his attention to more pressing problems at hand and soon had the satisfaction of seeing the First Brigade chase away the horsemen and overrun the fortifications. This bloodless victory won, the Second Division gave him the warmest response yet. "The men sprang to their feet," recalled a noncom of the 3rd New York, "and cheered till they fairly raised the old fellow, cigar and all, from his saddle."[16]

After seeing that the X Corps still seemingly did well, the General-in-Chief left the New Market Road and headed south by farm roads or cross country to ascertain what the left wing was doing. He rode up to Fort Harrison only minutes too late to meet Ord, who had gone to Deep Bottom to search for him. The failure of those two officers to confer left serious shortcomings in Grant's knowledge of events. Everything he had seen so far bespoke success. While there is no reason to think the adulation of the troops turned his customarily level head, there is no reason to doubt that their apparent success suggested that matters were progressing well. Now he saw at Chaffin's farm the most impressive victory yet. There the XVIII Corps had already seized a powerful fort, its curtains, and its armaments. Now it seemed to be carrying the fight to the next lines of defense, so far as Grant in Fort Harrison could infer from the sights and sounds of battle near the Osborne Turnpike and the artillery duel between Cook and Hardaway. Neither the distressing sight of Stannard's heavy casualties in taking the fort nor Butler's disturbing failure to come to the camp to co-ordinate his converging wings caused the Illinoisan to revise his appraisal. Ord, the one general who could have alerted him to the paralysis that now gripped the XVIII Corps in the wake of lost opportunities, was no longer present. Heckman, in contrast, spoke mostly of his intention to convert Harrison to a light-artillery work and evidently ignored more basic issues. It may, indeed, be doubted that the junior officer even grasped—let alone could relate—the true state of affairs.

Grant, therefore, turned from viewing the fighting, sure that he knew what needed to be done. He walked over to a little traverse south of the Great Traverse, sat down, and prepared the necessary dispatches. The ensuing scene, as recorded by one of his staff, was a classic case of Grant's fixity of purpose and imperturbability in the face of danger:

> He . . . seated himself on the ground, with his back to the parapet, to write the order. While he wrote, a shell burst immediately over his head, and instinctively, everyone around him stooped, to avoid

the fragments. Grant did not look up, his hand was unshaken, and he went on writing his order as calmly as if he had been in camp.[17]

The practical consequences of his writing, unfortunately, proved less spectacular than his bravery. Confident that the Army of the James could exploit its initial victories more fully, he ordered both wings to keep attacking. He may simply have told Heckman to press on, but he definitely wrote Birney at 10:35 to "push forward on the road I left you on." He further assured the major general that the XVIII Corps "is now ready to advance in conjunction with you."[18] Unaware that the faltering left wing was incapable of executing its mission, he made no personal effort to revitalize its attack. Instead, he wrote a dispatch to Washington on the morning's success and then left the front via the Varina and Kingsland roads for New Market Heights to look for Butler. Like Ord's quest earlier, his search in the rear proved vain since the man sought had gone up the New Market Road to the X Corps's front. Like Ord, too, he abandoned the effort in favor of simply corresponding with the officer and returned to Deep Bottom, a central location in communication with Meade as well as Butler. His unwitting failure to accomplish more at Fort Harrison destroyed the last chance of mounting a vigorous assault against Ewell's weak center.[19]

The Federals' main hope now rested with Birney on the New Market Road. His relatively late entry into this phase of the battle was inevitable. Both Federal wings had attacked their initial objectives virtually simultaneously. But because those first targets were so far apart, whereas the common second goal, the Fort Maury–Fort Gilmer line, loomed immediately before the left wing but remained still distant from the right wing, the two corps were almost inevitably unable to act in conjunction against it. Butler the planner failed to anticipate this result and unwisely allocated less strength to the left wing, which would have to strike the inner forts first. Such force as was available, moreover, Ord, and even more so Heckman, misused. But it was too late now to change all that. If the initial breakthrough were to be exploited, Birney's arriving troops would have to do it.

The Second Division led his renewed advance. Its capture of the Exterior Line on the New Market Road west of Clyne's house looked encouraging but was really meaningless. The XVIII Corps's breakthrough farther south had already rendered those works untenable. The Secessionists made a stand at Clyne's not to fight for the defenses but to force Foster to stop and deploy. Their objective achieved, they conceded him the works and fell back along the New Market Road 1¼ miles to Laurel Hill Church. The Yankees played along with this delaying action by taking a short rest at Clyne's. When they resumed marching, moreover, they likely moved more cautiously now that they knew the Butternuts were disposed to resist.

Foster had yet to discover just how disposed they were. Videttes' reports alerted Ewell to the new danger. At about 9:30, he risked weakening his own line to send his cavalry brigade back to meet it. The delay at the Exterior Line apparently gave Gary time to arive and deploy his dismounted troopers astride the New Market Road atop Laurel Hill. To cover the approach up this commanding height, he relied on frontal fire from the Third Richmond Howitzers on his battle line plus enfilading fire from two guns in Fort Gilmer and a third elsewhere in the Intermediate Line south of the hill. Thick woods running east from the foot of the hill masked this position from the unsuspecting Bluecoats. Only as Daggett emerged from the woods did he discover, too late, the danger. The Richmonders' 12-pounders ripped his ranks "with terrible effect," while Gathright's Goochlanders enfiladed his left. Such fire doomed efforts to deploy the First Brigade into an attack column of battalions and soon sent it fleeing into the shelter of the woods.

With his vanguard knocked back on its heels, Foster judged it necessary to deploy Colonel Galusha Pennypacker's Second Brigade and behind it Colonel Louis Bell's Third Brigade to support the New Yorkers. The reserve units, themselves suffering from the shelling, found it hard to form column in the woods and ravines and had to content themselves with echeloning to Daggett's right rear. The difficult terrain threw even those formations into disorder, as individual regiments broke out of line and clambered to the front. Somehow the 169th New York of the Third Brigade came forward to join the 3rd New York of the First. Foster himself was with the 3rd, vainly urging it to charge. Only when he reassured it that he would not reprimand it if it lost its colors while attacking did it agree to advance. The 169th and probably the rest of the First Brigade joined in, and the remainder of the division followed up the hill. Gary, outflanked to the north and outnumbered to the east, wisely did not wait to come to grips with the foe. He expeditiously retreated up the New Market Road, leaving his dead and a considerable amount of ammunition on the field. Despite the inelegant precipitance of his withdrawal, he achieved his objective of seriously delaying a whole Yankee division without jeopardizing his own brigade. His skillful operations compelled the enemy to take two hours to travel barely a mile from the Exterior Line to the church. Farther south, Ewell and Gregg put this time to good use to beat off Heckman's last thrusts and then take a breather before having to meet the X Corps.[20]

Both sides now disengaged on the New Market Road. Gary continued up the highway two miles to where it entered the Intermediate Line. He

left his battery there and led his horsemen north to meet Kautz's
raiders. The Second Division did not pursue. It had discovered from
Gathright's fire the proximity of a more important and more formidable foe, Fort Gilmer. Foster and Birney felt it unsafe to move farther
west with this stronghold in their left rear. The Indianian, accordingly,
deployed along or just south of the road eastward from the church to
face this new threat. He did not attack it right away, though. In the
tangled, bramble-infested woods, his Unionists simply waited. Once
more, delays of minutes stretched into half hours and then longer. For
two hours, the Second Division remained idle.

The difficulty of deploying in the rough terrain helps explain the
delay. So does the need to await the arrival of Birney's main body.
Only the 29th Connecticut of the Negro brigade of the X Corps and
two of Jackson's batteries now remained to secure New Market
Heights. The rest of the troops set out for the front sometime after
9:30, first Paine, then William Birney, and finally Terry. Now that
Foster had cleared the way, the main column made relatively good
time, suffered little straggling, and entirely reached the Exterior Line
by noon. Paine moved just beyond the works, and the X Corps elements halted in Clyne's field. There the troops got a little rest and
nourishment—for some the first food all day.

Yet beyond these legitimate causes of delay, more censurable factors
played a role. Chief among them was the fact that the Second Division,
the spearhead of the attack, had virtually withered away by the time it
took the church. A tiring march and a trying duel with a well-managed
rear guard depleted Foster's ranks by the thousands, who now straggled over the countryside from Bermuda Hundred to Laurel Hill. Not
just privates but also over fifty noncoms and even ten officers fell from
the ranks. The most egregious straggler was a regimental commander,
Captain Isaac Hobbs of the 4th New Hampshire. The Indianian, outraged at his men's dereliction, and Birney, furious at both subordinate
general and soldiers, now postponed attacking in order to permit at
least some skulkers to return to the colors and to allow those who
remained a little rest. Some men did rejoin, even as others had returned
to the First Division earlier in the morning, and some men did get a little rest. But with the sun's rays and the Goochlanders' shells beating
down on them and with only limited drinking water available (muddy
at that), the men could hardly recuperate. Nor did many stragglers return to duty. Foster's effective force thus remained pitiably weak. Out
of a potential 3,600 men, no more than 1,400 were still in the ranks
when fighting resumed.

Birney, furthermore, contributed to the delay himself. His dangerous
personal reconnaissance of the front under enemy shelling, which

nearly cost his Chief-of-Artillery his life, understandably took time. One suspects the Pennsylvanian, less defensibly, wasted time coming up with a plan. Despite his proven competence as a general of division, he had not yet displayed the same sure hand in maneuvering a far-flung corps, especially over difficult terrain. Loss of control, hesitancy, inordinate delay in attacking, and inability to exploit initial advantages repeatedly marred his generalship since June. Such factors evidently also affected him at midday on September 29. Then, too, once he did settle on a plan, that same inability to rise to the responsibilities of his office again led him to employ only a fraction of his force against a formidable objective. To pinch off the Fort Gilmer salient, he relied on just Foster, attacking south from the New Market Road, and William Birney, striking west from the Varina Road. Paine, however, was only to remain near the church as a reserve for the Second Division. Plaisted received no more than a comparable mission in respect to William Birney; the colonel, indeed, did not even move up behind the Negroes until just before they attacked. Terry's other two brigades, moreover, were left back in Clyne's field, entirely out of the operation. Even worse, the major general did not co-ordinate the two prongs, an omission all the more glaring since his entire strike force numbered less than 3,200 men.

His earlier hesitancy, moreover, now gave way to equally regrettable rashness. Tired of delays, he demanded that the Second Division attack "within ten minutes from the receipt of this order." Whether this directive originated with him or, more characteristically, with Butler is not clear. The army commander apparently accompanied the main body of the right wing to the front and now maintained field headquarters on the south side of the New Market Road just east of the Exterior Line. Anxious to strike, he had assured Grant at 12:50 that "Birney is at this moment making his attack." When the "moment" ran into minutes and no attack came, the Massachusetts man himself may have enjoined the X Corps to charge. In either case, it was unsound for Birney and Butler not to make sure the USCTs were ready to co-operate before issuing such a command. But Foster knew only that the instructions were peremptory. At about 1:35, he began carrying them out.

Nearly six hours thus elapsed between when the XVIII Corps and the right wing began attacking their second objective. By early afternoon most of Heckman's men, long since fought out, were in no condition to co-operate. Nor was the rest of Birney's command in position to assist the Second Division. Once more, a weak Union force was being hurled against strong works, unsupported.[21]

But once more, too, those strong works were only lightly manned, primarily by forces facing east toward Heckman, rather than north to-

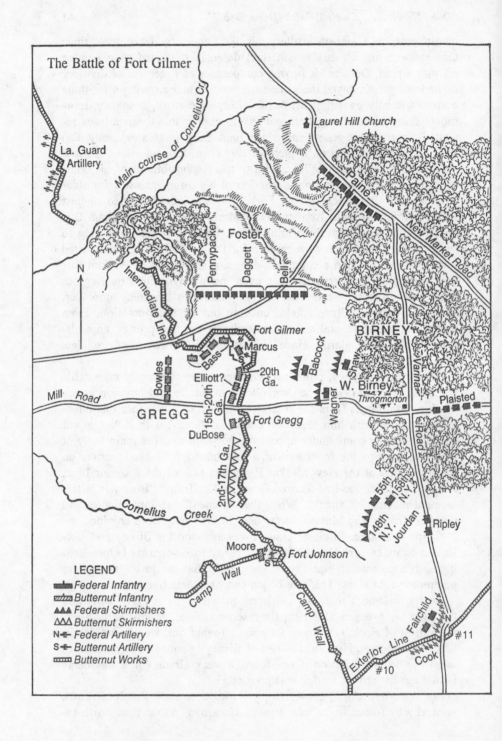

The Battle of Fort Gilmer

La. Guard
Artillery

Main course of Cornelius Cr

Laurel Hill Church

Paine

New Market Road

Foster

Pennypacker
Daggett
Bell

Intermediate Line

N

Fort Gilmer

Marcus

Bass

20th
Ga.

Elliott?

Babcock

BIRNEY

Shaw

W. Birney

Throgmorton

Varina

Plaisted

Bowles

Mill Road

GREGG

15th-20th Ga.

DuBose

Fort Gregg

Wagner

Road

2nd-17th Ga.

55th Pa.

158th N.Y.

Cornelius Creek

148th N.Y.

Jourdan

Ripley

Moore

Fort Johnson

Camp Wall

Camp Wall

LEGEND

Federal Infantry
Butternut Infantry
Federal Skirmishers
Butternut Skirmishers
N— Federal Artillery
S— Butternut Artillery
Butternut Works

Exterior Line

Fairchild

N

#11

Cook

#10

ward the new danger. The most southerly force that could help meet this new threat was Griffin's gun in the left flank of Fort Gregg, possibly his only piece that Cook had not disabled. Northward along the one-eighth mile of curtain from that redoubt to Fort Gilmer stretched part of the 15th Georgia and then the 20th Georgia, the latter having shifted northward by this time. In the more northerly stronghold were five more companies of the 15th plus fragments of Guy's, Bass's, and Elliott's forces that had fled there from the outer defenses—roughly 200 men under Captain Madison Marcus of the 15th.

The guardian of the most pronounced salient on the Intermediate Line, Fort Gilmer was the key to the Confederate left. In many ways, however, it was even less suited to the role cast upon it than Fort Harrison. A strong profile, a moat ten feet deep, two lines of abatis on its northern side but none on its eastern side, and a palisaded gorge wall of bastioned trace admittedly enhanced its defensibility. Unfortunately, the bastions were all on the gorge wall, not the front and flanks. Built like one giant bastion, the main part of the fort had no bastions of its own; except for a little re-entrant salient and a minimal right flank, it could enfilade virtually no portion of its own front. To make matters worse, it was not designed as an artillery emplacement and mounted only two heavy guns (one a 64-pounder), still manned by Gathright's Goochlanders. Worst of all, it could be easily outflanked to the west.

There the curtain of the Intermediate Line ran straight west, without any re-entrant, from Gilmer's left flank about 120 yards, then cut back southwest 145 yards, next ran west about 170 yards across a northward-flowing branch of Cornelius Creek, and finally ran almost due north across a country lane and along the left bank of the natural moat that the branch formed nearly to the main stream itself. The prolonga-

COMMENTARY

1. This map horologically telescopes Federal attacks against the Intermediate Line. Foster, in fact, struck first; then the 9th, 8th, and 7th USCT each charged, in that order; and finally, Jourdan engaged.

2. Bowles is shown arriving on the field and marching toward his sector to Bass's left, presumably the works on the left bank of the creek branch.

3. The 97th Pennsylvania held Foster's right; the 9th Maine is thought to have held his left; and the 142nd, 117th, 3rd, and 112th New York, right to left, formed Daggett's line in the center.

4. The positions of Paine and Plaisted are shown only symbolically.

5. Except for Marcus' and Moore's detachments, DeBose's units—and Elliott, too—are represented only symbolically.

6. The locations of the guns west of Cornelius Creek and of any of Stark's other pieces reinforcing Hardaway in this area are not certain.

tion of this line beyond the main stream, covering the Osborne Turnpike, had little bearing on this phase of the battle. The north–south
sector from the lane to just north of the main creek, in contrast, was
well suited to raking any force attacking south from Laurel Hill. Yet
virtually no troops guarded that important sector of works: just the
Louisiana Guard Artillery and one other battery (either the First
Rockbridge Artillery or perhaps some of Pemberton's men) west of
the branch and possibly, though doubtfully, D/17th Georgia immediately left of Fort Gilmer. If Foster could forge ahead on his present
axis from the New Market Road, he might well penetrate the nearly
vacant works west of Marcus and roll up the whole line southward.

A small garrison, a poorly designed stronghold, a position inviting
penetration—it seemed to be the story of Fort Harrison all over again.
This time, though, the defenders were alerted to the new threat and
ready for the foe. Most, moreover, were sturdy veterans, well braced
for the contest. Then, too, additional reliable troops were available
from other quarters, no longer threatened by Heckman. DuBose now
rushed part of the 2nd and 17th Georgia north from Fort Johnson to
bolster Marcus and probably also to strengthen the curtain between
those two redoubts. Those trenches needed reinforcing, for Gregg himself yanked the 3rd Arkansas and then the three Texas regiments out of
there and sent them hurrying for the vacant trenches just west of Fort
Gilmer. Though exhausted from eight hours of fighting, Bass's stalwart
veterans drew upon the reserve strength of their battle-hardened bodies
to race for the works. In a desperate dash, they reached the trenches
only minutes ahead of the advancing Bluecoats. As his own brigade
lined the parapet west to the branch, Gregg could see that he would be
ready for the Unionists this time.[22]

The division commander could not have known it, of course, but
problems the attackers faced gave them less prospect of success than
Stannard had enjoyed that morning. The striking force, for one thing,
further dwindled as exhausted men fell out of its charging line. The
Second Division's deployment, in addition, was ill suited to troops
rushing into battle unsupported. Foster had little experience in forming
such a large command to carry a position. Dragged along from one pe-
ripheral front to another the first three years of the war, he had seen
little field combat above the regimental level. Much of his initial service on returning to Virginia in 1864, moreover, had been staff duty or
line assignments on quiescent sectors. Although his command of a brigade at Second Deep Bottom had been promising, he had yet to prove
himself on the divisional level. In this, his first real trial, he chose a
poor formation for his men: not a massed column such as overran Fort
Harrison but a long, thin line with no reserves. The 97th Pennsylvania

held his far right; then came Pennypacker's other three regiments. Daggett prolonged the line eastward: 142nd, 117th, 3rd, and 112th New York, in that order. The 169th New York of the Third Brigade likely adjoined the 112th's left. Three more of Bell's regiments came next, and his 9th Maine probably held the far left. To encourage this thin blue line, Foster and his brigadiers strode bravely into the fray with their men, though both Pennypacker and Daggett were soon slightly wounded. However, heroism alone, when not the tool of tactics, no longer decided battles.

The weak line that moved south from the New Market Road, moreover, encountered neither open fields nor "blind spots" such as had facilitated Stannard's attack. This time several ravines—four on Daggett's front, three elsewhere—cut across its path, difficult ravines at that: overgrown, bramble-infested, in two cases penetrated by marshy tributaries of Cornelius Creek. From the last ravine an open cornfield, bare of protecting cover, stretched south to the abatis. The mile of such forbidding terrain by itself made many Unionists lose hope of success. Yet their commanders urged them on, so with grim determination they gripped their rifles a little tighter and moved to the attack.

They took few casualties from Hardaway's initial fire and quickly reached the sheltering ravine of the Laurel Hill tributary. Tearing their way through its swampy thickets, however, threw them into some disorder, so Foster halted briefly to dress ranks. Then he led them across the next ridgetop toward the next depression. Once his line emerged from cover, the Louisiana Guards and the other battery near them enfiladed his right, and the Goochlanders blasted his front. Staggered, the Bluecoats dashed for the shelter of the next ravine, only to find it offered no protection against the sweeping fire from the west. Still, they heroically clambered up its southern slope and braved the shelling plus a little musketry as well until they could "tumble" into the last creek-bottom north of the cornfield. There Foster again paused briefly to dress ranks and let his men catch their breath. Yet few could truly rest amid such scenes. "Death fairly reveled in that third ravine," wrote a soldier of the 3rd New York. "Shells hissed and exploded about our ears incessantly, and crushed heads and mangled bodies thickly strewed our pathway."[23] Despite the carnage, some men from at least the 115th New York refused to leave the minimal protection of that bloody depression. At their general's command, though, the more stalwart survivors bravely burst forth from the ravine, cheering, in a final rush for the works themselves. Hardaway now greeted them with canister. Gregg's riflemen, too, now blazed away in earnest. Even the 20th Georgia on the far right joined the shooting, though it was too far south to hit Bell. Marcus, Bass, and Hardaway, however, had perfect

range. Their deadly raking and ripping fire cut down Federals by the
score and stopped them far short of their objective. Inexperienced
troops might have returned such fire, but Foster's veterans knew better
than uselessly to expose themselves to this leaden hail. Without stopping to shoot back, they broke for the rear, presumably for the cover of
the nearest ravine.

There they found that their chiefs did not share their willingness to
call off the attack. Foster and his brigadiers desperately rallied them
for another attempt. To add weight to it, corps headquarters reinforced
Bell with the 5th USCT of Draper's brigade—just one battered regiment of the whole supporting division, yet another case of how Birney
fought with too little, too late. But they were all the help he would
give. The blacks, moreover, took further loss from Confederate shelling
just in tearing their way through the last two ravines. Once they finally
reached the front, though, the whole Northern force again pressed forward. The Graycoats, heartened by their initial success, again poured
devastating fire into the Second Division. The ensuing scene seared itself into the memory of one of Daggett's men:

> The hissing and howling and screaming of the missiles, mingled
> with the shouts of the attacking party, the yells of the rebels, and
> the groans of the wounded, were horrible beyond description. The
> leaves of corn, cut by flying shot, floated before our eyes con-
> tinually, and fell to the earth in showers. Many a poor fellow near
> me was struck the second time before he reached the ground with
> his first wound. We had passed a little log house, and were within
> forty paces of the abatis of the fort, when a whirlwind seemed to
> rush across our front. The line disappeared as though an earth-
> quake had swallowed it. The fatal hissing increased in volume a
> hundred fold. Perfectly bewildered, those who remained standing
> halted. The ground was covered with our slain, and we had come
> thus far with fixed bayonets and without firing a shot. Every one
> recoiled, and Foster, who was still with us, ordered a retreat. The
> rebels stood in crowds upon the parapet of their fort, shouting at us
> in derision.[24]

In futile fury, a few soldiers of the Third Brigade braved even this inferno as far as the frise but could not cross it. Nor could they endure
this fatal fire long. The whole Second Division now faltered. At least
the 115th New York of Bell's brigade vainly sought shelter behind a
little log cabin in the field. The Negroes meantime pressed on "with a
blind desperation" past the 115th to within a hundred yards of the
works. But then they, too, were stopped. To find cover from the deadly
fire, they threw themselves on the ground.[25] The open field, of course,

afforded no protection, so the 5th slowly and in good order pulled back
to the ravine. Foster now ordered his division, too, to withdraw, and
Bell took it on himself to issue comparable instructions. Pennypacker's
men, who had suffered relatively little on the far right, retired in good
order. The other two brigades, however, were badly shaken by their ordeal and withdrew in some disarray.

Denied victory, the soldiers strove to preserve honor by bringing off
their flags. Most succeeded, often by extraordinary efforts, but the
banner of the 3rd New York and a guidon of the 9th Maine were left
on the field. Left behind, too, were the dead and seriously wounded in
the cornfield. Those downed farther north, however, escaped capture,
as skirmishers of the Third Brigade now ranged out to cover their rescue. Many there were to save. Foster lost roughly 400 men, at least 35
per cent of those he took into battle. About 100 more USCTs reportedly fell during that fatal charge. Such staggering losses ruined the
right prong of Birney's pincer for the rest of the afternoon. Foster's
men could only regroup along the New Market Road and watch others
challenge the valiant defenders of the Intermediate Line. The X Corps's
inauspicious entry into this part of the fray achieved no more than to
illustrate what the XVIII Corps had already proved: the most effective
way to nullify numerical superiority is to attack in detail.[26]

Half-past two, Thursday afternoon, hardly saw the Confederates
meditating on such lessons in tactics. They had just won another splendid victory at minimal cost: a handful of men killed (probably
Gathright among them) and yet another big cannon dismounted by its
own recoil, this time in Gilmer. Now they leaped atop the parapet to
fire parting shots at the fleeing foe and to rend the air with a mighty
cheer. It was a shout of rejoicing and exultation, of course, and also a
shout of derision at the flying Yankees. But most of all, it was a cheer
of thankfulness, for as the Bluecoats retired, more Southern troops
rushed to the Intermediate Line just west of the branch of Cornelius
Creek to hasten them on their way. These were not some exhausted
units from Ewell's right but Major General Charles Field with the vanguard of reinforcements from Petersburg. These troops, Law's Alabama Brigade under Colonel Pinckney D. Bowles, had detrained west
of Drewry's Bluff, then double-quicked for five miles from the rail sid-
ing to Fort Gilmer, with only brief respites for walking instead of
rushing. Just before 2:30, they finally reached the front. Ewell's men
had won the time Lee needed to reinforce the Northside, and now they
cheered the fresh soldiers who came to share their burden.[27]

Field's leading brigade arrived just in time to help meet a new danger. Now that the Second Division had been repulsed, William Birney
at last attacked the eastern face of the Intermediate Line. This lack of

co-ordination again suggests that corps headquarters did not effectively control its units. Even though David Birney may have had no discretion about ordering the white troops into battle prematurely, he had little excuse for not committing his brother's command at the same time. The Negro brigade remained back at the Exterior Line for two hours. Not until 2:00 P.M. did it even begin moving toward the front. The 8th USCT led it west along the New Market Road a short way. Then the brigade faced left, formed brigade column of battalions (the 9th USCT now in front, followed by the 8th and then the 7th USCT), and advanced into the woods south of the highway. As it came opposite the Gregg–Gilmer sector, regiments peeled off westward toward those works. The 9th moved across the Varina Road and deployed in a depression facing the curtains between those redoubts. Only after that regiment subsequently attacked did the 8th take position farther south astride the Mill Road. Finally, the 7th, after some difficult maneuvering through the dense woods, came up on the 8th's right. By the time the blacks at last got into place, the Second Division was reeling back in defeat. Yet again, a fresh Federal unit was challenging Ewell by itself.

The elder Birney, moreover, now diminished his prospects still further. A citizen soldier like his brother, he too had served since the spring of 1861 but with less distinction and experience than David. The third year of the war William spent away from the front successfully recruiting Negro units in Maryland, a useful but hardly vital task. Armies are not welfare organizations nor just recruiting depots. Their generals must ultimately be judged on how they handle troops in camp and battle. Here William Birney fell short. His return to the field in March 1864 brought him little experience and less laurels. His strict and critical nature, furthermore, incurred the animosity of many of his white officers, though his unimpeachable abolitionist credentials stood him in good stead at army headquarters. He had, in sum, yet to earn the general's stars that now glittered on each shoulder. He would not prove claim to them on this day, either.

Whereas his brother had had difficulty in handling a whole wing in battle, the Jerseyman now proved unable to hold even a brigade together. That he left two of his units back at the junction of the New Market and Mill roads is understandable: the raw 2/45th USCT, only four days in the war zone, and the 29th Connecticut, arriving late from New Market Heights, likely as escort for M/1st U. S. Artillery. Nor may he necessarily be criticized for not using Plaisted, who probably now moved down from Clyne's to his support but who may not have reported to him. But the general must be held accountable for misusing the three veteran regiments he did send into action. Just what he intended them to do is not clear, for he wrote no wartime report, and his postwar polemic is absurdly incredible. What is clear is that he attacked not by brigade, not even by regiment, but in most cases by battalion, committed piecemeal.

Even before his whole line deployed west of the Varina Road, he hurled his leading regiment, Captain Edward Babcock's 9th USCT, against the curtain between Forts Gilmer and Gregg. Babcock promptly formed his available force (not counting the one company on provost duty at brigade headquarters) into the desired deployment of four companies of voltigeurs, supported by five in line of battle. Then he led it up out of its shallow depression into the cornfield, which stretched away to the eastern as well as the northern face of the Intermediate Line. Hardaway, no longer pressed on other sectors, turned his fire on both flanks of the regiment. Though "shaken" by this lethal enfilade and by having to charge so far, the Negroes still managed to get halfway across the field. Farther, Babcock felt them too weak to go. He therefore ordered them to hug the ground while he returned to the intersection of the Mill and Varina roads to inform William Birney of the unfavorable situation. The brigadier, unfazed, ordered the subordinate to press ahead and storm Fort Gilmer. Unknown to them, however, Captain Hugh Thompson, acting commander in Babcock's absence, had already concluded that waiting under fire was unendurable and took it on himself to resume attacking. By the time Babcock rejoined his men, they were falling back to the woods in defeat—clear testimony of the efficacy of Hardaway's fire and the unwisdom of ordering such a charge.

The general, however, was undaunted. Now he tossed Major George Wagner's 8th USCT against Fort Gregg. Wagner, evidently in compliance with orders, advanced a battle line of only four companies into the open field. More combat-tested than its black comrades who had just struck farther north, this battalion surged to within 250 yards of Fort Gregg. But there Griffin's deadly fire brought it, too, to a standstill. The Negroes at least bravely held their ground until Wagner, at his chief's order, could bring up four more companies to spearhead a renewed advance. Yet even this combined force, the major realized, was too weak to carry the fort. He accordingly secured the brigadier's permission simply to remain in the forward position and keep up light-infantry fire on the Salem Flying Artillery.

Reducing the 8th's mission, however, did not spare the last fresh unit, Colonel James Shaw's 7th USCT, from the ordeal. The rear of the original column of march, this regiment did not even begin deploying on the brigade's center west of the Varina Road until Babcock and Wagner had been checked. The Virginians' shells overshooting the charging 9th, indeed, struck around Shaw's force as it maneuvered into position. William Birney initially ordered the colonel to storm

Fort Gilmer in regimental line of battle. Before the 7th could advance,
however, Captain Marcellus Bailey, the brigade assistant adjutant general, delivered another order, allegedly in these words:

> The general commanding directs you to advance with your whole
> force and attack the work in your front, which is firing. You will
> throw forward four companies of your command as skirmishers.[28]

This seemingly clear directive generated much heated controversy after
the battle. The brigadier and his staff officer asserted that Shaw ignored
the adjective "whole" and mistook the second sentence as an amplification of the first: that only four companies in skirmishing order, not the
entire regiment, were to attack. The Rhode Islander and several of his
subordinates countered that the captain only told them to charge with
four companies and, to the colonel's protest that the original order
called for the whole regiment to attack, answered: "Well, now the Gen.
directs that you deploy 4 co's. as skirmishers to attack the work that is
firing."[29] Available evidence does not indicate whether it was regimental or brigade headquarters that ordered a mere battalion to charge
Fort Gilmer, although historical example and number, credibility, and
integrity of advocates make Shaw's case more plausible. Yet beyond
the intrinsic value of establishing the truth, resolving the dispute is
meaningless. Ten companies could no more have carried Fort Gilmer
that late in the day than could four. Leaving six out of action, at whoever's order, at least reduced casualties without affecting the outcome.
If the course of the whole day's operations had not made clear that a
few hundred men could not storm the works, then the fate of the little
battalion of the 7th that did charge should have at least reoriented subsequent controversy.

Whatever the errors of their superiors, the 9 officers and approximately 189 men of that battalion unquestionably covered themselves
with glory. Under no illusion about the outcome, Captain Julius Weiss
dutifully deployed his battalion and led it out of the swale into the
cornfield. Once more the guns of Gilmer blasted the attackers' front.
Once more, too, Griffin, not silenced by Wagner, enfiladed their left.
This time, though, the Maryland Negroes absorbed their losses and,
without stopping to fire, quick-timed onward. As it became clear that
Hardaway could not stop this charge, Southern infantry trained their
rifles on the approaching line. Marcus kept his men in check until the
7th was almost upon them and then blasted it with a devastating volley.
From the curtain to his right more of DuBose's men raked the USCTs'
left. From the west the Texans and even the Alabamians, not so scru-
pulous about getting the range, at least discharged their guns at the voltigeurs overlapping the fort from the north. Veteran troops would

never have remained exposed to such lethal fire, but these inexperienced blacks knew no better than to endure. Already at least 61 attackers had fallen, perhaps as many as 77. Still the survivors pressed on. Now, three quarters of the way to the fort, they broke into a run. Now, with no abatis to stop them, they poured into the moat itself.

Farther they could not go. Without ladders they could not effectively crown the ramparts; without reinforcements they could not even maintain their position. Nor did they dare leave their temporary refuge in the fosse to retreat to the woods. Of the few who tried to get back, only one survived. Like Sadler at Fort Johnson that morning, Weiss now found the moat a trap for his 120–140 men. At least, his soldiers bravely tried to fight their way into the fort. One crawled through a culvert, only to be killed as he emerged. Others clawed their way up the rampart or boosted comrades to the top. But unlike at Fort Harrison, the defenders, even the second-class Virginia troops, now stood firm and put a bullet through every head that appeared above the parapet. Three times the Unionists pushed an assault wave up the exterior slope; three times waves of bleeding bodies tumbled maimed or lifeless back into the fosse. Weiss himself fell wounded in the first wave. Another leader—not a commander, to be sure, but a paladin renowned for his prowess in battle—was apparently a certain "Corporal Dick"; at least, the Confederates remembered it that way:

> "Surrender, you black scoundrels!" shouted the commander of the fort.
> "S'rendah, yo'seff, sah!" came the reply in a stentorian voice. "Jess wait'll we'uns git in dah, eff yer wanter." Then they began lifting each other up to the top of the parapet, but no sooner did a head appear above it than its owner was killed by shot from the rifles of the infantry.
> "Less liff Caw'pul Dick up," one of them suggested; "he'll git in dah, suah," and the corporal was accordingly hoisted, only to fall back lifeless, with a bullet through his head.
> "Dah, now!" loudly exclaimed another of his companions; "Caw'pul Dick done dead! What I done bin tole yer?"[80]

This incident provided laughs for the defenders for days and weeks, years and decades to come. Many derived sheer joy from killing the Negroes. As word spread that a big "Blackbird shoot" was under way, Butternuts ran up from nearby works to join in the fun.

The Bluecoats returned this fire for a time. However, as their ranks steadily dwindled, they sought refuge along a blind face of the fort, which could not be enfiladed from the works. A few enterprising Seces-

sionists then lay atop the parapet and sniped at the foe. Marcus judged
this method too slow, so he ordered a Goochlander to lob a hand grenade, made from a shell with a short fuse, into the moat. First one and
then a second grenade burst among the USCTs with deadly effect. The
survivors, less than 100 men, many badly wounded, could stand no more
and finally surrendered. The garrison then pulled them up into the fort
and rushed them to the rear. White troops who had fought that bravely
would have been accorded the respect due worthy foemen, but the
blacks in arms, with few exceptions, encountered only hatred. Several
were killed on the spot, though there was no wholesale massacre;
others were abused; and many of the rest were consigned to the slow
death of prison, where two thirds of the survivors eventually perished.
Yet what the victors would not acknowledge, history can accord: The
physical courage of the Negro battalion stands out in spite of the ineptitude of its brigadier. But valor, unchanneled by generalship, does not
win battles. Weiss's battalion had been wiped out, and over 100 other
brave USCTs had fallen to no avail. Now even William Birney chose
not to risk additional men in foolhardy jabs at a strong line.[31]

Hardly had fighting around Fort Gilmer subsided before it broke out
anew before Fort Gregg. With tragic consistency Charles A. Heckman
—the officer who could not co-ordinate his first attack with Stannard's,
who could not co-ordinate his own brigades with each other, and who
could not co-ordinate the elements of the corps that had passed under
his command—of course, failed to co-ordinate his efforts to execute
Grant's order to "advance in conjunction with" the X Corps. Only
when all Birney's thrusts had been beaten back did the junior officer
hurl his last fresh brigade, Jourdan's, from the lower Exterior Line toward the redoubt on the Mill Road. The 55th Pennsylvania spearheaded
this drive, with the 158th New York echeloned to its right rear and the
148th New York skirmishing to its left rear. Its diagonal advance
northwestward exposed its left to a heavy enfilade from DuBose's right.
Hardaway, moreover, now concentrated on it the fire of all his guns
between Forts Gilmer and Johnson: at least five pieces, perhaps as
many as fifteen in the unlikely event that Griffin had more than one
gun operable and that the Louisiana Guard Artillery and the Mathews
Artillery reached this sector in time to open on Jourdan. The result
was predictable: The small Union force forged bravely ahead until the
deadly fire at last stopped it short.

This time, though, a small party, led by the color bearer of the 55th,
dashed forward and apparently even penetrated the Confederate works.
Any who got inside were easily overwhelmed by DuBose's men except
for one valiant corporal of the 158th, who managed to escape with the
flag of the 20th Georgia. Meantime, another noncom saved the Penn-

sylvanians' banner, which had gone down before reaching the moat. Such isolated acts of bravery, however, could not offset the basic fact that the First Brigade, too, was repulsed and forced to fall back to the Exterior Line.[32]

A few men of the 148th briefly lingered in the cornfield. Farther north the 8th and F/7th USCT stayed in the field nearly until dark. Sniping by these three forces now proved more effective than their comrades' battle lines as they silenced at least one and perhaps more guns in the Intermediate Line. Four 12-pounders of Battery M/1st U. S. Artillery meantime unlimbered on the New Market Road and hurled some heavier lead into Fort Gilmer. Hardaway ignored the Regulars but did bring the First Rockbridge into Fort Gilmer and the Third Richmond Howitzers to the works about 300 yards west of there to fire on the sharpshooters. He may also have transferred the Louisiana Guards into Fort Gregg and put the newly arrived Mathews Artillery of Stark's Battalion into Fort Johnson to relieve Griffin's and Dance's battered units. For the next two hours only the desultory firing of these batteries and marksmen punctuated the inactivity that settled over the field north of the lower Exterior Line.

The armies waited for their commanders to decide on some new course of action. Yet for the Yankees few options remained but to preserve the existing stalemate. Grant, to be sure, had written Butler from Deep Bottom at 1:35 P.M. that "if General Birney has not been successful in carrying the works in his front, I think it will be advisable to move out to" the Darbytown Road. Signal reports from the Army of the Potomac that Confederate reinforcements were en route to the Northside from Petersburg, the lieutenant general added, showed "that all must be done to-day that can be done toward Richmond."[33]

The trouble with such advice was that once Birney was repulsed, few fresh troops remained to carry it out. Terry's two brigades in Clyne's field plus the 1/4th Massachusetts Cavalry were available, however. Sometime between two and two-thirty, probably once Foster's defeat became evident, the army commander sent them north, most likely via the Strath Road, which entered the Darbytown Road about half a mile west of the Exterior Line. Near 3:00, Plaisted, too, was pulled out of tactical reserve and ordered to follow Pond. The First Division was apparently expected to join Kautz in overrunning the middle reaches of the Intermediate Line but was not to attack those works by itself. The troopers, however, had left the Darbytown Road hours before, and Terry could not ascertain their whereabouts. All he netted were a few stray Southerners plus a rumor (probably false) that strong Confederate forces confronted him. He, accordingly, halted and deployed across the highway to await developments, while scouts searched for the missing horsemen. No threat materialized; no Cavalry Division was found. So Terry remained idle for the rest of the afternoon within sight of the spires of Richmond just three miles away, too justifiably cautious to attack and too brave to retreat. Once more the Yankees used too weak a force to develop a potentially advantageous course of action.

While the First Division operated farther north, Birney's main body remained quiescent in front of Fort Gilmer. He may have been waiting for the expeditionary column to create a new opening. However, the absence of any effort to reinforce Terry plus redeployment already taking place on the XVIII Corps's sector suggest a far different conclusion. The Northerners had evidently already abandoned hope of accomplishing anything more that day and were simply keeping up a bold front to gain time to consolidate their initial gains.

As early as noon the General-in-Chief had advised Butler:

> If our troops do not reach Richmond this afternoon, my opinion is that it will be unsafe to spend the night north of the enemy's lower bridge. I think it advisable to select a line now to which the troops can be brought back to-night, if they do not reach Richmond.[34]

Barnard and Comstock started marking out such a line right away. When the X Corps's repeated defeats revealed that the line would be needed, army headquarters probably ordered sharpshooters to keep firing, not so much to cripple the Intermediate Line as to cover some of the redeployment necessary to take up the new line. Creating such a defensive position, of course, did not rule out renewed attacks on the morrow; Grant and probably Butler, indeed, remained committed to resuming the offensive on Friday. The decision to go on the defensive did, however, signify Yankee recognition that all the rich opportunities that had awaited them Thursday morning would still have to await them the next day if they were to be attained at all. By 3:00 P.M. the Confederates could well boast that their brilliant and heroic defense had plugged the hole in their works between the New Market Road and the James that had gaped so wide when the Stars and Stripes first rose over Fort Harrison a mere eight hours before.[35]

Establishing defensive stability, however, was not enough for Robert E. Lee. Throughout the day he had urged Ewell to recapture the fort. By midafternoon the subordinate at last felt able to send reassurance that "we will take the offensive as soon as troops come up." Yet the department commander did not follow through on his promise. He may not have remained at Chaffin's to carry it out but may instead have heeded Richmond's suggestion that he supervise efforts to defeat Kautz and leave Anderson in command of the main front. That possibility, however, does not explain why the I Corps commander did not counterattack with his left. Lack of available leaders becomes an even less plausible explanation due to the presence of Lee himself at and near Mrs. Chaffin's after midafternoon. As repeated threats by the Army of the Potomac failed to materialize into a real onslaught, the Virginian finally felt safe in leaving Dunn's Hill for the Peninsula. He even ordered his headquarters broken up and re-established on the Osborne Turnpike. Without waiting for that shift, he rode off to the active front. He may have arrived with the Alabamians and was definitely present by 3:00. There was, in sum, no lack of senior generals anxious to counterattack.

A better explanation of why they did not strike may lie in the proviso of Ewell's promise that he would attack "as soon as troops come up." Only one brigade had yet arrived from Petersburg, troops the generals may have felt needed to remain on guard west of Fort Gilmer. Field's second brigade, Brigadier General John Bratton's South Carolinians, did not reach the Intermediate Line until late afternoon. The rest of the troops from the Southside did not come up until night or next morning. Such forces as were available, three fresh brigades (including Montague) plus the exhausted men who had battled all day, may just have appeared too weak to justify counterattacking. Yet the Southern high command may have misread the situation or may even have been guilty of that lack of co-ordination that, when practiced by the Yankees, had so aided the defenders that day. The Butternuts did not mass their reinforcements for a concerted counterattack against either flank. Instead, they left Montague to fight his own battle on the far south and kept Bowles out of action altogether. Bratton and some of the 4th Texans, moreover, did no more than make several reconnaissances against the Union skirmish line sniping at the Intermediate Line about 5:30. One thrust provoked a brisk fire fight. Under mounting Confederate pressure, the 8th USCTs' left flank, low on ammunition and disgraced by a cowardly company commander who fled his post, threatened to crumble. Wagner, however, counterattacked with a company from his right and after a sharp fight forced the Secessionists to withdraw. William Birney then shifted the 7th down to relieve the 8th in renewed sharpshooting on the Mill Road and reinforced the 9th with the 29th in case the Southerners attacked again in greater strength.[36]

But no attack came. Under cover of this bolstered skirmish line, Foster, William Birney, and Paine at last fell back safely to a good, ready-made defensive position along the Exterior Line at the end of the afternoon. By early evening, the First Division, which Birney had recalled, rejoined the corps and bivouacked in Clyne's field. In the wake of the withdrawing Bluecoats, Southern voltigeurs ranged over the cornfield to gather arms, ammunition, the two abandoned flags, and booty from the fallen; to capture the grievously wounded; and to establish a skirmish line. Going over that bloody field made one South Carolinian exult that earlier in the afternoon "our men everlastingly slayed the Negro tribe; the Battle Field was covered with the Black rascals as well as the Whites." Some of his comrades allegedly still kept up the "everlasting slaying" by bayoneting some of the wounded USCTs on the field, but there was no general slaughter. Beyond throwing out this skirmish line, the Confederates made no effort to disrupt the withdrawal or to pursue.

The X Corps's delaying action, if such it was, also allowed Heckman to take up his new position without difficulty a little earlier in the afternoon. By then, he had at last concentrated his own three brigades around Batteries No. 10 and 11—united them not to attack but to withdraw. They were no longer needed there, since the right wing sufficed to hold all the works from the New Market Road to just right of Fort Harrison. He accordingly shifted them south of the fort to try to refuse the army's left flank. One small division, of course, could not extend all the way from Harrison to the river, but it offered at least some protection to the vulnerable line of communications along the Varina Road to Aiken's Landing. Covered by Birney on the north and Stannard to the southwest, the Second Division moved into its new sector without difficulty.

Not even Confederate naval forces caused that division much trouble. Battery Semmes had already proved itself no threat. When it belatedly received Pickett's request for support and opened fire on the Varina Road around 2:00 P.M., defective ammunition and powder invariably caused its shells to fall far short for the rest of the afternoon. The James River Squadron fared little better, even though the redoubtable *Virginia II* at last joined its firing line. The flagship had taken until 1:00 P.M. just to get into fighting trim. Then when she tried to weigh anchor, she found her chain entangled with that of the supply schooner *Gallego,* moored alongside. Another half hour was consumed disentangling the two vessels. Finally the ironclad set off downriver at 1:30, leaving the poor little *Gallego* to sink under the excess weight transferred to her from the *Virginia II.* Delayed too long already, Shepperd left her to her fate and kept on toward the front. After a brief stop just below Chaffin's Bluff, he finally got to Graveyard Reach at 3:30. Another seventy-five minutes elapsed before he opened fire. Hardly had he started shooting before Mitchell ordered the little *Drewry* to cease firing to preserve what little gunpowder remained. Neither ironclads nor gunboats did much damage, for they persistently overshot the Second and First divisions.

Such overshooting, in fact, made rear areas more dangerous than front lines. Ben Butler himself got caught in such an unintentional barrage on the Varina Road and had to gallop unceremoniously to the cover of the woods—a heroic deed in his own eyes but a ludicrous sight to his men. Some of Cook's guns dueling Hardaway from near Battery No. 11, likely the Pennsylvanians and Rhode Islanders, were not as fortunate as their general. At about 4:00 P.M. a shell from the fleet burst among them from the rear with lethal effect to man and horse. A naval fire spotter may then have called in more shots on the vulnerable companies; in any case, Mitchell's ensuing barrage definitely forced the Napoleons to limber up and withdraw. Yet even such an achievement, though gratifying to artillerists, had little impact on the battle. The failure of the Federal infantry to carry the Intermediate Line made meaningless the unavailability of some of their guns to shell that position. Mitchell's inability to damage Fort Harrison substantially, furthermore, not only obscured this one little coup but also gave Cook no qualms about placing more guns in that sector. He deployed half of his Regular battery there around 2:00 P.M. and posted three rifles of K/3rd New York Light Artillery in that area about the time A/1st and F/1st withdrew.[37]

Such long-range shelling plus light skirmishing marked operations in the camp from midmorning to late afternoon while fighting raged farther north. But shortly before dark, after Birney's sector too had become quiescent, heavy action once more erupted near the Osborne Turnpike. In the last Federal offensive of the day, at least the 58th and 188th Pennsylvania of Cullen's brigade attacked Laffoon's outwork, Fort Hoke. By then, Maury's Battalion had turned over the redoubt to other troops, likely a work detail of the 10th Virginia Heavy Artillery Battalion from Signal Hill. These ill-trained troops, unworthy of the trust Allen had bequeathed them, abandoned the fort to the onrushing Yankees. This victory, though, netted Stannard no more than the earthwork itself, its cannons, and a few prisoners. Between him and the James still stood Fort Maury, covered by Stark's company in Battery No. 1 plus a gunboat (either the *Beaufort* or the *Roanoke*) below the bluff. Such a barrier, the general judged, was too strong to be attacked.

Indeed, far from continuing the drive, the Vermonter, either on his own or on Heckman's orders, soon took steps to fall back to Fort Harrison, the First Division's sector of the army's new defense line. For Raulston such a move entailed simply pulling his skirmishers back to the stronghold. The Second and Third brigades, on the other hand, had to disengage from the enemy and also to disable the Diagonal Line before abandoning it. They, accordingly, spiked six guns, probably carried off those of Battery x, and presumably did at least marginal damage to the three redoubts they held along that line.

Before Stannard could complete these measures, the Butternuts counterattacked. Perhaps the loss of Fort Hoke precipitated their move; perhaps they struck as part of a larger plan. Whatever the initial objective, the presence nearby of Lee himself, the persistent advocate of the offensive, assured that the attack would be pressed to the fullest. Paucity of resources, doubtless, dismayed but did not daunt the army commander; he would make good use of whatever forces were on hand. The second-class units (possibly including the 3rd Local Defense Regiment and 4th Local Defense Battalion, which may already have arrived from Richmond) he left in charge of the works. Doing that freed the available veterans to attack: Montague as the nucleus, the experienced 44th and 63rd and presumably 25th Tennessee, even some of Laffoon's musketeers, who had won their spurs only that morning. By 5:30, his preparations were completed. He then ordered the ships to cease firing and the foot soldiers to charge. The infantry sprang over the parapets and swooped down on Fort Hoke. Cullen's vanguard, outnumbered and committed to retreating anyway, evidently put up little resistance and soon yielded the redoubt to the attackers.

Stannard, too, saw no point in contesting possession of an outwork he had intended to abandon. Yet he could not simply ignore this new danger and had to throw out a rear guard to oppose it. The onrushing Graycoats outflanked this new line's left, came close to capturing the flag of the 92nd New York, and chased the force up the Diagonal Line. They could not, however, overtake the principal part of the First Division. Their advance, indeed, only "materially accelerated our speed towards the main body by a severe fire of musketry in our rear," according to a soldier of the 21st Connecticut. Even so, they did take about 60 prisoners and reoccupied most of the Diagonal Line, including Battery x. Montague then tried for the big prize, Fort Harrison itself. That coveted objective the Federals would not yield him without a fight. The First Division now formed a strong line across his path, and three Napoleons of H/3rd New York Light Artillery sent canister ripping into his ranks from the fort. If he had had more men—say, the South Carolina brigade—or perhaps if he had not made some now unknown tactical error, the colonel might have overcome such odds. But as matters worked out, he had to fall back before H's fire, though actually suffering only "small loss." His abortive drive toward the fort closed fighting for the day.[38]

The sun thus set with the Northerners in possession of their original conquests but no more: Fort Harrison, the New Market Line, and consequently the Exterior Line below the New Market Road. Ewell's thin gray line had denied them the fuller fruits of those first victories, which had appeared so attainable in early morning. More than that, gathering twilight saw that Confederate line striking back in short, sharp jabs portending what might come on the morrow when all reinforcements from the Southside had arrived. Yet the desire to exploit the initial breakthroughs remained strong in the Bluecoats, who themselves contemplated resuming the attack on Friday. September 29, in sum, had opened with events too disruptive of the strategic equilibrium for either side to accept the indecisive results with which it had closed. Both armies recognized that renewed fighting lay ahead, and they spent the night trying to make sure that the thirtieth would bring them more clear-cut victory.

CHAPTER IV

——◆——

"Hold the Intermediate Line
at All Hazards"

The main armies near Chaffin's spent the night preparing to renew battle on September 30. Far to the northwest, however, Union cavalry raiders prolonged fighting until midnight: the final phase of Kautz's day-long dash for Richmond.

The Badener's operations initially progressed well. He began crossing from Jones's Neck to Deep Bottom at about 6:30, Thursday morning. Once New Market Heights were taken, he passed through the X Corps to the New Market Road. With the Second Division blocking passage westward, he likely spent little time on that highway but presumably continued northward on the first available lane along the western part of the heights. He soon reached the Darbytown Road, an open thoroughfare to the capital. Few troopers rode with Kautz that morning; his nominal division of fifty companies and two batteries totaled barely 2,200 men. Yet mobility, not strength, underlay Butler's expectations for him: Hard-riding horsemen on an open road could surely reach and overrun the Intermediate Line near Richmond, then enter the city itself before sufficient force could assemble against them. The Cavalry Division at first seemed to justify such hopes. In the absence of any resistance, it made reasonably good time and reached the fortifications just two miles from the city at around 10:00 A.M.

In those works the Confederates finally made a stand. Neither infantry from the city nor cavalry from Gary's Brigade held those defenses. The only force there was the permanent garrison, about 100 men (per-

haps B and C Companies) of Major James Hensley's 10th Virginia
Heavy Artillery Battalion of Lieutenant Colonel John Atkinson's First
Artillery Division. The defenders were few and inexperienced; the
fortifications lacked both slashing and frise; the armament may have
consisted of as few as six guns, certainly no more than fourteen. Yet
the gunners, alerted either by Gary's videttes or by general precautionary orders, were at least on guard against attack. They were, therefore, ready when the 5th Pennsylvania Cavalry of Colonel Robert M.
West's First Brigade led the Union advance into the clearing in front of
their works. The Virginians blasted the troopers with massive artillery
fire. Such shelling inflicted casualties; even more important, it created a
show of resistance. Since army headquarters had stressed outflanking
rather than overwhelming resistance, Kautz did not challenge the 10th
but withdrew the reeling Pennsylvanians to the cover of the woods
without even shooting back. A few corpses left in the road were all he
had to show for his first effort to penetrate the defenses of Richmond.

The Badener could not, of course, have known how few Confederates were pouring forth such heavy fire. Nor can he be fairly criticized for carrying out Butler's orders. Yet one cannot help wondering
what would have happened had "Fighting Phil" Sheridan or James
Harrison Wilson led the Cavalry Division that morning. Would they
too have retreated into the forest, or would they have massed their
force, stormed the works, and ridden into the city? But these able, daring generals were not present, only the cautious, oft-defeated Kautz,
who now followed the safer course of seeking an opening farther north.

The German initially sheltered his men in a ravine of one branch of
Almond Creek, presumably while he took time to reconnoiter. Then he
emerged from cover, came briefly under Confederate shelling, and set
off northward. Over six hours before Terry arrived to look for him he
thus left this sector. The horsemen no longer galloped in quest of an
opening. Earlier rapidity now gave way to extreme caution as they consumed three hours before again going into action on Charles City
Road, barely one mile to the north. Not until 1:00 P.M. or a little later
did they once more attempt to cross the works on that highway.[1]

By then the fortifications were much more heavily manned. Brigadier
General Patrick T. Moore's Virginia Local Defense Brigade had moved
to the sector on the New Market Road even before Hensley went into
action. Tidings of the threat on the Darbytown Road led the general
to transfer his brigade to the more northerly highway. Soon thereafter
Gary, withdrawing from his rear-guard action at Laurel Hill Church,
arrived to fill the gap on the New Market Road and probably to
assume over-all command of the Intermediate Line east of Richmond.
Once it became apparent in midafternoon that Foster was not pursuing

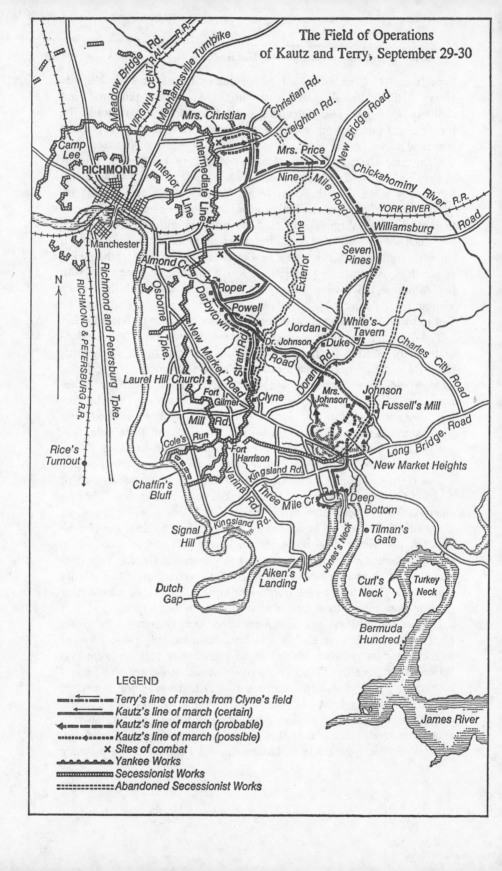

The Field of Operations
of Kautz and Terry, September 29-30

LEGEND

- Terry's line of march from Clyne's field
- Kautz's line of march (certain)
- Kautz's line of march (probable)
- Kautz's line of march (possible)
- **×** Sites of combat
- Yankee Works
- Secessionist Works
- Abandoned Secessionist Works

beyond the church and that Terry was advancing along the Darbytown Road, Ewell ordered the gray troopers, too, to join the Locals and Hensley. Even earlier, the 7th Sound Carolina Cavalry may have moved up to picket the sector where the Charles City Road ran into the Williamsburg Road just east of the Intermediate Line. Pemberton himself had direct charge of the several batteries of the 10th and 19th Virginia Heavy Artillery battalions on the Williamsburg Road. Earlier in the day, while in Richmond, he had been apprehensively "excited" over the vulnerability of his sector. The arrival of the 7th presumably helped allay his concern. Still farther north, other troops took position. Both Moore and also Major General James L. Kemper, commanding general of the Virginia reserves, who had charge of defending the city, were particularly concerned with securing the northeast approach via the Mechanicsville Turnpike. They, accordingly, rushed Colonel John B. Danforth's 1st Virginia Militia and probably Colonel Thomas J. Evans' 19th Virginia Militia, both evidently brigaded under Evans, into position astride that highway.

As these units closed off one avenue after another before the Bluecoats could reach them, Kemper could draw satisfaction that he had forestalled the greatest danger. Still, uncertainties troubled him. Concern over where the highly mobile foe of unknown strength might strike next proved especially worrisome. Lack of horsemen for much of the day and use of the Cavalry Brigade to help hold the works once it did arrive precluded locating the Northerners, known to be lurking near the city. Lack of sufficient troops, moreover, prevented him from covering every approach. Without direct permission from Ewell, he dared not shift the few available forces from east of town to the virtually vacant works north of the city west of the Mechanicsville Turnpike. Then, too, even where soldiers were available, he could not be

COMMENTARY

1. This map shows the field of operations of Terry and Kautz during the first day of the battle. The route of the infantry seems certain, except that some doubt exists about how far northwest along the Darbytown Road they went. More uncertainty concerns the horsemen. Their route from the New Market Road to the Darbytown Road is not known for sure. Kautz's course from Dr. Johnson's to the Nine Mile Road is clear, but there is some doubt about whether he made his final attack down the Creighton Road or the Christian Road. His return route has had to be conjectured on the basis of plausibility, in the absence of any other facts than that he did not retrace his original course and that he halted at Duke's and Dr. Johnson's.

2. Kautz fought heavy artillerists at every point as well as Gary on the Charles City–Williamsburg roads and militia on Mrs. Christian's farm.

sure that such mostly second-class troops would stand their ground
against serious attack. The line he threw together was the last barrier
between the raiders and the capital. To Moore and presumably to his
other principal subordinates, the major general made clear that they
were to "hold the Intermediate Line at all hazards."[2]

The second challenge to this tenuous line came on the Charles City
Road near 1:00 P.M. Colonel Samuel Spear's Second Brigade, proba-
bly dismounted, led the Federal attack there. This time Kautz also
committed his other three regiments. His division easily drove in the
South Carolina skirmishers but again had little stomach for taking on
Pemberton's big guns. Atkinson's heavy but not particularly destructive
frontal and enfilading fire once more sent the Unionists scampering for
cover in the woods between the Charles City and Williamsburg roads.
With his dragoons repulsed, West now opened counterfire with the 4th
Wisconsin Battery. Six ordnance rifles in the open, however, could
hardly silence at least eight to ten mostly heavier cannons in prepared
earthworks. After about an hour of noisy but ineffective shelling, the
Yankee guns, too, pulled back into the forest. This sector also now fell
silent.

Again the Bluecoats had failed to force the defenses. Again a brief
flurry of fighting gave way to prolonged inactivity. For over three hours
Kautz remained quiescent in the apex of woods between the two highways. Possibly he spent the time reconnoitering. Or he may have hoped
to deceive the Butternuts into thinking he had left so they would shift
forces elsewhere and allow him to resume attacking under more favorable odds. This hope proved vain; although Pemberton did reassure the
War Department at 4:30 that "I do not think the danger is much on
this line at present," the Southerners did not weaken their forces there.
More plausibly, the Badener—unperceptive to begin with and made
even more cautious by months of unbroken defeat—simply did not
know what to do upon finding inapplicable Butler's master plan for
him to keep probing northward to the Williamsburg Road in search of
an opening. He now spent hours trying to think of something.[3]

Not until near sunset, 5:30, did he finally resume moving, again in
search of an opening farther north. Dashing across the Williamsburg
Road temporarily exposed his men to Secessionist shelling, but thereafter he encountered no opposition. He planned to turn west along the
Nine Mile Road, 1¾ miles farther north, but he unwisely failed to
supervise the advance and discovered, too late, that Spear had overshot
that avenue and pushed on another 2 miles to either the Creighton
Road or more northerly Christian Road. Unbeknownst to the general,
the latter two roads were located only about a mile southeast of the
sally port on the Mechanicsville Turnpike, well within Danforth's de-

fense perimeter. Yet for all Kautz could tell, his chances of breaking through were as good on Mrs. Christian's farm as on the Nine Mile Road. Since it was already a few minutes past midnight by the time he could halt the Second Brigade, regroup, and deploy, he decided to waste no more time but to make his last big push there. The cloudy night helped conceal his advancing force from the defenses. Unfortunately, the darkness also concealed the works from him. His dismounted units could find only entangling slashing—and each other. In the inherent groping and confusion that makes even the best troops dread night attacks, his men accidentally fired on each other. Their shots, in turn, alerted the militia, who blazed away blindly into the darkness. Kautz had at last found the works, manned and apparently ready to receive him. For yet a third time he called off the attack rather than seriously challenge the show of resistance.[4]

Friday thus opened with no better results than on Thursday. For roughly fifteen hours Kautz had tried, albeit ineptly, to execute army headquarters' instructions to outflank serious opposition, only to have each thrust blocked. This latest failure at Mrs. Christian's led him to abandon hope of reaching Richmond. Even he knew better than to risk getting trapped against the Chickahominy by continuing farther to the Southern left. Nor dared he bivouac his small force in its isolated forward position and then seek new openings after sunrise. There was no alternative, he judged, but to try to get back to the main army and safety. They were tired men on tired horses who picked their way along strange roads through dark woods that cloudy night. A slashing counterattack would have scattered them. Understandably, however, Gary did not venture from his works to seek out a foe of unknown strength, so the Federals wound their way south without opposition. They probably followed the Nine Mile Road to Seven Pines, then moved south over the headwaters of White Oak Swamp to the Charles City Road at White's Tavern, and finally reached the Darbytown Road at Dr. Johnson's plantation, immediately southeast of the Exterior Line. Not until 7:30 in the morning did the missing horsemen rejoin the main army at Johnson's, much to the relief of worried Butler and Grant. There the Cavalry Division at last halted to rest, await orders, and protract the X Corps's outposts picketing the army's right flank and right rear.[5]

Kautz was thus gone from the main army for twenty-three hours on a ride of approximately thirty miles, about one forth of which distance was northward along the Intermediate Line. His raid cost virtually nothing, perhaps twenty-seven casualties, but it gained virtually nothing, either. Taking a handful of prisoners, turning loose Mrs. Christian's livestock, and perhaps diverting to the immediate defense of the city a few forces that would surely not have affected the outcome even had they instead gone to Chaffin's were all he could show for his effort. Lack of initiative and of sufficient troops made him signally fail to achieve his main objective of reaching the capital. He did not even succeed in disrupting the mobilization of the city's manpower. Clearly, his expedition was the least productive of any operation made by the Army of the James on September 29.[6]

His failure to penetrate the Intermediate Line gave Confederate authorities opportunity to muster the might of Richmond. Such mobilization began early Thursday as first word of Butler's crossing led Lee and Ewell to recommend calling out the infantry brigade and cavalry battalion of the Local Defense Force (LDF). The Locals were workers in government agencies and war-related industries who turned out only for emergencies. Four such "emergencies" since March, however, made mobilization virtually commonplace, so the War Department evidently initially treated this latest call as if it were almost routine. No sense of urgency marked efforts to turn out the brigade at about 7:00 A.M. Telegrams from Chaffin's and Dunn's Hill announcing the Federal breakthrough at Fort Harrison shattered this sense of complacency. General Samuel Cooper, the Adjutant and Inspector General, well summarized the reaction of the Confederate high command in a confidential letter just four days later: "The city is now being pressed by the enemy in a manner I have never before witnessed or expected. . . . And yet we do not despond, but we have never yet been so hard pressed in regard to the capital."[7]

The leaders did more than assess the danger; they also acted to meet it. From Dunn's Hill, Lee now dispensed with recommendations and formalities and simply told the nominal General-in-Chief, Bragg, to "order out the locals and all other troops" to assist Ewell.[8] The authorities in Richmond, awake at last to the unprecedented seriousness of the situation, took vigorous measures of their own. In the absence of President Jefferson Davis in Alabama, Secretary of War James A. Seddon, assisted by Bragg and Cooper, personally took the lead in obtaining needed manpower. They readied for action such few "other troops" as were in the city. Pemberton's five artillery battalions, 1,300 strong, were alerted to the threat, and most of his 200 additional men detailed on prison guard duty at Belle Isle were returned to him. Danforth's and Evans' militia regiments were also turned out, and the 3rd Virginia Reserve Battalion was presumably transferred from Manchester to the capital.

Yet few such organized forces could actually be spared to reinforce Chaffin's. The imminent peril to the capital itself required most to remain near the city. Even then, many of these troops were youths, elderly men, or foreigners with little commitment to the Confederacy,

weak in numbers, weaker still in effectiveness. Such outfits gave little
assurance of even being able to save Richmond, let alone to go recapture Fort Harrison. To obtain the needed manpower, the government
met the drastic crisis with drastic measures. Fragmentary forces below
the level of combat units, like the handful of men in the camp of the
Maryland Line, were called out. Thirty-two Virginia Military Institute
cadets then in the city also rallied as a provisional company under
Cadet Captain Andrew Pizzini—a fitting but ironic response to the crisis since that very day the institute's Board of Visitors rejected Seddon's request of September 27 to place the entire cadet battalion on
duty at Richmond until school could reopen.

Besides such units, all individual officers and soldiers then in town
on duty, on furlough, on sick leave, or on their way elsewhere were ordered to report for action. Military hospitals, which had already
yielded 700 able-bodied men in midmonth, were again screened for
anyone capable of fighting. Convalescents too weak to be ordered to
the front, moreover, heeded calls to volunteer for combat duty in the
so-called Hospital Corps—better known, because of the feeble condition of its soldiers, as the "Hospital Corpse."[9] Even the Confederate
military prison, Castle Thunder, turned out a company (subsequently
raised to a battalion) of 110 carefully chosen convicts who were promised (and would earn) pardons in exchange for faithful service. Nor
was this all: All male civilians in town between ages sixteen and fifty-
five who were not manifestly incapable of bearing arms or who did not
have an exemption from Kemper were ordered impressed into the
ranks.

The clangor of the tocsin summoning home guards to the colors
brought many curious citizens into the streets. A number of civilians,
knowing something was terribly wrong, volunteered to serve. Those
who hung back and could not hide in time were forcibly reminded of
their duty by Major Isaac Carrington's 700 provost guards, themselves
combed from the military hospitals in midmonth. By Sunday, some of
these guards themselves would be placed in the works, but for now
they were used to dragoon the populace into the ranks. Carrington's
dragnet sweeping the streets plus fear of Yankee invasion disrupted the
life of the city. Business came to a standstill; all newspapers but the
Whig ceased publishing; even farmers bringing produce to market
risked having themselves and their slaves pressed into service to fight
or to entrench. Rumor of impending disaster thrived in such circumstances, fed by refugees fleeing the threatened countryside east of town,
underscored by the ever-nearing boom of artillery. The possible consequences of such danger were all too clear to the citizenry: destruction
of war industry and transportation, seizure of government records, ig-

nominious capture of the capital, and release of 6,600 Union prisoners of war, who now inferred from the turmoil in the streets that their deliverance was at hand. Compounding such rational concerns was the irrational fear of what would happen if "the Beast of New Orleans" broke into the city.

Then came the roar of artillery on the Darbytown Road: The Yankees were at the gates. Tensions rose to fever pitch. Just as rapidly they subsided as firing ended in a few minutes. Each new probe by Kautz farther north produced new peaks of alarm, soon followed by new respites of relief. Not until late in the day, however, with the release of Ewell's message of 3:00 P.M. that victory at Fort Gilmer had turned the tide, did Richmond really feel safe. By then the city was almost a ghost town. The chaos of morning had given way to the order of a vast armed camp. Church bells were silent; business was paralyzed; streets were empty, save for the ever-present provost guards; and the manpower of the capital was under arms. Many days would elapse before Richmond returned to normal. But she would have those days. Her valiant defenders from Fort Maury to Mrs. Christian's were winning them for her.[10]

Sweeping the city of approximately 4,500 fighting men, including 1,800 provisionals the first day alone, was only the initial step in obtaining such defenders. The soldiers also needed to be organized, equipped, and assigned missions. The Locals, of course, were already organized; all they needed was a commander. In the absence of their official leader, Brigadier General G. W. Custis Lee, with the President in the Deep South and of young Lee's designated successor, Brigadier General William N. Gardner, inspecting Salisbury and Danville prisons, command of the brigade temporarily devolved on its senior regimental commander, Lieutenant Colonel D. E. Scruggs of the 2nd Virginia Locals. Both Dunn's Hill and Richmond, however, wanted a more experienced officer in charge. After considering Pemberton and Kemper, the authorities finally settled on Moore, Commandant of the Rendezvous of Reserves in the city. Moore's former command, the reserves and militia, were already organized, too, though a brigade headquarters may now have been created for the militia, presumably under Evans.

Far different were the soldiers and civilians gathered from the streets, depots, train stations, hospitals, and prisons. Few were armed; roughly one third lacked military experience; and none were now serving with trusted comrades in functioning units possessing the tactical cohesion that comes only with drill and shared danger under fire. Before they could do any good, they had to be transformed from a mob into a militia. Brigadier General Seth M. Barton drew this assignment.

As the provost guard sent individuals to him at the Confederate States Barracks at the northwestern corner of the city, he provided them with guns, ammunition, accoutrements, and eventually rations, though no uniforms for men in civilian clothing. Then they were told off into companies of about 100 men each, some homogeneous such as being composed entirely of convalescents or convicts, others completely heterogeneous. Such companies were grouped into battalions or regiments; at least four infantry regiments and perhaps a cavalry regiment were created on September 29. At each echelon, officers, impressed like their men, were assigned to command. Colonel Meriwether Lewis Clark, Major G. W. Alexander, Lieutenant Colonel R. S. Bevier, and Colonel Thomas H. Owen were put in charge of the 1st, 3rd, and 4th Infantry regiments and the Cavalry Regiment, respectively. Barton himself took charge of all the provisional regiments as "Barton's City Brigade."

Perhaps as early as Thursday, certainly by Saturday, the general was promoted to command a division consisting of the City and Local Brigades. His own brigade, in turn, passed to its able senior regimental commander, Clark. Barton did a good job creating the provisional units, and he was about the only available officer to lead the division. Yet his mediocre combat record in the West and at Chester Station made clear that he was not the man to co-ordinate over-all defense of the city on September 29. That responsibility rightly belonged to Ewell, but his absence at the main front necessitated selecting someone else. Several senior officers were then available in the city without assignment, but for various reasons none were chosen. Colonel Abraham Myers, the former Quartermaster General, for instance, chose to enter the ranks as a private. Brigadier General Thomas Jordan, in contrast, offered his services but was turned down, presumably because of the War Department's long-standing dislike of him and his former chief, G. T. Beauregard. Another general, Robert Ransom, who had twice before helped save the capital, did not even tender his services this time. Seddon turned rather to a general already on duty in Richmond, Kemper. That officer met his responsibilities reasonably well, though his crippled condition and his sense of nominal subordination to Ewell may have handicapped his efforts. Bragg, seemingly dissatisfied with the major general, evidently took a hand in co-ordinating the defense of the city himself. The General-in-Chief also urged, apparently in vain, that the department commander turn over the main front to Anderson and assume personal command around Richmond in late afternoon.[11]

Bragg was not the only one distressed by the lack of experienced senior officers to command the city's defense. A girl visiting the Ewells who dropped by department headquarters downtown that day vividly described the scene there: "Terrible excitement . . . Such a time—cannon booming, couriers rushing here and there—telegrams arriving at intervals of every 5 minutes with any amount of yelling and screaming that is always supposed to be necessary at Headqrs." Despite this apparent confusion, though, the generals managed to place their men athwart Kautz's avenues of advance. Moore's Locals, the militia, and presumably the reserves joined the heavy artillery in the works just east of town on Thursday. A few provisionals apparently also helped man the threatened ramparts, but most (including the 3rd and 4th City regiments) remained at the barracks or in town. Now that the immediate threat to the capital had diminished at least slightly, this most inexperienced unit—many of its members not even soldiers—could better spend its time organizing in the rear than guarding at the front. Still, the City Brigade and all other second-class forces were now available to help Pemberton meet any new threat to Richmond on September 30.

Defending the seat of government was, however, only one reason for the mobilization. All along, Lee and Ewell expected—and Bragg promised—that at least the Locals would also help recover ground lost at the main front farther southeast. To that end, the 3rd LDF Regiment and perhaps the 4th LDF Battalion moved to Chaffin's farm during the day. After dark and prior to 10:00 P.M., the 2nd LDF Regiment and possibly the 1st LDF Battalion came forward to relieve Bowles west of Fort Gilmer. The 4th evidently joined the 2nd there overnight. All these Locals at the front except the 3rd presumably reported to Scruggs, since Moore himself remained in his old sector near the city with the 5th LDF Battalion and other second-class troops. Holding the defenses close to Richmond and freeing experienced troops from minor sectors nearer the front were about all the Locals could do. To retake Fort Harrison, seasoned soliders were needed. Throughout the night thousands of such combat veterans from Petersburg poured into the entrenched camp.[12]

These reinforcements from the Southside had been en route to the Peninsula all day. Initial tidings of the Union crossing led Lee to take the sensible precaution of ordering one of his two reserve divisions, Field's of the I Corps, to Chaffin's. Then when word of the fall of Fort Harrison alerted the army commander to the true gravity of the situation, he sent far more troops to Henrico County: Hoke's Infantry Division of the Department of North Carolina and Southern Virginia, Major General W. H. F. ("Rooney") Lee's Third Division of the Cavalry Corps, part of the Light Division of the III Corps, and twelve light batteries. Intelligence that most of the Yankees had left Bermuda Hundred, moreover, induced him to dispatch Montague to the Northside.

Ordering such transfers was easy; carrying them out was not. A primitive logistical network greatly handicapped movement of troops. No military railroad, comparable to what Meade enjoyed, permitted lateral shifting of forces along the works. Still worse, the commercial line linking Richmond and Petersburg was a single-track railroad of limited cars and limited sidings that could carry only one brigade at a time even when, as now, it canceled all regular traffic. Its southern reaches, moreover, curved so far east as to come within range of Hancock's guns and thus were unusable. Between the threatened sector on the Peninsula and available reinforcements around Petersburg, in sum, stood a great logistical bottleneck that threatened to constrict seriously, perhaps fatally, the flow of help to the imperiled capital.[13]

First to enter this bottleneck was Field. Army headquarters sent him marching orders at 6:30 A.M. Calling his men from breakfast, breaking camp, perhaps assembling outlying detachments, and getting ready to move took nearly three hours. Not until near 9:00 did he set out from Whitworth's farm on the Cox Road west of Petersburg. Marching about three miles into town, crossing pontoon bridges over the Appomattox, continuing up through Chesterfield County to Dunlop's just south of where the railroad crossed Swift Creek, and awaiting the cars consumed much of the rest of the morning. From Dunlop's north, the track was usable. The problem now was that Montague was already using it, so Field could not entrain until the Virginians cleared the line. Not until shortly after noon did Bowles get aboard for the run up to Rice's Turnout near Drewry's Bluff, whence he marched over the river and reached Chaffin's near two-thirty. Once the Alabamians detrained, Bratton followed and arrived about three hours later. The remaining brigade, Brigadier General George T. ("Tige") Anderson's Georgians, boarded the cars at four, got off at six, and reached the front after dark. All three brigades proceeded to rejoin Gregg and DuBose holding Ewell's left. Field thus consumed over twelve hours, from when Dunn's Hill ordered him to move until when the Georgians arrived, to travel twenty-one miles. Primitive logistics made such slowness unavoidable, yet it would likely have proved fatal to Richmond had not Ewell's determined resistance and Heckman's incompetence given the reinforcements time to reach the Peninsula.[14]

Field's use of the railroad, in turn, blocked the next division. Despite the gravity of the crisis, Lee evidently feared it would exhaust, if not wreck, the infantry to make them march all the way through dry Chesterfield County, so he kept first the Kentuckian, then Hoke, south of the railhead awaiting the cars. Nor was logistics all that delayed the second division. For one thing, Dunn's Hill wanted Hoke's large, fresh division, not Johnson's readily available command, to follow Field, and it took time for the two units to change places. Johnson's men now found that the eagerly awaited respite from the trenches that had started only the day before was all too short-lived. Around 11:00 A.M., they filed back into the earthworks to relieve Hoke. Even then, the North Carolinian could not carry out Lee's initial orders to set out for the Peninsula. With Federal shows of force, reconnaissances, and cavalry raids around Petersburg that morning ominously portending an attack by the Army of the Potomac as well, the Virginian temporarily used Hoke to counter this new threat. On leaving his works, the major general did not yet cross to Dunlop's but remained close to Cockade City, presumably as a grand-tactical reserve. Indeed, he soon discarded initial instructions to conceal his movements and conspicuously paraded back and forth near Blandford's Cemetery Hill between 1:00 and 1:30 to deceive Union lookouts into thinking that Petersburg was still held in force.

Not until about 3:00 P.M., now that Field was on the verge of clearing the railroad and now that no serious Northern threat had materialized around Petersburg, did Hoke finally begin leading three of his brigades to Dunlop's. The Georgians, evidently his rear, did not reach there until around 6:00. Meantime, at 2:00 P.M., Brigadier General Alfred M. Scales's North Carolina Brigade of the Light Division left its works on the Weldon Railroad south of Petersburg to reinforce him. Then after dark, Hoke's remaining brigade, Brigadier General Johnson Hagood's South Carolinians, which delayed leaving Petersburg until night, rejoined him at the railhead. Even in Chesterfield County Hoke may have continued demonstrating. Some Butternuts definitely feigned crossing the lower Appomattox into the II Corps's right rear; they probably belonged to his command if they were not Thomas' Brigade.

Getting to Dunlop's did not solve Hoke's problem. He now faced the same logistical bottleneck that had hampered Field. Not until 6:00 P.M. did his first brigade, Clingman's North Carolinians under Colonel Hector M. McKethan, entrain. For some reason—perhaps logistical, perhaps strategic—a considerable gap ensued before his other brigades followed: the Georgians at ten, the Tarheels an hour later, the South Carolinians at midnight, and Scales at some indeterminate time. Such delays, in turn, retarded his arrival at Chaffin's, where his van marched in at 10:00 P.M. and his rear at daylight on Friday. Unlike the I Corps troops, Hoke's arriving men massed in reserve along the Osborne Turnpike just north of the entrenched camp, presumably so they could reinforce any threatened sector from Battery X through Fort Gilmer to Richmond. As with Field, Hoke's delay in getting to the Northside was a problem more hypothetical than real, since events proved he was not needed on Thursday after all. Still, his men—weary from the long move, some without any sleep—would not be in good shape to meet or deliver a renewed onslaught at sunrise on September 30.[15]

As things turned out, however, the Bluecoats did not strike right away on Friday. Nor did Lee renew counterattacking that early. He probably wanted to allow Hoke to rest and definitely desired to await the arrival of still more reinforcements. These additional troops, the other two brigades of Major General Cadmus M. Wilcox's Light Division at Petersburg, had been under marching orders almost all day on September 29. Concern over what Meade might do, however, prevented them from accompanying Scales in midafternoon. Not until 7:30 P.M. did they finally break up their field hospitals. Two and one-half hours later their ambulances became the latest in a long series of wagons to head for the Northside that day. No sooner had Wilcox's ambulances neared Drewry's Bluff, though, than they were ordered to bivouac for the night. Two hours later they were recalled to Petersburg. By the time they got back, near 10:00 A.M., they learned of still another change of plan. An hour before, the Light Division itself had set out for Dunlop's. These were the troops Lee awaited on Friday morning. Developments on the Southside that day, however, again altered Confederate plans. Before he could entrain, Wilcox had to countermarch to meet the Federal attack below Petersburg. He soon became so embroiled there that he never did reach the Peninsula.

Comparable developments in Dinwiddie County on Thursday prevented "Rooney" Lee from going to Chaffin's. He duly set out for there that morning, presumably because Dunn's Hill feared that, as in July and August, a strong Federal mounted arm accompanied the strike on the Northside. Word of Union cavalry incursions toward the army's communications below Petersburg, however, led Wade Hampton to halt the division on the Boydton Plank Road just southwest of the city. That afternoon young Lee turned south to counterattack the raiders and spent the rest of the battle fighting on the Southside.[16]

The Yankee threat to Cockade City also explains why Lieutenant Colonel William J. Pegram's Light Artillery Battalion did not carry out its initial instructions to cross the James. However, the III Corps was able to spare one of Pegram's batteries, the Fredericksburg Artillery, plus Clutter's Richmond Battery of Lieutenant Colonel David McIntosh's Battalion. These two companies, grouped under Major Marmaduke Johnson, McIntosh's second-in-command, turned over their duties south of town to other batteries at about 12:25 P.M., headed north through Chesterfield County during midafternoon, and reached the Northside overnight. The works east of Petersburg, too, yielded several artillery units to aid Ewell. Colonel Hilary P. Jones, commanding the Artillery Brigade of the Department of North Caro-

lina and Southern Virginia, rushed the Richmond Fayette Artillery of
the 38th Virginia Light Artillery Battalion and E/1st North Carolina
Artillery of Lieutenant Colonel Edgar F. Moseley's Battalion on a
forced march through Chesterfield to the Peninsula. Major John C.
Haskell of the I Corps also removed his three batteries—the Second
Palmetto Artillery, F/13th North Carolina Light Artillery Battalion,
and the Nelson Artillery (the last a mortar company)—from behind
the Crater and hurried them north in late afternoon. These seven batteries brought approximately thirty guns from the Southside to Henrico
County before fighting resumed on Friday. To take personal command
of all these pieces and the artillery already there, Brigadier General
Edward Porter Alexander, acting Chief-of-Artillery of the army, transferred his headquarters from south of the James to Mrs. Chaffin's
house on the night of September 29.

The Georgian kept the fresh artillery in reserve through the night
and used only batteries originally on the Northside to relieve the fatigued and battered cannoneers who had held the Intermediate Line all
day. The steadfast but hard-hit Salem Flying Artillery, for instance, fell
back into reserve after dark and left the Louisiana Guard Artillery in
exclusive control of Fort Gregg. Alexander also strengthened the command structure on the Northside by making the able Hardaway responsible for Stark's Battalion as well as his own. The Louisiana Guards,
moreover, presumably began reporting to Stark at this time if they had
not already done so. Pemberton, who held the anomalous position of
sharing artillery command north of the river with Alexander, also
sought to improve command sometime Friday by placing the head of
his Second Division, Lieutenant Colonel James M. Howard, in charge
of the post of Chaffin's Bluff: Maury's Battalion and probably also the
artillery work details from Signal Hill.[17]

The fresh artillerists plus Field, Hoke, Montague, and Scruggs
amounted to roughly 11,700 men. The troops originally on the Northside, though exhausted by the day's fighting, had suffered only about
400 casualties and still numbered approximately 4,100 men at
Chaffin's and 4,600 more right around Richmond. Together, the nearly
16,000 soldiers at the bluff were almost 75 per cent as strong as the
field force of the Army of the James. Had "Rooney" Lee's, Wilcox's,
and Pegram's 5,600 men also reached the Peninsula by Friday, they
would have given the Confederates virtual parity with the enemy, odds
Lee almost never enjoyed. Beyond mere numbers, qualitative considerations also favored him. Many of his men who had battled on September 29 were second-class troops of no use in counterattacking,
whereas most of his first-class forces went into Friday's fight fresh. Virtually the whole Yankee army, in contrast, was worn out from a day of

marching and heavy fighting and a night of entrenching. Butler had suffered staggering casualties of 3,000 men in achieving his limited breakthrough, and many of his brigades had been hard hit. Only about 21,000 men remained with his field force at the front.[18]

In leadership and combat record, too, the Graycoats excelled their foes. Nowhere was the advantage of leadership more apparent than in the artillery. Hardaway had once more demonstrated his outstanding ability in the field on Thursday; Haskell's tactical and administrative competence marked him as an officer "with no superiors in merit & desert"; and Johnson, though of weak moral character, was a fighter who could earn the praise of Lee himself.[19] Excelling even these battalion commanders was the Chief-of-Artillery. Porter Alexander was a logical, incisive thinker, yet a man of action; a bold administrative innovator, yet a stern disciplinarian; an aggressive tactician, yet a master of the forces at his disposal who indulged in rashness neither on the battlefield nor off. Not a genteel and magnanimous Southern planter but a cold and unrelenting engineer by training and temperament, he displayed a vindictiveness and implacable enmity toward his foes—in blue and occasionally in gray—which set him apart from many of his brother officers but made him a formidable opponent in battle as well. Unceasing application of his innate skill rapidly called him to the attention of his superiors and brought repeated promotions. Less than two years' service in the long arm already made him the senior Confederate artillerist in terms of ability. Now his seniority in rank as well made him temporary Chief-of-Artillery of the army. Everything in his record suggested that he would fill that office with distinction.

Whatever the ability of Alexander and his subordinates, though, Civil War tactics denied their guns the major role in offensive operations that the artillery had played on the defensive on September 29. If Lee were to recapture the lost ground, his infantry would have to do it. Here he seemed to enjoy the greatest advantage. Of his eleven first-class infantry brigades, seven were completely fresh, and two others had seen only limited action on Thursday. Much in the backgrounds of these units, moreover, promised success, though cause for misgivings was not lacking. The sturdy, battle-tempered division of Field stood out among the foot soldiers. Four of its brigades had won imperishable renown under John B. Hood, and the remaining one, the South Carolinians, still upheld the proud record achieved under Dick Anderson and Micah Jenkins. Hood, however, was gone now, promoted beyond his ability. In his place was Charles W. Field, originally a compromise candidate for the coveted divisional command, whose steady, trustworthy leadership had long since demonstrated the wisdom of making him Hood's permanent successor. Two of Field's brigadiers were veterans, Gregg and "Tige" Anderson, the latter a sound if uninspired officer who had led his brigade in battle ever since the Peninsular Campaign of 1862. Two others, DuBose and Bratton, were able newcomers, elevated to posts left vacant by the first shock of attrition in the Wilderness. Only Bowles lacked extensive combat experience as a brigadier, yet even he was a hard-fighting regimental commander who showed promise of meeting his added responsibilities. Another acting brigadier of comparable potentiality was the combative Montague. The only reservation about his independent provisional brigade was that its regiments were unaccustomed to serving together.

Much greater lack of cohesion and far less able leadership marked the other division, Hoke's. A nonhistoric unit thrown together only during the crisis of the Bermuda Hundred Campaign, it contained brigades decidedly uneven in quality. Thomas L. Clingman's North Carolinians, singularly unfortunate, had been badly pummeled in virtually all their battles from Roanoke Island to Globe Tavern. Clingman's being wounded out, on August 19, 1864, was a step in the right direction. However, the inexperienced junior colonel who now led the brigade, McKethan, gave little indication of being able to raise its fortunes. The other Tarheel unit in the division was an even more uncertain quantity, for it had seen less combat than any other brigade in the Eastern Theater. One encouraging sign, though, was its renowned discipline, due considerably to its able and battle-tested commander, Brigadier General William W. Kirkland, and to his predecessor, Brigadier General James G. Martin. Famed alike for discipline, command, and fighting were Hagood's South Carolinians. Casualties of 90 per cent in their first three months in Virginia, however, greatly reduced their former striking power. Their last battle, August 21, had ended disastrously, and they had not fully recuperated from their terrible losses that day. Finally, the Georgians of the rather mediocre Brigadier General Alfred H. Colquitt had served well along the lower Atlantic Coast but had performed less creditably with Lee's army earlier in the war. In marked contrast to Hoke's own brigades was the attached outfit of Scales, which still upheld its magnificent tradition of sound leadership and hard fighting. Its one drawback was its lack of experience in serving in this division, which was already weak in tactical cohesion.

Nor was Hoke able to offset these disadvantages. Though an able regimental and brigade commander under Lee through Chancellorsville, he was promoted to head a division not because of any sustained excellence but because his recapture of Plymouth, North Carolina, so impressed Jefferson Davis that the President immediately elevated him to major general. Repeated tactical blunders later in the year, especially failure to co-operate with other divisions in combined attacks, constantly underscored the unwisdom of promoting him. Now, five months after that one moment of glory at Plymouth, his record ranked as the least successful of any division commander in the Tidewater. Lee and the general public, surprisingly, retained confidence in him, but their trust could not erase his proven inability to co-operate in large-scale attacks. How he would perform on September 30 remained to be seen.

Doubt could also be felt about the corps commander responsible for overcoming the infantry's weaknesses and translating its strengths into concrete results. Like Grant, Lee delegated control of tactical operations to ranking subordinates, although lack of executive officers worthy of such discretion now forced him to exercise closer personal control than in previous years. The operations officer on whom he would rely this time was the general originally charged with defending the Northside, Richard H. Anderson of South Carolina. Though a distinguished brigade and division commander under James Longstreet during the first part of the war, he had not sustained his reputation after being transferred to the III Corps. His promotion in May 1864 temporarily to succeed Longstreet resulted more from his long connection with the I Corps than from his own merit. Despite a promising debut at Spotsylvania, his subsequent record was disappointingly marred by lack of initiative, of boldness, and of capacity to co-ordinate large bodies of men. Nearly half a year after promotion he remained an able division commander entrusted with responsibilities beyond his capacity. Still, the terrible attrition of command left him the only one available to carry out Lee's orders.[20]

What those orders would be remained to be seen. Lee evidently did not rule out renewed Federal frontal attacks, so he left Bass, DuBose, Scruggs, and Elliott to secure the lower Intermediate Line. The two Tennessee demibrigades, which soon reunited under Hughs but not right after dark, plus Montague comparably held the far right. To guard against more wide-ranging strikes, the army commander kept Hoke in mobile reserve north of the camp. Through Anderson, he even double-checked at 3:30 A.M. that Mitchell would patrol the James above Howlett's to prevent a Federal crossing into Pickett's left rear. Such an inquiry offended the Flag Officer. On his own initiative seven hours before, he had sent the *Drewry* and later the *Fredericksburg* downriver for that very reason. Although Rootes's two ships did not drop below Battery Semmes lest they be ambushed from Signal Hill, they stood ready to rush farther downstream if the Yankees indeed attempted to outflank Pickett. The navy, in sum, was as prepared as the army to meet another Northern onslaught.[21]

Yet the army commander did not assemble 16,000 men, nearly one third of his whole force, simply to establish a strong line of defense. The commitment to the offensive that dominated the first three years of his Confederate service still ran strong even with his army pinned down at Richmond and Petersburg. Opportunities to take the strategic initiative came rarely now. Wresting the grand-tactical initiative from the Unionists who ventured out of their works to attack him, however, remained his favorite and oft-used means for countering their thrusts.

The Army of the James at Chaffin's farm was more than just another tempting victim for such a counterattack. It held the outer line of Richmond and posed a dire threat to the safety of the capital itself. Even though Ewell's victory ended the initial danger, the threat would revive as soon as many of the defenders returned to Petersburg. Lee would, therefore, either have to drive the Bluecoats back or else reconcile himself to leaving on the Northside a far larger counterbalancing force than he could afford. Logic and inclination alike suggested only one answer to this problem. From the outbreak of fighting he urged Ewell to counterattack. Now the army commander personally undertook great risks to hurl back the foe. Drawing twelve or even eight of the twenty-eight brigades from Petersburg so contracted his lines there as virtually to uncover his communications to Meade's almost inevitable attack on Friday. To lose those supply lines was to lose all justification for holding Petersburg itself. Yet the Virginian was willing to take that chance, was prepared to abandon Cockade City on September 30 if loss of its communications or a renewed Federal attack on the Peninsula rendered the rail center untenable. But he ran such risks in hopes of achieving far greater compensatory advantage on the Peninsula than simply guaranteeing defensive stability. He ordered fourteen brigades to the front to save the capital, true, but to save it by driving back the enemy.

Lee, however, restrained his intention to counterattack until he could assemble his whole force. Field, in contrast, wanted to seize the initiative right away, before the Northerners could fortify the gorge of Fort Harrison. Just before sunset he asked the army commander's permission to charge the stronghold. Lee, though, thought the time inopportune, so the subordinate dropped the proposal and allowed his men to rest. His Alabamians and perhaps other units, having outstripped their supplies, had to go hungry and thirsty, but at least his men could get some sleep. Not long after dark, however, Gregg reportedly told the major general that army headquarters wanted his division to storm Fort Harrison that evening, after all. Field then decided to leave the Texans, DuBose, and Scruggs in the works and to use his three fresh brigades in reserve. At about 10:00 P.M. he roused them, marched back to the

Osborne Turnpike, moved down it into the entrenched camp, and then pushed his way through the thick woods in Ewell's center to a position near the fort.

By 1:00 A.M. he had finished deploying and went back, as instructed, to check with his corps commander before attacking. To his astonishment, he found his superior sound asleep. On awakening, moreover, Anderson denied ordering an attack and directed the Kentuckian to fall back to Fort Gilmer and wait until morning. Field began withdrawing somewhat over an hour later, sick at heart as he distinctly heard the Federals strengthening their works throughout the night. Farther south, too, the 3rd Locals reinforced Snowden to counterattack the fort, but that force also was recalled without being sent into action. Who ordered this bizarre affair is not clear. Anderson obviously did not. Lee's unwillingness to attack in force at sundown on Thursday or at dawn the next morning—or to take any action against the slumbering lieutenant general—makes equally clear that the army commander did not authorize the operation. Perhaps Ewell remained sufficiently committed to his promise of midafternoon that he ordered the strike, only to have it countermanded at the last minute by Anderson and Lee. However that may be, the night operation was surely contrary to the army commander's wishes.

The attack force, accordingly, fell back. The Tennesseans then spent the night entrenching near Fort Hoke, and Field bivouacked near Fort Gilmer. Sometime after daylight many or all of these troops would have to advance again, this time with Hoke's Division to aid them—but this time, too, with the Bluecoats much better prepared and fully able to see them coming.[22]

While the Secessionists spent the night maneuvering meaninglessly in the camp, the Unionists devoted the time to readying themselves in case Lee should continue counterattacking in the morning. Such preparations centered around allocating forces and fortifying. These tasks were relatively simple for the right wing. There the Exterior Line, though far from ideal, provided a convenient, ready-made rampart sufficient for the apparently limited duration of the need. It required merely to be reversed and to have its right flank refused by digging a northward-facing retrenchment east across Clyne's field just north of the New Market Road. Despite lack of sufficient tools until Friday, work proceeded reasonably well during the night. Paine took charge of the left of these defenses, adjoining Fort Harrison, and William Birney extended the line rightward to the New Market Road. Foster's First and then Third brigades manned the works north of that highway and the left of the flank line, and Pond held the extreme right. Terry's other two brigades went into reserve in Clyne's field, near where wing and army

headquarters remained. Finally, outposts from the First Division picketed the abandoned Exterior Line northward to Dr. Johnson's on the
Darbytown Road, and Colonel Arnold A. Rand's 4th Massachusetts
Cavalry patrolled still farther north to the Charles City Road to cover
the right rear until Kautz returned. Such outposts, together with available works and immediate reserves, made Birney's position relatively
strong.[23]

The left wing's situation looked less encouraging. Unlike the Exterior
Line, Fort Harrison faced the wrong way, so Stannard had to build a
gorge wall along the southern and western crest of the hill to cover his
front, especially his left in case the Butternuts resumed attacking up the
Diagonal Line. To provide revetments and to clear the field of fire,
moreover, Maury's old barracks had to be razed. And to facilitate
movement within the stronghold, the ramparts separating Batteries
No. 8 and 9 had to be torn down, transforming the whole Fort Harrison complex into one big fort. Then, too, the infantry probably
helped Cook finish removing the captured artillery and ammunition.
Although the XVIII Corps had had to leave behind, spiked, six guns
on abandoning the Diagonal Line, it still held sixteen Confederate cannons. As soon as Heckman determined to convert Fort Harrison into a
light-artillery work, Cook began removing its armament. With
members of his own brigade plus big sling carts from the Siege Train,
he brought off six guns by 3:00 P.M. The remaining ten plus eight wag-
onloads and one captured caisson full of ammunition he removed overnight. He turned twelve of these pieces over to the Siege Train, but
three were apparently diverted elsewhere. The sixteenth, moreover, was
accidentally dumped into the James by an inexperienced crew that tried
to bring it from Varina to Bermuda Hundred by bridge instead of
barge. Despite this mishap, Cook managed to clear away the guns.

Unlike on Stannard's front, no captured cannon were available to be
removed from the Second Division's sector south of the fort. No captured works existed there, either, so the White Oak boys had to work
even harder in creating a new line. Barnard and Comstock initially
hoped to run this line through Childrey's yard to Cox's Ferry on the
James below the southern end of the Osborne Turnpike. Butler, however, feared that Pickett might cross the river into the left rear of such
a line. Two of Serrell's engineers, moreover, reported that a strong
Confederate force from Chaffin's (in reality, likely no more than a
small reconnaissance force) potentially threatened the line's left front.
Such considerations led Heckman to pull the line back southeast to
parallel more closely the vital communications link along the Varina
Road. The Second and Third brigades, right to left, began digging the
more northerly portion of this line, while Jourdan apparently remained

back at the upper intersection of the Kingsland and Varina roads as a small reserve for the corps.

Ripley and Fairchild could not begin to cover the more than two miles from Fort Harrison to Signal Hill. Army headquarters, particularly sensitive about the vulnerable left flank, therefore detached Pennypacker to patrol the far left as soon as he returned from in front of Fort Gilmer. Yet even his outposts stretching to Signal Hill could only detect, not deter, an enemy attack. To provide the extra manpower needed, Heckman shifted Stannard southward from the fort at about 9:00 P.M. and extended the Second Division farther south. Paine, who had just completed two moves of his own along the Exterior Line, in turn, replaced the First Division in Fort Harrison. These moves made the left more secure but critically weakened the center where William Birney had to hold the entire mile and a half of works between the fort and the New Market Road. To make matters worse, the Graycoats kept up such telling sniping on the center throughout the night that at least Paine's men dared not expose themselves to bring entrenching tools into Fort Harrison but had to dig in with their bayonets and coffee cups. Fortunately for the Northerners, Anderson did not go beyond sharpshooting and actually attack the four weak Negro brigades overnight. Then when daylight came, at about 6:00, the opportunity diminished as the X Corps commander perceived and partially reduced the attenuation of his center. He had his brother close up on the left, shifted his Second Division to just south of the New Market Road and pulled Plaisted from reserve to plug the gap between Bell and Pond.

The strength of a line, however, does not depend solely on equitable apportioning of sectors. Even more important is the combat effectiveness of the fighting men who must hold those works. To be effective, soldiers need food and rest. Food they received that night. Although their commanders would not yet authorize bringing forward their main supply camps or even their knapsacks, they did at least get two days' worth of rations overnight, including one of fresh beef. But rest was another matter. Digging in and moving out all night long hardly improved the tone of Butler's soldiers. Such activities kept all units of the left wing and probably most of the right wing (except for Abbott and Plaisted) from getting the sleep they so desperately needed. Years later Ripley still recalled the ordeal:

> The instant we halted the men dropped in their tracks as though shot. In a few moments along would come the order "side step to the right and close a gap with such a Brigade." We would kick, prick, and pound the almost insensible men up, and side-step, halt and drop. Then would come another order from the other direction, "side step to the left" or "march forward" or "backward"

until at last we got the engineers satisfied and we thought we were
going to sleep. Instead of that shovels and pickaxes were passed
along, and we dug like beavers all night, until by morning for two
miles or more we presented to the enemy a fairly strong breastwork with five redoubts in it manned by light batteries.

The Vermonter, if anything, gave the exhausted men too much credit.
Far from creating "a fairly strong breastwork with five redoubts in it
manned by light batteries," the soldiers were able to throw up no more
than a rudimentary trench south of Fort Harrison. Nor did they complete the gorge wall of the stronghold, tear down more than a few
buildings west of it, or finish reversing the Exterior Line. Darkness,
lack of sufficient tools, and—above all—fatigue prevented them from
creating more than a primitive defense line that night.[24]

The night's arduous labor and the lack of sleep, moreover, only intensified the soldiers' exhaustion. Marching and fighting all day Thursday had already worn many of them out. Their heavy casualties made
matters worse. The right wing had lost an estimated 1,767 men—fully
14 per cent of its force; excluding its four brigades that saw little action
raises the proportionate loss for its other six brigades to 22 per cent.
The left wing suffered almost as much. Its estimated 1,183 casualties
represent 15 per cent of its strength; its two infantry divisions, which
did most of the fighting, lost 17 per cent. Adding casualites overnight
(principally 16 Negroes) plus Kautz's 27 men meant that Butler would
resume fighting on Friday with fully 3,000 men less than he had the
first day. One of his infantry brigades, Ames's, had been mauled; nine
more had been hard hit; and only six of the sixteen (Terry's three,
Pennypacker, Ripley, and Holman) had come through with negligible
or even limited casualties. Little, moreover, could be done to make
good these losses before fighting resumed. At least 193 of Paine's recruits from Deep Bottom and some X Corps stragglers, to be sure, did
come forward by morning, though other laggards remained in the rear.
No systematic effort, however, was made to scour detached commands
like Potter's and Marston's brigades for what few men they could
spare. Nor would City Point allocate to the Northside reinforcements
from the Army of the Potomac, itself slated to attack on September 30.
Unlike the Confederates, the Yankees, in sum, received no fresh troops
to share their burden, which grew progressively heavier the more their
numbers dwindled.[25]

About the only significant addition to the Army of the James, in fact,
was not men but a man. Butler had gone into battle without the presence of his Chief Engineer, friend, and protégé, Brevet Major General
Godfrey Weitzel, who had sailed to New Bern on September 24, osten-

sibly to survey its defenses but really to reconnoiter Fort Fisher preparatory to Grant's originally projected attack of October 5. The subordinate departed there for Virginia three days later, lucky to have barely escaped the yellow fever epidemic that left New Bern a quarantined city of death. Wednesday and again Thursday, Butler sent word to hasten him to the front. Before 4:20 P.M. on September 29, the junior officer reached Bermuda Hundred, and soon thereafter he presumably executed orders to join army headquarters in the field. What Butler originally planned for him is not clear; likely the Massachusetts man simply desired the presence of his trusted friend during the crucial operations. The fall of Ord and Heckman's subsequent blundering, however, created an obvious opening for an experienced general. The army commander may have initially refrained from filling the vacancy, though, until the Marylander's fate could be ascertained. Perhaps not until he met Grant at Deep Bottom at 5:00 A.M. on Friday did Butler learn that Ord, out of touch with department headquarters, had obtained thirty days' leave directly from his friend the General-in-Chief and was on the verge of setting out for home. Now that he was sure Ord was out of the way, the army commander no longer delayed assigning Weitzel to command the XVIII Army Corps, too late to have any bearing on the first day of battle but in plenty of time to affect the second.

Butler promoting Weitzel was an old story. Two years before, the junior officer had been only a lieutenant in Butler's army in Louisiana. Time and again since then the Massachusetts man had elevated him until now he headed a corps. It seemed a strange association. Weitzel, though a Bavarian immigrant, had lived in the United States since infancy and was a career officer. Yet he violated a cardinal principle of burgeoning American military professionalism by maintaining close working and personal relations with the arch political general, Ben Butler. Some, indeed, charged that Weitzel owed his promotions solely to Butler's friendship, and Weitzel himself acknowledged his obligation to the senior officer. The German was not, however, devoid of ability. At the head of an independent brigade and then division of the Army of the Gulf, he had shown himself a competent, resourceful, tactically skillful commander. His debut in Virginia, in contrast, had ended in disaster at Second Drewry's Bluff. Even so, his subsequent service at army headquarters, first as Chief-of-Staff and then as Chief Engineer, had only increased Butler's respect for him. The Ohioan had, to be sure, not yet earned corps command. With either commendable self-appraisal or paralyzing self-doubt, he himself had some misgivings, perhaps as yet unspoken, that he was qualified for so high an office.

Yet now it was thrust upon him by an army commander who probably knew that a replacement for Heckman was imperative, who likely wanted to advance his friend further, and who surely also hoped that the promise first shown along Bayou LaFourche would now rise to the greater demands of the higher office.[26]

The assignment of Weitzel caused Heckman to resume command of the Second Division. Several brigades, too, received new leaders overnight. Roberts may have nominally resumed command of his brigade, though Lieutenant Colonel Stephen Moffitt of the 96th New York apparently exercised actual operational control of it. Cullen, in any case, definitely went back to the Second Brigade, First Division, XVIII Corps, to command it vice Donohoe, who had been severely wounded in the right hip in late afternoon. Of Stannard's brigadiers only Raulston escaped being reshuffled, and even he was only a temporary appointee dating from Thursday morning. Casualties caused changes among X Corps officers, too. Pennypacker, slightly wounded, momentarily turned over operational control to Major Isaiah Price of the 97th Pennsylvania but resumed command right away. Daggett, in contrast, was too painfully wounded to remain on duty and had to entrust his brigade to Lieutenant Colonel Albert M. Barney of the 142nd New York for the duration of the battle. With the exception of Weitzel these changes simply involved reassigning officers already with the troops, not bringing in new leaders at the head of fresh regiments. The alterations emphasized all the more that only those who had survived the ordeal on September 29 would be available to renew the battle on Friday.[27]

Even so, these exhausted troops, battered by a day of fighting, worn out by a night of entrenching, were expected to resume combat by attacking on September 30. The Federal leadership went into Thursday night committed to renewing the offensive the next day. Signal reports from Petersburg at noon and 3:30 P.M. and perhaps also from Bermuda Hundred in early afternoon that heavy Confederate reinforcements were heading for the Northside left Grant undaunted. Unaware that Field, Montague, W. H. F. Lee, and Wilcox were moving to or at least slated for Chaffin's, he accepted Meade's understandable but erroneous intelligence estimate that the troops sighted were only Hoke's Division, reported to be in reserve. Confident the Army of the James could handle such opposition, the lieutenant general advised Butler at 3:50 P.M. on September 29 to ". . . hold all the ground we can to-night, and feel out to the right in the morning. This is not intended to prevent as rapid a push forward to-night as can be made." Fifty-five minutes later, just before leaving Deep Bottom for City Point, the Illinoisan specified to his ranking subordinate that "if the enemy do not re-enforce by more than a division we will give them another trial in the morning, flanking instead of attacking works."

There matters rested for the next four hours. In the absence of further word from the Northside or from the Army of the Potomac, either, the General-in-Chief could actually take a few minutes from the operations at hand to deal with the deteriorating situation in the West. At 8:00 P.M., he demanded that the VII Corps in Arkansas get a new quartermaster. One hour later, he readily seized on a pretext to try to ruin the career of one of his archenemies, Major General William S. Rosecrans, commanding in Missouri.

Butler, however, soon recalled his attention to the Virginia campaign. Justifiably proud of achieving what he probably already considered "the most brilliant movement of the war," the Massachusetts man had welcomed the orders of 3:50 and 4:45. Although he wisely interpreted the earlier message in light of the later one and of the condition of his troops and of the Southern resurgence near sundown to rule out attacking after dark, he remained committed to the offensive well into the night. A few doubts, admittedly, disturbed him. Since 9:00 A.M., he and Potter had been concerned that Pickett might overrun Bermuda Hundred, now stripped of most of its defenders. Besides ordering the abortive show of force there, the army commander directed the brigadier to have his troops under arms from 4:00 A.M. to sunrise as a precaution against such an attack. Now after dark the Massachusetts man may have returned Cook himself to the Hundred to oversee the artillery there. Butler was less worried, though, that the Virginians would attack the Provisional Brigade than that they might cross the James into the XVIII Corps's left rear. He, therefore, appealed to City Point at 9:10 P.M. for one of Meade's corps to secure that flank. The General-in-Chief, however, turned him down nearly two hours later, lest the Army of the Potomac be weakened on the eve of its own attack below Petersburg. Grant, though, did promise that "If the enemy has detached largely [on the Southside, Meade] may be able to carry Petersburg. If so, I can send [you] two corps, using railroads and steam-boats for the infantry." The major general accepted this refusal in better grace than he would show the following night and contented himself with redeploying his own troops to protect his left.

The line he took up and so laboriously fortified that night must be understood in this context. The works he dug, far from expressing a defensive strategy aimed at repelling an inevitable counterattack, were merely temporary means to secure the day's gains as a base for renewing his own advance. Defensive benefits of the trenches were coincidental, though, of course, he would enjoy them should the Graycoats strike first. However, barring such a counterattack, which he felt would

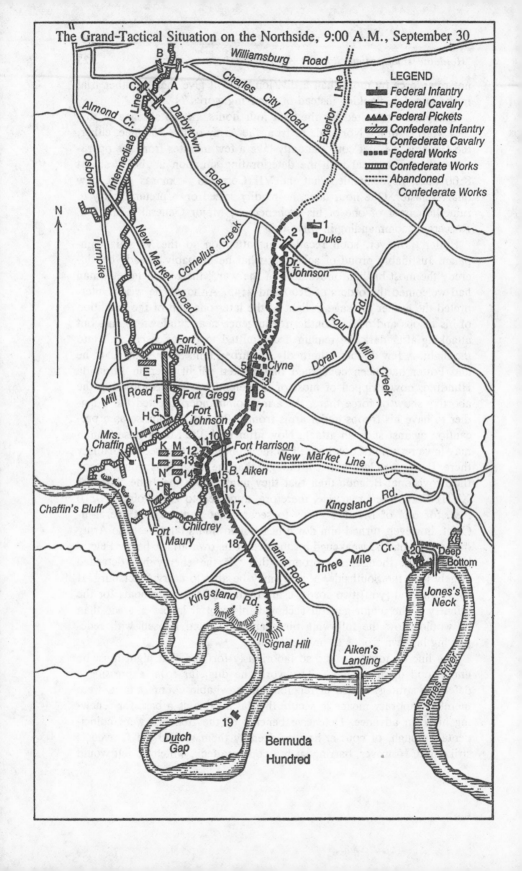

The Grand-Tactical Situation on the Northside, 9:00 A.M., September 30

Army of the James - BUTLER

Cavalry - KAUTZ
  1 - Spear
  2 - West

Right Wing - BIRNEY

TERRY
  3 - Abbott
  4 - Pond
  5 - Plaisted

FOSTER
  6 - Bell
  7 - Barney

W. BIRNEY
  8 - W. BIRNEY

PAINE
  9 - Draper
  10 - Holman
  11 - Ames

Deep Bottom
  20 - Moore

Left Wing -WEITZEL

STANNARD
  12 - Cullen
  13 - Moffitt
  14 - Raulston

HECKMAN
  15 - Jourdan
  16 - Ripley
  17 - Fairchild

Independent
  18 - Pennypacker
  19 - Strong

Southern Forces - LEE

Dept. of Richmond - EWELL
  A - Gary
  B - Barton
  C - Moore
  D - Scruggs
  Q - Hughs

I Corps - R.H. ANDERSON

FIELD
  E - Gregg
  F - DuBose
  G - Bowles
  H - G.T. Anderson
  J - Bratton

HOKE
  K - Colquitt
  L - Scales
  M - McKethan
  N - Hagood
  O - Kirkland

Independent
  P - Montague

COMMENTARY

1. This diagram makes clear how much the situation has changed in 24 hours. Butler is now on the defensive within his conquests, and Lee is preparing to attempt to recover his losses of Thursday.

2. It is probable but not certain that all three of Field's reserve brigades were north of the camp wall.

3. The position of Hoke's Division and the relative order of his brigades is probably correct.

4. The relative order of Hugh-Montague and of Cullen-Moffitt is not certain, nor is the position of those two Southern brigades definite.

5. The locations of Fairchild's left and of Pennypacker's line are highly approximate.

6. Raulston subsequently moved to Ames's left, and Abbott replaced Bell, who then shifted to Barney's left to permit William Birney to begin relieving Paine.

7. The location of Gary is not certain.

come at night if at all, he remained committed to the offensive. At 10:00 P.M. he requested Grant to meet him at Deep Bottom at 5:00 the next morning to discuss prospective operations. "I would not say this early" for getting together, the major general explained, "were it not that any move should be made early."[28]

As the two Northern commanders, eager to renew the attack, arranged to confer, their counterpart across Chaffin's farm, R. E. Lee, saw Hoke's vanguard coming in to join Field's Division and continued offensive preparations of his own. If both sides adhered to their intentions, a mobile, bloody, perhaps decisive battle in the open field seemed inevitable.

CHAPTER V

———◆———

"We Mowed Them Down like Grass"

The mobile field battle that looked so probable the night before did not, however, take place. Either in the wee hours on Friday morning, or at the Deep Bottom conference itself, one or both senior Federal generals concluded that resuming the offensive was no longer practicable, after all. Perhaps Butler finally grasped how heavily his army had suffered in the first day's fighting and the night's entrenching. He thus perceived that, ironically, digging works to promote an offensive strategy left the soldiers too tired to carry out that strategy. If so, he may have advised against attacking.

Or maybe it was Grant who had lost interest in striking again. Fear of encountering heavy Confederate forces in the open would not have produced such a change. Union intelligence still failed to reveal the magnitude of the Southern buildup in Henrico, and he thought the situation there that morning looked "quiet." He may rather have felt a strategic defensive on the Northside to be a useful if not necessary complement to Meade's concurrent onslaught at Petersburg. Or, with less deliberate analysis, the Illinoisan may have simply not fully made up his mind as to the advisability of maintaining the offensive all along such a far-flung front. The sustained pressure that he applied grand strategically against the Confederacy had not yet found its grand-tactical counterpart in simultaneous attacks by his two armies based on City Point. Here as so often before in the war, his generalship evolved only through long experience. From the time he settled down to beleaguer Petersburg following the First Battle of the Weldon Railroad, his conduct of operations consisted of a series of two-pronged attacks—first a heavy feint, then the main blow—that progressively tended toward striking simultaneously but did not actually reach that stage until late October. A month earlier, whatever lip service he paid to attacking all along the line, he may have just not yet gotten to the point where he thought it advisable to commit his whole force at the same time.

But whatever the explanation, the two generals, during the three hours they spent at Deep Bottom, definitely decided not to renew the offensive on Friday morning. Never confident that this drive would carry him into Richmond, the General-in-Chief now abandoned the effort and relegated the Army of the James to the defensive. He still did not permanently rule out a new attack, at least not consciously. Indeed, at around 9:00 A.M., shortly after returning to City Point, he recommended to his senior subordinate:

> Reconnaissances might be made toward the Charles City Road, and preparations made to move out that way in a day or two if thought advisable, breaking for a time all connection with the river. I do not say this will be advisable, but get such information as you can about roads, &c.

What would make this move advisable, more than anything else, was a breakthrough at Petersburg. September 30 was Meade's day to attack; Butler now had only to solidify his defensive position.[1]

The works he had thrown up overnight thus stood him in good stead, after all. No longer a mere step to promote an offensive strategy, they now became the key element in maintaining the new defensive strategy. He, accordingly, kept his men laboring to improve the fortifications throughout the morning. Much entrenching remained to be done. Still, what had already been achieved gave the Yankees a big head start in the developing contest to see whether Federal defenders or Confederate counterattackers could complete their preparations first. To lend weight to the line, the kind Hardaway and Allen provided so effectively for Ewell the day before, both Cook and Jackson placed more guns along the front. The major had pulled his Pennsylvanians, Rhode Islanders, and the 16th into reserve overnight. Now he brought them back to join half batteries of H, K, and the regulars in holding the works. At least half of K/3rd and perhaps the rest of H/3rd and F/5th, however, remained in reserve. The Irishman, too, moved more guns to the front, where M/1st presumably remained. The 4th New Jersey Battery and possibly D/4th bolstered the battle line before fighting resumed, and his Rhode Islanders and C-D/1st U. S. Artillery joined him in late afternoon. In the morning, however, C/3rd remained near New Market Heights, and C-D was still on Jones's Neck, along with the 1st Connecticut Battery, the 5th New Jersey Battery, and E/3rd U. S. Artillery. Finally, E/1st Pennsylvania Light Artillery stayed at Deep Bottom.

Even more importantly, the infantry redeployed to provide more balanced distribution of force along the earthworks. The army's center just north of Fort Harrison, whose attenuation had caused so much concern around sunrise, still looked too thin, even after Birney's first effort to bolster it. Around 8:00 A.M., Butler, therefore, ordered Foster and William Birney to close up rightward toward the New Market Road. Such concentration helped that sector but uncovered the whole line from the fort to a ravine of Three Mile Creek 400 yards right of the Varina Road. To plug this gap, Paine's men, much to their disgust, were ordered out of the stronghold on which they had labored so hard most of the night and shifted northward into the trenches. Ames held the left of the new position, and Holman, then Draper, prolonged the line rightward. Stannard, in turn, re-entered Fort Harrison and posted his First, Third, and Second Brigades, left to right. Like the Negroes before him, he concentrated on incorporating the three batteries of the old complex into the new Fort Harrison and on manning and fortifying the left part of the gorge wall covering the Diagonal Line. In contrast, he paid little attention to guarding the northwestern approach from Fort Johnson. In the meantime, Jourdan's brigade may have moved up from reserve to help occupy the First Division's former sector south of Harrison. Heckman's other brigades also seem to have shifted rightward to help fill the hole.

These moves eliminated the danger of an attenuated center. That center had been thinned the previous evening, however, in order to stretch leftward toward the river. Now that four fifths of the army had closed up to the right to bolster the middle, the space between the left and the river became as gaping as before. Butler, who could plan major operations with some skill but who had trouble conducting their intricacies, evidently did not perceive this inevitable consequence until his troops had already taken up the more contracted line. But if he did not foresee the new weakness, at least he attempted to solve it once it appeared. Rather than shift his army south yet again, he proposed a more far-reaching rearrangement in the orders he issued at 9:55 A.M. to announce and implement City Point's new defensive strategy. Essentially he broke up the temporary wing structure under which the army operated on September 29, reconstituted the three official "corps elements," and charged each with defending a distinct sector of his new line.

Kautz, back at last from his raid, was ordered to maintain his position on the Darbytown Road as a forward stronghold from which any enemy attack could be "resisted firmly." Although he allegedly did not receive this directive until afternoon, he took up the desired position on his own initiative. At least his First Brigade and its battery remained at Dr. Johnson's plantation, right on the highway. The Regulars and perhaps Spear's whole command, moreover, occupied a formidable outer position at Duke's, half a mile northeast of Johnson's and less than a quarter mile north of Pioneer Church. From this position the horsemen could not only blunt any enemy drive down the Darbytown Road but could also patrol the army's right flank and right rear. More immediate responsibility for securing that flank rested with the X Corps. Birney now terminated Paine's authority over the bridgehead at Deep Bottom and the recent conquests at New Market Heights. Garrisoning that post and picketing that sector were entrusted to Colonel John Moore with his 203rd Pennsylvania and the eight guns in the *tête-de-pont*. The main body of the X Corps meantime took charge of the whole trench line from Clyne's field down through the camp wall north of Fort Harrison. To help man this longer sector, the army's last reserve brigade, Abbott's, took over Bell's works just south of the New Market Road. The Third Brigade, in turn, shifted to Barney's left to begin relieving the colored brigade. William Birney was then directed to replace Paine astride the Varina Road and down to Fort Harrison. Then, too, Pennypacker, on being relieved, was expected to return from the extreme left to help hold the X Corps's line. Birney initially counted on him rejoining Foster but subsequently promised him to Terry. Stannard and Heckman were to remain in place during all these changes. However, Paine, once relieved, was to report back to the XVIII Corps and occupy its vulnerable far left. Weitzel would thus have nine brigades, not six, to hold Fort Harrison and extend toward the river.

Despite its belated origin, it was a good plan. It floundered, however, on a legacy of the old wing structure. With channels of command in such flux, word did not reach Paine that he was supposed to move from the center to the far left. He therefore refused to yield his trenches to William Birney's arriving van, the 29th Connecticut. Precious hours ticked away as protests filtered up one command line and down the other. Not until early afternoon did Paine finally receive orders he would honor. By then, signs of Confederate attack on his sector were so ominous that he dared not leave the center. Should that blow indeed fall near the Varina Road, having all four black brigades there would be a piece of good fortune. But if the Secessionists were just feinting on the center and really sought to turn the extreme left, where only Pennypacker's picket posts patrolled, the delay in shifting the Third Division south might prove fatal.[2]

Deciding where and when to deliver that blow were the problems Lee faced while the Yankees rearranged their line on Friday morning. Unlike the Northern high command, he remained committed to the offensive. Preparatory to attacking, he and his two senior subordinates rode through the entrenched camp to scout the enemy position. "Old Bald Head" did not make the trip unscathed. The I Corps Chief-of-Staff describes what happened:

> When [in June] Ewell, one leg gone, was forced to relinquish field work and take leave of his corps, the old warrior insisted on other duty, and was assigned to command of the inner line of defenses about Richmond. General Lee, with Ewell, Anderson, and a number of other officers, and some of our staff, was examining a new line of defense [sic] with that trained engineer's eye of his, Ewell riding by him. The latter was so good a horseman that his one leg was equal to most riders' two, but his horse stumbling, down came both—an awful cropper. I made sure the General's head and neck were cracked. He was picked up, no bones broken, but an "object" about the head; scratched, bruised, torn and bloody. Lee instantly ordered him back to Richmond and to stay there until completely well.
>
> In two or three hours he was again on the lines, and such a sight! Painfully comical it was. He had gone to the hospital, where the bald head and face were dressed. He returned swathed in bandages from crown of head to shoulders. Two little apertures for his piercing eyes and two small breathing spaces were all that was left open for the Lieutenant-General. Quite indifferent, however, to such mishaps, he was sharp about his work and lisping out directions as usual.[3]

Dick Ewell's accident and temporary absence concerned the army commander, of course, but did not disrupt his plans. The lieutenant general had served him well on the defense on Thursday, but for the impending counterattack chief reliance would be placed on Anderson and his fresh veterans, not on "Old Bald Head," anyway. So Lee and the South Carolinian continued their observations.

What they saw and what they learned from other sources suggested a number of tempting targets. The reconnaissances they apparently made down the Osborne Turnpike overnight may have revealed that the Union left flank was in air. Could Lee roll up that flank, he would drive the enemy away from the James, sever their communications with the

Southside, and perhaps even create the opportunity to destroy them. Such a bold stroke was risky, however. Were Butler, perhaps reinforced by the Army of the Potomac, to counterattack the flanking columns marching visibly through the narrow field of maneuver along the pike, he could easily drive them into the river. The Virginian had once taken such risks for such gains, but the deterioration of his army's offensive capabilities over the past year justified him in not chancing the loss of his capital and one third of his army on such a doubtful venture.

Turning the opposite Federal flank in Clyne's field would be less perilous for the striking force, but doing so would entail the added difficulty of overcoming the Union cavalry's strong forward position at Dr. Johnson's. Gary, moving east along the Darbytown Road and then bivouacking on that highway, had apparently already detected the blue troopers there. This discovery he presumably reported to army headquarters. Besides the danger from Kautz, the use of the defenders of the entrenched camp for such a move would once more uncover the Confederate center to a renewed Northern onslaught. But if the Graycoats themselves remained in the camp and attacked the exposed Fort Harrison salient, they would risk neither loss of Chaffin's farm nor annihilation of the striking force. Such a frontal blow was less promising than a flank attack, yet if successful, it would at least recover the outer face of the camp wall and might well pierce and scatter the Union center. Whether or not Lee weighed the prospects of these three plans is not known, but there is no doubt that he settled on Fort Harrison as his initial objective.

Not long after sunup, orders went out from Mrs. Chaffin's for the striking force to assemble opposite Fort Harrison. Field once more left Gregg, DuBose, and the Virginia battalions to confront the X Corps and used his three reserve brigades to attack. His Alabamians led the way around 6:00; "Tige" Anderson followed, and Bratton set out about 8:00. These units moved straight south from the vicinity of Fort Gilmer, past Fort Gregg, and masked themselves along the northern face of the camp wall west of Fort Johnson. Hoke meantime broke camp on the pike and marched into the upper center of Chaffin's farm, south of but not adjacent to Field. McKethan headed the column at 6:00, and Hagood brought the rear into position three hours later. Alexander, too, moved the fresh batteries brought from Petersburg into place near noon. He also alerted one of Griffin's guns, presumably all four pieces of the Mathews Artillery, and three of Hardin's cannons that bore on the fort to stand ready. All told, about forty pieces were massed against Harrison.

As the troops neared the front, they divested themselves of haversacks, knapsacks, and blanket rolls. A rifle, a cartridge box of ammunition, and a canteen were all the gear they would need. Most Butternuts, of course, brought their own munitions, but at least the 6th South Carolina of Bratton's Brigade had exchanged its cartridges for the superior ones of the dead and captured USCTs around Fort Gilmer. The blacks had not used their bullets in attempting to storm a fort on Thursday. Now the Secessionists could use them—or try to, anyway—in an assault of their own against another stronghold. Whether they would fare any better than the Negroes they could not tell. But they could at least see that there was bloody work ahead. All night they and their comrades in Anderson's corps had wondered what the morning would hold in store. Now as they closed in on Fort Harrison and stripped down to combat readiness, they could tell what their mission would be.

They had nearly half a day, in fact, to meditate on the odds they faced, for they did not attack until after noon. Little if any preliminary skirmishing and sniping diverted their thoughts from what lay ahead, for Lee did not want to disclose his force prematurely, and Weitzel was too busy entrenching to provoke a fight. For several hours, Anderson's divisions remained idle, sweltering in the heat and humidity of a rapidly beclouding day that threatened to add rain to the hardships that were in store. Why the army commander delayed striking so long is not clear. Perhaps he awaited the Light Division and sent his troops into action only when he learned it would have to return to Petersburg to help oppose Meade's attack. In any case, he did not initiate even preliminary fighting until about 11:00 A.M.[4]

At that hour, Mitchell's three ironclads opened the ball by shelling Fort Harrison. An hour later, the *Drewry* joined the fight. Whether or not Shippey's ship entered the fray is not clear. Mason, detached to resupply Battery Semmes, definitely remained out of action, and as on Thursday, the *Hampton* and the *Nansemond* stayed back to cover the bridge. Also as on Thursday, weak charges and limited elevation caused their shots to fall short. Increasing the charge merely succeeded in bursting one of Rootes's guns on its third discharge. Shepperd's maneuvering into new position closer to Chaffin's Bluff at 1:30 did little good, either. Porter Alexander's effort at fire control, moreover, only drew naval shelling down on his own spotter party; he barely escaped with his life. Other shells began dropping dangerously close to the Southern infantry. Clearly the ships were doing more harm than good; except for the *Richmond,* they soon slackened their fire virtually to nothing.

Alexander's own artillery was in better position to accomplish something. He posted his fresh field pieces opposite Fort Harrison at about noon and ran them forward to open fire an hour later. To the north Hardaway's nearby cannons and to the south the mortars of the Nelson

Artillery plus three of Hardin's big guns joined the bombardment. For twenty minutes the gray cannoneers fired deliberately; for the next twenty-five they shelled intensively. All their artillery gave them, for once, a distinct preponderance over their Federal counterparts—a "right pleasant" change, thought a gunner of the Second Palmetto Artillery. Yet this numerical advantage did little good. Alexander's fire produced much noise and much thick, acrid smoke, which, with no wind stirring on this muggy afternoon, hung over the field like a pall. His shells produced little effect, though, because they generally overshot Weitzel. Once more, troops in the rear, this time the 1st New York Engineers, were in more peril than the front-line forces. Serrell now hastily moved his camp back from Childrey's field to escape the barrage. The colonel in the rear and the XVIII Corps commander at the front could see that they were passing through the ordeal unharmed. Then when the Georgian ceased firing at the appointed time and the smoke began to clear, the Butternuts, too, realized that the Union line—works, infantry, and artillery—remained undamaged. If Lee were going to recapture Fort Harrison, the full burden would have to fall on his foot soldiers.[5]

The experienced army commander, of course, did not count on the artillery to destroy the XVIII Corps's position. Even while the shelling continued, he had Anderson bring the infantry into place. Field now crossed into the camp and took position in the woods west of Fort Johnson. Bowles formed just south of the curtain wall that ran southeast from that redoubt toward Fort Harrison, and "Tige" Anderson and then Bratton extended the line of battle farther right. Corps headquarters, however, did not intend to dash this division against the fort in such a long, thin line. Once they began charging, the Georgians were to halt halfway toward Harrison and allow the South Carolinians to catch up and form in their rear. The Alabamians were to move forward simultaneously to cover their left. Hoke meantime was to mass his division farther south, opposite the fort's center and left: McKethan and probably Hagood and Kirkland in the front line, left to right; Colquitt behind McKethan and likely Scales just right of the Georgians, in support. Dick Anderson thus hoped to converge two battle lines of five brigades in front and three behind, 8,800 strong, against barely one fourth that number in Fort Harrison. Only five other brigades plus the miscellaneous independent battalions were to remain out of action containing the rest of the Union army.

The plan looked promising, yet it was not without risk. Because they would attack concentrically, the two divisions could not form a united battle line beforehand lest their lines intermingle while advancing. Only after they began charging could they attempt to come together. Con-

verging at the point of fighting is tricky at best. The ground west of
Fort Harrison made matters worse. To reduce casualties, both divisions
wanted to launch their attacks as close to the stronghold as they could
find cover. The valley of Cole's Run, which rose just west of Fort Harrison and flowed southwest along the western base of the fort's hill before turning northwest through the camp, afforded Hoke such cover.
Between noon and 1:00, he moved up it and deployed in a dry gully
north of it about 400 to 500 yards from the Yankee position, masked
by a hill between the gully and the head of the creek. Field had no
such gully but had to advance from Fort Johnson down the northeastern camp curtain running along the open ridge that was the watershed between Cole's Run and Three Mile Creek–Cornelius Creek. He
dared not expose himself prematurely on this open ground but had to
remain in the woods 1,000 yards northwest of Harrison. To bring both
divisions into unison, the left wing, which had twice as far to go, was
ordered to advance first. "Tige" Anderson was to lead the way at 1:45
and then halt and lie down in a small brushy depression above the
head of Cole's Run (not adjacent to Hoke's men but about as far from
Stannard as they were). Bratton was then to hurry into position behind
the Georgians. It was assumed that the South Carolinians could get
into place within fifteen minutes, so both division commanders were
told to launch the main attack at 2:00. Hoke in particular was cautioned not to risk outdistancing the left wing by committing his forces
before that hour.

The complicated plan thus hinged on timing and tactical skill to
offset the dangers of concentrating distant columns at the actual point
of battle. Lee, who reportedly devised the plan himself, felt sure his
veteran infantry had that skill. Though he entrusted its execution to
Anderson, the army commander remained on the field to see it carried
out and to take charge of exploiting the expected breakthrough. First
from Fort Gilmer, then from even closer to the front, he viewed his
foot soldiers moving into action. At the appointed time of 1:45, they
began advancing. In a compact line of battle, with no men detailed as
skirmishers, "Tige" Anderson emerged from the woods and headed
southeast toward Fort Harrison. The big push to undo Butler's success
of September 29 and to punish him for his temerity was under way at
last.[6]

The Georgians' advance hardly took Weitzel by surprise. Alexander's
shelling and the sight of Southern infantry massing promptly led him to
notify army headquarters that a Confederate attack seemed imminent.
These tidings may have caused Butler to order William Birney to resume moving south to reinforce Paine's threatened sector. At about
1:30, in any case, the 7th and 2/45th USCT occupied positions behind

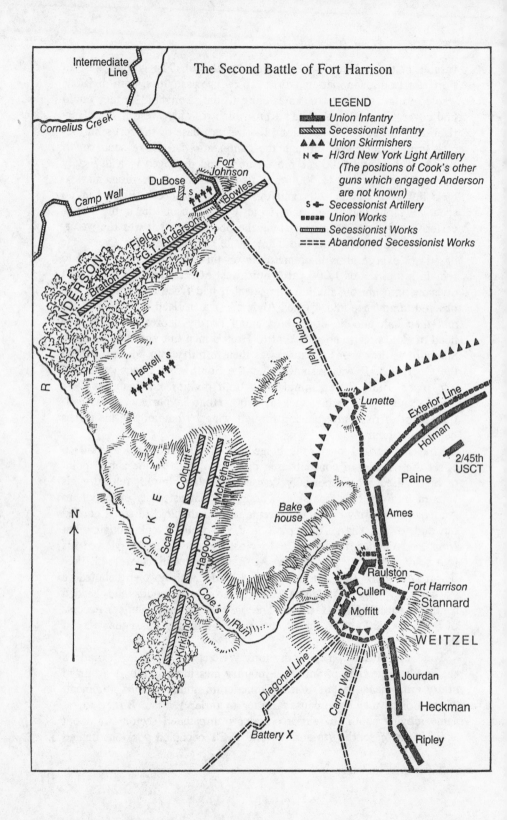

The Second Battle of Fort Harrison

LEGEND

Union Infantry
Secessionist Infantry
Union Skirmishers
N ← H/3rd New York Light Artillery
  (The positions of Cook's other
  guns which engaged Anderson
  are not known)
S ← Secessionist Artillery
Union Works
Secessionist Works
Abandoned Secessionist Works

Draper and Ames, respectively. The corps commander or Stannard also took steps of his own to meet the new peril by transferring most of Raulston's brigade from the left to the right sector of the gorge to connect with Ames's left and confront Field. Cullen and then Moffitt meantime closed up on the First Brigade's left. Only a picket line from the 21st Connecticut and from the First Brigade remained to hold the fort's new left face and adjoin Heckman. Defenses, unfortunately, could not be shifted like manpower. Almost all previous entrenching on the gorge had been to guard against attack from the southwest up the Diagonal Line. The Yankees, especially Raulston's men, now discovered to their dismay that virtually no works had been erected on the right, where the real danger loomed. Frantic digging in the twenty or so minutes remaining before the attack produced merely a slight parapet of logs and earth barely a foot high. For all practical purposes they remained exposed. In a fort without fortification, they would have to rely on an old-fashioned, stand-up fire fight to hold their position. Grimly they concentrated into a phalanx three ranks deep and stood ready to meet the Southern infantry now coming into sight near Fort Johnson.[7]

With steadfast determination Stannard's men viewed the approaching Graycoats. With keen expectation Confederate commanders observed the same brigade. But then the Southerners' anticipation turned to dismay. The Georgians did not halt and lie down in the depression as expected but broke right into the charge, unsupported. "Tige" Anderson had reportedly neglected to explain the plan beforehand, and now that his troops were moving, he found he could no longer control them. Brigadier and brigade had been together nearly three years, yet attrition had so gutted the lower echelon of command that the general dis-

COMMENTARY

1. This diagram represents the tactical situation about 1:30 P.M., just prior to the Confederate attack. The separation between the wings of Anderson's corps is well revealed.

2. Fairchild on the left and Draper and the X Corps on the right (all off the map) extend the flanks of the Union army.

3. One of William Birney's battalions is arriving behind Paine's line.

4. The positions of Hagood, Kirkland, Scales, and Jourdan are thought but not known to be correct.

5. Bowles's location is shown only approximately.

6. Haskell's position is probably correct; the location of Alexander's other guns is not known.

7. Bratton deployed the Palmetto Sharpshooters, 6th South Carolina, 1st South Carolina Volunteers, 2nd South Carolina Rifles, and 5th South Carolina, right to left.

covered himself as lacking a medium through which to exert his will over troops in motion as if he were still at the head of the untrained volunteers of '61. All he could do was go along with his armed mob and hope for the best. This breakdown of control, in turn, forced Field's hand. Rather than sacrifice the Georgians, he ordered his other two brigades forward in hopes of assembling the main column of attack ahead of schedule. The effort proved vain. Bowles, moving along the camp wall, was temporarily stalled by Holman's pickets around a little lunette 1,900 feet down the curtain from Fort Johnson. Moreover, the South Carolinians, rush though they did, were unable to get into position behind "Tige" Anderson before he engaged. Even worse, Hoke drew the opposite assessment than the other major general and refused to commit his division before the appointed hour of 2:00. Surprisingly, corps and army headquarters seemingly made no effort to stir the North Carolinian into action and appear, justifiably or not, to have almost helplessly watched the Georgians hurry forward alone.

Stannard, too, was not pleased by what he saw. He did not, of course, know of the breakdown of Southern tactical cohesion and could only discern that the Butternuts were now attacking a position that lacked both fortifications and artillery support. Some of Cook's guns, though not hurt by Alexander's bombardment, deliberately withheld their fire. Worse still, the only pieces actually in Fort Harrison, three Napoleons of H/3rd New York Light Artillery, had received no ammunition overnight and had used up their limited supply in the preliminary shelling. Now that the Confederate infantry was coming into range, the half-battery commander reported himself out of ammunition. Disgustedly, Stannard ordered the 12-pounders wheeled out of the fort and appealed for reliable replacements. Weitzel promised him a fresh company, but before it could arrive, the Georgians charged. To meet them, Stannard would have to rely on his infantry and them alone.

Perhaps needlessly, the Vermonter cautioned his veterans not to fire until the Secessionists emerged from the brushy depression at the head of Cole's Run, well within range. As the Bluecoats stood poised for action, yet not allowed to fire at the rapidly nearing foe, tension mounted. With both infantry and artillery now silent, the ominous quiet before the impending storm seemed almost oppressive. The psychological pressure finally became too great for one Union soldier. Suddenly, to relieve his pent-up emotions, he sang out in deep, rich tones that great old song of war "The Battle Cry of Freedom":

> Yes, we'll rally 'round the flag, boys, we'll rally once again,
>   Shouting the Battle Cry of Freedom,
> We will rally from the hillside, we'll gather from the plain,
>   Shouting the Battle Cry of Freedom.

At the thrilling sound, the color bearers unfurled and planted their banners, and the troops joined in to send the stirring chorus resounding down the lines:

> The Union forever, hurrah! boys, hurrah!
> Down with the traitor, up with the star,
> As we rally 'round the flag, boys, rally once again,
> Shouting the Battle Cry of Freedom.[8]

The singing abruptly stopped as "Tige" Anderson entered the chapparal-covered ravine 100 to 200 yards from Fort Harrison. Now at last the Yankees had the final, ultimate release from prebattle tensions. With terrible fury they blasted his line as it emerged from the depression. No sooner had the front ranks unleashed this fire than the rear rank passed them loaded guns. The regiments with Spencer repeaters needed not even that assistance to keep up the fire. Ames and Holman from the east and Moffitt from the southwest added enfilading fire against both flanks. Ripped in front and side, the Georgians reeled and staggered. They dared not long pit their single-shooters against this unceasing hail of lead. Nor could they even maintain their order. A few hugged the earth for what slight protection it might offer; the rest broke for the rear in complete disarray. Neither the entreaties nor the curses of their brigadier could stop them until they reached the protective cover of the woods near Fort Johnson.

The fleeing Georgians further disrupted Bratton's already disorganized line and swept some of his men to the rear. Vainly hurrying forward to get into position had tired his men, broken up his formations, and compelled his rightmost regiment, the Palmetto Sharpshooters, to drop out of line. Passing through the refugees and through Maury's abandoned barracks now caused more of his soldiers to fall out. Still, four of his regiments managed to press on into the brushy ravine and attack Fort Harrison. Stannard was waiting for them. His men, encouraged by their initial success, felt more confident about holding their ground. Moreover, the three rifles of Battery K/3rd New York Light Artillery already at the front had now shifted into the fort to replace H. His acting ordnance officer, furthermore, drove up a fresh wagonload of rifle bullets just in the nick of time to replenish the cartridge boxes nearly emptied in repulsing the first charge. And over to the right William Birney, continuing to arrive, posted the 9th to Shaw's left and Wagner to the 2/45th's right, all in close support of Paine, just in case. A few of Babcock's men even left their reserve position to join Paine's men in the trenches.

Thus bolstered, the defenders again reserved their main fire until Bratton neared. Then they blasted him with devastating effect. One of his colonels, James R. Hagood of the 1st South Carolina Volunteers, vividly recalled this fire:

> No musketry was used until we got within 200 yards of the fort; but now there issued forth from the frowning parapet a furious storm of bullets such as would appall the stoutest heart. The noise sounded like the magnified roar of a thousand kettle drums. On three sides of us this *feu d'enfer* poured its remorseless fury and its effects were soon discovered in the wilted state of the troops who breathed it.[9]

The leaden hail halted the brigade in the brushy ravine and broke it up into a series of regiments acting on their own. Apparently all the colonels now ordered charges; few, though, succeeded in moving farther. The 2nd South Carolina Rifles on the left center refused to budge. The 5th South Carolina on the far left, feeling abandoned by the Rifles, decided to retreat. Only on the right center did Hagood manage to lead about thirty men of the 1st and 6th South Carolina to within roughly sixty yards of the fort. His handful, however, proved no match for the First Division in a fire fight, and he soon took refuge in a blind spot at the base of the hill. From there he urged his comrades to join him from the brushy ravine for a renewed charge, but the Graycoats had no heart for a second attack. Soon the whole brigade, including the advance party, fell back up the ridge toward Fort Johnson, out of rifle range, where Bratton reformed it. As they withdrew, Hagood personally saved the colors of his regiment, but the flag of the valiant, hard-hit 6th was left where it had fallen. Fallen with it were over 300 Carolinians in the four regiments, staggering casualties of 30 per cent.[10]

While his main body initially dashed toward Fort Harrison, Bratton's rightmost regiment, Colonel Joseph Walker's Palmetto Sharpshooters, was unable to keep its place in line. The general, seeing this, ordered it to close ranks and move leftward to occupy the lunette on the camp wall between Forts Harrison and Johnson. He evidently mistook the Union picket line there for the principal Federal position and thought that capturing the redoubt would breach the main line. By the time the Sharpshooters came up, however, Bowles had finally cleared the Negro outposts from the curtain wall. Since division headquarters intended for his brigade to guard the left flank, not to storm the enemy position, he did not proceed beyond there in force. Part of his command, though, did jab feebly at Paine's true battle line in the lower Exterior Line, only to be handily repulsed. The Alabamians, checked and restrained, were regrouping around the lunette by the time Walker arrived. He could only join them there in their main duty of covering Field's left flank by opening annoying but not damaging sniping on the USCTs.

Bratton, however, continued regarding possession of that earthwork as the key to victory, so after his main body fell back, he rushed Hagood to reinforce the Palmetto Sharpshooters. Yet all the 1st Volunteers could do was to take part in the sniping.

A handful of his troops diverted to meaningless sharpshooting on the left, his other two brigades shattered—Field's whole column had been put out of action in just fifteen minutes. The broken, disjointed nature of his attack helped cause his defeat, but so had Hoke's failure to provide any assistance before the prescribed time. But now the appointed hour was at hand, and the junior officer dutifully moved out on schedule to engage a foe undistracted by Field, not appreciably weakened by the first two charges, and exultant over the seeming impregnability of their position.[11]

The only serious loss Field had, in fact, inflicted was that one of his South Carolinians had shot Stannard off his command post atop the Great Traverse during the second charge. Grievously injured by a bone-shattering wound that would cost him his right arm and end his service in the war zone, the Vermonter had to relinquish command to his senior subordinate, Cullen. The colonel managed to keep control of his enlarged command, confined as it was in such a compact sector, long enough to repulse Bratton. Still, grave doubts remained about the competence of a man of such limited experience, who had led only a regiment up to the previous morning. For that matter, his debut as regimental commander in a major battle, Second Cold Harbor, nearly four months earlier had not been auspicious:

> One of the youngest colonels in the service, E. M. Cullen, commands the 96th [wrote a brother regimental commander].
>
> He has ridden all day a light, roan horse; young, restive, unaccustomed to battle. Cullen commanded at Coinjock, while we were at Pungo, and though he was stationed in North Carolina hunting guerrillas, he too has never been in battle. Son of Dr. Cullen of Brooklyn, he has had every opportunity to inform himself, and no pains have been spared in his education. Nervous, intelligent, steeped to the lips in poetry and literature, he has become enamored of military glory, and wishes to distinguish himself in the field; but now Bellona, in all her terrible reality, in her Gorgon terrors clad, stares him in the face. Far different her appearance now from when he saw her first in imagination, at his home of ease and luxury in Brooklyn. He becomes embarrassed, grows pale; his horse dashes about in an ungovernable manner. Riding furiously up to Col. [Frederick F.] Wead, he said: "Do you think they intend to take us in battle to-night?"

"I have no doubt of it," said Wead.

"What, after marching all day as we have done!" exclaimed Cullen.

"Certainly," said Wead.

Cullen rode back; informed his men that they were going to fight; exhorted them to keep in line, obey orders, and preserve presence of mind. When the order to advance was given, he became sick, fell behind, and let his regiment go. He was not a coward; the fault was in his nervous constitution. We saw him often afterwards, during the summer's campaign, on fatigue, in skirmish and battle; his youthful cheeks became embrowned with exposure and sun, until he appeared like the female mummy in the Smithsonian Institute.

Some maturity as well as experience and sunburn came to the New Yorker in the four months since the battle of the first of June. Stannard, indeed, cited him for "gallant bearing" in the capture of Fort Harrison the day before. Yet his over-all record up to September 30 was such that still another regimental commander could describe him as "the youthful colonel of a New York regiment, of whom nothing was to be expected in any capacity."

A serious question thus existed as to Cullen's ability to command even a small division in battle. Before Hoke could put that question to a real test, a more reliable officer took charge of Fort Harrison. With all the fighting so far raging around that stronghold and Paine's sector, Weitzel felt justified in weakening his quiescent left to reinforce the fort. Accordingly, just as the Confederate right wing began advancing, Jourdan left his Pennsylvania regiment with Ripley and apparently led his two New York regiments into Harrison. As senior officer present, he assumed command of the First Division, thus elevating Guion to head the reinforcements and presumably causing Cullen to resume command of the Second Brigade. Moffitt, who had temporarily led the Second during Cullen's brief promotion, in turn, went back to the Third Brigade, vice Captain James Brown of the 21st Connecticut. Defense of the fort thus passed to Jourdan, a more qualified officer who, though lacking extensive combat experience, possessed the innate capacity for hard fighting and cool judgment that fitted him well for his added responsibilities.[12]

The Confederate high command unwittingly contributed to the success of his debut by allowing their assault to continue disintegrating disastrously. First Field had struck prematurely. Now Bratton, acting in the apparent void of leadership from division and corps headquarters, tried to co-ordinate operations directly with Hoke. Before detaching the 1st Volunteers to the lunette, he promised the major general to lead his whole brigade except the Palmetto Sharpshooters back into action in conjunction with the right wing. As matters turned out, though, the South Carolinians were unable to attack again, after all. Hoke, too, failed to prevent even his own division from falling apart, just as Field's had done. Whether intentionally or accidentally, he left his three rightmost brigades—4,200 strong, virtually half of Anderson's corps—thankfully out of the fray. Kirkland's men, spared battle once again, congratulated themselves on their "good luck," and a sergeant major of Hagood's Brigade, which had seen all too much action these past five months, sighed with relief that he did not have to attack "as I have lost all taste for charging Breastworks."[13]

The two brigades Hoke did commit, moreover, advanced disjointedly. Depending on whether one believes a Tarheel or a Georgian, either Colquitt failed to keep up with the leading brigade, or else McKethan outdistanced his support. In either case, the little North Carolina outfit, battered so hard so often, definitely plunged unsupported into the maelstrom—and the worst disaster of its inglorious career. McKethan's claim that his men went into action "confident of success" rings hollow.[14] Seeing what had befallen Field could hardly have encouraged the Tarheels. The brigadier, indeed, was reportedly unhappy about having to charge a fort that had just repulsed a whole division and tried to have the attack canceled. Hoke himself, for that matter, was allegedly so displeased by the lack of continuing effective artillery support as to urge calling off the charge. Nonetheless, the order stood.

McKethan's men, therefore, slowly picked their way out of the sheltering gully, then burst over the crest with a yell, and surged across the 450 yards of open ground that gently descended to the head of Cole's Run. Beyond the creek rose the hill crowned by Fort Harrison. For a brief moment no shots rang out from either side. Then the deep ranks in blue squeezed their triggers. The initial volley fell short and succeeded only in kicking up little puffs of dust along the ground. But as the Tarheels reached that telltale line of death, the bullets struck home with devastating effect. "We mowed them down like grass," exulted one Union officer. "Our line was entirely broken . . . literally from the men being cut down by piles by the terrific fire," agreed a Southern participant.[15] Now all the attackers' flags went down; now new color bearers raised them again; now they too were shot down. And still the brave North Carolinians pressed on. Still, too, Jourdan's men ripped them to shreds. Some Federals, by now coolly confident, picked them off with deliberate fire; others, conditioned by long service, blasted them with regular volleys; still others, gripped by the primal passion of combat, pumped their repeaters like automatons. The hundreds of bleeding bodies stretched out on the slope west of the run made clear that no one could long endure that fire and live. Lack of support from Colquitt made equally apparent that division headquarters no longer intended to press the attack. Battered and unsupported, McKethan's men got as far as the base of the Harrison hill but dared go no farther. Nor could they retreat without exposing themselves once more to the death-dealing fire storm still sweeping the open ground where their fallen comrades lay. The only alternative they could see was to press themselves against the ground in a slight, bramble-infested depression at the base of the hill where Jourdan's bullets could not reach them. There they waited for succor or night—or whatever fate the Northerners had in store for them.

Succor Hoke could not provide. Colquitt, to be sure, had charged out of the dry gully and had suffered heavily to no purpose. Perhaps seeing what befell the Tarheels led him not to rush so far forward. In any case, he was able to fall back to the cover of the gully. His men who ventured onto that bloody field would have resented accusations that they failed to support the leading brigade. "It was as bad a place as I ever was in," was how a private of the 27th Georgia described the reception the Yankees gave him.[16]

Colquitt's fate evidently convinced the Southern high command to throw no more men into the meat grinder. After two vain charges, he and McKethan seemed on the verge of losing approximately 222 and 528 men, respectively (including those trapped near the fort), and "Tige" Anderson, Bratton, and Bowles had needlessly sacrificed about 70, 377, and 25 more, respectively. The supporting troops, too, had taken a handful of casualties—say, 16—among them the able Snowden badly wounded. Over 1,200 irreplaceable infantry had already fallen to no avail. To mount more attacks or even to send out a rescue party would only incur more losses, perhaps in excess of the number of McKethan's soldiers who could be saved. Despite an urgent entreaty from the colonel, who personally ran the gantlet to appeal for aid, the generals refused to commit more troops. By 3:00 P.M., barely an hour after fighting resumed, the grand Southern counterattack was accepted as a dismal failure.[17]

All Lee could now do was to put up a bold front in hopes of keeping the Bluecoats under cover of their works long enough for Clingman's Brigade to escape, probably until after dark. The Virginian duly took a personal hand in rallying the survivors, though claims that he galloped around in the thick of the fighting at the head of Cole's Run and thrice sent Hoke's Division back to the attack may politely be termed "inaccurate." He may, however, have sufficiently exposed himself to have precipitated another "Lee to the rear" incident, comparable to the famous ones of May 6 and 12, 1864. In any event, he definitely regrouped his men, put the fresh troops on alert, and threw out sharpshooters to snipe at the XVIII Corps. He also arranged for the fleet, bolstered by the *Beaufort* at 3:30, to hurl a few more shells in the general direction of the foe. Except for the *Richmond*, though, the squadron continued shelling only slowly, just one shot per vessel every thirty or even every sixty minutes.[18]

Such firing and such other countermeasures proved ineffective. Stannard, Paine, and Cook had lost only about 88, 100, and 5 men, respectively. William Birney, who had suffered heavily from overshooting, took another 44 casualties, and the remaining three divisions lost an estimated 23 men. Butler's whole army thus lost only about 260 men in inflicting nearly five times as many casualties. Now, despite the sometimes annoying sharpshooting that enfiladed Fort Harrison from both flanks, it could not be restrained from reaping the fruits of its victory. To the north, the 22nd USCT sallied out of Holman's trenches to push the Alabama outposts back to the little lunette on the camp wall. The arrival of Bratton's other three regiments, however, enabled Bowles to check the Negroes' further advance.[19]

Within Fort Harrison Jourdan fared even better. Confident and unshaken, his men were even stronger than before, because the 55th Pennsylvania had reinforced them just prior to Colquitt's charge, though the new regiment evidently took little part in the final fighting. The vigilant garrison now made sure that the tempting prize at the base of the hill did not get away. Some Northerners heedlessly pumped their repeaters into any target available. "There was a fascination in using these rifles," an officer of the 118th New York acknowledged, "and it was difficult to stop firing even upon the outlying wounded when the enemy retired." Other Unionists kept watch on the brigade hiding just below them and cut down all but a few who tried to get away, undeterred by the spattering of fire that the Tarheels themselves kept up. The defenders, of course, more mercifully held their fire whenever a foeman waved a white cloth and attempted to come in and surrender, but those Butternuts, in turn, risked being shot as traitors by their own side. Most Secessionists, however, neither fired nor fled but simply hugged the earth awaiting the protective cover of darkness.

As one hour ticked into another and the gathering clouds and intermittent showers portended heavy rain and an early nightfall, it looked as if their plan might succeed. The Yankees, however, descended on them before night could. In the growing twilight Captain Enoch Goss's First Division sharpshooter battalion sallied out of the works and gobbled up all of McKethan's vanguard plus some other prisoners of

Dick Anderson's command and even a few of Maury's wounded who had lain between the lines since Thursday morning. With that supineness that paralyzes even brave troops stunned with disaster, over 200 Southerners surrendered virtually without firing a shot. All eight flags of McKethan's brigade plus the two of the 6th South Carolina were also lost; a few were destroyed by their own men at the last minute, but three to seven banners, including those of the 8th and 61st North Carolina, fell into Federal hands. Goss's sortie came close to wrecking Clingman's Brigade. Of 911 men whom McKethan had led into battle at 2:00 P.M., only 383 could be mustered that evening. Approximately 122 of his men had been killed, 203 more captured. Three of his 4 regimental commanders and 27 of his 40 company commanders were among the casualties. "The brigade is literally cut to pieces," bemoaned the sole surviving officer of the 31st North Carolina; "another such a fight will certainly wipe us out."[20]

Besides pushing one brigade to the brink of doom, Goss's raid brought home the magnitude of the debacle. Confederate flags floated over Fort Harrison as darkness fell but only to amuse their captors, who now tauntingly waved them at the battered Secessionist battle lines. Flags are symbols of an army, at best tangible manifestations of *esprit*. On their oft-torn folds are recorded the army's honor; behind their onward surge rush troops to victory; around their defiant stand rally soldiers in defeat. To lose one's flag is to lose one's honor; to allow the enemy to capture and mockingly wave one's flag is virtually to accept defeat.

Nowhere was the symbolism better understood than at Lee's headquarters. One staff officer there, with remarkable understatement, summarized the day's operations: "Our effort to retake [Fort Harrison] was not an energetic nor systematic one. We could & should have retaken it, but matters were not executed as well as they were planned." The general himself clearly shared these sentiments and more. The day had been disastrous for him. He had seen his urgent desire to drive back the enemy come to nought. He had seen a disgusting example of how his army's once-vaunted tactical cohesion had fallen apart. And he had seen his irreplaceable infantry vainly sacrificed in useless slaughter. These setbacks so affected him that, for once, not even his famed iron-willed self-control could conceal his disappointment from his soldiers and his generals. One of McKethan's adjutants reportedly detected the army commander "with a face on him as long as a gun barrel." And Porter Alexander definitely confided that "General Lee was more worried at this failure than I have ever seen him under similar circumstances."

Despite this setback—or perhaps because of it—Lee remained determined to retake Fort Harrison. Tactical exigencies, strategic necessities —indeed, pride and his whole philosophy of warfare—demanded that he recapture it. He would let his men recuperate overnight and then try again on Saturday. He apparently still did not realize that the well-led, well-armed, partially entrenched Federal infantry made the whole mission, in the words of General Bratton, "too much for human valor."[21]

CHAPTER VI

—◆—

"You Must Discard the Idea of Receiving Re-enforcements . . . "

Lee, though committed to counterattacking, knew he could not resume fighting overnight. As darkness fell on Friday, he therefore pulled Field's Division back to its starting point near Fort Johnson and withdrew Hoke's men about 600 yards to the center of the entrenched camp. There the Confederates spent a miserable night. Severe defeat always leaves the vanquished despondent. Hearing the anguished cries of their wounded comrades lying helplessly between the lines only made matters worse. Some of the fallen, mostly Field's men, could, admittedly, now be brought off under cover of night, but the stretcher bearers dared not advance as far as the ravine of Cole's Run to reach McKethan's casualties. An effort by Colquitt's skirmishers in late afternoon to cover such a rescue party of hospital corpsmen had been driven back by heavy fire from Fort Harrison. Except for a few unwounded Tarheels who at last managed to escape after dark, most of the North Carolinians had to be left where they fell. Their agonized screams pierced the night—until, for many, death mercifully came. Increasing the misery of wounded and survivors alike, the intermittent showers of the afternoon gave way to a drenching downpour about 6:00 P.M. that continued well into Saturday.[1]

The rain fell on both vanquished and victor. The Bluecoats also suffered from the storm, as the "Fighting Chaplain" of the 10th Connecticut later recorded:

On Friday it began to rain severely. Without shelter of any kind, and no bed save the soft clay of the traveled road, but comfortless sleep was secured during the drenching storm of the following night; and Saturday morning, when it came, gave only the opportunity to rise up, and take the rain perpendicularly instead of horizontally.[2]

Orders not to build cook fires only made matters worse. Then, too, the Unionists were hardly more oblivious than their foemen to the cries of the fallen Southerners. A few Federals, indeed, even crept outside Fort Harrison to share with the men they had cut down but a few hours earlier that most prized of luxuries on the field of battle, a drink of water. Most Yankees, however, spent the night not on errands of mercy but on readying themselves to kill still more Secessionists on Saturday, if necessary. Jourdan's soldiers labored to close Fort Harrison's gorge wall. To their right the X Corps improved its works sufficiently overnight to convince Birney, by morning, that his line was now "very strong."[3] The arrival of C-D/1st U. S. Artillery, which crossed from Jones's Neck at 5:30 P.M. and moved straight to the front, and of C/3rd Rhode Island Heavy Artillery, which came forward from New Market Heights, further strengthened his sector that night. Ordering up three days' fresh rations also made his men more combat ready. Even so, he still did not feel justified in encumbering his forward position with a full-scale camp, so he left most of his wagons and half his artillery back at Deep Bottom and Jones's Neck.

More than improve his own position, Birney also materially strengthened the XVIII Corps on September 30. For one thing, he returned to Weitzel the squadron of the 4th Massachusetts Cavalry that had temporarily served with its regiment since the previous morning. Much more importantly, once fighting ended Friday, Birney was at last able to place his brother's brigade in the works between Foster and Fort Harrison. On being relieved, Paine finally set out in late afternoon for the far left, and by early evening he was in position. Holman likely now adjoined Fairchild, who had extended southward himself, and the Second and Third Colored Brigades prolonged the line farther left in that order. Perhaps this early, certainly sometime overnight, Draper became too ill to remain on duty. Weitzel, therefore, transferred Ames to command the Second Brigade and allowed the Third to devolve on Major Augustus Boernstein of the 4th USCT. Ames, however, apparently continued looking after his old brigade as well as the Second. Under these new brigadiers, the blacks then began entrenching the more westerly line Serrell had originally selected the preceding evening. Even now they were unable to reach to the James; their left reportedly rested on a country lane running southwest from the upper Kingsland Road to Boulware's house, and only their pickets extended farther south over the lower portion of the Kingsland Road.

This condition apparently led Weitzel to refuse to obey Butler's order to stretch back northward from Fort Harrison to relieve the attenuation of Birney's line. Still, moving Paine to the far left went a long way toward plugging the gaping hole in that sector, covering the flank, and guarding the line of communications along the Varina Road. Having him there finally allowed Pennypacker to rejoin his own division around 10:00 P.M. on Friday. Once back, he went into reserve near Widow Aiken's behind William Birney's right. All these nighttime moves brought every brigade under its own corps commander, made Fort Harrison the dividing point between Birney and Weitzel, and left the Army of the James even better deployed, entrenched, and supplied than on Friday to meet any renewed Confederate attack on October 1.[4]

This conclusion about the army's capabilities, however, is more obvious to historians than it was to Ben Butler at the time. His evening was almost as troubled as the Southerners'. Problems developed for him more quickly than they could be solved. First came the inconvenience of bivouacking in the open during the downpour; this problem his staff solved by procuring some captured Southern tents, probably Hughs's. The staff was inadequate, though, to meet the next difficulty: securing all the prisoners whom Weitzel simply left at army headquarters. As hundreds upon hundreds arrived, they soon accumulated faster than they could be forwarded to Deep Bottom. Nor did Butler have anyone to guard them. His own escort company, I/3rd Pennsylvania Heavy Artillery, had not accompanied him from Point of Rocks. Though he now ordered most of it to join him, it was unable to set out until shortly before 11:10 P.M. and did not reach him until Saturday morning. In its absence, his staff officers were clearly incapable of handling so many captives. Fortunately for him, the Graycoats were too psychologically subdued to revolt, and they remained passive, even polite, until their opportunity passed with the arrival of sufficient guards, urgently requested from Birney. The rest of the night ticked away uneventfully, and at about 6:00 A.M. the prisoners were sent on to Moore, who kept them until 4:00 P.M. and then transferred them to Bermuda Hundred.

More pressing and less easily resolved was the problem of what the Butternut army would do after daybreak. Finding tents and providing guards were tasks for subordinates, but discerning and countering enemy intentions were functions of high command. Here Butler revealed one of his greatest shortcomings. It has already been seen how his aptitude for planning was not matched by skill in execution. He now demonstrated an even more serious weakness: infixity of purpose that left him buffeted by each succeeding development. For all his cleverness, he lacked the brilliance of Lee, the moral courage and resolution of Grant, the cool competence of Meade that permitted those able generals to master events and wage war on their own terms. Rather, events mastered Butler, and he could only react to succeeding occurrences.

His confidence of Thursday evening that he could continue attacking had given way the next morning to concern over the attenuation of his defense line. The outcome of fighting on September 30, however, caused his spirits to soar almost to euphoria. Neither proof that Field and the Locals as well as Hoke now confronted him nor a warning from City Point that initial Federal victories below Petersburg that afternoon might lead the enemy to abandon the rail center and concentrate against him gave him pause. He boasted to Grant at 7:50, Friday night, that if necessary he could withstand the entire Army of Northern Virginia until Meade could join him. The Massachusetts man, to be sure, alerted the XVIII Corps overnight to expect a renewed attack on Fort Harrison on Saturday morning. He also added in his 7:50 message to City Point that "we are much weaker than you suppose. I would be very glad of any re-enforcements."[5] Yet he apparently wanted more troops not to bolster his lines but to resume his attack. Encouraged by his victory Friday and by a refugee's report of panic in and prospective abandonment of Richmond, he even revived his original aspiration of striking along the Darbytown Road into the capital itself.

Grant encouraged these aggressive tendencies but only to the extent that they fitted into his over-all offensive, which persistently relegated the Army of the James to a secondary role. The lieutenant general learned Friday night that the effort to exploit early gains below Petersburg had been defeated by two Confederate divisions, that the Army of the Potomac had gone on the tactical defensive, and that Meade recommended remaining on the strategic defensive the next day. City Point partially acceded to the Pennsylvanian's suggestion but urged him to resume attacking and added at 9:40 P.M.: "We must be greatly superior to the enemy in numbers on one flank or the other, and by working around at each end, we will find where the enemy's weak point is. . . . I will direct him [Butler] to feel up the Darbytown road tomorrow." Then at 11:00 P.M. supreme headquarters informed the senior subordinate of developments on the Southside and observed: "This [the course of operations] would look as if no heavy force had been sent north of the James. I think it would be advisable for you to reconnoiter up the Darbytown road, and if there appears to be any chance for an advance make it."[6] The Illinoisan thus went along with Butler's hope to resume attacking but did not provide the reinforcements he thought necessary. His reference to most Secessionists remaining around Petersburg, indeed, seemed to rule out sending troops from the Army of the Potomac. The implication became even clearer fifteen minutes later when Grant authorized Butler to secure more men from Marston's brigade downriver, whose position the main army itself secured from attack, but again offered no help from Meade.

Getting more to do but not more with which to do it would hardly have pleased Butler under any circumstances. Such instructions particularly distressed him now, for in the ensuing three hours his mercurial disposition had plummeted from the euphoria of 7:50. The latest catalyst was testimony by prisoners, who evidently deliberately took advantage of his credulity, to the effect that not only Hoke and Field but also Wilcox and Heth confronted him and would renew the onslaught at daybreak. Such tidings utterly shattered his earlier confidence. All of Lee's army he could vanquish in his prideful imagination, but two thirds of it frightened him dreadfully. At 11:30, even before receiving City Point's authorization to resume attacking, he relayed the dire intelligence to supreme headquarters and asked for "a division or two," this time clearly to strengthen his defenses.[7] Grant correctly discounted the report and at last explicitly refused to send more men right away, although he did promise a corps from Meade in a day or two if the situation on the Southside remained stable. All he could offer now, though, were more recommendations, of limited utility, that Butler scour his own department (Bermuda Hundred and Deep Bottom) for reinforcements.

The major general, with typical willfulness, refused to accept the decision, disputed intelligence from the Army of the Potomac, and continued to argue his case. Lack of telegraphic connection between the two headquarters before daytime, Saturday, retarded conclusive communication and contributed to the two generals trading letters through the night. Finally the General-in-Chief had enough. Positive now that the whole III Corps plus Bushrod Johnson remained at Petersburg and that only two Southern divisions had gone to the Peninsula, he instructed his senior subordinate at 3:00 A.M. on October 1 that "under existing circumstances you must discard the idea of receiving re-enforcements, and if attacked make the best defense you can with the troops with you." This dispatch corked Butler in his bottle at last. Even he now ceased protesting and undertook to defend his left and reconnoiter on his right as best he could.[8]

Denied reinforcements from the Army of the Potomac, the Massachusetts man now reassessed his earlier denials to City Point that he had any spare troops in his own department and discovered that he could find some, after all. Before 6:00 A.M. on Saturday, he ordered forward the one experienced regiment of the First Separate Brigade, the 2nd New Hampshire. At the same hour army headquarters directed Marston himself to come forward to take over the First Division of the XVIII Corps. Filling that vacancy had concerned Butler and Weitzel ever since Stannard fell. Right away on Friday, the Ohioan recommended recalling a veteran general of division from leave, Brigadier General Adelbert Ames, to take command. The army commander did not want to wait that long, though, so at 3:50 P.M. on September 30, he asked Grant to provide a general. The Illinoisan instead offered a colonel, William Humphrey of the 2nd Michigan, a veteran brigadier of the IX Corps. It turned out, however, that Humphrey had mustered out of service that morning and left for home. Butler, therefore, had to search for a replacement in his own department and called up Marston. Again, his efforts proved unavailing. At 10:00 that very morning the Hampshireman became so ill with ague as to be unable to leave Fort Pocahontas for over a week. The generals thus had no choice but to leave Jourdan in charge for the time being. Wilson's Wharf, however, could at least spare the desired regiment, which reached Aiken's Landing late October 1 and then moved on to join the XVIII Corps.

The X Corps commander, meantime, ordered forward more stragglers who had regrouped at Deep Bottom. From Bermuda Hundred, too, army headquarters, through Weitzel, brought up more men, apparently undeterred by the fact that at least Steuart advanced his picket line overnight. Even before receiving Grant's suggestion to that effect, Butler directed the convalescing Ord to send forward individuals and camp guards belonging to units on the Northside. Since the camps themselves were not broken up, not all guards could leave them, but some did rejoin their outfits the first two days of October. Organized forces, too, crossed the James on Saturday: a battalion of the 11th Connecticut to join XVIII Corps headquarters, and the 5th Maryland and 12th New Hampshire to reinforce Weitzel's main line. The 5th may have rejoined Cullen right away, and the 2nd and 12th may have returned to Moffitt immediately, or perhaps the 12th to Ripley. However, those three regiments more likely constituted a temporary brigade under the Marylanders' commander, Major David B. White of the 81st New York, which remained in existence until October 7, possibly serving in Pennypacker's old sector on the far left. The last veteran regiment of the Provisional Brigade, the 40th Massachusetts, also received marching orders, Saturday, but they were canceled later in the day, presumably to leave Potter one seasoned regiment. Even without the 40th, approximately 625 to 750 men, the equivalent of a small but fresh brigade, joined the field army on October 1.[9]

Yet because none of these troops arrived until Saturday afternoon or evening, they were not on hand to help resist the expected attack at daybreak. Only the battered regiments that had operated on the Peninsula the last two days would be available to meet that blow. They braced themselves for such an assault, but no attack came. The wan morning light, spreading faintly over the battlefield beneath leaden skies from which downpours still fell intermittently all day, revealed contradictory signs as to whether the Butternuts would strike at all. Birney's immediate discovery that they had abandoned the lunette northwest of Fort Harrison and had apparently fallen back toward Fort Johnson suggested they might not renew fighting. But Alexander's early resumption of shelling, the assembling of Confederate troops inside the entrenched camp, and Weitzel's belief that Graycoats were trying to turn the X Corps's right at about 8:30 A.M. all seemed to presage another counterattack.

What Lee really intended is not clear. The only known account of his conference with his senior officers on Friday night, written after the war by the often erroneous I Corps Chief-of-Staff, asserts that Lee called off further fighting that early:

> [Pemberton] was present and, speaking of Battery Harrison, said with something like superior confidence, "I presume, General, you will retake the fort *coute que coute.*" Lee's sad, steady eyes rested on that unfortunate officer as he slowly said: "General Pemberton, I made my effort this morning and failed, losing many killed and wounded. I have ordered another line provided for that point and shall have no more blood shed at the fort unless you can show me a practical plan of capture; perhaps you can. I shall be glad to have it." There was no answer from Pemberton.[10]

This incident caused rejoicing among Pemberton's many enemies, ever ready to pounce on the victim of Vicksburg, but one questions that it really occurred on September 30. Wartime testimony from Alexander's headquarters indicates that Lee did intend to resume attacking on Saturday. Events seem to bear out the latter assertion. For one thing, the army commander summoned another council of war early October 1, probably though not definitely to go over plans for the forthcoming attack. More revealingly, he began concentrating troops against Fort Harrison. To open the fray, Hardaway and Haskell, including the mortar battery, resumed shelling the stronghold. At Lee's request, the *Drewry, Virginia II, Beaufort, Richmond,* and *Fredericksburg,* deployed downriver from Chaffin's Bluff in that order, added their firepower in midmorning. Then at about 11:20 A.M., Mason steamed upriver to a more advantageous firing position between Wall and Shepperd. Light and naval guns alike initially fired slowly to conserve precious powder and ammunition, presumably for the big bombardment likely to immediately precede the charge. As if to get ready for that advance, infantry began deploying inside the camp. Bratton's and McKethan's hard-hit units were spared the ordeal this time, but Colquitt was tapped again, probably along with Hoke's three fresh brigades and perhaps even DuBose.

Despite these preparations Lee decided to call off the attack. Reconciled for the time being to the fall of Fort Harrison, he now contented himself with containing further Federal breakthroughs by erecting new defensive works through the middle of the camp between Forts Johnson and Hoke. Most of his force now took position in that area and spent the rest of the day waiting for their commanders to slog through the mud laying out the new line. Only the Nelson Artillery and the increasingly restrained James River Squadron kept engaging the XVIII Corps. Even Mitchell, moreover, saw little point in continuing to expend precious powder and by the end of the day cut his rate of fire to only seven shots an hour from the entire fleet. His whole squadron likely fired only about seventy rounds all day. The mortars, to be sure, fired more vigorously and landed many shells right in Fort Harrison. Before they could bomb the infantry from the works, though, Cook's guns opened counterfire, especially all six guns of Battery K, now in the stronghold. Twice the rifles silenced the Virginians, to the resounding cheers of the Union foot soldiers. The New Yorkers suffered heavily in the process, however, and had to have two sections replaced in Fort Harrison by F/1st Rhode Island Light Artillery at about 4:00 P.M.

Besides this shelling, some ominous infantry maneuvering occurred opposite Jourdan at 3:00 and again at 3:45 P.M. Whether it portended a projected attack, a feint to counter the X Corps's operations farther northwest, or the transfer of two Southern brigades to Richmond is not clear. In any case, no heavy fighting developed in the camp that afternoon. Except for this maneuvering and shelling, the situation between the Mill Road and the river appeared almost tranquil in contrast to the fury of the past two days.

Soldiers who had recently been locked in mortal combat now spent their time throwing up earthworks, razing obstructions to fields of fire, bringing up needed supplies from the rear (such as one wagonload of shelter tents per regiment in the X Corps), building two signal lookout stations on the XVIII Corps's line, or simply standing watch in the rain. Sailors who had frantically battled to stop the drive to the James now concentrated on such mundane tasks as the *Nansemond* hauling ammunition to the front and the *Hampton* and the *Roanoke* raising the poor

Gallego. Even nearby civilians could begin to get back to normal. A passer-by, traveling down the Osborne Turnpike just north of the entrenched camp, noted the "surgeons busily engaged in their horrible work of amputation, in the house of Mr. James Taylor on whose farm the fight took place; while, strange to relate, a sorghum mill was busily grinding cane & Mr. Taylor [was] superintending the process of making syrup, as if nothing unusual was going on. Such is war."[11] Other civilians, less philosophical and more ghoulish, actually flocked to the front to gaze at the dead Negroes lying on the field east of Fort Gilmer. Black manservants in the Southern army joined the civilians at the ramparts to jeer at the fallen USCTs. Confederate authorities refused a Yankee request for a truce to bury those and other corpses between the lines on Saturday, and for days to come the fallen Negroes remained a major tourist attraction.[12]

A day opening with much promise of heavy fighting thus rapidly subsided into near quiescence. Why Lee canceled his attack is not clear. Perhaps the mud and the rain dissuaded him. Or perhaps he realized that the Bluecoats would be even better prepared to hand him another bloody repulse, which he could ill afford. Then again, he may simply have lost the initiative to Butler, whose thrust up the Darbytown Road once more threatened the capital itself.

While Lee was maneuvering and assessing the situation on his right front, the Northerners were going into action against his left. At 8:30 on Saturday morning, Butler began to execute City Point's plan by directing Birney to scout up the Darbytown Road with four brigades and to break through the Intermediate Line if possible. For some reason, perhaps to see if he would have to help defend Fort Harrison, the corps commander took nearly all morning to comply. He pulled Abbott and Pond out of the trenches around 9:30, shifted Plaisted rightward to replace them, and moved Pennypacker into the works to Barney's right. Not until just prior to 11:15, though, did the Pennsylvania general send the two reserve brigades northward to the Darbytown Road along Terry's route of Thursday. On the way, they discovered that the rumor of Graycoats north of Clyne's was groundless. At 1:25, they joined the cavalry on that highway and then struck westward in two columns. Spear and a section of the 4th Wisconsin Battery operated on the Charles City Road, and West (accompanied by Kautz himself), the other eight horse artillery guns, Abbott, and Pond (in that order) advanced on the Darbytown Road. Birney, though promising Butler to "personally superintend the movement as it advances," did not actually accompany the expedition, so Terry once more took charge. Acting Chief Engineer Michie rode along to help map the country penetrated and to verify the accuracy of a map captured on the body of Confederate Brigadier General John Chambliss on August 16. This little command of roughly 4,300 to 4,400 men was a reconnaissance party, indeed. Contrary to Grant's recommendation that the reconnaissance force might develop an opening where the army could attack, Butler equated the reconnoitering and strike forces, yet restricted its strength to the point where it had little chance to accomplish much.

Even so, Kautz's brigades alone had no trouble pushing back Gary's outposts and the few provisional cavalry, perhaps Owens' City Cavalry Regiment, who reportedly ventured into their path. The blue infantry, moreover, initially encountered no greater obstacle than mud, rain, and heavy fog. But when West at last neared the Intermediate Line between 3:00 and 3:30, he found Butternut skirmishers—Kemper's men and perhaps some of Gary's as well—making a real stand athwart his path. Rather than try to drive them in, he halted to let the First Division advance. Now would come the real trial of how much Terry's little command could achieve.[13]

The Southerners were much better prepared to meet this test than they had been when the Unionists first probed this area on September 29. Richmond was now an armed camp, with most of her businesses closed and most of her citizens under arms. Carrington's dragnet had continued sweeping the streets for those it had missed, for individual transient soldiers and unsuspecting farmers who only arrived in town on Friday or Saturday, and for anyone else without a pass or an exemption. Even the Confederate Attorney General and Postmaster General temporarily fell into the clutches of the provost guard on September 30—much to their outrage—but at least they soon secured their release. Most individuals were not so fortunate and were pressed into Barton's Brigade. More of his men were armed and equipped on Friday, and some of his troops actually began bolstering the defenses that day. One of his regiments in the morning and the 3rd Regiment after dark were sent to the works, likely to the sector west of the Mechanicsville Turnpike, which so concerned Kemper. Then from 10:00 A.M. till noon on October 1, the rest of the brigade trudged up the Meadow Bridge Road to reinforce the heavy artillery in the Exterior Line overlooking the Chickahominy. These moves were apparently only precautionary, for the City Troops were not placed in the works—let alone made to join the heavies on picket—but were allowed to enter vacant tents to take shelter from the rain.

Word of Terry's advance jolted Barton's Brigade out of its tranquillity around 2:00 P.M. Leaving the artillerists and militia to defend the fortifications north of Richmond, the provisionals hurried back down the Meadow Bridge Road toward the Williamsburg Road. From the Confederate Barracks, the VMI cadet company, too, headed for the eastern front. These troops rushed along to the clangor of the tocsin, yet one might well have sent to ask for whom the bell tolled. Most of the eligible manpower of the city was already under arms and at or on the way to the front. The 700 organized soldiers still in town, armed convalescents at that, had to stay behind to guard prisoners or perform provost duty, and only a handful of other men were still available. Among those fortunate enough to be exempt from even emergency service, moreover, curiosity replaced the chaos of Thursday as bolder citizens now climbed to the roofs or hilltops to catch glimpses of the firing. Except among the more fainthearted, mostly women, the tocsin and the shelling no longer seemed to sound the death knell of the city. Nor need even the timid have been alarmed, for Kemper and Pemberton were ready for the foe. Not only were Barton and Pizzini on the way, but also, many troops were already in place east of the capital. Atkinson was there, of course, and Gary, too. Part of Moore's command—including the 5th Local Battalion, the Richmond Ambulance Company, and probably the 1st Local and 3rd Reserve battalions and the detail from the Maryland Line—remained on the most threatened sector confronting Terry. The 1st Virginia Reserve Battalion, sent back from the main front just that morning in precaution or in disgrace, was with Moore, too, and at least the Surry Light Artillery of Lighfoot's field-artillery battalion apparently joined him during the day. In quality most of these units left much to be desired, but in quantity they were now able to confront the Northerners in force.[14]

More than that, Atkinson poured forth such heavy fire as to check the first Federal foot soldiers, likely West's men, dismounted, to emerge into Roper's open field stretching away to the works. As these Bluecoats fell back to the cover of the woods, the Regular battery and a section of the Wisconsin unit moved out into the field southwest of the Darbytown Road to open counterbattery fire. They apparently scored a direct hit on a 12-pounder of the Surry Light Artillery but could not begin to silence Hensley's pieces. The Union guns themselves soon ceased firing and withdrew into the forest, not driven off but ordered back by Terry, who could see that something else would have to be tried.

At least some Secessionists believed these two withdrawals marked another victory for them, as on Thursday morning. The Yankee high command, however, was not prepared to accept defeat. Birney sent word, prior to 4:35, to press the attack against any force outside the main works and perhaps also to develop what else "could be done." Either in response to this or on his own initiative before receiving the directive, Terry himself issued orders to advance. Ever a prudently cautious general, the Connecticut man did not recklessly hurl his whole force over difficult terrain toward strong and apparently well-defended ramparts. Rather, he kept West and Pond in reserve in the woods, ordered at least Battery B to resume firing, and then sent his Second Brigade forward as skirmishers, a deployment well suited for driving the enemy into their fortifications and then developing their position.

Abbott, accordingly, strung out his four infantry regiments, armed with Spencer repeating rifles—7th and 3rd New Hampshire, 7th and 6th Connecticut, left to right—astride the highway in a line a mile long, posted the 16th New York Heavy Artillery in supporting line of battle just right of the road, and moved out into Roper's field. Southern voltigeurs remaining outside the works offered no resistance, but the soggy cornfield proved quite an obstacle. "You have no idea how muddy it is," wrote a Hampshireman; ". . . when running accrost a corn field the mud would almost pull our shoes off." The Bluecoats, nevertheless, pressed on down into the wooded ravine of Almond Creek, a good place for enemy light infantry to make a stand. Still they met no riflemen. Again, the rain-swollen stream afforded more problems than the Secessionists, but Abbott managed to slosh across it and continue advancing. His right wing now had to slog over another cornfield and make its way through another overgrown creek depression; his left, on the other hand, had to cross only the one ravine, for the two creek gullies joined just west of the highway. Both wings then continued to the far edge of the gully thicket bordering the southeastern edge of the last open field. At the opposite end of the field, some 600 to 800 yards to the northwest, ranged the Confederate skirmishers, and behind them loomed the Intermediate Line.

Neither tactical objectives nor good sense required Abbott to drive the voltigeurs inside the fortifications. Simply reaching the ravine provided a good view of the works and established that the Butternuts would not fight outside them. The advance also made clear that the enemy would defend the ramparts in force. Unlike the gray skirmishers, Hensley's artillerists had battled the colonel almost as soon as he emerged from the woods. The Confederate works paralleling the Osborne Turnpike struck home first with enfilading fire against the Union left. The batteries astride the Darbytown Road soon added frontal fire, and as Abbott drew nearer, his right also was raked from the north. The Virginians, moreover, now stepped up their cannonade so much that not even the rain could prevent their cannon smoke from hanging over the field like a pall. Relatively accurate the shelling was, too, but difficulty of sighting due to the dark and stormy weather and also the Yankees' open order and good discipline kept their casualties low and their ranks well formed—so far. Losses would

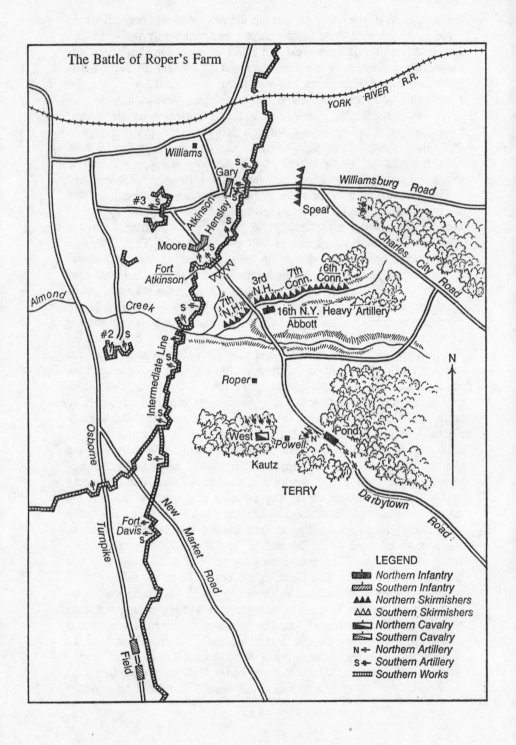

The Battle of Roper's Farm

YORK RIVER R.R.

Williams

Gary

Williamsburg Road

#3

Atkinson

Hensley

Spear

Charles City Road

Moore

Fort Atkinson

3rd N.H.

7th Conn.

6th Conn.

7th N.H.

Almond Creek

16th N.Y. Heavy Artillery

Abbott

#2

Intermediate Line

Roper

West

Pond

Powell

Osborne

Kautz

N

TERRY

Darbytown Road

New Market Road

Fort Davis

Turnpike

Field

LEGEND

Northern Infantry

Southern Infantry

Northern Skirmishers

Southern Skirmishers

Northern Cavalry

Southern Cavalry

N — Northern Artillery

S — Southern Artillery

Southern Works

mount rapidly, though, if the Second Brigade pressed on toward the main defenses. Terry realized the folly of sending a skirmish line to storm permanent earthworks bristling with five redoubts. He wisely ordered the brigade to halt and take cover in the edge of the woods and along the slope and floor of the gully.[15]

Seeing his main body checked could hardly have pleased the Connecticut man. Nor did available indications from the Charles City Road appear encouraging, even though lack of direct communication with the Second Cavalry Brigade prevented him from knowing the details of its operations. In fact, it had reached the scene of its fight of Thursday afternoon, dismounted, and trudged over the muddy fields to engage Gary's skirmishers, who did make a stand outside the works on this sector. Confederate resistance initially proved feeble as the panicky flight of one squadron of the 7th South Carolina Cavalry forced the rest of the regiment to fall back into the Intermediate Line. On that sector too, however, those works now checked the Bluecoats. The one section of ordnance rifles Spear now committed proved no match for Pemberton's emplaced guns and soon fell silent. The cessation of shelling on the Charles City Road probably alerted Terry that things were not progressing well there either.[16]

With his principal force stalled and presumably his right wing as well, the general now had to make a crucial decision. Should he content himself with developing the enemy's presence in force, or should he add his two fresh brigades to Abbott's and try to storm the ramparts? With darkness fast approaching, he lacked time to consult corps headquarters and had to reach his own conclusion. Confident that he had achieved all that could reasonably be expected of a reconnaissance force and concerned that he was too weak to carry a position that even now hurled defiance at him, he could see only one answer. Without committing Pond and West, he issued orders to disengage and fall back on the main army.

After lying under the trying but not telling fire approximately half an hour, Abbott began pulling out at about 5:00 P.M. Withdrawing over

COMMENTARY

1. This map depicts Terry's reconnaissance on Saturday afternoon. Abbott and Spear are skirmishing toward the Confederate works, and the other two Union brigades are symbolically shown in reserve.

2. Field's two brigades are marching up the pike to bolster the threatened sector. Clark, also, subsequently reinforced Gary on the Williamsburg Road.

3. The ten Federal guns are shown symbolically. Locating Pemberton's pieces with certainty is not possible, so only his emplacements are indicated.

the open fields again exposed him to the 10th's shelling. The Virginians seized on their opportunity to increase their fire and soon imagined that they had knocked apart an attacking force and driven it from the field in disorder. The Northerners, in fact, were falling back of their own volition. Their negligible casualties bear out their claim to have disengaged in good order, not in full rout. Once under cover of the woods southeast of Roper's, the brigade ployed and led the way back down the Darbytown Road. Pond, the artillery, and West fell in behind Abbott for the long, slow, trying march back to the Exterior Line. Farther north, Spear briefly resumed shelling at the end of the afternoon. This time he directed his fire not only against the works but reportedly also against the southeastern suburbs of Richmond itself, though claims that he actually hit Rocketts have not been verified. But then he too limbered up, remounted, and began retracing his steps along the Charles City Road, presumably in response to Kautz's order. This withdrawal of Terry's two wings represented the end not just of a skirmish and a reconnaissance or even of a battle but also of a whole effort. The retreating Federals did not know it at the time, but their probes that day marked the closest point Northern combat troops ever came to the Confederate capital from the outbreak of the Civil War to the day Godfrey Weitzel marched into the city, unopposed, over half a year later.[17]

Insights into history and into the tactical situation were also denied the commanders in gray that afternoon. Far from realizing that he had stopped the closest drive to Richmond, Atkinson did not even know that the fight was over. He therefore decided that the best way to prevent the supposedly concealed enemy from launching a new attack was simply to blaze away into the woods. No Yankees remained to endure his bombardment, but many a tree and an occasional farmhouse fell victim to his fire, and much precious powder and ammunition were combat tested. The roar of such shelling, moreover, shook the houses in Richmond and frightened inexperienced troops in other sectors. The sound produced a much different response from Pemberton, who not only ordered the cannonade to cease but also actually put his subordinate in arrest for violating long-standing prohibitions against firing at small bodies of Federals. The division commander evidently managed to clear himself and return to duty in a day or two, but by then complaints from Lee himself over the incident apparently caused him to be relieved again. The lieutenant colonel's conduct certainly appears unnecessary, almost foolish, in retrospect, yet the censure of his two superiors hardly seems warranted. His initial fire unquestionably checked the Unionists before they could come to grips with the same sort of inexperienced infantry who had failed to hold Fort Harrison. Even his later bombardment, moreover, represents an unwise but hardly inexcusable response of an officer who lacked any other means of ascertaining whether or not the foe remained in his front. Consideration of these points likely underlay his restoration to command on October 9.

The army commander, for that matter, certainly had little ground for criticizing others' understanding of Northern movements still in progress on October 1. Just as Atkinson did not know that Terry would break off the battle about five o'clock, so Lee did not realize that the Federal thrust did not represent a major attack on his weak left center, and he prudently took steps to bolster that threatened sector. It has already been seen that Barton's Brigade was ordered to move from north to east of town to confront the Federals, but as matters turned out, it failed to arrive in time to affect the fighting. Muddy roads and, even more important, the unseasoned nature and/or unwilling disposition of most of its members more than offset its initial proximity to the combat zone. The brigade literally fell apart en route to the front:

> The men were found to be deserting rapidly [complained the commander of the 4th City Regiment]. Provost guards were thrown out as skirmishers and they left also; non-commissioned officers were sent after them and doubtless got lost, as we never saw them again. The commissioned officers were worked to death, and when, at night, after a most wearisome march, we corralled our regiment . . . the captains and lieutenants were worn down and the command reduced by near two hundred men. We thought we were disgraced, until we learned that our regiment had been kept together better than either of the other three. . . .

The relatively few men who remained in the ranks probably did not file into the Intermediate Line (likely the sector crossing the Williamsburg Road) until shortly before dark, after the main Federal probes had been checked. Spear's final shelling, however, seemingly was still under way "much to the consternation and astonishment of some of the uninitiated [men of the City Brigade]," recalled one of Barton's veteran officers from the Army of the Valley; "it was richly amusing to witness the maneuvers of some of the uninitiated."[18] Many of the provisionals failed to see the humor and anxiously awaited the imminent attack that Atkinson's heavy shelling apparently portended. Down on the Darbytown Road, meantime, the VMI cadet company comparably arrived only in time to see the final bombardment. With these reinforcements may have come Barton himself. If he did not already have charge of Moore's brigade as well as his own, he surely turned the provisionals over to Clark and assumed such divisional command at this time.

Neither such dubious troops nor such castoff leaders satisfied Lee, though. He wanted Richmond's safety entrusted to first-class officers and men, and by midafternoon he felt it safe to send such forces from his main army at Chaffin's. Around 3:30, Dick Anderson pulled Bowles and Montague back to the Osborne Turnpike, grouped them under his best divisional commander, Field, and led them north to the threatened sector. Even these seasoned brigades, however, could not make good time on the muddy roads. They, too, did not arrive until about 5:30, when Atkinson was in full blast but Terry was long gone.

The corps commander now established his headquarters with Gary on the Williamsburg Road and assumed over-all charge of the eastern defenses of Richmond. Yet he, too, remained as uncertain as his predecessors over enemy intentions. True, troopers ranging out just before dark to raze houses that had helped shelter Spear encountered no Bluecoats there. True, too, Moore had not established contact on the Darbytown Road. Following the grand cannonade, he had finally sent out a reconnaissance party, Pizzini's company. After trading their smoothbores for the rifles of the nearby Richmond Ambulance Company, the cadets ventured warily out toward the last known location of the enemy. Helping trounce the likes of Franz Sigel the preceeding May had been one thing, but crossing swords with a general of the caliber of Alfred H. Terry was quite another, and the VMI boys had little eagerness for such work this time. No sooner did they get out of sight of the defenses than they began falling back again. Soon some Locals came forward to replace them on outpost, and the cadets pulled back into the works—to receive, within hours, the more suitable assignment of guarding Moore's person. Yet during their brief excursion eastward, they too had met no Unionists.

Even such tidings from both highways, however, did not convince Anderson that the Federal force had finished fighting. Like Kautz's cavalry on Thursday, it might continue probing elsewhere after dark. The South Carolinian, therefore, felt it prudent to remain in the area overnight. He put Montague and Bowles in the fortifications on the New Market and Darbytown roads, respectively, and alerted the militia on the Christian and Mechanicsville roads against a possible night attack. The Southern commanders, indeed, reportedly spent much time that night trying to increase the security of their vulnerable far left. Such precautions, though understandable, proved unnecessary. Terry really had fallen back, so no further fighting erupted near the city.[19]

While Field, Barton, and Moore spent the afternoon marching and/or garrisoning works, Scruggs's men alone of the second-class forces actually came to grips with attacking Yankees. His Locals, during DuBose's presumed absence in the entrenched camp, picketed the

Fort Gilmer sector, against which the X Corps feinted in Terry's behalf. Birney gave orders for the diversion prior to 2:00 P.M., but it was midafternoon by the time Foster could select and deploy a reconnoitering force. The Indianian, perhaps disgusted with his division's performance on Thursday, turned to his old brigade, now Plaisted's, for the needed troops. The choice fell on Colonel John Otis' 10th Connecticut, even though 162 of its members were back at Deep Bottom awaiting muster-out and only 153 men remained with the colors. Otis duly threw out skirmishers, backed them up with a little battle line, and at 3:00 P.M. moved along the axis of the Mill Road into the woods where William Birney had deployed Thursday afternoon. The New Englanders handily cleared the few Local videttes out of the forest, secured the line of the Varina Road, and pressed on to their designated objective: the eastern edge of the bloody cornfield stretching away to Fort Gilmer. Here Otis halted around 3:45.

Scruggs's skirmishers, too, made a stand in the field and even lashed back at the Union left but were beaten off by reinforcements from the 10th Connecticut's line of battle. The Confederate commander, likely Gregg in Field's absence, may also have rushed reinforcements of his own north to Fort Gilmer at about 3:45 (perhaps DuBose). Moreover, he definitely threw out an estimated regiment to attack Otis' more exposed right. The Graycoats, under heavy fire all the while, were again checked, but their mere presence in the cornfield clearly precluded renewing the Federal advance. Birney's seeming intention to press the diversion at about 4:35, accordingly, was apparently not even attempted. The two regiments spent the rest of the afternoon noisily but harmlessly popping away at each other.

Not until shortly after dark did Otis' skirmishers receive and execute the corps commander's orders to break off fighting, rejoin their battle line, and move back to the Exterior Line. The returning Connecticut men felt justifiably proud of their minor-tactical operations, including capturing two prisoners who confirmed Scruggs's presence in this area, but they had obviously failed in their principal mission: preventing dispatch of troops to oppose Terry. Yet because Field did not arrive in time actually to fight the First Division, this failure proved inconsequential and entitled the 10th to be judged primarily in terms of its own fight with the Locals. From that perspective the regiment, filing back into its trenches that night, could clearly count itself victor.[20]

Several hours after re-entering the earthworks, the 10th and Plaisted's other outfits shifted leftward to their former sector just south of the New Market Road to maintain connection with Foster, who had pulled in his right to make room for Terry. The brigadier then resumed reporting to the First Division. Between 7:30 and 9:00 Terry's

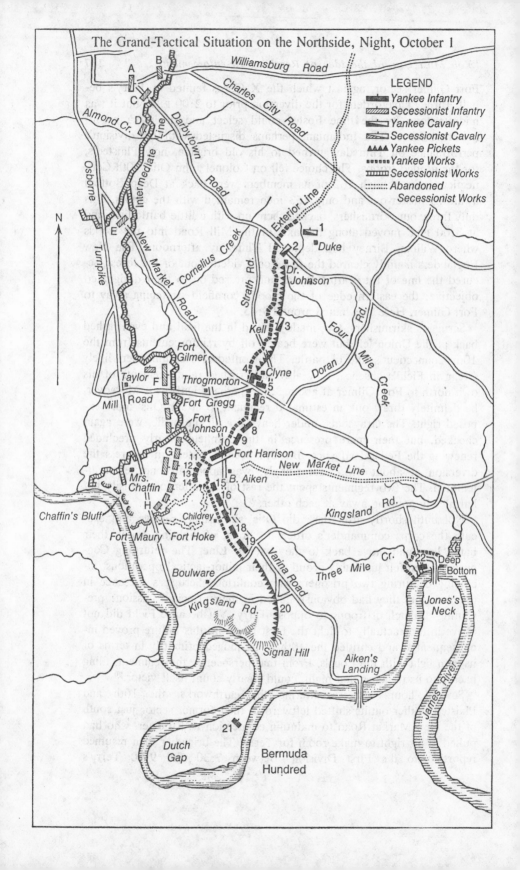

The Grand-Tactical Situation on the Northside, Night, October 1

Army of the James - BUTLER

Cavalry - KAUTZ
  1-Spear
  '2-West
  3-1st N.Y. Mounted Rifles

X Corps - BIRNEY
  TERRY
    4-Pond
    5-Abbott
    6-Plaisted
  FOSTER
    7-Pennypacker
    8-Barney
    9-Bell
  W. BIRNEY
    10-W. Birney
  Deep Bottom
    22-Moore·

XVIII Corps - WEITZEL
  JOURDAN
    11-Raulston
    12-Cullen
    13-Moffitt
    14-Guion
  HECKMAN
    15-Ripley
    16-Fairchild
  PAINE
    17-Holman
    18-Ames
    19-Boernstein
  Independent
    20-White
  Dutch Gap
    21-Strong

Confederates - LEE

Northern Sector - R.H. ANDERSON
  Cavalry
    A - Gary
  BARTON
    B - Clark
    C - Moore
  FIELD
    D - Bowles
    E - Montague
  Chaffin's Sector - LEE, EWELL
    F - Gregg
    G - Hoke
    H - Hughs

COMMENTARY

1. This map shows both sides settling down into a short-lived stalemate at the end of the day, Saturday.

2. Spear is thought but not known to have supported the Regular battery at Duke's.

3. The relative order of Jourdan's brigades is probably: Raulston, Cullen, Moffitt, Guion, right to left.

4. The relative order of Paine's three brigades is very probably correct, but the location of his left flank is only approximate. Not only the position but the very existence of White's brigade is speculative.

5. Gary's location is only approximate.

6. A hypothetical deployment of the eleven Southern brigades at Chaffin's (a theory with little corroboration) is, from left to right: Bass, DuBose, G. T. Anderson, Bratton, Colquitt, Scales, Hagood, Kirkland, and Hughs, with McKethan in reserve and Scruggs either on the far left or else south of DuBose.

drenched and exhausted infantry came plodding back to their former position on the far right: the First Brigade to hold the refused flank line in Clyne's field, the Second Brigade to go into reserve. "It was a dreary, tiresome night march back to camp," groaned Abbott's Chief-of-Staff, "and no particular relief when we got there—for we had to lie down in the mud and water, making the best shift of it we could, hungry, cold, and tired." Meantime, Kautz, with a shorter distance to go, reached his old bivouacs at Johnson's and Duke's by 8:00 P.M.

The safe return of the expeditionary force undoubtedly produced relief at army and supreme headquarters. Even while Terry's small force remained so potentially exposed that afternoon, Butler had apparently considered recalling it, but Birney had evidently dissuaded him by urging it be given a chance to succeed until dark. The corps commander kept his chief as well apprised of developments as practicable throughout the afternoon, and on learning the troops were returning safely, duly reassured army headquarters at 7:30 P.M. that they were now out of danger. However, the Massachusetts man, as after Kautz's raid of September 29–30, negligently failed to relay all this intelligence to City Point until prompted by Grant's inquiry of 8:30, whereupon he forwarded a relatively comprehensive summary at 8:55.[21]

These were the first tidings the lieutenant general had received from the Northside since visiting Butler's headquarters in midday. He planned to set out for the Peninsula at about 10:30 A.M. and was still with the Massachusetts man at least as late as 1:55 P.M. During these several hours at the front, he, of course, saw none of Terry's skirmishing, only the quiescence that progressively settled over the main armies, each secure in its breastworks. Word from below Petersburg suggested that the Army of the Potomac, too, had little prospect of attacking the Secessionists outside their defenses on October 1. Such intelligence decisively influenced Grant's planning. Ever one to profit, however slowly, from experience, he had learned in May and June the terrible cost of attacking the entrenched Army of Northern Virginia and subsequently avoided such battles. Only if he could turn or envelop a weak flank or catch the Confederates in the open would he precipitate fighting. Since all evidence suggested that they were no longer in the open, he saw no basis for continuing to do battle and came increasingly to feel that the whole offensive should be brought to a close. He, to be sure, did not peremptorily order its termination on Saturday and even yielded to Meade's urging that operations on the Southside continue into Sunday. Still, Grant apparently had little heart for prolonging the offensive and did not enthusiastically support subordinates' repeated requests to keep on attacking.

Whether he communicated this reassessment to Butler during their meeting in mid-Saturday is not clear. The change of plans, in any case, definitely became apparent at 11:00 that night, when the junior officer received City Point's instructions to lay out a new line for one corps covering either Deep Bottom or Aiken's Landing preparatory to razing the Exterior Line and perhaps Fort Harrison and falling back to the new position. Grant's principal concern in ordering this move was to refuse the exposed right flank currently at Clyne's lest the Army of the Valley, fleeing Sheridan, should swoop down on that vulnerable sector as "Stonewall" Jackson had done in the Seven Days' Battle. But at the same time his willingness to break contact, fall back, and leave just one corps permanently on the Peninsula, while the other remained there only temporarily as a strategic reserve, suggested his lack of intention to press the current offensive. Butler's initial response of 11:55 P.M. accepted the proposal and promised to lay out the new line on Sunday but asked that Grant specify its trace since Barnard and Comstock had reconnoitered the ground. The General-in-Chief from the start offered two staff officers as engineers and, on receiving the Massachusetts man's appeal, promised to send the two men requested. This last dispatch, written half an hour past midnight, also informed Butler that the Army of the Potomac would feel for openings after daybreak and significantly noted that the engineers' arrival should not "make any difference in your plans. . . ."[22] City Point thus conveyed an over-all defensive tone but did not preclude fighting on October 2. Neither encouragement, advice, nor reinforcements would Grant provide, but if Butler, like Meade, had "plans" of his own for attacking, the Illinoisan would not rule them out.

Butler, as usual, did not lack for plans. He and his two corps commanders spent Saturday night and early Sunday analyzing the implications of Terry's reconnaissance. They learned, for one thing, that Michie had been able to confirm the accuracy of the captured Chambliss map. More important still, the prisoners Otis took and the Confederates' failure to resist Terry outside their fortifications suggested that only second-class troops held the works west and north of Fort Gilmer. Against them Butler proposed to hurl the whole Army of the James along the Darbytown and Charles City roads on Monday morning. Gone now were the despair and fear of imminent destruction that had plagued him the preceding evening. The mercurial general's spirits were soaring again at the fancied prospect of new triumphs. Confident of his ability as an intelligence officer, he had no doubt that his force was sufficient to carry him into Richmond. To insure his success, however, he insisted that one of Meade's corps, tentatively promised him on September 30, arrive on Sunday night to replace his men presently confronting Lee on Chaffin's farm. As if to keep the army moving in the proper direction, he now added his first protest against falling back to the proposed new line for the reason that his own reconnaissance revealed no good position between the present position and the original footholds at Deep Bottom and Dutch Gap. The Massachusetts man set these thoughts down on paper and forwarded them to City Point at 9:45 A.M. on October 2.

Whether Grant learned of the proposal from the letter or from his personal conference with Butler (perhaps at Deep Bottom) on Sunday morning is not clear. The General-in-Chief, in either case, was momentarily impressed with the subordinate's plan—but only momentarily. Comstock and Barnard emphasized to him all its drawbacks: difficulty of reaching the capital, vulnerability of a position so far west, likelihood of heavy casualties, strategic fallacy of making the major drive east of Richmond rather than south of Petersburg. Then, too, there was the matter of reinforcements from the Army of the Potomac; the plan depended on them, yet they were clearly unavailable for at least one day. Grant was probably then unaware that his left wing, too, now favored the defensive. But even if he received Meade's telegram of 11:00 A.M. to that effect before responding to Butler, it probably only strengthened his determination to cease fighting. With no commitment of his own to prolonging the offensive, Grant readily acceded to these criticisms and rejected Butler's proposal.

The Massachusetts man continued to argue for his strike or some variation of it on Monday and Tuesday, but to no avail. As far as Grant was concerned, the Fifth Offensive was over, and plans had to be made for a wholly new offensive. Getting more men for that onslaught—from recruiting depots and from the Army of the Shenandoah—increasingly dominated his thoughts the first week of October and for much of the month and left him neither time nor sympathy for proposals to prolong the old offensive. His initial, conclusive rejection of Butler's planned continuation of fighting on Sunday morning thus marks the end of the Battle of Chaffin's Bluff.[23]

The Illinoisan had decreed the battle would begin on September 29; he could comparably ordain its close on October 2. But even as his junior officers and the enemy made the battle he ordered, so would they have to tidy up the fight he now terminated. Doing so was not difficult for the Army of the James. Although its senior officers chafed at the inactivity, they at least found it easy to implement City Point's new plan. Forbidden to attack, they now concentrated on defending their recent conquests. Barnard and Comstock spent October 2 tracing the new defense line north and northwest of Deep Bottom from Four Mile Creek on the right to a swamp on the James south of Three Mile Creek on the left, with a forward detached redoubt on New Market Heights. Michie duly began entrenching the new line the next day.

The main army meantime spent Sunday strengthening its forward position to make it more defensible for however long it would still be held. The basic gorge wall of Fort Harrison was completed that day (though much work remained to be done to make it permanent); Heckman and Paine continued digging in on the left; and the X Corps kept on reversing the Exterior Line. Further to bolster the field force, Cook pulled two batteries (A/1st and F/5th) into mobile reserve on the Northside, and Jackson advanced his Pennsylvanians to the front. The Irishman also moved at least the 1st Connecticut Battery and E/3rd U. S. Artillery (and perhaps the 5th, too) from Jones's Neck to Deep Bottom late Sunday afternoon. More convalescents, stragglers, and camp guards also rejoined the main army that day, and even a new unit from the North, the 127th USCT, reinforced the X Corps. The latest in a continuing series of Negro outfits being channeled into the Army of the James, the 127th had been scheduled to leave Philadelphia for the war zone on September 23, but had delayed its departure until Wednesday to secure enough officers. It reached Bermuda Hundred on October 1, was assigned to William Birney on Sunday, and was detached later in the day to dig the new line around Deep Bottom. It began work on October 3.[24]

Lee, too, spent the first two days of October strengthening his position. His engineers had traced the new line through the middle of the entrenched camp connecting Forts Johnson and Hoke on Saturday. After dark, his troops maneuvered into place on this new line, some like Bratton advancing to it, others like Hagood shifting leftward to their assigned sector. Inconclusive evidence suggests that, as finally arranged, his line ran: Hughs, Kirkland, Hagood, Scales, Colquitt, Elliott, Bratton, and "Tige" Anderson, right to left, with McKethan in reserve and DuBose, Gregg, and Scruggs still farther left in the lower Intermediate Line. The units inside the camp immediately began digging, and before Sunday closed, their trenches were defensible, though much work still needed to be done over the next four days. Federal sniping and shelling, never severe, annoyed but did not stop the entrenching, and Butler made no other attempt to disrupt efforts to seal off his initial breakthrough.

The Yankees were not the only ones to open cannon and sharpshooter fire on October 2. Gray marksmen harassed the Rhode Island gunners in Fort Harrison throughout the day, and Hardaway's pieces in Forts Johnson and Gilmer hurled heavier lead into Jourdan's stronghold. Artillery nearer Chaffin's Bluff plus Battery Semmes meantime threw a few shells toward the XVIII Corps's new southern flank near Boulware's farm. Mitchell's naval squadron, however, did not join in the fray this time. During the heavy fighting of the past three days, his ironclads had used up virtually all the shells, shrapnel, and fuses not only in their own magazines but even in the Richmond naval depots. His gunboats, moreover, lacked the necessary range to reach the Union position. With no compelling reason to expend what few munitions remained, he stayed quiet throughout Sunday and even continued his efforts to get the poor *Gallego* afloat again, this time with the help of the *Drewry* and the *Beaufort*. Finally, after dark, he led the *Fredericksburg, Richmond,* and *Drewry* down below Bishop's Landing to guard against efforts by those Bluecoats at Boulware's to cross the James into Pickett's left rear.

Confederate infantry, too, was curious about the XVIII Corps's intentions near the river on October 2. A seven-man reconnaissance party from the 17th North Carolina of Kirkland's Brigade found out the hard way that the Federals were there in force. Paine, apparently particularly conscious of the vulnerability of his position, had vigilantly patrolled his sector since at least the preceding evening, probably even earlier. Now one of his forward patrols, the 2nd USCT Cavalry, ambushed the Tarheels and captured them to the last man. Such precautions and probes by the Secessionists were understandable but, in the long run, unnecessary. Events were to show that Weitzel was only refusing his left toward the river and had no offensive designs.[25]

While the Confederate right thus confronted the XVIII Corps, other reconnaissances against the opposite Union flank precipitated Sunday's heaviest action. That region north of the New Market Road represented alike the greatest danger and the greatest uncertainty to the Butternut high command. With the whole country from New Market Heights to Roper's farm and north to the Chickahominy now open to the Bluecoats, there was no telling what force lurked in that area to mount yet another thrust at the capital on October 2. The Southerners could perceive that Terry was not in sight of the Intermediate Line that morning, but they did not know whether he still hovered nearby to strike again or had fallen back to Clyne's. Therefore, although a few of the feebler members of the "Hospital Corpse" had to be returned to their wards after enduring the cold, rainy night in the trenches and although some of the most vital members of war industry, such as Captain Charles Talcott's independent Virginia Local Defense Company from the Danville Railroad, had to be ordered back to their civilian jobs, the general economic and social life of Richmond remained disrupted. Her businesses stayed closed a fourth day; most of her citizen-defenders remained on the alert; and much of her populace continued greatly disturbed by the threat. One visitor to department headquarters confided after meeting many civilians on the capitol grounds: "Everything very blue and everybody blue as indigo too—I tremble for Richmond."[26]

To end this uncertainty, Anderson turned over the defenses to Barton's division and led Field's two veteran brigades reconnoitering east along the New Market Road. Gary simultaneously moved out in force with his main body on the Darbytown Road and the 7th South Carolina Cavalry on the Charles City Road. On none of these avenues did the Graycoats encounter any resistance west of Fort Gilmer. They thus discovered at last that Terry had fallen back to the Exterior Line.

Even now they kept on advancing. In late morning, Gary and at least Montague moved against the Unionists in their fronts. The horsemen easily drove in Kautz's outposts from the 5th and 11th Pennsylvania Cavalry on both northerly highways but did not challenge his main lines at Johnson's and Duke's. The infantry meantime pressed Terry's pickets astride the New Market Road. The Virginians soon turned the right of the First Brigade's outposts and forced them back, but Pond's reserves, in turn, checked Montague about noon and even took seventeen prisoners. While this skirmishing flared up, both Pond and Plaisted manned their main works in force, just in case the Butternuts tried to overrun Clyne's.

Federal headquarters, too, worried about what Montague's probe portended. Birney initially believed the Southerners were present in strong force between the New Market and Darbytown roads. Checking the Virginians and taking prisoners from all four regiments, far from dispelling his concern, only made matters worse, for the captives obligingly reported that behind them massed a heavy strike force under Ewell, including reinforcements from the Department of North Carolina and Southern Virginia. The corps commander forwarded this intelligence to army headquarters either at 11:35 A.M. or 12:35 P.M. Butler replied at 1:10 that if the threat materialized, Birney should refuse his right eastward down the New Market Road, perhaps even fall back southward toward the Kingsland Road, and keep Kautz on the enemy's left flank.

"Ewell's" attack, however, never took place. The infantry and cavalry probes sufficed for Lee's purpose, whatever it was. He may simply have been completing the reconnaissance eastward from the Intermediate Line to ascertain whether the enemy he had finally located would resist or withdraw at the least pressure. Or he may have intentionally jabbed the Bluecoats to keep them off balance and on the defensive and not allow them time to mount another major drive for the capital. Then again, he may even have hoped to convert these probes into a full-scale attack, only to cancel it in order to guard against a renewed Northern advance below Petersburg on October 2. He definitely alerted at least Scales's Brigade on Sunday to be ready to return to Cockade

City, and he may have comparably refused to commit his other reserves on the Peninsula that day.

Whatever the reason, he soon broke off the engagement and pulled back his troops. Anderson retired within the Fort Gilmer–Fort Maury line and established his headquarters at Ball's house near the Randolph plantation "Wilton" just above the entrenched camp. Gary meantime withdrew to the Military Road northwest of Dr. Johnson's. This cessation of skirmishing, in turn, shortly convinced the Federals that their right flank was in no danger. They were content to let fighting end and did not pursue.[27]

With this little action near Clyne's and the few other probes and patrols on October 2, the Battle of Chaffin's Bluff sputtered to a close. Unlike the corresponding operations that weekend on the Southside, which were launched by both sides in quest of major results, operations on the Peninsula on Saturday and Sunday were but the tail end of a battle virtually concluded on September 30. Neither the fateful drama of Richmond's fight for survival on Thursday nor the primal passion of the savage battle for Fort Harrison on Friday marked occurrences over the weekend. Casualties the last two days were minor—perhaps 100 Yankees, maybe 70 Southerners—and tactical results appeared the same.[28] Yet October 1 and 2 were not without strategic significance. Unfavorable weather and terrain and formidable ramparts convinced both Grant and Lee on Saturday that prolonging the battle would prove unavailing; events Sunday only confirmed their judgment. Neither commander yet renounced his basic objective—for the lieutenant general, to seize Richmond; for the Virginian, to drive the Northerners from Fort Harrison and the Exterior Line. Both officers, however, now realized that such results could be attained, if at all, only through a wholly new battle. They knew the Battle of Chaffin's Bluff was over, and they now concentrated on consolidating their present positions, giving their men rest, and preparing for new operations.[29]

Both rest and preparation were needed. Each army had fought hard and lost heavily. Butler suffered about 3,350 casualties, and Lee lost approximately 1,700 men.[30] Such sizable losses, however, had brought neither side decisive victory, so new operations had to be planned. The Federals, to be sure, had breached the forward Southern lines, seized a major sector on the Peninsula, and bloodily repulsed efforts to drive them back; they had, however, fallen far short of fully exploiting their initial advantage. The Graycoats, by the same token, had stopped the Army of the James short of Richmond but had signally failed to recover the considerable area they originally lost. Thus, despite all its opportunities—realized and unrealized—despite all its fury and its fallen, the Battle of Chaffin's Bluff was ultimately indecisive.

Yet the battle involved so great a threat to Richmond that it forced Lee to weaken Petersburg to save his capital. From the beginning, Grant counted on such a development, and hardly had fighting started on the Peninsula before he unleashed the Army of the Potomac south of the Appomattox. Meade's objectives were to cut the gravely imperiled lines of communication leading south and west into the Southern heartland, perhaps even to capture Cockade City itself. To accomplish this, he knew he would have to fight his way past the outer Confederate defenses running just west of a little country meeting house called "Poplar Spring Church."

CHAPTER VII

◆

"The Whole Army Will Be Under Arms Ready to Move . . . "

To the soldiers in blue, Federal fortifications around Petersburg were earthen ramparts to protect them from infantry and artillery fire. To the commanders in blue, those fortifications were key instruments in an offensive strategy. Just east of town, for two miles southward from the lower Appomattox to the Jerusalem Plank Road, the trenches pressed close to their Confederate counterparts literally to fix Lee in place. He constantly had to keep heavy counterbalancing forces in that sector to make sure that the Yankees, who almost incessantly sniped at and shelled his works, did not also pour over the short no-man's-land, often only several hundred yards wide, and break into the city. Beyond Fort Sedgwick on the plank road, the Union works ceased grappling Lee and shot southwestward and westward, below firing range, for three miles like a lean, muscular arm to clutch one of his life lines, the Weldon Railroad. At Globe Tavern, two miles south of the Petersburg defenses, the fist of this arm held a mile-long sector of track. Then the works doubled back eastward, facing south and southeast to guard the Federal rear. Now this mighty arm flexed itself to jab even deeper into Confederate territory to grasp still more enemy supply lines west of the Weldon Railroad.

That westerly country teemed with Secessionist communications. The Federal presence at Globe Tavern denied uninterrupted use of the Weldon Railroad and the parallel Halifax Road straight into Cockade City, but the Graycoats did continue running trains as far north as Stony

Creek Depot, about eighteen miles below town, and then transshipped freight by wagon into Petersburg. The main wagon route ran northwest from the depot via the Flat Foot Road to Dinwiddie Court House, thence northeast along the Boydton Plank Road to Cockade City. To shorten this circuitous twenty-eight-mile course, the Southerners built the Military Road connecting the Flat Foot Road to the Quaker Road, which entered the Boydton Road one mile southwest of where the plank road crossed Hatcher's Run at Burgess' Mill, thus cutting off the court house. The Military Road also gave access to a still more easterly course via the Vaughan, Duncan, and Harman roads to the plank road only three miles southwest of Petersburg. All these routes eventually led into the Boydton Plank Road, which thus became a key objective for a new Federal offensive. Beyond that highway was the even more coveted Southside Railroad, the last track running uninterruptedly into the city from the interior. Taking these two arteries would provide the "push" that Grant felt sure would shake the Southerners out of Petersburg itself that autumn.

Plenty of routes offered the Bluecoats access to this country. The Halifax Road ran straight south from Globe Tavern to Stony Creek Depot—and straight north from the tavern to Petersburg. Five other roads led west from that highway toward the other lines of communications. Three quarters of a mile north of the Federal foothold the Vaughan Road branched off on a twelve-mile course southwest, west, and southwest again over Hatcher's Run at Cummings' Ford to Dinwiddie Court House. From Globe Tavern itself the Poplar Spring Road ran nearly two miles straight west across the Vaughan Road, past Poplar Spring Church, to the key intersections around William Peebles's farm. From the western end of the Poplar Spring Road, the Squirrel Level Road headed north for two and a half miles to the works of Petersburg and south for two miles to E. Wilkinson's farm on the east–west portion of the Vaughan Road north of Hatcher's Run. Just north of the intersection of the Poplar Spring Road and the Squirrel Level Road, the Church Road cut diagonally northwest for three miles to the Boydton Plank Road a mile west of the Petersburg defenses, and just south of Peebles's farm, Route 673 (to use its modern name) ran west for two miles from the Squirrel Level Road to the Duncan Road-Harman Road. The third great westward artery from the Halifax Road, the Lower Church Road, left it at Wyatt's Crossing, one and three-fourths mile south of the Globe Tavern defenses, led west half a mile to Colonel Edward A. Wyatt's plantation, and then continued northwest to J. Davis' on the Vaughan Road, a mile and a half southwest of the Union fortifications. From Wyatt's plantation the Wyatt Road ran straight west over a mile to McDowell's farm (sometimes called "Snyder's" or "Mrs. Davis'"), located on the Vaughan Road a mile south of J. Davis'. Three quarters of a mile farther south of Wyatt's Crossing, the Stage Road headed west on its five-mile course across Rowanty Creek at Monk's Neck Bridge to the Vaughan Road. Just east of the bridge another road entered the Stage Road from Reams's Station, situated on the Weldon Railroad nearly four miles south of Globe Tavern.

So many routes leading toward his communications forced Lee to take countermeasures to protect those supply lines. His original fortifications—constructed in 1862, revised east of town in June 1864—did him little good in that regard, for they simply ringed Petersburg south of the Appomattox and did not cover the communications. The loss of Globe Tavern in August, accordingly, not only deprived him of uninterrupted use of the Weldon Railroad but also diverted his precious manpower to containing the Yankees there, lest they cut the remaining lines of supply farther west. He therefore began building a trench line along the Boydton Plank Road as far right as a mile southwest of the Harman Road on September 16. Just four days later, moreover, he moved his construction parties eastward to erect another line southward along the Squirrel Level Road to Peebles's farm, thence southwestward to Route 673 at Hawks's house to block any Northern strike westward from Globe Tavern to the many routes fanning out from Peebles's. The late start on this construction plus the lack of available troops to dig these defenses—Field's three brigades on the Southside plus two of Major General Henry Heth's brigades were all that could be spared for the task—prevented finishing the fortifications before fighting erupted at the end of the month. The Squirrel Level Line was little more than an elementary trench, and the more westerly position no more than primitive logworks barely covered with earth. Even worse, no trenches whatsoever, no matter how incomplete, extended south of Route 673. Only outposts of Major General Wade Hampton's Cavalry Corps patrolled the country southeast from Heth's right to Reams's Station and Malone's Crossing to cover all the wagon routes in that sector. Finally, two brigades of garrison troops—mostly reserves—of Brigadier General Henry A. Wise's First District, Department of North Carolina and Southern Virginia, guarded the Weldon, Southside, and Danville railroads proper. Except for the Holcombe Legion of South Carolina at Stony Creek Depot, Wise's brigades were so far to the rear as to be useful only against cavalry raiders, not against Grant's main army.[1]

Numerous roads toward Lee's communications, and few troops and fewer defenses guarding that area—the country west of the Halifax Road and south of Petersburg was virtually a military vacuum. Into that vacuum—whose vulnerability had been considerably revealed by cavalry and infantry reconnaissances, lookouts, and deserters—U. S. Grant now prepared to strike. His original grand onslaught projected for October 5 would have occurred in that region, and now his hastened attack as part of the Fifth Offensive was aimed there, too. The main problem now was determining when to launch the blow toward the Southside Railroad. Simultaneous attacks all along the line were not his practice. At the end of September, as earlier in the siege, his two-pronged strikes against the Richmond–Petersburg lines were designed to knock the enemy off a balanced strategic defense and to permit one Union wing, if not both, to achieve a major success. The first blow of the Fifth Offensive was, as usual, delivered on the Peninsula on September 29. Meade's role that day was not to attack right away himself but to make such shows of force as would prevent Confederate reinforcements leaving Petersburg for the Northside. Should some Secessionists depart despite his efforts, he was to hold himself ready to drive for Lee's supply lines.

Initial orders from City Point on September 27 stressed that the Army of the Potomac was to use "every effort . . . to convince the enemy that the South Side road and Petersburg are the objects of our efforts." Evidently following through on Barnard's suggestion on how to improve Butler's prospects, Grant added at 9:00, Tuesday night, that "if troops can be moved to-morrow, so as to give the appearance of massing on our left, it would serve to deceive the enemy." This intended amplification actually left Meade uncertain whether the forces were to "mass" inside Union lines for a mere show of strength or "mass" outside the works for a demonstration against the Squirrel Level Line. His inquiry on the subject at 10:30 P.M. brought a reply forty-five minutes later that the troops were to move "within our lines, not openly, but so that the enemy will likely get glimpses of them and think there was a concentration on our left." Army headquarters now knew what was expected, and at 1:00 A.M. on September 28, Meade's Chief-of-Staff, Major General Andrew A. Humphreys, ordered Parke to transfer Brigadier General Robert B. Potter's Second Division, IX Corps, from its reserve position behind Hancock's center, just north of the Norfolk Railroad, to Dr. Gurley's house, about half a mile southeast of Globe Tavern, "as soon after full daylight as practicable . . . and in such a manner as to attract the attention of the enemy." With great fanfare—reveille was "beaten . . . with as much noise as possible," one soldier noted—Potter roused his two brigades and marched to the woods along the U. S. Military Railroad near Dr. Gurley's. On arriving, the troops remained under arms, ready to move at a moment's notice, for the rest of the day.[2]

Whether or not the Second Division's move succeeded in deceiving

Dunn's Hill is not known, but in any case it served the ultimately useful purpose of concentrating striking forces near the Weldon Railroad. Grant intended all along to hurl those forces into the largely open country west of the tracks when the time seemed right. His battle order of September 27 to Meade made clear that the Army of the Potomac was to do more than just stage a show of force:

> Should the enemy draw off [to oppose Butler] such a force from the defenses of Petersburg as to justify you in moving either for the South Side road or for Petersburg, I want you to do it without waiting for instructions, and in your own way. One thing, however, I would say: If the road is reached it, or a position commanding it, should be held at all hazards. If it becomes necessary to maintain the position against an attack, draw off from our present defenses what force you deem necessary, always keeping the garrisons detailed for the inclosed works on the line intact, however.

The General-in-Chief contented himself with issuing these general guidelines and deliberately avoided intruding upon his subordinate's prerogatives by specifying the composition and tactics of the projected column of attack. More than an act of official courtesy, this restraint on Grant's part testified to his confidence in the veteran army commander. This confidence proved well placed. Either upon first learning informally of the proposed move (September 24) or else on receiving official notice three days later, Meade promptly projected how he would operate, and once City Point clarified its intentions on Tuesday night, he took steps to implement his plan. He may, to be sure, have responded to his superior's trust by divulging the plan to him at supreme headquarters on Wednesday afternoon, but there seems little question that the Pennsylvanian authored the plan. He spelled out its initial phases to his corps and other independent commanders shortly before 7:30 P.M. on September 28, and they, in turn, passed it on to their subordinates throughout the night.

Meade designated the two reserve divisions of Parke's IX Corps, at least two divisions of Warren's V Corps, and most of Gregg's cavalry division as the striking force. To support them, he planned to call on his other troops, if necessary, and requested that "the whole army will be under arms ready to move at 4 a.m. of the 29th instant. . . ." Like Butler, he disencumbered his attacking column of such impedimenta as forage, supply, office, baggage, and sutlers' wagons, but unlike the Massachusetts man, he did authorize vital ammunition and medical wagons to accompany the troops initially. The men, he specified, were to have:

. . . four days' rations in the haversacks and sixty rounds of ammunition on the person. All trains and wagons will be hitched up, ready to move at the same hour [4:00 A.M.], supply trains with the prescribed number of rations (six days'), and all the trains with forage to the extent of their capacity. . . . The troops that move will take with them their intrenching tools, one-half their ambulances, and one medicine and one hospital wagon to each brigade, one-half the small-arm ammunition wagons and one-half the reserve ammunition wagons of the 12-pounder guns. The spring wagons and pack animals allowed for headquarters may also accompany the troops. . . .

Meade also withdrew the 50th New York Engineers from various construction and fortification projects to army headquarters at Birchett's house about 10:00 P.M. and then sent five companies of that regiment under Captain James McDonald to City Point to prepare the six pontoon trains there to move "at a moment's notice." The army commander wanted to be ready in case his drive achieved so big a breakthrough as to carry him all the way to the upper Appomattox above Petersburg.

Beyond preparing the troops, Meade could not yet go. City Point required his army to be "ready to move in any direction," so until either instructions from there or else intelligence of the weakening of Petersburg disclosed his objective, he could not yet commit his forces to the plan of operations he had in mind. Thursday would be Butler's day to define the course of events; the Army of the Potomac could only wait and watch with "special vigilance" for whatever openings he might create.[8]

For a time Wednesday night it looked as if the Butternuts, not the Army of the James, would define how events would go by beating the Yankees to the attack. The outbreak of heavy musketry just west of the Jerusalem Plank Road at about 9:00 P.M. suggested a Confederate raid there, perhaps even an attack. Nearby forces of both sides soon joined in the firing, and at least the First Division of the IX Corps, in reserve in that sector, turned out under arms. Federal headquarters from City Point to Globe Tavern meantime sent out a flurry of inquiries as to what the shooting meant. After much checking back and forth, the Union commanders finally found out it was only a false alarm, caused by relatively inexperienced Negro troops of Brigadier General Edward Ferrero's Third Division, IX Corps, who had drawn fire while changing pickets and had responded far more briskly than more seasoned troops would have done. Their fusilades, in turn, provoked artillery fire and counterfire that raged from their sector northward along the works to the Swift Creek Line. A probe by an estimated 200 to 300 of Hoke's men, probably from McKethan's brigade, against Battery No. 9 on Hancock's right center only intensified the shelling before being driven back by the 12th New York Battery. But as no further strikes developed there or elsewhere, artillery commanders eventually slackened and then ceased firing around 11:00 to 11:15. No serious battle, then, erupted around Cockade City on the night of September 28–29, only a minor affray escalated out of all proportion by the cause-and-effect relationship of fire and counterfire. Virtually the only casualty of the incident was sleep, what soldiers on the verge of battle so badly need.[4]

Finally, however, the guns fell silent, and the men were able to get a little rest—but not for long. Throughout the night supply trains and hospitals packed up and headed for City Point, where they would be out of the way. Some sutlers accompanied them; others prepared to "sell off cheap," come daylight. Nor did the combat troops get much more rest than the support elements. Early in the morning buglers, intentionally avoiding any effort to conceal the gathering of forces, sounded reveille. Some units were roused as early as 2:00 A.M.; others turned out at 3:00; and all the combat troops were ready by the prescribed time of 4:00 A.M.—although, it must be admitted, the generals at army headquarters itself, evidently taking advantage of their knowledge that the strike force would not attack right away in any case, did not get up until 5:30 to 6:00. By full daylight, in any event, all the Federal combat units were ready for whatever the day might bring.[5]

For some Yankee soldiers, daylight brought the "feverish excitement" that always grips even veteran troops who know battle is imminent. For one Union officer, Brigadier General Edward S. Bragg of the First ("Iron") Brigade, Third Division, V Corps, daylight brought fulfillment of an old apprehension. Experience had taught him that the arrival of a paymaster would be followed by a change of camp, and after that would come a rainstorm and a battle. The harbinger of battle had passed out pay on September 27, and Bragg's Iron Brigade had duly changed its camp. Now he could see that the standard sequence was continuing—that fighting would soon be at hand. He could hardly have known it at the time—apprehend it though he might—but a rainstorm would break before the month was over. Cycles and excitement the imminence of combat could generate, but only Grant or Meade could actually precipitate fighting. Until they gave the word to attack, the Army of the Potomac could only create shows of force to try to prevent Secessionist reinforcements from being sent to Ewell. Hancock's II Corps, though under arms and ready to move, accordingly did no more than man its trenches in force and even bolstered the Consolidated and Fourth brigades of Brigadier General Nelson A. Miles's First Division on its right center in midafternoon in the face of a Southern buildup across the way, on Johnson's sector. Even the V Corps, moreover, may have remained in its fortifications to help create a show of strength, and the white troops of the IX Corps, definitely in reserve, may have ostentatiously paraded behind the Union left in hopes of deceiving Confederate lookouts. Of all Federal forces, only ten of Gregg's eleven cavalry regiments actually struck out into enemy country on Thursday, and even their raids down the Halifax and Vaughan roads were only more demonstrations to mislead Dunn's Hill.[6]

All these efforts only partially succeeded in detaining Graycoats on the Southside. Initial tidings of Butler's crossing prompted Lee, at 6:30 A.M., to order Field's three brigades to break camp west of Petersburg, supporting the new Squirrel Level Line, and head for Chaffin's Bluff. Further word of the gravity of the crisis on the Peninsula led army headquarters to direct Johnson to take over Hoke's sector so the North Carolinian, too, could cross the James. At about 11:00 A.M. Johnson's men began filing back into the trenches they had left only the day before. Colonel John T. Goode's Virginia brigade took over Colquitt's sector next to the Appomattox; Colonel Lee McAfee's North Carolina brigade replaced McKethan to Goode's right; then came Brigadier General Archibald Gracie's Alabamians in Hagood's old sector; and Brigadier General William Wallace's South Carolina Brigade now manned Kirkland's former line holding the division's right. Thus relieved, Hoke fell back into reserve preparatory to marching to Dunlop's.[7]

Even ordering Field's and Hoke's seven brigades to Henrico County did not satisfy Lee, who pressed Powell Hill to give him still a third division. The choice settled on Major General Cadmus M. Wilcox's Light Division, presumably because its position on the far right, over two miles north of the V Corps, was least vulnerable to being carried by a *coup de main*. Yet with the Yankees at Globe Tavern, the vital sector crossing the Weldon Railroad could not simply be abandoned. Wilcox could issue orders early Thursday morning to break camp, draw rations and presumably ammunition, turn over the works to a weak trench guard, and prepare to march, but until replacements arrived, he could not actually pull out of the area behind the defenses.

Finding such replacements was no easy matter now that both reserve divisions (Field's and Johnson's) were committed to other tasks. Lee met the need in ways that the Confederate manpower shortage already made all too common. He returned "extra duty" men (cooks, clerks, fatigue details) to the ranks; he called second-class and small detached units to front-line service; and he extended the sectors of some first-class troops already in the works to permit other forces to be relieved. Petersburg now endured a milder version of the manpower drain that Richmond was experiencing that day. With the emergency on the Southside less urgent, no dragnet impressed civilians into the ranks, though some did voluntarily evacuate the area for the interior. Nor were soldiers operating the key railroads called from their jobs. But some convalescents in hospitals were returned to duty, and most of the organized second-class outfits in town—the City Battalion, the reserves, the militia—were turned out, grouped under Lieutenant Colonel Fletcher H. Archer of the 3rd Virginia Reserve Battalion, and rushed to report to Major General William Mahone's Division at the Confederate States Lead Works, where the Halifax Road passed south through the defenses. At least Mahone's provost guard also moved to the lead works, and other provost guards near the city, apparently including the 5th Alabama Battalion from III Corps headquarters, likely entered the trenches, too, perhaps in the same vicinity. The arrival of these small units—and possibly also the leftward extension of the trench guard of Wilcox's center brigade, Brigadier General Samuel McGowan's South Carolinians—may have been what permitted Scales to depart for the Northside between 2:00 and 2:30 that afternoon.[8]

Neither McGowan nor the Light Division's right brigade (Brigadier General James H. Lane's North Carolinians) nor the artillery could follow Scales, though, until still more troops arrived to replace them. Guns from the center of the line duly relieved Marmaduke Johnson on the right and enabled him to set out for the Northside, but it proved less easy to obtain replacements for the infantry: Heth's two brigades holding the left center between the Jerusalem Plank Road and the Crater (the great excavation blown out by Burnside's mine on July 30). To free Heth, in turn, to relieve Wilcox, army headquarters planned for Johnson and Mahone to take over the left center. Still, Lee had reservations about attenuating one division so far, and he asked rather than directed Johnson if he could stretch rightward to replace Brigadier General John R. Cooke's North Carolinians. Johnson, already charged with holding with four brigades a sector once guarded by eight, evidently shared his chieftain's concern. But conscientious soldier that he was, he grasped the significance of an inquiry underlined with the warning that "the case is urgent," and he dutifully answered, "I have simply to state that I will relieve Cooke's Brigade. . . ."

However, Ewell's initial victories at Chaffin's or logistical considerations or signs of a possible advance by the Army of the Potomac then intervened to make Lee feel that transferring Heth and relieving Wilcox were not so urgent or so desirable, after all. He, therefore, requested that the moves be postponed until dark. Before orders could filter down to Johnson, though, he extended Wallace south of the Crater to replace Cooke at about 3:00 P.M. The Tarheels then dropped back to the cover of a sheltered ravine, presumably west of Cemetery Hill, where they prepared two days' rations and awaited developments. Even in such obviously tense conditions, Cooke's men had a "tremendous time" exulting that they were at last out of the trenches. Their comrades in Heth's Division, Brigadier General Joseph R. Davis' Mississippians in Rives's Salient (the great southeastern angle where the Jerusalem Plank Road passed through the works), did not share this luxury, though. Lee's new instructions, passing through one less intermediate headquarters than the orders to Johnson, reached Mahone in time to prevent him from relieving Davis until around dark, after all. Mahone did keep his forces well in hand, however, and may have moved his own Virginia brigade under Colonel David A. Weiseger out of the trenches, preparatory to replacing Davis, if it were not already in reserve.[9]

All these forces were moved for two fundamental reasons: to save the capital and, if possible, also to retain the rail center. Some troops definitely remained to defend Cockade City, and even units slated for the Northside at least temporarily stayed around Petersburg. The logistical bottleneck along the railroad in Chesterfield County, it has been seen, delayed Field and then Hoke, but that factor does not explain why the North Carolinian—and even more so, Hagood—remained so long at Petersburg before moving to Dunlop's. Nor does it account for the decision to keep two of Wilcox's brigades on the far right until dark. Their retention near the city was more likely due to concern that all the signs of activity in Union lines portended an attack on the Southside, too. Meade's shows of force definitely kept "Rooney" Lee and Pegram at Petersburg and probably also delayed Hoke's and Wilcox's departure. Yet Lee did not supinely keep all these units quiescent. As long as they had to remain near the city, he apparently put them to good use by making shows of force of his own—manning the trenches in strength on the center and left, marching and countermarching and doubling back still again all along the lines, even feinting along the lower Appomattox on the Chesterfield side. Neither army sought battle at Petersburg on September 29, and both sides actively demonstrated to bluff the other into not moving.

Lee's shows of force succeeded as well or even better than the Yankees' and thoroughly confused Northern observers. Throughout the day lookouts of Major Benjamin Fisher's Union Signal Corps spotted contradictory signs. They could see Confederates moving into town and still other columns heading north behind the Howlett Line. But they also observed forces moving west from the city, marching back and forth near Cemetery Hill, and even heading south along the Squirrel Level Line. At around 7:00 A.M. the trenches west of the Weldon Railroad looked empty, but elsewhere later in the day they appeared to have the usual garrison or even to be manned in force. The hazy, smoky atmosphere further interfered with observation, and from a distance even the direction in which dust clouds moved—usually telltale marks of marching columns—could not be discerned for sure.

Other indications appeared no more conclusive than what the Signal Corps detected. A party of black troops, timidly feeling forward just west of the Jerusalem Plank Road before noon, mistook Southern outposts for the main line and reported the works only weakly held (as a picket line indeed would be), but when Ferrero, dissatisfied with this report, sent the whole 27th USCT into that area on a reconnaissance in force, he discovered Mahone's main line "filled with troops." Rather than press on and risk provoking a fight with even the outposts, let alone the main line, the Negroes then fell back to their own fortifications. From the far left, comparable tidings came in from Gregg that he initially encountered little resistance but soon met the enemy in heavy force. Even on the army's rear line, Confederate cavalry pickets— though not aggressive—confronted Union videttes in greater strength than usual. Most ominous of all, if true, was the discovery by an officer of Hancock's rightmost brigade that some of Johnson's men appeared to be moving from east of Petersburg into southeastern Chesterfield County as if to recross the lower Appomattox into the II Corps's right rear. Whether all these moves were ruses, shifts of force toward the Peninsula, regrouping of troops around the rail center, or even portents of a Confederate offensive at Petersburg, Union intelligence simply could not tell for certain. All that was clear was that no conclusive reduction of Secessionist force, sufficient to justify attacking, could be detected.[10]

Most of these intelligence reports came to Birchett's, where Meade could analyze them. Just after 9:30 A.M., however, he and Humphreys turned over their base camp to Brigadier General Seth Williams, the Assistant Adjutant General of the army, and rode out to V Corps headquarters at Globe Tavern to view the situation firsthand and to be in the staging area if the strike force should be committed. Stopping en route with first Hancock and then Parke delayed Meade's arrival at the tavern until 1:30. Nothing the army commander saw along the way suggested the advisability of attacking; indeed, signal reports that Williams forwarded to him plus word of Ferrero's reconnaissance only increased the uncertainty over Confederate intentions. Nor did Grant provide specific instructions on whether or not to attack. Meade and Williams duly kept City Point informed of developments throughout the day, but whether or not Parker forwarded the morning's intelligence to the General-in-Chief on the Peninsula in time to influence his assessment is not known. Grant, in any case, obtained sufficient perspective during his visit to the Army of the James at least to recommend what to do on the Southside. On first reaching New Market Heights he, admittedly, did no more than inform Meade, at 9:30, of the initial breakthrough and offered no guidance. But once he visited Chaffin's and then returned to Deep Bottom, he saw enough to advise the Pennsylvanian, at 1:30, that "re-enforcements are beginning to come from Petersburg [but] I doubt whether it will be advisable for you to make any advance this evening, but this I leave to your judgment." Before concluding this message, however, the lieutenant general received more intelligence reports, probably from Bermuda Hundred, of "large forces moving from Petersburg toward Richmond." He then revised his recommendation to say that "if this continues it may be well for you to attack this evening."

The army commander, though, did not share his chief's assessment of the situation. Neither signal reports, the Negroes' reconnaissance, nor Gregg's probes gave conclusive evidence that Petersburg was being significantly weakened. Most information received by early afternoon, indeed, suggested that the city was still held in force. Meade, accordingly, surmised that the troops sighted moving north through Chesterfield must have been only Hoke's Division, which Union intelligence had rightly identified as being in reserve as late as Wednesday before losing track of it among several contradictory reports. The Pennsylvanian relayed these developments and estimates to supreme headquarters at 3:30 and then drew the obvious conclusion: Apparent Southern strength plus the lateness in the day ruled out an advance on September 29. He did promise, though, to "be prepared to advance at daylight to-morrow." The lieutenant general, who accorded him much discretion and who knew that he (Grant) could not judge the situation as well from Deep Bottom and City Point as could his subordinate at the front, accepted Meade's assessment and began working on plans to co-ordinate operations on both sides of the James on Friday.[11]

The Army of the Potomac, accordingly, made only a few minor moves that did not precipitate battle that afternoon but that did put it in better position to engage the next day. About fifteen minutes after Meade arrived at Globe Tavern, when it looked as if the strike force might advance, after all, he authorized Warren to call in his pickets east of the Weldon Railroad to prepare them for action. Then at 4:00 P.M. Brigadier General John F. Hartranft's First Division, IX Corps, marched west from its reserve position just west of the Jerusalem Plank Road to Dr. Gurley's to join both Potter and also four IX Corps batteries, which had moved there between 3:00 and 4:00 A.M.

Meade even went so far as to send a reconnaissance west from Globe Tavern toward Peebles's farm at about 3:00 P.M. Intelligence reports earlier in the month indicated the existence of the Squirrel Level Line, the presence of a redoubt with four guns at Peebles's, and the service there of two of Heth's brigades: Brigadier General James J. Archer's and Brigadier General William MacRae's. Now Meade desired to see if Heth still barred his path there or had fallen back toward Petersburg. As local commander, Warren furnished the reconnaissance force, the garrison of Fort Dushane: the 39th Massachusetts, 104th New York, and 11th, 88th, and 90th Pennsylvania of Brigadier General Henry Baxter's Second Brigade, Third Division, V Corps. Leaving the nearby First Brigade, First Division, V Corps, responsible for his stronghold at the southwestern salient of the Federal works, Baxter moved westward astride the Poplar Spring Road. His force, led by the 39th as voltigeurs, soon encountered Confederate pickets (possibly from Colonel Joel Griffin's cavalry brigade) and drove them back a mile. As he passed beyond Poplar Spring Church and neared Peebles's farm, however, Southern artillery opened on him, and many skirmishers and a line of battle (perhaps Archer's) advanced toward his right flank. Once more a Northern probe had developed the presence of Butternuts in strength. Doing so fulfilled Baxter's mission; he therefore did not wait to engage the foe seriously but fell back without loss to Warren's earthworks before 5:00. The Secessionists, hardly looking for a fight around Petersburg that afternoon, did not pursue him far and contented themselves with re-establishing their pickets and then returned to their own lines.[12]

But if the foot soldiers and their senior generals did not seek battle on the Southside on September 29, the same could not be said of the Federal and Confederate cavalry, which were extensively engaged all day. Meade's general battle order of September 28 required Gregg's Second Cavalry Division to concentrate on the Weldon Railroad at Robertson's house, a mile south of Fort Dushane, and to be ready to move out by 4:00 A.M. on Thursday. Late Wednesday afternoon Gregg began preparing his two brigades for action. He cut them down to fighting trim by sending sick and weak men and horses to the rear and by limiting the number of wagons that would accompany his column. Each of his troopers also drew sixty rounds of carbine ammunition, twenty rounds of pistol ammunition, three days' rations, and two days' forage. To facilitate setting out in the morning, camps were broken up on Wednesday evening, and the soldiers simply bivouacked for the night.

Most important of all, the far-flung cavalry outposts concentrated overnight at the base camp of Colonel Charles H. Smith's Second Brigade on the Jerusalem Plank Road just south of the rear line. Over half that brigade was already there, and it was not difficult for its remaining regiments, the 13th and most of the 4th Pennsylvania Cavalry, to abandon their outposts between the Weldon and Norfolk railroads below the rear line and rejoin their comrades. Also reporting to the Second Brigade at 9:00 P.M. was Battery H-I/1st U. S. Artillery, which Gregg had requested from the Artillery Reserve of the army. Brigadier General Henry E. Davies' First Brigade, patrolling farther left from the Norfolk Railroad to the James, had a harder time getting to the plank road. It initially drew in its pickets—10th New York Cavalry, 6th Ohio Cavalry, and 1st Pennsylvania Cavalry—to its own base at Prince George Court House, two miles east of army headquarters. Once these outposts arrived, the whole brigade set out south for the plank road at about 2:00 A.M. En route, Davies' men beheld, dimly silhouetted against flickering campfires, the army preparing itself for battle—a sight that "served to keep the men awake and filled them with suppressed excitement." Even so, six miles of night marching could not help but fatigue the First Brigade. It spent most of the night moving and arrived only a little before dawn.

By then army headquarters expected Gregg to be at Robertson's; he himself had planned at least to set out for there at 4:00 A.M.; but, in fact, he had not even left the plank road. He delayed still longer to give Davies' troopers a little rest. But shortly before daybreak he issued orders to get ready. By the time the men could gulp down a hasty breakfast, complete final preparations, and form column, it was already between 5:00 and 5:30, and the sun was beginning to light the eastern sky. Such delay, however, proved inconsequential, because the subsequent inactivity of the main army obviated the need to adhere rigidly to the original schedule. The late start, indeed, was useful, for it enabled Gregg to assemble his powerful striking force of ten regiments and two batteries, approximately 4,350 strong. Only a handful of his 4,900 men stayed behind—100 of Smith's videttes, which still patrolled west of the Weldon Railroad from Wyatt's Crossing to Flowers' house west of Fort Wadsworth, plus Lieutenant Colonel John K. Robison's 16th Pennsylvania Cavalry, also of the Second Brigade, which remained on the plank road to cover the army's rear in conjunction with infantry outposts thrown out by Brigadier General Henry W. Benham's City Point garrison on the far left. These few troops kept on picket were thought sufficient to cope with guerrillas hovering in the area and at least to warn of any greater danger.

There was, however, little likelihood that strong Confederate forces could operate east of the Weldon Railroad if the Army of the Potomac threatened their sensitive supply lines west of those tracks. The first force scheduled to probe toward those communications, appropriately enough, was the Second Cavalry Division, and now it duly moved out—

to the stirring strains of "The Battle Cry of Freedom," "Kitty Wells," and "Yankee Doodle," courtesy of the mounted band of the 1st Maine Cavalry, recently transferred to Smith's brigade from the 1st D.C. Cavalry. Gregg initially marched inside Meade's lines to Globe Tavern and then turned south along the Halifax Road. As his fine body of horsemen trotted past Fort Dushane and out of the Union fortifications at about 6:30 A.M., they formed a "grand sight" for an admiring artillerist in the nearby works. Just beyond the fort and while still inside Warren's picket line, Gregg halted to let his column close up and to permit the Second Brigade to take the lead.[13]

It was no coincidence that the division commander moved the Second Brigade into the van. Not only was it fresher than Davies' men, who had marched all the way from Prince George Court House and beyond, but also it was the unit on which Gregg had increasingly relied to spearhead his advance these past two months. The First Brigade had not fared well leading his attacks in late July, but the Second Brigade had repeatedly performed well in that capacity the following month. Now the general evidently wanted the proven Second in the lead again. That brigade took orders from Smith, colonel of the 1st Maine Cavalry. Although he was nominally only the temporary successor of Colonel J. Irvin Gregg, who had been wounded in the running battle along the Charles City Road on August 16, Smith's hard fighting at Second Reams's Station marked him as a promising brigadier. By the end of September he was already well on the way to earning permanent brigade command. His fellow brigadier, Davies, in contrast, had had both a brigade and a star for over a year and had won an enviable record as a battle commander. Qualified judges, admittedly, questioned his qualifications to exercise independent cavalry command above the brigade level, but none doubted that he was an inspiring leader and a master of minor tactics so telling in close cavalry combat.

Co-ordinating both these brigades was David M. Gregg, the last and —save for Buford—the best of the high-ranking officers initially associated with the cavalry of the Army of the Potomac. All the others were gone now: Bayard, Davis, and Buford—dead; Cooke, Emory, Stoneman, Averell, Kilpatrick, and Pleasonton—transferred; John Farnsworth—resigned. In their places were ex-infantrymen, "interlopers" from other theaters, and the "boy generals" and the promising colonels who were winning their spurs and their stars as the Union cavalry came into its own from 1863 on: Torbert, Sheridan, Wilson, Merritt, Custer, Devin, Chapman, McIntosh, Gibbs, Stagg. Gregg alone remained—the highest form of the old order, which could not quite mesh with the new. Not the thundering cavalry charge, the bold strategic raid, the massed attack of a quasi-independent cavalry corps for Gregg. He was a horse soldier better suited to serving right with the main army, screening its advance, locating its enemy, patrolling its rear, and moving into battle on its flank—either joining its attack or helping secure its defense. In such roles the bushy-bearded Pennsylvanian had repeatedly proved his ability and had compiled a proud record at Brandy Station, Middleburg, Upperville, Second Deep Bottom, Second Reams's Station, and—above all—the third day at Gettysburg. This service earned him the trust and respect of superior, subordinate, and soldier alike. "I can state with confidence that I have seen no officer whom I would prefer [over Gregg] to have with me . . ." acknowledged the masterful combat commander Hancock, with whom the cavalryman had repeatedly served. "He has a fine knowledge of the country, so necessary in a cavalry commander in ordinary service. In battle, he is cool, tenacious, brave, and judicious. I could not give higher qualities to any person." Yet these very qualities set him off from the brashness, braggadocio, and bravado of those archetypes of the new order, Sheridan and Custer. He may have been uncomfortable with these new men and have preferred the present situation, where the bold blades were off in the Valley and he alone directed Meade's cavalry. Some have even surmised that he felt so strongly on the matter that it prompted his resignation when faced with the prospect of Sheridan's return in 1865—although, in fact, the "imperative demand for my continued presence at home" provided at least the pretext, if not the total explanation, of his resignation. But such matters were far in the future. At the end of September he still held the independent command he so enjoyed. And now he was moving out to meet his old adversary, Wade Hampton, once more.[14]

Hampton was a South Carolina grandee—the foremost example of the Southern planter whose social prominence and instinct for command made him a leader in war as in peace. Although he lacked formal military training and although he opposed secession, he lived up to his social duties and to his family's martial tradition, once war actually came, by raising and leading to Virginia the legion that bore his name. From his first battle atop the Henry House Hill onward, his preeminent natural ability overcame his lack of formal training and marked him as a hard-fighting combat leader, an able tactician, and a trustworthy reconnaissance officer. He consistently met the growing responsibilities that befell him as the ranking brigade and then the ranking division commander in the expanding cavalry branch of the Army of Northern Virginia. After the head of that corps, "Jeb" Stuart, fell at Yellow Tavern on May 11, 1864, Hampton stood first in the line of succession. Army headquarters, however, hesitated to choose between

him and the candidate of the so-called Virginia clique, Fitz Lee, and
delayed selection. Over the next three months Hampton went on to win
what his rank and past service had earned. His operations at Trevilian
Station, Samaria Church, and First Reams's Station showed him ready
for corps command, and on August 11 he received the coveted appointment. In the following seven weeks, the new laurels he won at
Second Deep Bottom, Second Reams's Station, and Sycamore Church
only underscored the wisdom of promoting him. His entire record from
First Manassas through the Great Cattle Raid marked him a worthy
general and a dangerous foe.

On first taking over the corps, Hampton had had eight brigades at
his disposal. But Fitz Lee's immediate departure for the Valley and
Rosser's transfer there on September 27 now left him only five brigades, including one from the Department of North Carolina and
Southern Virginia. On paper this corps numbered approximately 6,900
officers and men present for duty, far more than Gregg had. But the
loss of horses in the four months of arduous campaigning this year, the
inability of animals from South Carolina and Georgia to regain their
strength in the customary "recruiting" (recuperating) sections of
southwestern Virginia, and the Confederacy's primitive system of
requiring soldiers to furnish their own mounts or risk transfer to the infantry cut heavily into his strength. Only about 4,500 of his men were
actually mounted—approximately the same strength as Gregg's strike
force. Fully 35 per cent of the Confederate Cavalry Corps lacked
horses by the end of September 1864. Rather than lose them altogether, Hampton grouped them into companies and battalions of foot
dragoons. Those with good prospect of being remounted stayed with
their brigades. Those with less chance made up a provisional foot brigade under Major Henry Farley. These dismounted men were useful
for garrisoning key points along Hampton's extended line covering the
army's communications, but their lack of mobility clearly handicapped
their ability to resist cavalry raiders. To deal with Gregg, Hampton
would have to rely principally on his small mounted units.[15]

The largest of his horse commands, relatively speaking, was Major
General W. H. F. ("Rooney") Lee's Third Division. Young Lee, second son of the army commander, was a big, hard-fighting man, distinguished in all his battles. This distinction arose not from grandeur and
nobility like his father's. Nor did "Rooney" possess the swaggering cavalry bravado of his cousin Fitz, the intellectual attainments of his
brother Custis, or the competence in strategy and grand tactics of
Stuart and Hampton. "Rooney" Lee's strength rather lay in leading
combat troops in small actions where he could survey, control, and
inspire his battleline. This was just the duty his divisional command

required. Other officers could exercise the higher arts of generalship—and then count on him to carry out their plans. He, in turn, relied on the two brigades that made up his division, one from North Carolina, the other Virginian. Both were excellent combat outfits with proud traditions; the Virginians, in fact, had originally been his own brigade. Yet the two units differed markedly on one key point: leadership. The Tarheels were in good hands under hard-hitting Brigadier General Rufus Barringer, but the other outfit languished under Colonel J. Lucius Davis of the 10th Virginia Cavalry, who could write about horsemen better than he could command them. He had only taken over the brigade on the death of the able John Chambliss on August 16 and had yet to earn the office to which only his rank entitled him.

Death among the high command had elevated several officers in Hampton's other division, too. Whenever the general exercised corps command, officially or otherwise, after Stuart's death, his own First Division passed to Brigadier General Matthew C. Butler. A fellow South Carolinian, Butler was Hampton's favorite officer. They had gone off to war together, had almost continuously served together, and would remain close associates, in peace as in war, for the rest of the century. Yet the junior officer was more than just the protégé of the grandee. Butler ably commanded the cavalry arm of the Hampton Legion, soon expanded to become the 2nd South Carolina Cavalry, until losing his right foot at Brandy Station; he won additional credit leading a sturdy new South Carolina brigade that came to Virginia only in May 1864; and he competently directed Hampton's Division whenever the major general exercised higher command. The army commander, to be sure, originally had reservations about the junior officer's fitness to lead a division, but by autumn—in fact, the very day the Fifth Offensive broke out—he acknowledged that Butler "should be promoted Maj. Genl. Since he has had command of Hampton's old Division he has shown great gallantry and so far as I am able to judge managed his troops with skill." Butler's elevation, in turn, caused command of his own South Carolina brigade to pass to Brigadier General John Dunovant. Hard-fighting and hard-drinking, Dunovant had been cashiered from Confederate service for drunkenness in 1862. His excellent family connections, however, enabled him to get another regiment, which he led much better in Virginia in 1864. Still, his almost reckless dash suggests that he may have been trying to atone for his earlier dereliction. The division's other brigadier general felt no such guilt. Pierce Manning Butler Young considered himself a highly meritorious officer who deserved, more than Butler, to succeed Hampton. Young's distinguished combat service, first at the head of the cavalry of Cobb's Legion and now in charge of a basically Georgia brigade also containing five Alabama and three Mississippi companies, lent credibility to his appraisal, if not to his pretensions.

Three other commands rounded out Hampton's force: Farley's foot dragoons, Major Robert Preston Chew's three batteries of horse artillery, and Brigadier General James Dearing's mixed Georgia, North Carolina, and Confederate brigade from the Department of North Carolina and Southern Virginia. Dearing had already earned an enviable record as Pickett's artillery officer, and this year he was achieving even greater distinction at the head of horse soldiers. But unfortunately for the Graycoats, he fell ill in late September and had to turn over his brigade to Colonel Joel Griffin of the 8th Georgia Cavalry, a political appointee ill suited to such high command. Perhaps to keep watch on this doubtful force as well as to gratify the brigadier general's desire for promotion, corps headquarters assigned Young to lead a demidivision consisting of his own and Griffin's men, still under Butler's over-all charge. The Georgia brigade then temporarily passed to the competent Lieutenant Colonel J. Fred Waring of the Jeff Davis Legion.[16]

Thus organized, Hampton's men were strung out from Peebles's farm to the vicinity of Reams's Station and Malone's Crossing on the Weldon Railroad to guard the supply lines between Stony Creek Depot and Petersburg. Griffin's men served closest to Cockade City, and the two divisions alternated guard duty farther south. At the end of September Butler's patrols were at the front—the South Carolinians on his left, the Georgians on his right. Only outposts manned this picket line. The bulk of all three brigades, though ready to bolster the outposts, were encamped farther back—Joel Griffin on the Squirrel Level Road north of Peebles's farm, Dunovant near the junction of the White Oak and Boydton Plank roads immediately south of Burgess' mill, and Waring near where the Vaughan Road crossed Gravelly Run, four miles northeast of Dinwiddie Court House. "Rooney" Lee's men meantime provided a more general reserve—the Virginians on Chappell's and Gresham's farms on Goose Creek about two miles northeast of the court house, the Tarheels on the Military Road near the stream Stony Creek, just east of the county seat.

Since the Third Division was not presently on duty at the front, Hampton decided to review it on September 29. Reviews had once been common in the days of the flamboyant Stuart, but the change in command and the press of active campaigning made them less frequent by the fall of 1864. The prospect of reviving the old ways created some excitement in camp, as the men looked forward to what would be "a very pretty sight" of massed troopers wheeling in parade, their sabers gleaming, their guidons fluttering. Yet the review would also be a sobering reflection of attrition, one Virginian thought, a parade "not so grand as those we had in Culpeper as there will not be so much cavalry present." Such troopers as there were, however, duly formed ranks in a large field, first for standing and then for marching inspection. Before Hampton could review them, though, the far-reaching impact of the Battle of Chaffin's Bluff penetrated far down into Dinwiddie County to cancel the event. Pennants and serried ranks would have to wait for another day; now the Third Division had to rush to the Northside to help stop Ben Butler's onslaught. The two brigades, accordingly, formed column of march; the attached Second Stuart Horse Artillery joined the procession; and the whole force set out along the Boydton Plank Road toward Petersburg. Before "Rooney" Lee could even reach Cockade City, let alone the Peninsula, however, corps headquarters received even more alarming news from the other flank: Gregg's Union horsemen were driving in Matthew Butler's outposts as if to presage a grand attack on the Southside, too—aimed at the army's vital lines of communications.[17]

Gregg, after massing his division just south of Fort Dushane, prepared to strike the Confederates in the unfortified country south of Peebles's farm. There he could drive in the Butternut pickets and threaten, if not actually cut, the supply routes from Stony Creek Depot. This move would satisfy his immediate objective of diverting the Secessionists' attention from Chaffin's Bluff to Dinwiddie County. It would also place him in good position to co-operate with the infantry if Meade decided to expand the demonstration into a full-scale attack.

To get to that open country, the Second Cavalry Division marched down the Halifax Road to its intersection with the Lower Church Road at Wyatt's Crossing. There Smith turned off to the right and sought to reach the Vaughan Road. The First Brigade meantime continued straight south toward Reams's Station. The 1st New Jersey Cavalry spearheaded Davies' drive; the 1st Massachusetts Cavalry and the 6th Ohio Cavalry provided close support; and the 10th New York Cavalry and the 1st Pennsylvania Cavalry backed them up in general reserve. So few Southerners served in this area, though, that Major Myron Beaumont's Jerseymen initially needed no help in handling them. His regiment reached the junction of the Stage and Halifax roads, about a mile north of Reams's, without difficulty. One battalion then dashed into the station itself, easily drove off a handful of outposts from the 7th Georgia Cavalry, and chased them for a mile—whether south toward Malone's Crossing or west toward Monk's Neck Bridge, the records do not indicate. At the same time another of Beaumont's battalions pressed other videttes southwest along the Stage Road toward the bridge. Along or just east of the creek, though, resistance stiffened, perhaps due to the possible arrival of the Cobb's Legion Cavalry. Beau-

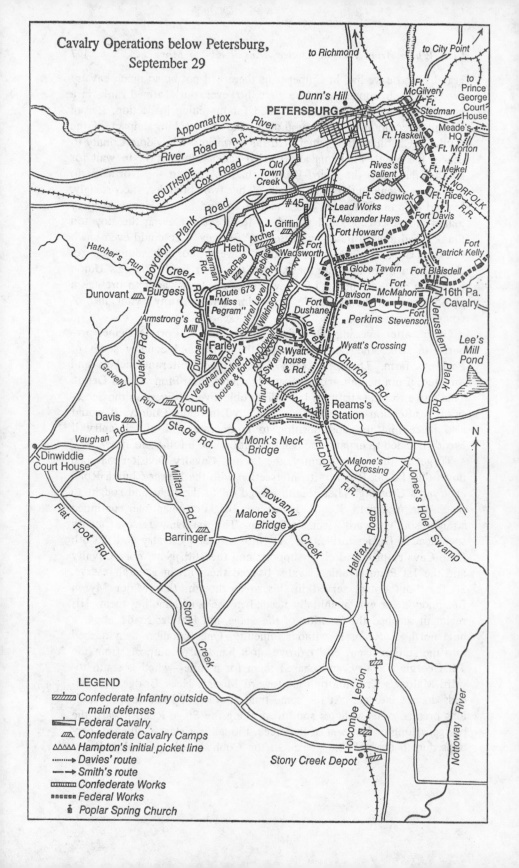

Cavalry Operations below Petersburg,
September 29

to Richmond

to City Point

to Prince George Court House

Dunn's Hill

Ft. McGilvery
Ft. Stedman
Meade's HQ

PETERSBURG

Ft. Haskell

Ft. Morton

Appomattox River

River Road R.R.

Rives's Salient

Ft. Meikel

NORFOLK R.R.

Old Town Creek

SOUTHSIDE Cox Road

Boydton Plank Road

#45

Ft. Sedgwick
Lead Works

Ft. Rice
Fort Davis

J. Griffin

Archer

Ft. Alexander Hays
Fort Howard

Fort Patrick Kelly

Heth

MacRae

Harman Rd.

Fort Wadsworth

Peebles Yd.

Globe Tavern

Fort Blaisdell

Hatcher's Run

Creek Rd.

Dunovant

Burgess

Route 673 "Miss Pegram"

Fort Davison

Fort McMahon

16th Pa. Cavalry

Armstrong's Mill

Squirrel Level

Wilkinson

Fort Dushane

Perkins

Fort Stevenson

Jerusalem Plank Rd.

Quaker Rd.

Gravelly Run

Duncan Rd.

Vaughan Rd.

Cummings' house & ford

McDowell

Arthur's Swamp

Farley

Young

Lower Church Rd.

Wyatt's Crossing

Wyatt house & Rd.

Lee's Mill Pond

N

Davis

Vaughan Rd.

Stage Rd.

Reams's Station

Dinwiddie Court House

Military Rd.

Monk's Neck Bridge

WELDON R.R.

Malone's Crossing

Jones's Hole Swamp

Flat Foot Rd.

Rowanty Creek

Malone's Bridge

Barringer

Stony Creek

Halifax Road

Holcombe Legion

Nottoway River

Stony Creek Depot

LEGEND

Confederate Infantry outside main defenses
Federal Cavalry
Confederate Cavalry Camps
Hampton's initial picket line
Davies' route
Smith's route
Confederate Works
Federal Works
Poplar Spring Church

mont did not challenge the Georgians further but threw out a strong skirmish line to face them and pulled his main body back to the Halifax-Stage Road junction and to Reams's Station. More of the First Brigade now joined him—the Massachusetts men to help skirmish, the 10th and the 6th to assist in fortifying the southerly and northerly intersections, respectively. Such a limited demonstration sufficed for Davies' purpose, and he pushed it no farther. By the same token, the Secessionists, who had few forces there and not many more available, were unable to counterattack. With both sides thus content with the situation, no more than light skirmishing flickered on in this sector for the rest of the day.[18]

Gregg reportedly deplored the absence of heavier resistance there, because he would rather have met the Confederates near Union lines instead of deep in enemy country. Yet the campaign-tested general recognized all along that only by penetrating nearer the sensitive supply lines farther west could he fulfill his mission. From the beginning he intended to send the Second Brigade—rather to lead it, for he judged its mission the more important—along the Lower Church Road into the region west of the Weldon Railroad. By 7:00 A.M. his men were moving along that lane in search of a crossover to the Vaughan Road, down which they could move toward the Secessionist communications. Should no crossover be found, Gregg advised army headquarters at 7:00, he would continue up the Lower Church Road and "demonstrate toward Poplar Spring Church or wherever I find the enemy." Before Humphreys could warn him—probably unnecessarily—that Heth's stronghold on Peebles's farm would bar any advance beyond the church, the horsemen found the desired connecting route, the Wyatt Road from Wyatt's plantation to McDowell's on the Vaughan Road. Gregg, the 1st Maine Cavalry, and reportedly Smith now remained at the plantation to be in a convenient central location and to cover the right rear. However, the other four regiments, spearheaded by the 13th

COMMENTARY

1. This map shows the entire field of operations south of the Appomattox River where the Battle of Poplar Spring Church was fought. On it are traced the routes of Gregg's two Federal cavalry brigades on September 29.

2. It is probable but not positive that Davies advanced as far west as Monk's Neck Bridge.

3. How far northeast from Wyatt's the 1st Maine Cavalry moved is not clear.

4. The locations of Young's, Davis', and Barringer's camps are not certain.

5. The course of Hampton's initial picket line is only approximate.

Pennsylvania Cavalry, continued farther west into enemy country. As their vanguard reached the main stem of Arthur's Swamp about three quarters of a mile west of Wyatt's house, they finally made contact with the foe. Only Dunovant's outposts, a mixed detail under Lieutenant Colonel Robert L. Jeffords of the 5th South Carolina Cavalry, stood watch that far east, though—brave men but hardly a match for a brigade. The stubborn Butternuts at least yielded ground only reluctantly. They took advantage of the heavy woods bordering the roads to put up an effective rear-guard fight. Still, the Yankees slowly but surely forged ahead, past McDowell's and then westward along the Vaughan Road. By 9:30 they were ready to attack the detachment clinging to the southern end of the Squirrel Level Road at E. Wilkinson's. Within seventy-five minutes they had overrun that position, too, and pushed on to Hatcher's Run.[19]

There they found a foe willing to make a real stand. Hatcher's Run formed a natural moat for the camps and communications of Dinwiddie County lying south and west of it. Rising west of the Boydton Plank Road, it flowed east across that highway at Burgess' mill, then southeast across the Duncan and Vaughan roads at Armstrong's mill and Cummings' Ford, respectively. About two miles below the ford, at a point where Arthur's Swamp joined it from the north, it cut back west a mile to combine with Gravelly Run (a stream that flowed roughly due eastward) to form Rowanty Creek. A quarter mile below the confluence, the Rowanty flowed under the Stage Road crossing of Monk's Neck Bridge and then continued southeast five miles to cross the Halifax Road about half that far north of Stony Creek Depot. Two miles farther southeast it emptied into the Nottoway River. Hatcher's Run, the uppermost part of the Rowanty, though fordable for infantry in most places, nevertheless formed a major tactical obstacle to strikes westward. Although the Graycoats had not yet fully developed its defensive possibilities, they already appreciated its advantages sufficiently to erect rifle pits on the right bank of the four crossings from Burgess' to Monk's Neck. Into those trenches at Cummings' Ford and Armstrong's mill, Hampton now placed a force to oppose Gregg. First into position at both sites were Farley's foot dragoons, who were stationed nearby, to begin with. At least the Jeff Davis Legion, 20th Georgia Cavalry Battalion, and 7th Georgia Cavalry of Waring's brigade, alerted for action soon after breakfast, arrived shortly to bolster the troops at the ford. Jeffords' outposts and rearguard also rallied on the fresh forces there, and the rest of the South Carolina brigade, too, moved to the threatened sector, perhaps to Armstrong's mills. Virtually the whole of the First Division (excluding Griffin farther north and the Georgians facing Davies) thus barred the Pennsylvanians' path by the time they reached Cummings' Ford. Young, Butler, and Hampton themselves, moreover, took charge of the threatened sector. If Gregg was looking for a fight, they would give it to him.[20]

A fight was just what the Unionists did not want. Meade required them to demonstrate against Southern communications, not to provoke a full-scale battle before he was ready to commit his infantry. Once the Secessionist buildup blocked their advance along the Vaughan Road, they did not allow the light skirmishing with Farley there to reach battle proportions but carried out Gregg's original intention of shifting westward in hopes of outflanking the Confederate left and reaching the Boydton Plank Road. Some Bluecoats, perhaps the 8th Pennsylvania Cavalry, had to remain southwest of E. Wilkinson's to mask Butler, but the others marched out along a little country lane running westward above the left bank of the run to the Duncan Road at Armstrong's house, a quarter mile north of Armstrong's mill. At 11:00 A.M. the telegraph line along the Duncan Road went dead—sure evidence that the Federals had reached there and cut the wires. The horsemen also tore down eight telegraph poles, made off with the wire, and intercepted the only freight wagon passing their way, a private vehicle of a blockade runner. But when they turned south to the creek itself, they once more found Butler barring their path. Checked there, too, the Pennsylvanians again left a force to confront him and then moved northward up the Duncan Road in hopes of finding an opening to the plank road that way. However, these repeated rebuffs and the attendant detachments from the strike force appeared to foredoom the venture. As reports of these events reached Gregg, he warned Birchett's as early as 12:12 P.M. that "a strong effort is being made to reach the road (plank), but I do not think we will reach it, having tried as much as possible."

The general's assessment proved accurate. The raiders got no farther than where the Duncan and Harman roads, Route 673, and a lane running east from the plank road came together around Watkins' farm (an area that Gregg's grossly inaccurate map of the largely uncharted region mistakenly called "Miss Pegram's"). There they learned, presumably from local citizens, that Confederate infantry lay a short way "beyond." Whether the intelligence referred to Heth in the lower Squirrel Level Line (as Gregg supposed) or to alleged forces in the log works near the plank road the Union horsemen did not bother to check out. Convinced they were too weak to venture deeper into enemy country, they fell back southward to rejoin the rest of the brigade facing Butler at about 1:00. Yet nothing was to be gained from simply sitting, exposed, near Armstrong's and Cummings'. Gregg, accordingly, left only a picket line observing the First Cavalry Division and carried out his earlier intention of withdrawing the main body to the western part of Wyatt's plantation, a strong position whose heights overlooked the main stream of Arthur's Swamp.

Once the Pennsylvanians returned, the general sought a new opening by sending the 1st Maine Cavalry reconnoitering up the Lower Church Road toward Poplar Spring Church in early afternoon. In that direction, too, the Bluecoats made little progress in the face of Joel Griffin's heavy picket patrols and numerous road barricades. The Maine men soon called off their advance and pulled back to a position on the road just north of Wyatt's. By early afternoon the entire Second Brigade had fallen back on the defensive in the area between Cummings' and Wyatt's. Gregg summed up conditions for army headquarters at 1:45: "I . . . do not think any further results can be produced in this direction." This dispatch, along with earlier ones by which the conscientious division commander kept him fully posted, contributed to Meade's conclusion that the Graycoats were too strong to justify him attacking on September 29.[21]

As if to bring home that point, Wade Hampton did not share his counterpart's intention of breaking off the fight. The corps commander had initially worried that the cavalry probes portended a major Federal onslaught toward the supply lines, but Gregg's repeated refusal to accept battle and the absence of any Northern infantry attack dispelled such apprehensions. Now the South Carolinian determined to find out just how many Bluecoats really faced him across Hatcher's Run; at about 4:00 P.M. he ordered Butler to challenge the enemy line near Mrs. Cummings' house. Waring's probe discovered a mere picket screen, which easily caved in and fled to Gregg's main position. The Georgians, soon followed by the South Carolinians from Armstrong's mill and house, rapidly but not rashly gave chase. As the pursuers neared the principal Federal position beyond McDowell's, the prudent Butler did not allow them to blunder on into a potential trap but halted them and threw out sharpshooters to engage the Pennsylvanians. This pause gave Dunovant a chance to come up and deploy to Waring's left and also allowed the division commander and his scouts to reconnoiter the ground. Among the first to locate the foe was one Roger A. Pryor—fire eater, former U.S. congressman, former C.S. congressman, former Confederate colonel and brigadier general, who had resigned his commission the previous year after twice being stripped of brigade command and who was now only a private serving as a scout.

Pryor's task was made easier by the fact that the Northerners hardly tried to conceal themselves. Lieutenant Frank Reynolds' section of H-I/1st U. S. Artillery readily revealed Smith's position by opening fire on the gathering Graycoats. A section of Captain James F. Hart's

Washington Artillery of South Carolina soon unlimbered on the heights of McDowell's farm west of the stream and replied. The South Carolina company had not always fared well in such artillery duels. Fighting the 3rd New Jersey Battery at White House on June 20, 1864, it had had one of its caissons blown up, with the loss of three men. Now Chew urged his cannoneers to avenge themselves; within five shots, he said, they must knock a Yankee piece "into a cocked hat." Hart's gunnery corporal did not need that many tries. His third shell arched across the creek valley and struck a Federal limber chest, which exploded with a deafening roar, disabling one gun and sending up a great pillar of smoke visible as far away as Globe Tavern.

This brilliant little success was just the impetus his men needed, Butler judged. "Remember White House!" he shouted and led his line down into the valley, thence up toward the Union line. To pave their way, the Washington Artillery turned its attention from the crippled Regulars to the cavalry and nearly drove off the center astride the Wyatt Road, perhaps held by the 4th Pennsylvania Cavalry, even before Butler could engage. The earlier collapse of the picket line had, however, caused Smith to recall his own regiment into tactical reserve in Wyatt's yard, and now he rushed its Third Battalion forward to bolster the shaken center. With all but two battalions now at the front, the Second Brigade stood ready to meet the division rapidly moving up the hillside from the creek bottom. The ensuing clash was no encounter of compact lines of mounted men riding side by side with sabers drawn. Such battles as that were rare in the Civil War. By this period of the conflict the cavalry of both armies almost always used horses only as means of swiftly reaching the battlefield. Once there, they dismounted, left one man in every file of four out of action holding the horses, and went into combat on foot. They had become quite adept at this, and with their breech-loading carbines (a few of them repeaters), many cavalry units could put up a good fight even against infantry. Against each other they waged dandy battles in the best tradition of true dragoons. As the two dismounted lines met in late afternoon, the Secessionists pressed Smith hard but could not push him from the heights. All day he had not sought battle, but now that battle had come to him, he resisted firmly. Unable to drive him, the exhausted Butternuts had to fall back a short way themselves about 5:10.[22]

This attack made clear to Gregg that the Confederates were present "in considerable force" yet left him confident that he could hold out. Still, he, doubtless, welcomed news from Humphreys that help was on the way. As early as Wednesday night army headquarters notified Warren to support the cavalry the next day if they wanted it. Now even without an appeal from Gregg, Meade took it on himself to send reinforcements. The sight of the exploding caisson aroused concern among him and others at Globe Tavern. He, accordingly, directed Warren to look to his own defenses—Baxter duly manned Fort Dushane—and also to dispatch troops to Wyatt's. The corps commander then pulled Colonel Edgar M. Gregory's Second Brigade, First Division, out of the fortifications and rushed it down the Halifax Road toward the battlefield at about 5:00 P.M.[23]

The Northerners were not the only ones to bring up reinforcements. Hampton had thus far used only his First Division to battle the Yankees, but his Third Division, too, was at his disposal. On first learning of Gregg's probes south and west toward the supply lines, the corps commander took it on himself to countermand orders from army headquarters to send the Third to the Peninsula. For most of the day he kept that unit waiting on the Boydton Plank Road near the upper end of the Church Road, where it could either move to join him or resume marching toward the Northside, as necessary. Since Dunn's Hill did not insist the horsemen continue across the James, they remained at the South Carolinian's disposal. Now in late afternoon he ordered young Lee to leave Davis and the artillery on the plank road and to bring the Tarheels to McDowell's. These reinforcements reached the field just before sunset and took position, dismounted, on the far right: the 2nd North Carolina Cavalry, supported by the 5th North Carolina Cavalry, in the spearhead, the 1st North Carolina Cavalry in reserve, and the 3rd North Carolina Cavalry as skirmishers.

In the gathering darkness the new brigade charged Smith's left; Butler simultaneously surged forward again toward the Union center and right. Barringer's fresh troops tore into the weary blue regiments, crumpled the 4th and 13th Pennsylvania Cavalry, and captured the 4th's commander, Major James Peale. This victory, in turn, outflanked the Federal center and right, which had still held off the First Division up to then. The Maine battalion then withdrew from the center on its own initiative before it could be cut off. The 2nd and 8th Pennsylvania Cavalry, however, stood their ground so long that they were nearly captured. The 3/1st Maine Cavalry, seeing their plight, then counterattacked and rescued them. This nighttime sortie did not stem the tide of battle, though; it only allowed the front line to pull back eastward from the heights above Arthur's Swamp to the field works thrown up around Wyatt's yard. In those defenses Smith's battered brigade rallied on the two fresh Maine battalions plus Gregory's sturdy infantry, who had arrived by then. Hampton swept across the plantation after the retreating Northerners but did not seriously challenge their inner stronghold now that night had fallen. As a result no more than light skirmishing continued flickering around Wyatt's house.[24]

Even that did not last long. At about 9:00 P.M. Hampton broke contact, pulled back westward, and re-established his picket line along the right bank of Arthur's Swamp. Butler's main body continued on to its camps beyond Hatcher's Run, and Barringer rejoined Davis on the plank road, where the whole Third Division now bivouacked. As the hard-fighting Butternuts trotted back to their camps and bivouacs, they could take pride in having clearly carried off the honors of the day. They had, for one thing, suffered fewer casualties, roughly thirty-seven men to the foe's estimated fifty-six. Even more important, they had checked the raiders, preserved virtually all the supply lines, and driven the Unionists from a strong position all the way to Wyatt's house.[25]

The Yankees—tired, hard hit, but still busy—had little time or inclination that evening to worry about questions of laurels. At about the same hour that the Southerners broke contact, Gregg made his final dispositions for the night. Unlike his opponents, he could not simply withdraw to his starting place without disrupting army headquarters' possible plans for renewing the battle on Friday. He therefore elected to stand his ground in his final defensive positions around Wyatt's yard and Reams's Station. Gregory no longer remained to help him. Prior to 8:00 the colonel received orders from the V Corps to return to Globe Tavern, presumably to rejoin the strike force; by 9:00 P.M. he was back in Warren's lines. With the foot soldiers gone and Smith so used up, Gregg clearly needed fresh troops at the front, so he brought forward his First Brigade. Leaving the New Jersey regiment at Reams's and the eastern end of the Stage Road, Davies either set out or arrived with his main body at about 10:00 P.M. He duly took position just west and south of Wyatt's yard and threw out skirmishers who chased off the handful of Southern videttes and stragglers still east of the swamp. His outposts then picketed the left bank of the stream. Now that the First was in position, Gregg and the exhausted Second Brigade rode back to Perkins' house on the Halifax Road about half a mile south of Fort Dushane, where they could unsaddle, rest, and recuperate. Nearly as tired as their comrades, the First Brigade, right up to its general, bivouacked on Wyatt's plantation.[26]

The day of raiding and fighting, reconnoitering and probing, demonstrating and bluffing was over. For the weary soldiers on both sides, day's end brought a welcome opportunity to sleep. But for their commanders night was the time for assessing the day's results, for sifting bluff from substance, and for making plans for the morrow.

CHAPTER VIII

———◆———

"The Enemy Must Be Weak Enough . . . to Let Us In"

The principal task facing the Confederate high command in late afternoon and evening on September 29 was to complete the redeployment of troops and then fundamentally assess the defensibility of the contracted position. At about 5:00 P.M. orders at last reached Joseph Davis' men to prepare to turn over Rives's Salient to Weiseger. After dark—perhaps around 7:30—the Virginians finally moved into those works, annoyed but not impeded by the sharpshooting and mortar fire that once more raged along the Jerusalem Plank Road that night. On leaving the trenches, the Mississippians, like Cooke before them, did not execute the original mission of replacing the Light Division on the far right of the main works but instead remained in reserve behind the left center. Hill did not go so far as to distribute Cooke's four regiments behind each of Johnson's salients, as the major general requested, but the corps commander at least kept the two brigades in the area overnight.

He left them there not only because Johnson and Mahone needed support but also because other replacements had now reached the far right: the rest of Heth's Division from the Squirrel Level Line. So great was the pressure on Lee to save Richmond that he decided even to abandon those forward defenses covering his army's communications. Field's three brigades left that outer area early Thursday morning. Now Archer, MacRae, and their attached battery were withdrawn as well. In late afternoon, after confronting Baxter's reconnaissance, they turned over their trenches to Dearing's Cavalry Brigade and marched up the Church Road, thence east along the Boydton Plank Road. About sunset they entered the main works. Some Graycoats expected that they would soon continue to the threatened Northside, but, in fact, they were already at their destination. Their commanders, accordingly, bivouacked them in the woods behind Battery No. 45 and Wilcox's old sector. Withdrawing all forces except a weak cavalry brigade from the forward line was risky. It was also unavoidable. Federal demonstrations and probes on September 29, as well as Grant's past practice, strongly suggested that the Army of the Potomac, too, would shortly take the offensive. There seemed little point in exposing Heth's 2,700 men on Peebles's farm to this inevitable onslaught.[1] Yet more was involved than just the security of two brigades and an outer line. With Field gone to Chaffin's, Hoke en route there, and Wilcox ordered to follow, Hill's ability to hold even the main works of Petersburg themselves became questionable. Withdrawing Archer and MacRae to the main line, however, helped replace the departed forces and made the lieutenant general's position less insecure. As an additional benefit, the two brigades were transformed from a vulnerable target near Poplar Spring Church into a ready reserve for counterattacking any Union drive westward. Hill was, in effect, cocking his powerful right arm for a counterpunch in case the aggressive foe should lower its guard.

Counterpunching, striking back, looking—hoping—for an opening and all the while trying to fend off the Northerners' blows: To such measures was Lee now reduced. The master of offensive warfare no longer possessed the manpower and the command personnel to carry the war to the enemy in a strategic sense, and almost without exception in the Petersburg operations to date, he had to allow Grant to strike first and then hope to counterattack successfully. The Fifth Offensive proved no exception. The Illinoisan initiated the operation with Butler's attack, to which Lee could only respond. On the Southside, too, the Federals dominated the strategic situation on September 29–30, and until they made their move, the Butternuts could only take defensive precautions and wait.

Placing all four of Heth's brigades in tactical reserve, flexibly responsive to developments, was one such precaution. Another was Mahone's extension rightward at least to the Weldon Railroad (the second-class troops may have gone even farther west) from 9:00 to 11:00 P.M. He thus drastically thinned his whole line to the point that the most attenuated sector, the right, could muster only one man every three paces. Even so, his move relieved the last of the Light Division's trench guards between the tracks and Battery No. 45. Now all men of Wilcox's two brigades as well as Heth's four would be available for any need—to join the concentration on the Peninsula, to bolster the defenses of Petersburg, or to counterattack Meade's expected advance. But once more, Southern actions were contingent on the Federals' initiative. These reserve troops would not move in any direction until Lee and Hill could learn if the Army of the Potomac would strike for the supply lines on September 30.[2]

Those supply lines along the Boydton Plank Road and the Southside Railroad were now especially vulnerable. Where twenty-seven regiments and two battalions of infantry, 5,800 strong, had recently stood guard, only three weak cavalry regiments and a horse battery now served—a mere 1,500 men, barely enough to provide a token force for the Squirrel Level Line, even with the interior line immediately south of the plank road left completely unoccupied. The exigencies of active campaigning with limited manpower had previously forced Lee to entrust his works to dismounted cavalry, but never before had he left a line at once so exposed and so important to horsemen alone. Yet the course of operations on September 29 afforded him no choice. The Battle of Chaffin's Bluff not only threw Richmond into mortal peril but also, in its impact, extended deeply into the Southside virtually to uncover the army's communications as well.

Indeed, Butler's breakthrough made Lee fear for the safety of Petersburg itself. Should the supply lines, already almost stripped of defenders, be cut, there would be no point holding the city any longer. Then, too, it was by no means certain that the main works around the town themselves, now manned by a much reduced force, could withstand direct assault. And, of course, a renewed onslaught toward the capital could necessitate transferring the remaining troops from Petersburg for a final stand in Henrico and Chesterfield counties. The Cockade City's position was, in sum, precarious, and a major attack by either Federal army on September 30 could render it untenable. Lee recognized this fact, and overnight and on into Friday morning he prepared to abandon his entire position south of the Appomattox, if necessary. He reportedly ordered government stockpiles removed from town. He, moreover, definitely had a new pontoon bridge constructed across the Appomattox a mile above town, presumably to facilitate withdrawing his right wing. Most revealingly of all, early Friday morning, his Medical Director, recognizing the "pressing military necessity," ordered all military hospitals in Petersburg broken up and their patients transferred far into the interior (Burkeville, Farmville, Danville, even Raleigh) "in anticipation of a change in the position of the Army of Northern Va." Just what "change" was projected is now lost in the dearth of extant records. It is doubtful that Lee would have abandoned his position on the James River altogether and pulled back into the hinterland. Perhaps he would have done what City Point feared: given up Petersburg in order to concentrate his whole force against the Army of the James in a grand effort to cripple the foe and regain the strategic initiative in the Tidewater. The fact that he did not make such a bold move suggests, however, that he no longer played for such high stakes. Most likely he would have done something akin to the contingency plan he is known to have entertained in mid-October: to withdraw north from Petersburg, send some forces to the Peninsula, and use the rest to man a new defensive line in Chesterfield County, perhaps along the left bank of the Appomattox, perhaps farther north behind Swift Creek or Proctor's Creek just below Drewry's Bluff.[3]

Abandoning his rail center for a last stand around his capital would not have immediately doomed Richmond itself. That city could still have been supplied via the Danville and Virginia Central railroads and the James River Canal. The latter two routes, though, were of dubious value—interior to one state with a major army at each end. Principal reliance would had to have rested on the Danville Railroad and connecting lines—a single railroad (one of the worst railroads at that, even by notoriously low Confederate standards). Still greater than these logistical difficulties would be strategic problems. Yankees following him into Chesterfield from the south would interpose themselves between him and the Confederate heartland. There they could easily raid westward to sever the last rail line. Still worse, they would be in excellent position not only to cut off his capital but to trap his army as well. Yet despite all the disadvantages of abandoning Petersburg and withdrawing into Chesterfield, Lee had to project such a move, so great was the need to counter the threat to Richmond on the Northside. Butler's victory thus not only smashed down the front gate to the capital but bade fair to unlock the back gate, too.

The Southern chieftain was, however, understandably reluctant to be forced into such a predicament if he could avoid it. Joe Johnston, in comparable circumstances, would likely have equated probability with certainty and would have fallen back overnight with masterful skill to some new defense line north of the Appomattox. Lee's approach to warfare was bolder. He made the requisite preparations for withdrawing if necessary, but until that necessity became irresistible, he would cling to Cockade City and its supply links to the rest of the nation. By bluff if he could, by battle if he must, he would attempt to save his rail center as well as his capital.

Prospects for doing so did not look hopeless. The repulse of later Union attacks in Henrico on September 29 reduced the pressure to transfer still more troops from the Southside. Barring a renewed Yankee drive for Richmond on Friday, the main reason for gathering

Secessionist units north of the James would not be to stop Butler's attack but to drive him back. Then too, powerful forces remained to defend Petersburg. Lee managed to redeploy nearly 17,500 men in and around the main defenses of the rail center on Thursday—approximately 20,200, counting Wilcox. Another 6,900 cavalry were available farther south, including Joel Griffin's 1,500 men holding the Squirrel Level Line. Altogether, some 27,000 men still defended Cockade City. It would take a mighty Union attack, indeed—or great pressure at Chaffin's Bluff—to dislodge them. Lee gambled that he could forestall or resist such blows. So while he initiated tentative measures to abandon Petersburg on September 30, he worked actively to save it.[4]

With his own presence diverted to the still more vital sector on Chaffin's farm, he had to entrust the safety of the city and its communications to its regrouped defenders and their commanders. During his comparable absences from Petersburg earlier in the siege, General G. T. Beauregard, commanding the Department of North Carolina and Southern Virginia, took charge on the Southside. But Beauregard, uncomfortable in his subordinate role, had left on September 20 to inspect the defenses of Charleston. He would not be back. On October 3, he was assigned to command the Military Division of the West. At the end of September, however, he still had a number of troops nominally in his department in and around Petersburg: Hoke's and Johnson's divisions, Dearing's Brigade, and Wise's district. These forces would be absorbed into the Army of Northern Virginia within the next five weeks, but for now they continued reporting to the functioning headquarters he left behind. This headquarters, under Lieutenant Colonel John Otey, was, however, no more than a medium for transmitting instructions. It lacked an officer of Beauregard's rank and importance to exercise over-all command south of the Appomattox.

That command and the attendant responsibility to save Petersburg, accordingly, passed to the senior subordinate of the Army of Northern Virginia, the commander of the III Corps: Ambrose Powell Hill. Hill was a man of strange contrasts: bold often to rashness, yet occasionally too hesitant; highly sensitive of his own honor, yet protective of the honor of his friends; deeply devoted to his men, yet at times negligent of their true interests. His military career was as varied as his personality, and now he was in the third and final stage of that career. He initially reached the level of executive officer in May 1862, when army headquarters entrusted him, a promising brigadier, with command of the newly created Light Division. With this six-brigade outfit he more than lived up to expectations, and in the following twelve months he won undying glory and a pre-eminent position among all the illustrious major generals of that halcyon period of the Army of Northern Virginia. His fine combat record earned him promotion to lieutenant general and the command of the newly organized III Corps in May 1863. No man showed greater promise for corps command than he; no man proved more disappointing. In this second and most regrettable phase of his career he seemed to shun his added responsibilities—and even to lose his former ability to handle troops in battle. His record for the next year stood marred with a sorry series of lost opportunities, rash assaults, and ill-co-ordinated maneuvers. Slowly and almost imperceptibly, however, he rose from the nadir of Second Bristoe and the Wilderness and passed into the third phase of his career as the Campaign of 1864 progressed. Now more accustomed to handling a corps and to exercising responsibility, he came into command maturity. Added experience, the relatively stable situation at Petersburg, and the limited amount of troops involved in any given sortie all contributed to his improvement. The distinction he had already earned in the siege—and the laurels he was yet to gain—marked him a successful general once more. Although he would never again win the renown that had been his between the Seven Days and Chancellorsville, he was still a good commander, the best then available to Lee.

From his new command post at Lee's former headquarters, Dunn's Hill, the Lieutenant general took charge of both artillery brigades and all fifteen infantry brigades defending Petersburg.[5] The leftmost portion of the artillery was situated on the Chesterfield side, where detachments of Batteries B, G, and H/1st North Carolina Artillery and part of the 34th Virginia manned Fort Clifton at the confluence of Swift Creek and the Appomattox to block a naval advance up the river to Cockade City. Also on the left bank between the fort and the town, the equivalent of a battery each from the two artillery brigades at Petersburg enfiladed Hancock's right south of the river. Then in the main works east of the city Colonel Hilary P. Jones's Artillery Brigade of Beauregard's department stood guard: Major Francis Boggs's 12th Virginia Light Artillery Battalion, Lieutenant Colonel Edgar Moseley's Battalion, and Major James Coit's Battalion rightward in that order from the river to the Crater. The brigade's remaining outfit, Major John Read's 38th Virginia Light Artillery Battalion, comparably held the second line rightward from the river at least as far as the rear of Gracie's Salient, where the Norfolk Railroad passed through the works. South of Coit, Major William Miller Owen's 13th Virginia Light Artillery Battalion served from the Crater to just north of Rives's Salient. Jones may have taken charge of this I Corps unit as soon as Alexander succeeded Pendleton on September 28. If not, the colonel was surely responsible for it by September 30, after Haskell departed for the Peninsula.

To Owen's right, Colonel Reuben Lindsay Walker's Artillery Bri-

gade of the III Corps defended the works between Rives's Salient and
Battery No. 45. Lieutenant Colonel Allan S. Cutts guarded the vital
southeastern angle with Lieutenant Colonel Charles Richardson's Bat-
talion in the salient itself and his own 11th Georgia Light Artillery
Battalion under Major John Lane in the works across and near the
highway, including the famous Fort Damnation. Next came an attached
I Corps unit, Lieutenant Colonel Benjamin Eshelman's Washington
Artillery Battalion of Louisiana, in Batteries No. 30–35. Finally,
McIntosh and then Pegram extended the artillery west to No. 45. Both
Walker and Jones were able, experienced veterans of the Army of
Northern Virginia. They and their ten battalions could be counted on
to make a determined defense of the city if worse came to worst. None
of the problems that beset Maury's Battalion at Chaffin's Bluff would
weaken these gunners at Petersburg.[6]

Even so, artillerists need infantry support to secure their works from
capture. And counterattacks in the Civil War relied almost exclusively
on foot soldiers. The four infantry divisions at his disposal, accordingly, formed Hill's main reliance for saving the city. Johnson's Division held his left, from the lower Appomattox to south of the Crater.
Like Hoke's Division, this was a heterogeneous and nonhistoric command growing out of the crisis of the Bermuda Hundred Campaign. Its
left consisted of Wise's Virginia Brigade, an outfit that had served in
what would be West Virginia and in many places along the Atlantic
coast but that had only briefly acted in conjunction with Lee's army before June 1864. The absence of its ambitious, carping, but not altogether inept commander, Brigadier General Henry A. Wise, at the head
of the First Military District of Beauregard's department left the brigade under its senior colonel, J. Thomas Goode of the 34th Virginia.
South of Goode was Ransom's North Carolina Brigade, a hard-fighting
unit that had served with Lee from the Seven Days through Fredericksburg but that had been shunted around in less crucial fronts after that
until returning to Virginia in May 1864. It, too, lacked its proper commander, Brigadier General Matt W. Ransom, still recuperating from a
wound received at Wooldridge's Hill, and was now led by Colonel Lee
McAfee of the 49th North Carolina. Next in line to the right was Brigadier General Archibald Gracie's Alabama Brigade, whose constituent
units had served in the West until May 1864, where their finest day had
been at Chickamauga. It was a reliable, hard-fighting body of men,
tempered into an effective combat force by the sure, steady hand of its
able brigadier. Army headquarters itself praised the brigade's "general
appearance [which] reflected great credit on the commander and gave
evidence of the ceaseless energy for which he is distinguished." Less
impressive were the men holding the right flank, Wallace's South

Carolinians. They were called "the Tramp Brigade" because they had served on so many fronts around the Confederacy: from South Carolina to Second Manassas and Antietam to Southwest Creek to Jackson and back to Charleston before returning to Virginia in May 1864. Something of tramps in spirit as well as in travels, they lacked the *esprit* of a successful combat unit. They were not a poor body of fighting men, but—doomed until 1864 to battle against heavy odds under mediocre leadership—they had suffered a long series of defeats. Better odds and much sounder leadership had improved their combat record during the past five months, yet they had already lost their two ablest brigadiers—W. S. Walker and Stephen Elliott—and were now under the inexperienced Wallace, who had only taken command on September 25. Whether or not this promising former regimental commander could meet the test of battle remained to be seen.

Leading these motley brigades was an officer as strange to the Army of Northern Virginia as were they. Bushrod Johnson had served in the West for the first three years of the war, where he had proved himself an engineer of dubious value but a brigade and division commander of considerable merit. Wreathed with the laurels of Shiloh, Murfreesboro, and Chickamauga, he had come East in May 1864 to win more renown at Port Walthall Junction and Second Drewry's Bluff—and the permanent divisional command to which his sound ability entitled him. He met his added responsibilities well when the occasion demanded, yet from June onward his presence on relatively inactive fronts gave him less combat service—certainly less aggressive service, anyway—than any other division commander in the army. His sector, to be sure, was anything but quiet. Its proximity to the II Corps's line enabled Federal shelling and sharpshooting to take a small toll from his ranks almost daily. Permitting only guns stationed in his inner line just east of the Jerusalem Plank Road, not those with his infantry in the front line, to shell the Union position lest the forward guns, if engaged, draw return fire upon the foot soldiers merely reduced but did not eliminate this attrition. Then, too, there was always the danger that the Bluecoats would take advantage of their closeness to his lines to expand their desultory firing into another grand attack like that of July 30. Countermining and careful observation of suspicious excavations in the Union lines to guard against another Federal mine continued up through September. Only a week before the Fifth Offensive began, in fact, no less an officer then Porter Alexander felt that the next great Yankee attack would fall on Johnson—not a mine but a grand bombardment and assault. Against such dangers, the division commander always had to remain ready. Though his duties usually proved unspectacular, they were important. In the ensuing operations his infantry and Jones's supporting artillery, more than any other units, bore immediate responsibility for safeguarding the most direct approach to Petersburg.[7]

From Johnson's right to the Weldon Railroad was Mahone's Division, a historic command whose antecedents ran all the way back to Benjamin Huger's Norfolk garrison and to Joseph E. Johnston's army at Centreville. His left brigade, Weiseger's Virginians, guarded Rives's Salient. Mahone himself had originally led this brigade—it still bore his name—and he often called on it to perform his hardest tasks, this despite the fact that he and Weiseger were usually at loggerheads. Sanders' Alabama Brigade manned the ramparts to the Virginians' right. This unit had once been Cadmus Wilcox's hard-fighting outfit, but his promotion and the death of his two able successors, Abner Perrin and John Sanders, had deprived it of sound leadership. Lee and Hill had not yet found a suitable successor for Sanders, so they left the brigade to its senior colonel, J. Horace King of the 9th Alabama, a mediocre officer who would not win its permanent command. West of the Alabamians, in Mahone's center, were the four fine Mississippi regiments of Brigadier General Nathaniel H. Harris, a sound though not brilliant commander. To his right was Brigadier General Joseph Finegan's Florida Brigade. Finegan himself was an outsider who served in Florida until May 1864, when he led the equivalent of three regiments to Virginia, where he reinforced and took command of the fine but tiny Florida Brigade that had served so well under Edward Perry. Even with these additional troops his brigade was still woefully understrength—six regiments aggregating a mere 678 men. Finally, Wright's Georgia Brigade, under Colonel William Gibson of the 48th Georgia, extended Mahone's line to the Weldon Railroad. This unit had a fine heritage, but with Ambrose R. Wright gone, with Victor Girardey dead, and with the stigma of its rout at Fussell's Mill still upon it, it had declined badly, and Gibson, superior and subordinate alike recognized, was not the man to revive it. "We all like Col. Gibson very much," one of his men wrote, "but he has no military genius. He will do very well to command the brig. during stillness, but when active operations commence I don't think there is hardly an officer in the brig. that would be willing for him to lead them in a fight." To make matters worse, most of Gibson's regimental and battalion commanders were even more incompetent than he was; the brigade inspector, indeed, branded the commander of the 10th Georgia Battalion as "mentally incapacitated for officership." Such poor leadership had reduced the unit's effectiveness so much that Hill regarded it as "almost worthless." Of equally little use were the attached second-class troops from Petersburg, a force incapable of attacking and even unreliable in defending any position. Yet the reserves could at least give the appearance of

1. David B. Birney

2. Robert S. Foster

THE X ARMY CORPS

3. Richard H. Jackson

4. William Birney

MHRC

5. Edward Otho Ord

MHR

6. George J. Stannard

THE XVIII ARMY CORPS

7. Charles A. Heckman

MHRC

8. Godfrey Weitzel

MHR

9. Edgar M. Cullen

10. James Jourdan

THE XVIII ARMY CORPS

11. Charles J. Paine

12. Harrison S. Fairchild

13. Alfred H. Terry

14. August V. Kautz

RECONNOITERERS TO RICHMOND

DEFENDERS OF THE NORTHERN SUPPLY LINES

15. Gilman Marston

16. Joseph H. Potter

MHRC

NA

17. John Gregg

18. Dudley M. DuBose

INITIAL DEFENDERS OF THE NORTHSIDE, SEPTEMBER 29

19. Martin W. Gary

20. R. Bogardus Snowden

MHRC

CV, v. VI, p. 248

21. John K. Mitchell

22. Robert Archelaus Hardaway

DEFENDERS OF CHAFFIN'S FARM

23. Mark B. Hardin

24. George E. Pickett

25. Braxton Bragg   MHRC

26. James L. Kemper   MHRC

DEFENDERS OF RICHMOND

27. Seth M. Barton   MHRC

28. John C. Pemberton   MHRC

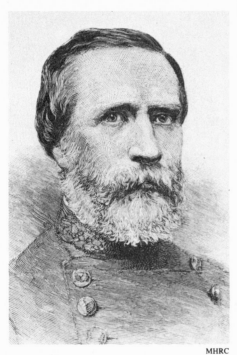

MHRC

29. Richard Heron Anderson

MHRC

30. Charles W. Field

CONFEDERATE COUNTERATTACKERS

31. Robert F. Hoke

MHRC

32. Edward Porter Alexander

VSL

manning the trench line in hopes of deceiving Union lookouts, and if worse came to worst and they were attacked, experience had already shown that Fletcher Archer, one of the heroes of the Battle of the Ninth of June, would get whatever fight was possible out of them.

Although the division thus had officers and troops of greatly varying quality, its commander was a soldier of much merit. Unlike many, William Mahone excelled when given added responsibility and rose from a below-average brigadier of long service and little promise to an outstanding division commander. From the time he succeeded Dick Anderson in May 1864, he led his division superbly, and he served with distinction in every operation of the siege that occurred on the Southside to date. Claims—originated by himself, accepted by some later historians—that he was the one great and flawless major general at Lee's disposal in this final autumn of the war are exaggerated, but there is no doubt that army and corps headquarters often turned to him to deliver key attacks. Almost as often, he succeeded. Like Hancock's corps in the Union army, however, his hard-fighting command was to sit out the ensuing battle on a relatively quiet line and would come into action only if directly attacked or if the course of others' operations required it. Meantime, his mission was to secure the vital Rives's Salient and also to guard the line running west to the lead works. With Grant's first offensive since his extension to the Weldon Railroad now under way, Mahone had to be ready in case the Yankees struck north, not west, from their August conquests.[8]

Available to counterattack such a westward advance or any other blows were the remaining divisions of the III Corps: Wilcox's on the far right flank and Heth's in grand-tactical reserve. Viewed at its second echelon, Wilcox's was the soundest division defending Richmond and Petersburg. The nucleus of Powell Hill's old Light Division, it still retained its great corps of brigadiers, all of whom were pre-Gettysburg men and one of whom had led his unit since just after the Seven Days' Battle. Unlike all Lee's other historic divisions, which had lost brigadiers heavily at Gettysburg and since, this command kept its high-quality leadership, for although each had been wounded during the year, all were now back on duty. Lane, indeed, had just returned from convalescence on August 29 and was still not fully recovered. Unfortunately, the division itself did not serve as a unit, for Thomas' Georgians were stationed on the Swift Creek Line and Scales's North Carolinians had gone to Chaffin's Bluff. The two outfits that remained, though, were excellent. The South Carolina brigade, which had adjoined Mahone's right before going into reserve, was a superb combat unit, worthy material for its hard-fighting commander, Brigadier General Samuel McGowan. Originally extending west from McGowan to

Battery No. 45, where the incomplete line along the Boydton Plank Road left the main line, but now also in reserve were the five reliable North Carolina regiments of another experienced and highly competent brigadier general, James H. Lane.

Despite these reliable officers and hard-hitting men, the division had one weakness: its commander, Cadmus Marcellus Wilcox. Although he had temporarily led a division in the Second Manassas Campaign, he had won his claim to promotion at the head of an Alabama brigade, which he had directed solidly but not brilliantly until after Gettysburg, when he had succeeded the great Pender in office but not in performance. Wilcox never quite excelled as a major general, and he frequently proved unable to wield the outstanding material at his disposal to best advantage. Yet flashes of excellence did come to him on occasion. At such times he could transcend the limitations of his normal stolidity, and—with rapid yet accurate analysis, planning, and execution—discern and react to the essence of a given tactical situation. These "moments of excellence" came to him only infrequently—but when they did, he at last became a general worthy of his troops.[9]

Hill's remaining division was Heth's, the newest of the historic divisions of the Army of Northern Virginia. Dating only from the post-Chancellorsville reorganization, it consisted of two brigades taken from the Light Division and three brought from North Carolina and Southside Virginia. The former two, Field's Virginians and Archer's Tennesseans and Alabamians, were now consolidated into one brigade, with the little 2nd Maryland Battalion added. Both had once been fine fighting units, but under a long succession of poor colonels and transient brigadier generals—John Brockenbrough, Robert Mayo, Heth himself, "Mud" Walker, Birkett D. Fry—their combat capacity had appreciably diminished. At last they had a good commander again—James J. Archer, who had returned in August after his long captivity—but he was a dying man who could only slow, not reverse, their decline. Inept leadership also plagued another of Heth's units, Davis' Brigade, the blame for whose poor combat record and indiscipline rests largely on its commander, the unskilled and negligent nephew of the Confederate President. These two brigades contrasted diametrically with Heth's other two outfits, which flourished under excellent leadership. One was a fine North Carolina brigade that had won its place in the main theater of the war after arriving late. Led satisfactorily when under Johnston Pettigrew and then William Kirkland, it rose to excellence under its present commander, William MacRae, who tempered it on the drill field and tested it on the battlefield until it became one of the best assault units in the army. Yet even it does not rank as high as its fellow North Carolinians of Cooke's superb brigade, renowned veterans of all Lee's campaigns except for Chancellorsville and Gettysburg. These hard-fighting soldiers, too, owed their meritorious record to their outstanding commander. "Cooke's brigade I found in excellent order, as it always is . . ." reported the Assistant Inspector General of the army. "I consider the high state of perfection it has reached attributable more to the energy and devotion of its commander than any other cause. Other brigades have as good material, but few brigades have so watchful and skillful a commander." The historian may even go beyond the inspector and assert that of all the fine generals of brigade still remaining in Lee's army—Wofford, Conner, Cox, Grimes, Thomas, McGowan, Lane, MacRae—John Gregg alone ranks as high as John Rogers Cooke as a combat leader; as a disciplinarian, Cooke stands pre-eminent.

In this division, also, its weak point was its commander. Virginia gentleman, loyal patriot, close friend of Robert E. Lee, Henry Heth was a devoted, well-meaning soldier, long beset with misfortune: Lewisburg, Chancellorsville, Gettysburg, Falling Waters, Second Bristoe, the Wilderness. Most of these setbacks, however, were due to causes at least partially beyond his control. They certainly did not indicate that he was incompetent. To the contrary, he possessed all the technical know-how of a solid division commander—though not the brilliance of a great one—and under the right circumstances he could handle his forces creditably. Yet all too often, circumstances had not been right for Harry Heth. Of all Lee's major generals, his past record was the most checkered, his future conduct the most unpredictable.[10]

Even more than in Heth's brigades did the influence of leadership on combat effectiveness manifest itself in the remaining brigade in the trenches, Dearing's cavalry in the Squirrel Level Line. A hodgepodge of Georgia and North Carolina companies grouped into mostly heterogeneous regiments and of regiments formed into a conglomerate brigade, it only came together early in 1864 as part of the Confederate resurgence in eastern North Carolina. Half a year later it had still not coalesced, but Dearing, an able ex-artillerist who now proved himself a hard-hitting horse soldier as well, managed to keep the brigade together almost single-handedly by force of example and skill of direction. Performing such a role hardly pleased him, and he longed to return to some high-quality combat unit. "I'll get killed yet trying to make these people of mine fight," he confided in November; ". . . I want to get out of this concern"—an ironic statement since he was to be killed in action, all right, but only after he got his wish and left his old, unreliable force to lead the famed Laurel Brigade. Death was still over half a year in the future at the end of September, however, and transfer, too, was over four months away. For the present Dearing was

still responsible for getting his "people" to fight. Whatever his distaste
for the task, he did the job well enough to earn praise from Lee himself.

The army commander was all the more anxious to keep Dearing as
brigadier for fear that his two ranking colonels, political appointees
Joel Griffin of the 8th Georgia Cavalry and Dennis Ferebee of the 4th
North Carolina Cavalry, were incompetent to handle a large force. The
army commander was sufficiently powerful to protect his choice from
the pressure of the colonels' influential supporters, but not even Lee
could save him from the elements. As fate would have it, the cam-
paign-seasoned brigadier chanced to fall sick in late September and had
no recourse but to relinquish command to Joel Griffin. Though Hampton attempted to offset this decline in leadership by requiring Young to
look after Dearing's Brigade as well as his own, Gregg's incursion toward Hatcher's Run diverted the demidivision commander's attention
as well as his presence farther south. The demands of the campaign
thus left the care of the Squirrel Level Line to one brigade; the
demands of nature left the care of that brigade to its senior colonel—
and nothing in Joel Griffin's record suggested that he could make his
unsteady forces meet their responsibilities. The security of the forward
line—and the communications it covered—could hardly have been
placed in less trustworthy hands. Yet pressures from other quarters—to
save Richmond and drive back Butler, to secure Petersburg itself, to
block Gregg—left Lee no alternative but to weaken the Squirrel Level
Line. With the fate of both cities hanging in the balance on September
29–30, he had no other choice.[11]

And so the Virginian massed his strike force at Chaffin's Bluff,
regrouped his defenders around Petersburg—and hoped for the best on
Friday. First signs seemed encouraging. The busy night brightened into
day, and still no attack came on either front. Perhaps the Bluecoats
would remain quiescent, after all. The army commander even felt
justified in ordering the Light Division to start marching for the Peninsula at 9:00 A.M. to join his counterattack against Fort Harrison.[12]

Wilcox's departure, however, proved premature. The Army of the
Potomac was far from quiescent on September 30. Like its counterpart
in gray, it had spent the night regrouping, gathering its strength, and
preparing for operations on Friday. For some Yankees the night passed
pleasantly, even joyfully. Blue soldiers on the left were initially startled
to hear a great shout come ringing down the line toward them from the
right. But when they were mustered and told of the capture of Fort
Harrison, they joined in with three cheers of their own and sent the
huzzahs resounding farther to the left.[13]

All was not gladness and rejoicing in Union lines that evening. Butler's very victory that so thrilled the rank and file increased their gen-

erals' concern that Lee might seek to offset it either by moving troops from Petersburg to the Northside or possibly even by attacking the Army of the Potomac. Front-line Federal commanders, accordingly, redoubled their vigil, and at least the Third Division, II Corps, kept half its men awake and under arms overnight to be ready for any contingency. The senior brigadier of that division, perhaps reflecting his superiors' views as well as his own, felt that developments on the Peninsula that day would likely force the abandonment of Petersburg. "Big work is in prospect," he concluded, and he kept his soldiers alert to be ready to take part in it.

His and Hancock's other watchful men, as usual, became embroiled in fire fights with Johnson. Sharpshooting flickered along the Jerusalem Plank Road all night, and at about 7:30 one of Jones's mortar batteries picked a fight with Fort Sedgwick. Major John Hazard, Chief-of-Artillery of the II Corps and commander of all field guns in Hancock's works, moved four mortars of his own (belonging to D/4th New York Heavy Artillery) into Battery No. 20 and replied. Their brief exchange produced much noise but little damage beyond disturbing the repose of nearby infantrymen. Between 10:00 and 11:00 heavier exchanges of shelling—and brisk musketry as well—broke out between Miles's right and Goode and McAfee. Some common soldiers felt these flare-ups portended heavy fighting that night. Even responsible commanders believed the firing formed part of some larger design by the foe. Johnson thought that Miles provoked the later affair to draw return fire and thus reveal whether the Confederate line east of town had been weakened. The New Yorker and his immediate superior, in contrast, worried that the Butternuts initiated the shooting in preparation for attacking the Federal right. Miles had been apprehensive about such a blow since midafternoon. Hancock, unconcerned at first, gave greater credence to the threat on learning of the reported enemy buildup along the left bank of the Appomattox below his right. He first promised to fulfill Miles's request for the last reserve artillery unit, the 14th Massachusetts Battery, should the First Division actually be attacked. Now the major general checked with his junior division commander to see if the late-night firing marked the expected assault. But no attack came. The fact that the responsible commanders on both sides thought that the enemy started the fight, indeed, suggests that the incidents were not part of some broader plan at all, only the customary clash between troops in proximity. Even so, the Confederate return fire had the effect of showing that Lee had not stripped his lines.

Elsewhere the same conclusion could be drawn from opposite intelligence. The extreme quiet that prevailed west of the Jerusalem Plank Road—"the calm before a storm," one of Ferrero's officers perceptively observed—gave no evidence of any Southern moves in that area, either.[14]

No official confirmation of Confederate inactivity that night reached army headquarters until Hancock reported to that effect at 8:16, Friday morning, in response to Humphreys' inquiry. Even so, the very absence of any indication that some Secessionists were withdrawing that evening likely displeased Meade. He returned to Birchett's sometime between 8:20 and 10:30 P.M., not at all satisfied with developments during the day. Almost every index he received showed that he succeeded so well in pinning down at Petersburg Graycoats who might have moved to Chaffin's that the prospects for success of his own strike toward the supply lines on Friday appeared negligible. His lookouts, to be sure, had spotted an estimated 7,000 infantry and four batteries marching toward Richmond, but they also thought they saw another 5,000 infantry and 200 cavalry reinforcing the Confederate right. Ferrero's and Baxter's reconnaissances, moreover, seemed to reveal that the enemy held both the main defenses of the city and also the Squirrel Level Line in force, and Gregg's raid, far from penetrating even to the Boydton Plank Road, drew down upon itself a heavy concentration of Butternuts. Though the careful outpost officer Gregg conscientiously advised his superior at 8:00 P.M. that he thought only Southern cavalry, not infantry as well, opposed him, he added that they were "very strong in my front and on my left flank" during the battle. That evening Warren and Hancock, too, provided more contradictory evidence on whether or not Petersburg had been appreciably weakened. At 8:25 P.M. word arrived at Birchett's from Globe Tavern that deserters testified that Lane and Scales were preparing to move "north of Petersburg." Second Corps headquarters, in contrast, reported at 8:16 P.M. that a strong force of Confederates was maneuvering in Chesterfield County as if to cross the lower Appomattox into the II Corps's right rear. Then to make matters worse, Meade feared that he lacked adequate manpower to overcome the heavy force he thought remained in his front. In a message written at 10:30 P.M. and dispatched forty-five minutes later, he summarized most of these developments for Grant and then added:

> I do not see indications sufficient to justify my making an attempt on the South Side Railroad. . . . I can throw a force out to Poplar Spring Church, and engage the enemy, if you deem advisable, but this will only be extending our lines without a commensurate object, unless engaging the enemy is so deemed.

The army commander thus came close to recommending that the whole attack south of the Appomattox be canceled. Lee's daring plan of masking his extreme vulnerability with deceptive shows of force seemed on the verge of paying off.

The Virginian's strategy did not succeed, however, because the ultimate decision on challenging it did not rest with Meade. The major general, something of a perfectionist of the old school, could fight hard and well for grand goals when conditions were right but preferred not to fight at all when objectives seemed minor or conditions not all that might be desired. Like his good friend and Chief-of-Staff, Humphreys, Meade likely considered launching an offensive at this time "premature." The army commander no longer had the final say in such matters, though, and could only recommend his views to the much different general who controlled operations from City Point. Grant, to be sure, neither advocated blundering blindly into battle nor fighting for no greater reason than just to kill some Southerners. Yet he was not an all-or-nothing man either and was willing to strive for even penultimate objectives in hopes that later, if not sooner, they would provide the opening to more complete success. He responded to his subordinate's report in that light.

Well into Thursday night the lieutenant general counted on continuing the offensive on both sides of the James at daylight. As late as 11:00 P.M., in fact, he informed Butler that the Army of the Potomac had good prospects of carrying Cockade City itself, provided that "the enemy have detached largely." Within half an hour, however, Meade's report of 10:30 that the Graycoats had not "detached largely" arrived to alter his plans. The General-in-Chief accepted the data it contained but not its implicit recommendation and simply restricted rather than abandoned his goals on the Southside. He did go so far as to agree that the Army of the Potomac should not try to reach the railroad at this time "unless a very considerable part of the enemy is drawn across the James, and then only when we are able to withdraw Butler's force rapidly and send it to you"—something not likely to happen soon since he had promised Butler, less than half an hour before receiving Meade's message, that the Army of the Potomac would reinforce the Northside if it carried Petersburg on Friday. Yet just because "a very considerable part of the enemy" seemed not to have gone and because the Army of the James was not immediately available, Grant did not allow the Army of the Potomac to remain inactive. At 11:30 P.M. he told Meade not to strike at daylight as first intended but to hold his men ready to move out at about 8:00 A.M., by which time the lieutenant general expected to be back from Deep Bottom with a better perspective on how many Graycoats had gone to Chaffin's. He made clear that Meade would still have *some* active role to play:

When you do move out I think it will be advisable to maneuver to
get a good position from which to attack, and then if the enemy is
routed follow him into Petersburg, or where circumstances seem to
direct.

The hard-hitting Grant left no doubt that "engaging the enemy" was a
"commensurate object"—not for the purpose of killing a few Confederates but rather for the purpose of seeking out initial advantages that
might lead to the ultimate goals he sought in common with the perfectionists.[15]

Fifteen minutes after midnight Meade, accordingly, passed on the instructions to his three corps commanders and Gregg that they should
hold their men ready to move at the prescribed hour. Warren, Hancock, and presumably Parke had previously ordered their forces to be
prepared by much earlier times—5:30 for the V Corps, 4:00 for the
other two. Now they had to issue new directives. Some copies of the revised orders took so long to filter down through the chain of command
that some troops of the IX Corps turned out in compliance with the
original instructions hours before the new starting time. Other commanders, however, received the orders in time to give their men a little
more, much-needed rest before sending them into battle.

Whenever the officers finally roused their men, they had little more
to do than form ranks. The greatest part of the strike force had already
assembled on the far left by September 29, and such men of the V
Corps as remained in the trenches could easily pull back into mobile
reserve after dark. A powerful strike force it was. Warren contributed
to it virtually his entire First and Second divisions. Even camp guards
reported back to their regiments for duty, though the camps themselves
were left standing. Only about 700 pickets—approximately 170 outposts of the First Division just east of the Vaughan Road northward
from the Poplar Spring Road to Flowers' house, 30 horsemen at the
house, and 500 pickets of the Second Division from Flowers' east to
the railroad—remained in place west and northwest of the works to
cover the defenses and protect the right flank and right rear of the
force driving westward. More than offsetting the absence of these
pickets, the Third Brigade, Third Division, V Corps, temporarily joined
the Second Division on September 29 for the impending operation. To
provide artillery support, the five reserve batteries of the V Corps—
B, D, and L/1st New York Light Artillery, the 15th New York Battery,
and B/1st Pennsylvania Light Artillery—plus H/1st New York Light
Artillery from Battery No. 26 prepared to take the field: a total of
twenty-four guns. The IX Corps, too, contributed all its reserve artillery, the eighteen pieces of the 7th Maine Battery, the 19th and 34th
New York batteries, and Battery D, Pennsylvania Light Artillery. To

the guns Parke added all but three regiments of his two white divisions. Twelve infantry brigades and ten batteries (forty-two guns), in sum, thus poised around Globe Tavern and Dr. Gurley's that night—20,000 men prepared to be unleashed wherever Meade might direct. Farther south, from Wyatt's plantation to Reams's Station, 4,300 more soldiers, veteran cavalry, stood ready to lend their support.[16]

Over 24,000 troops clearly constituted a formidable striking force. Yet equally clearly, they did not come close to approximating Meade's whole strength the way Butler's columns embraced virtually the entire Army of the James. The Massachusetts man, required to garrison only Bermuda Hundred and Marston's three posts down the James, could afford to send most of his army into the field. Meade, in contrast, shared the same burden as Powell Hill: the need to man the works immediately east and south of Petersburg in order to protect the army's supply lines, prevent the foe from severing troops on the far southwest from those north of the Appomattox, and—in the Yankees' case—retain possession of the foothold on the Weldon Railroad. Grant, who imposed this requirement on the Pennsylvanian, admittedly, authorized the subordinate on September 27 to send part of the garrison into the field if necessary to maintain control of the Southside Railroad, but he still directed that at least the forts along the works be held. Even this extreme permissible degree of stripping the defenses, moreover, could be carried out only after the original striking force reached the railroad and overcame or at least pinned down any mobile Confederate troops that might otherwise attack Hancock. Intelligence reports of the alleged concentration against the II Corps's right on September 29, doubtless, emphasized the potential danger to that sector and confirmed Meade's original intention of September 27 to send only four infantry divisions into the field and to man the old works in strength. In fact, he allocated 38,000–39,000 men to such garrison duty.

Nearly 11,000 of those troops held the fortifications west of the Jerusalem Plank Road, which Warren and Parke were leaving. Since the strike force, moving westward, would cover the north–south retrenchment west of the Weldon Railroad, only the 700 pickets in that sector plus the garrisons of three forts would have to remain there. Baxter, back from his reconnaissance toward Peebles's farm, resumed his customary duty of manning those three forts. The 94th New York and the 5th Massachusetts Battery held the far left in Fort Davison, a mile and a half east of the tracks, the only redoubt that the V Corps garrisoned on the rear line. Next rightward, at the southwestern salient, Fort Dushane, the five regiments that had probed toward Peebles's on Thursday, plus the 9th Massachusetts Battery and D/5th U. S. Artillery, all under Colonel Richard Coulter of the 11th Pennsylvania, stood guard. Baxter's remaining three regiments, the 16th Maine, 97th New York, and 107th Pennsylvania, forming a demibrigade under Colonel Thomas F. McCoy of the 107th, joined C-E/1st New York Light Artillery and B/4th U. S. Artillery in garrisoning Fort Wadsworth, the northwestern salient. Coulter's men had entered their stronghold late Thursday afternoon after sighting the ominous pillar of smoke from the cavalry battle at Wyatt's. Now his troops and Baxter's others actually moved their camps inside the forts as well, just in case—admittedly, remote—they should have to make a last stand in their enclosed strongholds.

Demibrigades in redoubts sufficed to hold the retrenchments. The three miles of the east–west front line running rightward from Fort Wadsworth to Fort Davis and facing Mahone required a stronger garrison. Bragg's Iron Brigade of the V Corps manned the left third of that line from McCoy to just west of Fort Howard. The IX Corps held the balance of the works. The 29th Massachusetts of that corps's Third Brigade, First Division, plus the 11th Massachusetts Battery garrisoned Howard itself. Then came Colonel Ozora P. Stearns's First Brigade, Third Division, in the trenches between Howard and Fort Alexander Hays, a mile farther right. The 79th New York and 51st Pennsylvania of the First Brigade, First Division, plus the 27th New York Battery defended the more easterly redoubt. Finally, Colonel Charles S. Russell's Second Brigade, Third Division, extended rightward to connect with the II Corps holding Fort Davis, immediately west of the Jerusalem Plank Road. All these IX Corps troops reported to their Third Division's commander, Ferrero, who now transferred his command post to Parke's headquarters at Jones's house, just west of the plank road. The V Corps forces were, in turn, under the head of their Third Division, Brigadier General Samuel W. Crawford, who comparably moved into Warren's headquarters at Globe Tavern. Even though the corps commanders themselves and some of their staff would be absent from these buildings during the attack, much of their permanent staff remained in the old headquarters to assist the two subordinates in directing the garrisons. Jones's house and the tavern, moreover, had far superior telegraphic communication with the rest of the army than the division headquarters had. Further to facilitate control of the forces left in the defenses, Meade placed Crawford in charge of the entire garrison left of Fort Davis at 12:30 P.M. on Friday.[17]

North from that fort another 28,000 men were on duty. Hancock, from his headquarters at Shand's house, controlled the bulk of these forces: the 20,000 men of his reinforced II Corps. Brigadier General Gershom Mott's Third Division held the left half of his line from Fort Davis to just south of Fort Morton. His Third Brigade under Colonel Robert McAllister garrisoned Davis and manned the trenches from the

Norfolk Railroad north to Fort Morton. Between McAllister's divided command stood Brigadier General P. Regis DeTrobriand's First Brigade. Mott's remaining brigade, Brigadier General Byron R. Pierce's Second, camped in reserve on the Jerusalem Plank Road. North of the Third Division, Major General John Gibbon's Second Division held three-fourths mile of line from Fort Morton to just left of Fort Stedman: Colonel Mathew Murphy's Second Brigade, Colonel Thomas A. Smyth's Third Brigade, and Brigadier General Thomas W. Egan's First Brigade, left to right. Finally, the remaining mile of defenses from Fort Stedman to the lower Appomattox was manned by Miles's First Division. Lieutenant Colonel William Glenny's Fourth Brigade held Miles's left, and Colonel James McGee's Consolidated Brigade and Colonel James Lynch's First Brigade extended rightward in that order.

Hancock's proximity to the Confederate works and to Petersburg beyond led to a disproportionately heavy concentration of artillery on his sector, both to lend weight to his defense line and to bombard the enemy works and city. Parts of four artillery brigades served there: Hazard's fourteen batteries of the II Corps, Captain William Harn's six batteries of the VI Corps that did not serve with their comrades in the Shenandoah Valley, two batteries from the Army's Artillery Reserve, and Major Albert Brooker's six heavy batteries of the Siege Train—a total of eighty field pieces, thirty-six mortars, and twelve siege guns. September 30 found the artillery posted as follows, left to right (the parent corps is indicated parenthetically; mortars and siege guns are denoted with an "m" and an "s," respectively):

WORK	GUNS	UNIT
Davis	4	B/1st New Jersey Light Artillery (II)
	4	6th Maine Battery (II)
Sedgwick	4	H/1st Ohio Light Artillery (VI)
	4	E/5th U. S. Artillery (VI)
	4	3rd Vermont Battery (Reserve)
No. 21	4	3rd New York Battery (VI)
No. 20	4m	D/4th New York Heavy Artillery (II)
Rice	4	E/1st Rhode Island Light Artillery (VI)
	2	3rd Maine Battery (Reserve)
No. 19	2	3rd Maine Battery (Reserve)
Meikel	3	A/1st New Jersey Light Artillery (VI)
No. 18	1	A/1st New Jersey Light Artillery (VI)
No. 16	4	3rd New Jersey Battery (II)
Morton	4	G/1st New York Light Artillery (II)
	2m	D/4th New York Heavy Artillery (II)
	4m,2s	A/1st Connecticut Heavy Artillery (Siege)
	4s	M/1st Connecticut Heavy Artillery (Siege)

No. 14	4	10th Massachusetts Battery (II)
No. 13	4	1st New Hampshire Battery (II)
Haskell	4	C-I/5th U. S. Artillery (II)
	2	4th Maine Battery (VI)
No. 12	13m	L/1st Connecticut Heavy Artillery (Siege)
No. 11	2	4th Maine Battery (VI)
Stedman	4	A-B/1st Rhode Island Light Artillery (II)
	2	F/1st Pennsylvania Light Artillery (II)
No. 10	2	F/1st Pennsylvania Light Artillery (II)
	4m	K/1st Connecticut Heavy Artillery (Siege)
No. 9	4	12th New York Battery (II)
	3m	K/1st Connecticut Heavy Artillery (Siege)
McGilvery	2m	K/1st Connecticut Heavy Artillery (Siege)
	4	K/4th U. S. Artillery (II)
	2	11th New York Battery (II)
No. 6	2	11th New York Battery (II)
No. 5	4m,3s	E/1st Connecticut Heavy Artillery (Siege)
No. 4	3s	I/1st Connecticut Heavy Artillery (Siege)

Up until September 28–29, the rightmost redoubt also contained the most famous artillery piece of the whole Siege of Petersburg, the huge 13-inch seacoast mortar known as "The Dictator," but on the outbreak of the Fifth Offensive it was sent back to the Siege Train's depot at Broadway Landing. Also behind the lines was the remaining company of the II Corps, L/4th New York Heavy Artillery, which had charge of the corps munitions trains. All the front line light artillery of the VI Corps and the Army Reserve reported to Harn, and he, in turn, was subordinate to Hazard. The major, moreover, closely co-operated with Brooker in co-ordinating the heavy guns. All these pieces, in sum, made up a mighty artillery arm to support Hancock's position. Brigadier General Henry J. Hunt, Chief-of-Artillery of the Army, admittedly resented this arrangement that left him complete control of only the two batteries of the Army Reserve not at the front (one of them a supply unit with no guns) and forced him to share operational control of most of the artillery with his archenemy, Hancock. Even so, this allocation and control of armament were necessary for conducting the siege effectively.[18]

Besides Hancock's mighty force of artillery and infantry, another 2,400 men served north from the Jerusalem Plank Road—mostly miscellaneous detachments and small units. Meade's staff and guards (the Oneida Cavalry Company of New York) were there at Birchett's house on the road to Prince George Court House behind Hancock's right. Near army headquarters were six companies of Lieutenant Colonel Ira

Spaulding's 50th New York Engineers, Captain Franklin Harwood's U. S. Engineer Battalion, and most of Brigadier General Marsena R. Patrick's Provost Brigade: the 114th Pennsylvania, six companies of the 68th Pennsylvania, all but one company of the 3rd Pennsylvania Cavalry, K/1st Indiana Cavalry, and C and D/1st Massachusetts Cavalry (the latter squadron, Meade's escort). Also in the area were most of Major Benjamin Fisher's detachment of the Signal Corps and what was left of Captain Calvin Shaffer's Army Artillery Reserve, his own F/15th New York Heavy Artillery plus the 14th Massachusetts Battery. And, of course, the 16th Pennsylvania Cavalry still patrolled the rear after Gregg's other units moved west.

Immediately down the Appomattox from the II Corps's right was Battery No. 5, and a mile inland east of that redoubt was Battery No. 4, both part of Hancock's artillery to try to silence the guns enfilading that flank from the Chesterfield side. The next two positions, over four miles farther down the river, Fort Converse and the camp of Colonel Henry L. Abbot's Siege Train at Broadway Landing, were part of the defense complex anchoring the left flank of Bermuda Hundred and so are not counted in Meade's total strength. The army commander was, however, responsible for defending the main supply depot and supreme headquarters at City Point, another four miles east of Converse. Such an important base, of course, deserved protection. Underscoring that need was its isolated condition and extreme vulnerability. Confederate guerrillas constantly hovered in the area, and just two weeks earlier, four of Hampton's brigades penetrated deeply into that sector. His daring raid led to a heavy Federal buildup around the point, and now some 6,100 men from both of Grant's armies served there. Benham, commander of the Engineer Brigade of the Army of the Potomac, was charged with defending the hamlet. His 3,400 men consisted of five companies of the 15th New York Engineers, five companies plus the depot platoon and the recruits of the 50th New York Engineers, the 200th and 205th Pennsylvania, the 2nd Maine Battery, and VanRaden's provisional battery of the 2nd New York Heavy Artillery. Besides Benham's men numerous other outfits served in and around the depot. Patrick's remaining units—the 80th New York, four companies of the 68th Pennsylvania, and B/3rd Pennsylvania Cavalry—guarded prisoners and administered passes at the point. Also present were the 22nd Massachusetts of the V Corps, the 10th USCT of the XVIII Corps, the dismounted cavalry of Gregg's division, the 210th Pennsylvania (which only arrived from its recruiting depot on September 29), and Grant's headquarters guards: five companies of the 4th U. S. Infantry and three companies of the 5th U. S. Cavalry.[19]

The forces at City Point plus Hancock's and Crawford's commands and the miscellaneous units thus totaled approximately 39,000. Comparing this number with the 24,000 men of the strike force makes clear that Meade left over 60 per cent of his men inside his original lines. Even if the numerous staff, engineer, and artillery units of the garrison —troops not well suited to attacking—are dropped from consideration and only infantry and mounted cavalry are counted, the column of attack still amounts to only 42–43 per cent of Meade's whole command. The Pennsylvanian could have varied the totals by a few thousand men —a few percentage points—either way, but the basic approach of committing only part of the army while the rest remained in the trenches originated at City Point.

Observers then and since have criticized Grant for apparently leaving so many men out of action and not striking with the entire Army of the Potomac. Such criticism, however, ignores two key factors governing his conduct of the siege and of the war in Virginia that summer and autumn. To begin with, his army had lost so many able leaders and veteran soldiers, May 5–June 18, that it now lacked the mobility it had enjoyed the preceding spring. The survivors needed rest; the replacements needed seasoning. Until both could be obtained, the army could simply not function effectively in mass maneuvers and bold strategic penetrations of the heartland. Short, sharp jabs by part of the army reaching out only a small way were all that the Bluecoats could still attempt. Even such jabs could produce major results: They nearly secured Richmond on September 29 and now offered good prospect of taking Petersburg the next day. But because they could only function in the grand-tactical domain, not the broad-strategic arena, they could never be conducted far from their base on the James or far from the two cities they sought to capture. Hence, part of the Federal forces had to remain in their works to protect that base and to confront those cities. But—and this was the second governing factor in Grant's conduct of operations—those troops in the fortifications were not really inactive, as critics charged. Those breastworks were not just defenses for the depot, nor were they parallels of a true Vaubanian investment. They were instead the ramparts of a great entrenched camp from which some of Grant's forces sallied against the enemy's communications while others remained behind not only to protect his own base but also to pin down the defenders of Petersburg. So long as the entrenched camp beleaguered the city, the Graycoats could never draw off their full strength to fight for their supply lines, lest the Yankees from the entrenched camp pour straight into the rail center itself. The Northern troops who stayed in the works thus did not cease affecting the course of events but rather, as a potential reserve to the striking force and as a direct threat to Cockade City, themselves had an important role to play. Meade, accordingly, directed most if not all of them, too, to be under arms, ready to move by 8:00 A.M. on Friday in case developments required them, also, to go into action.[20]

Such opportunities, however, first had to be won by the mobile columns, which clearly received the major assignment. How well they would carry it out depended not only on the number of men called from the works to form them but even more on the quality of those men and of the officers who led them.

Foremost of the responsible officers was, of course, George Gordon Meade himself. Dour, uninspiring, touchy, often short-tempered with his subordinates, he yet managed to redeem his frequently unattractive personality by his qualities as a general: patient yet steadfast resistance while on the defensive, devotion to duty and the highest interests of his country, the capacity to fight hard and well when he felt circumstances justified giving battle. He, to be sure, lacked other, probably higher, military attributes. The broad grasp and bulldog tenacity of Grant, the bold imagination of Sherman, the reckless bravado of Sheridan, the irresistible onslaught of Thomas were not the hallmarks of Meade. Yet he takes his place in the "Big Five" of the Federal high command on the basis of his excellent service as a brigade and division commander in the old Pennsylvania Reserves, on the basis of his brief but promising direction of a corps, and, above all, on the basis of those three July days in 1863 when he sought out the enemy, then stood, fought, did not retreat, and stopped Robert E. Lee at Gettysburg. Meade never again won the renown that he achieved in that battle, and the Overland Campaign of 1863 soon demonstrated his limitations as an independent army commander: reluctance to take chances plus a certain lack of initiative and perseverance, not so much in precipitating but in following through on offensives. Even so, he managed to serve well during the operations in 1864, in which he was relieved of some of the ultimate responsibility and became, in effect, Grant's principal executive officer, charged with supervising the minor-strategic and grand-tactical operations he was so well suited to handle. Such an arrangement was uncomfortable for the Pennsylvanian. His acute sense of professional propriety and dignity made him particularly sensitive to supposed slights or neglect on the part of the General-in-Chief. Then, too, the layered command structure not only restricted Meade's professional independence as nominal commander of the foremost Union army but also allowed his superior to receive all the public credit for victories while *he* drew the public criticism for setbacks. Grant, it must be emphasized, did not intentionally slight the junior officer. Nor did the Illinoisan set Meade up as a mere decoy for abuse. The General-in-

Chief not only came genuinely to respect his subordinate's many fine
qualities as a general but also sought to give them full play—and at the
same time recognize the importance of the major general's high office
—by allowing him as much discretion as possible. Yet there was no
doubt which of them made final decisions. It seems equally clear that
such an arrangement, however painful for the man, was better for the
country, since the Pennsylvanian was a better subordinate than a
supreme commander.

Backing Meade up at army headquarters was his brilliant Chief-of-
Staff, Major General Andrew Atkinson Humphreys. A distinguished
engineer of long-standing reputation before and during the Civil War, a
hard-fighting commander of an infantry division, a capable staff officer,
Humphreys ranks as one of the best all-around generals of the whole
Union army. He was, in fact, so well qualified to direct troops that one
cannot help wondering why Grant and Meade retained him in his present post—important as it was—for so long. Not until November 25,
1864, did they finally give him command of a corps, which he had so
long craved and for which he was so well suited.

Another officer of Humphreys' brilliant intellectual caliber was
Gouverneur Kemble Warren, commander of the V Corps. Also an engineer of high standing, this New Yorker had led infantry more frequently than had Humphreys. He had originally served with the old 5th
New York and then had led a brigade of New York volunteer Zouaves,
which deserved its place in Sykes's division alongside the Regulars. But
his finest day had been as an engineer at Gettysburg, when he had spotted the crucial importance of Little Round Top and had rushed troops
up to hold it just in the nick of time. This achievement first earned him
command of the II Corps, with which he won a sparkling little victory
at Second Bristoe Station during the Overland Campaign of 1863, and
then command of the V Corps, which he had generally led well during
the battles of the 1864 campaign. Yet certain defects somewhat offset
his unquestioned ability as an engineer and as a tactical commander.
Two of those shortcomings directly related to his professional performance. For one thing, despite his fine service once fighting actually
started, he was excessively cautious about precipitating a battle. Then,
too, he frequently had difficulty co-operating with others in a co-ordinated attack. His other two faults involved his relations with other
officers. Like Meade, he was high-strung, sensitive, and touchy, and
like several other Union corps commanders, he had an aggravating
tendency to instruct his superiors how they ought to conduct operations. These drawbacks would eventually ruin his career only nine days
before Lee surrendered. That tragedy, though, was far in the future.
Just now this able soldier, who had seized the Weldon Railroad, was
again spearheading the drive to the west.

His subordinates were generally sound men, too. Charles Griffin was a bluff ex-artillery officer, who led a fine if ill-fated battery at First Manassas, an artillery battalion in the first part of the Peninsular Campaign, an infantry brigade up through Antietam, and an infantry division ever since then except when ill during Gettysburg. With this background he believed in the close co-ordination of infantry and artillery in battle, and he always fought his men and guns so well that he ranks as one of the most outstanding division commanders in Grant's entire army group. Another former battery commander now ably leading Warren's Second Division was Romeyn B. Ayres, a hard-hitting tactician whom Grant himself praised as "a capital commander . . . one of our best officers. . . ." None doubted that Ayres was worthy to lead the division that included the U. S. Regulars who, two years earlier, had been the bedrock of the army.

Griffin's and Ayres's brigadiers were less distinguished than their chiefs. Not one of them had won his stars, although several deserved them. In the First Division, the respective commanders of the Second and Third brigades, Colonel Edgar Gregory of the 91st Pennsylvania and Colonel James Gwyn of the 118th Pennsylvania, were both able, experienced combat leaders, whose veteran brigades included most of the remaining volunteer regiments that had once made up the old V Corps before the great reorganization of March 1864. The remaining brigadier of that division, Colonel Horatio G. Sickel of the First Brigade, was a newcomer to the post but a man with historic ties to the army. He had served in the old Pennsylvania Reserve Division, had passed out of the main army during that division's Washington interlude, had emerged in the Army of West Virginia during the Cloyd's Mountain Campaign, and, just six days before the Fifth Offensive started, had at last returned to the Army of the Potomac at the head of the 198th Pennsylvania, a new regiment some of whose members had served in the old Reserves. Most new outfits reaching City Point after September 14 were assigned to the Army of the James, but Meade himself intervened to secure the services of his old comrade and the 198th. Warren promptly put them in Griffin's new, nonhistoric First Brigade, command of which Sickel then assumed.

Ayres's brigades were not in such experienced hands. Two other regiments that descended more directly from the Pennsylvania Reserves plus three regiments of garrison troops that had only served with the Army of the Potomac for the past four months made up his Third Brigade, under Colonel Arthur Grimshaw of the 4th Delaware, a reliable regimental commander but an untested brigadier. Also new to his post was the promising Lieutenant Colonel Elwell S. Otis of the 140th New York, the temporary commander of the First Brigade, which included the 15th New York Heavy Artillery plus all that was left of the old

Regular Division. With less historic bonds to the old corps but slightly
more combat experience as brigadier was Colonel Samuel Graham of
the Purnell Legion, commanding the Second (Maryland) Brigade,
which had only joined Meade's army in July 1863. Officers of such inexperience left the performance of Ayres's second echelon of command
an uncertain factor. Fortunately, however, he had attached to his command a leader of proven ability, Colonel J. William Hofmann of the
56th Pennsylvania, whose Third Brigade of Crawford's division represented the old I Corps in the approaching battle. Another combat-
tested veteran directed Warren's artillery, Colonel Charles S.
Wainwright, a sharp-tongued patrician War Democrat from New York,
who detested most of his brother officers when in camp but who co-
operated with them admirably when in battle. His long record as an artillery brigadier—initially in the I Corps, then in the V Corps—gave
every promise that he would direct well the guns supporting the drive
against Hill's position.[21]

Acting in conjunction with the V Corps was the IX Corps under
John Grubb Parke, the ranking corps commander of Meade's army.
Ever since the genesis of the IX Corps during the North Carolina
Sounds Campaign of 1862, his name had been inseparably linked to it
only less so than that of Burnside himself. After the unfortunate Rhode
Islander left the army following the Battle of the Crater, Parke succeeded to the corps command he had briefly held twice before. His
long association with the corps, however, had mostly been as its Chief-
of-Staff, and even this late in the war he lacked extensive combat experience on the corps level. Although he was capable of controlling the
minor tactics of a battle on a limited front, his capacity for the higher
arts of an army executive officer remained untested. Could he handle
his corps as a unit without losing control of some of his forces? And
with how much initiative would he respond to a rapidly developing situation? By the conclusion of the war his increased experience would
earn him favorable answers to those points, but now, at the end of September 1864, his ability to command a corps in battle was an open
question.

His ranking subordinate was another officer long identified with high
command in the IX Corps, Brigadier General Orlando Bolivar Willcox.
He had been the acting corps commander at Fredericksburg, had in
effect directed it during its superb counterattack against Mahone on
that overcast Friday at Globe Tavern, and had commanded a division
in it on many other occasions from the Maryland Campaign of 1862
onward. He, too, was a competent soldier who could fight well. After a
seventeen-day leave of absence, he got back to Fort Monroe on Thursday night and then hurried forward to resume command of the First

Division the following morning on learning that a "move" was imminent. He thereby displaced Brigadier General John F. Hartranft, a hard-hitting Pennsylvanian, the best combat officer the IX Corps ever produced. Also on September 30, two competent veteran brigadiers of the First Division, Colonel Benjamin Christ (50th Pennsylvania) of the First Brigade and Colonel William Humphrey (2nd Michigan) of the Second Brigade, mustered out of service. Division headquarters initially planned to let the Second pass to Colonel William C. Raulston of the 24th New York Cavalry (dismounted), a promising officer whose able brother John was then leading a brigade in embattled Fort Harrison. However, another regimental commander in the Second Brigade, Colonel Charles DeLand of the 1st Michigan Sharpshooters, turned out to be senior to Raulston. Rather than allow the Michigander to take charge, Hartranft assumed command of it himself instead of returning to his own First Brigade. With the general diverted and Christ, too, mustered out, leadership of the First then devolved on Colonel Samuel Harriman of the 37th Wisconsin, a relatively new regiment raised that spring and only assigned to the main army in June. During all these changes, the Third Brigade remained under Colonel Napoleon Bonaparte McLaughlen of the 57th Massachusetts, an able veteran regimental commander but one lacking extensive experience as a brigadier.

Parke's other division had more seasoned leaders. Its commander, Robert B. Potter, was the rising man of the corps—along with Hartranft, with whom his name was first paired in glory in the storming of Burnside's Bridge at Antietam. Unlike Parke and Willcox, who started out near the top, this citizen-soldier began the war as a militia private and then as a major and won his way up to the command of a division and even a corps during the Knoxville Campaign—a record that amply attests to his merit. He and his able, experienced brigadiers—Colonel John I. Curtin (45th Pennsylvania) of the First Brigade (a nephew of Governor Andrew G. Curtin of Pennsylvania) and Brigadier General Simon G. Griffin of the Second, the former colonel of the renowned 6th New Hampshire—formed a combat-tested team long accustomed to handling the division well in battle.

All of Parke's brigadiers, unlike Warren's, directed units containing many regiments with ties embedded deep in the heritage of the corps. New outfits were then added to veteran brigades from time to time, but only McLaughlen's command contained a preponderance of these relatively new regiments—and even two of those outfits, the 57th and 59th Massachusetts, boasted descent from troops that had served in 1862 and 1863. This sound approach to organization meant that the corps, despite many reorganizations, contained white divisions of roughly equal balance. Only in terms of freshness did Potter enjoy even a slight advantage. Unlike Willcox's troops, who had fought hard in mid-August, the Second Division had not been engaged since the Battle of the Crater. Indeed, as of September 30, it was the freshest white division in Grant's entire command.

Like the foot soldiers, the IX Corps artillery contained a good mix of veterans and newer men. Its commander, Lieutenant Colonel J. Albert Monroe, unfortunately belonged in the latter category. Though he had been associated with light artillery throughout the war, he possessed no combat experience above battery level. His earlier service in the siege as nominal Chief-of-Artillery of the corps was purely a staff assignment, since the batteries were parceled out by battalions among the infantry divisions. Not until August 30 were six of those companies drawn together in a corps artillery brigade. A mere month of quiescent experience with this brigade did not daunt the Rhode Islander's brash self-confidence, but it was self-confidence grounded in self-esteem rather than in solid achievement. Rank, not record, brought him charge of Parke's guns. Of all the brigadiers in the field force of the IX Corps, he was the least promising.[22]

This, then, was the Union high command—not uniformly brilliant but, on the whole, a sound, competent, and above-average officer corps with, however, some weak spots. A greater liability to Meade's plan than the quality of his subordinates was the caliber of his men. Staggering casualties and also the high muster-out rate of many experienced soldiers—indeed, of many experienced regiments—over the past five months literally vitiated the fighting tone of his army. By autumn, the hauntingly melancholy words of the camp song rang all too true: "Many are dead and gone/Of the Brave and True who've left their homes/Others been wounded long." Many historic, veteran units remained on the rolls, to be sure, but attrition, which Grant's armies not only inflicted but also suffered, caused fewer and fewer veteran *soldiers* to fill their ranks. Most outfits were worn down to the size of a full company or two, while other regiments maintained respectable strength only by filling the places of those fallen "Brave and True" with conscripts, bounty men, bounty jumpers, and foreigners with little heart for or commitment to the Union war effort. Most new regiments, moreover, consisted almost entirely of such material. Some of those men were worthless scoundrels; others were potentially good soldiers who simply lacked proper training as yet. Whatever their future potentiality, such men were of doubtful value for the present and had, in fact, already wrecked the vaunted II Corps at Second Reams's Station. They might do the same to the V and IX corps, too, for they infected both outfits, right down to Otis' Regulars themselves. But only the test of battle would reveal how they would affect those two corps.[23]

The Fifth Offensive brought that test to hand. By Friday morning, the Army of the Potomac had completed all its preparations for attacking. Its surplus wagons and supplies had now reached City Point, and its field wagons stood ready to join the strike force when called. The soldiers themselves had drawn four days' rations and sixty rounds of ammunition. They had turned out early and had eaten breakfast. All they now awaited were orders to move.[24]

Their superiors to the highest echelons awaited those same orders. At first, even Warren and Parke did not know whether they should move out at 8:00 A.M. or should await orders from Birchett's. The IX Corps commander initially asked what his colleague would do and subsequently informed Globe Tavern that he would not advance without authorization from army headquarters. At 7:25 A.M. the New Yorker sought guidance from a more knowledgeable source, Humphreys. The Chief-of-Staff replied thirteen minutes later that the infantry should not move without further instructions. Humphreys did not specify it, but Meade himself was waiting for the go-ahead from Grant. The scheduled time came and passed, and still no orders arrived, so the whole army—from private to major general—kept on waiting. Then, at 8:25, word clicked over the wires from City Point. The lieutenant general was now back from his early-morning conference with Butler at Deep Bottom and had devised his plans for the day. He revealed them to Meade in a succinct dispatch that not only authorized attacking but also epitomized his conduct of the siege to date:

> General Butler's forces will remain where they are for the present, ready to advance, if found practicable. You may move out now and see if an advantage can be gained. It seems to me the enemy must be weak enough at one or the other place to let us in.

Now that Birchett's at last had permission to advance, it acknowledged Grant's message at 8:50 and passed on its own battle plan to Warren, Gregg, and Parke at 8:50, 9:00, and 9:09, respectively. Meade had already discussed at least the broad outlines of his plans with his subordinates on Thursday, if not on Wednesday. Now he put down in writing what was to be done. The directive that IX Corps headquarters received at 9:20 best summarizes the projected attack:

> General Warren is ordered to move out the Poplar Spring Church road and endeavor to secure the intersection of the Squirrel Level road. The commanding general directs that you move out after and co-operate with him in endeavoring to secure a position on the right of the enemy's position. Try to open a route across the swamp to vicinity of Miss Pegram's, below Poplar Spring Church, and take post on Warren's left. Gregg will be directed to move out to [E.] Wilkinson's.

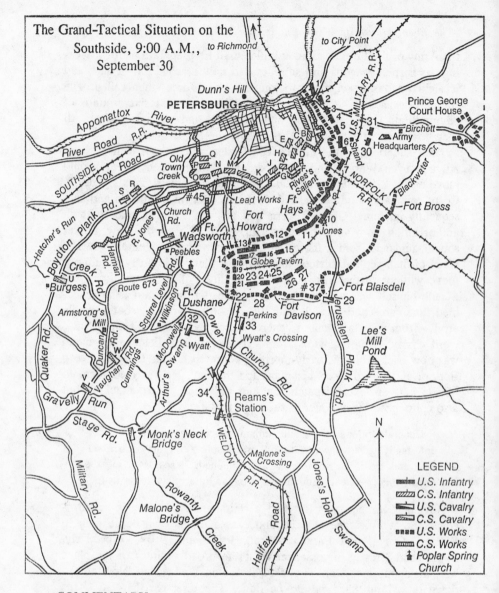

The Grand-Tactical Situation on the Southside, 9:00 A.M., September 30

COMMENTARY

1. This map reveals the profound impact of the Battle of Chaffin's Bluff on the situation south of the Appomattox. Hill has had to send off most of his reserves and to call back his remaining infantry to the main defenses of town, leaving only cavalry to guard the communications against which Warren and Parke are now moving.

2. Of Hampton's corps, only Dearing and Farley are located with certainty.

3. Wilcox is shown starting for the Peninsula.

4. The location of Archer and MacRae is approximate, and their relative order is not certain.

5. The relative order of Ayres's brigades is not certain. The relative order of Miles's brigades is correct, but their sectors are only approximate.

Army of the Potomac - MEADE	Confederates - HILL

Army of the Potomac - MEADE

GARRISON

II Corps - HANCOCK

MILES
1 - Lynch
2 - McGee
3 - Glenny

GIBBON
4 - Egan
5 - Smyth
6 - Murphy

MOTT
7 - McAllister
8 - DeTrobriand
9 - Price (of McAllister)
10 - Pierce

Independent

FERRERO
11 - Russell
12 - Stearns

CRAWFORD
13 - Bragg
Baxter
14 - McCoy
22 - Coulter
28 - 94th N.Y.

Miscellaneous
29 - Robison
30 - Spaulding
31 - Patrick

STRIKING FORCE

V Corps - WARREN

AYRES
15 - Hofmann
16 - Graham
17 - Grimshaw
18 - Otis

GRIFFIN
19 - Sickel
20 - Gregory
21 - Gwyn

IX Corps - PARKE

POTTER
23 - Curtin
24 - S. Griffin

WILLCOX
25 - Hartranft
26 - McLaughlen
27 - Harriman

Cavalry - GREGG
32 - Davies
33 - Smith
34 - Beaumont

Confederates - HILL

III Corps - HILL

HETH
E - Cooke
H - J.R. Davis
N - J. Archer
O - MacRae

MAHONE
F - Weiseger
G - King
J - Harris
K - Finegan
L - Gibson
M - F. Archer

WILCOX
P - McGowan
Q - Lane

JOHNSON
A - Góode
B - McAfee
C - Gracie
D - Wallace

Cavalry Corps - HAMPTON

W. LEE
R - J.L. Davis
S - Barringer

BUTLER
U - Dunovant
V - Young

Independent
T - J. Griffin
W - Farley

These instructions thus focused on overrunning Peebles's farm. Federal intelligence had still not learned of Heth's departure from there late the previous afternoon—indeed, it thought he had been reinforced on Thursday morning—so it understandably marked his supposed stronghold as the chief barrier to be overcome in order to reach the supply lines. The way of achieving this goal, however, seems peculiar—if interpreted literally. Moving the IX Corps southwestward for a mile and a half through densely wooded country to Westmoreland's [Miss Pegram's] would virtually place Parke out of the battle, not put him in position to co-operate with Warren against Peebles's farm. The Yankees were not aiming for Westmoreland's, though. Rough drafts of this directive make clear that they equated Miss Pegram's with Watkins' at the western end of Route 673, a position that their grossly erroneous maps showed as only one and a quarter miles west of Poplar Spring Church and three fourths of a mile west of the Squirrel Level Road— half the true distance. The map thus suggested that the IX Corps could easily cross the swamp south of Warren, deploy along the entire length of Route 673 between the Squirrel Level and Duncan roads, and then strike northward. Its right would join the V Corps in overrunning Peebles's farm, and its left would move up the Harman Road to the Boydton Plank Road. That is how Meade read his map and planned; that is how Parke read his map and understood what was expected. Hence, the army commander, far from scattering his troops over the countryside, skillfully concentrated them to turn and storm Peebles's farm. While the foot soldiers thus breached the outer Confederate line, Gregg was to reoccupy the southern end of the Squirrel Level Road to cover their left rear and to be ready to join in the general drive for the communications.

The cavalry general and the two corps commanders knew they were to advance toward those supply lines if they overran the forward works. Meade, admittedly, did not spell out this follow-up in his initial orders. Required by City Point to try to press on "into Petersburg or where circumstances seem to direct," he chose to await the outcome of his first attack before specifying later objectives. Even so, on Thursday he had evidently given his senior subordinates a general idea of what was expected of them beyond capturing the Squirrel Level Line. The absence of any formal, written statement of later goals was thus of little moment—provided that sufficient control from army headquarters or sufficient initiative at the corps level kept the attack going once the initial objective was secured.[25]

What Warren and Parke received on Friday morning was, therefore, less an introduction to Meade's plan than an authorization to begin carrying out a mission on which they had already been briefed. For over an hour they had awaited such permission. Now that it had at last arrived, they sent couriers speeding to set the waiting ranks in motion. For them and their comrades the time for reconnaissances, cavalry raids, and watchful waiting was over. The mighty Army of the Potomac was marching into battle once more.

CHAPTER IX

———◆———

"Rolling over the Field like a Large Wave"

For hours the V and IX corps had awaited permission to move. Some of their rear and support units evidently became so tired of waiting that they stacked arms, but the lead elements remained ready to march at a moment's notice. Now that authorization had arrived, and the great column of 20,000 men finally got under way. Close to 9:00 the V Corps led the march south along the Halifax Road, thence west on the Poplar Spring Road toward Poplar Spring Church and Peebles's farm. First came a small cavalry detachment (presumably the detail from the 4th Pennsylvania Cavalry that served as Warren's escort, perhaps reinforced by the comparable detachment of the 3rd New Jersey Cavalry from IX Corps headquarters). Behind the horsemen marched Gwyn, Gregory, Sickel, and Captain Robert B. Rogers' Battery B/1st New York Light Artillery, in that order. Next in the column were Ayres's four brigades (probably Otis, Grimshaw, Graham, and Hofmann, front to rear), and then came Wainwright's other five batteries. No supply wagons brought up the rear. Contrary to Meade's initial orders, Warren left all his vehicles—including ammunition wagons, ambulances, and supply wagons carrying six days' rations—inside his works. "The movement will determine very soon whether or not the wagons, &c., will be needed," felt Warren; "they can then be sent for." Leaving the impedimenta behind not only disencumbered the V Corps of it but, better still, prevented it from delaying the IX Corps. Even as it was, Warren's combat troops alone took over an hour just to clear the Hali-

fax Road and pass out of the fortifications. Not until 10:00 did the IX
Corps begin to move out from Dr. Gurley's to join the main column,
and not for another half hour did it actually start following
Wainwright. Curtin led Parke's column, and then came Simon Griffin,
the 19th and 34th New York Batteries, Hartranft, McLaughlen, Harriman, and Monroe's other two artillery companies. By the time the
final guns were set in motion, the hands of one of their officers' watches
pointed to noon.[1]

A difference of approximately three hours thus separated the starting
times of the front and the rear units. Logistical difficulties, opposite to
those that plagued Butler on September 29, partly caused this delay.
The Army of the James, that is, attacked in two wings on widely separated roads and, therefore, had trouble co-ordinating the second wave
of its onslaught. The Army of the Potomac, in contrast, initially
remained concentrated on the only available road—thus causing its
own van to delay the advance of its rear. That Meade had no practical
alternative to assigning all twelve brigades and ten batteries, 20,000
strong, to one road excused but did not eliminate the resulting delay.
Logistical problems alone accounted for any delay experienced while
marching westward on the first three-quarters mile of road beyond the
Union works. The lane itself ran through open fields reaching from the
fortifications nearly to the Vaughan Road and, even more importantly,
was covered by the pickets Griffin and Ayres left in place. But at or
just east of the Vaughan Road the Bluecoats passed beyond their outposts into enemy country. To make matters worse, dense woods now
closed in about the good but narrow Poplar Spring Road from a point
about one-quarter mile east of the Vaughan Road all the way westward
to the church, half a mile beyond the north–south highway—woods
that could conceal the lurking foe. No longer just difficulties in logistics
but also fundamental problems in grand tactics now confronted the
Federals.

Prime responsibility for meeting these problems, of course, fell upon
the commander of the lead corps, Gouverneur Warren. This proficient
engineer-turned-tactician met the technical demands of the new situation well. He had already concentrated all his pioneers near the front
of his column. Now he sought to solve the logistical problem of being
confined to one narrow road by setting them to building another route
alongside the Poplar Spring Road. The problem of security now that he
was west of his original picket line he comparably met by throwing out
his lead regiment, the 18th Massachusetts, as skirmishers. Once his
cavalry advance drew fire from Confederate outposts, moreover, he
pulled the horsemen aside and pushed forward the 18th, soon reinforced by parts of Gwyn's next three regiments, the 1st Michigan, 20th

Maine, and 118th Pennsylvania. The corps sharpshooter battalion, temporarily attached to the First Division, likely also went on the skirmish line at this time. Thus the major general again met all demands of the minor operational level with his accustomed competence.

But successful generalship is not a function of expertise alone. Technical know-how is no more than the complementary means of executing that vital element of command variously called will, or drive, or initiative. In that higher aspect of generalship the New Yorker once more revealed his shortcomings. The lack of such drive goes a long way toward accounting for the delay in moving westward that morning. Part of the caution that now dominated his operations was, admittedly, the sort of praiseworthy prudence required of officers operating in wooded and potentially dangerous country. Both theory and his own experience these past five months made clear that he could not afford to plunge recklessly ahead. Army headquarters, moreover, may have compounded his problems by warning of the hazards potentially awaiting him. He was likely aware of Meade's misgivings, Thursday, that the Confederates were weak enough to be attacked successfully. For all the New Yorker knew, Heth still held Peebles's farm in force, and enough potential reinforcements remained up in the works of Petersburg to cause the army commander himself to doubt the prospects of victory.

But beyond these understandable restraints on his forward movement, there existed within Warren's personality certain influences that expertise could not offset nor extraneous factors explain. His hesitancy to force a battle on September 30—far from reflecting unique circumstances—was almost characteristic of his conduct on semi-independent missions during the last twelve months of the war. Such conduct, despite its many fine features, drew unfavorable comment from others, including Grant himself. The General-in-Chief later attributed the subordinate's shortcomings to a tendency to "see every danger at a glance before he had encountered it." A letter the corps commander wrote to Meade just the following evening initially seems to bear out the lieutenant general's analysis. Presumably with Friday's experience fresh in his mind to underline his more general conclusions, Warren complained that the over-all approach of striking with only limited force made "the commander at each point apprehensive of being greatly outnumbered by the enemy, which is always practicable for him to do . . . and thus inevitably produce[s] want of boldness and vigor on our part, unless we neglect more than any of us are willing to do." Despite such apparent confirmation, the General-in-Chief's estimate, while accurate in itself, does not get to the root of the problem. Nor does the New Yorker's desire for perfection more than complement, if not stem from, the basic cause. Warren was hesitant not just because he feared danger, not just because he feared imperfection, but also because he feared responsibility. Not the responsibility for minor tactics—his technical know-how made him justifiably confident there; nor was it the responsibility for meeting an emergency, which summoned forth his latent talent without leaving time for self-doubt. What bothered Warren was the responsibility for grand tactics, that realm of military art dealing with movements just outside the actual field of combat. Making the awesome decision to precipitate battle and concerning himself with potential enemy responses beyond the site of fighting were what made him hesitant. The same day that he complained to army headquarters of the fear of being outnumbered, he gave voice to this deeper concern by confessing to his wife how the "anxiety of responsibility" had borne down on him on September 30.[2]

To make matters worse, the officers who could have freed him from much of that responsibility were nowhere near the potential combat zone when their strike force moved out. Meade and Humphreys remained way back at Birchett's until after issuing the orders to advance. Not until between 9:00 and 9:15 did they turn over army headquarters to Williams and set out for the front. Their decision to travel by horse instead of by train and their willingness to stop en route— perhaps with Ferrero, definitely with Hancock, whose company Meade and the army staff found "irresistible"—delayed them so long that they did not reach Globe Tavern until noon. During those three hours the army commander and his Chief-of-Staff were virtually out of touch with the column of attack and even with their own headquarters.

Before leaving Birchett's they received two or three signal reports that few Confederates were visible around their camps and that the only Southern forces spotted in motion were ambulances heading west. Some Signal Corpsmen who made these sightings privately concluded that they perhaps portended evacuation of the city. The observers, however, did not report these conclusions to their superiors, and no evidence has been found that the top commanders made the same assessment of what appeared as routine reports. The generals also got word from II Corps headquarters that the situation east of town looked quiet and that an escaped contraband reported that Heth had left Petersburg for the Northside overnight and that other troops had departed on the Southside Railroad on Thursday. Subsequent interrogation by John Babcock, the chief intelligence officer, disclosed, however, that the unperceptive Negro now claimed that only one regiment had moved from Cockade City to Chaffin's Bluff on September 29, but that a brigade had gone to Lynchburg on Wednesday. Williams duly forwarded this revised report to his superiors at 10:25 A.M., but it may be doubted that it reached Meade until much later. The Pennsylvanian

definitely did not receive until midafternoon a signal report of 9:15
A.M., also forwarded at 10:25, that wagons were seen moving north
through Chesterfield County and that few Butternuts were spotted in
the works between the Jerusalem Plank and Halifax roads but that
many were seen just east of and behind Battery No. 45.

Meade and later Williams conscientiously kept City Point abreast of
this intelligence, but they made much less effort to inform the front-line
commander, Warren. The Assistant Adjutant General, to be sure, sent
Globe Tavern the report of the sightings between Rives's Salient and
No. 45, but if that message traveled as slowly as the copy to Meade, it
would not have reached the corps commander in the field until late in
the afternoon. Nor did the one intelligence summary that Meade did
receive and that did reach the tavern at 11:00 A.M. amount to much.
Babcock's report that the Light Division was still at Petersburg was
hardly new, for Warren himself had gathered that information the preceding evening. The only concrete news it contained, that Rosser had
left for the Valley, moreover, was of little moment to the infantry general, since the V Corps would probably not have to fight cavalry, anyway. Birchett's, in sum, contributed little to revitalize Warren's drive.

Meade and Humphreys exercised little more control. Beyond rou-
tinely reminding the New Yorker at 8:45 A.M. to keep them posted on
the identity of units from which he took prisoners and asking him at
9:00 A.M. to leave word on how they could reach him in the field, they
did not contact him again until 11:30. At that time Humphreys wrote
both him and Parke to "push forward your reconnaissances and ascertain the strength of the enemy." Such an order sounds impressive, but
no evidence has been found that this message, not telegraphed but
carried all the way along congested roads by couriers, actually reached
the corps commanders in time to affect their operations. Writing letters
from afar thus proved an uncertain means for controlling operations.
As long as Meade himself was not on or near the field, his corps
officers would continue acting largely on their own.[8]

The army commander's willingness to let responsible subordinates
exercise responsibility and the executive officer's hesitancy to use that
responsibility thus produced a failure of generalship that retarded the
advance of the lead division. That delay, in turn, blocked the other
three divisions behind Griffin and thus brought home the logistical drawbacks of moving 20,000 men over one road. Until the vanguard could
force its way through the mile of logistical bottleneck east of the church,
the whole striking force was slowed to a snail's pace. With corps headquarters providing little leadership, the responsibility for pressing
through those woods centered on Gwyn's skirmishers. The men in the
ranks neither knew the strategic factors nor shared the personal charac-

teristics that together restrained Warren, but, veterans that they were, the voltigeurs themselves knew enough to move slowly. "We advanced cautiously through the thick brush and undergrowth," wrote a soldier of the 1st Michigan; "one could scarcely see two rods, not knowing what moment we should receive a volley from the concealed foe. Our boys had had a taste of this in the Wilderness and were pretty cautious." No volley yet blasted them, but the crackle of musketry revealed the presence of at least some Graycoats in those woods. Who could say how many more lay concealed there?

Gwyn and his superiors, of course, could not answer that question, but Joel Griffin could. The knowledge of Confederate strength that the Unionists understandably lacked must have been all too painfully clear to the Georgian as he received reports that strong Northern forces were closing in on his sector. Little is known of how the brigadier responded to the impending conflict; some doubt, in fact, exists that he even alerted his superiors to developments. What does seem clear is that he realized he was too weak to make a stand outside his main works on Peebles's farm and, therefore, used only his pickets to oppose the Yankees east of the Squirrel Level Road. Such outposts, of course, could not hold off Gwyn by themselves. And without Dearing to inspire them, they reportedly made little effort to stand up to the foe. Once the slow-moving Northerners actually neared the picket line, it, therefore, offered little resistance and fled past the church to the ravine of Arthur's Swamp west and north of that building. There, too, the outposts put up little fight and, except for their comrades south of the Poplar Spring Road, fell back into Peebles's field just in front of Joel Griffin's defenses.[4]

In those works the colonel made his stand. His position itself was strong. Its left flank rested just east of the road that gave the Squirrel Level Line its name about half a mile south of the main defenses of Petersburg. From there the line, facing basically eastward, ran roughly southwest a little over three miles before terminating on Route 673 a mile west of the Squirrel Level Road and about three-quarters mile east of the Duncan Road. A little redoubt, possibly called Fort Cherry, stood guard where the fortifications crossed the Squirrel Level Road at W. W. Davis' house about a mile and a half down the road from the main defenses of the city. From that plantation the trenches extended southward just west of the road for half a mile to Fort Bratton, a small, enclosed, square work on Chappell's farm a little over three-fourths mile east of north from Poplar Spring Church. South of there the works formed a vast re-entrant angle to cover the key intersections around Peebles's farm. The curtain ran more sharply southwest half a mile from Fort Bratton to the main stronghold on the farm, Fort

Archer, an enclosed, pentagonal work located immediately east of where the Church Road passed through the trenches about half a mile northwest of the church. The infantry parapet then extended west half a mile through the field just north of Peebles's deserted farmhouse to the woods along the northwestern fork of Arthur's Swamp. There the trench turned south, crossed the stream, and ran nearly due south through the woods almost half a mile to a lane that led northwest from the eastern end of Route 673 to Wilkinson's house, a building over three-fourths mile west of Peebles's house. The earthworks thus formed a right angle along the middle-northern and far-western edges of Peebles's field, which could open a crossfire on any troops debouching onto the farm from the western end of the Poplar Spring Road. From Wilkinson's lane the curtain cut back sharply southwest five-eighths mile to its southern terminus on Route 673, a little redoubt called Fort MacRae, situated just northwest of J. Smith's farm and just east of J. Hawks's house.

The trace of the Squirrel Level Line was good. The works were new, however, and by no means finished. On the crucial site of Peebles's farm, no slashing had been laid, and a frise a hundred yards outside the works had been planted only in front of and possibly west of Fort Archer itself. That redoubt also had a moat ten feet deep and fourteen feet wide, but the curtains on both flanks apparently had only a shallow fosse—if any at all. Those trenches northeast of the fort, moreover, were of weak profile, only two to three feet high, but the much stronger ones to its right had parapets as high as a man's head. The redoubt itself lacked gun platforms, though cannon could, nevertheless, be emplaced in it, and its ramparts themselves were complete. Such shortcomings were handicaps but hardly fatal weaknesses. The infantry had accomplished enough in the nine or ten days they had labored on the line to make it formidable, despite its remaining imperfections.

What the line needed, September 30, was not more engineering work but a strong, brave, well-led garrison. Therein lay its greatest weakness. The huge manpower drain of September 29 had stripped it of its infantry defenders and left in their place one small cavalry brigade—a unit, moreover, not renowned for its stamina. And to make matters worse, it was now led by an officer of doubtful competence. Even when faced with the obvious danger to his right center, Joel Griffin apparently kept the 4th North Carolina Cavalry along his unthreatened left at and north of Chappell's and concentrated only his other two regiments and his artillery on Peebles's farm. Captain Edward Graham's Petersburg Battery, supported by a detachment of the 7th Confederate Cavalry under Major Jesse H. Sikes, garrisoned Fort Archer itself. Griffin's own 8th Georgia Cavalry plus the rest of the 7th manned the curtains on the farm. Together, these two regiments and the battery totaled only about 1,000 men. In the woods east of them were gathering some 20,000 Yankees. By midday on Friday, the lack of substance of Lee's great bluff to save his supply lines appeared all too evident.[5]

Yet what is now clear to historians and must have been apparent then to the Southerners was by no means obvious to the Federals. The heavy fire of case shot that Graham now directed toward the church at least created the impression that the Secessionists were willing to put up a fight, even though it overshot the Yankees and did little more damage than to drive the frightened pastor and his family to shelter. The same dense woods between the church and Peebles's that prevented the horse battery from taking better aim also prevented Warren from readily perceiving how weak the enemy really was. Nothing, in sum, signified to the Union commander that he should proceed less cautiously than he had previously done. He had already taken two hours to push his leading division as far as the church. Now he took another two hours to complete his dispositions to attack Peebles's farm.

His personal hesitancy to precipitate battle probably continues partially to explain the delay. Another key factor in slowing the attack was the terrain, which was even more difficult west of the church than east of it. The dense woods north of the Poplar Spring Road gave way to a small clearing three-eighths mile west of the Vaughan Road. In that clearing stood the church: It was a little wooden building that some Bluecoats mockingly called "stately" but that was, in fact, an unpainted, dilapidated, totally unimpressive structure, lacking both steeple and bell—withal, hardly an edifice worthy of lending its name to a great battle. Opposite the church and below a fringe of trees south of the Poplar Spring Road was an even larger open field, Widow Smith's farm. Those clearings, however, gave way to more woodlands farther west, in the rough ravines through which flowed several branches of Arthur's Swamp. This tributary of Hatcher's Run, along whose middle reaches Gregg had fought on Thursday, had three principal forks near Peebles's. One rose west of Chappell's house and flowed straight south through the Confederate works a quarter mile east of Fort Archer, across the Squirrel Level Road, and into the woods northwest of the church, where a second branch joined it from the northeast. The two branches plus that road enclosed Pastor Job Talmage's farm, and the northeastern fork plus the combined stream, respectively, bordered the northern and western edges of the clearing around his church. The combined stream then ran southward through a partially drained millpond formed by a dam on which the Poplar Spring Road crossed the creek just east of the Squirrel Level Road. From there the swamp continued southward to the southwestern end of Widow Smith's farm,

where it was joined by a third fork coming in from the northwest parallel to and southwest of the Church Road. Along all these branches
were dense woods and tangled undergrowth.

These thickets not only blocked Warren's view of Peebles's farm but
also delayed his troops taking position. Griffin, for instance, found it
no easy matter to move his division up the ravine of the combined
stream west of the church. Wainwright, by the same token, readily
spotted no place from which he could reply to Fort Archer. And by the
time the colonel finally located a slight clearing amid the pines northwest of the church and dragged a section of Battery B/1st New York
Light Artillery there, he found that the First Division had occupied the
ravine in his front. The foot soldiers did not thereby mask him, but for
some reason—perhaps fear of drawing Graham's fire down on them,
perhaps concern that his own shells might drop on them—their presence caused him to hold his fire. That ravine thus slowed the infantry
and neutralized the artillery, yet it also had its advantages. It provided
Griffin's men with a natural covered way from which to mount their attack. They, accordingly, filed across the dam, spread north along the
depression, and then lay on its western slope, annoyed but not hurt by
the Confederate case shot passing over their heads. Even lying under
Graham's fire proved "most trying" to the new 198th Pennsylvania, but
the veteran soldiers and their experienced commanders readily appreciated the advantages that the ravine provided. Those warwise troops
also knew better than to leave their knapsacks behind, but the inexperienced 198th dutifully stripped to what was thought to be fighting trim
and naïvely left its packs untended in the ravine.[6]

Bringing up and deploying his First Division in difficult terrain helps
account for Warren's delay in attacking. So does his decision to await
the arrival of the IX Corps. Once his van reached the church, the New
Yorker at last took steps to unblock the logistical bottleneck that had
so long retarded Parke's advance. In solving this problem, the junior
officer could do nothing about the paucity of roads, nor did he feel he
could hasten his First Division's progress. His solution was rather to
remove his Second Division from the procession by now shifting it a
short way north on the Vaughan Road and deploying it astride that
highway facing northward. There Ayres could protect the right flank of
the striking force against any effort to cut it off from the Weldon Railroad. Even more importantly, moving the Second Division aside at last
cleared the road for Parke to come up behind Griffin to the clearing at
Widow Smith's, where the Pennsylvanian could finally begin carrying
out his own mission of crossing Arthur's Swamp, moving to Watkins',
and turning the Confederate right. As soon as Ayres moved to his new
position, the IX Corps duly advanced, and its van reached the church a

little after noon. Once Parke himself arrived, he and Warren further modified the original plan to permit the IX Corps to be used more effectively. Instead of sending Potter's whole force into the widow's field simply to wait for a new road to be cut across the swamp, they kept it right around the church—Curtin facing west astride the road, Simon Griffin to his right facing north, and Willcox coming up from the east. That way Parke's Second Division and his First, too, could readily support Griffin until the new road was ready for them.

Only Potter's engineers, the 7th Rhode Island of the First Brigade, actually moved down to Widow Smith's to begin cutting the passage. The 7th came under artillery fire overshooting Griffin and soon discovered as well some Butternuts still holding out in the thickets along the creek south of the Poplar Spring Road. The Rhode Islanders now deployed as skirmishers, and Curtin backed them up with the 21st Massachusetts and 48th Pennsylvania. The Yankees pressed on over the field and through the brush and thickets, expecting heavy resistance. The Secessionists, however, proved only to be outposts, who fled before this determined advance without firing a shot. The Union skirmishers reached their target, a hill near the stream, without opposition. To guard against further interference, the reinforcements remained at the widow's house. The 7th, meantime, made initial preparations to start cutting the road. Whether assigning so few troops to carry out the important first phase of Meade's projected turning movement was wise is difficult to say. As matters worked out, though, leaving the bulk of the IX Corps near the church placed it in just the right position. Before the acting engineers could actually begin working on the road across the swamp, the slow-moving developments around Peebles's farm finally reached a climax at about 1:00 P.M.[7]

It is not certain that Warren and Griffin desired to precipitate fighting even then, before Ayres too could reach the front. Most available information for early afternoon pertains to the generals' actions rather than their intentions. The division commander definitely reinforced his skirmish line with part of the 155th Pennsylvania of his Second Brigade and then pushed all the voltigeurs up the western slope of the ravine into the woods along the southeastern part of Peebles's farm. Edward Graham's heavy fire of case shot plus "furious enfilading fire from an unseen foe lurking in the woods on the left front" (evidently Confederate outposts on Wilkinson's farm) stopped the Northern skirmishers there. The Yankees then took cover behind trees and in a shallow depression and returned the fire. Griffin meantime chose not to press their advance until he could finish deploying his main body along the bottom of the ravine, safe from the torrent of shells soaring overhead. After much difficult maneuvering through the thickets and sev-

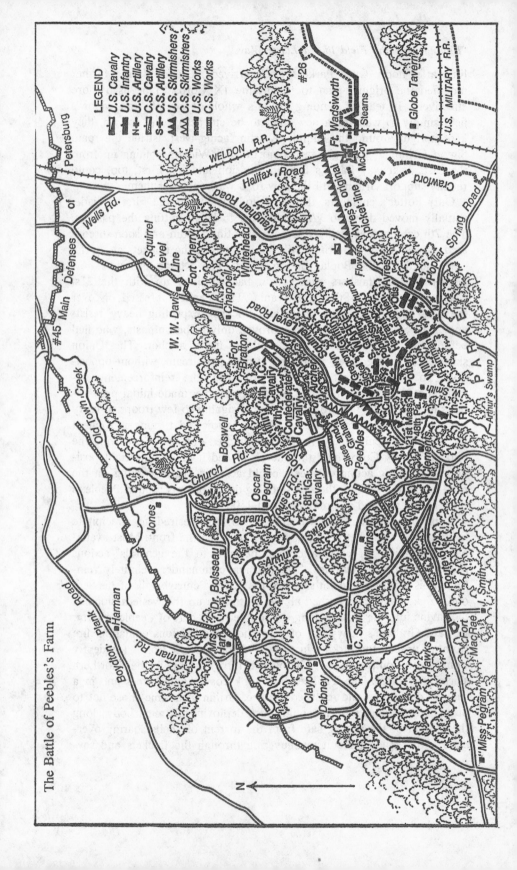

The Battle of Peebles's Farm

LEGEND
U.S. Cavalry
U.S. Infantry
N— U.S. Artillery
C.S. Cavalry
s— C.S. Artillery
U.S. Skirmishers
C.S. Skirmishers
U.S. Works
C.S. Works

eral repositionings of individual regiments, he finally managed to stretch his force out in a single line of battle north of the Poplar Spring Road. Sickel held the left of this line with his own regiment on the far left and the 21st Pennsylvania Cavalry (dismounted) next to it. Adjoining the First Brigade's right was Gregory, who probably posted the 32nd Massachusetts, 91st and then 155th Pennsylvania, left to right. Next came the 20th Maine and then the 118th Pennsylvania, which originally held Gwyn's far right and right center, respectively, but which now manned his far left and left center, respectively. His remaining three regiments not on the skirmish line—the 44th New York, 16th Michigan, and 83rd Pennsylvania—prolonged his line rightward, in that order.

The ravine necessarily forced this long, thin line to face west, virtually on an extension of a hypothetical southward prolongation of the trenches between Forts Cherry and Bratton. Should the First Division actually attack along this axis toward Wilkinson's, its right would be disastrously enfiladed by Fort Archer and both of its curtains. The experienced Griffin was not about to expose his troops to such danger, though. He, accordingly, directed that as soon as the soldiers advanced from the shelter of the ravine, each brigade would execute a half-right wheel that would shift its axis northwestward toward Fort Archer. Gwyn would then follow the skirmishers; Gregory would move up behind him; and Sickel would take position behind the Second Brigade. Once under way, the whole First Division would, in sum, ploy into a column of three brigade lines aimed straight at Sikes's stronghold. Like Charles Field and Richard H. Anderson about the same hour that day some twenty-four miles away on Chaffin's Bluff, Griffin thus massed his forces to capture an enemy fort and sought to achieve that success through a complicated maneuver to be executed once the charge was in motion.

COMMENTARY

1. This map depicts the terrain over which the Battle of Poplar Spring Church was fought. Note the key intersections around Peebles's farm.

2. Troop dispositions show the tactical situation in the Battle of Peebles's Farm, just prior to the Northern attack about 1:00 P.M. Griffin is in the creek bottom, ready to ploy into column of brigade lines. Potter supports him; Willcox is moving forward; and Ayres is still to the right-rear.

3. Ayres's position is highly approximate. It cannot be proved that he deployed in that formation.

4. The two Yankee guns at the front were probably Robert Rogers'. The location of the other Union batteries is only approximate.

5. The relative order of Joel Griffin's three regiments is probably correct.

Also like those Confederate officers, the Federal general encountered difficulty carrying out the involved plan. The ensuing breakdown of execution is what creates the uncertainty over whether he and Warren intended attacking as early as 1:00 P.M. Some sources declare that some men in the ranks, impatient at the delay and tense at remaining under Secessionist fire, spontaneously broke into the charge and drew the rest of the division in after them. Other accounts maintain that the units attacked in obedience to orders. What may have happened is that the division started moving at Griffin's command but got out of control due to a breakdown on the skirmish line. The general, that is, apparently reinforced the voltigeurs with the rest of the 155th Pennsylvania just before attacking and definitely ordered the balance of the 20th Maine to such duty just as the division began advancing. The 20th duly moved up to the skirmishers and, finding them reluctant to leave the sheltering depression, swept on past them and broke into the charge itself. The sight of that one regiment attacking evidently prompted other outfits to join in on their own.[8]

As one regiment after another began charging—some right away, others only after understandable uncertainty and delay—the beautiful formation Griffin had projected disintegrated into a number of smaller lines that surged over the field like a great blue torrent. The 44th New York, starting late, lost its place in line and apparently had to shift to the Third Brigade's left center. The 118th and 16th meantime closed the gap thus created and pressed on, side by side. North of the Michiganders, the 83rd too initially held back but soon came forward on the far right. To Gwyn's left, Gregory and his officers at first attempted to halt their men to ploy them behind the Third Brigade. The soldiers would have none of that. Their comrades were charging, and they would charge, too. The 32nd and 91st pressed on until they came abreast of Gwyn's left. Both brigades then swept up their waiting skirmishers and kept on advancing, side by side. Sickel, on the other hand, apparently tried to keep his assigned place behind the Second Brigade, only to have the clumsy new 198th Pennsylvania completely misunderstand orders and drop back into the woods to the left rear. His assistant adjutant general, however, brought the regiment back to join the 21st behind Gregory shortly after Gwyn's van reached the works.

Seeing his division advancing that way could hardly have pleased the sturdy old Regular Griffin, yet it did not disturb him either, now that the troops were on the proper axis toward Fort Archer. Two years' service at the head of those stalwart veterans made him confident that, even partially disorganized, they could still accomplish their task. "Never mind about keeping the men in line," he reportedly exclaimed;

"tell them to go and they will go if only you will let them."[9] Go they did: up out of the creek bottom, over the Squirrel Level Road, across the southeastern part of the field, down into a little depression east of and around Peebles's abandoned plantation house, then up toward the earthworks. From ravine to ramparts was only some 600 to 800 yards —short enough, the troops felt, to justify them rushing. Unlike Stannard's deliberately restrained columns advancing against Fort Harrison on the previous day, Griffin's men intentionally ran toward the Southern line in hopes of reducing the duration of their exposure to enemy fire.

The Graycoat skirmishers greeted them with one blast of musketry and then fled into the main defenses in order to unmask those works. The Confederate parapets now crackled with carbine and rifle fire of Joel Griffin's dismounted troopers. Graham's four guns discharged a few more solid shot and then sent canister ripping into the blue ranks. This fire, though still high on Graham's part, cut down some Unionists, checked the 21st Pennsylvania Cavalry, and forced at least the 83rd Pennsylvania to pause briefly for cover in the swale in the field. Griffin's main body, however, kept right on coming. Pioneers from the 16th Michigan and 118th Pennsylvania now rushed forward to hack paths through the frise wide enough for eight men. Through these openings many of their comrades poured. Elsewhere, other units penetrated or even leaped over the abatis—"not . . . much of an impediment," the senior subordinate of the 1st Michigan later chuckled.[10] Still elsewhere, some outfits simply worked their way around to the curtains, in whose front no frise was emplaced. As these seemingly unstoppable Northerners neared the works themselves, many Butternut cavalrymen panicked and fled—mostly up the Church Road, a few northward along the trenches toward Fort Bratton. Graham, too, managed to discharge only two or three blasts of canister before he began limbering up as he saw the Federals crossing the abatis. Other Confederates, including Sikes's garrison, however, stood to their posts for the final struggle. It soon broke around them.

The Bluecoats, streaming through or around the obstructions, now jumped into the moat. Some, burdened down with their knapsacks, had difficulty getting out. Many more, though, soon clambered up the exterior slope and planted their flags on the ramparts; among the first banners raised were those of the 83rd and 155th Pennsylvania. The first unit actually to cross the parapet was the 20th Maine on the far left. Almost immediately afterward the 16th Michigan surged over the salient of the redoubt. Colonel Norval E. Welch of the 16th, separated from his main force by the disorderly advance, meantime hurried to the crest of the unfinished ramparts a little to the Union right of the fort.

"Forward, men," he called out to those behind him; "a commission to him who first mounts this parapet with me." Before his comrades arrived, though, some defenders still in the area got to him and sent his lifeless body plummeting back into the moat, with two bullets in his head.[11] Angered, not daunted, by the death of their leader, his men pressed on to avenge him. Though the strange Lindsay rifles—guns that fired two bullets from one barrel—that they were combat testing were now out of ammunition, the Michiganders wisely did not stop to reload them but pressed on to capture the northeastern curtain with clubbed musket and bayonet alone. With that sector cleared, the 16th and 83rd then swung around in rear of the fort to cut off Sikes's retreat. Gwyn's remaining units, now reinforced by Gregory's, meantime continued swarming over the front of the redoubt. Even Sickel's two regiments finally came forward to join the onrush. In a matter of minutes the whole First Division surged over Fort Archer and overwhelmed or drove off the last defenders.

Most of the garrison—including the 7th's bannerman, his flag ripped with eighteen bulletholes—managed to escape before the Northerners could sweep across their front and the 16th and 83rd could cut off their retreat. About fifty, though, fell into Union hands near the sally port, among them Sikes himself, who surrendered to the commander of the 83rd. Two of Graham's cannons, too, were able to flee the fort just in the nick of time. A third one, however, was almost taken and was only saved when a hard-fighting postillion, armed with a whip, unhorsed a pursuing Yankee officer who attempted to saber him. The remaining piece, a 3-inch rifle, was not so fortunate. As its crew started to pull it off, Lieutenant Albert Fernald of the 20th got the drop on its driver and forced him to halt. Some cavalrymen then tried to free the gun by shooting the Maine man but only managed to hit the poor artillery horses and thus permanently immobilized the piece. Seizing this gun was particularly welcome for the Bluecoats; it was the first cannon the V Corps had captured since the great campaign of 1864 began nearly five months before. Taking this one piece, moreover, was especially appropriate, for it was not a real Virginia rifle at all but one the Secessionists themselves had captured from the 10th Massachusetts Battery at Second Reams's Station on August 25. The gun was promptly hauled back to Globe Tavern—home at last.

Even before the cannon was moved east, the Federal commanders headed west amid the turmoil to the captured fort. Colonel Gwyn did not quite make it. As he attempted to ride up the exterior slope, his horse slipped and fell on him, injuring him so painfully that he had to relinquish command to Major Ellis Spear of the 20th Maine. Though the junior officer himself would be wounded later in the afternoon, he apparently remained in charge of the Third Brigade for the rest of the day. General Griffin meantime fared better, and as he entered Fort Archer, his men greeted him with loud cheers. Within ten minutes Warren himself, who had viewed the battle from the woods back near the church, rode out over the field, also to be met with resounding huzzahs.

Before the major general arrived, the division commander congratulated his men on their sparkling victory, but he reminded them that they still had work to do. From the stronghold he could see some Graycoats, including two of Graham's guns, rallying in a little lunette at the northwestern corner of the field, where the Church Road enters the woods between Peebles's and Oscar Pegram's farms. He promptly sent his veterans to capture that earthwork, too. The 1st Michigan and 18th Massachusetts accidently diverged north toward Chappell's farm, but the main body surged on toward the lunette. All semblance of order was gone now; to one of Gregory's men, the First Division just seemed to go "rolling over the field like a large wave."[12] Spearheaded by the 155th Pennsylvania, this wave washed over the lunette and swept away all resistance after a brief but fierce encounter. The two cannon and the defenders now continued their flight up the Church Road. Behind them, the lunette and Fort Archer and all the works on Peebles's farm remained in Federal hands.

This was as much as Griffin could accomplish. He now regrouped his men around and just beyond Fort Archer to let them rest and refit, while his superiors decided what to do next. The First Division deserved that rest. It had captured one cannon, nearly sixty prisoners, and, above all, the key position on the entire Squirrel Level Line. Well could Warren exclaim that "the Fifth Corps has done splendidly today; principally Griffin." By 1:15 or 1:30 P.M. at the latest, the division had called Lee's bluff, punched right through his outer defenses, and opened the way to the Boydton Plank Road itself. Now all that was needed were fresh troops to press on to seize it.[13]

Such fresh troops were certainly available: Parke's five brigades at Poplar Spring Church. Indeed, Curtin's men, forming column, had actually hurried out toward Peebles's field during the V Corps's charge and had nearly been raked by Graham's last cannonball as they crossed the dam over Arthur's Swamp. Only timely ducking by the entire 35th Massachusetts allowed the shot to pass harmlessly overhead rather than to slaughter the regiment. The First Brigade, including the 21st and 48th from Widow Smith's, did not arrive in time to help storm Fort Archer, but it did now press northward up the Squirrel Level Road in line of battle. By then, however, that area too had been overrun by Griffin's skirmishers. The colonel merely advanced in their

wake through the woods to Chappell's field and Fort Bratton. There he
halted and took up a defensive position from the fort southwest toward
the V Corps's sector. Nor did Potter's Second Brigade accomplish any
more. It followed Curtin as far as Peebles's farm and then occupied the
captured works on the northern part of the field west of Griffin. Behind
Simon Griffin came more fresh troops, Willcox's—again right along the
Poplar Spring Road rather than via the now-abandoned route the
Rhode Islanders had been cutting across the swamp. Contrary to
Parke's subsequent report, the First Division, too, initially did no more
than continue prolonging the line to the left. Hartranft extended southward and southeastward through the woods on the western part of the
farm from the Second Division's left nearly to Clements' house, just
north of where Route 673 entered the Squirrel Level Road from the
west. Harriman, facing south, then completed the line back to the main
stream of Arthur's Swamp by deploying along the left bank of that
creek's northwestern fork. McLaughlen and at least three IX Corps
batteries—the 34th, the 7th, and D—meantime went into general
reserve near Peebles's house, and one of Wainwright's batteries perhaps
soon joined them. Battery B/1st New York Light Artillery, in contrast,
actually took position along the curtain west of Fort Archer, and Battery H/1st New York Light Artillery of the V Corps and possibly also
Monroe's remaining company soon unlimbered there, too. Also coming
up from the rear at this time was Griffin's original picket line, which no
longer needed to remain along the Vaughan Road south of Flowers'.
The pickets, too, simply rejoined their regiments and did not move beyond Peebles's.

This, then, was how the Unionists used their fresh troops to follow
up Griffin's breakthrough—not to pursue and seek out new advantages
but to take up a vast defense perimeter to secure their initial conquest
on Peebles's farm.[14]

From this stronghold they sent out no more than probes and pickets
to develop the new enemy position. Hartranft, for instance, dispatched
the 2nd and 20th Michigan under Lieutenant Colonel Byron Mac
Cutcheon of the 20th south to Clements', thence west along Route 673
or the Wilkinson lane in a vain search either for the Butternuts or even
for Simon Griffin's pickets. The Hampshireman's pickets were out, all
right—Curtin, for that matter, advanced some, too—but the Michiganders simply failed to locate them. Harriman fared slightly better.
When an initial reconnaissance disclosed no Secessionists south of the
northwestern fork, he crossed that branch to the eastern end of Route
673. There he posted four regiments astride the Squirrel Level Road,
kept the other two in reserve, and detached scouts along Route 673.
The reconnaissance party went as far west as Fort MacRae, which it

occupied, without encountering any Confederates. From the redoubt the outposts finally spotted a few mounted gray videttes hovering still farther west. Nowhere south or southwest of Peebles's, though, did the Yankees locate the enemy in strength.

Things were different northwest and north of the farm. There, ironically enough, it was Griffin's men, who had fought so hard at Fort Archer, who continued carrying the attack to the Southerners. Some of his troops who had stormed the lunette now continued through the woods onto Oscar Pegram's farm in skirmishing order and at least confronted, if not fought with, Dearing's Brigade regrouping there. Even before then, part of the 1st Michigan plus the 18th Massachusetts accidentally diverged northward from the main body during the final charge on the lunette. Alone now, they deployed as skirmishers to cover the division's right and to protect themselves and then moved through the woods to Chappell's farm to see what they could find. They found Fort Bratton and part of Ferebee's 4th North Carolina Cavalry. The Tarheels, though, lacked either the strength or the stamina to resist even skirmishers and soon fled up the Squirrel Level Road to Fort Cherry. There they rallied on some more of their regiment plus infantry pickets and a brass gun at about 1:15. But when the infantry and artillery support shifted elsewhere about forty-five minutes later, the 4th by itself again proved no match for the two Yankee regiments, which soon overran W. W. Davis', too.

Confederate resistance finally stabilized north of the plantation—initially because the 1st and 18th at last ran out of steam. Curtin's brigade had by now moved up in their wake as far as Chappell's but gave them no help on the fighting line above Fort Cherry. Again it fell to Griffin and Spear to keep up the action. The 16th Michigan and 83rd Pennsylvania, soon reinforced by the 44th New York, came forward to join the two regiments north of W. W. Davis'. But by then, more than a small detachment was needed in that sector. As early as 11:45 A.M., Archer and MacRae, on learning of the threat to Joel Griffin, had struck their tents and shifted a little way left—presumably to the woods behind Battery No. 45—to be ready if the threat actually materialized. Now that that danger had been realized and was spreading up the Squirrel Level Road toward Petersburg itself, Butternut infantry at last moved out to meet it. Southern skirmishers—perhaps from Heth's two brigades, perhaps Mahone's sharpshooter battalions—finally challenged the Yankees north of Fort Cherry. Even when reinforced to five regiments, Spear's men found their hands full simply resisting the counterjabs of the increasingly aggressive Graycoats. If the Unionists were to overcome this opposition, they would clearly need more than one demibrigade.[15]

Such support, eight brigades of it, was readily available back on Peebles's farm—and there it stayed. The IX Corps remained preoccupied
with holding the defense line and with scouting along Route 673.
Griffin's main body, too, stood on the defensive astride the Church
Road. The V Corps troops understandably needed time to rest and
regroup. Most soldiers put this time to good use, catching their breath,
but a few knaves among them took advantage of the respite to plunder
their own comrades' knapsacks that the 198th had naïvely left back
in the ravine. Even veteran troops who only now laid aside their packs
suffered from the pillagers. And in the immediate aftermath of the capture of Fort Archer, while fighting still raged around the lunette, one
Maine captain went so far as to murder a captured Confederate
crouching in the redoubt—much to the disgust of most Federals present. Most prisoners, though, were safely carried off to Globe Tavern,
glad to be removed from the battlefield. Stealing, too, eventually came
to an end. And slowly the First Division regained its formation. But
even then it was kept on the defensive, reversing the captured earthworks. For over an hour the strike force remained busily inactive.[16]

Several factors apparently account for this delay. Griffin's need to
regroup after his disorganized charge was genuine. Equally legitimate
was the necessity to take some security precautions against counterattack—a blow that the course of the siege these past three months
suggested was almost inevitable. Beyond guarding Peebles's farm itself
against such a strike, the expeditionary force also had to maintain its
security back to Globe Tavern. The last time the V Corps had ventured
west from Meade's works in mid-August, it had nearly been cut off by
an attack against its right flank. Warren now guarded against any similar danger. Even before receiving at 1:45 Humphreys' suggestion of
1:00 P.M. that he maintain connection with the original works, the
corps commander had posted his Second Division on the Vaughan
Road. There Ayres not only unblocked the IX Corps's route but also
lent support to his 500 pickets still in place between Flowers' and Fort
Wadsworth. On learning from that same dispatch of 1:00 P.M. that
Meade had pulled the Iron Brigade, too, into reserve, Warren requested that it move west to prolong the outposts from Flowers' to Peebles's and thus enable Ayres and the last three batteries to join the
other three divisions at the front.

Before 3:00, however, the corps commander received word that
Ayres's original picket line itself had pushed up the Vaughan Road
from Flowers' to beyond Whitehead's and had linked up with Spear's
skirmishers east of W. W. Davis'. The major general, therefore, instructed Crawford at 3:30 that Bragg should remain at Globe Tavern;
the New Yorker even added that Hofmann would probably rejoin the

Third Division after dark—moves clearly designed to make sure that the Secessionists, if they struck still farther east, would not recapture the Weldon Railroad itself. Still more importantly, the presence of a continuous skirmish line between Forts Wadsworth and Cherry permitted Warren to order Ayres to rejoin the main body. The division commander, accordingly, detached the 146th New York of his First Brigade to move up the Vaughan Road to support the cavalry outposts above Flowers' and then led his main body west along the Poplar Spring Road to Peebles's, thence up the Squirrel Level Road to Chappell's. Not until sometime around 3:00–3:30 did his leading brigade, Otis', finally relieve Curtin around Fort Bratton to permit the Pennsylvanian to resume advancing. Even then, Ayres's other three brigades were still coming up.

All these reasons help explain the delay following the storming of Fort Archer: the need to maintain security at Peebles's farm and back to Fort Wadsworth, the need to regroup Warren's First Division and bring forward his Second Division. Yet one questions that the whole strike force had to be tied down on the defensive and that no forces but five of Spear's regiments could try to exploit the victory right after it was gained, while Southern resistance was necessarily weakest. At least as influential as the foregoing reasons were the same misgivings, concerns, and fears of ultimate responsibility that had slowed Warren east of Poplar Spring Church all morning. He admittedly promised army headquarters at about 1:45–2:00 that "I will push up as fast as I can get my troops in order toward Petersburg on the Squirrel Level road." His actions make clear, however, that worry over being counterattacked outweighed his commitment to renewing the advance. Parke's conduct throughout the afternoon, moreover, reveals him even more hesitant than the New Yorker in his unaccustomed role of corps commander. These personal shortcomings of the two responsible generals plus their worry about strong Confederate forces reported to have been in the area earlier in the week completely paralyzed their strike force for a crucial hour following the breakthrough at Fort Archer. By giving rise to these fears in the Yankee leaders, those phantom forces from outdated Union intelligence reports did a far better job than Joel Griffin's shaky troopers of retarding the Federal advance and guarding Lee's supply lines in early afternoon.

That the corps commanders lacked up-to-the-minute intelligence of the enemy is understandable. They did not, however, lack awareness of what Meade expected of them. Despite the limited scope of his original written instructions that morning, he had previously made clear to both subordinates that they were to press on beyond Peebles's to the Boydton Plank Road, perhaps even to Petersburg itself. What the junior officers lacked now was not directives but direction—firm and effective control by one commander with the authority and the will to infuse action into his executive officers. Had either Parke or Warren commanded the strike force instead of acting as coequals, they might at least have achieved a greater measure of co-ordination—though their individual hesitancy would likely have still retarded the advance. Better yet, Meade himself or at least Humphreys should have come to the front by now to take charge of the second stage of the attack. The need to assess the priority of possible targets plus the desirability of being on hand to meet the potential enemy response to thrusts into such sensitive sectors were sufficient reasons for one or both officers to have joined the striking force by the time it overran Peebles's farm. Once there, they could also have made sure that their subordinates devoted more energies to advancing than to taking up defensive positions. By not coming to the front, army headquarters thus shares with the corps commanders blame for the delay that settled over the expeditionary force following Griffin's victory.[17]

Meade and Humphreys instead remained back at permanent V Corps headquarters at Globe Tavern, where they had arrived at noon. At least, they were hardly idle there. From that fixed spot on the western end of the telegraph line, they kept in touch with the far-flung units of the entire Army of the Potomac, not just with the strike force. News they received from those other outfits as they rode to and stayed at the tavern was sufficiently important, they felt, to justify them remaining at the railhead rather than moving on to Peebles's.

The most far-reaching tidings came from Gregg. The cavalryman had turned out his troopers at 3:00 A.M. and had them ready to march by daybreak to be prepared for whatever day might bring. When daylight came and several hours passed without a renewed Confederate onslaught, he informed Birchett's at 8:45 that Secessionist videttes faced him on the Halifax, Wyatt, and Lower Church roads, but that Hampton had not attacked him. Soon thereafter he received Humphreys' orders of 9:00 A.M. to advance west to E. Wilkinson's to secure the lower end of the Squirrel Level Road. Smith's battered brigade, badly pummeled on Thursday, could hardly lead this advance, so it was scattered on relatively minor assignments. The 2nd Pennsylvania Cavalry took over far-southern outpost duty from the 1st New Jersey Cavalry at and around Reams's Station, and the 8th Pennsylvania Cavalry, too, went on picket. The other three regiments, led by Smith and Gregg themselves, rode back to Wyatt's near 10:00 A.M. The 4th remained there throughout the day, but the 13th later moved on to support the First Brigade. The Maine men meanwhile marched up the Lower Church Road to try to establish contact with the strike force.

While the Second Brigade scattered itself out for nearly five miles, Davies' four relatively fresh regiments moved out to execute Humphreys' directive. Without waiting for Beaumont, who rejoined them only sometime after they had started moving and just as they were about to enter a fight, they struck west along the Wyatt Road and handily chased the few Confederate videttes in their path back to the Vaughan Road. Immediately east of that key intersection and west of McDowell's house, the Bluecoats briefly halted to throw up light works commanding the junction. Some of Davies' men, including part of the Jersey unit when it arrived, remained in those defenses, backed up by the 13th from just east of the main stream of Arthur's Swamp. At least the 10th New York Cavalry, closely supported by the 1st Massachusetts Cavalry, however, shortly resumed moving west on the Vaughan Road, and the 6th Ohio Cavalry and 1st Pennsylvania Cavalry either went with them or soon joined them. Beaumont's main body, too, reached them before long. The 10th now found out what Smith had learned the previous day: Butler's outposts could make a determined stand in the heavy woods through which the road ran near E. Wilkinson's. Their resistance was sufficient for Gregg to call it to Meade's attention at 12:10 and to report that the whole Confederate Cavalry Corps might lie farther west on the Vaughan Road, where it had fallen back on Thursday night. This dispatch or another, more explicit one, now lost, caused Lieutenant Colonel Orville Babcock, Grant's liaison officer with Meade, and presumably the army commander himself to infer at 12:45 that "Gregg . . . has a very heavy force in his front."

Developments in early afternoon, however, led the Northern high command to much different assessments. Whether due to weakening of the Secessionist force or to simple inability to withstand continued pressure from the New Yorkers and Massachusetts men, resistance north of Hatcher's Run collapsed, and the outposts fell back virtually to the left bank of the stream, where they resumed skirmishing in behalf of the works on the far side. Gregg followed them as far as Mrs. Cummings' and evidently again sent detachments over to the Duncan Road at Armstrong's. At both ford and mill he now detected strong forces in the trenches on the right bank—too strong to be overcome, he judged. Unlike on Thursday his current mission was not to raid, yet it was not really to seek battle either. Protecting the left rear of the expeditionary force and locating and observing Hampton sufficed. The Pennsylvanian, accordingly, contented himself with finding at least some Graycoats along the stream and did not try to force his way across. Indeed, he soon withdrew his more westerly party to the Vaughan Road, where his First Brigade continued keeping an eye on the Secessionists. The apparent collapse of resistance north of the run, his ability to remain in his forward position unchallenged, and the absence of any other signs of the enemy's main force now convinced him that Hampton's corps remained south of that stream.[18]

Such an assessment hardly reassured Meade when it reached him shortly before 2:25. He understandably but inaccurately inferred from that report and the one of 12:10 that the entire Southern Cavalry Corps had fallen back behind Hatcher's Run. Yet he correctly realized that all those troops would hardly remain inactive during a major Union offensive. If they were not in Gregg's front and could not be detected north of the creek, they might just move around his left and strike the Federal army's vulnerable, generally unguarded rear somewhere east of the Weldon Railroad. Hampton's daring cattle raid all the way to the James River below City Point only two weeks earlier demonstrated the feasibility of such a move and underscored its danger. The virtual absence of any defenders on the rear line and the inability of the Second Cavalry Division, now out of defensive position west of the Weldon Railroad, to provide anything more than warning of a raid east of the tracks made the problem all the more acute. The army commander, therefore, spent part of his time at Globe Tavern making sure his infantry commanders would be ready if the enemy struck.

Four hours before this problem arose, the careful Meade took steps to provide more adequate protection for his rear than the 16th Pennsylvania Cavalry could offer. He ordered Williams to send troops from Birchett's to secure two key points opposite the II Corps and to help patrol the area north of the Jerusalem Plank Road. Promptly on receiving these instructions at 10:30, the staff officer relayed them to Spaulding and Patrick. The engineer, in turn, sent Major Wesley Brainerd with parts of Companies B, E, and G of the 50th New York Engineers to man Fort Bross and its adjacent curtains, where the Norfolk Railroad passed out of the rear line about two miles northeast of the Jerusalem Plank Road. The Provost Marshal General comparably dispatched his available infantry—the 114th Pennsylvania and six companies of the 68th Pennsylvania under Colonel Charles Collis of the 114th—to hold and continue fortifying the incomplete redoubt commanding the key intersection at Prince George Court House. Patrick also sent his available horsemen—at least the 3rd Pennsylvania Cavalry and K/1st Indiana Cavalry under Major James Walsh of the 3rd (but apparently not the other three mounted escort companies, which evidently accompanied Meade westward)—to help the 16th patrol the guerrilla-infested region north of the plank road. Meade ordered these moves, more immediately, to oppose irregulars and, more generally, to serve as precautions against some possible major attack. The reported threat from Hampton later in the day now made such precautions seem justified.

Yet even they did not satisfy the army commander now that a major incursion into his rear appeared distinctly possible. Rather than send the remaining three companies of the 50th plus the U. S. Engineer Battalion from Birchett's to the rear line, he notified the infantry commanders in the works to be ready to meet the potential raid. At 2:25 he informed supreme headquarters of the danger and requested that Benham patrol the approaches to City Point, particularly the road running eastward from the main outpost at Old Court House. Grant duly forwarded the message to the brigadier, ordered him to post strong picket forces on that route, and offered to lend him the battalion of the 5th U. S. Cavalry from the headquarters escort to help cover his front. The engineer had vainly sought the Regulars earlier in the month, but now he apparently declined them, presumably because some other horsemen, likely B/3rd Pennsylvania Cavalry from the provost detachment at City Point, patrolled his sector. He did, however, alert and bolster his engineer pickets on his far left and also Colonel Joseph Mathews' 200 and 205th Pennsylvania at Old Court House, as required.

Alerting Benham and posting Collis and Brainerd helped secure the left half of the rear lines but did not provide for the safety of the center rear, which Robison's troopers could not hope to defend against a determined attack. Meade had already directed II Corps headquarters, during his stop at Shand's in midmorning, to have its reserves ready to cope with any threat to the rear. Now that such a danger seemed real, he requested Hancock at 2:30 "to keep a lookout for the [Jerusalem] plank road, so as to meet such a movement if attempted." On receiving these instructions seventy minutes later, the subordinate borrowed a section of the last remaining reserve artillery combat unit, the 14th Massachusetts Battery, to send to Battery No. 37 on the rear line immediately west of the plank road. He also dispatched Colonel John Pulford's 5th Michigan of Mott's reserve Second Brigade to garrison that and nearby redoubts—presumably No. 36 and Fort Stevenson just to the west, No. 38 on the re-entrant covering the highway, and Fort Blaisdell on the plank road itself. The major general, in addition, transferred two of Miles's reserve regiments from the northern sector to the Norfolk Railroad between Avery's and Shand's houses to put them closer to the potentially threatened sector. Hancock further directed that if firing actually broke out around No. 37, Mott should rush the rest of Pierce's brigade there immediately and should even begin pulling out "such regiments from the front line as can be easiest withdrawn." Miles, under the same circumstances, was to go still farther:

He was to send his other five reserve regiments to join the two near corps headquarters and to strip his curtains of all but a skirmish line, leaving only the garrisons of redoubts intact. Gibbon's large reserve— 1,800 men, mostly from Murphy's brigade behind Fort Morton—was likely also alerted to reinforce the rear line if necessary.

Prior to 4:05 Hancock notified his superiors of his response yet pointed out that his primary mission of holding his front prevented him from actually committing his reserves to the rear line prematurely. That restraint, in turn, imposed the risk that, should the Graycoats overrun the 16th, they might be able to penetrate the works themselves before he could get enough reserves to the threatened sector to stop them. Could not Russell's brigade west of Fort Davis, he inquired, help defend the rear line west of the plank road?[19]

No reply from Humphreys has been found, but his silence, if genuine, was as eloquent as any answer could have been. The Negroes' line was now too attenuated to be reduced for other purposes. At 12:30 P.M. the Chief-of-Staff had placed the USCTs under Crawford's overall direction and ordered them to stretch west from Fort Howard to McCoy's right in order to relieve Bragg. Within the next thirty minutes or so, Stearns duly extended leftward, and Russell probably also stretched west to relieve some of the Negro First Brigade's attenuation. By the time Hancock's request arrived at 4:05, Ferrero was thus responsible for the entire line of curtains over three miles long between Forts Davis and Wadsworth—a task that ruled out sparing any men for the rear. Nor did the Iron Brigade assist Hancock. Even before it left the trenches, Bragg and Crawford—in a rare act of co-operation—used the resumption of active operations as a pretext for delaying compliance with City Point's order to transfer the famous old 19th Indiana to the II Corps, to be absorbed into the 20th Indiana. Once the brigade withdrew from the works, moreover, it did not move to the back line but simply remained in general reserve at its old camp near Dr. Gurley's after Warren made clear at 3:30 that he no longer needed it at Flowers'. Baxter, too, did no more than perhaps to increase the vigilance of the troops manning his own rear once Crawford learned from Humphreys of the possible cavalry raid.

Not even new troops the V Corps received from City Point were used to hold the rear line. The 210th Pennsylvania, 760 strong, reached the point on Wednesday evening, was assigned to Butler as usual, and actually moved to Bermuda Hundred the next day. Meade's particular desire for this outfit—his brother-in-law, Colonel William Sergeant, commanded it—plus Grant's decision to begin funneling all new units into the Army of the Potomac, however, caused it to be recalled to supreme headquarters almost immediately. It remained there overnight, and after much correspondence between logisticians, midday Friday, it left for Globe Tavern by special train shortly after 1:40 P.M. It might then have been used to garrison Fort Stevenson or even to reinforce Warren in the field, but the army commander himself earmarked it to enter the trenches just east of Fort Wadsworth and thereby permit Ferrero to draw in his overextended left. Results if not replies must have made clear to Hancock that army headquarters was not going to give him any support from Crawford.

The responsible, trustworthy II Corps commander apparently accepted this result in good grace and contented himself with extending his operational control over the small, independent units on the rear line and even at Birchett's. If they were going to be the only troops available, they could at least be used more effectively if brought under a single command. Officially he did not yet have charge of them, but practically he found out what forces were available where and then expressed his "wishes" concerning them to Williams—wishes that the staff officer promptly translated into orders. Now that he knew where the troops were, the major general could start issuing instructions of his own if the rear line actually came under attack. As yet, his outposts detected no signs of such an attack that afternoon, he reported, but should one occur, he was going to try to be ready for it.[20]

Having the reliable Hancock in charge must have reassured Meade, who clearly worried about the danger of being raided. The senior officer, in a sense, thus showed the same concern for defensive preparations while at Globe Tavern that afternoon that Warren and Parke were displaying at the same time out on Peebles's farm. Such precautions were understandable—indeed, necessary—under the circumstances. One wonders, though, if they really required the personal attention of Meade himself and could not have been satisfactorily handled by Humphreys or even Seth Williams.

The army commander, to be sure, also devoted his attention to other reports more closely related to the progress of his main attack. At 2:00 P.M. he received Warren's report of 1:30 that his First Division had stormed Peebles's farm. Twenty minutes later, the New Yorker's effusive dispatch of 1:45–2:00 arrived to amplify the first one and give signs that the V Corps was getting ready to press on toward its next objectives. The latter prospect may have convinced the Pennsylvanian that now was the time for him to go forward. After passing on the good news to Grant at 2:25 and to Hancock and Williams at 2:30 and after taking a little time to set in motion preparations to defend the rear line of works, Meade at last started for the front. Not until 2:45–3:00 or later—roughly six hours after he had ordered the striking force to move out—did he finally join it.

Whether or not the "Old Snapping Turtle" denounced his ranking subordinates for not exploiting the victory is not known. He probably did not, for he apparently found the IX Corps on the verge of going forward along an axis either paralleling the Church Road or else running northwest across country from Peebles's to the northern end of the Harman Road. Since that unit was already on and around Peebles's farm, he saw no point in making it adhere to the original plan of moving via Route 673 and the Harman Road. He instead accepted its new line of advance and sought to expedite its progress by issuing his own orders for it to press on to the Boydton Plank Road. He also ordered Warren to push Griffin forward abreast of Parke's right and to use Ayres (whether offensively or defensively is not known) farther to the right. Hardly had he issued these orders before the IX Corps resumed advancing at about 3:00.[21]

A little over an hour later the army commander, at Grant's suggestion, also finally took steps to use his cavalry as an integral part of the main striking force. After returning from Deep Bottom that morning, the lieutenant general stayed at City Point all day to remain in touch with both his embattled armies. Until well into the afternoon, however, he received no news from the Peninsula at all and scarcely any more from the Southside. The only dispatches he received from the Army of the Potomac were the message of 8:50 that the striking force was being launched, plus intelligence and signal reports that Williams forwarded to City Point as well as to Humphreys at 9:15, 9:30, 11:00–11:15, and 12:30–1:00. Most such reports were conflicting and relatively inconsequential, save for the last one to the effect that refugees claimed the Graycoats had laid five or six pontoon bridges over the Appomattox "to facilitate the falling back to a new line about three miles to the rear of the river."

Whether or not the General-in-Chief chafed at being kept in the dark by both Meade and Butler is not known, but there can be no doubt that when Grant at last received more substantial reports from them late in the afternoon, he found the news well worth waiting for. Even before learning of Weitzel's victory at Fort Harrison, the lieutenant general got word of Warren's breakthrough—first from Orville Babcock's telegram of 2:10, then from Meade's telegram of 2:25. Such tidings from Globe Tavern, coupled with the intelligence gathered prior to and during the Fifth Offensive, made him feel that a prize much bigger than a fort or a crossroads was within his reach, and he urged Meade not to let it elude him. "If the enemy can be broken and started, follow him up closely," he wrote the army commander at 3:00 P.M.; "I can't help believing that the enemy are prepared to leave Petersburg if forced a little." To help "force" the Confederates, he added fifteen minutes later that "if the enemy's cavalry has left Gregg's front he ought to push ahead, and if he finds no obstacle turn [the right flank of the enemy's] infantry." Hampton's apparent absence—to Meade a potential threat to his rear on the Jerusalem Plank Road—was to Grant a potential opportunity to threaten the Confederates' own rear on the Boydton Plank Road. Even more vitally, the General-in-Chief's keen instinct had penetrated his opponent's bluff and had discerned the essence of Lee's dilemma: Compelled to choose between saving his capital or his rail center, the Virginian would abandon Petersburg if he lost its lines of communications or if he needed its defenders to rescue Richmond.

Discerning the heart of a strategic situation does not, however, guarantee that either means or will are available to carry perception into effect. Executive officer Meade's doubts that his striking force was strong enough to carry Cockade City had all along restrained his will to try for grander objectives. It may be questioned that even the breakthrough at Peebles's farm caused him to share City Point's feeling that the rail center itself could be taken at this time. He did, however, conscientiously try to achieve at least the limited gain of reaching the Boydton Plank Road. To that end, he sent word at 4:15 P.M. for Gregg to leave one brigade to patrol the left rear of the expeditionary force and to send the other one west to Armstrong's house, thence north on the Duncan and Harman roads to cover Parke's left and cooperate in the drive toward the plank road. Also at 4:15 Meade notified supreme headquarters that the horsemen were ordered forward and that the IX Corps was already in motion.[22]

By midafternoon, after a delay of over an hour, the infantry and cavalry were at last moving out to try to reap the fruits of Griffin's initial victory. The interlude of cautious planning, precautions, and preparations seemed about to end. The grand onslaught appeared getting under way once more.

CHAPTER X

----◆----

"Push On . . . Without Reference to Any One Else"

To spearhead his advance, Parke chose his Second Division, the best-rested white division in the Army of the Potomac. Simon Griffin led the column north through the thin belt of woods separating Peebles's and Oscar Pegram's farms and on past Pegram's house. Curtin followed the Second Brigade as soon as Ayres relieved him around Fort Bratton; the colonel also called up the 7th Rhode Island from Widow Smith's to rejoin him on Pegram's. Hartranft, too, recalled his two detached regiments, but he apparently did not leave Peebles's to move up into Potter's left rear until they returned to him. McLaughlen followed Hartranft into the Second Division's right rear, and Harriman formed the rear of the column. The Wisconsinite set out before his scouts in Fort MacRae could get back. When they finally came in and reported seeing a few Confederate horsemen farther west, some Union troopers—perhaps the 1st Maine Cavalry—were dispatched to take their place on outpost on Route 673. By patrolling the southwestern sector, the mounted forces thus helped free part of the IX Corps to advance. Monroe, in contrast, provided no support; all his guns remained on Peebles's farm. As yet, only infantry moved forward over Pegram's toward the Boydton Plank Road in midafternoon.[1]

The IX Corps now occupied a large open field, which will be called "Pegram's farm," encompassing that farm plus those of Dr. Alfred Boisseau and J. D. Boswell. Woods surrounded the clearing on all sides. On the south a thin fringe of trees divided it from Peebles's farm.

On the east a heavy forest almost entirely covered the area between the Church and Squirrel Level roads. About one-fourth mile north of Pegram's house and from one-fourth to one-half mile north of the southern woods, another thicker line of trees separated Pegram's farm and Robert Jones's farm. Finally, almost impenetrable thickets marked the western edge of Pegram's farm, along the upper reaches of the northwestern branch of Arthur's Swamp. The Church Road ran along the eastern edge of Pegram's farm in its two-mile course from the Squirrel Level Road to the Boydton Plank Road. At the farm's southeastern corner the Pegram House Road branched off from the Church Road and slanted northwest for almost one-half mile to Pegram's farmhouse, then headed due north over a bald ridge and down through a depression before turning back east into the Church Road just north of the woods on the southern end of Jones's farm. From Pegram's house another lane cut southwest across Arthur's Swamp and eventually entered Route 673. Still a third lane ran west from the Pegram House Road for almost one-half mile from the southern edge of the northern woods to Dr. Boisseau's house, immediately east of Arthur's Swamp. Just above this last road, and northeast of the house, was a large field of sorghum, grown high enough to block all vision to the northeast. Almost one mile east-northeast of Dr. Boisseau's was Boswell's house, located in a small clearing on the east side of the Church Road slightly south of the woods on the northern end of Pegram's farm. From the vicinity of Boswell's a country road headed straight east through the forest for almost a mile from the Church Road to the Squirrel Level Road at Chappell's house.

North of the trees in the depression along the upper end of this large clearing of Pegram's farm was the open, undulating country of Jones's farm. Jones's plantation house itself stood just west of the Church Road a little over one-quarter mile north of the woods. Another quarter mile beyond that, the headwaters of the upper fork of Old Town Creek, a tributary of the Appomattox, flowed eastward through a ravine crossing the Church Road. Still another quarter mile north of the creek the road forked left and right to enter the Boydton Plank Road itself. Only a few incomplete log works on the height just north of the creek, part of the new inner line begun in mid-September, barred the way to Lee's vital artery. Along the western edge of this clearing the Harman Road ran due south, and from it a country lane headed east from Mrs. Hart's to the vicinity of Dr. Boisseau's. The eastern side of Jones's farm was bordered by additional heavy forests. Through them the lower fork of Old Town Creek flowed north from its source in the almost impenetrable swamp that lay between the Church Road and the Pegram House Road in the wooded depression north of Pegram's farm.[2]

Over this country the IX Corps now advanced. Simon Griffin continued leading Parke's column through Pegram's farm on the Pegram
House Road. As the Hampshireman passed beyond the V Corps's
outposts near the Pegram house, he threw out the 2nd New York
Mounted Rifles (dismounted) as skirmishers. Growing resistance from
gray voltigeurs (presumably from Dearing's Brigade) just north of the
house led Potter to order him to give his skirmishers more backing.
The brigadier duly deployed the 6th and 11th New Hampshire, left to
right, in line of battle at the head of his column and pushed the
Graycoats back toward the northern woods. About a quarter mile
north of the house they rallied and opened on him with Graham's battery. Again pursuant to instructions from the division commander, he
deployed his whole brigade in line of battle and pressed into the forest.
With so many troops to back them up, the Mounted Rifles were able to
clear out the woods and force the Secessionists up onto Jones's farm.

Before continuing after them in force, Parke stopped to perfect his
deployment. Simon Griffin kept on holding the front from the swampy
thickets where the lower fork of Old Town Creek rose to west of the
Pegram House Road. The Mounted Rifles remained on his skirmish
line, and behind them stood two lines of battle: the 2nd Maryland and
6th, 11th, and 9th New Hampshire, left to right, in the first line, and
the 179th New York, 56th Massachusetts, 32nd and 31st Maine, and
17th Vermont, left to right, in the second. To protract this line westward, Potter brought up his other brigade. Curtin entered Pegram's
farm on the Church Road, deployed right away, and moved northwest
with his right resting on the Pegram House Road until it reached Boisseau's lane and until his left extended to the doctor's house. Now Potter ordered the colonel to swing forward his right until it was abreast of
Simon Griffin. Thus posted, the First Brigade, too, was in two lines:
the 51st New York, 58th Massachusetts, 45th Pennsylvania, and 35th
Massachusetts, left to right, in the front, and the 36th and 21st Massachusetts and 48th Pennsylvania, left to right, behind. Curtin's two
Rhode Island regiments meantime remained farther in the rear near
Pegram's house—the 7th because it was just coming up with its engineer tools, and the 4th because it was assigned relatively easy provost
duty in appreciation of the fact that its 130 "loyalists" stayed on duty
for the operation under way despite the fact that their terms of service
had expired that morning. Except for these two detached regiments, the
Second Division thus concentrated into a powerful spearhead of
Parke's attack.

The First Division, in contrast, was widely dispersed with no greater
mission than supporting Potter and covering his flanks. Willcox entrusted his best subordinate, Hartranft, with the most crucial assign-

ment: operating directly with the Second Division to guard its vulnerable left flank. After moving up from Peebles's farm, Hartranft's brigade occupied a position facing almost straight west from Boisseau's to Arthur's Swamp opposite Pegram's house. From there the brigadier could see some Confederate horsemen occupying a line of works to the west—part of the Third Cavalry Division in the incomplete inner line that crossed the Harman Road near Mrs. Hart's. He wisely sent a skirmish line across the creek to observe them and to determine how easily this swamp could be crossed—getting through the tangled creek bottom proved quite difficult—but he did not advance his main body west of the stream. He thus remained in position to support the Second Division. When it began moving northward into the woods, he, preserving his formation, shifted northward by the right flank behind it. As its left brigade swung up northward and out westward, he made a right wheel so as to come into position facing north along a line running straight east from the swamp to just north of Boisseau's house. The 20th Michigan held the left of this line, and the 2nd Michigan, 60th Ohio, 46th New York, 24th New York Cavalry (dismounted), 50th Pennsylvania, and 1st Michigan Sharpshooters extended his line rightward in that order; details of skirmishers covered his front. He thus took position *en échelon* to the First Brigade of the Second Division, his right being overlapped by its left 150 yards to the front and his left extending beyond its exposed flank—the standard formation for covering the flank of an advancing line.

McLaughlen comparably moved forward in line of battle through the woods east of the Church Road to cover Simon Griffin's right and sent the 100th Pennsylvania ahead as skirmishers to connect with Potter's pickets. Finally, Willcox posted the 109th New York to guard the road leading southwest to Route 673 and deployed Harriman's other five regiments just west of Pegram's house to act as the general reserve to either Potter or Hartranft. All these infantry units continued operating without any artillery support. Monroe still left all his pieces back on Peebles's and committed none either to accompany Potter or to wait with Willcox in easy call.[3]

Getting these troops into position, of course, took time. But more than deploying his men now caused Parke to hesitate. He worried about those repeated sightings of Secessionist cavalry beyond his left, and he was concerned with the strength of the ramparts and garrison of the inner line of works that barred his way to the plank road. Defenses that the Butternuts, close up, knew were pitifully weak looked strong to the Yankees from afar. Obviously uncertain in his unaccustomed role of corps commander, the Pennsylvanian evidently allowed these worries to paralyze his advance. For the third time that day, delay settled over the Union strike force—this time for two hours. Ironically, Warren, who had delayed all morning himself, now rode up to Pegram's to urge his colleague forward. The junior officer managed to slap down the brash Monroe, who (as the observing Wainwright put it) "had neither the good sense nor the modesty to hold his tongue until his opinion was asked," but he achieved no results with the IX Corps commander himself. After making a determined but vain appeal, Warren abandoned the effort and returned to his own lines.[4]

This was a nice gesture on the part of the V Corps commander. He would have been more helpful, however, had he offered men as well as advice. Parke certainly expected him to unmask Charles Griffin's division and move it up to Potter's right, and Meade reportedly counted on about the same thing. Warren did not do this, though, so his First Division continued to rest back at Peebles's farm all the while. Ayres, also, apparently did no more than to bring his own Third and Second brigades into position across Chappell's farm east of the Regulars. The batteries he escorted forward, meantime, joined most of the other artillery in general reserve on the Peebles's house knoll. The V Corps, in sum, contributed nothing to the advance toward the Boydton Plank Road.

As the crisis of the battle approached, a dangerous lapse of command thus flawed the Union effort. The IX Corps was being allowed to threaten one of Lee's most sensitive sectors—a move sure to provoke heavy resistance—all by itself, while available reinforcements did virtually nothing right under the eyes of their corps commander and of the army commander himself. Meade contented himself with issuing orders from Fort Archer for the three divisions to advance and then moved into Peebles's house at about 4:15 "to wait developments," as his aide called it.[5] But he evidently did nothing to revitalize Parke or to make sure the V Corps joined him. A dilatory strike commander, an uncooperative support commander, an over-all commander who failed to exert a unifying influence at the most crucial time—these failures of leadership boded ill for the impending Yankee advance toward the plank road.

Only the test of battle, however, would reveal how dangerous these shortcomings might be. That test finally came late that cloudy afternoon. Shortly before 5:00 P.M. Parke at last directed his men to attack. Confident that Hartranft would cover his left and that Charles Griffin would protect his right, the corps commander requested his Second Division to strike straight ahead. As Potter later put it: "I was ordered to push on with my whole force as rapidly as practicable, without reference to any one else." "Without reference to any one else"—that was a dangerous expression. Potter, in fact, needed to advance in reference to four other officers: Hartranft and Charles Griffin, the supposed guardians of his flanks, and also Wade Hampton and Cadmus M. Wilcox, whose Confederate reinforcements had at last arrived to counter this threat to Lee's vital communications.[6]

Probably the first high-ranking Southern officer to learn that the outer defense line had collapsed was Hampton, who received news of the Federal onslaught just after reaching Dearing's headquarters on the Squirrel Level Road north of Peebles's farm on an inspection tour. Although he arrived too late to save Fort Archer, the South Carolinian was at least in position to co-ordinate initial efforts to contain the breakthrough. His role in establishing a new defense line near W. W. Davis' is not clear, but he unquestionably took steps to block the enemy's other line of advance up the Church Road. He definitely rushed both brigades and two guns of "Rooney" Lee's Division from their temporary camp on the Boydton Plank Road to occupy the incomplete works south of that highway, and he probably also helped rally Joel Griffin's men in those defenses astride the Church Road just north of Jones's house. The corps commander presumably also sent word to Hill that the Yankees had stormed the advance line.

Whether or not his supposed message arrived in time to affect the lieutenant general's planning is not clear. It is not known whether news of Fort Archer's fall or perhaps simply earlier reports from Joel Griffin that the enemy threatened Peebles's farm were what led Secessionist headquarters to order back to Petersburg Wilcox's two brigades, which were north of the Appomattox but had not yet entrained for Rice's Turnout. Whether Hill or only Lee himself issued those instructions, for that matter, remains uncertain. What is clear is that sometime shortly before 2:00 P.M.—while Field's and Hoke's infantry completed their deployment on the Northside, while Alexander's and Mitchell's gunners finished bombarding Ben Butler's lines, while Stannard's defenders braced themselves in Fort Harrison for the imminent onslaught —the last of the Confederate reinforcements Lee had summoned from Petersburg to counter the Army of the James reversed their march and quick-timed back to Cockade City. Now the Light Division would not be available to exploit any breakthrough on the Northside that afternoon or to renew any Southern attack or parry any Yankee thrust the next day. Even as Butler on Thursday had created an opening for Meade, so now on Friday Meade relieved the pressure on Butler.

By about 3:00 Wilcox's troops were back in the vicinity of Battery No. 45. There they waited for approximately one hour, presumably to see whether the Yankees would move along the Church Road toward the plank road or straight up the Squirrel Level Road toward Petersburg itself. A courier from Hampton dispelled this uncertainty about an hour later. He informed Wilcox that the Federals threatened the plank road. The division commander reacted promptly to the crisis. He dutifully passed the news on to Hill, and then, fearing that too much time would elapse before the Virginian could reply, he took it on himself to march his two brigades down the plank road to oppose Parke. As soon as the lieutenant general received the dispatch, he sought additional reinforcements for Hampton, not merely to block the Union advance but also to hurl it back. Though he presumably lacked time to refer the problem to Lee, he was evidently sufficiently aware of his superior's general views and past conduct to know that he was expected to counterattack the Federals, and he now began assembling a striking force for that purpose.

Heth and his two brigades already near the threatened area, Archer's and MacRae's, now received marching orders to follow Wilcox and counterattack the foe. At the same time the rest of the Virginian's division set out from behind the center for the vicinity of Battery No. 45 to replace the troops sent from there and also to provide potential reinforcements to join the counterattack. Word that the main Yankee blow was aimed up the Church Road apparently made Hill feel that he could afford to weaken the main defenses north of W. W. Davis', so he hurried Heth forward before Cooke and Davis arrived. The corps commander further bolstered his mobile column at the expense of the city's works by shifting some of Walker's companies—including C/11th Georgia Light Artillery Battalion—from left to right to replace three batteries (twelve guns) of Pegram's Artillery Battalion: Captain Thomas Brander's Letcher Artillery, the Crenshaw Artillery, and probably the Purcell Artillery. On being relieved the gunners joined Heth's command. To insure that they would be used effectively, the lieutenant general sent their chief-of-battalion to command them.

Few who knew Pegram before 1861 would have marked this shy, scholarly university student as a man of war. Yet the inscrutable alchemy of battle had transformed him into a true military leader— brave, heroic, inspiring, yet possessed of sound tactical insight. Long renowned as commander of a battery and then of a battalion who ran his guns in close and fought them long and hard, he had emerged as the greatest artillerist of Lee's III Corps and one of the most outstanding of the entire Civil War. He had already become Hill's most trusted artillerist. Throughout the entire Siege of Petersburg (save only for the First Battle of the Weldon Railroad) the corps commander called on him to help check all Federal thrusts south of the city. Another such attack was now under way, and the lieutenant general once more had Pegram sally forth to meet it.[7]

As Pegram's cannons rumbled along behind Heth's infantry, Wilcox's soldiers were already moving down the Church Road to support Hampton's men in the breastworks north of Old Town Creek. By the time the Light Division arrived, the IX Corps was slowly beginning to advance again. The 2nd New York Mounted Rifles had by now moved onto Jones's farm and were driving the gray troopers from the plantation house. The opposing skirmish lines presently faced each other on the northern part of Jones's field. Behind the New Yorkers, Potter's main line was coming into view in the woods between Jones's and Pegram's. Such developments made Wilcox fear that the Second Division would reinforce its voltigeurs, press right over the Southern cavalry, and seize the log works themselves. To forestall this threat, he placed his own infantry in the fortifications—Lane on the right, McGowan on the left—and moved the horsemen farther to the right. Further to check the danger and to cover his own deployment, he threw forward his own skirmishers, Captain William Dunlop's Sharpshooter Battalion of the South Carolina Brigade and Major Thomas J. Wooten's Sharpshooter Battalion of the Tarheel Brigade. These fine commands splashed over the upper fork of Old Town Creek, briefly concealed themselves in the ravine through which it flowed, then burst forth upon the New Yorkers. Graham's gunners added their fire to the attack. The Mounted Rifles had previously had things their own way. This unexpected counterattack clearly took them by surprise, and most of them precipitously fled back to Potter's main line. Those who tried to make a stand in Jones's house were first pinned down and cut off by Wooten, then overrun and captured by Dunlop's hard-fighting South Carolinians. This handsome little raid netted the Butternuts a major and at least thirty other prisoners.

More than that, it helped make clear to Wilcox that the great Union juggernaut was not as formidable as it seemed from afar. From his position north of the creek, he surveyed the whole field. Stimulated by the crisis to generalship far above his average, he now discerned the essence of the tactical situation. The Yankees had failed to block his counterjab, and their main body had not come forward to retrieve the capture of Jones's house. To the contrary, that main body could be seen throwing up light works along the northern edge of the woods between Jones's and Pegram's. Nor had the Bluecoats managed to fire more than a few random bullets into his main line—though one of them had mortally wounded Colonel William Barbour of the 37th North Carolina. All signs, in sum, revealed considerable vacillation by the Union high command. Bold marching had brought Wilcox to this spot; keen perception had shown him this weakness. Now he followed through with decisive execution. He determined to exploit the Northern hesitancy by seizing the initiative himself and knocking the IX Corps back on its heels. Possibly his counterattack could even carry him right on to regain Peebles's farm itself.

He accordingly moved his two brigades down from the works to the south bank of the creek and posted them under cover of the ravine. The 33rd North Carolina held Lane's right, and the 37th North Carolina prolonged his line leftward to a little rivulet flowing north into the creek. The 28th, 7th, and 18th North Carolina, right to left, extended eastward from the rivulet to the Church Road. McGowan meantime took position in the ravine and in the pine thickets just south of the depression left of that highway in the following order: 1st South Carolina (Provisional Army), 14th South Carolina, 1st South Carolina Rifles, 13th South Carolina, and 12th South Carolina, right to left. Here the troops waited for Heth's men to join them.

Heth himself rode up about this time and evidently approved the way Hill's order to counterattack had been anticipated. He also promised to add his own two brigades to the striking force as soon as they arrived—MacRae *en échelon* on Lane's right rear and Archer *en échelon* on McGowan's left rear. As ranking officer present, the Virginian assumed general command of the operation and turned his own division over to Archer, whose brigade, in turn, passed to Colonel William McComb of the 14th Tennessee. Heth further entrusted immediate direction of all four infantry brigades of the striking force to Wilcox, presumably in order to free himself to exercise more general supervision and co-ordination of the counterattack. The senior infantry general now arranged with his cavalry coequal, Hampton, for the horsemen to hit the Bluecoats' left at the same time the Southern infantry attacked their front. For this operation, Heth and Hampton had 5,500 infantry and artillery just brought down or on the way from Petersburg plus 3,200 to 3,700 cavalry now assembled in the area. This aggregate force of 8,700 to 9,200 men was six times as strong as the weak brigade that had been the sole guardian of Lee's communications just four hours earlier. The Secessionists had clearly made good use of the Yankees' earlier delays to build up a force adequate to save the plank road, perhaps even sufficient to recover the Squirrel Level Line. The consequences of Parke's hesitancy, Warren's lack of co-operation, and Meade's failure to take personal charge of the operation were about to become apparent.[8]

Ironically, now that caution would at last have served the Unionists well, they finally acted boldly and thereby precipitated the next phase of heavy fighting. Before Heth's own brigades could deploy behind the Light Division, the Yankees advanced onto Jones's farm in force. The Mounted Rifles, of course, had already been there and had been driven back again. During the skirmishers' fight around Jones's house, Simon Griffin's main body had moved north out of the ravine of the lower fork of Old Town Creek to the fence along the northern end of the woods. There the battle line halted. Some Federals now threw up light works along the fence, and others simply lay down to avoid enemy fire overshooting the voltigeurs around Jones's house. Before long, Curtin moved up to the fence to prolong the line leftward. He, too, now halted there. Only after Potter learned that the First Brigade was in position did he order both brigades forward. By now, the 2nd had been defeated; Dunlop and Wooten had recaptured Jones's house; and Wilcox was readying his principal force to counterattack.

Simon Griffin duly ordered the 2nd New York Mounted Rifles forward again as skirmishers and now moved his first line of battle—the Marylanders and Hampshiremen—up behind them. However, he still left his second line back in the woods—a surprising decision since he not only knew the enemy in his front was strong enough to recapture the plantation house but also was aware or soon discovered that no other brigades guarded his flanks. Only as he began advancing did the 100th Pennsylvania finally come up to connect with his skirmishers' right. The "Roundheads," as they were called, almost immediately pulled back, however, and McLaughlen's main body never did arrive. Parke, concerned that the cavalry spotted around Mrs. Hart's threatened his left flank, now withdrew McLaughlen's men from the far right to a position just west of Pegram's house, where they could better meet any danger from west of Arthur's Swamp. The major general counted on the First Division of the V Corps to replace the Third Brigade on the right front, but he apparently made no effort to ascertain that the replacements were actually moving into position. Simon Griffin, in contrast, was all too aware of the absence of the 100th or anyone else on his right flank. He conscientiously "pointed out"—indeed, probably protested—the danger of moving forward with his right in air. Potter, himself under orders to "push on . . . without reference to any one else," felt that he could not or need not heed these warnings. Unjustifiably assured by corps headquarters that Charles Griffin would cover the right, the division commander peremptorily ordered his senior brigadier to keep advancing.

Nor was Simon Griffin's left more secure. A peculiar breakdown of command caused both him and Curtin to lose control of two regiments where their lines connected, so neither officer made sure those units advanced. As the First Brigade initially moved up through the woods to the fence, its right front element, the 35th Massachusetts, somehow became sandwiched between the left of the Second Brigade's two lines: the 2nd Maryland in front and the 179th New York behind. Then as

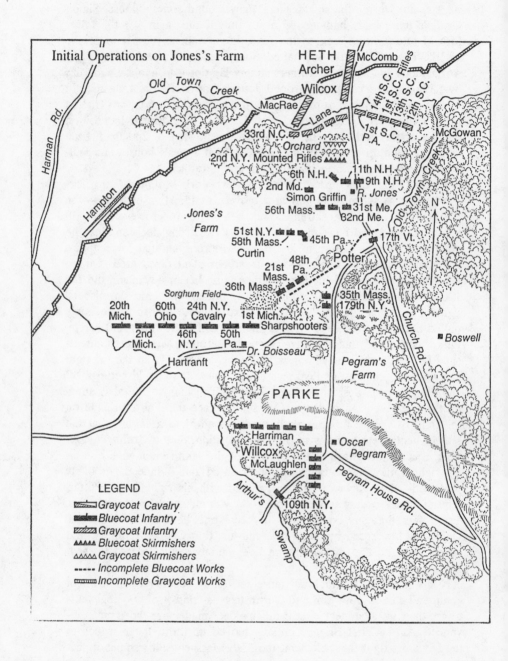

Initial Operations on Jones's Farm

HETH
Archer
McComb

Old Town Creek

Wilcox

MacRae

14th S.C.
1st S.C. Rifles
13th S.C.
12th S.C.

Lane

McGowan

Harman Rd.

33rd N.C.

1st S.C.
P.A.

Orchard

2nd N.Y. Mounted Rifles

Hampton

6th N.H.   11th N.H.
2nd Md.   9th N.H.
Simon Griffin   R. Jones

Jones's
Farm

56th Mass.   31st Me.
                82nd Me.

51st N.Y.
58th Mass.   45th Pa.   17th Vt.
Curtin

48th
21st   Pa.
Mass.   Potter
36th Mass.

Old Town Creek

Sorghum Field   35th Mass.
                           179th N.Y.
20th   60th   24th N.Y.
Mich. Ohio   Cavalry
              1st Mich.
2nd   46th   50th   Sharpshooters   ■ Boswell
Mich. N.Y.   Pa.

Dr. Boisseau   Church Rd.

Hartranft   Pegram's
                         Farm

PARKE

Harriman
Willcox   ■ Oscar
McLaughlen   Pegram

                         Pegram House Rd.
Arthur's
        109th N.Y.

Swamp

the Southern sharpshooters drove the New Yorkers from Jones's house, Potter ordered Curtin to bolster Simon Griffin with a regiment, and the colonel duly detached the 35th. Now that the Second Brigade was advancing in earnest, the Hampshireman ordered the reinforcements to move forward, too. The 35th's two rightmost companies obeyed, but the others stood fast. Major John Hudson, commanding the 35th, had not received word of the reassignment. He regarded himself as still in the First Brigade, declined to recognize Simon Griffin's authority, and refused to budge. The brigadier general accepted the protest at face value and left the regiment behind. Curtin, however, thought he had taken it and ceased sending orders to it. Hudson's men thus simply remained in the woods, unclaimed by either officer; behind them, the 179th stayed in place, too.

The Pennsylvanian at least perceived that the 35th's inactivity created a gap between his right and the Second Brigade's left, so he shifted his other three front-line regiments rightward to close it. A much more serious gap, however, soon developed and remained unclosed, because his brigade advanced neither as soon nor as far as Simon Griffin's. The colonel, too, left his second line idle along the southern end of Jones's field just north of the fence and moved only his three front regiments forward. Since he did not keep abreast of the troops farther east and since he could not observe what was occurring near Jones's house, he saw little advantage and much danger in continuing to advance. He accordingly halted about halfway across the field—far to the Second Brigade's left rear—and swung the 45th Pennsylvania up by a half right wheel to refuse his right along another fence. Then

COMMENTARY

1. This map makes clear how greatly the Federal thrust had fractured by the time it reached Jones's farm. Only the IX Corps had moved beyond Peebles's farm; only Potter had moved onto Jones's farm; only Simon Griffin had continued advancing; and only half of his brigade had yet reached Jones's farmyard. Such a feeble probe offers a tempting target to Wilcox, who now prepares to strike back with his own division, without waiting for Archer's two brigades to get into position.

2. The positions of Curtin's front line, MacRae, and McComb are approximate.

3. Whether or not Pegram was yet in position—and just where Edward Graham's guns were posted—is not clear.

4. Harriman's line probably ran: 13th Ohio Cavalry, 1/38th Wisconsin, 37th Wisconsin, 8th Michigan, and 27th Michigan, left to right.

5. Lane's line ran: 18th, 7th, 28th, 37th, and 33rd North Carolina, left to right.

he rode off alone reconnoitering to the left to make sure that no threat lurked in that direction.

Hartranft was, of course, expected to cover that flank. But neither Potter, Willcox, nor Parke informed him that the Second Division was advancing, and the sorghum field blocked his own view of the forward movement. He therefore stayed in place just north of Dr. Boisseau's, unaware the attack was resuming. The rest of the First Division plus the two Rhode Island regiments remained even farther to the rear on Pegram's farm. And Monroe and Charles Griffin were still back on Peebles's farm. Twenty thousand Union foot soldiers had struck west from Globe Tavern at nine that morning. Just eight hours later the expeditionary force had fragmented so badly that only half of one brigade—a mere twelve hundred to thirteen hundred men—actually took part in the final drive for the plank road itself.[9]

Despite its weakness, Simon Griffin's front line at least managed to make good progress against Dunlop's and Wooten's marksmen. A heavy plank fence just south of Jones's house forced the Bluecoats to enter the farmyard by the gate, where they made tempting targets. The fence along the west side, however, was only picket and proved virtually no barrier at all. The Yankees soon retook the plantation house and pushed the sharpshooters back through an orchard toward the ravine of the upper fork of Old Town Creek. The Butternuts, always brave and now especially stiffened by the knowledge that support lay close behind, rallied just south of the ravine and fought back obstinately. The Unionists then halted in the orchard and returned the fire. By now the outbuildings of the farm, the terrain, and the pace of advancing had disrupted Griffin's line. The 2nd Maryland had dropped off, and the 6th New Hampshire now held the left. As it closed in on the Confederate skirmishers, the 6th obliqued rightward to avoid a farm building on its left. In swinging right, it squarely exposed its left flank to Lane's soldiers waiting, concealed, in the ravine. Against this tempting target Wilcox now launched his counterattack. As soon as he saw the Second Division advancing, he determined to strike whenever a favorable opening occurred, without awaiting the arrival of MacRae and McComb. The Hampshiremen's exposed left flank, perpendicular to his front, provided that opening. On Colonel Robert V. Cowan's own initiative, his 33rd North Carolina now erupted from the ravine and overwhelmed the 6th. The 37th North Carolina joined Cowan immediately, and Lane's remaining three regiments soon rushed forward too, to roll up the Federal left. At the same time McGowan's long line advanced from east of the Church Road against the Union right. And Graham, perhaps soon joined by Pegram, added brisk artillery fire to the attack.

Startled though they were to be caught in a double envelopment, some Federals could not help begrudging the Confederates praise. "The rebels . . . were bearing down on us, like a fleet of war ships—in front and on both flanks," officially recorded the adjutant of the 11th New Hampshire; "they advanced in splendid, unbroken lines."[10] The responsible Northern generals shared the lieutenant's surprise, but they lacked time to experience his admiration as they busied themselves meeting the crisis. Potter attempted to realign his whole division but did not have time to do so before Wilcox closed with him. Simon Griffin, however, at least managed to bring the 17th Vermont from his second line to the fence along the southern edge of Jones's field and to shift it to face northwest to try to meet the South Carolinians' threat to his right. He also ordered up his two Maine regiments and the 56th Massachusetts to bolster his front line around the house itself. Such halfway measures proved inadequate. The reinforcements only succeeded in sharing the front line's fate. By now Lane had swept the orchard clear of Bluecoats and was forcing them back toward the plantation house. As he kept eating up the Union line from its left, the South Carolinians began closing in on the opposite flank. Most Northerners did not wait for the pincers to snap shut on them but panicked and fled in complete disorder. Knapsacks, oilcloths, blankets—anything that could slow their flight—were discarded; some men even cut the knapsacks from their shoulders in order not to delay in taking them off. Some Federals, admittedly, stayed long enough to fire a volley or two, but then they joined the headlong rush for the rear. Only a brave but foolhardy few sought to make a last stand in the plantation house, especially its brick basement. Like the Mounted Rifles a short time earlier, they found the protection of their citadel illusory. They were soon overwhelmed, driven off, or forced to surrender. One Tarheel alone took sixty-one prisoners there. Then both of Wilcox's brigades closed in to open a deadly cross fire on the refugees "running the gantlet" back to the woods. Such fire "piled the ground with their bodies," exulted one of McGowan's men.[11]

To make matters worse, the 17th Vermont, back in the woods, mistook the main body of its own brigade for Secessionists and briefly opened fire on it before the regimental commander could stop the shooting. Coming under fire from all sides further demoralized many Yankees, who refused to heed their generals' appeals to rally. Potter and Simon Griffin repeatedly exposed themselves to danger in trying to regroup their men—both their horses were wounded at this time—but to no avail. Of the few men whom they did manage to rally in the light works along the northern edge of the lower woods, most were swept to the rear by their panic-stricken comrades fleeing to Pegram's farm.

Such survivors from Jones's as withstood even the refugees, moreover, proved no match for Wilcox's soldiers surging into the forest in hot pursuit. The South Carolinians caught the 17th Vermont in the act of fixing bayonets, sliced the regiment in half, and forced it to withdraw, leaving its commander, Lieutenant Colonel Charles Cummings, mortally wounded on the field. In retreating over the swampy headwaters of the lower fork of Old Town Creek, the 17th fell into confusion and ceased functioning as a tactical unit. The Butternuts comparably cleared the few regrouping Unionists from their works in a short, sharp fight. Now entirely used up, the whole Second Brigade fled toward Pegram's field in total rout. Potter, who had remained calm and collected throughout the debacle, now accepted the battle for Jones's farm as lost and sought to salvage what little he could. He ordered his two Rhode Island regiments to rally the refugees near Pegram's house, and he sent Curtin word to withdraw there.[12]

The colonel, however, did not receive this message, because he was still away from his command, reconnoitering. His brigade, therefore, remained in place to face the onslaught that had just crushed Simon Griffin. This onslaught now broadened its targets as Wilcox changed tactics from the double envelopment that had overthrown the Second Brigade to a divergent, two-pronged attack. His main body, all of McGowan's regiments and four of Lane's, battled its way through the woods and followed the refugees southward along the Pegram House Road. The major general's other wing—Cowan's regiment, soon reinforced by part of MacRae's Brigade (including at least the 26th North Carolina), which was just coming up—meantime wheeled west to continue clearing the Federals out of the woods between Jones's and Pegram's. The Tarheels' drive rightward, amazingly, took parts of Curtin's second line completely by surprise. The Bluecoats had previously come under long-range shelling that overshot their comrades around Jones's house, and they had heard the heavy firing in that quarter. "The crash of musketry," indeed, sounded "frightful beyond even that of the wilderness" to a soldier of the 36th Massachusetts on the left rear.[13] But the men on that rear line actually had no idea of what had befallen Simon Griffin until they saw the Secessionists bearing down on their right. First to detect the danger was the 179th New York, whose position down the slope of the ravine of the lower fork enabled it to see under the foliage, which blocked the view eastward of most of the second line. Spotting the legs of an onrushing battle line greatly disquieted the New Yorkers—all the more so because most of the regiment was unarmed. As soon as they came under fire, one of their number cried out, "Let's get out of here!" His comrades harkened to his call, and the whole outfit abandoned their stacked knapsacks and fled southward without resisting.[14]

Seeing the 179th retreat, for no apparent cause, in turn, alarmed the 35th Massachusetts in its front, and some men from that unit, too, began drifting rearward. Hudson, still unaware of the threat, told his soldiers to lie back down and remain calm. Not until the Graycoats burst on his right flank did he at last become aware of the danger. He now ordered his soldiers to rise up and withdraw westward through the sorghum field. Falling back over difficult terrain before a charging foe was no easy matter for seasoned troops. For the 35th, it was particularly difficult. The regiment was numerically the largest and qualitatively the weakest outfit in the entire division. Fully two thirds of its men were new recruits who had only reached the front early in September. To make matters worse, most of the new men were German immigrants barely off the boats, who could not understand the English language. Many veteran New England Yankees in the regiment ridiculed and despised these newcomers and suggested that the outfit's name should be changed from the "35th Massachusetts" to the "1st Hamburgers." What now befell the "Hamburgers" hardly made the veterans relish them more. The recruits could hardly understand Hudson's commands and fell back in considerable disorder. The next regiment leftward, the 48th Pennsylvania, tried to rally them without avail. Not even the 48th's commander, Lieutenant Colonel Henry Pleasants, flailing the refugees with his saber, could stop them from passing right through his regiment, disrupting its alignment. Soon it, also, had to pull back toward Boisseau's in the face of the onrushing North Carolinians. This retreat, in turn, uncovered the 21st Massachusetts. That brave little regiment, only three companies strong, managed to keep its alignment and actually skirmished with Cowan, but it, too, had to fall back. Finally the Southerners reached the 36th Massachusetts on the far left. It, also, could not redeploy to meet them and had to retire westward across the sorghum field. The Tarheels' advance thus caused Curtin's whole second line to crumble from right to left.

As the remnants of the First Brigade streamed out of the field, Hartranft, though slightly wounded in the process, managed to rally them on his right in a position almost perpendicular to Curtin's front line, which was still out in Jones's field. Their arrival was the general's first warning of the disaster on the right. From his position atop the watershed between the Albemarle and Chesapeake systems just north of Boisseau's, he had previously seen nothing more alarming than the Butternut troopers off to his left. He could hardly believe that the Second Division had been overcome. Even more surprising was the arrival of one of Humphreys' aides who galloped up with instructions for him to retreat. The Chief-of-Staff, who had led infantry in battle before and who still yearned to direct combat troops again, had not remained back on Peebles's farm with Meade but had ridden to the front to take part

in what he soon came to regard as a "pretty little fight."[15] There he
learned what had befallen the Second Division's Second Brigade, realized the peril to Hartranft, and ordered him to withdraw.

The hard-fighting brigadier, however, had been in no action himself
and could not see through the sorghum field to learn what had happened around Jones's house. He therefore saw little point in abandoning the attack and, as he later put it, "obeyed this order very slowly."[16]
He retired only about a hundred yards and then formed a new line of
battle still north of Boisseau's house. To guard against the horsemen
to the west, he now moved Cutcheon's two Michigan regiments across
to the right bank of Arthur's Swamp, where they faced west and refused the brigade's left flank back to the country lane leading to Mrs.
Hart's on the Harman Road. To help plug the gap between the 2nd
west of the swamp and the Ohioans on the left of his main line, he
transferred the 1st Michigan Sharpshooters westward from his right to
an intermediate point between the 60th and the left bank of the
stream. Northeast of the sharpshooters, his main battle line, still facing
north, guarded his center. And to his right rear, refugees from the First
Brigade regrouped and faced east in a depression open at the northern
end. The brave 21st moved right up to the eastern rim of the swale to
make its stand. The 48th formed a hollow square to protect itself on all
sides. The 36th, too, took position, and the 35th at least managed to
rally. Thus deployed, Hartranft stood his ground to find out if all was
really lost.

He soon received his answer. Since his position was the only link between Curtin's front line and the main Union army, the Confederates
moved rapidly to pinch it off. On his right the North Carolinians threw
themselves against the refugees in the depression to precipitate a furious battle. From this naturally strong position most of the regrouped
Yankees—the 36th, the 48th, and, above all, the 21st—fought well.
The 35th, however, continued to be of marginal value, as Hudson himself conceded:

> Many of my men readily took an advanced position here, and only
> left when regularly ordered back by me as I saw the lines receding
> on both sides, but I do not claim that the regiment was of any serv-
> ice whatever here on the whole. The rather dense formation and
> the want of experience in drill which we labored under were so un-
> favorable to our usefulness that but for example's sake and the evi-
> dent propriety of suffering generously with the rest, I could consci-
> entiously have withdrawn all my men without any attempt at
> forming them to resist the enemy.

The "Hamburgers" at least succeeded in "suffering generously with the rest." "Men fell on all sides like autumn leaves," noted the regiment's deputy commander.[17] Despite the 35th's sacrifice and its comrades' resistance, however, the Tarheels rapidly gained ground on them. At the same time, danger developed from the opposite direction, too, as some of Hampton's troopers—possibly the 2nd and 3rd North Carolina Cavalry or the 13th Virginia Cavalry—drove in the skirmishers west of Arthur's Swamp and menaced Hartranft's left flank.

These threats from both sides alerted the Pennsylvanian to the danger at last. Finally, he issued orders for his regiments to pull out from left to right down the line and then to fall back. Before he could break contact and withdraw, however, his position began collapsing. Cowan's and MacRae's men now swung around to occupy the mouth of the depression and poured enfilading fire southward into the refugees' left flank while continuing to press their front. Such cross fire killed the 21st's commander, Captain Orange Sampson, and shattered the refugees. Already shaken by their initial defeat in the woods and the sorghum field, these soldiers from the Second Division now gave way completely and fled in disorder. As a captain of the 36th put it: "A lively scattering over the fences and through the grounds of the Boisseau house ensued, each man doing his level best to preserve a life for future usefulness to his country. . . ."[18] Some of these troops headed down the left bank of the stream and eventually regrouped around Peebles's house. Others—especially the 35th and apparently also part of the 48th—clambered through the thickets to the right bank of Arthur's Swamp. Some found safety west of the stream, as they made their way down to the abandoned southern end of the Squirrel Level Line or Route 673, and others, including the Pennsylvanians, soon recrossed to the left bank farther south. Hampton's horsemen, however, dashed in to catch up with most of the "Hamburgers" and captured 124 of them. Taking so many new immigrants in their first battle was quite a coup for the Confederacy and furnished excellent material for its propaganda on the source of the North's manpower.

Hartranft hardly had time right then to worry about furnishing fuel for enemy propaganda. The flight of the refugees threw at least the 50th Pennsylvania on the right of his own brigade into some disorder. The difficulty of withdrawing through the undergrowth along the left bank of Arthur's Swamp disrupted the order of the 1st and the 60th on the opposite flank, too. Confederate voltigeurs heightened the confusion by closing in to open a telling cross fire on the Yankees retreating southeastward across Boisseau's farm. This firing and the attendant disorder took their toll. The brigade lost nearly two hundred men at this time, of whom two thirds were captured or missing. Among the pris-

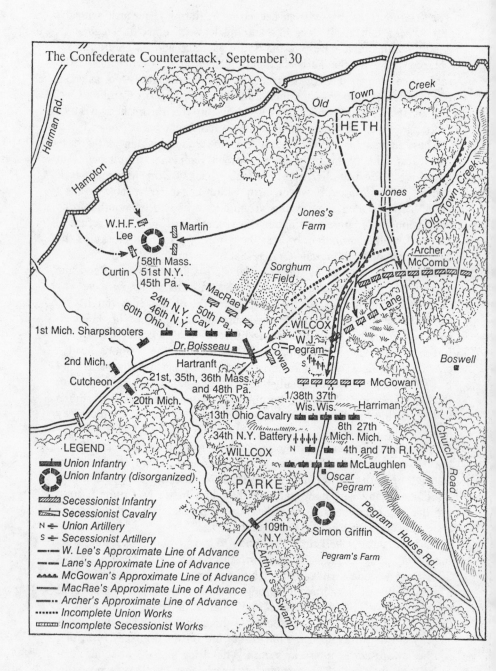

The Confederate Counterattack, September 30

Harman Rd.

Old Town Creek

HETH

Hampton

Jones

Jones's
Farm

W.H.F.
Lee — Martin

Curtin
58th Mass.
51st N.Y.
45th Pa.

Sorghum
Field

Archer
McComb

MacRae

24th N.Y.
46th N.Y.
60th Ohio. Cav.
50th Pa.

Lane

1st Mich. Sharpshooters

WILCOX
W.J.
Pegram's

Dr. Boisseau

Cowan

Boswell

2nd Mich.

Hartranft

McGowan

Cutcheon

21st, 35th, 36th Mass.
and 48th Pa.

20th Mich.

1/38th 37th
Wis. Wis.   Harriman

13th Ohio Cavalry

8th 27th
Mich. Mich.

LEGEND

34th N.Y. Battery

N

WILLCOX

4th and 7th R.I.

McLaughlen

Union Infantry

PARKE

Oscar
Pegram

Union Infantry (disorganized)

Secessionist Infantry

109th
N.Y.

Simon Griffin

Secessionist Cavalry

N— Union Artillery

s— Secessionist Artillery

Pegram's Farm

W. Lee's Approximate Line of Advance

Lane's Approximate Line of Advance

McGowan's Approximate Line of Advance

MacRae's Approximate Line of Advance

Archer's Approximate Line of Advance

Incomplete Union Works

Incomplete Secessionist Works

Church Road

Pegram House Rd.

Arthur's Swamp

oners were the two ranking colonels of the brigade, DeLand and Raulston, plus much of the skirmish line, which was so far forward that it was cut off before it could escape. Yet the splendid brigadier, himself perhaps unhorsed by this time, knew that his primary mission now was not to fight back but to get his main body to safety before Wilcox's and Hampton's battle lines could join their skirmishers and overwhelm him. His gamble paid off. At the price of not being able to return the cross fire, he led his men out of the potential trap, across the enfiladed depression, to Willcox's position around Pegram's house—and did it, despite the inevitable confusion, in relatively good order. Unlike Potter's brigades, Hartranft's brigade came out of the fight still able to function as a tactical unit.

One of his regiments, though, barely managed to escape. His order to withdraw was delayed in reaching the 20th Michigan, so it remained out on the far left after the 2nd Michigan and all the other units on its right retired down the left bank of the creek. By the time the instructions finally reached Cutcheon, the Confederate infantry had overrun Boisseau's yard and thus blocked his prescribed line of retreat. Both the general's order and also his own good sense told him he had to get back to the left bank somehow, so he withdrew along the right bank and then attempted to recross farther southeast. Floundering through the briars and brambles along the swamp was no easy matter even under favorable conditions; doing so in the midst of battle was particularly difficult and dangerous. Some of Hampton's troopers spotted the 20th bogged down in the tangled undergrowth and slashed in at this tempting target. They killed the regimental adjutant, inflicted fairly heavy casualties, and forced some Michiganders to abandon the effort to ford the swamp there and to withdraw southeastward to Route 673

COMMENTARY

1. This map reveals the divergent routes of the Confederate counterattack. Lane and McGowan executed a double envelopment at Jones's, then made a slashing right wheel through the woods, and finally emerged on Pegram's farm. McComb belatedly moved straight down the Church Road to again create a second prong for Wilcox's drive. Cowan meantime continued farther west and joined MacRae in overrunning Dr. Boisseau's, which some horsemen also threatened from the west. Hampton's main blow, however, fell farther north, where "Rooney" Lee cut off and helped capture the three regiments Martin was pursuing. MacRae also later doubled back northward to help trap Curtin's front line.

2. The identity of the cavalry facing Cutcheon is not known.

3. The relative order of Cowan and MacRae is probably correct.

4. The positions of Curtin, Cutcheon, and Lane are only approximate.

and thence to the Squirrel Level Road. The 20th was not like the "Hamburgers," though—a defenseless mob ripe for capture. Cutcheon's main body had sufficient tactical cohesion to be able to defend itself against the thrust and then to continue crossing the stream and rejoin their brigade west of Pegram's house.[19]

Overrunning Boisseau's marked the final phase of Wilcox's grand flanking movement, which had rolled up the whole Union line from Jones's house to Arthur's Swamp in only about half an hour. Now the Southerners plucked the fruits of their victory: Curtin's front line, which had been unable to escape because the Yankee right and rear had collapsed so rapidly. The three regiments out in Jones's field had not stood idle as their comrades were swept from the area. As the Butternuts overran Jones's yard and then struck southward to attack the 17th Vermont in the woods, the First Brigade at last realized that something was amiss. The 51st New York now shifted from the 58th's left, facing north, to the 45th's right, facing northeast. Then as they spotted a Confederate force heading south toward the woods, the New Yorkers charged it and actually rolled up its right flank element. The troops thus attacked proved to be the 52nd North Carolina, moving up with the rest of MacRae's Brigade to join the other Tarheels in the forest. Their general kept moving south with three regiments, but his right-center outfit, Colonel William Martin's 11th North Carolina, now turned west to help the 52nd against the 51st. The Secessionists counterattacked and drove the New Yorkers back on the Pennsylvanians.

At about this point Curtin finally returned from his reconnaissance and at last located the enemy—not off to the northwest somewhere but rolling up the right of his second line and attacking the right of his first. His front line soon gave way, too, and all three regiments fled westward. The brigadier bravely tried to rally his men. Twice they halted to fire a volley; twice Martin drove them back again. By this time Cowan and MacRae had overrun Boisseau's to cut off the last escape route southward. From the doctor's place the 26th North Carolina and probably MacRae's other two regiments now turned northward to help Martin chase Curtin.

Then from the west the fleeing Yankees came under artillery fire. During the initial fighting at Jones's, Hampton led at least Davis' brigade and a section of Captain William McGregor's Second Stuart Horse Artillery down the Harman Road to man the works across the western part of Jones's field and to be ready to strike if the Federals exposed their left. Now that Curtin's men were nearing that sector, one of McGregor's pieces moved forward and shelled them vigorously. The Bluecoats still had fight left in them, though, and kept on coming toward the gun. As they neared, the Virginians abandoned the piece and fled toward the works. The Butternuts, however, were not about to let refugees capture their artillery. "Rooney" Lee personally led the dismounted 9th and 10th Virginia Cavalry forward to save the gun, and McGregor advanced his other rifle to provide close artillery support. These long lines of Virginians sweeping down from the northwest delivered the *coup de grâce*. Their well-aimed fire completely shattered the Yankees. Part of the 45th Pennsylvania tried to make a stand in a log barn but was overwhelmed by Davis' own regiment. Even some of McGregor's gunners rushed in among the refugees to seize prisoners. Surrounded on all sides, the Union force now went to pieces and was captured almost to the last man. Only a handful of Unionists got away —eleven men of the 58th, sixteen of the 51st, and twenty-six of the 45th—and even of these, the New Yorkers were initially captured and then escaped from custody after dark. Curtin, too, made his escape just in the nick of time. His swift Kentucky Thoroughbred enabled him to outdistance his pursuers. Just as he was leaping a fence, the poor animal was killed, but the brigadier flew right on over the horse's head and over the fence and kept on going to safety.

Most of his troops did not make it. Approximately six hundred men from his first line were taken prisoner, including all three regimental commanders: Lieutenant Colonel Theodore Gregg of the 45th, Major John G. Wright of the 51st, and Major Everett S. Horton of the 58th. Curtin's second line, Simon Griffin, and Hartranft lost about seven hundred more captives. Lost, too, were the flags of the 51st, destroyed, and of the 45th and the 58th, captured. Well over a thousand rifles plus much booty were also taken from the three brigades. Prisoners, flags, rifles, loot—these were all trophies of the Confederates' elegant victory. Wilcox, Heth, and Hampton had not only parried the enemy drive toward the supply lines but also had hurled it back, wrecking two Union brigades and pummeling a third. Now if they could just exploit their success, the Butternuts might well overrun Pegram's farm, too, and even regain the Squirrel Level Line itself.[20]

Wilcox's main body moved to achieve these goals even while Cowan, Martin, and Hampton were overrunning Boisseau's and the western parts of Jones's farm. The major general sent McGowan's Brigade, four of Lane's regiments, and perhaps some of MacRae's straight south after the refugees retreating down the Pegram House Road. Both front-line brigades had by now become somewhat disorganized by their victorious advance. Lane's right, moreover, was disrupted by MacRae's intermingling outfits. Still, McGowan "thought it best not to dampen the ardor of victorious pursuit by stopping to reform."[21] His men and the Tarheels, accordingly, surged down toward Pegram's house. Willie Pegram, ever in the thick of the fray, temporarily left his guns behind and rode along with the infantry. Wilcox meantime ordered Archer, who was just reaching the battlefield, to continue straight south on the Church Road with McComb's brigade in order to turn the right flank of any force McGowan might encounter.

The South Carolinians, indeed, encountered some forces. As they poured out of the woods between Jones's and Pegram's farms, they met Northern reinforcements moving up to bolster the crumbling front. Even while the Second Division fought on Jones's, Parke ordered his two reserve brigades to support it. Potter's line, however, collapsed before the First Division could reach it. McLaughlen, indeed, made little effort to advance. As his command came under Southern artillery fire overshooting the Yankees in the woods to the north, he merely shifted westward a slight way into a thicket on the reverse slope of a small hill to get out of range. There he massed his force in close column of battalion and simply stayed in place. Harriman, in contrast, remained in line of battle, extended eastward to the Pegram House Road, and then moved northward. Monroe meantime finally provided some artillery support. But instead of massing his whole brigade to sweep the field with cross fire, he left three companies idle on Peebles's farm and brought forward only Lieutenant Thomas Heasley's 34th New York Battery—armed with four 3-inch ordance rifles, at that, pieces well suited for precise long-distance shelling but not as good as Napoleons for close-range antipersonnel fire. Perhaps the lieutenant colonel ordered up the battery when there was still a need to shell the Graycoats north of Jones's house, but by the time it crossed Pegram's, the enemy was already much closer at hand.

Harriman had by now reached a rather high east–west bald crest midway between Pegram's house and the northern woods. There his line halted briefly: the 13th Ohio Cavalry (dismounted), 1/38th Wisconsin, 37th Wisconsin, 8th Michigan, and 27th Michigan, left to right. Out of the woods ahead of him poured the remnants of the Second Division. They made no effort to rally but rushed around and through his ranks and continued southward, somewhat disrupting his brigade. Right behind them came McGowan. To make matters worse, Monroe now rushed the 34th up atop the ridge and unlimbered it in front of the 1/38th Wisconsin—a rash and foolhardy exposure of the battery. The New Yorkers came under musketry fire immediately, but they managed to shot their pieces and send canister ripping into the gray ranks. Undaunted, the Secessionists pressed on toward the crest. Receiving eight rounds of canister in fifteen minutes did not stop them; closer and closer to the guns they came. Potter himself, seeing the danger, now ordered the battery to withdraw before it was too late. Disengaging was no easy matter, but Heasley and his two section chiefs handled their pieces superbly and succeeded in limbering up and galloping to the rear just in the nick of time. Their guns plunging through the infantry again threw Harriman's men into some disorder, but the 37th Wisconsin moved up to cover the withdrawal and slowed the Confederate onrush a little, thus giving the cannoneers some badly needed time.

McGowan's soldiers, though slowed, were far from stopped. Denied at least temporarily the rifles, they now closed in on the First Brigade. After a short, sharp fight they pushed it off the crest onto the southern slope. There the Butternuts enjoyed the advantage of attacking downhill. Their fire proved too much for the Unionists. Most of the 13th Ohio Cavalry panicked and—as Willcox himself branded it—"fled ingloriously from the field," sweeping the 1/38th Wisconsin along with them.[22] Harriman's other three regiments, however, preserved their formations and retired in good order to the northwestern part of a fence enclosing Pegram's yard.

Their retreat once more exposed the 34th New York Battery, which was still galloping across the field toward the yard. Responsibility for saving the guns now passed to Lieutenant Colonel Percy Daniels' 7th Rhode Island, Curtin's engineers. A battle line of four companies of that regiment under Captain George Wilbur was already in the field north of the house vainly attempting to rally the refugees. Daniels now led his other six companies out into the field to try to stay the Confederate onrush. He, too, succeeded in rallying only a handful of refugees —perhaps a few of Harriman's men, even some of Potter's, including part of the 17th Vermont. So few joined the lieutenant colonel, though, that he basically had to face Wilcox's force by himself. A battalion taking on a division was a sight that stirred Potter. "For God's sake," the general cried to his refugees, "move up and help that little Seventh Rhode Island."[23] The refugees, shattered and demoralized, did not respond, and the 7th was left to face Wilcox alone. Its brisk fire at least managed to give the Butternuts pause as they poured down from the bald crest. That delay earned Heasley time to reach the yard, even though one of his pieces crashed into the gatepost and had to be extricated by hand. With the guns saved, Daniels himself fell back to the farmhouse in the face of a renewed Secessionist advance. Wilbur, on the other hand, was unable to get away and had to fall back a short way and then hide his men in the cornfield northeast of the house—a no-man's-land between the two armies.[24]

While Daniels, Harriman, and Heasley vainly contested control of the northern part of Pegram's farm, a new line of resistance began coalescing around the house. Major credit for forging this line rests with Willcox, who was now in the forefront of the action. He lost his horse and his commissary of musters in the process, but he managed to set up the new defense perimeter. His Second Brigade, escaping from Boisseau's, now came in to take position west of Pegram's house. Here Hartranft again fronted the Secessionists and, with two volleys from the 1st Michigan Sharpshooters, beat off some horsemen who pressed him too closely. Just before dark Cutcheon recrossed Arthur's Swamp, rejoined the brigade, and prolonged its line southwestward from the 60th Ohio to the 109th New York, still guarding the left rear. The Pennsylvanian faced more serious problems on his right as another horde of refugees, this time the 13th Ohio Cavalry, plunged through his line and swept the 50th Pennsylvania along with it to the rear. To replace the 50th, however, the brigadier managed to rally the 1/38th Wisconsin. Thus regrouped, the Second Brigade made its stand.

To its right Harriman's other three regiments reformed behind a rail fence just north of the farmhouse. They promptly converted the fence into a log breastwork and prepared to meet the oncoming Graycoats. Farther east, also behind the fence, were the remnants of the Second Division: the 4th Rhode Island, Daniels' six companies, and such few survivors of the debacle on Jones's farm as Parke, Potter, and their staffs had rallied—"a repulsed and disordered mass," a captain of the 36th called the latter. Potter himself was there "sitting gloomily on his horse."[25] Dejected as he was over his defeat, he was too good a soldier to neglect his responsibilities. He soon perceived that his own men could not prolong the line to the Church Road, so he sent a staff officer to ask Willcox for reinforcements to cover that sector. As soon as the Michigander learned of the need, he personally ordered the IX Corps's last reserve unit, his Third Brigade, into position there. McLaughlen, by this time, had moved out from behind the shelter of the brushy hill. When the debris of the Second Division first started streaming across Pegram's farm, he sought to stop them by deploying his column rightward into line from his rear regiment, the 3rd Maryland. This maneuver not only succeeded in rallying such of the refugees as did halt but also spared the 3rd the complicated evolutions his four veteran regiments executed. The 3rd was veteran, too, but like the 35th Massachusetts it had just been filled with new recruits and could hardly maneuver. But now Potter's plea and Willcox's instructions caused the 3rd and the regiments to its right to shift eastward, then left-face, and charge northward with fixed bayonets to come up abreast of Potter's right.

Even bringing McLaughlen to the front did not prolong the IX Corps's line to the Church Road. But he did not need to reach that far, for his right almost immediately connected with the left of other troops covering that highway—troops on whose kepis was emblazoned the red Maltese cross. The V Corps had moved up to help Parke at last.[26]

Somewhat over an hour earlier, at about 4:00 P.M., Warren began reconcentrating his First Division on his left by recalling Spear's five regiments from the vicinity of W. W. Davis' to Peebles's farm. Even though these regiments double-quicked back to Griffin, they apparently changed sectors not in order to enable the First Division to join the drive toward the Boydton Plank Road but simply to tidy up the V Corps's lines. The Second Division, that is, was now assuming responsibility for covering the Squirrel Level Road, so Spear's detachment no longer needed to serve there and could return to its own command. Otis, of course, was already in position astride that highway at Fort Bratton. Grimshaw then came up to protract this line rightward across Chappell's farm, and Graham, in turn, prolonged the line still farther eastward into the woods where rose the northeastern fork of Arthur's Swamp. Hofmann, however, did not accompany the Second Division but evidently remained back on Peebles's with Wainwright's last three batteries, which he had escorted forward to rejoin the artillery brigade. Even without the extra troops, Ayres held a strong position, and he now made it stronger by erecting a new line across Chappell's right through Fort Bratton, facing north.

To replace Spear's five regiments and to cover this entrenching, he threw forward a heavy skirmish line, consisting of at least the 1st and 4th Maryland, 3rd Delaware, and 17th U.S. and perhaps also the 15th New York Heavy Artillery and the 11th and 14th U.S. The voltigeurs found it no easy matter to press through the woods north of Chappell's. The terrain itself posed quite a problem, as the 3rd's adjutant recounted:

> [The skirmishers] deployed in a field & then advanced through a thick undergrowth of woods & briars such as I would never think of going into if I were out gunning & were sure of a good covey there. Now people at home think we advance in a beautiful line and fire off our guns. . . . No. No. Down we lay in a field the shells whizzing over and around us. Up rides an aid to brigade commander whispers a few words & dashes away. Attention 3d Brigade. Forward and away we go, come to the briars, go through head long over stumps, bushs & all not in a nice line of battle but like a big flock of stray sheep—officers shouting, men halloing & growling, "Swing up that left back on right. Keep by those colours." "Hold on those, two men are enough to carry off that man, Steady men ["] and so we go till we reach the edge of the woods. "Halt! Officers form your companies!" Again we form a decent line. "Fix bayonets." *We* know what that means. "Forward" "Yell boys" Yeh! Yeh-Yeh! Double quick and away we go shouting as loud as we can and, you may not believe it, but the cheering is half the battle when we charge.[27]

To make matters worse, some of Mahone's men—likely his sharp-shooters, perhaps also the 48th Georgia of Gibson's brigade—had either recaptured or at least reoccupied Fort Cherry at around 4:00 P.M., and some of Ferebee's troopers ventured still farther south toward Chappell's farm. These forces now contested the Federals' advance. However, neither Ayres, Warren, nor Meade sought battle on this sector while the main Union force was driving northwest, so the Second Division contented itself with covering its own sector, guarding the right rear, and attracting enemy attention. The Northerners, accordingly, made no effort to retake W. W. Davis'; many, indeed, simply lay down to avoid the fire. Mahone inferred from this inactivity that the Bluecoats on the Squirrel Level Road were weak, but he was weak, too, and could not afford to attack them. Therefore, no more than desultory skirmishing, occasionally punctuated by Walker's shelling, occurred on this sector for the rest of the afternoon.[28]

The sector northwest of Peebles's farm was hardly that quiescent, as Spear's men who had returned from the Squirrel Level Road soon found out. Those troops and the rest of the First Division, admittedly, initially remained idle in the field just north of Fort Archer, standing in line or even lying on the ground. However, the outbreak of heavy firing on Jones's farm and the ever-approaching sound of battle warned the waiting soldiers that fighting might once more reach their sector. Surely enough, about 5:30 Warren—whether on his own initiative or on Meade's command is not clear—directed his First Division to move northwest from Peebles's and try to stem the Confederate onrush across Pegram's. His fresh troops had not advanced from Peebles's in time to help the IX Corps try to penetrate to the heart of the enemy's position. Now they were finally ordered up for a last desperate effort to prevent the enemy from penetrating to the heart of their position. Griffin, accordingly, double-quicked his Third Brigade toward the front, shifted it leftward, and then rushed it through the fringe of trees between the two farms. The reinforcements soon met some of Parke's refugees streaming to the supposed safety of Peebles's—a sight that disgusted rather than demoralized the fresh troops. Unshaken by the encounter, the brigade pressed on to a ridge astride the Church Road just south of Boswell's house.

Atop that ridge Griffin made his stand. The ridge was bald on its western reaches, where the 16th Michigan and—to its right—the 118th Pennsylvania went into line. Farther east, where the 20th Maine and then the 83rd Pennsylvania stood guard, right around the road itself, a scattering of trees grew. Still farther right, where Spear's other three regiments served, the thick forest east of the highway covered the height. Moving Spear there secured the Church Road itself. To strengthen this position still more, Griffin apparently used his First Brigade to prolong the line farther eastward through the woods. Even more importantly, he brought his Second Brigade up to occupy the bald crest of the ridge left of Spear. The 155th apparently held Gregory's right, connecting with the 16th Michigan. To its left came the 32nd Massachusetts and then probably the 91st Pennsylvania. Gregory's left was initially in air but only briefly. Before Wilcox could strike the Pennsylvanians' front, a line came charging up from their left rear, with bayonets fixed: McLaughlen plugging the gap between Potter and Griffin. The Yankees' efforts had been fragmented all afternoon, but now they managed to put together a united defense line at last. From the 109th New York on the far southwest, through Hartranft, Harriman, Potter, McLaughlen, Gregory, Spear, and Sickel, a solid line of Federals stood guard between Arthur's Swamp and the Church Road to bar the Secessionists' drive. This was the last credible defense line. If it too gave way, the Army of the Potomac would lose everything it had gained that day.[29]

To protect against that danger, the Unionists tried to scrape together another line back at Peebles's. Meade himself was now alert to the problem. The outbreak of heavy firing around 5:00 initially made him think the IX Corps was breaking through to the plank road. As the sound of battle drew progressively nearer, though, he realized that something was terribly wrong, so he returned to where the Church Road passed through the Squirrel Level Line immediately west of Fort Archer in case his presence was required at the front. He may have played some role in ordering the First Division of the V Corps to Pegram's farm, but he apparently saw that Warren was handling things so well as to obviate the need for his personal intervention. Gone now were the hesitancy and misgivings that had troubled the corps commander in midday. Meeting the crisis of the battle left him no time for self-doubts. His latent talent now shone forth as he helped forge one defense line and created another. He not only saw that his First Division got up to the ridge but also directed his Deputy Chief-of-Artillery, Major Robert H. Fitzhugh, who had charge of the guns during Wainwright's temporary absence on Pegram's farm, to send Griffin a battery. The major selected Captain Charles E. Mink's H/1st New York Light Artillery. To save time, Mink promptly limbered up, mounted his gun crews on the limber chests, and left his caissons behind. Soon his four Napoleons were speeding up the Church Road to join the infantry, the gunners clinging to the limber chests for dear life.

As an added precaution, Warren ordered Wainwright, who now just returned from Pegram's, to create a new artillery line on Peebles's. The colonel duly unlimbered his four reserve batteries on the commanding knoll at Peebles's house and moved their caissons out of the way behind the hill. He also directed Battery B/1st New York Light Artillery to remain alert along the Squirrel Level Line west of Fort Archer. The 19th New York Battery, too, now took position along those works, if it were not already there. The brigadier was, however, distressed to see the other two fresh IX Corps batteries simply parked in front of his field of fire. He eventually found Monroe, though, and persuaded him to post them also along the captured defenses. Wainwright was even more incensed to discover the 34th New York Battery fleeing from Pegram's farm while Mink was advancing. Hardly had Heasley unlimbered in Battery H's former position along the curtain west of Fort Archer when a courier from Parke arrived with orders for him to return to Pegram's house. This directive the lieutenant refused to obey, because Monroe had instructed him to remain in the redoubt and not to leave without new orders from artillery headquarters. Meade said nothing during this curious exchange, but he, doubtless, made a mental note of Monroe's performance. Warren and Griffin may have been more outspoken in ridiculing the lieutenant colonel to his face for pulling the 34th out of battle and sending it so far to the rear. And Wainwright definitely denounced Heasley for according greater weight to instructions from a brigadier than from a corps commander. By now the lieutenant began to see the light, so he limbered up and returned to Willcox's line.

The 34th's departure left 34 guns in place on Peebles's farm: sixteen Napoleons, twelve ordnance rifles, and six 10-pound Parrotts. This massed artillery looked formidable, but it lacked one thing to make it truly effective: supporting infantry. Admittedly, Hofmann's brigade was probably still on the farm, but within minutes it too would receive orders to reinforce Griffin. When the colonel departed, the only available foot soldiers were Potter's regrouping refugees, shattered and ineffective, plus perhaps the V and IX corps provost troops: a battalion each of the 5th New York and 8th U.S., respectively. Such a handful could not protect the guns. If the Graycoats could breach the line on Pegram's and then press right on after the fleeing Yankees, they could overrun the artillery before it could fire more than one salvo. The strength of the inner line was thus illusory. A successful defense, if it were to be achieved at all, would have to be made by the infantry line on Pegram's. Seven Union defense lines had already given way in the last forty minutes: Simon Griffin's two, Curtin's two, Hartranft's, Harriman's, and Daniels'. If Cadmus Wilcox could defeat this line, also, he could reconquer everything that had been lost west of the Squirrel Level Road.[30]

The major general now sought this final, decisive victory. The South

Carolinians continued spearheading his advance. These brave troops again charged gallantly, but by now the spear was blunted, its shaft shattered. Casualties, exhaustion, the inevitable disorganization of victory, the well-known Confederate propensity to fall out and plunder had all taken a progressively heavier toll during the advance from Jones's house to the ridge north of Pegram's yard. The brigade no longer had the punch it possessed earlier in the afternoon. As it moved forward, McLaughlen's men, charging up to their sector between Potter and Gregory, opened a heavy fire on it. Harriman added his own fire, and Hartranft's right units, such as the 1/38th, may also have joined in the shooting. In the face of this stiff resistance, the Confederate wave, now largely foam, could only lap up against the Federal line and then recede in defeat.

To soften up the Federal breaker, McGowan called on Willie Pegram for artillery support. But when one Confederate battery rumbled toward the front, Willcox's infantry blasted it so devastatingly that the battalion commander had to pull it back before it could even unlimber. Although he would not sacrifice his beloved guns, the young Virginian had no fears for his personal safety. As the infantry were retreating, he seized one of their flags and galloped on to the front. One of his comrades, in an account somewhat embellished by friendship and admiration, later described what ensued:

> When forty or fifty yards in advance of the whole line, placing the color-staff on his stirrup and turning half way round in the saddle, he dropped the reins on his horse's neck and shouted out in tones sweet and clear as a bugle, "Follow me, men!" It was a scene never to be forgotten—the glorious sunset, the lithe, boyish form now sharply cut against the crimson western sky, then hid for a moment by the smoke of battle, the tattered colors, the cheering lines of men. With a rousing yell, the sturdy brigade closed up and never after gave back a single inch. The color-bearer ran out to him, the tears standing in his eyes, and cried out: "Give me back my colors, Colonel! I'll carry them wherever you say!" "Oh! I'm sure of that," he answered cheerily, "it was necessary to let the whole line see the colors; that's the only reason I took them."[31]

Pegram succeeded in rallying the brigade, but neither he nor anyone else could get it to charge again as a unit.

The 1st South Carolina (Provisional Army) and the 14th Carolina, however, did return to the fray. This time they surged right up to the farmyard gate. The artillery battalion commander, too, now managed to get a battery into position and opened fire on the little 4th Rhode Island. Being legally out of service afforded the Rhode

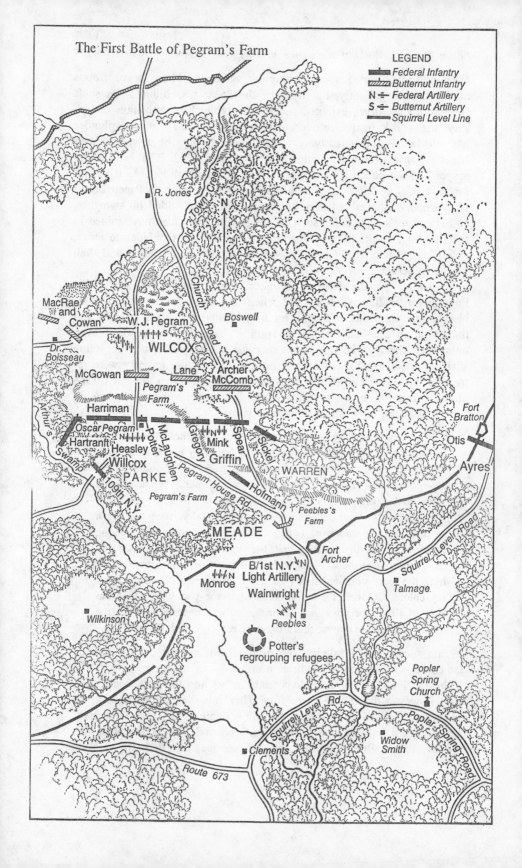

The First Battle of Pegram's Farm

R. Jones'

Old Church Road

Town Creek

N

Boswell

MacRae and Cowan

Dr. Boisseau

W. J. Pegram
S

WILCOX

McGowan

Lane

Archer
McComb

Pegram's Farm

Harriman

Oscar Pegram

Potter

McLaughlen

Gregory

Mink

Spear

Sickel

Fort Bratton

Otis

Ayres

Hartranft

Heasley

Griffin

WARREN

Willcox

109th N.Y.

PARKE

Pegram House Rd.

Hofmann

Pegram's Farm

Peebles's Farm

Arthur's Swamp

MEADE

Fort Archer

Squirrel Level Road

Monroe
N

B/1st N.Y.
Light Artillery
N

Wainwright

Talmage

Wilkinson

Peebles
N

Potter's
regrouping refugees

Poplar Spring Church

Squirrel Level Rd.

Poplar Spring Road

Widow Smith

Clements

Route 673

Islanders no protection from this fire. Nor did the fence that supposedly sheltered them do much good. Confederate shells turned the fence into a shower of lethal splinters, which forced the regiment to fall back a short way. Daniels, to the 4th's right; Harriman, and McLaughlen, however, stood firm. The 34th New York Battery, too, had returned to the front by now and opened a heavy fire of its own: 168 rounds of canister in a matter of minutes. "Our batteries put grape and canister into them like rain and killed a great many of them," exulted a soldier of the 48th Pennsylvania, who finally had something about which to cheer.[32] Against this heavy fire of canister and musketry, Pegram's fire availed little. The 1st and 14th, too, could go no farther and now sought shelter at the front rather than risk retreating to the main body. That main body meantime remained back on the bald ridge, unable to move farther south.

A little beyond McGowan's left, Lane's Tarheels now jabbed in toward the crucial junction between the V and IX corps. In advancing to the bald ridge, they nearly discovered Wilbur's place of concealment in the cornfield. But before they could stumble across the hidden battalion, let alone reach the main Northern line, they were beaten back by Spear's, Gregory's, and McLaughlen's determined defenders. The 18th North Carolina renewed the drive to within 100 yards of the Bluecoat brigades, but, alone and unsupported, it was easily stopped. Their every effort checked, the Secessionists now sullenly abandoned the attack. Shortly before dusk, their main body fell back to regroup along the fence bordering the northern edge of the woods between Pegram's and Jones's farms, where Potter had tarried in midafternoon. Even there they were under musketry and artillery fire, but the woods and depression afforded them some protection. Only the two South Carolina regiments pinned down near the gate, Pegram, and the two sharpshooter battalions still remained near Pegram's house to keep up the fight. With some Butternut units now fixed in place and others with-

COMMENTARY

1. This map portrays the situation after McGowan drove Harriman from the ridge north of Pegram's house and after Parke and Griffin created their final defense line across Pegram's farm. Heasley's battery is shown in the position to which it probably returned after retreating from the ridge to Fort Archer. Hofmann is shown approaching the front line.

2. The positions of Sickel, Lane, and Willie Pegram are approximate.

3. Monroe had 14 guns (three batteries) on Peebles's farm. Wainwright had 16 guns (four batteries) on the Peebles's house knoll plus Rogers in the works west of Fort Archer. The captain subsequently reinforced Griffin just before fighting ended for the day.

drawing, Wilbur, who had remained between two battling commands virtually unscathed, was at last able to leave his cover and fall back to the safety of the farmyard.[33]

The Bluecoats had halted Wilcox's main striking force at last. Their own generalship in finally forging a line through Pegram's yard and their hard fighting in holding that line entitles them to much of the credit for this success. Yet their victory was unquestionably made easier by Confederate shortcomings. Not only had the main Butternut column lost much of its punch in defeating four brigades farther north, but also it launched its final attacks unsupported on either flank. Cowan, Martin, and Davis were so busy bagging Curtin that they provided no assistance on the right near Arthur's Swamp. Hampton's other troopers, too, were still grinding up the "Hamburgers" west of the stream and made only minimal efforts to engage the main Federal line, probes that Hartranft easily fended off.

McGregor, too, did little more than engage in a curious duel with a Yankee sharpshooter. The marksman, perched high in a tree, spotted a promising target: three horsemen gathered in conference. They proved to be no ordinary horsemen, either, but "Rooney" Lee, Barringer, and one of the Virginia colonels, either Davis or Richard Beale of the 9th. The sniper took aim on them, fired, and killed a nearby private. Again he fired; this time he almost hit another enlisted man near the cluster. The riders did not wait for him to zero in on them but looked around for countermeasures. The major general lacked marksmen of his own, so he called on the Second Stuart House Artillery. In his first shot McGregor blasted the sharpshooter out of the tree. This unusual contest provided the subject for camp lore, and it perhaps saved the lives of some able cavalry leaders. But it contributed nothing to Wilcox's effort to overrun Pegram's farm and recapture the Squirrel Level Line.[34]

Confederate troops on Wilcox's opposite flank, the left, admittedly played a much more active role than the cavalry. The problem there was that they engaged only after McGowan and Lane had been checked. This force, McComb's, had originally been slated to support the South Carolinians back at Jones's. They, however, had charged before he could come up, and the farther south they went, the more they pulled away from him. The gap widened still farther as his men bogged down in the thickets along and south of the upper fork of Old Town Creek. The Light Division had passed that ravine with ease, but the supporting brigade encountered much difficulty. The commander of the 55th Virginia, Major Robert B. Fauntleroy, later reported:

> On the evening of the 30th of September we moved forward by the flank, right in front, encountering difficult and boggy ground,

tangled with brush and strong, matted undergrowth. Emerging
from thence we formed line of battle, but owing still to the intrac-
table nature of the ground in front were moved by Colonel
McComb by flank farther to the left, formed, and were ordered
forward, but the difficulties of ground still increasing, we were
compelled to move by flank to extricate us from the almost impassable jungle of tangled briers, grape-vines, and alder bushes.[35]

After finally extricating itself, the brigade paused briefly to deploy.
The 14th Tennessee held its right, and the 7th Tennessee, 1st Tennessee (Provisional Army), 13th Alabama, and 2nd Maryland Battalion
prolonged the line leftward. Then came three Virginia units, and either
now or after passing through the next thicket, the 55th held the far left
of the battle line. The brigade sharpshooter battalion ranged still farther east to cover that flank. McComb exercised direct command of
these men, but Archer went along to oversee operations. The general,
captured at Gettysburg, had been in Yankee hands for about a year,
and this was his first battle after being exchanged.

He soon saw plenty of action to make up for that lost year. As he
moved southward over the eastern part of Jones's field, he received
word from Wilcox not to follow the main body but to continue straight
down the Church Road to outflank Parke's right on Pegram's farm.
The Marylander dutifully plunged into the woods just east of the
source of the lower fork of Old Town Creek. Some light works there,
apparently still held by a few of Potter's refugees, proved no barrier
and were easily overrun. The swampy headwaters again turned out
to be the real obstacles. The Secessionists lost more valuable time
floundering through them. On finally emerging from the marsh, they
did not halt to dress ranks but simply tried to reform them (with only
partial success) while continuing to advance past Boswell's house and
onto Pegram's farm. Moving through the woods and swamps so delayed them that Wilcox's main body was checked before they really
engaged. The major general admittedly later reported that he broke
off the battle only because he mistook their advance for a Federal
force threatening his left, but the IX Corps clearly played a bigger
role in forcing him to fall back than did this misapprehension. Even
more significantly, by the time the fresh brigade finally reached the
front, it no longer found itself able to outflank the right of the Bluecoats in Pegram's yard. By now those Northerners connected with
the First Division of the V Corps, which had moved up from Peebles's
farm and seized the crest across the Church Road, right astride
Archer's path, just in the nick of time.

As the Confederates moved south from Jones's, some of them
evidently stopped long enough to scavenge among the wreckage of

Simon Griffin's brigade, for as they burst forth on Spear's front, many
of them were wearing various items of blue uniforms. Their somewhat
disorganized ranks further contributed to their appearance. In the rapidly fading light, many Union officers mistook them for more of
Parke's refugees and called on their men to hold their fire. But the junior officers and soldiers in the ranks were not deceived. They could tell
that these grimly determined figures rapidly closing in on them—every
one firmly clutching his rifle, many already firing them—were not
panic-stricken Unionists at all but attacking Secessionists. Therefore,
just as McComb's men came rushing down toward the ridge, Griffin's
battle line blasted them with a devastating discharge of lead. This murderous fire ripped through the Butternut ranks and slammed them to a
halt. Yet Archer's veterans stood up under it and shot back at the sheet
of fire blazing away along the crest. East of the highway both sides
battled in heavy forest. West of the road the Northerners stood exposed, while at least some Confederates were protected along the edge
of a point of woods, though others were in the open cornfield.
Valiantly the Southerners pressed on toward the summit. The Virginians made little progress through the trees toward Spear's right and
Sickel, but the Marylanders and Alabamians almost made it to the
Union battle line. Farther west some Tennesseans, probably the 1st,
actually closed with the 20th Maine in hand-to-hand fighting. For a little over thirty minutes the two lines were locked in mortal combat.

Both sides stood up well to their task, despite rapidly mounting casualties. Spear himself was wounded at this time, though he apparently
retained command. One of his regimental commanders, Captain James
Wheaton of the 1st Michigan, was killed, and a Confederate battalion
commander, Captain Ferdinand Duvall of the Maryland outfit, was
critically wounded. The 16th Michigan, which had already lost its
colonel earlier in the afternoon, continued to be particularly hard-hit.
Just as it deployed, Pegram exploded a shell in its ranks, causing it to
reel "like a drunken man."[86] To make matters worse, the experimental
Lindsay rifles that it was combat testing now proved more dangerous to
users than to intended victims. These curious weapons were supposed
to fire two bullets from one barrel, but several hours of use had so be-
fouled them that both bullets now fired simultaneously—thus causing
the breech to blow up in the user's face. Despite all these handicaps the
regiment stood by its comrades and fought as best it could. Perhaps
some of the Michiganders already began discarding the treacherous
rifles for usable guns of the fallen. Federals all along the line unquestionably searched the cartridge boxes of the casualties for more ammunition with which to keep up the fight. Griffin, all the while, added

his own intangible contribution as he personally supervised his embattled line, directing his officers and reassuring his men:

> And then amid it all [wrote one of Spear's men of the tumult], General Griffin came along, resolute, heroic, impressive, with assuring words and comforting promises of help. The wavering lines stiffened; strong men were strengthened and the weak made strong. From now on it was his fight, and his presence in inspiring the men was almost equal to the promised support of his batteries.[37]

"Almost equal" to artillery support the general's contribution may have been, but he knew better than really to substitute himself for his guns. His qualities of leadership and generalship were already slowly beginning to tip the balance in favor of the Bluecoats. The arrival of Hofmann's brigade to support his left shortly before 6:00 added further to his advantage. But what really hastened that tendency and conclusively turned the tide against Archer was the magnificent Northern artillery. Battery H, ordered forward by Warren, now came galloping up the Church Road through a hail of bullets overshooting the First Division. The fire was so heavy that many gunners feared they could not survive passing through it. But pass it they did—only to discover that Griffin demanded still more of them. An ex-artillerist himself with a long record in both branches of running his guns in close, he was not about to let his line of battle mask his artillery the way McComb was now blocking Pegram's field of fire. The general, accordingly, directed the New Yorkers to unlimber right on the battle line itself. Getting in that close made even the stouthearted Mink a little wary, and he exclaimed to the division commander:

> "My God, General, do you mean for me to put my guns out on that skirmish line?"
>
> "Yes [replied Griffin], rush them in there; artillery is no better than infantry, put them in line, and let them fight together."[38]

The captain, therefore, pushed one section into line between the 118th and the 16th and put the other one on Gregory's sector, where the 155th simply lay down to uncover its field of fire.

Once his Napoleons actually "joined in the awful music," the one-armed captain rapidly warmed to the occasion. "The old fellow enjoyed the fight amazingly," Wainwright duly noted, "especially the taking of the 9th Corps's place."[39] Mink was less pleased, though, to see his limber chests rapidly being exhausted of canister. Finally, when he got down to a mere three rounds per gun, he actually had to cease firing and gallingly stand idle until he could secure more ammunition. Only if the Southerners threatened to push the Yankees off the ridge

would he fire his last twelve charges. But the blue infantry was in no
danger of being driven and held firm until the battery caissons could
bring up more canister from Peebles's. Foot soldiers now eagerly lent
the gun crews a hand in passing out the ammunition. Mink used these
charges to good advantage and tore the Confederate ranks horribly.
Desperately the Graycoats tried to silence him. Once they charged to
within fifty yards of his guns. But they could not reach him or stop
him.

Nor could they hold out for long, alone and unsupported. They had
no alternative but to fall back to the southern edge of the woods near
Boswell's. From the protection of those trees, Archer's men continued
firing on the exposed Unionists on the open portion of the ridge west of
the highway. Federal riflemen replied, but again it was Northern artillery that proved decisive. Mink now double-shotted his guns and raked
the woods with ghastly effect. He was joined in the effort by Battery B
of his regiment, which Wainwright personally led forward in response
to Warren's call for more guns. Though slightly injured en route, the
colonel managed to bring up the fresh company and add it to the battle
line. It only got off six shots at Archer, though, because Battery H and
the First Division had already decided the outcome before it arrived.
The Yankee fire was just too devastating. The Southerners could stand
it no more. Some under orders, some not—they abandoned the struggle
and withdrew northward out of range, leaving some of their dead and
wounded on the field.[40]

Darkness had already fallen. Still the fighting sputtered on. Wilcox's
combat brigades had pulled back by now, but his belligerent sharpshooters kept on sniping—and were answered in kind from the blue
lines. The pop-pop-pop of the marksmen's fire was broken now and
again by the dull thud of an artillery report as Pegram dueled
Wainwright and Heasley. The Union infantrymen, who had so welcomed Mink to their sector when they needed his help against the
Tennesseans, were not so glad to have him around now that he—and
those around him—had become targets for Southern guns. Beyond
making the foot soldiers understandably apprehensive, though, the Virginians did no real harm. Soon even the shelling and the skirmishing
fell silent.[41]

"Night put an end to further operations," read Heth's characteristically disingenuous one-sentence report of what happened south of
Jones's farm on September 30.[42] Yet it was not really night at all but
hard-fighting Northerners who ended the combat there—and ended it
in a fashion that deserved more than a one-sentence summary. The
fighting that raged on the crest across the Church Road was the most
severe of the whole day. For the Federals it was also the most decisive.

Just as Wilcox's victory on Jones's farm—the Confederate high point —prevented the Yankees from reaching the Boydton Plank Road, so did Parke's and, even more so, Griffin's victory on Pegram's farm prevent the Secessionists from recovering their losses of early afternoon. Wilcox had thrown in his last fresh unit, and it had failed. The last Union line had held. The first day of the Battle of Poplar Spring Church was over.

CHAPTER XI

———◆———

"Damn Dunovant!"

Heavy fighting on September 30 entailed heavy casualties. Approximately 600 Confederates fell that day: 273 of Wilcox's men, an estimated 217 of Heth's, and approximately 106 horsemen. Federal casualties were 3½ times as great: 1,928 in the IX Corps, 316 in the V Corps, and around 12 in the cavalry—a total of 2,256. Approximately 1,400 of those Bluecoats were missing in action, of whom roughly 1,300 were actually captured. Such losses represent 9 per cent of the entire Union striking force, including cavalry and artillery. For hard-hit Potter and Hartranft the proportions were much higher: a staggering 29 per cent. Some Southern units, especially in Archer's Brigade, had been severely battered, too. The little 2nd Maryland Battalion, for instance, lost 43 of its 149 men. "If this continues," lamented a survivor, "there will be none of us left to tell the tale."[1]

Despite the frightful losses, the tactical results remained indecisive. The Yankees managed to seize an important outer enemy line but did not reach their main goal, the Boydton Plank Road, let alone the Southside Railroad or even Petersburg. The Graycoats, in turn, succeeded in hurling back the thrust at their communications but did not recover the key intersections around Peebles's farm. Each side's inability to achieve its full objectives made resumption of combat virtually inevitable. Yet for a time darkness provided a welcome respite from the fighting. Like two giants who had grappled all day, both sides now pulled apart to lick their wounds, to rest, and to plan and prepare for another round on the morrow.

Heth and Wilcox regrouped their scattered columns—MacRae, Martin, Cowan, and the troops who had fought on Pegram's farm—in the woods along the southern edge of Jones's plantation. For three hours their gray battle line stood vigil, just in case Meade launched a surprise night attack. The Southern commanders might well have surmised that the Yankees they had hammered so hard in late afternoon would be in no condition to attack again that day. They might have drawn the same conclusion from the musketry and shelling that the IX Corps hurled in their general direction. Shielded from this random and largely ineffectual fire by the bald ridge—even though one shell did grievously wound Martin in the left leg—they could well have inferred that it was basically a defensive fire to keep them away, not an offensive fire to presage another Northern blow. Still, with the fate of Lee's vital communications in their hands, Heth and Wilcox were taking no chances: They kept their weary infantrymen in line.

At last, nature gave the exhausted soldiers the respite their commanders would not permit. Shortly after fighting on the Church Road ended, the severe rainstorm that had so drenched Lee's and Butler's men on Chaffin's Bluff earlier that evening also broke on the Southside. The cloudbursts turned the fields to mud, across which no Federal line of battle could attack at night. What Meade's lack of activity might have suggested to Heth, the downpour confirmed: The Yankees would not charge that evening. The Southern leaders, accordingly, pulled Dunlop's and Wooten's sharpshooter battalions back from Pegram's to picket the woods and withdrew their main body to the vicinity of Jones's house at about 9:00 P.M. They made this move, Wilcox said, in order to be near a good supply of water—as if his drenched men did not have water enough already. More plausible reasons for the disengagement were to break contact with the enemy, provide a greater measure of security for resting, and prepare for the morrow. For now, though, the North Carolinian simply bivouacked his own two brigades on the spot, except for such individuals as had already been sent to Petersburg for medical attention or for escorting the hordes of prisoners. Hampton, too, moved at least his Third Division and probably Joel Griffin as well back between 9:00 and 10:00 to the temporary camps on the plank road, where they arrived at about 11:00. This time the cavalry corps commander bivouacked right with his men rather than return to his headquarters south of Hatcher's Run.[2]

Archer, MacRae, and most of Pegram, on the other hand, did not yet get their much-needed rest. A. P. Hill had other plans for them. The lieutenant general apparently spent most of the day at Dunn's Hill and Petersburg. Only after fighting ended did he finally reach Jones's

farm, too late to conduct direct operations against the Unionists. His
visit to the front, however, at least helped him plan for the morrow.
He, accordingly, spent the night arranging to give Meade a dose of his
own medicine. The Federal commander and Grant, too, constantly
relished the prospect of catching Hill outside his earthworks. But now
that the Federals had exposed themselves outside their own trenches,
the combative Virginian thought in the same terms. Though vigilant
against the danger that Northern reinforcements from east of the Cockade City might bolster the strike force to renew the Union drive, he
determined to retain the initiative he had seized in late afternoon. A
mere twenty-four hours earlier he and his chief had seriously considered abandoning Petersburg. Now the city seemed safe, and he devoted his attention not to retreating but to hurling back the foe.

The memory of the Battle of Globe Tavern may have been strong in
his mind as he drew up plans for October 1. On the first day of that engagement, also, the Unionists had come out of their works to threaten
Lee's communications, only to have Heth hit their left and stop them
cold. The following day Heth had again threatened their left, but this
time Mahone had rolled up their exposed right. Only Hill's lack of
reserves plus the timely arrival of Willcox's reinforcements had saved
Warren from disaster on August 19. Now six weeks later, history
seemed to repeat itself. Once more the Bluecoats had marched from
their defenses, seized an intermediate position, and then received a severe rebuff as their left advanced farther. As the second day of the Battle of Poplar Spring Church approached, might not the Yankees once
more pay most attention to their supposedly threatened left and neglect
their right? Intelligence from Mahone at W. W. Davis' that the
Unionists on the Squirrel Level Road appeared weak suggested that
they would. Here Hill again saw his opening. He moved promptly to
capitalize on this supposed Federal blunder.

At the same time he sought to avoid the mistake he had made on the
second day at Globe Tavern: On October 1, he would attack in
strength. Lack of available manpower again handicapped him as he assembled his striking force—what with Field, Hoke, and Scales committed to Chaffin's Bluff and with Mahone and Johnson guarding Petersburg itself against a direct attack. Still, the corps commander gathered
what units he could. He at last utilized the grand-tactical reserve that
he had assembled the previous evening. Cooke's and Joseph Davis'
fresh brigades, already in the vicinity of Battery No. 45, were readily
available to attack down the Squirrel Level Road. To strengthen their
column, the corps commander shifted the weight of his mobile force
from right to left. When Heth and the Purcell Artillery and Crenshaw
Artillery withdrew from the woods at 9:00 P.M., Hill did not leave

them on Jones's farm but moved them back to the Boydton Plank Road, thence toward the city.

The lieutenant general, however, did not yet go so far as to transfer his main striking force outside his works. He allowed Archer to camp near the upper end of the Church Road, permitted Cooke to bivouac along the plank road about half a mile southwest of Battery No. 45, posted Davis and possibly MacRae near that fort itself, and kept only outposts (Ferebee's and perhaps Mahone's skirmishers, too) at W. W. Davis'. Still, he had already taken the major step to concentrate his column of attack. Early Saturday, he completed these preparations by rousing Archer's Brigade at about 3:00 A.M. and bringing the whole force together near No. 45. As Cooke's men retraced their steps toward the city, they congratulated themselves that they had been spared fighting and were now returning to the relative safety of the town. The halt near the fort, shortly followed by their transfer down the Squirrel Level Road, dashed these hopes. They now realized that they were heading for the combat zone, after all. Indeed they were, for Hill had forged their whole division plus Pegram's two batteries into a powerful striking force of approximately 4,750 men.

To increase its prospects, the corps commander directed the troops still at Jones's, Wilcox's two brigades and Brander's battery, nearly 2,400 strong, to feint against Meade's front on Pegram's farm on October 1. While Wilcox distracted the Yankees, Heth would strike straight south on the Squirrel Level Road and roll up the Federal right even more effectively than Mahone had done against Crawford on August 19. At the same time Hampton's men on the plank road were to return to their former sector and co-operate against the Union left as opportunity permitted. Butler in the meantime would try to regain control of the Vaughan Road at least through McDowell's, if not farther. Thus Powell Hill planned his battle. He would make history repeat itself. Indeed, he might even outdo his fine performance of August 19 and cut the Yankee strike force off from its main defenses to the east.[3]

But there were other students of history in Southside Virginia that evening, veteran officers in blue. They learned from their mistakes— and they remembered that there had been a third day of heavy fighting at Globe Tavern. They, too, made plans for October 1.

The Federal generals, at first, thought only of defending what they had seized. The stiff Confederate resistance of late afternoon initially made them abandon hope of reaching the plank road and caused them to concentrate on resisting the expected onslaught by Hill on Saturday. Warren, indeed, actually went so far as to reinforce his old stronghold around Globe Tavern, lest the Southerners should try to recapture the Weldon Railroad itself and thereby undo the Union gains of the past six weeks. Though he could not keep his afternoon promise to give Hofmann back to Crawford, the V Corps commander did feel safe in sending three batteries back to his base to bolster Dresser's companies already there and to be ready to reinforce Flowers'. To support the field force, Wainwright left the two batteries that had fought with Griffin plus Lieutenant Lester Richardson's Battery D/1st New York Light Artillery, all under Fitzhugh. The other three batteries the brigadier led back to the tavern, where he parked them in reserve on his old drill ground before 9:00 P.M. Attentive to his horses like the good artillerist he was, he then had his teams unhitched so they could rest for the night. Still, he warned his subordinates to be ready to move out again at daylight and to be prepared to rush to the ramparts without awaiting orders, should the Butternuts attack.[4]

With these matters arranged, Wainwright gladly sought relief from the cold rain in the warm, comfortable tavern. Before nine o'clock he was joined by Meade, who had ridden back from the front after fighting ended. The army commander expected a train to meet him, but, through some error, none had arrived. Most of his staff then trotted on to army headquarters, but he, Humphreys, and an aide, all of whom had had enough of the blustery weather, determined to wait in the tavern for the train.

As Meade sat there, he thought over the day's developments. Not sanguine of a major success to begin with, he was now sure his initial analysis was correct. At 9:00 P.M. he wired Grant news of the afternoon's operations, reported that Heth and Wilcox were still on the Southside, and then drew his own conclusion: "I do not think it judicious to make another advance tomorrow unless re-enforced or some evidence can be obtained of the weakening of the enemy."[5]

Such tidings must have surprised the General-in-Chief. After returning from Deep Bottom in the early morning, he had remained at City Point all day and thus depended on dispatches from subordinates to keep him posted. Such messages just six hours earlier had left him confident that "the enemy are prepared to leave Petersburg if forced a little." Neither of Williams' routine messages to him at 6:30 and 8:00 P.M. changed this assessment. The later one reported the sighting of an estimated Confederate regiment moving up from the enemy right to camp just southwest of Petersburg. The earlier telegram indicated that 2,000 to 3,000 Confederates had been spotted marching south through Chesterfield at 2:00 P.M. Although Union intelligence did not realize that those troops were the Light Division returning from Dunlop's, not reinforcements from the Howlett Line or the Peninsula, the Illinoisan apparently attached no significance to their movement. Not until he received Meade's telegram of 9:00 P.M. did he realize that all was not proceeding well with the Army of the Potomac. Even so, such a change of prospects did not leave him downcast or desirous of finding a scapegoat. Grant had a war to win, and to do that, he had to deal with realities, not hopes, in search of such victory. That quest briefly made him consider calling off the attack below Petersburg and seeking victory on the Northside by transferring one of Meade's corps there over the weekend if the Cockade City continued to be held in force. Still, he was not yet prepared to concede that nothing further could be gained south of the Appomattox. Accordingly, at 9:40, he sent new instructions to the Pennsylvanian in line with the revised grand-tactical situation:

> You need not advance tomorrow, unless in your judgment an advantage can be gained, but hold on to what you have, and be ready to advance. We must be greatly superior to the enemy on one flank or the other, and by working around at each end, we will find where the enemy's weak point is. General Butler was assaulted three times this afternoon, but repulsed all of them. I will direct him to feel up the Darbytown road tomorrow.[6]

Once again Grant revealed his fine technique of command. In essence, he deferred to the opinion of his ablest executive officer, whose knowledge of conditions at the front exceeded his own. Yet he seemed subtly to suggest that the Army of the Potomac ought to be more active on Saturday than Meade planned for it to be. In his first sentence, the lieutenant general did not insist on pressing the attack. At the same time, however, he encouraged the subordinate to strike anyway if "an advantage can be gained" and further advised him, no matter what, not to renounce the idea of attacking but to be "ready to advance." That such an advance was likely became clear in the second sentence, which revealed that Grant still hoped to turn one of Lee's flanks "and by working around at each end, we will find where the enemy's weak point is." The Army of the James would definitely have a role trying to "work around" one flank on October 1. The whole tone of the dispatch suggested that the Illinoisan would like for the Army of the Potomac to operate against the other flank.

Meade had predicated a new advance on receipt of considerable reinforcements or positive news of Confederate weakness. Grant could give him neither, although around 10:30 P.M. he did advise the Pennsylvanian to use the three new regiments just assigned him to relieve veterans to join the field force. At 11:30 the major general replied that he had previously earmarked them for that purpose and that the 210th had already helped replace the Iron Brigade. Meade did not go on to say it, but 2,100 raw recruits were hardly the reinforcements he had in mind. Veterans Grant would not provide, nor would he dispatch cold, harsh, peremptory orders to govern a situation he could not fully know from City Point. What the General-in-Chief did send was more important: a single message that showed his confidence in the essence of Meade's judgment and yet considerately but effectively managed to arrange that his own plans would be carried out.[7]

Meade evidently got the hint (if such it was), for by the time his train finally brought him back to his headquarters just before 10:30, he had decided to resume the initiative. At 11:45 P.M. he ordered Parke and Warren to advance a strong, well-supported line the next morning to develop the Confederate position. Fifteen minutes later he informed City Point of his intentions. Meantime Grant apparently passed along Butler's report of 7:50 that Hoke and Field were definitely on the Northside and that Heth was ordered to go there. Although this intelligence reached Birchett's at 10:00, Meade evidently did not read it until near midnight. But when he did, he realized its significance, so at 12:15 A.M. Humphreys gave the two corps commanders on Peebles's farm a greatly expanded mission:

> General Butler has Field's and Hoke's divisions and part of Pickett's before him. Lee may send away more troops from this side of the Appomattox. If your reconnaissances show the enemy to have left your front, and the indications are that he has sent off more troops against Butler, it is advisable that you get onto the Boydton plank road. If you deem it practicable, advance to and make a lodgment on it.

Meade and his Chief-of-Staff, of course, disbelieved—indeed, scorned—Butler's reports, especially the ones of 11:30 P.M. and 12:30 A.M., which City Point forwarded at 3:00 A.M., to the effect that Heth and Wilcox as well were already in his front and that only Johnson and Mahone remained at Petersburg. "Abou Ben Butler had quite a stampede last night," snickered one officer at Birchett's; "having got so far away from home, he conceived that the whole Southern host was massed to crush him, and communicated the same with much eloquence, by the instrumentality of the magnetic telegraph; whereat Major-General Humphreys, Chief-of-Staff, had the brutality to laugh." Humphreys and Meade knew all too well where Heth and Wilcox were, and at 9:00 and again at midnight they provided Grant enough proof of this for him to "cork Butler back in his bottle." Nevertheless, the intelligence reports and Grant's comments now caused Birchett's once more to think of attacking.

Army headquarters, moreover, took steps to add greater weight to its striking force. At midnight Humphreys at last made the hard-fighting dragoons an integral part of the column of attack. He directed Gregg to march from the Vaughan Road to Parke's left at daylight and then scout and, if necessary, fight westward along Route 673, then northward on the Harman Road in co-operation with the infantry's advance. At about the same time the Chief-of-Staff also began carrying out Grant's suggestion of late afternoon that one division of the II Corps be transferred from the quiet right to the field force just prior to striking a new blow.[8]

The heavy fighting that had raged west of the Weldon Railroad and north of the James that day did not embroil Hancock's and Crawford's sectors. Even darkness brought no more than the customary flare-ups of picket and artillery fire. At about 5:30 P.M. Miles's men and Gibbon's right stirred up a brief fire fight with Goode and McAfee. Neither side sought battle there, though. The Virginians, indeed, deliberately held their fire to be ready in case the Yankees charged in earnest. After just fifteen minutes both sides let the firing die down. Then near 7:00 the Graycoats demonstrated against Gibbon's right. Miles responded with artillery fire, and other guns down the works to just west of the Jerusalem Plank Road added their fire. Pickets on Mahone's left and Ferrero's right then became engaged, too. For thirty to sixty minutes the skirmishing and shelling flickered along the line. Then they too subsided.

Such firing sufficed to demonstrate to each side that the enemy remained across the way in force. Hancock noted only the withdrawal of two Confederate heavy guns but could detect no other weakening of Southern lines. Johnson, too, realized that the Unionists were still present in strength, although later in the night Northern deserters informed him that the II Corps was spreading itself thin. Despite this basic continuation of the status quo, neither side took any chances. For instance, Hancock, concerned that the First Division's unauthorized shelling at 7:00 portended a serious attack, moved the last reserve artillery unit of the whole garrison force, a section of the 14th Massachusetts Battery, into the works near Fort Morton. But when he learned the cause of the firing, he sought to give himself a new mobile reserve to meet new threats, including those from cavalry against his rear. Accordingly, just after midnight, he transferred the 3rd Vermont Battery from front-line duty in Fort Sedgwick to a virtual reserve position in Battery No. 17, a detached work between the Norfolk Railroad and the Baxter Road in rear of Fort Meikel. Further to provide a reserve and strengthen the rear, approximately 150 to 200 dismounted cavalry came forward from City Point and bivouacked about half a mile behind Fort Patrick Kelly on the rear line.

Shifting platoons, companies, and battalions provided Hancock some increase in security but not much. Four minutes after midnight, however, Humphreys gave him a bigger reserve, with a more important mission. The Chief-of-Staff ordered him to withdraw a whole division from his lines that night, prepared to join the field force should Meade so direct. The foot soldiers, however, were not to move to Peebles's farm right away. The army commander apparently preferred awaiting the results of the strike force's reconnaissances in the morning before bringing the reinforcements forward. Still, the troops were at least ready for his call.[9]

Meade thus planned to reconnoiter in force and, if circumstances permitted, to attack in strength on October 1. The two corps commanders who were to execute this plan, however, did not share their superior's optimism as they looked forward to Saturday. Throughout the night both Warren and Parke continued to believe that the army should concentrate on holding its limited gain.

Meade, of course, had agreed with them while still at the front in early evening. Concerned then that his strike force was vulnerable to a frontal or flank attack or to being cut off from the Weldon Railroad, he overruled Griffin's desire to remain on Pegram's farm and directed all three divisions to fall back to Peebles's farm. That position, less exposed, nearer to the Globe Tavern works, possessed of ready-made defenses of its own (the Squirrel Level Line), offered his army much greater security. Humphreys duly issued this order at 7:45, but Parke and Griffin remained on Pegram's farm several hours longer. Like Wilcox and Heth north of the woods, they stood guard against a surprise night assault, an attack that seemed all the more probable when their scouts detected Dunlop and Wooten in the woods south of Jones's. But when these shadowy figures in gray had not charged by late evening, Parke and Warren apparently concluded that fighting was over for the day and pulled their men back at about 11:00. To cover their withdrawal, Willcox, Potter, and probably Griffin left at least the 24th New York Cavalry, 1/38th Wisconsin, 6th and 9th New Hampshire, part of the 31st Maine, 18th and 32nd Massachusetts, and apparently 17th Vermont to picket Pegram's farm. Warren, moreover, directed Hofmann's whole brigade to dig in near the Pegram house, a grand guard indeed. With the Federals retiring southeast and the Secessionists already withdrawn northwest, the two sides were now effectively disengaged. Only their pickets kept quiet vigil on the no-man's-land of Pegram's farm.[10]

As soon as they reached Peebles's, the Bluecoats worked hard to secure their position. On the far left Harriman returned to his general location of early afternoon near the Clements house, where he covered Route 673 and the southern approach up the Squirrel Level Road. Two hours after leaving Pegram's, Hartranft took position to the First Brigade's right to extend the line north toward Fort Archer. Both brigades then entrenched that night. McLaughlen meantime thought he was supposed to plug the gap between Harriman and Potter. The Massachusetts man discovered, however, that the Second Brigade already adjoined the First and that, even so, his line could not extend all the way to the Second Division. He accordingly took position on low ground to Hartranft's right and then advanced slightly to more favorable terrain and threw out pickets 150 yards to his front. There the colonel simply bivouacked. He had had enough of aimless nighttime maneuvering in the rain and did not want to lay out a line of works until he could carefully examine the ground in the daylight. The First Division thus formed a flank line facing west and southwest to cover the army's left but not connecting, by the length of a brigade front, with the troops in the captured defenses, facing north.

North of Willcox, Simon Griffin's regrouping refugees held the left portion of the Squirrel Level Line on Peebles's farm, and Curtin's brigade extended Parke's line to the western edge of Fort Archer. Warren's line began in the fort itself and ran northeast along the old Confederate trenches to Chappell's farm. Sickel adjoined the IX Corps, and Spear, then Gregory prolonged the line rightward. Both Potter's and Griffin's men spent the night refacing these works to guard against attack down the Church Road from Jones's, across Pegram's. To add weight to this position, Robert Rogers' guns apparently took position in Fort Archer, and Battery H and the 19th and 34th New York batteries bolstered Potter's sector. The 7th Maine Battery, however, now dropped back to join Monroe's other company in reserve on the Peebles's house knoll, and Richardson's battery, too, remained in support behind Ayres's works.

This powerful line across Peebles's farm barred a frontal assault from the northwest. But what would happen if Hill should try to roll up the Federal right or even cut the expeditionary force off from the Weldon Railroad? What would happen if he should attempt a flank attack south along the Squirrel Level Road? This time the Union commanders were alert to those dangers; they had learned their lesson on the second day at Globe Tavern.

While Humphreys was still at the front, he directed Warren to entrench a line back to Crawford's position, facing north. Throughout the night the V Corpsmen tried to erect this trace. The Union generals still devoted more manpower, armament, and effort to defending Peebles's farm, but they also made sure that Hill could not surprise their right.

Ayres's division was already in position facing north across Chappell's farm to help cover the right and also to threaten Hill's main line west of the Weldon Railroad. Warren now directed it to concentrate on refusing the flank eastward from Griffin's right. Accordingly, at about 9:00 P.M. Ayres called up the 146th New York from the Vaughan Road and sent only the 10th and 12th U.S. and light details from his other two brigades to replace the heavy skirmish line in the woods between Chappell's and W. W. Davis'. The voltigeurs who had relieved Spear's regiments that afternoon then rejoined their brigades and helped dig defenses on Chappell's. The men, of course, could not create an elaborate system of fortifications in only one dark, rainy evening, but they did manage to throw up enough earth to protect themselves—"a light line of breastworks," their general called it.[11] Behind this parapet Otis posted the 15th New York Heavies and 11th U.S. left of Fort Bratton, the 5th and 146th New York in the fort, the 14th U.S. to its right, and the 140th New York and 17th U.S. in reserve. Grimshaw extended the line rightward across Chappell's field just east of the Squirrel Level Road, and Graham prolonged the line into the woods along the headwaters of the northeastern fork of Arthur's Swamp. By daylight their line was sufficiently fortified to constitute a formidable barrier to Heth's advance.[12]

Ayres's men, however, could not stretch all the way to the Halifax Road or even to the Vaughan Road. Warren, therefore, requested Crawford to reach out to meet them. Far from returning Hofmann to Globe Tavern, the corps commander now judged that he needed with the field force all available veteran infantry. Baxter's fixed garrisons could not be withdrawn from their forts without Meade's permission. Nor was it felt advisable to move Bragg's outposts picketing from in front of Fort Howard westward to the vicinity of the Weldon Railroad. The main body of the Iron Brigade, however, had been in reserve since midday. At 9:00 P.M., Warren sent word for it and two of the batteries returned from Peebles's to take position at Flowers' house on the Vaughan Road by dawn. The New Yorker suggested that the troops march at 5:00 A.M., but Crawford set them in motion by 3:00. Accompanied by the 15th New York Battery and L/1st New York Light Artillery, they marched across country to Flowers'. In a drenching downpour they deployed across the Vaughan Road there, facing north, and began entrenching. Bragg's skirmishers meantime ranged out from this new battle line to connect with Graham's outposts on the left and with Ayres's original skirmish line, still covering the sector west of Fort Wadsworth, on the right. The First Brigade's main body did not adjoin either the Marylanders or McCoy, yet it did fulfill its mission of bolstering the picket line that linked Warren to the railroad.[13]

To replace this outfit as Crawford's reserve, the corps commander, at 9:00 P.M., authorized the Pennsylvanian to retain any new regiments that reached the tavern. The 210th, of course, had already arrived, but other such units were more difficult to obtain, though several were potentially available. Both the 2/38th Wisconsin, 500 strong, and the 185th New York, 850 strong, had anchored off City Point on Thursday night. Along with 190 men of two New York companies, they reported for duty the following morning. The two companies, fragmentary units not combat-effective, were kept at the point, but the other two outfits became available for service at the front. The Wisconsinites were obviously slated to unite with their First Battalion in Harriman's brigade. They received travel orders at noon but did not actually take the train west until late afternoon. By the time they reached their station, nightfall and the absence of instructions made it difficult for them to join the strike force. They therefore spent the night in Crawford's sector, possibly at Globe Tavern, more likely at Jones's. Come morning, though, they would move on to the front.

The other new regiment, moreover, provided not even that limited measure of support to Crawford. Although Meade, as early as Thursday night, had indicated that he wanted it in his main army as soon as all its companies had debarked, he did not specify which corps would receive it. Some other cause of delay, perhaps the late arrival of the second transport carrying part of the unit, compounded the problem. As a result, Williams did not even begin inquiring where it should go until 3:45 P.M. on September 30. By the time the army commander could designate Crawford as recipient, it was 5:13, and nearly another hour elapsed before his instructions could pass through Birchett's to City Point. By then, no transportation to the front could be even tentatively promised to the regiment earlier than 9:00 P.M. And as matters worked out, it did not reach Globe Tavern until Saturday morning. Meade's assurance to Crawford that reinforcements would reach him after dark thus went unfulfilled, and the division commander had to pass the night without any permanent reserves.[14]

Yet his problem was small compared to those of the troops in the field. Already exhausted by a day of marching and fighting, they now had to spend the night fortifying. Lack of food, of fresh clothing, and of tents made matters worse. Some units would not get fresh, dry uniforms for days to come. Virtually everyone, moreover, was exposed to the elements. Except for a few senior officers who found shelter in nearby buildings—Griffin and Ayres in Pastor Talmage's home; Warren, Parke, and probably Willcox and Potter in Peebles's house—everyone from brigadier down had to bivouac in the rain and mud. Such conditions were hard enough for the V Corps, exultant over its victories. For the battered IX Corps, they only compounded the despair of defeat. Hundreds of Potter's men still straggled over the countryside from Fort MacRae to Fort Wadsworth. Some were conscientious soldiers, temporarily cut off from their units. Others were shirkers and coffee boilers, not at all anxious to get back to the battle line. Initial efforts now began to return such men to duty, though little was accomplished before daylight. Officers also began scouring camps and details to turn up such few men as remained from the three regiments destroyed on Jones's farm. To spare the 179th New York similar annihilation, it was now excused from combat duty, though presumably not from fatigue duty, until it could be armed. Potter's men who remained at the front, moreover, were chagrined and dismayed by their defeat. The general himself appeared "disconsolate" on into Saturday, and his soldiers looked and felt no different. "Miserable in body and mentally filled with regret and anger, we sullenly counted the hours of that dreary night," wrote a member of the 32nd Maine. The 35th Massachusetts agreed; "to say that there was a general feeling of shame and disgust . . ." declared one, "would weakly characterize the expressions used."[15]

Despite all these handicaps, though, the two corps managed to throw up a formidable barrier to Confederate counterattack. Yet it was almost too strong, for it unduly emphasized the defensive. To the survivors of the IX Corps, who were hardly in the mood to advance again, it offered a welcome refuge. It conduced even more to the attitudes of Parke and Warren. Like his men, the IX Corps commander got his fill of offensive operations that afternoon and preferred to stand on the defensive on Saturday. Concern that the strike force, now numbering only about 16,000 to 17,400 men for duty, was too weak to attack again further restrained him. Warren, too, did not favor another attack. Like so many engineers, the New Yorker abhorred the uncertainties of war and wanted to arrange everything perfectly before acting. Yet an attack, unless made in overwhelming force, could not help but generate uncertainty and disarray—witness the IX Corps's operations on Jones's farm that afternoon. The defensive, on the other hand, was his kind of battle. He could construct his works and deploy his troops perfectly and then invite the enemy to fight on his terms. Gouverneur Warren had a natural affinity for the line his men erected that evening.

Neither general was happy, then, to receive, about 5:00 A.M., Humphreys' orders of 11:45 P.M. and 12:15 A.M. to reconnoiter in force and be prepared to move toward the Boydton Plank Road. Of course, neither officer could directly disobey it, but they were not enthusiastic to carry it out, either. Fifteen minutes after Parke's copy arrived, he protested that his heavy losses on Friday, the presence of Confederates north of Pegram's farm, and the incomplete condition of his own lines made him "much prefer making ourselves secure in our present position." Although he dutifully promised to "do the best I can to acquire the desired information," the whole tone of his dispatch made clear that he would rather remain on the defensive. If Warren, too, replied, his message has not been found, but his actions of early morning confirm that he shared Parke's view. Without Meade or Humphreys present to prod them into action, the two corps commanders were not going to show much initiative when day broke.[16]

The Union cavalry commander, on the other hand, did display willingness to attack again. Willingness alone, however, counted for little on the part of an officer now subordinated to the defensive-minded Parke. Meade himself, for that matter, at first assigned Gregg only a defensive role for October 1. In his initial analysis after fighting ended on Pegram's farm and before Grant stirred him to attack again on Saturday, the army commander thought of using his cavalry only to help guard the defense line he was creating around Peebles's and Chappell's farms. At 8:15 that evening Humphreys, accordingly, directed Gregg to withdraw all of the First Brigade from the Harman Road to the Vaughan Road except for one regiment, which was to picket Parke's left around Fort MacRae. Both mounted brigades were then to concentrate at the key junction of the Vaughan and Wyatt roads at McDowell's farm to block any Confederate incursion up the Vaughan Road toward the infantry's left rear.

Much of Smith's force plus part of the 1st New Jersey Cavalry remained near that intersection throughout Friday, picketing and fortifying. Virtually nothing had disturbed them there; the 8th or possibly the 4th handily beat off a demonstration by some of Butler's outposts (perhaps from the 5th South Carolina Cavalry) along a lane running north to Wyatt's in late afternoon. Neither that probe nor one by an estimated battalion of Cobb's Legion, which temporarily drove in the pickets of the 2nd Pennsylvania Cavalry on the Stage Road that afternoon, only to be checked by the picket reserves, disturbed Gregg. He recognized them as feints and accorded them no more attention than needed to parry them. Still, he did have to keep part of his Second Brigade on guard against them. The rest of that brigade, apparently including the regiment sent up the Lower Church Road to connect with the strike force, he now concentrated around McDowell's. That close to the front the troopers could not unsaddle that evening but simply had to stake their saddled mounts to be ready for action.

Besides regrouping Smith's men, the general had to locate and recall Davies. On Friday morning part of the First Brigade, it will be remembered, had pressed along the Vaughan Road to the Cummings house, near which it had intermittently skirmished with Young throughout much of the day. Although most of his troops had joined him by late afternoon, Davies apparently remained stalled there when he received Meade's order of 4:15 P.M., relayed by Gregg before 5:20, to move up the Duncan and Harman roads and co-operate with Parke's advance toward the Boydton Plank Road. By the time these instructions arrived, the sound of firing told the brigadier that the IX Corps was being driven back, so he decided not to risk losing his whole brigade by marching to the plank road. On the other hand, this fine general did not want to return without accomplishing something. He therefore determined to reconnoiter north on the Duncan Road to see if he could at least gather some intelligence for his superiors.

He already had some information, of course—that Secessionists in some strength barred his path. Before he could find out more, he had to fight his way through that force. By the time he resumed advancing, the Butternut line had been weakened somewhat. In the intervening lull the Jeff Davis Legion, minus the attached 20th Georgia Cavalry Battalion, moved off southeast to relieve Cobb's Legion confronting the Unionists at Reams's Station. Waring accompanied his battalion, so command of the brigade likely either passed back to Young or possibly went to Colonel Gilbert J. Wright of Cobb's Legion, who returned from court-martial duty by October 1, if not by Friday. Even without Waring, Young still had plenty of men to meet the new threat. In the rapidly fading daylight the Bluecoats pressed his outposts back a little but could not break their line. Alarmed by this new flare-up, Butler moved Dunovant's Brigade, which had done much marching but little or no fighting thus far Friday, east along the crossroad running southeast from Armstrong's house toward the Vaughan Road. On nearing the front, the brigadier sent the 4th South Carolina Cavalry into action on foot and kept his main body in mounted reserve. Committing such a small force sufficed to check Davies' advance in that quarter, too. When the approach of night ended hostilities, the Southerners were still holding their own.

Then, almost unbelievably, the Confederate line, which had performed its counterreconnaissance mission so well in the face of the enemy, completely dissolved once fighting ended. Dunovant simply remounted the 4th and pulled his whole brigade all the way back to his camp on the Boydton Plank Road just south of Burgess' mill. Young, too, may have retired across Hatcher's Run via the Vaughan Road; he certainly made little effort, in any case, to picket his left or to keep an eye on Davies.[17]

Henry Davies was a soldier who needed to be watched, for initial setbacks left him undaunted. Even as the Southern line fell apart, he lurked in the woods near Mrs. Cummings' house, awaiting the opportunity to move. Just before dark, he determined to try again, so he led the 10th New York Cavalry, most of the 1st New Jersey Cavalry, and one squadron of the 6th Ohio Cavalry west on the crossroad toward Armstrong's house. To mask the Georgians and prevent them from striking his rear, he left the rest of the 6th plus the 1st Massachusetts Cavalry and 1st Pennsylvania Cavalry in breastworks along the edge of the woods. This time no Secessionist battle line barred his way. Only a few Confederate pickets briefly exchanged shots with his dismounted skirmishers, the Ohioans, before mounting and fleeing. The road to Armstrong's house was open at last. Along it pressed the mounted Jerseymen, followed by the 6th, then the 10th.

Davies, however, gained this advantage too late. Pitch darkness now closed in on his little column. Almost blindly the Bluecoats groped through the dense forests. The rainstorm—now torrential, now only misting—added to the discomfort and confusion. Several times the troops lost their way and wandered off the road. Only by lighting a candle, just briefly lest its light betray their location, could they find their way back. At least once, Beaumont's regiment mistook these lost men for Butternuts and fired on them as they tried to regain the road. To minimize this danger in the future, Davies kept the Ohioans on foot and dismounted the New Yorkers as well so they could keep to the road better as they trod along behind the mounted Jerseymen. As a further precaution, he subsequently shifted the horsemen behind the two dismounted units. All of these factors—darkness, rain, travel by foot—increased the normally cautious pace of a column penetrating enemy country at night. Davies consequently consumed nearly five hours traversing the one and a half miles between the Vaughan and Duncan roads.

As his men neared Armstrong's house from the east, they heard another column coming along the Duncan Road from the north: John Dunovant's Brigade. Its earlier withdrawal from the front evidently displeased, if not angered, Butler, not because it uncovered the Northerners but because it interfered with his plans to regain control of the east–west stretch of the Vaughan Road on Saturday morning. The division commander wanted the South Carolinians closer to the front on Friday evening so they could attack right after daybreak. Between 9:00 and 10:00 P.M. his messenger instructed Dunovant to move to Armstrong's mill, where the brigade could easily support Young. The South Carolinian rapidly called his men to horse and moved out. He could have traveled about half a mile south along the plank road, a little over two miles southeast to Dabney's mill, and then one mile northeast on the Duncan Road to Armstrong's mill, so Hatcher's Run would have shielded his entire march. Instead, he immediately crossed the stream and plunged east and southeast along the Creek Road for two miles until he struck the Duncan Road nearly one mile north of Armstrong's house. On reaching the Duncan Road, he turned south toward the mill. Familiar with the countryside, his men made reasonably good time, despite the rain and darkness that occasionally caused a few hapless troopers to collide with trees.

That evening Dunovant was supremely confident, not to say, oblivious to danger. Not only did he select a risky line of march north of the run, but he also traversed it with no vanguard except his own staff. Just after he left Burgess', he did use Captain M. A. Sullivan's ten camp guards to ride the point, but he soon dismissed Sullivan's warnings of peril and took the lead himself. "There is no danger on this road," the general proclaimed; "I will be the advance guard myself tonight."[18]

As Dunovant approached Armstrong's house from the north, the Federal column neared it from the east. Both sides were surprised to find a strange brigade on the road. The Federals reacted to the encounter with wise precautions. The 6th hurried off leftward to deploy across the Duncan Road, facing north. The 10th, accompanied by Davies himself, meantime formed line of battle astride the crossroad. Finally the 1st, still mounted, shifted ahead to support the Ohioans. In contrast, the Confederates reacted with bullheaded obstinacy.

"Halt!" shouted Captain E. S. Austin of the 6th Ohio Cavalry, "Halt, or we fire!"

This challenge upset the South Carolina aristocrat. Who did Young's pickets think they were, anyway, to interfere with a full brigadier general in the Confederate army? "I am Dunovant; let me pass."

"I don't know you," shot back the Yankee. "Dismount, one of you, and advance and give the countersign."

"I tell you I am Dunovant," the general repeated. "Let me pass."

"Damn Dunovant! We don't know you; if one of you do not dismount and come up here and let us know who you are, we will fire."

By now almost every South Carolinian at the head of the column knew their brigade had run into Federals. The only man who failed to grasp the point was the one who counted, John Dunovant.

The brigadier directed a staff officer, Captain Andrew Pickens Butler, cousin of the division commander, to go down and convince those troublesome Georgia pickets that they were stopping friends. The captain instead tried to persuade his general that the pickets were not Confederates.

"Are you afraid, sir?" scoffed Dunovant.

That made it an affair of honor, not reason. No Butler could permit the integrity of his family to remain impugned. Immediately the captain dismounted and trudged down the road, all too aware of the fate awaiting him. "I am not afraid," he made clear to the brigadier, "but I am gone up."

Pick Butler was a big man, over seven feet tall. As his shadowy figure loomed up in the darkness, the Federals thought that he was still on his horse.

"Dismount, I say," demanded the Bluecoat, "or I will fire into you."

"I am dismounted! I am a very tall man, and I am leading my horse."[19]

After this exchange Butler entered the Union lines. His arrival confirmed that the Northerners had encountered Graycoats, so Austin immediately seized him and then ordered his Ohioans to blast the Confederates. Beaumont's troopers, too, galloped forward to fire at the South Carolinians. This volley panicked the Butternut vanguard and sent it fleeing madly back up the road. As it burst upon the head of the column, those troops too gave way in disorder. In the wild scramble, Lieutenant Colonel Lovick Miller, commanding the leading 6th South Carolina Cavalry, was unhorsed and nearly dragged to death. Only three things saved the Southerners from complete disaster. First, Butler shrewdly veered off to the left of the road as he approached, so when the Yankees fired in the direction from which he had come, they missed hitting the main body. What they did do was to frighten some men and stampede their horses. Fortunately, some farsighted Confederate officers had warned their men beforehand to be ready for the shock, so when it came, these units provided a firm nucleus around which others could soon rally. They had time to do this, moreover, for the darkness prevented the Jerseymen from effectively pursuing them. Beaumont, who obviously believed that the pen was mightier than the sword, later relied on writing instruments to conjure up a fabulous tale of how he routed and rode down the Secessionists. In fact, in the darkness, he never even closed with them.

Indeed, in this whole affair Dunovant lost only one man, Captain Butler, perhaps fewer than the Unionists, who reportedly shot several of their own men by mistake. The general himself lost something else, however. The sound reputation that he had painstakingly built during the past five months now seemed eclipsed by this one instance of folly. A new tarnish marred his escutcheon, one almost as black as that which had nearly ruined his military career in Charleston over two years before. His subsequent actions suggest that he desperately felt the need to remove this new blot; if he ever got the chance, he would have to efface it by one bold act.

But there would be time for that when next he went into battle. Right now he had to regroup his brigade. Thanks to the steadfast efforts of his perceptive subordinates, he was able to rally his men fairly easily. Then he led them off to the right, presumably around Armstrong's house to the mill, and eventually made contact with Young's outposts—the real ones this time. At last he let his weary troopers get some rest. But did he too sleep—or did he think of how he must redeem himself when day broke?

Henry Davies was still thinking of what he must do yet that evening. The incident at Armstrong's made clear that the country teemed with Confederates. Those he had routed would surely summon reinforcements, and his luck might not hold out next time. He concluded that he could not safely proceed north on the Duncan Road or even remain where he was, so he decided to move back to the Vaughan Road and retire all the way to Gregg's position. Even before the South Carolinians regrouped and resumed their circuitous march southward, he abandoned his ambush at Armstrong's house and hurried back down the crossroad. Probably about the time he rejoined his detachment near Mrs. Cummings', he received Gregg's orders to withdraw to McDowell's, thus confirming the decision he had already made. His return march was swifter and easier than his advance. Possibly his men were just more familiar with a good highway like the Vaughan Road. Or possibly Pick Butler lighted the way for them: "We were happy to grope our way back," recalled a New York captain, "illuminated by the sulpherous atmosphere emanating from our prize captain's conversation."[20]

When the exhausted troopers reached McDowell's about 2:00 A.M., Gregg let them catch a few hours of much-needed sleep. He saw no need to put them in position to attack again at dawn, since army headquarters, according to latest communications, intended for the cavalry to remain on the defensive at McDowell's. Not until nearly daybreak did he learn that Meade planned to use him in the major movement toward the plank road that day. Somewhat after 5:00 A.M. a courier who had groped his way all night through the inky darkness finally brought to Gregg, Humphreys' order of 11:50 P.M. to reconnoiter along Route 673 and the Harman Road and co-operate with the IX Corps.

At 6:00 A.M. the division commander informed Birchett's of the night's activities and added that Pick Butler reported that Hampton had fought the V and IX corps on Friday. Gregg also reported that he would carry out the new orders "as soon as possible," though he did note that he had not yet issued forage and rations. Whether or not he took time to distribute those provisions is not clear. In any case, he soon assembled his men and moved out. At least the 4th Pennsylvania Cavalry and 8th Pennsylvania Cavalry of Smith's brigade led the column; Davies came next; and the 1st Maine Cavalry brought up the rear. Since Gregg now abandoned the junction of the Wyatt and Vaughan roads, he called in his outlying pickets from that sector and moved his field hospital from the Perkins house up the Halifax Road into Baxter's works. Only the patrols at Reams's Station remained in place, a duty that the 13th assumed from the 2nd sometime Saturday.[21]

The cavalry commander thus moved promptly to participate in the impending advance. Unfortunately, Parke and Warren did not share his enthusiasm, and they, not he, would determine the course of Union operations that day. These two infantry officers still resolved to remain on the defensive. They thereby forfeited the initiative to A. P. Hill.

CHAPTER XII

——◆——

"It Was an Awful Time . . . Charging . . . in the Rain"

The rain subsided in the wee hours on Saturday, but the day dawned lowery, with evident promise of a new downpour. Manmade tempests also threatened that morning. All night Powell Hill had forged his thunderbolts. Now he moved swiftly to hurl them. At about daylight his main column marched down the Squirrel Level Road from Battery No. 45 to roll up the Federal right. On reaching W. W. Davis', some of Heth's men, probably MacRae's Brigade, deployed in line of battle north of the old Confederate advanced works that crossed the road there. Southern skirmishers then ranged down to the farmhouse itself and out southeast of the trenches to cover the front, left, and left rear of this battle line. Ferebee's troopers, on being relieved by the voltigeurs, likely shifted eastward to help patrol the left. By 6:45 A.M., these forces were in position. Now Heth paused to perfect his arrangements, to reconnoiter, and to allow Hill's right wing time to get into position.

Wilcox, also, moved forward about 7:00 A.M. His left column, McGowan's Brigade, followed Archer's route of the day before as far as where the Church Road left the southern edge of the trees between Pegram's and Jones's. On the right, the division commander led Lane's Brigade along the Pegram House Road to the southern edge of those woods. Farther west Brander unlimbered his four Napoleons near Dr. Boisseau's. The heavy woods, the crest north of the Pegram house, and the sorghum field east of Boisseau's hid these movements from the ad-

vanced line of Federals, who remained unaware of the impending onslaught. As Wilcox secretly observed the Yankees from the doctor's
farm, he rejoiced to see that they were busying themselves digging rifle
pits, not standing in line of battle ready to resist him. They would pay
for their incaution, he promised himself. But he would not attack until
he heard Heth's guns. In the meantime, he had the Tarheels throw up
temporary works, tear down a fence obstructing their advance, and
complete other final preparations.

Beyond his right Wade Hampton prepared to participate in the impending attack. Shortly after daylight he roused "Rooney" Lee's sleepy
troopers and moved them back to the incomplete line of works west of
the Harman Road. The Second Stuart Horse Artillery reoccupied its
initial position of the previous afternoon, and Davis' men deployed
just behind where they had served on September 30. Barringer guarded
farther to the right, and at least his 2nd Regiment even pressed up
Route 673 all the way to Fort MacRae. They occupied the redoubt
without resistance, since such of Curtin's refugees as had regrouped
there on Friday and the Federal outposts as well had already rejoined
their commands by early Saturday morning. Most or all of Dearing's
Brigade, too, helped young Lee hold the line covering the Boydton
Plank Road.

Within a few hours all of Hill's forces were in place. Now they
readied themselves for the grand counterattack that they hoped would
equal or exceed their flank attack of August 19.[1]

The two Union corps commanders on Peebles's farm, of course, did
not know every move Hill made. Ayres's pickets, however, did alert
them to the danger on the Squirrel Level Road. Signal Corpsmen on
Crawford's and Hancock's lines also spotted the Butternut buildup
around W. W. Davis' and duly notified Globe Tavern and Birchett's.
Crawford likely relayed this report to his chief. All this intelligence
suggested to Warren and Parke that the Southern leader would renew
his attack of the previous afternoon.

This was just the information the V and IX corps commanders
wanted. They evidently reasoned that if Hill felt himself strong enough
to attack, he could not have reinforced Chaffin's Bluff during the evening. And since Meade had predicated renewing the advance that day
on a weakening of Hill's position, the subordinates now felt justified in
not taking the offensive. They did not even throw forward strong reconnaissance parties to ascertain just how formidable the gray columns
really were. No, they now had their pretext for not attacking. Let Hill
try whatever he wanted; Parke and Warren would concentrate on per-
fecting their defensive arrangements.

Parke's most important move was virtually to plug the hole between

Willcox's right and Potter's left. The corps commander presumably approved the new position of McLaughlen's brigade, so instead of pulling that unit back into line, he shifted Hartranft rightward. Between 7:00 and 8:00 A.M., the Second Brigade moved north to prolong the line from the colonel's right to Peebles's house, thus narrowing the gap between McLaughlen and Simon Griffin. To replace Hartranft, Willcox's other two brigades stretched along the line until they joined. All the IX Corps infantry then worked to dig new earthworks or to strengthen existing ones. Monroe meantime posted all his available guns to bolster the line. He pulled Heasley back to unlimber with the Maine men and one section of D on the Peebles's house knoll. Another section of Pennsylvanians deployed along Willcox's line just southwest of the building, and the remaining two ten-pound Parrotts stood guard where the Squirrel Level Road passed out of Harriman's southwestern salient. The 19th, all the while, remained on Potter's sector.[2]

The Yankees, however, could not long continue their defensive preparations undisturbed. At about 7:00 A.M., Heth's skirmishers began tangling with Ayres's pickets in the woods north of Chappell's house. The main Confederate force meantime crossed the old trenches at W. W. Davis' and deployed in two lines in the field to the south. MacRae and Archer evidently held the front line, right to left, while Davis and Cooke apparently formed the second line, right to left. As yet, these lines did not advance to support the skirmishers.

Soon after 8:00, however, Heth sent his battle lines forward. The brunt of his attack fell on the 140th New York and 17th U.S., under Captain John P. Wales of the 17th, which had just relieved the 10th and 12th U.S. on Otis' picket line. Hard pressed, Wales soon abandoned his outer works just south of W. W. Davis' and fell back to the principal picket line behind the abatis in the woods between that farm and Chappell's. There he put up fierce resistance. At least the 10th and likely also the 12th U.S. soon returned to join his valiant fight. Valiant it was, but also hopeless; voltigeurs alone could hardly stop a whole division. As it began enveloping both their flanks, they had to withdraw to Otis' main line, in good order but not without the loss of about forty prisoners. Grimshaw's skirmishers, in contrast, offered virtually no resistance but retreated at the mere sight of the Butternuts. The left part of Graham's skirmish line, too, retired without a struggle, but his right plus Bragg's voltigeurs, farther east than the main Confederate drive, stood their ground.

This general Yankee withdrawal from the woods between W. W. Davis' and Chappell's gave Heth an early success. His victory proved hollow, however. Instead of having driven in Federal flankers and gotten astride the Union right, he had merely forced back a picket line and now found a strong Northern battle line, well entrenched, barring his way at Fort Bratton. Likely surprised by this discovery, he halted in the forest to give himself time to reconnoiter the enemy's position. He found it strong enough to justify advancing Willie Pegram to soften it up. The Southern artillery, however, apparently accomplished little more than to induce Fitzhugh to run forward one of Richardson's sections on either side of Fort Bratton and open counterfire. For over half an hour, the booming artillery report and crackling rifle fire resounded across Chappell's farm. Still, Heth hesitated to launch his real attack.[3]

Cadmus Wilcox acted more promptly. For about an hour, he had awaited the sound of firing on the Squirrel Level Road. Now that the shooting finally started, he sent his men into action. Brander unmasked his battery at Boisseau's and devastatingly enfiladed the Union lines around the Pegram house. On Wilcox's other flank Dunlop's sharp-shooters raced ahead of McGowan's main line on the Church Road and overran some advanced Federal rifle pits, 250 yards in front of the main Northern line on Pegram's. At this first sign of danger, Warren and probably Parke directed their forward line to fall back to the principal position on Peebles's. Most Bluecoats eagerly obeyed this welcome order. Few offered much resistance to the South Carolina skirmishers scampering over the scarp to expedite their withdrawal. In the absence of the Devil, Dunlop took the hindmost—more prisoners, in fact, than he had soldiers. The majority of Northerners, however, managed to reach safety.

Warren's orders did not get to Hofmann's left, however, so the units there kept on fighting. As the course of the battle rapidly became apparent, many Yankees—in the tradition of the independent-minded American soldier—decided that they could render the cause better service back on Peebles's farm and betook themselves there posthaste. But others, including Lieutenant Colonel James Warner and about fifty men of Hofmann's leftmost 121st Pennsylvania, felt honor bound to make a last stand. Still other Unionists, among them some men of the 9th New Hampshire, simply feared to expose themselves to Brander's fire, so they just crouched in their rifle pits, awaiting the lesser of two evils.

The time of reckoning soon came. While Dunlop enveloped the Federal right, Wooten's sharpshooters secretly crept along the ravine of Arthur's Swamp that led beyond the Yankee left. Now the Tarheels burst upon the surprised Northerners and gobbled up Warner's men, about sixty more of Hofmann's soldiers, and some of Simon Griffin's soldiers with virtually no fighting. As the handful of North Carolina sharpshooters rushed their prisoners to the rear, the horde of Bluecoats so outnumbered them that their movement looked like an overwhelm-

ing Federal counterattack to the astonished Brander. He therefore
opened fire on them, killing a few Unionists, wounding three Secessionists, and throwing Wooten's men into disarray. One shot, moreover, barely missed Wilcox himself, who was riding to the front at the
time. Fortunately, the captain learned of his error and ceased firing before he inflicted worse damage.

Despite this regrettable incident, the affair in general once more
demonstrated the worth of the Light Division's fine sharpshooter battalions. They captured about 190 defenders plus an estimated 50 more
wounded men and the flag of the 9th New Hampshire that had fallen
on Friday and simply lain on the field all night. The voltigeurs also
completely cleared the other Federals from Pegram's farm before
Lane's and McGowan's main lines could even engage. But this was as
much as the skirmishers or even Wilcox's whole force could accomplish. His men could hardly dash themselves against the main Union
line on Peebles's farm. Nor were they supposed to, for Hill simply
required them to distract attention from Heth's flank attack. Wilcox,
accordingly, continued to feint by sending Dunlop and Wooten into the
woods between Pegram's and Peebles's to skirmish with Potter's and
Griffin's divisions. Later the Confederate major general ran up
Brander's cannon to exchange occasional shots with the Northern artillery. Lane's and McGowan's main lines, however, stayed in reserve in
the old Federal works near Pegram's house, the Tarheels on the right,
the South Carolinians on the left. There they were almost entirely out
of Federal range except for a few stray overshots. Before those two brigades could press the attack, Heth would have to open the way by
rolling up Warren's right.[4]

While Wilcox repositioned his men and Heth perfected his arrangements, Parke and Warren prepared for the battle Hill had thrust upon
them. Both Northern generals grasped the seriousness of the situation.
"I expect a hard time," Warren warned Birchett's at 8:00 A.M. The
Federal corps commanders, accordingly, braced themselves for the imminent attack. Parke redeployed his retreating skirmishers to cover his
front on Peebles's. He also kept his main line digging in. Hartranft's
men in particular rushed construction of their parapets as fighting
raged across Pegram's farm toward them. To cover such redeployment
and final preparations and to check pursuit, the 19th New York Battery and the right section of Pennsylvanians shelled the woods between
the two farms and also fired a few shots at the Letcher Artillery. Warren meantime presumably posted Griffin's skirmishers in front of the
First Division's works. The V Corps commander did not leave Hofmann's brigade on Peebles's farm, however. As soon as it regrouped,
he returned it to Ayres to bolster the threatened northern front. The

general of division used it to prolong the Marylanders' line rightward, likely all the way to Bragg's left.[5]

Besides strengthening their own position, the two Union corps commanders also worked Gregg's division into their defensive system. The cavalrymen came up the muddy Vaughan Road early that morning and crossed on the Poplar Spring Road to the Squirrel Level Road. Davies' patrols, now in the van, then led the way out Route 673 toward J. Hawks's. They soon observed some of "Rooney" Lee's men in the incomplete works around Fort MacRae, but without infantry support the Bluecoat troopers hesitated to attack entrenchments.

Parke and Warren took great pains to assure Gregg that such infantry support would not be forthcoming. Indeed, even before Heth delivered his main attack, the two senior officers convinced the cavalry general that he need not even bother to carry out Meade's orders to reconnoiter the Confederate right. "The object of the intended reconnaissances has been fully accomplished—the enemy found," Gregg explained to Birchett's at 8:30 A.M.[6] He therefore decided to post some troops on the IX Corps's left (perhaps the 4th Pennsylvania Cavalry) and move his main force back to McDowell's, where he could guard the left rear of the expeditionary force.

The need to return there soon became urgent, for in the Northern cavalry's absence, Butler was threatening that key intersection. Soon after daybreak, the South Carolinian struck eastward from Hatcher's Run. Young's Brigade (minus Waring's battalion) led the way. Since Davies no longer barred the road near Mrs. Cummings', the Georgians advanced without opposition to the junction of the Wyatt and Vaughan roads at McDowell's. By the time they reached the intersection at about 9:00 A.M., the main body of Union horsemen had already marched north to join Parke. Only the rearguard, the 1st Maine Cavalry, remained to confront them. Most of the regiment temporarily manned the works at the intersection while its pickets skirmished with the Graycoats. With their comrades gone, however, the Maine men were not about to make a last stand. When Young's Brigade, supported by a section of Hart's battery, pressed them, they readily abandoned the junction and followed the Second Cavalry Division northward. Within a matter of minutes the Butternuts occupied McDowell's.

The ease with which he regained the entire east–west section of the Vaughan Road apparently surprised Butler. The Yankee division had obviously left this area, he may have reasoned, but where had it gone —east toward the Halifax Road, or north toward its infantry? Wherever it was, he decided not to send his few battalions after it, presumably lest the main Federal infantry force around Poplar Spring Church cut them off. He instead directed Young and Hart to fortify McDow-

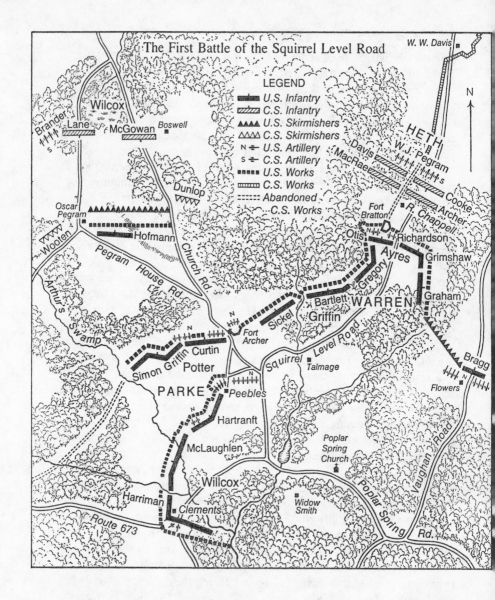

The First Battle of the Squirrel Level Road

LEGEND
U.S. Infantry
C.S. Infantry
U.S. Skirmishers
C.S. Skirmishers
U.S. Artillery
C.S. Artillery
U.S. Works
C.S. Works
Abandoned
C.S. Works

ell's and ordered Dunovant and Farley to join them. The division commander was seemingly content to consolidate his limited gain and hesitated to seek out the Bluecoats without positive orders from Hampton.

The Bluecoats, however, had no hesitancy about seeking him out. On learning of the fall of McDowell's, Gregg resolved to return there, not just to cover the left rear but also to drive off the Confederates. Once more the horsemen were heading into combat, but once more,

COMMENTARY

1. This map shows the situation early Saturday morning. Heth has driven Ayres's skirmishers from the woods between Chappell's and W. W. Davis' and is now reconnoitering the main Federal line. Wilcox meantime is just preparing to attack across Pegram's farm.

2. At least the 31st Maine, 18th and 32nd Massachusetts, 6th and 9th New Hampshire, 24th New York Cavalry, and 1/38th Wisconsin served along with Hofmann on Pegram's farm. The individual regiments subsequently fell back to in front of their divisions' main lines, but the brigade rejoined Ayres and took position to Graham's right.

3. The relative order of Griffin's and Heth's brigades is probably correct.

4. The location of Pegram's 12 guns (Brander with Wilcox, Ellett and Hollis with Heth) is only schematically representational. The Federal pieces can be placed somewhat more surely. The 15th New York Battery served on Bragg's left, and L/1st New York Light Artillery presumably bolstered his right; Richardson had a section on either side of Fort Bratton; and Robert Rogers served in Fort Archer. Mink probably also served on the Squirrel Level Line, perhaps on Potter's front, where the 19th New York Battery was definitely posted. The 7th Maine Battery and two guns of Pennsylvania D were at Peebles's house, and the rest of D and the 34th were on Willcox's line.

too, they were diverging from integral participation in the main combat zone to their semi-independent sector on the Vaughan Road. However, before Gregg got word of the First Cavalry Division's advance and before he could carry out his announced intention of securing McDowell's, heavy fighting at last broke out on Chappell's farm. He therefore delayed his departure to await its outcome.[7]

That major combat erupted on Chappell's farm is certain; why it did so is less clear. Heth's personal reconnaissance of the Second Division's position convinced him that the whole Confederate battle plan centered on a false premise: Not a vulnerable flank but an apparently strong, well-defended retrenchment rested on the Squirrel Level Road. The line, indeed, looked so formidable that he seemingly did not feel justified in trying to storm it. Instead, he ordered at least MacRae's Brigade to make a reconnaissance in force, presumably to develop more fully whether or not Ayres's position was too strong to justify a full-scale attack.

Just after 9:00, the North Carolinians moved forward. A crack outfit they were—renowned for their discipline. Yet now their discipline failed, a weakness becoming distressingly common in Lee's once-vaunted infantry. As in Field's Division before Fort Harrison the previous day, some of them—the 44th Regiment and probably the 52nd on the right part of his line—supposed they were actually to storm the enemy position at the first rush. Right away they raised the high-

pitched Rebel Yell and broke into the charge. MacRae ordered them to
slow down, to no avail; then he commanded them to halt, still to go
unheeded. The Tarheels who had scattered Curtin's brigade the day before were determined to overrun Ayres as well. Their general could do
no more than give them free rein and hope for the best. He even lacked
time or inclination to bring up his other three regiments farther east as
he accompanied his overeager right wing.

Nature greeted the North Carolinians' onslaught with savage fury.
The skies, which had threatened rain all morning, now opened with a
driving downpour that soaked the soldiers and deepened the mud in the
fields over which they were charging. The Union ramparts, too,
consisted mostly of mud, hardly an imposing or formidable barrier.
They remained good enough to stop a bullet, though—to shield the
grimy but determined foot soldiers who formed the real barrier across
Heth's path. Whatever the Yankees lacked in comfort and appearance,
they made up in command and experience. Their brigadiers, Otis and
Grimshaw, handled them well. Even better direction came from their
superb division commander, who had ridden "to the front at full
speed" as soon as his picket line came under attack and who remained
right with them on the battle line, commanding them personally, setting
a good example in the process—and "enjoying the fight hugely" all the
while.[8] The veterans of the Second Division appreciated and benefited
from their leaders' control, but they had been in enough fights to know
what to do in the immediate scope of personal combat. They aimed
their sights low and ripped the onrushing battle line with terrible effect.
Heroically, the North Carolinians tried to brave this fire, but, outgunned and unsupported, they could not reach the ramparts. Nor dared
they remain in the open for long. Within minutes they went reeling
back to the cover of the woods north of Chappell's house, the 44th
coming out of the fight "the worst cut up they have been in the whole
campaign."[9]

Soon after MacRae fell back, Archer and Davis moved forward.
Whether Heth initially intended for them to participate in the reconnaissance in force or only committed them later in hopes of salvaging
something from the Tarheels' error by converting it into a real attack is
not clear. What is certain is that they engaged only after MacRae had
been checked—still another of the piecemeal efforts that marred Confederate attacks so much of late. Nor did the two brigades manage to
co-operate with each other or even to hold their own lines intact. The
front-line unit obliqued rightward across the Squirrel Level Road, perhaps to try to close the gap between it and the 44th North Carolina.
But before it could reach the Tarheels, it collided with the Mississippians moving up from the rear. The resulting confusion disrupted

THE CONFEDERATE HIGH COMMAND

33. ·R. E. Lee

34. Richard S. Ewell

35. Ambrose Powell Hill

36. Ord's pontoon bridge across the James from Bermuda Hundred (foreground) to Aiken's Landing (far side). Note on the horizon the wooded ridge on which Donohoe encountered Hughs's outposts.

37. The center of the entrenched camp, as seen from a point one-third of a mile south of Fort Johnson, looking south and west toward the James. Most works shown were built after September 29, but the forest, far more extensive than shown, concealed the hole in the Confederate center that day. On the far left is the Fort Maury hill, with the Osborne Turnpike seen crossing it. The double bastioned White Battery is on the left-center edge of the dark ground, and Fort Hoke is faintly visible behind it. The three buildings on the far right belonged to the Negro Pierinan. The next building, between two clumps of trees, is thought to be Mrs. Chaffins' house.

38. Fort Harrison: The fort is thought to be in the left foreground, and the view apparently looks southeast across Childrey's field to the remains of Cox's woods (center distance) and the forested swamp along Three Mile Creek (left distance). The Varina Road appears as a white strip between the woods and the blur in the center. The upper crest of the "blind spot" is on a line with the coatless soldier's head. The tents were not pitched there until after the battle.

39. Fort Harrison as seen from the far western part of Childrey's field, looking north. From right to left along the horizon are the Great Traverse, the new sallyport and new (low) rampart built by the Yankees, the much higher rampart of the fort's original right flank, and the entrenched camp's outer wall. The abatis east of that curtain and the parapet closer to the tents were thrown up by the Federals.

40. The moat of Fort Johnson's east face, from south to north. The fosse shown is deeper than when Sadler was trapped in it on September 29. Beyond the moat is seen the field over which Ripley and Jourdan charged. The lower end of the Intermediate Line is seen running north to Fort Gregg on the horizon. Fort Gilmer, farther north along that line, is out of view.

41. Fort Johnson as seen from the south. The fort is on the horizon, just left of the solitary tree. The rampart, moat, and frise in the foreground were thrown up after September 29. Rightward from the fort along the horizon can be seen the northeastern curtain of the entrenched camp, running southeast toward Fort Harrison.

42. The same angle as the preceding picture but taken from one-third of a mile south of Fort Johnson. Most structures shown were built after the battle; only those along the horizon existed on September 29. Along the left distance is the upper camp wall, facing north. The fort is on the center horizon, immediately left of the lone tree. Rightward from the tree runs the northeastern camp wall toward Fort Harrison. Beyond that northeastern curtain is the ground over which Fairchild attacked. Over the northeastern wall is where Moore counterattacked him. And down the axis of the wall toward Stannard is where Field charged on September 30.

43. Although the works and abatis shown were built after the battle, this height is thought to be the position from which Haskell bombarded Fort Harrison on September 30. This scene looks east toward the fort, which is vaguely visible on the horizon.

44. The V Corps advancing west from its defenses on the Weldon Railroad toward the woods along the Vaughan Road on the morning of September 30.

Frank Leslie's, Oct. 22,

Frank Leslie's, Oct. 22,

45. The IX Corps marching west past Poplar Spring Church toward the Squirrel Level Road on the afternoon of September 30.

46. Griffin's division storming Peebles' Farm on the early afternoon of September 30.

47. Mott's division reaching Globe Tavern by military railroad on the afternoon of October 1.

MHRC

48. Ulysses S. Grant

THE FEDERAL HIGH COMMAND

49. Benjamin F. Butler

NA

50. George G. Meade

MHRC

the "beautiful order" in which at least Archer's line had gone forward and knocked at least the 2nd Maryland Battalion out of position. The Marylanders managed to regroup behind some farm buildings and from there to open fire on Ayres's works, but they advanced no farther. Other men of that brigade, with less excuse, also hung back. The 22nd Virginia Battalion, long disgraced by a poor, even poltroonish record and shaken by its repulse Friday, simply refused to make what appeared a hopeless effort. Neither its brigadier's entreaties, orders, nor threats could induce it to charge. Worse yet, the battalion's officers sympathized with their craven men and "stood listlessly looking on" while the general, unaided, tried vainly to revitalize the outfit.[10]

The soldiers of the 22nd could take little pride in their cowardly action, but they may have felt a certain perverse satisfaction as they beheld the fate of their braver comrades. Most of the brigade, though jarred by its defeat on the thirtieth, nevertheless made a greater effort than these two battalions and duly pressed on toward Fort Bratton. For their trouble, they could show much heavier casualties but no greater results. Some of Archer's units went all to pieces under the devastating fire and fled in disorder, leaving their dead on the field. Even a regimental commander was left where he was killed: Captain Robert P. Davis of the 40th Virginia. Soon the whole brigade had to abandon the struggle and withdraw northward into the woods.

The Mississippians, too, could make no headway against the straight-shooting Bluecoats. Attacking across mud into such an inferno during a rainstorm had a nightmarish horror about it that vividly impressed itself on one of Joseph Davis' men:

> Oh, it was an awful time Saturday charging the Yankees in the rain through the woods and swamps and thickets, and the balls flying, thick and fast in every direction, and men getting killed, and wounded hollering all over the woods.[11]

An awful time it was; that brigade, too, was stopped short of the Federal ramparts. Soon it, also, had to fall back.

Cooke's sharpshooter battalion, apparently moving abreast of Davis, was also compelled to withdraw. Cooke's main body, moreover, was not even ordered to advance. His 48th Regiment, emerging from the woods into the field, took light losses from stray bullets overshooting the attackers. To protect themselves from such fire, his 27th Regiment and presumably his other outfits simply lay down on the ground. None of his four regiments was actually directed to charge.

The fate of these thrusts, even more than his own reconnaissances, resolved Heth's uncertainty about the vulnerability of the Yankee position. Twice his men, once more urged on by the gallant Pegram himself, had charged to within about forty yards of the works. Twice they had been severely repulsed. All they had to show for their efforts were bleeding bodies left behind, stretched out in the mud. South of them the Federal line remained unbroken, its fire still blazing undiminished over its parapets. If the Virginian were, indeed, only reconnoitering the Union position in force, he now knew that it was held in strength. If he were actually trying to storm it, he could perceive that he had failed. Renewed efforts, he feared, would only bring more casualties. He therefore did not send his three battered brigades back into the fray or commit the main body of Cooke's fresh outfit. Instead, he broke off the fighting—and with it the whole effort to roll up the Union right and re-capture Peebles's farm—and retired north to the old works near W. W. Davis'.[12]

In his wake came the Bluecoats. They had passed through the battle virtually unscathed except for a few key officers. Lieutenant Thomas D. Urmston, commanding the 12th U.S., had been killed, presumably at this time. Otis, too, suffered a grievous face wound; it was first thought to be mortal, but he eventually recovered and went on to serve thirty-eight years in the Regular army, reaching the rank of major general. He would see no more action in the Civil War, though, and had to turn his brigade over to his senior subordinate, Major James Grindlay of the 146th New York. The major, along with Grimshaw and Graham, now sent forward their light troops "howling like fiends" to re-establish their picket lines. These voltigeurs drove off the Confederate rear guard, regained the picket line, and resumed skirmishing with the sharpshooters covering Heth's withdrawal. Ayres did not pursue the Secessionists in force, however, so the front rapidly quieted down to the deadly but limited level of sniping. Within less than half an hour Heth's entire division had been totally repulsed and thrown back on the defensive.[13]

This brief battle entailed relatively few casualties: about 128 Unionists (with perhaps 226 more Yankees lost on Pegram's farm) and approximately 400 Confederates (412 including Wilcox's casualties).[14] Although the losses were light and, in the aggregate, nearly equally balanced, the results were far-reaching and one-sided. The battle set to nought Powell Hill's plan to pursue his initial successes of September 30 until he had recovered all Joel Griffin had lost. It also confirmed Federal possession of their newly won foothold on Peebles's farm. In light of the over-all way Grant's entire offensive of September 29–October 2 worked out, this engagement on the Squirrel Level Road ranks as the most decisive phase of the Battle of Poplar Spring Church.

Decisive though the combat at Chappell's proved in retrospect, it did not end fighting on October 1. To the contrary, Gregg's decision to return to McDowell's precipitated the heaviest cavalry clash of the whole battle. As soon as the victory at Fort Bratton ended the immediate threat to the Union infantry position, he left Peebles's farm and marched back to the Vaughan Road, thence toward McDowell's. Confederate outposts north of the intersection caused "some resistance and embarrassment" but could not stop him. Between 10:00 and 10:45 A.M. he closed in on the main body of Georgians. His return to McDowell's evidently surprised them more than his departure had done. They were not prepared to resist. A squadron of skirmishers from Davies' leading brigade, probably from the 10th New York Cavalry, sufficed to drive them off and retake the farm. Young's troopers then retreated west to E. Wilkinson's, where the Squirrel Level Road ran into the Vaughan Road.[15]

Between those two farms, Wilkinson's and McDowell's, the opposing cavalry battled savagely all day. Both plantations were located on hills rising about thirty to forty feet above the intervening country. On the easterly hill was the intersection of the Vaughan and Wyatt roads; on the westerly height was the lower end of the Squirrel Level Road. Although these two junctions were half a mile apart, the crests of the two hills extended toward one another until they were only approximately 500 yards apart. Halfway between the two crests and 300 yards south of the Vaughan Road, yet another fork of Arthur's Swamp took rise and flowed north for 1,100 yards, across that highway, to a larger branch. That branch, in turn, ran east for 1,000 yards to the main stem of the stream north of McDowell's. From the wooded crest of Wilkinson's hill the open ground sloped gently down to the little fork of Arthur's Swamp, 250 yards to the east. Along the creek in the valley floor, trees and heavy undergrowth offered formidable obstacles to advancing troops; only a narrow corduroyed causeway for the Vaughan Road provided unimpeded access through the tangled vegetation. East of the creek, though, the trees once more gave way to open fields, which gradually ascended to the crest of McDowell's hill, 250 yards east of the swamp. Near the top of that height, around the farmhouse just north of the Wyatt Road, stood another woods. Also on McDowell's hill west of the dwelling place was the key intersection of the Vaughan and Wyatt roads. This was the terrain over which the two sides would fight.[16]

The Yankees moved immediately to secure the entire field. Davies' skirmishers, flushed with victory, followed Young west across the swamp to try to drive him from Wilkinson's, too. The Georgians, however, rallied in existing breastworks crowning the western hill and easily checked their pursuers. The Graycoats, in turn, counterattacked on foot and pressed the skirmishers back across the creek and up the west-

ern slope of McDowell's hill. By this time most of the First Brigade
had arrived to bolster its voltigeurs. Davies quickly dismounted his
men, sent the horseholders to the rear, and rushed his troopers into line
across Young's path. The 1st Pennsylvania Cavalry held his left; the
10th New York Cavalry prolonged the line rightward to the Vaughan
Road; the 6th Ohio Cavalry served just north of the highway; and the
1st Massachusetts Cavalry occupied the right. One battalion of the 1st
Maine Cavalry supported his right, while the rest of that regiment (as
well as the 1st New Jersey Cavalry once it arrived) stayed in reserve.
Although the remainder of the Second Brigade was probably not yet up
and was certainly not engaged, Davies now felt strong enough to attack. His front line surged down on the Georgians and slowly forced
them back toward Arthur's Swamp.

The Confederates' failure to retake McDowell's disturbed their generals. Young blamed his own men. From the safety of the Wilkinson
hill, he denounced them mercilessly as they stubbornly retired before
the Yankees. "Young was cursing and storming in that stentorian voice
of his, which could be heard for half a mile," recalled one of
Dunovant's troopers:

> "Hold your ground down there, you damned scoundrels," was one
> of his mildest expressions. The men were fighting gallantly against
> heavy odds, as we could plainly see, and I remember well how in-
> dignant I was at General Young, much as I admired him, for curs-
> ing them so outrageously.[17]

Butler preferred resistance to recrimination, so he sought reinforcements for his hard-pressed troops. Such assistance was now at
hand, for about this time his other brigade finally reached Wilkinson's
after a long, slow march during which it had halted at least twice. The
division commander immediately explained the situation to Dunovant
and directed him to attack the Federal right.

The brigadier promptly dismounted the 4th South Carolina Cavalry
and 5th South Carolina Cavalry, right to left, and led them down the
hill and through the swamp north of the Vaughan Road. As his men
moved up the gentle slope of McDowell's hill toward the Union right,
he began to worry about his own exposed right flank, which did not
connect with the Georgians' left. To watch out for Federal penetration
between the two brigades, he ordered up a few videttes from the 6th
South Carolina Cavalry, the rest of which remained in reserve, presumably back on Wilkinson's hill. The wisdom of this precaution soon
became evident. Some Bluecoats, probably the 6th Ohio Cavalry, either perceived or stumbled across the gap in Butler's line, entered it,
and swung north to cut off Dunovant. Their trap closed prematurely,

however. Before they could get in his rear, some of their comrades, likely the 1st Massachusetts Cavalry, outflanked the 5th's left and drove back both Confederate regiments. Dunovant and Lieutenant Colonel William Stokes, commanding the 4th, initially hoped to rally their men in the woods east of the creek. But when the 6th South Carolina Cavalry's vigilant videttes warned that the Ohioans were moving down the swamp toward the 4th's right, Dunovant retreated all the way to the works atop Wilkinson's hill. Young's men, too, fell back there.

Once more the Unionists held the initiative. A squadron of the 10th New York Cavalry and probably the Ohioans followed the Southerners across the creek. There they deployed under cover of the woods, then charged the breastworks on the crest. As earlier in the morning, Butler's soldiers regrouped in their logworks and repulsed the Bluecoats. Although Davies fed in two more troops of the 10th and finally the remaining eight, his men could not stand up under the Confederate fire and had to fall back about 200 yards.[18]

A stalemate then settled over the front for several hours. The New Yorkers strengthened their advanced position on the eastern slope of Wilkinson's hill with light works. Northeast of them, at least part of the Ohio regiment refused the right flank back to the creek. Davies regarded their position as a *tête-de-pont* and an advanced line of defense only. Should they be attacked, he would not reinforce them; he directed, instead, that they hold their ground as long as possible, then retire to the east bank of the creek, where the 1st Massachusetts Cavalry was entrenching a stronger line. In case this second position, too, proved untenable, the brigadier's remaining outfits readied a third line atop McDowell's hill by strengthening the fortifications they had thrown up west and south of the farmhouse on Friday. To back up these lines, Lieutenant William N. Dennison's four-gun Battery A/2nd U. S. Artillery unlimbered on a rise just northeast of the house.

The Secessionists meantime strengthened their own parapet with fence rails. From those works they glowered down on the enemy lines on the valley floor. More than glares came from the westerly hill as Hampton ordered up another battery, presumably Graham's, to help Hart shell the Federals. Chew's Union counterparts at first paid no heed to his shells bursting around them. The Regulars, however, could not long ignore the slow-paced but ever-nearing shots, and they opened counterfire. Battery A's entry into the fray did not prevent Chew from also turning some fire on Davies' forward line, "making it decidedly uncomfortable" for the Bluecoats there.[19] The New Yorkers became still more uncomfortable as they discovered themselves dangerously low on bullets. Their initial heavy firing used up most of their ammunition, and their forward position and heterogeneous armament—three

different types of carbines for one regiment—made it difficult to secure
more. They nevertheless put up a bold front with their revolvers and
with "taunts and jeers."[20] This, together with the absence of any Confederate intention to attack, enabled them to pass the crisis until more
bullets could be brought up.

They soon found good use for the ammunition, firing at Butternuts
who were not above hurling taunts of their own. Just two weeks earlier
the Union cavalry had failed to prevent Hampton's corps from stealing
2,500 beef cattle from deep inside Yankee lines. Now the handful of
Dunovant's men who had participated in that raid gloated over their
success:

> The men were bellowing like bulls [recalled one of Dunovant's
> couriers], and shouting over to the Yankees, "Good, fat beef over
> here; come over and get some," and then a fellow would jump up
> and bellow, and by the time he dropped, bullets would be whistling
> over our heads and rattling on the rail piles.[21]

But these shouts and counterjeers, like the accompanying shots from
carbine and cannon, little influenced the course of the battle. They
merely highlighted how the heavy action of the morning had tapered
off by midday.[22]

As the two sides rested and prepared to renew fighting, the opposing
commanders analyzed the situation. Gregg apparently felt that recapturing the road junction at McDowell's farm sufficed to guard the rear
of the infantry's position on Peebles's farm. Since Parke and Warren
had already told him they would not attack that day, he saw no reason
to force his way toward Hatcher's Run and thereby risk getting cut off
by the III Corps. He would instead simply hold his present position
about McDowell's with Davies' brigade, the 1st Maine Cavalry, and
Dennison's battery.

His remaining regiments, moreover, would cover the First Brigade's
flanks and rear. Some troopers served as videttes to link Davies with
the foot soldiers farther north. Smith's main body, however, guarded
the opposite flank back across Wyatt's plantation to the Weldon Railroad: the 2nd on returning from Reams's Station, the 8th, presumably
Battery H-I/1st, and perhaps the 4th if it had not remained with the IX
Corps. Further to secure the left rear, the 13th drew in its defense perimeter closer to the Halifax Road. The good sense of such precautions
was underscored on the most southerly sector about noon. Although
Waring, too, originally remained on the defensive there to guard
against a reprisal raid on his picket line, he was disappointed in his expectation of receiving an attack. After spending most of the morning
positioning new outposts of his own, he moved east on the Stage Road

prior to 12:45 P.M. to seek out the foe. But by then the 13th had pulled back near the tracks—too far east, the legion commander judged, for him to venture. He therefore retired without engaging. His probe, nevertheless, made clear to Gregg the wisdom of covering his left rear in force.[23]

The division commander reported these arrangements to army headquarters at 12:45. Keeping Meade informed was, of course, necessary but by no means easy. Messages between the cavalry and him took so much time in transit as frequently to make their contents out of date—or at least "out of hour"—by the time they were received. Gregg's initial report of 8:30, that instead of attacking toward the Boydton Plank Road he was returning to McDowell's to guard the infantry's left rear, required two and a half hours to reach the army commander. Still unaware of it and still committed to the offensive, the senior officer, at 10:00 A.M., renewed his orders to Parke to attack with the cavalry, Willcox, Potter, and Mott as soon as the II Corps troops arrived. However, the IX Corps commander, not realizing his superior thought the original instructions of midnight remained operative, assumed that Birchett's had countermanded Gregg's decision of 8:30. Parke, accordingly, forwarded the directive of 10:00 to the cavalryman and told him to report in person at Peebles's as soon as Mott arrived. This dispatch, in turn, did not reach McDowell's until after Gregg wrote army headquarters at 12:45. By then the situation on the Vaughan Road was so inconsistent with what the infantryman proposed that the division commander personally rode back to IX Corps field headquarters to protest abandoning his present position lest the Graycoats "follow him directly up the Vaughan Road" and get into the infantry's rear. Parke, evidently impressed with this argument, almost immediately forwarded it to Humphreys at Globe Tavern at 2:50.

By then the Chief-of-Staff had received the communications of 8:30 and 12:45 and had concluded that the cavalry division could remain on the Vaughan Road. It was still to attack as part of the army's general advance that afternoon, he wrote Gregg at 2:00 P.M.; it could simply do so from its present position against forces in its own front instead of returning to Route 673. "If you can occupy an equal or greater force of the enemy than your own, and keep them from joining those we attack, it will be equivalent to joining the attack here," Humphreys wrote and then gratuitously added, "particularly if you beat them."[24] This order had clearly not reached Gregg at 2:50. He learned of its substance a few minutes later, however, when he, Parke, and Warren conferred with Meade and Humphreys, who had just reached Peebles's. The cavalry commander thus at last received instructions without experiencing a time lag. But to do so, he had to place himself out of

touch with his own troops. By the time he could get back to them
(probably shortly before 5:00 P.M.), he would find this directive, too,
outmoded: His men would be in no position to drive the Confederates
anyplace.[25]

What changed things, not surprisingly, was Wade Hampton. The
Northerners' reconquest of McDowell's farm that morning both
alarmed and pleased him. He, of course, worried that they might drive
to or across Hatcher's Run, yet he also saw in their advanced position
the opportunity to deal them a heavy blow. He would repeat his successful movement of Thursday by transferring a force from his own
quiet front near the Harman Road to cut off or cripple the Unionists
on the Vaughan Road. Indeed, their forward position near Wilkinson's
made them especially vulnerable to a flank attack down the Squirrel
Level Road. Around midday he put infantry into the fortifications to
relieve the 9th Virginia Cavalry and 13th Virginia Cavalry, remounted
those two regiments, and then personally led them toward the Vaughan
Road. Lucius Davis accompanied him as the immediate brigadier,
while "Rooney" Lee took charge of the troopers remaining near the
Harman Road.

Hampton's reinforcements made poor time slogging along the narrow
country lanes from the Harman Road to the Squirrel Level Road, lanes
in bad condition to begin with and now made almost impassable by the
heavy rains. Nor could they travel much faster on the Squirrel Level
Road itself lest they reveal themselves prematurely or even blunder
into an ambush. Dismounting part of the brigade on reaching the
north–south highway further slowed movement. Because of all these
delays, the Virginians did not reach the general area of E. Wilkinson's
until near 3:00 P.M. At least they encountered no opposition en route.
A hasty reconnaissance, moreover, revealed that the Yankees west of
Arthur's Swamp still did not suspect the threat to their right flank. "So
far, so good," Hampton concluded; now he could plan his minor tactics. Davis' brigade—mounted saber companies in front, dismounted
carbineers in the rear—would deliver the main blow: a crushing flank
attack down a farm lane to roll up the Bluecoats' right, capture or scatter their horses, and cut the isolated foot troopers off from McDowell's.
As the Virginians advanced, they were to raise the Rebel Yell. When
Butler's Division heard this cry on its left, it was to hit the Federal
front with a dismounted line, backed up by horsemen. This powerful
pincer should crush at least the two Union regiments west of the creek
and might well carry the Secessionists on to McDowell's. At about
3:00 P.M. Hampton launched his attack.

Slowly, resolutely, Davis moved south. Now mounted videttes spotted him and galloped back to warn of his approach; his saber com-

panies raised a yell and thundered after them. Too late: An opposing line of battle was already forming across his path. Very well, then, his regiments would charge the foe. As the Virginians neared this battle line, they perceived something strange: Their "opponents" wore gray. Within that battle line Matthew Butler holstered his pistol with an air of disgust. Just as he was preparing to hit the Yankees, his videttes had galloped up to report an enemy column advancing against his left. Desperately he pulled regiments out of his own strike force to meet this threat. He himself rode to the endangered flank and took aim at a leader of the attacking column—and then he recognized that officer as a Virginian. Hampton's concentric columns had converged all right but not at the proper place. Instead of diverging onto the farm lane toward the Ohioans, Davis had stayed on the Squirrel Level Road all the way to E. Wilkinson's. As a result, he barely avoided rolling up Dunovant's left, not Davies' right.

This fiasco ruined Hampton's basic plan. His men, nonetheless, did manage to force the Northerners across the swamp. Although some of Butler's men turned to confront the Virginians, his other troopers (presumably Young and perhaps Farley) swept down frontally against the 10th New York Cavalry and the 6th Ohio Cavalry. By now at least the Regulars were alerted to the danger and turned their guns on Davis (though they overshot him). The two forward Federal regiments were probably aware of the peril, too. In any case, they did not seriously resist Butler but began falling back on the 1st Massachusetts Cavalry, just east of the stream. The throng milling across the narrow causeway provided a tempting target. As a gap opened up there between the 6th and the 10th, mounted Confederates galloped down on the opening and gobbled up forty-six Ohioans—the sole fruit of Hampton's grand flank attack. Other Yankees were cut down resisting, but most made it across the creek, either on the bridge or through the thickets. Once on the right bank, they regrouped on the 1st and beat off their pursuers.[26]

The Secessionists rallied in the old Yankee works west of the stream and engaged in a brisk fire fight with Davies' new front line. Over the ravine soared artillery shells as Hart and Graham engaged Battery A. But for about half an hour, neither side actually attacked. The commanders needed time to plan anew. Butler, of course, did much of the Confederate planning. A good general, he hesitated to sacrifice many irreplaceable men by assaulting straight across the swamp once his personal reconnaissance disclosed how strong the Union position on the right bank was. "Could he not turn this line?" he asked. Dunovant could not answer, but that fine officer Major Farley promptly reported that the Southerners could easily outflank the Union left. The division commander then shifted his mounted reserve unit—the Phillips Legion or possibly the 13th Virginia Cavalry—to the right and sent scouts to ascertain if the horsemen could, indeed, move around the head of the swamp and hit Davies' flank.

Dunovant objected to this plan: He desired to attack straight ahead. Possibly this rash brigadier was just flushed with his initial, if limited, success. But something more basic may have driven him. Did he consciously or subconsciously wish to win new laurels for himself, to redeem his blunder of the previous evening and prove once again that he really was a good officer? Whatever his reason, he urgently importuned Butler to let him advance straight ahead. An orderly at brigade headquarters described the ensuing scene:

> Butler at once turned to Dunovant and said, "General, move the brigade by the right flank down this creek until you get that position [beyond Davies' left], then attack." During this conversation I had noticed that Dunovant had seemed to be very impatient, and when Butler gave him this order, he saluted and replied: "Oh, General, let me charge 'em, we've got 'em going and let us keep 'em going." Butler said, "General, I am afraid I will lose too many men." "Oh, no we won't," answered Dunovant, "my men are perfectly enthusiastic and ready to charge, an' we've got the Yankees demoralized, one more charge will finish 'em. Let me charge them." Then I saw Butler's face change. He had been calm and unmoved till then, but as Dunovant said this, his face flushed, his eyes seemed to grow darker (I was looking him directly in the face not five feet from him) and in a voice short, sharp, and stern, he called to Dunovant, "Charge them, sir, if you wish."[27]

A frontal charge was just what the brigadier wished. He called to his troopers to attack. They belied his claim about their enthusiasm by refusing to budge. With more emphasis, he commanded them to attack. This time they scrambled over their logworks and rushed down to the creek. The brigadier, mounted on his chestnut horse, galloped ahead to · lead them. On the right Young's men, too, surged forward.

Davies was ready for them. Just minutes before, he had scouted west along the highway. He immediately drew fire from the nearby foe. Alerted to just how close they were, he told his forward line to be on guard for an imminent attack. Thus forewarned of the danger, it blazed away at the Graycoats when they came. Straight into this leaden hail rode Dunovant. As he thundered across the causeway, a bullet tore into his chest. By the time his body hit the rough bridge John Dunovant was dead. Butler tried to keep his death secret from his men, but they had seen him fall. Many guessed that his wound was fatal, and they pulled back, horrified and demoralized.

A few, though, still hoped he could be saved. A courier galloped back to Wilkinson's hill to report the casualty to Hampton. The major general immediately sent his corps Medical Director, Dr. John B. Fontaine, to treat the brigadier. Fontaine, long accustomed to being in the thick of the fray, summoned his orderly and promptly rode through the Confederate batteries toward the front. Just as the doctor got beyond the guns, one of Dennison's shells burst over his head and mortally wounded him. By the time another doctor could reach him, Fontaine, too, was dead.

More than a brigade commander and the corps Medical Director fell in this charge. Confederate prospects of success, slim at best, were completely ruined by Dunovant's death. The demoralized Secessionists were bloodily repulsed and forced to fall back, though in good order, to the New Yorkers' old line on the west bank.[28]

The exhausted soldiers on both sides sought shelter in the muddy rifle pits from enemy fire. and the drizzling rain that left the men "soaked to the skin . . . and shivering all the time with cold."[29] At least Hart's battery, perhaps Graham's, too, now joined the dragoons on the forward line. Even such proximity to the foe, however, did not enable Chew to blast the Bluecoats out of position. Once more the dull boom of artillery and the crackling fire of carbines and rifles marked the stalemated interlude between attacks. Once more the Confederate generals had to seek a new way to dislodge Gregg's tenacious troopers.

With their misgivings about a frontal assault confirmed, Hampton and Butler returned to the original plan of outflanking the Yankee left. The corps commander moved Davis' brigade into position north of the Vaughan Road, facing the Federal right, and shifted Butler's Division south of that highway. This movement placed the South Carolina brigade opposite Davies' left and put Young's Brigade beyond the head of the swamp, where it potentially outflanked the Union left. This redeployment did not satisfy Hampton, though. To assure victory, he wanted additional forces. He accordingly ordered "Rooney" Lee to turn over command on the Harman Road to Barringer and to lead two more regiments from there to the Vaughan Road, perhaps the 10th Virginia Cavalry and the 1st North Carolina Cavalry. These reinforcements were presumably intended to go into action north of Davis' left to turn Davies' right flank.

For approximately an hour Hampton held his brigades in check, awaiting the reinforcements. While he waited, the South Carolina brigade again endangered his plan. Already badly shaken, the outfit now suffered from poor leadership as well. Its new commander, Stokes, was so inexperienced that he confessed to an enlisted man, "I never had command of a brigade before, and I don't know what to do in here. I

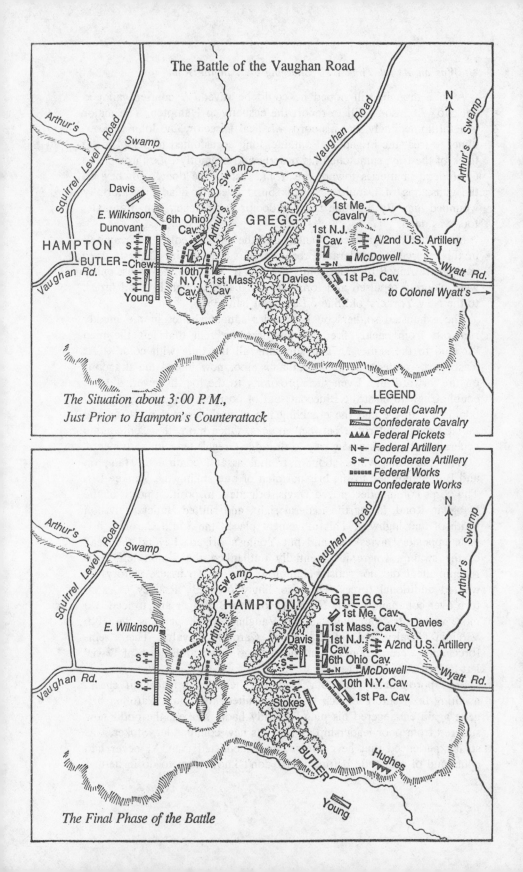

The Battle of the Vaughan Road

The Situation about 3:00 P.M.,
Just Prior to Hampton's Counterattack

LEGEND
Federal Cavalry
Confederate Cavalry
Federal Pickets
N Federal Artillery
S Confederate Artillery
Federal Works
Confederate Works

The Final Phase of the Battle

COMMENTARY

1. The relative positions of Chew's two batteries, Hart's and probably Graham's, are not known.

2. Stokes's position in the lower map is probably correct.

3. The locations of Young Hughes, and the battalion of the 1st Maine Cavalry in the lower map are only schematically representational.

4. In the lower map, the 1st New Jersey Cavalry subsequently took position between the New Yorkers and Pennsylvanians to help meet Young's attack.

5. By the time Young struck that sector, the 7th Georgia Cavalry had been detached. The Jeff Davis Legion, moreover, did not serve with him at all.

6. Farley's position in each map is not known.

will go back and ask General Butler what he wants us to do."[30] Perhaps while he was away, some of his men, for some now unknown reason, suddenly bolted for the rear. He and Butler soon rallied them, however, and sent them back into line.

Hampton could not afford to worry about the South Carolinians' temporary flight. More important problems concerned him. All day he had seen his plans fail: Butler had not held McDowell's; Davis had blundered the flank attack at Wilkinson's; Dunovant had squandered lives to no avail in the frontal charge; and now young Lee proved slow in arriving. As the minute hand of his watch ticked on toward 5:00, the corps commander realized he could await the reinforcements no longer. If he wished to win the battle before darkness ended fighting, he would have to attack with only three brigades. Between 4:30 and 5:00 he ordered his available units to charge.[31]

Once more his dismounted men rushed against the Yankee line east of the swamp. This time, however, it offered little resistance. Davies had learned that the Georgians were moving from the south to cut off his forward position, so he ordered it to fall back before Butler could close with it. The three Union regiments, accordingly, conducted a determined rear-guard action and slowly withdrew up the hill and through the woods to Gregg's reserve position around McDowell's house.

As they reached these works, the 1st Massachusetts Cavalry and the 6th Ohio Cavalry took positions north and south, respectively, of the 1st New Jersey Cavalry. One battalion of the 1st Maine Cavalry continued supporting the far right, while the rest of that unit remained in reserve. All four regiments were north of the Wyatt Road, looking west. To their left the trenches bent back nearly at right angles and faced south. The New Yorkers filed into this refused line adjacent to

the Ohioans, and the 1st Pennsylvania Cavalry prolonged the line eastward. Dennison planted one 12-pounder between the 10th and the 6th
to sweep the Wyatt-Vaughan Road and kept his other Napoleon and
his two 3-inch rifles on the slight rise just northeast of the farmhouse,
about 100 yards behind the works. Here Gregg and Davies braced their
men for Hampton's imminent assault. Their two outer lines were gone;
their vidette line to the IX Corps would soon be severed, if it were not
already cut; and now their main line was about to come under attack.
It was their last position. If it fell, they would lose control of the
Vaughan Road and have to retreat at least as far as Wyatt's plantation.
The final, decisive phase of the battle was at hand.

Hampton did not long delay forcing the issue. After gaining control
of the right bank of the creek, he probably paused briefly to reform.
Then he detached the Georgians on another flanking movement toward
the new Yankee left rear. In the meantime, he sent his main body up
the western slope of McDowell's hill and through the woods against the
Union front. As he emerged from the forest, he found the Federals
waiting for him in the clearing around the farmhouse.

So far, only the Regular battery challenged his advance. Though surprised by the front-line gun, which hit them like a masked battery, his
men remained unshaken. On they kept coming—Davis toward the west
face, Stokes swinging up toward the south face. Still the Northern
dragoons remained at the ready. Only when the attackers closed to
within fifty yards of the works did the Bluecoats open fire. With their
single-shot breech-loading carbines, their pistols, and their canister-
shotted field pieces, Gregg's men sent a leaden hail ripping into the
gray ranks. "Canister . . . rattled through the underbrush like hail-
stones," noted a trooper of the 9th Virginia Cavalry.[32] He and his comrades reeled under this fire and staggered to a halt. Desperately Davis,
Farley, and Stokes urged their soldiers on. With equal determination
Gregg, Davies, their senior staff officers, and their subordinates encouraged the defenders to maintain their fire. The Southern officers
brought their artillery up close to blast their way through. The
Northerners endured this fire and continued pumping lead into Hampton's men. Now the Confederate colors moved forward to set the pace,
wrote one Graycoat, and "the men seemed about to follow when a volley more terribly [sic] than the last was poured into their
ranks. . . ."[33] This latest blast was more than the Butternuts could
stand. At last they recoiled to the refuge afforded under the brow of
McDowell's hill.

There they rested for approximately half an hour. Then they surged
forward again. Again Davies' determined defenders hurled them back.
Still a third time Stokes's men charged the breastworks; still a third

time the Yankees repulsed them. As the Secessionists fell back, the Jerseymen and the New Yorkers poured over their parapets to counterattack. Despite strong resistance, they slowly forced the enemy back
about 200 yards and may even have captured some Virginians.
Satisfied with this success and unwilling to press their luck, Davies'
men then fell back to their works. In their wake, Butler reoccupied the
entire forest. Exhausted, his troopers then slumped down to rest. They
were fought out, and they knew it. The men in the ranks simply decided that they had had enough and refused to attack again. All they
would now do was to post themselves along the edge of the woods and
engage the Federals in a fire fight.[34]

The battle was not over, though, for Hampton still had fresh troops
available. While his principal force assaulted the enemy's right, the
corps commander sent most of Young's Brigade to turn the opposite
flank. Just before nightfall Young's main body (now minus the 7th
Georgia Cavalry as well as the Jeff Davis Legion) at last neared the
Union position. Then his unit emulated the service of Hampton's other
two brigades on the field that day: At a crucial moment it blundered.
On approaching Gregg's right, his soldiers encountered Lieutenant
William Hughes's Company C/1st New Jersey Cavalry, which picketed
that sector. Young drove in these videttes so swiftly that evidently he
unknowingly cut their grand guard off from Davies' works. That
reserve then regrouped, drew its sabers and pistols, and tried to cut its
way through to safety. Its attack from the rear so surprised the Georgians that it was able to break through. During the ensuing confusion
Young, who had gone ahead to reconnoiter, barely escaped being captured. The Jerseymen tell the story this way:

> Sergt. Charles Watts, of Company C, seeing a group of men
> dressed apparently like our men, rode up to one who proved to be
> General Young and asked him, "How in thunder are we going to
> get out of this?" The general seemed to be as much puzzled as
> Watts. . . . Private Miles Downey, seeing that they were the
> enemy, seized upon Captain [John] Jones, assistant adjutant-
> general to General Young, and brought him in a prisoner.[35]

The Butternuts have a much different version:

> On the 1st of October, 1864 . . . General P. M. B. Young rode
> with one aide down a road in front of where his command was
> fighting. He halted, being some distance from his men, and intently
> observed the enemy through his field glasses. Happening to look
> back, he saw a group of Yankee officers in the road between him
> and his men. He saw in an instant that it was important for him to

regain his command as soon as possible. Putting spurs to his horse (he was always splendidly mounted), he dashed at full speed, hoping to pass them. They saw him coming and, when near, with level pistols called him to surrender. Not halting, they [sic] greeted him with a shower of bullets. When passing one of these Yankee officers near enough to touch him, he was called upon to surrender. "Surrender hell," said Young, and passing him like the wind, he gave the Yankee a cut across his face with his riding switch (he had no weapon), and was soon safe among his men. Some days after, we learned from prisoners that the officer cut by General Young bore the mark across his face and was much ridiculed by his brother officers.[36]

In either case, there is no doubt that the general had a close call, that his brigade was thrown into disarray, and that the Northern company got away.

Hughes's men then galloped on to Gregg's lines. Once there, Jones, despite his chagrin, struck up a curious conversation with the Federal brigadier. The staff officer, according to the commander of the 1st Pennsylvania Cavalry, could only think to say that it was "fearfully bad weather for moving about and for cavalry fighting. Davies replied, 'Yes, you people were not content in your camps, but must come out here for a fight, and I guess you got one.' "[37] Gregg meantime prepared to give them still more of a fight. Alert now to the threat to his left, he immediately readied the forces holding that sector, recalled his counterattacking troops, shifted the Jersey regiment down to confront this new danger, and turned Dennison's guns toward the threatened point. By the time Young could regroup and advance, these troopers and artillerymen were ready for him. They easily repulsed his feeble charge. He then fled so fast that he left his dead on the field.

The Georgians attacked weakly because they had not yet recovered from the shock of Hughes's dash. No one was more disconcerted than Young. He magnified the little Union troop into a large force threatening his rear, and he passed the "bad news" on to Hampton. The South Carolinian accepted the report and redeployed units to protect the rear. By the time the major general realized that no danger existed, night had put an end to fighting. The corps commander made much of this error and later contended that if only Young had not misled him, his brigades would have captured McDowell's farm. Here Hampton misled himself. He had clearly lost the battle before receiving the false report. Not Pierce Young but David Gregg ruined Confederate plans that day.[38]

The Southern rank and file knew they had been beaten. Even the combative Major Farley conceded it. Hampton acknowledged as much by ordering a pullback about dark. His men, with difficulty, gathered up most of their dead and wounded and slogged back through knee-deep mud and water to the west side of Arthur's Swamp. From Wilkinson's hill they kept wary vigil on the Northerners over on McDowell's.[39]

The Battle of the Vaughan Road was over. At the cost of about 90 men, over half of them captives lost in the retreat across Arthur's Swamp, Gregg had inflicted approximately 130 casualties. More importantly, he had repulsed repeated Confederate efforts to capture the key road junction at McDowell's. In his hands the Federal left rear was secure.[40]

In achieving this, he sustained the confidence of an old friend. Earlier in the day, some officer (probably Humphreys or Crawford) had passed on to Hancock news of the initial cavalry operations. A little later, at 1:30 P.M., as the corps commander informed army headquarters of the condition of the division he was sending to Peebles's farm, he paused to think of this message about the horsemen. He recalled how often and how well they had served with him. These memories so overcame him that he could not help changing the subject to jot a little postscript on his dispatch to Meade: "I will add that Gregg's cavalry will fight remarkably well dismounted, holding a defensive position." Throughout the day David Gregg and his troopers lived up to Hancock's compliment.[41]

CHAPTER XIII

———◆———

"This Delay Is Unpardonable"

Gregg's victory on the Vaughan Road secured the left rear of the Federal forces near Poplar Spring Church and kept the cavalry of both sides away from their foot soldiers. While the horsemen battled all day, those infantry divisions spent most of October 1 reacting to the outcome of the morning's fight at Chappell's. The senior generals of each army, of course, could not know beforehand that fight's decisive place in the over-all course of the battle. Rather, they could rely on only their military instincts as veteran commanders and their predilections as men to determine the engagement's significance.

To Powell Hill it was another Battle of Globe Tavern, all right, but it was a repetition of August 21, not of August 19. Like that final Sunday on the Weldon Railroad, fighting on October 1 sealed Yankee retention of yet another sector in their apparently relentless drive westward. By midmorning, Hill realized that their strength and his weakness precluded recapturing the key road junctions around Peebles's farm. He therefore ceased trying. Much as this combative Virginian must have hated to do so, he abandoned the initiative he had seized the previous afternoon, conceded the Union gain, and concentrated on preventing them from extending any closer to the Boydton Plank Road. On all sectors except McDowell's, his troops ceased to exert real pressure on the Northern line. They relied instead on feints, diversions, their mere presence, and the continuing rainstorm to forestall a new Federal attack.

On Pegram's farm Wilcox ordered his sharpshooters to pull back from Peebles's farm closer to Lane's and McGowan's main line and to continue skirmishing less briskly. Those two brigades remained in the trenches near the farmhouse despite the annoying but "not very active" Yankee skirmishing and artillery fire and the even more bothersome rain. Brander meantime occasionally exchanged a few shots with the Union artillery. These Southern forces, however, were just a potential threat and a forward line of defense; they did not intend to attack. They spent much of their time, in fact, gathering booty from their earlier successes, rather than seeking new victories.

Over on the Squirrel Level Road Heth also went on the defensive. His voltigeurs, to be sure, continued skirmishing vigorously with the Bluecoat pickets, even managing to wound Richardson. His artillery, too, kept on engaging Battery D/1st New York Light Artillery. Neither Butternut sharpshooters nor cannoneers, though, did the Federals much harm. Indeed, Pegram's most effective shot was his single bolt that cut down a tree eight inches in diameter—a spectacular but hardly decisive blast. Such fire, moreover, counted for little as long as Heth's main body remained back in the old works around W. W. Davis', faced with no more pressing task than regrouping and trying, in vain, to dry out around fires during intermittent slackenings of the storm. With the outcome of his operations against Fort Bratton fresh in mind, he had no intention of assaulting again.[1]

Behind these advanced positions Powell Hill shifted some of his troops (perhaps Finegan's and King's main bodies) in the right and center sectors of the main defenses of Petersburg. At 11:25 some of his forces were spotted moving west on the Boydton Plank Road. Two hours later another 1,500 Graycoats were detected heading from Mahone's sector to the woods west of Battery No. 45. Sometime in between, another column marched to the Southern left, then doubled back to Gibson's sector just before 1:15. Hill may have made some of these moves to free the 9th Virginia Cavalry and 13th Virginia Cavalry to go to E. Wilkinson's. Or he may have been seriously trying to strengthen his lines. So much marching and countermarching, however, suggests that he sought primarily to deceive Northern lookouts. Intermittent rain and dense fog made it hard enough for Federal Signal Corpsmen to detect what he was really doing. The few glimpses they did catch of so much maneuvering, moreover, served very nicely to keep them in doubt.[2]

To divert Meade's attention even more, Hill sent several parties to feint against Crawford. At about 12:15 P.M., a strong skirmish line, probably from Gibson's brigade, ranged south along the east side of the Weldon Railroad and tangled with the right of Ayres's original picket line. Within an hour the threat to Globe Tavern intensified as a full battle line moved south behind these voltigeurs until it occupied some abandoned works (built just after the August fighting) one-half to one-quarter mile north of the Union fortifications. Farther east other Secessionist pickets clashed with Ferrero's outposts by 12:45.

Fighting had at last come to the original lines east of the Weldon Railroad during full daylight. At least some Bluecoats in the ranks likely feared that it presaged a major battle there. Crawford, however, did not share their concern, even when the Graycoats began probing the area east of Fort Howard where they had routed him on August 19. He, to be sure, took the necessary precautions with his own artillery and infantry. As soon as skirmishing broke out, he moved his last reserve cannon company, the Pennsylvanians, into Battery No. 26. He further charged Wainwright to keep a direct eye on the guns in the threatened sector. Beyond that, the general apparently also called up the big new 185th New York—such as it was. It was not much. Despite army headquarters' promises that it would join him overnight, it evidently did not reach the railhead until around 9:00 A.M. Even then, it brought only men and guns. Tents, rations, even ammunition remained back at City Point. Repeated efforts by Crawford and Williams on Saturday seemingly failed to secure these supplies even by night. But at least the men themselves, with weapons, were available—the only infantry reserve. Presumably supplied from the Third Division's ammunition stocks, the regiment joined the 210th in the trenches just east of Fort Wadsworth, apparently at this time.

Despite these countermeasures, Crawford made no appeal to corps or army headquarters for reinforcements as if he feared being attacked in force. More importantly, he took it on himself to find out how strong the Southerners really were. At about 1:15, he sent out a skirmish line to challenge them, likely the Iron Brigade's original picket line, which had not accompanied Bragg's main body to Flowers'. His ploy worked. The Union force handily pushed the Confederate voltigeurs back to their supporting battle line in the old August works. The lack of serious resistance made clear that the Butternuts had come only to demonstrate, not to attack.

Crawford's front then quieted down for four hours. At about 5:20, though, some of Mahone's men, probably including the 11th Alabama of King's brigade, jabbed toward the Negro sector east of Fort Howard. This time they apparently drove in some of Stearns's pickets. However, Ferrero, from his new, more central headquarters at Aiken's, had repeatedly cautioned his brigadiers that afternoon to be vigilant against probes of their long, thin line. The main USCT battle line was, accordingly, ready for the danger and promptly opened up on the Confederates. Once more, they did not stand up to such fire but immediately retired out of range. Their feint ended fighting in this sector for October 1. Mahone's operations by daylight thus proved little different than his maneuvers after dark: mere jabs and sorties to distract and annoy the Yankees. Like Heth and Wilcox farther west, he had no intention of attacking in strength.

Indeed, the only Southern troops around Petersburg to engage in serious combat after Heth's repulse were Hampton's horsemen on the Vaughan Road, and they were fighting a private battle that formed no integral part of Hill's new plan. All the infantry units had lapsed back into the strategic and grand-tactical defensive. The necessity for doing this was the conclusion the lieutenant general drew from the failure on Chappell's that morning.[3]

Parke and Warren made a remarkably comparable analysis of the battle's impact on Federal operations. Repelling the Secessionist attack confirmed their predisposition to remain on the defensive. Now that fighting had ended, they busied themselves strengthening their position. Throughout that rainy, foggy morning, their three divisions on the left concentrated on completing their entrenchments and abatis. At least the 7th Rhode Island even ventured out into the woods between Peebles's and Pegram's to cut logs for revetments. Fire from Wilcox's voltigeurs, however, soon forced it to withdraw, but Pennsylvania Battery D, in turn, trained its guns on the skirmishers and silenced them. The engineers then resumed their woodcutting. Potter's main line plus Griffin's First and possibly Third brigades meantime continued their random firing into those woods, with much noise and little effect.

Farther northeast, Ayres's soldiers worked on the east–west retrenchment that formed Warren's right. Confederate sniping on that sector was more telling. When it proved too annoying, Northern skirmishers, backed up by a section of D/1st New York Light Artillery, drove Heth's sharpshooters a short way up the Squirrel Level Road in late afternoon. Even so, the Second Division, V Corps, did not counterattack in force. It, too, spent the rest of the day shoveling mud, not fighting. Further to strengthen the division's line, Hofmann extended its works southeastward from Graham's right toward Flowers'. Around Flowers' itself, the Iron Brigade took up the defense. Told by Bragg to hold that position "at all hazards," it worked with extra zeal to erect works, slash abatis, clear a field of fire for its two accompanying batteries, and build a crossroad between Flowers' and Fort Wadsworth. As it labored, some skirmishers covering the far left of Heth's attack had lapped against its front, only to be easily checked. Now voltigeurs from the 143rd and 150th Pennsylvania ranged out to drive them back.

Those Bucktail light infantry, of course, were fresh, but the pickets adjoining their right, the 500 original outposts the Second Division had left in place, were now exhausted after three days of picketing. Concerned for their welfare and combat effectiveness, Ayres requested that they be relieved that evening and allowed to rejoin him. Warren approved that recommendation and, at 5:00 P.M., instructed the Third Division commander to provide 200 replacements. Despite Crawford's initial determination not to call on the Iron Brigade's original picket force for this quota, he subsequently decided to extend it leftward to the Weldon Railroad. Baxter contributed the remaining outposts to prolong the line westward from the tracks to Bragg's new position. That evening these replacements duly relieved Ayres's exhausted pickets, who at last rejoined their division.

Crawford also sent forward a number of men from within his own lines. The 2/38th Wisconsin joined its sister battalion at Clements' that afternoon. Also, shortly after 12:45 P.M. he sent the 88th Pennsylvania through his camps to round up V Corps and IX Corps stragglers and to call up cooks and clerks. Getting even a few men helped rebuild the shattered ranks of the three regiments destroyed on Jones's farm, but over-all, the dragnet turned up few soldiers to be sent to the front. Most of the stragglers and routed men had gone no farther east than the woods around Poplar Spring Church, and from there many more returned to duty on Saturday. Also returning to the field that day from sick leave was the hard-hitting, reliable Brigadier General Joseph J. Bartlett, who passed through Globe Tavern sometime October 1 en route to resuming command of the Third Brigade of Griffin's division.[4]

No additional troops followed Bartlett up the tracks from City Point to help replace those Crawford forwarded. At around 10:30 A.M., to be sure, Grant did tell Birchett's that another large new regiment was available at the supply base to join the 185th and 210th. Repeated inquiries from Williams in midmorning and midafternoon, however, disclosed that no such unit was on hand. Perhaps the Illinoisan had mistaken the two provisional New York companies for the vanguard of a new regiment. Or perchance he had in mind the 127th USCT, which did reach the point sometime on Saturday but which was earmarked for the Army of the James. Thus no additional organized units were available for Benham and Patrick to send into the field.

Indeed, all that the engineer and the provost officer at the point, Colonel Theodore B. Gates of the 80th New York, provided army headquarters on October 1 was another headache. The problem arose when the General-in-Chief, ever sensitive to the security of the big supply base, called on Benham to report how many men, other than those of the Engineer Brigade, were on guard there. The junior officer replied that he had 1,837 men but that Gates would not report his strength. The colonel thrice ignored Benham's requests for a report and then explicitly refused to recognize orders from anyone but Patrick. Always touchy, the Connecticut man took umbrage at this rejoinder and thrust the whole problem upon Birchett's. Humphreys had to take valuable time from field operations to resolve the matter. Fully alive to the need for a unified command, he decided in Benham's favor and told Patrick to reprimand his overly independent subordinate. The resulting unity of command was obviously desirable, but its absence during the preceding two weeks had hardly been fatal, and the matter certainly did not need to be resolved in the midst of battle.[5]

Supply officers at the central depot proved more co-operative and forwarded extra arms and ammunition that the V Corps needed. Local ammunition trains at Globe Tavern, too, rumbled out the Poplar Spring Road to help replace the depleted stocks. Dutiful headquarters officers even saw to it that ranking commanders would have tents and bedding to enable them to spend Saturday night in less discomfort than the previous one. Junior officers and men in the ranks fared much less well. Muddy and drenched, they lacked both shelter from the rain and also fresh, dry clothing. Even food was lacking for some outfits, such as the 60th Ohio, which had already consumed the rations in their haversacks. Other units had food but could not always get it. Many men of the 4th Rhode Island, for instance, reminded their superiors that they were no longer in the Union army. They had stayed on an extra day to fight, but they were not about to remain a second day to wallow in mud. Potter took them at their word. Since they were no longer in service, they were not entitled to government rations. Loss of their food quickly brought them to terms, and throughout Saturday and on into Sunday they rejoined their "loyalist" comrades of the 4th at the front. Less sulky regiments meantime endured the hardships, appreciated such supplies as they did receive, and continued to fortify their recent conquests.[6]

Retrench, reinforce, resupply—these were the requirements Warren and Parke set for their men. Reconnoitering and resuming the attack had no place in their plans. The fog of war, far denser than the natural fog that obscured the Virginia countryside that day, closed in around their headquarters once fighting ended, and they decided to sit tight rather than grope through it. More than that, the V Corps commander sought to convert army headquarters to his point of view. At 11:30 A.M., he informed Birchett's of recent operations, then went on to say:

> It is, in a measure, a necessity to occupy the line we hold, and that leaves no force to attack with. The quiet of the enemy may indicate that he is intrenching a new line or preparing to attack. We are not strong enough to act offensively, in view of the uncertainty of the enemy's positions, numbers, and movements, but we keep

feeling them. A mistake on our part might enable the enemy to
reoccupy the points we have taken. We, therefore, are waiting further developments and securing our position. I would be pleased to
know if our course meets the approval of the general commanding.[7]

This dispatch did not overtake Meade and Humphreys for quite a
while, since it initially traveled by courier (the telegraph line would not
be extended to Peebles's house until shortly before 2:00 P.M.) and
since they spent much of the day away from their headquarters. By the
time it finally reached them at Globe Tavern just prior to 2:00 P.M.,
the army commander had already decided what he wanted done.

Meade, in fact, never renounced his decision of the previous evening
that the army should renew the attack on Saturday. He reaffirmed his
intentions throughout the day. Early that morning, to be sure, gloomy
intelligence reports did make him waver a little. Parke's pessimistic dispatch of 5:15 A.M., the sighting of Confederates moving south along
the Squirrel Level Road ninety minutes later, and Hancock's report of
7:00 A.M. that deserters from Gracie's headquarters reported that two
enemy divisions still served in the main defenses of Petersburg all
suggested that the Graycoats remained present in force. Later reports
from John Babcock before 9:20 and before 10:30 and from Williams
at 11:45 strengthened Meade's belief that only two divisions had gone
to the Peninsula and four still confronted him on the Southside, most
of which might take the field against him. At 8:00 A.M., the army commander forwarded the first three reports to City Point and added that,
before finally ordering an advance, he would await the results of the reconnaissance he had ordered Parke, Warren, and Gregg to make. Even
so, he let the Illinoisan know that he still thought of attacking. His dispatch surely never got farther than Grant's headquarters, but if he had
sent it in the old days—back when he could report directly to
Washington—Mr. Lincoln would have framed it in gold. Its final sentence promised exactly what the Chief Executive had repeatedly urged
his generals to do in the earlier years of the war: "If I advance, I will
send up Hancock's division, and put in all the troops I can get hold
of."[8]

So strong, indeed, was Meade's commitment to advancing that even
Warren's ominous report of 8:00 A.M. that the enemy would attack imminently could not shake it. The army commander suspected that the
Confederates were just bluffing, so he assured Grant, at 9:20, that he
would resume advancing as soon as Mott's reinforcements reached the
front. One hour and ten minutes later he again expressed this intention
to the lieutenant general. The Pennsylvanian, of course, misread the initial intelligence, which did portend a real attack against Chappell's.

But by the time he received Warren's report, at 9:20, that attack had been repulsed and all further demonstrations were, indeed, feints. Hence, Meade's attitude of calling the bluff by attacking showed better understanding of the tactical realities of midmorning than did the defensive outlook of his two corps commanders.

Meade, for that matter, was even more oriented to attacking than the General-in-Chief himself. Grant had other things on his mind on October 1. Failure by the Northern populace to support the war effort more fully upset him greatly. He made clear to Bartlett, as the junior officer passed through City Point en route to the front, that he "was disgusted with the manner in which men were allowed to leak away after quotas were filled & wished the Presidential Election any where but in the hands of the people this fall."[9] His whole day was not spent in bitter brooding, though. He indulged much more jovial sentiments in consequence of the actions of a supply officer at the point who:

> . . . made a bet with an old Irish soldier (50.$) that he could not make Genl. Grant laugh. Paddy got 2 8 week old pups in Darkie town and got permission to present them to Genl. Grant. We sat under chf. [?] Correspondent's fly & saw the General receive the mick & the pups. The pups were let down upon the ground & began to play their pup antics. Genl. Grant began to laugh & was thrown into immoderate laughter, much to the delight of all who saw him [especially] to the mickey who was winning the $50.00.[10]

More than hoi polloi and happy puppies captured the Illinoisan's attention that day. He was principally concerned with the viability of the Fifth Offensive itself. Not how to attack but whether to attack was the question he pondered. Some hint of his mounting doubt may appear in his response to Meade's messages of 8:00 and 9:20. This reply, which reached Birchett's at 10:30, contained no order, nor even any encouragement, to press the advance. The lieutenant general would say only that "you will be able to judge best as to the propriety of further offensive operations."[11] This dispatch may simply represent deferral to the front-line commander, but it may also reflect growing lack of commitment to continuing the attack. His trip to the Northside in late morning intensified, if it did not create, these doubts about the desirability of prolonging the offensive. He evidently concluded from his visit that the Army of the James could accomplish little that day, and he presumably decided that the Army of the Potomac could not achieve much, either. Gone was his earlier enthusiasm for pressing the attack. By early afternoon, if not sooner, he came increasingly to believe that the Fifth Offensive had already netted as much as it ever would and need not be continued. Probably around 2:00 P.M., he accordingly wrote Meade from Foster's front to "correct and strengthen your line and advance no farther unless a very favorable chance presents itself."[12]

Whether the Pennsylvanian received this dispatch in the afternoon or not until evening is not known, nor does it matter. Unlike his chief, he remained committed to attacking. Assessing the attainability of strategic objectives like capturing the capital or its rail center he admittedly left to City Point. A great tactical objective, however, he felt was still within reach. At long last he had forced the Confederates out of their fortifications into the open field, and he still hoped to smite them there if there were any prospect of success. He therefore informed Grant at 2:30 that "I shall see Warren and Parke and then determine what I will do, being most desirous to attack unless I should not deem it judicious to do so."[13]

This, then, was Meade's frame of mind when, at 2:00 P.M., he received Warren's letter of 11:30 A.M., asking if his defensive plan "meets the approval of the general commanding." Since the Pennsylvanian had made clear ever since midnight that he favored advancing and since he had informed both front-line corps commanders as recently as 10:00 A.M. that he desired the whole force to attack as soon as Mott arrived, the senior officer hardly granted his approval to Warren's latest effort to have his own way. At 2:00 P.M. the army commander had his Chief-of-Staff set the New Yorker straight on this matter:

> Your dispatch of 11:30 a.m. received. Your course, as preliminary to the arrival of Mott's division, is approved by the commanding general. As soon as Mott gets up, dispositions must be made to attack.[14]

Meade thus remained determined to advance. He, of course, could not formulate a specific battle plan before reaching the front, but he did develop a general idea of what he wanted done. Gregg (still thought to be at Peebles's) and Mott (on arriving) were to report to Parke and take position to Willcox's left, Meade informed the IX Corps commander at 10:00 A.M. Then all three divisions plus Potter and Griffin were to pin and turn the Confederate right on Pegram's farm. In the meantime Ayres, at Warren's insistence, was to continue guarding the right flank and right rear, which the V Corps commander felt would be attacked again that evening. Four hours later, on learning of the cavalry operations on the Vaughan Road, the army commander decided to let Gregg continue fighting where he was and to reinforce Parke with infantry only.[15]

As Meade developed these plans, he made his daily journey from Birchett's to the front. He and Humphreys set out around 10:00–10:30

A.M., again by horse. Again, too, they spent much time at II Corps headquarters, conferring and presumably trying to expedite the Third Division's departure. Not until sometime between 12:45 and 2:00 P.M. did they reach Globe Tavern. They remained with Crawford at least one hour in order to engage in major correspondence with Grant, Warren, and Gregg and apparently also to make sure that Mott was finally arriving. At last, just before 3:00 P.M., they left for Peebles's farm. Thus a more aggressive commander finally reached the front to offset the cautious conduct of Parke and Warren. Yet even Meade did not attack right away. His whole plan, as repeatedly expressed to superior and subordinate, depended on the arrival of reinforcements. And Gershom Mott was a long time coming.[16]

The first call for Hancock to get some troops ready to move had gone out from Birchett's just after midnight. "The lateness of the hour at which your order was received," the corps commander forewarned Humphreys at 1:00 A.M., would potentially cause delay by making "it a difficult matter to execute it before daylight." Even so, the subordinate promised to take "all steps in my power" to carry out the instructions.[17]

Hancock's first problem, of course, was selecting which unit to send. An excellent tactician led the First Division, but Miles's brigadiers lacked the experience and the ability to translate his commands into results. Gibbon, if anything, gave the Second Division even better direction than the First enjoyed. Two of his brigadiers, Egan and Smyth, moreover, were hard-hitting combat leaders. Yet the presence of these three officers in that division, like that of Miles in the First, could not offset the spreading cancer that threatened to vitiate both units. The divisions were being consumed by their own glory. They had fought so long, so hard, so well, so often that they were now just shells of their former selves. Too, too many men who had earned fame for these outfits were now dead or wounded out; far inferior—or, at least, far more inexperienced—soldiers presently bore the proud banners. They had fought poorly, even disastrously, in August. Now, five weeks later, Hancock hesitated to commit them to battle. His Third Division, on the other hand, had been battered less severely than the others throughout the past five months and had avoided the debacle of Second Reams's Station. Besides being the freshest and strongest qualitatively, it was also the strongest numerically, with several hundred more men than the First Division and several thousand more than the Second.

Then, too, on balance, it possessed the best commanders. Gershom Mott himself, to be sure, ranks nowhere near Miles and Gibbon in ability. Indeed, Mott's initial handling of a division, at the Wilderness and the first part of Spotsylvania, was so poor that his unit was broken up and he was demoted to brigade command. He profited from the renewed experience as a brigadier, for by the time Birney rose to corps command in July, Mott had won the right to be his permanent successor. Even so, no gleam of brilliance, no flash of inspiration, no dazzle of flamboyant personal magnetism highlighted his record. He was and would always remain just a dull, plodding soldier—but he had learned how to handle a division. Hancock like this; he sensed that Mott contributed a measure of effective leadership that made his entire division stronger than the sum of its parts. Yet those parts themselves were relatively well led, too. DeTrobriand, a dashing French nobleman become American citizen, combined long experience with considerable natural ability to give the First Brigade sound direction. The Third Brigade, too, performed well in the highly competent hands of the dour old Calvinist citizen-soldier, McAllister. The remaining commander, the bushy-bearded Michigander Pierce, was also an able officer, although not as skilled as DeTrobriand and McAllister. These men unquestionably formed the best team of senior commanders then available in the II Corps.

Able leadership, freshness, numerical strength all contributed to the division's impressive combat effectiveness. Yet the unit benefited from another factor as well. Its men fought hard because they were the sole guardians of a proud tradition. Twenty-three of its twenty-six regiments had served in the old III Corps. That corps no longer existed, but these men remained its children. They still strove to live up to the glorious heritage bequeathed them by Hooker and Kearny and Humphreys and Birney and all the other greats of the old "Diamond Corps."

As Hancock looked for a division to send to Peebles's farm, he knew he could rely on Mott's to serve well. At 1:00 A.M. on October 1, he ordered Miles and Gibbon to extend leftward along the entire front and relieve the Third Division, which was then to mass in the rear.

The picket line, including Mott's outposts, remained in position to cover the redeployment. A major redistribution it was. Of the front-line forces, the only outfits to remain in position were the artillery and some of the garrisons of the strongholds, such as the 140th Pennsylvania in Battery No. 5, the 61st New York in Fort McGilvery, part of the 69th New York in No. 9, and the 148th Pennsylvania in Fort Stedman. The garrisons of the other six forts and the troops in the curtains all moved. The Fourth Brigade drew the heaviest assignment: to extend leftward from Fort Stedman through Fort Haskell to relieve Egan's brigade and at the same time to stretch rightward along the curtains north of Stedman to replace virtually all of Miles's other units except the four garrisons named above and 260 pickets along the lower Appomattox. Glenny posted some of the 7th New York Heavy Artillery, the 66th New York, and the 53rd Pennsylvania in No. 11, No. 12, and Fort Haskell, respectively, and strung other regiments out along the trenches. In the meantime the Consolidated Brigade, on being replaced in Miles's original center, shifted to his new center, from the Fourth's left to just south of Fort Morton, thus relieving Gibbon's other two brigades. McGee assigned the rest of the 69th New York that had not stayed with its comrades in No. 9 to hold No. 14 and Morton, and put the 111th New York in No. 13. Miles's remaining brigade, at the same time, moved from far right to far left and replaced DeTrobriand's garrison in Fort Meikel plus McAllister's right demibrigade. The First Division thus held with three brigades the entire two miles of works from the river to the Norfolk Railroad, a sector previously manned by seven brigades. Such a heavy commitment of his manpower forced Miles to put some of his reserves in the fortifications, to place musicians and some extra-duty men in the ranks, and probably to attenuate his troops in the curtains to the open order of a skirmish line. Even so, he did manage to keep 800 of Lynch's men behind Fort Morton as a general reserve against attacks on the front and rear lines.

Gibbon, with far fewer troops, received a much lighter assignment: merely to relieve DeTrobriand's main body and the garrison of Fort Davis. Murphy took over the right of this line along the trenches from the First Division's left to Fort Rice, then halfway beyond toward Battery No. 21. Egan posted the 1st Minnesota and 36th Wisconsin in Rice itself, the 19th and 20th Massachusetts and 59th and 152nd New York and later the 7th Michigan in the trenches from Murphy's left to No. 21, part of the 19th Maine from that battery to Fort Sedgwick, and the rest of the 19th, 60 men of the 184th Pennsylvania (supported by the rest of that regiment), and the 12th New Jersey (of the Third Brigade) in Sedgwick itself. Smyth took up the line leftward from there through Fort Davis. Some 760 of his men anchored the Second Division's left in that stronghold, among them the 10th New York and 69th and 106th Pennsylvania. In occupying this short sector, Gibbon probably did not have to attenuate his line like the First Division. Even so, he used virtually all his soldiers just to hold the works and had no reserve.

Getting these units into position on a dark, rainy night was no easy matter. Some, in fact, did not make it. The 7th Michigan lost its way and lost its commander en route and did not rejoin its brigade, first in Fort Sedgwick, then in the curtain right of there, until morning. Those troops who did reach their new sectors, moreover, experienced further difficulty in occupying trenches flooded by the downpour. The resulting delays seriously concerned Mott, who was conscious of the need to effect the transfer promptly, while darkness still afforded cover. He initially got word to his units by 2:00 A.M. to be ready to move on being relieved. When two hours elapsed and still no replacements came, he instructed his brigadiers to pull out without awaiting the Second Division. At least three regiments from McAllister's right evidently did this, but his 11th New Jersey did not leave that sector until just before daybreak. Gibbon was probably present by then, for he definitely relieved the First Brigade, farther left, at that time. Nevertheless, the most westerly force, the 5th–7th New Jersey and 11th Massachusetts in Fort Davis, had not been replaced by 7:15 A.M. But over the next forty-five minutes, Smyth took over their position, too. By 8:00, Hancock could inform Birchett's that the whole operation was completed.

Although he had experienced annoying delays, he had managed to pull the Third Division out of line in time, since Meade was not yet ready to call for it, anyway. Mott's men, therefore, simply tried to conceal themselves in the rear. McAllister's four right regiments marched back to the Trestle Station, where the U. S. Military Railroad crossed Blackwater Creek just south of the Petersburg and Norfolk tracks. There his detached force from Fort Davis rejoined him. Pierce's detached regiment in Battery No. 37, on the other hand, did not return to him despite Hancock's order of 10:30 A.M. that it do so. However, the main body of the Second Brigade, which was in reserve behind Mott's left to begin with, simply moved down the Jerusalem Plank Road to the Chieves house, three quarters of a mile north of where the highway crossed the U. S. Military Railroad at Hancock's Station. Most of the First Brigade probably joined Pierce there, but its right apparently marched to the Trestle Station.[18]

That was about where army headquarters wanted the troops. By midmorning, Meade had allayed his few remaining doubts and decided to resume advancing. At 9:30 A.M., his Chief-of-Staff ordered Hancock to forward the reinforcements to Parke at Peebles's farm. Humphreys added that he wanted only infantry. He declined Hancock's offer of 8:00 A.M. to send the 3rd Vermont Battery, too, a company that had left Fort Sedgwick late Friday night (before Mott's movement was ordered) to take up a virtual reserve position in Battery No. 17. Then at 10:15 A.M., the staff officer forbade provision trains to accompany the Third Division, either. He therefore suggested that the men draw rations from those wagons before leaving. Only absolutely indispensable ammunition, medicine, and headquarters wagons, he went on, could go with the troops. Even the pared-down medical train, it turned out, got no farther than a point between Gurley's and Globe Tavern and did not move on to join the V Corps and IX Corps field hospitals at Poplar Spring Church and Peebles's farm, respectively. The earlier order may not have reached Hancock until around 10:15. But within the next fifteen minutes he had received both directives. At 10:30, he summarized them for Mott.

Birchett's divested the Third Division of so many wagons more to prevent congestion on the Poplar Spring Road than to free its march from impedimenta. No matter how many were selected, the wagons moving west along the corduroyed military highway to the Halifax Road would not accompany their troops. The combat infantry would long precede them, borne virtually to the front by the U. S. Military Railroad.

The rail line from Cedar Level Station to Globe Tavern had been completed only on September 12. Now, for the first time in American military history, probably in world military history, the high command was using a railroad to facilitate grand-tactical movement in the midst of battle. Trains, of course, had long been used for logistical support and had played an often significant and occasionally brilliant role in strategic and grand-strategic movement of forces. But this was the first time they were employed to transfer troops laterally from a quiet sector of a battlefield to a railhead barely a mile from the firing line. It was a bold and innovative use of new technology by Meade and Humphreys to take advantage of old tactics about the benefits of massing one's forces against the enemy. The entire rolling stock of the line, sixty cars, was to pick up the division at Trestle and Hancock's stations and rush it to Globe Tavern. Marching that far on a rainy day, thence on to Peebles's, nearly six miles altogether, would take all afternoon. But riding most of the way by train would get the troops to the front soon enough and fresh enough that they could spearhead the renewed attack yet Saturday. This new means of speeding forces into battle looked like just what Meade needed to jolt his corps commanders into action and revitalize the attack.

Unfortunately for him, the approach was still too new. The perceptive grand-tactical planning outstripped logistical support. Quartermasters, unaccustomed to transporting thousands of combat soldiers into battle, introduced new elements of delay in transferring the division. Earlier delays had been inherent in the situation: the inclement weather, the dark night, the strategic uncertainty of early morning. Now, however, a far more serious delay occurred—and it was solely man-made. Somehow the chain of command broke down among the Chief-of-Staff; the Chief Quartermaster of the Army of the Potomac, Colonel Richard N. Batchelder; and the Chief Quartermaster at City Point, Colonel Perley P. Pitkin. The supply officers had no trains waiting or readily available to pick up the Third Division at the stations. Instead, most or all of the cars were back at City Point! So everyone simply waited: Mott's drenched men, who were just standing out in the rain; Hancock and his staff and perhaps Humphreys as well, who were trying to send them off; and, above all, General Meade, who counted on these reinforcements to spearhead his attack. This logistical failure brought the entire Army of the Potomac to a standstill.

Humphreys was furious. "This delay is unpardonable," he snorted to Batchelder at 11:45 A.M., and he directed the quartermaster to send forward any cars he could get.[19] The colonel had evidently previously reached the same conclusion on his own and had ordered Pitkin to dispatch whatever rolling stock was available. A little before noon, the first three trains, totaling forty-seven cars, finally chugged into Hancock's Station. A fourth train, with twelve more cars, followed shortly. The sixtieth car apparently never did arrive.

Nonetheless, enough cars were now on hand to start transporting the division. At Batchelder's order, Colonel Luther H. Peirce, Chief Quartermaster of the IX Corps, took charge of getting the reinforcements to the front. Yet even now, some delay ensued. Not until around 12:30 did the first contingent, the greatest part of the Second Brigade, led by its brigadier but also accompanied by DeTrobriand and at least some of his brigade, begin boarding the cars. Once it started moving, though, it made good time on the 3½-mile journey and reached Globe Tavern at about 2:00. Meade himself was awaiting it and personally ordered it on to the front, while Humphreys sent word ahead to IX Corps headquarters at 2:00 that the reinforcements had finally arrived and were starting for the front. Unaware of these tidings, Parke, at the same hour, had anxiously asked Crawford where the fresh division was. Although the junior officer did not formally reply until 3:30 that it was en route, the corps commander became aware of that fact long before then. About 2:30 to 2:40 P.M., Pierce's contingent, guided to the front by one of Crawford's staff officers, finally reached Peebles's farm. At 2:50, Parke duly reported the arrival to army headquarters. Even before the Michigander reached Peebles's, a much larger contingent of about 3,000 men followed; Mott, satisfied that the movement was progressing well, accompanied them. By 3:30, they arrived at the tavern; half an hour later, they too reached the IX Corps. Finally, McAllister policed up the remaining 600 men of the First Brigade, 700 of the Second, and 125 of the Third and set out for the railhead aboard a third group of trains. By 3:00 P.M. all the troops were under way.[20]

Their departure at last freed Hancock from the burden of sending them off. His cares were hardly over, though. With his much-reduced force he still had to guard the right and the rear. True, the Butternuts east of Petersburg did not actively threaten him. Humphreys, indeed, had reassured him at 10:00 A.M. that they were probably weak, too, with most of their comrades sent to Jones's or Chaffin's. True, too, the cavalry attack on the rear had not materialized. Robison spotted no more than a few videttes, who, he reported on Wednesday, "make no unfriendly demonstrations."[21] Still, the corps commander took some necessary precautions. At 1:30 P.M., he repeated to Miles that if the Southerners did attack the rear line on the Jerusalem Plank Road or the Norfolk Railroad, Lynch's mobile reserve should move to Avery's house, and most of the troops in the curtains should join him. The division commander, in that eventuality, was to take charge of all troops on the back line, while Gibbon would become responsible for the entire front line from Fort Davis to the lower Appomattox. Unless such an attack occurred, though, the infantry would remain in place. Not until late at night did Hancock actually move some foot soldiers to increase his combat mobility. At 10:00 P.M. Egan began extending northward to Lynch's left, thus permitting Murphy's whole brigade to drop back into mobile reserve.

Even before then, the corps commander provided artillery support to the back line in response to Humphrey's request. Sometime that afternoon, the Chief-of-Staff told Hunt to send two guns each to Prince George Court House and Fort Bross. The artillerist, once commander of a mighty force, now had only one company at his disposal, and it was a supply unit with no cannons. "I have not a gun," he confessed. Even more gallingly, he had to seek help from his archenemy, Hancock, and Hancock's man, Hazard. In a message sent at 3:30 P.M. and received at 4:45 P.M., he asked the major to "spare" him the battery sent the II Corps on Friday.[22] One section of the 14th, however, was already on the rear line, in No. 37, so only its other two guns were available. These the Rhode Islander duly transferred from the First Division's left to the Norfolk Railroad. To reinforce the courthouse after dark, he sent two rifles of the 3rd Vermont Battery, no longer earmarked to accompany Mott. Now guns as well as infantry and cavalry stood guard against a possible raid by Hampton.

Lonely outpost duty in the rear during the rain, often without even the shelter of tents, was hardly comfortable, but it was necessary. What the back line now needed was not more tents or more guns but an over-all commander. Patrick had done little in that regard at best, and now he was gone to more healthful climes at City Point. Collis, Spaulding, Robison, and Pulford thus remained independent of each other and most everyone else. Hancock, however, already began exercising operational control over all of them, even without official authorization from Birchett's. That splendid soldier sensed the need for such unity of command and conscientiously started sparing Meade of the necessity to concern himself with the back line any longer.[23]

The army commander was, doubtless, grateful for such help. He still had enough pressing problems of his own about which to worry.

Throughout the early morning he had seen hesitant subordinates at the front refuse to take the initiative. Despite all the prodding from Birchett's, Parke remained unenthusiastic. As late as 3:00 P.M., with Pierce already at hand, the IX Corps commander was still reluctant to budge. He admittedly did not think the Graycoats held Pegram's in strength, but he may have worried that stronger forces of them were again concealed in the woods to counterattack him. And he was definitely troubled about the unfavorable weather, the resulting muddiness of the field of advance, and the lateness of the hour. He therefore warned his superiors that "any advance that we may be able to make this evening may result in the taking of the Pegram house, but I think nothing further." Even that limited gain, moreover, he made dependent on the availability of Mott's division.

Hence the greater the delay in bringing up those reinforcements, the greater the delay in renewing the attack. No one appreciated this fact more than Meade, for unlike his corps commanders he was anxious to attack. Yet like them he was unwilling to commit to battle piecemeal the fragments that dribbled into Peebles's farm in midafternoon. Only when the entire Third Division was available would he strike. And as the minutes ticked on into hours and one delay after another slowed the unit's arrival, he gradually realized that it would not arrive in time. By the time McAllister's final contingent at last moved out the Poplar Spring Road between 5:00 and 5:30, darkness had virtually fallen. En route, these reinforcements passed Meade going the other way, his mind reluctantly made up that he could achieve nothing that afternoon. All his reinforcements could do now was to bivouac for the night in Peebles's open field and the woods near the church.[24]

Shifting fresh troops westward only to allow them to go to sleep looked like an insignificant achievement for October 1. The army commander, of course, had hoped for much more. From late Friday night on through the day, he had urged, encouraged, and ordered his strike force to resume advancing. However, nature and men—men who were hesitant or cautious or willful or even incompetent—had thwarted his plans. His army was no nearer the enemy supply lines on Saturday night than it had been the previous evening. In fact, its pullback from Pegram's in early morning even made it a little farther away from those communications.

Yet the day had not been without advantage to the Bluecoats. They had confirmed their grip on the important intersections around Peebles's farm and had blocked Hampton's efforts to get into their left rear. Equally important, Meade had significantly redistributed his manpower. The 2,300 new troops who joined him from City Point and the North on Friday and Saturday virtually offset his 2,700 casualties thus far in the battle. More than just replace the losses, though, he had actually strengthened his striking force at the expense of his garrisons by the night of October 1. About 61 per cent of his army had remained in the lines east of Forts Wadsworth and Dushane when fighting erupted in earnest on Friday morning. By Saturday night, he had drawn them down to the point that only around 31,000 troops now served there: a little over 10,000 with Crawford, approximately 15,500 north of the Jerusalem Plank Road, and about 5,300 at City Point. The attack force, despite its heavy casualties, had been correspondingly strengthened. Crawford had sent it nearly 2,800 men, and Mott's first three convoys added about 5,800 more. Then overnight 230 of the Jerseyman's 300 pickets were relieved from Hancock's front when Gibbon and Miles extended their own outposts leftward to correspond to their trench sectors. Those 230 pickets then set out for Peebles's. If they arrived by daylight, they would have made the strike force 30,000 strong. Virtually half the Army of the Potomac was now mobile, poised near the front, and ready to attack the first thing on Sunday.[25]

Meade, moreover, remained determined to resume advancing. The day's disappointments had not fazed him. Nor was he daunted by an intelligence report, apparently received shortly before 7:00 P.M., that some of "Tige" Anderson's men confronted him on the Southside. Both he and City Point, admittedly, accepted this information at face value as indicating that the enemy was dividing divisions and even brigades to try to create a show of force everywhere. They did not realize that the report referred to the 8th Georgia Cavalry of Dearing's Brigade, not the 8th Georgia Infantry of Anderson's Brigade. Still, the army commander did not allow the foot soldiers' supposed presence to dissuade him from striking. He formulated his specific plans for attacking after returning to Globe Tavern just after sundown. As he drew up these battle orders, two assumptions continued to dominate his thinking: first, that he could still reach the Boydton Plank Road, if not the Southside Railroad, and second, that he could still attack the Confederates in the open field, outside their fortifications. How he would react if either assumption proved false remained to be seen. What mattered now was that he was going to attempt to advance again.

At 6:45 P.M., Humphreys dispatched Meade's orders to the IX Corps commander. Parke's three infantry divisions were to advance "as soon after daylight tomorrow as practicable," preferably by a modified right wheel. They were to defeat or outflank the force on Pegram's, then press on to the plank road. Parke was also to take charge of Gregg's division and either send it west along Route 673 or else let it resume fighting on the Vaughan Road. Fifteen minutes later the Chief-of-Staff instructed Warren, too, to be ready to advance the next morn-

ing. Other than telling him to strike with his whole corps except for
Crawford's men at Globe Tavern, the Pennsylvanian gave him only
the imprecise order to "move forward and attack." The New Yorker
could learn all the details of Meade's plan by reading Parke's copy of
it, Humphreys told him. Why army headquarters did not send comprehensive orders to the V Corps commander is not known.[26]

Although Warren did not receive complete instructions, he had no
hesitancy about lecturing the army commander and the General-in-
Chief at great length on how to campaign. The New Yorker was in a
relaxed mood that evening. He had gotten over his apprehension of
early afternoon that the Southerners might attack his Second Division
after dark, and he sighed with relief that not he but Meade would bear
the supreme responsibility during the advance on Sunday. The emotional exuberance of this freedom from responsibility may have overcome his better judgment, for sometime Saturday evening he presumed
to instruct the Pennsylvanian that Grant's whole conduct of operations
was wrong:

> Major-General Meade:
> General: From what I know of our and General Lee's relative
> strength I do not think we can extend our lines further around
> Petersburg without great risk. If we design, by such continued ex-
> tensions, ultimately to make him abandon Petersburg, and if the
> complete envelopment of it from river-bank to river-bank is prac-
> ticable, I think it altogether to be expected that when we reach our
> fullest development he will, by a concentrated effort, break our
> lines and compel us to fall back to the James with much loss of
> material. If Petersburg is worth the efforts we are making, it is
> worth that effort from General Lee, and he will make it before
> evacuation of the place. Now, I would propose the establishment of
> a very strong position on the Weldon railroad, with a supply of
> stores and competent garrison, and then, assembling all our force,
> place ourselves on the South Side railroad and destroy it. This
> would undoubtedly bring on a general battle, which would decide
> whether General Lee could keep the field against us or not. If he
> could not, we should thus compel him to retire within his defenses,
> and a siege proper could begin. If he beats us, we can retire upon
> the position on the Weldon railroad or upon the James. This last is
> a supposition which our calculations do not admit of. If it be said
> General Lee might refuse us battle and come out between us and
> our base and fortify, we could prepare several roads to the James
> on which to retire for supplies if necessary; or we could attack him
> or Petersburg, one of which would be held by half or less of his
> force. If we go on as we are going, with our ultimate point of occu-

pation so distant, we shall finally become powerless for offensive operations, perhaps before it is reached, all our forces being required to hold our lines against attacks from the front or cavalry raids in our rear. We need time to get our new levies in order, and no matter how great the pressure, we cannot succeed with them till they have at least acquired the knowledge of the rudiments of their drill and discipline. Another effect of our operating at the same time on two such distant flanks is to make the commander at each point apprehensive of being greatly outnumbered by the enemy, which is always practicable for him to do at one or the other, and thus inevitably produce want of boldness and vigor on our part, unless we neglect more than any of us are willing to do. Then, I would again urge, let us give up all our investing line, except one point at most, and again take the field with our whole army. I do not wish to urge my views for any personal object, nor wish them to be considered as finding fault with other plans, but I am so convinced of the justness of what I advance and of its importance to our corps that I present them to you at all hazards, and you are at liberty to make use of this communication in any way you please to.

Respectfully submitted.

Warren's essential arguments are sound; as a classroom exercise in strategy, they are compelling. Even so, his letter was out of place in the midst of active operations and probably out of place under any conditions. Had he tactfully suggested this plan to Meade during a personal conference on some quiet day, it might have been appropriate. But the New Yorker was wrong to put down in writing—cold, stark, formal, cutting, even galling—his implicit denunciation of his army commander and, through Meade, Grant. The Pennsylvanian's reaction to this criticism is not recorded, but, so far as can be determined, he "pleased" not "to make use of this communication" but to ignore it. At least, he ignored its arguments. He may have remembered Warren's presumptuousness. This remarkable letter was probably yet another step in the long progression by which the corps commander drained the reservoir of good will he had accumulated for service at Little Round Top. Within half a year to the day from this Saturday, October 1, he would have so antagonized his superiors that they would not save him from the merciless wrath of Phil Sheridan.[27]

Although Meade could ignore his subordinate's recommendations, he could not dismiss Grant's. The General-in-Chief mistakenly supposed that Hill had found Crawford quiescent that afternoon and had, therefore, reinforced Wilcox and Heth with some of Mahone's men. To offset this, the Illinoisan suggested that on October 2 almost all of Crawford's force, except for a weak trench guard and presumably the garrison of the rear line, should advance north to compel Mahone to remain in the fortifications or else to capture them. The supreme commander also requested that Hancock make a comparable move against Johnson. Thus, even before receiving Meade's promise of 7:00 P.M. to renew the drive toward the Boydton Plank Road, the lieutenant general took steps of his own to keep his offensive alive into Sunday. Though believing that his onslaught was coming to an end, he was not so set in his conviction as not to respond to supposed opportunities.

The army commander hastened to point out at 8:00 P.M. that, far from being weakened, the Confederate center had skirmished so aggressively as to suggest that it had apparently been reinforced on Saturday. Even so, he promised to advance Crawford up the east side of the Weldon Railroad to threaten Mahone and actually to attack if the opportunity arose. Meade's written instructions to the junior officer were less explicit, though. Crawford was simply told to "watch the enemy in his front and take advantage of any opportunity that may present itself, in conformity with previous instructions, either to attack or maneuver so as to compel the enemy to keep a force in his front."[28] The army commander, however, probably elaborated on these instructions verbally and definitely relayed to Crawford a copy of Grant's telegram. The commander at Globe Tavern unquestionably knew that he was expected to move forward, not merely to observe the Secessionists.

Ordering Crawford to advance was easier than finding troops for him to use. Most of his own division was tied down somewhere: Baxter in Forts Wadsworth, Dushane, and Davison; Bragg at Flowers' house, and Hofmann with the Second Division. Only the two new undrilled regiments and the pickets remained near the tavern—pickets, moreover, weakened by the departure of Ayres's 500 men for Chappell's farm overnight. Such as were available the division commander dutifully ordered to arise at 4:30 A.M. and to be ready to move forward at daylight. Yet even when alerted, his white troops were clearly too few to threaten Mahone seriously. Meade, therefore, authorized him to advance one of Ferrero's brigades, too, presumably the First.[29]

Army headquarters thus worked Crawford into the projected attack. City Point's suggestion that the II Corps, too, advance was apparently ignored, though. Months before, Meade had learned that frontal attacks on prepared works north of the Jerusalem Plank Road were disastrous, and he had no intention of sacrificing more men in that sector. The troops he now wanted to mesh into his plan for Sunday were not those on his right but those on his left: the cavalry. Though he heard the outbreak of heavy firing around McDowell's at 5:00 P.M., he felt enough confidence in the horsemen's ability to stand firm that he decided to return to Birchett's before learning the outcome. The difficulty of securing rail transportation, however, delayed his departure from Globe Tavern for about three hours. Before leaving, he managed to arrange the role of the Second Cavalry Division on October 2, after all.

The main step in this process came shortly before 10:00 with the arrival of Gregg's long-awaited dispatch of 6:30 that he had held his ground on the Vaughan Road. At about the same time Meade received a second message from the junior officer that four Confederate cavalry brigades confronted him. These tidings resolved the problem of what Gregg should do on Sunday. At 10:00 P.M., the army commander directed him to brace himself against renewed efforts to capture McDowell's after daybreak and to summon infantry support from Parke if necessary. The IX Corps commander, alerted by Humphreys to the possible danger, turned out DeTrobriand's brigade, moved it a short way, and sent word to Gregg at 2:00 A.M. that these reinforcements were available if he wanted them. However, the cavalryman, confident that he could hold his own after sunup, did not call for help, so the foot soldiers were soon allowed to return to their bivouacs. Except for this offer of assistance, Parke had already renounced much of his tenuous control over the horsemen by leaving their operations on Sunday to Gregg's discretion. Since Meade himself now instructed the Second Cavalry Division to stand fast on the morrow, its mission was settled: It would continue to defend the left rear at McDowell's and would not participate in the main advance toward the plank road.[30]

On learning that Gregg was safe, Meade hastened to pass the good news on to City Point at 10:15. Unlike Butler, the Pennsylvanian understood Grant's concern about the safety of imperiled detachments and kept him fully informed. Secure in the knowledge that the troopers were out of danger and that plans were layed for the next day, the army commander shortly afterward caught the train back to his own headquarters, where he arrived at about 11:30. Apparently no midnight planning sessions cut into his rest this evening. Tonight he could sleep well and then be refreshed for the busy day ahead.[31]

Not even the outbreak of a potentially serious threat shortly before daylight disturbed his repose—for the very good reason that the responsible generals on the endangered sector, who might have alerted him, were themselves unaware of the incident. Indeed, the only senior general with any knowledge of what was occurring was not a Yankee at all but Billy Mahone. In late afternoon, he had pulled the 48th Mississippi of Harris' Brigade out of the trenches, not only to enable it to support his center but also to use it to gobble up the far right of Ferrero's picket line. The major general thereby expected to net some prisoners, of course, but he was hardly attacking in strength. The whole regiment totaled only 139 men, and the raiding party may have numbered closer to 100. This move was just another of the feints he had made all afternoon against the Union center in hopes of discouraging Birchett's from sending more troops to Peebles's farm.

Shortly after 3:00 A.M., the raiders moved out. Walker held his fire so as not to endanger them and alert the enemy. Slowly they groped their way forward through the rain and thick darkness. Not until just before daylight did they reach the picket line immediately west of the Jerusalem Plank Road. Their arrival startled the Negro outposts. Instead of challenging them or even firing a warning shot as pickets are supposed to do, the blacks in one or two threatened pits simply fled to the Second Brigade's works. A few were killed, but none were captured, and most escaped unhurt. Perhaps they at least told their comrades of the danger on reaching them. Or perhaps Ferrero's or Russell's officer of the day detected the threat. In any case, nearby picket posts farther west, who remained in place, and the picket reserve opened fire on the threatened sector. With all possibility of surprise now gone and with the 48th itself taking a few casualties, the Secessionists abandoned the effort and withdrew to their own lines.

Two Mississippians, however, lost their way in the darkness and wandered around until they stumbled into the garrison of Fort Davis. They tried to pass themselves off as deserters but were soon unmasked as raiders—much to the dismay of Smyth, who thereby learned for the first time that part of the picket line supposedly covering his left flank had given way. The brigadier's previous unawareness of what was occurring typifies the state of knowledge of the Federal high command. Neither Hancock, Crawford, nor even Ferrero had any idea that something was amiss on the outpost line. Russell, content with promptly reestablishing his picket line, apparently did not even bother to inform his division commander of the incident. Word of Mahone's probe thus did not at first get beyond brigade level, let alone all the way to Birchett's. As a feint to divert Bluecoats from Peebles's, it failed even more surely than as a raid to capture the picket line.[32]

Thus ended the strange affair west of the Jerusalem Plank Road. The strangest thing about it was the essential fact that it involved a Confederate advance, albeit limited. Everywhere else that night, the Southerners broke contact with the Yankees and fell back.

Down on the lower Vaughan Road, the opposing cavalry warily confronted each other from their respective hilltops for over an hour after fighting ended. Some Unionist skirmishers ranged out, perhaps as far as the little branch of Arthur's Swamp, to observe the foe but not to attack. Then they pulled back to their stronghold on McDowell's to bivouac and to brace themselves for the expected Butternut onslaught at daybreak. Hampton, however, had no intention of attacking there then.

In early evening he moved back westward and northwestward. His First Division withdrew along the Vaughan Road, surely as far as Mrs. Cummings', more likely to the right bank of Hatcher's Run at Cummings' Ford (but not to Burgess' mill). The regiments from the Third Division meantime apparently returned to or near to their former bivouac on the Boydton Plank Road, where McGregor rejoined them. On reaching their campsites, the exhausted Southerners threw themselves onto the ground and, despite the mud and the light rain, soon fell sound asleep.

Whether the cavalry commander retreated simply to permit his tired soldiers to rest in less exposed positions than E. Wilkinson's or whether Hill ordered him back is not known. In either case, the Virginian surely approved of the withdrawal, because that evening the lieutenant general recalled almost all his mobile columns from the immediate presence of the Federals to or toward the main defenses of Petersburg. His main strike force, Heth's Division, fell back up the Squirrel Level Road just after dark, leaving only a skirmish line of Mississippians to confront Ayres from W. W. Davis'. Cooke and apparently MacRae then simply bivouacked in reserve behind Battery No. 45. Davis and probably Archer, however, continued down the plank road to Jones's farm. Ferebee likely accompanied the latter brigades if he had not already gone there. The horsemen rejoined Joel Griffin (apparently in the trench line) whenever they arrived, and the infantry relieved the Light Division at about 7:00 P.M. By then Wilcox had recalled his whole force, including his skirmishers, from Pegram's farm to Jones's. Now that replacements had arrived, he pulled out for the main defenses of the city. The need to transport his many spoils on a dark, inclement night evidently delayed his progress, for not until about 9:00 did he file into his old works: McGowan extending west from Mahone's right and Lane prolonging the line to Battery No. 45. At about the time Wilcox reached his destination, Barringer had his 2nd Regiment turn over Fort MacRae to his 3rd Regiment. The 2nd then set out on a three-hour march to Perkins' mill on Gravelly Run.

Why the Tarheel cavalry were sent to a quiet region so far south of the main combat zone is hard to understand. Even more baffling is Hill's decision to have Wilcox change places with half of Heth's command instead of simply leaving the Light Division on the Church Road and Heth's whole force on and near the Squirrel Level Road. Indeed, the whole Confederate strategic outlook that evening is only imperfectly understood. It seems that the victory at Jones's farm on Friday and the absence of a renewed Union onslaught the next day convinced Southern headquarters by October 1 that Petersburg could be held, after all. The failure to recapture Peebles's farm on Saturday, moreover, apparently dissuaded the Graycoats from renewing their counterattack. Together, such conclusions may have suggested to them that the Battle of Poplar Spring Church, though not yet over, was drawing to a close.

That inference, were it made, helps explain several developments on Saturday. It definitely accounts for the reopening of the military hospitals in Petersburg that day. Most patients there were apparently transferred to Danville on Friday, as first ordered. However, the presence of men unable to travel, the large influx of wounded Confederates and captive Federals due to two days of heavy fighting, and, most of all, the fact that "the pressing military necessity for the abandonment of all these hospitals has also been somewhat removed" explain why the medical-treatment centers were re-established in the Cockade City sometime on October 1.[33] The absence of any intention to continue counterattacking on Sunday, in addition, could account for the withdrawal of the six infantry brigades that had fought the Northerners during the day. Then, too, the belief that the danger had diminished and that the situation was under control would have allowed Confederate commanders to allocate troops to other tasks. With the need to preserve the army's supply lines still operative but not all-consuming, a mounted regiment could well be spared to go to Perkins' mill for what the generals judged a good and sufficient reason. The supposed imminent end of the battle, in sum, could explain these unusual developments.

The prospect of a renewal of the Battle of Chaffin's Bluff, underscored by Terry's probes so close to the capital that afternoon, could also account for some of these occurrences. Hill's whole force might have to rush back to Richmond. If so, it could get away better if it were disengaged. Short of that, he might have to send more reinforcements to the Northside. Relocating Heth's reserves nearer Petersburg would enable them to cross the James if necessary as well as to respond to threats to the town. The potential need to bolster Chaffin's, for that matter, may explain why the 48th Mississippi dropped back into reserve late Saturday afternoon, rather than to prepare for their raid on the Negro picket line. Some of McAfee's deserters, moreover, even told Union intelligence officers that Johnson extended his three rightmost brigades northward to enable Goode to leave the trenches on the night of October 1–2—though their claim is doubtful. But numerous reserves, in any case, were definitely built up near the city.

This creation of mobile reserves and pullback of front-line forces do not mean that the Secessionists were oblivious to the possibility of another flare-up on the Southside. The reserves, after all, could just as well meet such a threat as move to the Peninsula. And the two infantry brigades and two cavalry brigades left on guard in the light works across the Church Road and Route 673 continued forming something of a barrier between the Bluecoats and Lee's lines of communications.[34]

Still, it was a barrier much weaker than that forged on Friday. That day and overnight, 60 per cent of Hill's force—7,100 infantry and artillery and 6,750 cavalry and horse artillery—had concentrated around Peebles's farm and its left rear, not merely to block the Yankees but also to drive them back. Now that force was almost entirely broken up. A mere 16 per cent continued in the immediate presence of the Unionists: 1,900 foot soldiers and about 2,350 horsemen. Hampton's remaining 4,300 troopers—half of them mounted, half artillerists and dragoons—were on guard in the open country farther south or in reserve. Hill's other 17,300 men were again drawn tightly around the Cockade City itself, either in its earthworks or in immediate support. As on Thursday night, the pressing exigencies of trying to defend two fronts with inadequate manpower compelled Lee to concentrate most of his strength at Richmond and Petersburg and to leave only a few weak units to cover his communications. His first such gamble had paid off on September 30. If he were correct in supposing that the Battle of Poplar Spring Church had virtually ended, his second gamble might succeed, too. But if he were wrong—if the Federals intended renewing their drive for his supply lines on Sunday—then he risked losing everything he had retained the past few days: his communications, his rail center, perhaps even his capital itself.[35]

And, of course, he was wrong. Meade did still plan to drive for the plank road, come daylight. His heavily strengthened strike force, moreover, was no longer back at Globe Tavern but was massed on Peebles's farm, just two miles from that highway. His advance on October 2 against greatly outnumbered defenders seemed sure to bring on major fighting—certainly bloody, maybe decisive.

The men in the ranks, who would do that fighting, did not fully grasp what the morrow held in store. The rain, which had resumed after dark, was their big worry. It troubled Willcox's pickets, who had been on outpost duty all afternoon and then had to stay out in the elements all night, prepared to start skirmishing in the morning. The downpour bothered Mott's men even more, fresh from the camps and bombproofs they had held since mid-August. They reportedly wanted to exchange "their field camp for their more comfortable bunks in Fort Hell, even though there was a possibility of making a bed fellow of a bursting mortar shell." Their generals, however, knew that rain, fatigue, and discomfort were as nothing compared with the dangers ahead on October 2. "We bivouac for the night in a large woods, surrounded by big fires kindled everywhere," DeTrobriand noted in his diary; "we go to sleep prepared for the following day—and a battle which will probably put a goodly number of us to sleep for their final sleep."[36]

CHAPTER XIV

"I Shall Not Attack
Their Intrenchments"

The storm of weather abated overnight. Sunday dawned hot and dry—
still overcast with lingering ground fog, to be sure, but with ever-
increasing warmth and light that gave promise of sunshine for a
change. The storm of war held no such promise of clearing away.
Great blue warclouds, supercharged with power during Saturday's
buildup, now threatened to unleash their thunderbolts against the
Southern supply lines.[1]

Mightiest of these thunderbolts was Mott's fresh division. To it went
the first summons to action. Before 5:00 A.M., Parke ordered it to be
ready to move by 5:30. By the prescribed time, it was massed under
arms, prepared to strike. But as so often happens in war, the soldiers
had hurried, only to wait. For an hour and a half, it was left in place
on Peebles's farm, awaiting orders. To ascertain those directives, Mott
rode up to corps headquarters at about 6:00. He found Parke unwilling
to issue instructions until his other two division commanders arrived,
and they were not required to report until 6:30. Willcox and Potter
likely reached Peebles's house shortly after the appointed time, whereupon all four generals went over to Warren's nearby headquarters.
There the Pennsylvanian explained his plan:

The Second Division, IX Corps, was to move straight forward onto
Pegram's farm and confront whatever Confederate force remained
there. To Potter's left, Willcox was to concentrate his spread-out brigades and, pivoting on his right, was to wheel forward onto Pegram's.

The Michigander was also to make sure that at least his skirmishers maintained contact with the Third Division to his left. That unit played the key role in Parke's plan. While the other two divisions simply engaged head on, Mott was to turn the Graycoats' right on Pegram's by marching west along Route 673 and then swinging north toward the Harman Road. The 7th Maine and 34th New York batteries stood ready to support Parke's right wing, but no guns were to accompany the flanking column. Mott's lean, sturdy infantry would have to accomplish their mission by themselves.

After the Pennsylvanian revealed his plan, Warren may have indicated what his soldiers would do. The New Yorker did not have much to tell, though. At least Ayres and presumably Griffin, too, were not present to receive orders, and not until 7:45 would instructions be issued even for their troops to get ready for a movement. Just what that movement would be was apparently rather indefinite. The V Corps would simply reconnoiter all along its front and then react to whatever it discovered. If Heth still potentially threatened the Second Division from W. W. Davis', the Bluecoats would probably strike north along the Squirrel Level Road. But if the danger there had diminished, then at least the First Division could move up to Potter's right on Pegram's farm. Meantime, other V Corps troops back at Globe Tavern were also to advance north. Army headquarters, however, worried about letting Crawford go forward. Concerned about either the weakness of his force or the weakness of his competence for independent command, Humphreys sent him word at 8:00 A.M. on Sunday to "communicate with General Warren, before making any serious movement, upon the appearance of a favorable opportunity." Thus Warren's one division that was ready to move would not be allowed to do so without going through the time-consuming process of communicating, and his other two divisions, which were already in close communication, were not yet ready to move early in the morning. The V Corps, in sum, was not likely to provide effective support to the IX Corps's initial operations. Despite this, Parke determined to advance right away. After his subordinates received their orders, they rode back to their men and prepared to move out.[2]

Since the mobile left column, the Third Division of the II Corps, had to march farthest to get into place, it started first, shortly after 7:00. At the head of the column Pierce threw out the 1st U. S. Sharpshooters and 84th Pennsylvania as voltigeurs. On reaching Route 673, his 141st Pennsylvania prolonged the 84th's skirmish line leftward. Behind these three regiments advanced his strong line of battle—the 1st Massachusetts Heavy Artillery, 57th Pennsylvania, 93rd New York, and 105th Pennsylvania, right to left. McAllister's force, deployed in col-

umn of battalions, closely supported the Michigander. As the Second
Brigade wheeled toward the northwest through the woods of J. Wilkinson's farm, the colonel constantly threw forward regiments of
skirmishers to cover its left south of Route 673. First the 5th–7th New
Jersey advanced abreast of, though not adjacent to, Pierce's left. Then
the 120th New York extended the skirmish line leftward; and finally
the 11th New Jersey, deployed in column of companies with one company of flankers farther south, moved down to guard the far left. Parts
of these regiments formed into line to provide close support for their
voltigeur companies, and, in more general support, McAllister backed
up his skirmishers with the 11th Massachusetts and 6th–8th New Jersey in line of battle, left to right. Behind the Third Brigade came De-
Trobriand's men. Some, perhaps the 20th Indiana and/or the 2nd U. S.
Sharpshooters, ranged south of Route 673 as flankers to cover the left
flank. Others, either the 73rd or 86th New York, remained behind to
guard the intersection of Route 673 and the Squirrel Level Road. But
his main force served chiefly as a general reserve for the front line.

Mott's soldiers soon encountered the pickets of the 3rd North Carolina Cavalry. The Tarheels fired a shot or two, then scampered back to
the lower end of the old Squirrel Level Line, principally Fort MacRae
itself. The Bluecoats scrambled through the thickets after them.
Pierce's men found no break in the forest until they got to the trench
line. McAllister, however, discovered that the woods gave way to a
clearing around J. Smith's farm, which extended up to Route 673 and
Fort MacRae. On reaching the field, the colonel left only flankers
south of that farmhouse to cover his left and shifted his main force
rightward toward the enemy. The 5th–7th and the 120th moved northward along the eastern border of the clearing until they closed up on
Pierce's left. They then formed line of battle, and at least the two
Jersey battalions even reported to the Michigander. Behind these outfits
came McAllister's main battle line. Farther north, Pierce, too, strengthened his front by placing half the 105th on the left of the 141st and by
using the rest of the former regiment to support his skirmish line. Once
both brigades were in place, they moved out to the attack: the 120th
toward the fort, the 5th–7th just north of there, and the Second Brigade toward the trench line across J. Wilkinson's farm.

It was a well-built line these Yankees rushed, with a good profile,
well-constructed redoubt, and formidable slashing. But it was a line
garrisoned even more weakly than its northward extension on Peebles's
farm had been on Friday. From it now spattered only a ragged fire.
The heavily outnumbered North Carolinians knew they could not stop
this powerful blue line. They resisted only briefly and then fled northward and westward toward the works beyond the Harman Road. By the

time Pierce's and McAllister's men picked their way through the abatis and surged forward with a shout, no Secessionists remained to contest control of the fortifications. All of the lower Squirrel Level Line was in Federal hands once more. And this time the occupying force was not Harriman's outposts, Potter's refugees, or Davies' patrols but the spearhead of a mighty attack.[3]

This spearhead, though, had been aimed at transfixing and destroying the main enemy force, thought to be holding the front line. But virtually no resistance had been offered there, so the spear had hurtled harmlessly through the air and buried itself deeply into the ground. The Unionists had come prepared for heavy fighting, only to discover that no enemy could be found. Their easy conquest troubled the victors as much as the vanquished. Gershom Mott, in particular, worried over the implications of the initial fighting: Where were the Butternuts? he wondered. Was the whole Northern battle plan misdirected? What should he do next?

His first move was obvious. He regrouped his regiments, which had partially lost their formation passing through the abatis. Deciding the more fundamental question of where to go was more difficult. His original orders from the IX Corps were now irrelevant, and no new instructions had been received. Even worse, the Confederates, having broken contact, were mobile again and could potentially launch a surprise counterattack in the woods. Yet he could hardly just stay put at Fort MacRae. He accordingly determined to feel forward to ascertain what lay ahead but to do so with great caution. Continuing westward from J. Smith's to the northern end of the Duncan Road in isolation seemed far too risky. He therefore shifted his axis from west to northwest along a little country lane running for nearly a mile from Fort MacRae and Hawks's, past C. Smith's, to Claypole's on the Harman Road, about three quarters of a mile south of Mrs. Hart's. Doing this should enable him to turn the right not only of Pegram's farm but also of the inner enemy line that Potter had failed to carry on Friday. It would also allow the Jerseyman to narrow the gap between his right and Willcox's left. Pierce's skirmishers already connected with Harriman's, but now the main bodies of the two divisions would be closer together as they moved toward the plank road.

As part of this redirection, Mott shifted his force rightward along the captured defenses. Then the 1st U. S. Sharpshooters, as skirmishers, followed by the 1st Massachusetts Heavy Artillery in line of battle, picked their way forward through the woods southwest of the northwestern branch of Arthur's Swamp. The 84th, 141st, and 105th, however, did not accompany them. Except for a few companies each, the three Pennsylvania outfits were no longer on the skirmish line but had been concentrated into line of battle. For some reason, they and Pierce's other regiments did not go forward with the sharpshooters and heavies but remained in or a little northwest of the old Southern works for several hours. The main body of the Second Brigade did not move abreast of the Massachusetts outfit until nearly noon.

Pierce's retarded advance set the pace for the Third Brigade. The aftermath of the initial fighting saw that unit spread out from Fort MacRae to the southern end of J. Smith's field, where all of the 11th New Jersey had joined its flankers on the skirmish line to meet a reported enemy advance against the Union left. That danger, however, did not materialize, so McAllister began concentrating his dispersed voltigeurs into a line of battle, preparatory for the renewed advance. He reduced the number of skirmishers to a company or more per battalion and formed his other companies into a battle line by closing up on his right in the Confederate fortifications. Then when the Second Brigade moved to the right along the trenches, he followed, and when its main force finally advanced, he went forward on its left. Its slow movement and frequent halts along the way, in turn, retarded his advance.

As Mott's front line pivoted on its right and swung northwest, DeTrobriand moved abreast of the Third Brigade to help cover the exposed left flank. Maintaining that position on the far left proved no easy matter. Keeping in place as the tail unit of a wheeling line is hard enough under optimum conditions. Conditions here were far from optimum. The recent rain left the ground muddy and the little tributary of Arthur's Swamp that flowed eastward from C. Smith's to Clements' brimming. Even worse, the storm had ushered in a warm front, and as the clouds cleared away and the sun came out about noon, the day became "hot and sultry, and the men perspired as much as in the hottest weather of summer." A still greater obstacle was the dense woods. "We had to get through the thickets after the manner of wild boars," recalled DeTrobriand, ". . . by breaking the branches to make way. . . ."[4] Yet the same hindrances that impeded him also delayed the other brigades and enabled the First to keep abreast of the Third without even having to rush.

Confederates, probably troopers from Barringer's Brigade or Dearing's Brigade, sought to add to the delay by making a stand in light works at and east of C. Smith's farm, located almost three quarters of a mile north of Fort MacRae and only a third that far south of the Harman Road. The few Graycoats, however, again proved no match for a whole division and once more fell back before the onrush of its skirmishers. The horsemen likely contributed little to delaying Mott. Such halts as he did make were probably in order to correct his disrupted alignments, not to deal with the foe. The difficult ground and uncertainty over the location of the Secessionist force were the real barriers. Along with his caution and with the Second Brigade's delay near the Squirrel Level Line, they so slowed his advance that he did not near the works on and just west of the Harman Road until about noon.[5]

Despite the heavy woods, Mott could surely have traveled one mile more rapidly than he did. Yet his caution was justified. Neither orders from Parke nor a "clear and present opportunity" required him to plunge rashly forward and thereby risk suffering what had happened to Potter on Friday. For that matter, Mott's restrained advance exceeded his superiors' expectations. The absence of serious Southern resistance on the front line confounded the Union high command even more than it did him.

Parke expected to face major opposition on Pegram's farm. To overcome it, he threw forward all five of his own brigades from Peebles's. Shortly before 8:00 A.M., a strong, fresh skirmish line (not the tired pickets from overnight, after all) led the way. Behind it came his powerful battle line. Curtin on the far right and Simon Griffin to his left advanced directly ahead. In the middle, Hartranft made a right wheel that aimed his right straight toward Pegram's house. The 60th Ohio skirmished for his brigade, and behind that regiment came his double line of battle: the 20th and 46th in front, left to right, and the 24th, 1st, 2nd, and 50th in the second line, left to right. McLaughlen, too, right-wheeled forward in a double line, with the 100th Pennsylvania ranging ahead as voltigeurs. The course of the northwestern branch of Arthur's Swamp and the woods near it prevented Harriman from continuing the First Division's right wheel. He had to make a separate march northward to get into position on the far left, extending toward the stream. Once there, the 109th and 37th, left to right, formed his front line, and the 13th and 1/38th, left to right, held his second line. The 27th, backed up by the 8th, prolonged the 100th's skirmish line westward across the First Brigade's front and across the creek to connect with Pierce's voltigeurs. To support these foot soldiers, the 7th Maine and 34th New York batteries stood ready to advance. Only Monroe's other two companies, the raw 2/38th Wisconsin, presumably the unarmed 179th New York, and perhaps a few other men remained to hold Peebles's.[6] Virtually all the rest of Parke's First and Second divisions were being hurled against the supposed Southern stronghold on Pegram's.

Skirmishers from these divisions soon found, however, that this stronghold did not exist, that no major Secessionist force remained around Pegram's house. This discovery disrupted Parke's plans. He could hardly attack an enemy that was no longer present. Nor would he boldly strike northward toward Jones's farm. His customary caution and probably also his recollection of what had befallen him Friday initially caused him to halt his main line in the woods between Peebles's and Pegram's. He would not send it further until his skirmishers could confirm that the Graycoats did not lurk in ambush nearby. Not until 9:30 A.M. did he feel it safe to advance as far as the Pegram farmhouse. Potter moved up to a line running eastward from the building toward the Church Road. West of him, Willcox occupied the sector from the dwelling to the swamp. The First Division initially formed a straight line, but Harriman soon dropped back *en échelon* along the creek to cover the left flank and to be closer to Mott, who had not yet come abreast of him.

Parke's main line stopped there, but his skirmishers ranged over the northern part of the farm. Although they stirred up some resistance from small Butternut patrols, perhaps Joel Griffin's, they did not develop the presence of a large Confederate force. The Pennsylvanian did not know what to make of this situation. Conditions had changed so drastically from what the original plans presupposed that he hesitated to plunge on toward the Boydton Plank Road without new orders from Meade. Until the army commander could reach the front, the IX Corps would go no farther.[7]

Warren, too, was confused by the Confederate withdrawal. Griffin's skirmishers reported that no Graycoats confronted the First Division. Opposite the V Corps's center Ayres located only the small body of Mississippians at W. W. Davis', where Heth's whole force had been the previous day. To determine whether any troops backed them up, the Second Division commander ordered Grimshaw to make a reconnaissance in force toward Fort Cherry. The colonel left the 3rd Delaware to hold his works and sent forward the 157th, 190th, and 191st Pennsylvania in line of battle, supported by the 4th Delaware. These troops moved out at about 9:00 but took considerable time before striking. Not until nearly 10:00 did they actually begin attacking, covered by Hazelton's shelling. On first emerging from the woods north of Chappell's, they drew fire. The color bearer of the 157th went down, but his comrades easily absorbed their losses and pressed up the Squirrel Level Road toward the enemy trenches. The small force of Graycoats had no intention of contesting control of those works but soon broke and fled. However, they shortly rallied around a big barn immediately north of Davis' house. The Yankees did not pursue beyond the abandoned works and contented themselves with shelling and shooting at the Butternuts around the barn. Capturing the more southerly trenches sufficed to tell Ayres what he wanted to know: The

Confederates were no more looking for a fight at Davis' than at Pegram's or Wilkinson's-Smith's. About ninety minutes later, Warren received additional confirmation of this conclusion: a report made by his observers in the watch tower at Globe Tavern at 8:00 A.M. that few Secessionists remained near Fort Cherry.

That same signal detachment also discovered the only large Southern force sighted in the area—Mahone's and Wilcox's men in Hill's main line of entrenchments on both sides of the Weldon Railroad. Their presence there apparently convinced Crawford that he need not demonstrate against the Georgians and the Floridians. He therefore stayed in place, still ready to advance but not actually moving unless the enemy opposite him should be weakened. Besides keeping his Negroes inactive, he also worked the Iron Brigade back into his own defense system. Until late Sunday morning, that unit had been outside both his operational control and Ayres's. The Pennsylvanian's uncertainty over who had charge of it prompted Humphreys, at 11:00, to tell Warren to resolve the matter. Fifty minutes later, the corps commander directed that Crawford remain responsible for the outfit since it would withdraw to the Weldon Railroad if attacked. Warren implied, though, that he wanted it left in place at Flowers' except to avoid disaster. Surely enough, there Bragg stayed, fortifying and standing guard but making no other move than to send a fresh picket detail to replace his original outposts east of the tracks.

Bragg and Crawford thus saw no opportunity to advance in the face of the strong, fortified Confederate units spotted near the city. No such enemy concentration was detected near Warren's field force, however, so he felt safe in joining the IX Corps on Pegram's farm. Ayres and Hazelton, of course, had to remain on Chappell's to cover the right rear. Fitzhugh's other eight pieces, moreover, may have continued garrisoning Peebles's. But the First Division, at least, could move up to Potter's right. At about 9:30, shortly after discovering that no Graycoats faced him, Griffin advanced. To place his best troops near the Church Road, where fighting might erupt, he transferred Gregory from the right to the left flank and then moved him and Bartlett abreast of Curtin. Sickel meantime probably dropped back into reserve or else was echeloned to the Third Brigade's right rear. Before 11:30 A.M., the First Division was in place on Parke's right. By then Warren himself came forward to reconnoiter the situation on Pegram's. However, neither his scouting nor the arrival of these reinforcements fundamentally altered the state of affairs there. In the absence of major opposition, Griffin's men, too, could only halt and await their superiors' orders.

Thus far, the Unionists' grand offensive had accomplished virtually nothing. Except for negligible opposition at Forts MacRae and Cherry, the five Northern divisions had not even located the foe. How could they conquer their way to the Boydton Plank Road when no Butternuts were around to be conquered? In less stark terms the corps commanders passed the news on to army headquarters—Parke chiefly at 9:30 A.M. and also about 11:20–11:30 A.M., Warren before 11:00 A.M. Their reports profoundly altered Meade's thinking.[8]

The army commander originally anticipated fighting a heavy battle outside the main Confederate fortifications. He thought, moreover, that this combat would open up the area west of the Weldon Railroad as the principal zone of future operations and might even break up the stalemate of summer and restore the mobile warfare of spring. To be ready for such an opportunity, he ordered his permanent headquarters at Birchett's dismantled at 11:00 A.M. and moved westward to be nearer the new scene of action, perhaps even to be prepared to take the field again if necessary. He also initially planned for most of his headquarters troops to get ready to follow him. Preparing them for the field entailed withdrawing the infantry and engineers and also Hancock's four guns from Prince George Court House and Fort Bross and leaving only the 3rd Pennsylvania Cavalry on the rear line. But when Hunt and Williams notified Shand's of this projected redeployment at 8:00 and 8:30 A.M., respectively, the corps commander vigorously objected to stripping the eastern works, the object of such solicitude earlier in the battle. Hancock converted Meade to his views during their subsequent meeting, and at 9:00 the army commander issued revised orders that Collis' two infantry regiments should move only from the court house to Fort Bross, where the Massachusetts section would remain. All three units plus the horsemen were now formally put under the control of II Corps headquarters. The Vermont guns meantime returned to Battery No. 17, and Brainerd rejoined his regiment.

At least the engineers thus became mobile again. All three battalions of the 50th and probably the U. S. Engineer Battalion, too, began moving in late morning to Jones's house just left of the Jerusalem Plank Road, under orders to be ready to continue westward if necessary. Significantly, the battalion from City Point brought the army's six pontoon trains. Their teams had remained in harness on Thursday, Friday, and presumably Saturday, ready to move. Now they headed back toward the front to be prepared in case the expected breakthrough carried the Yankees across even the Southside Railroad all the way to the upper Appomattox.

With such prospects in store, Meade did not wait for Williams, Spaulding, and Harwood to complete these transfers. The major general desired to command his men personally in the big battle ahead, so he set out with his field staff for the front a few minutes after 8:00, far earlier than his departures on the two preceding days of battle. Also unlike on Friday and Saturday, he did not linger long en route, but he did take a little time to survey his right and center. Hancock evidently reported his sector quiet and definitely relayed the deserters' report that Johnson's sector, too, had been thinned out. How the army commander evaluated the North Carolinians' testimony in light of a Federal signal report that the Confederate left appeared to have been slightly strengthened during the night is not known. There is no question, though, that he believed the two Mississippians who had blundered into Fort Davis that morning, claiming to have just captured without resistance part of the Negroes' skirmish line immediately west of there. That he had not previously been informed of the 48th's reported success likely upset him. When he found, on subsequently reaching Aiken's, that Ferrero, too, was unaware of the affair, he apparently "chewed out" the division commander. Once Meade had vented his spleen and ridden on, the IX Corps general checked with Russell to learn what had actually occurred. The brigadier soon replied that although heavy firing had erupted at daybreak, the USCT pickets had generally stood fast and that his line was now intact. Ferrero then passed the news on to headquarters and even indulged himself in the concluding remark that the army commander "must have been misinformed." Fortunately for himself, he sent this dispatch to Crawford, not Meade.[9]

Likely before the touchy subordinate's report reached Globe Tavern, Meade and Humphreys got there at about 10:15. They immediately became absorbed in a problem far greater than a minor nighttime picket raid. Only now did they receive the full impact of the news from the front that no battle had developed. These reports drove Meade to a crucial decision. Since his field force could not locate the Secessionists and since his Signal Corps reported that many of them were in Petersburg's principal defenses, he concluded that he could no longer engage them outside their works, after all. Nor would he risk assaulting their entrenchments. On May 18 at Spotsylvania, at Cold Harbor, as late as First Petersburg on June 18, he and Grant had been willing to charge well-defended fortifications, but not anymore. Those battles had given the Pennsylvanian a healthy fear of attacking breastworks, and for the past 3½ months he had made no such assaults. He would not order one now. More than that, he decided not even to attempt to seize the Boydton Plank Road. His reasons for this are not so obvious. He apparently just did not feel strong enough to extend that far west; he may have believed that his left flank would be too weak to resist Hill's inevitable counterattack.

Meade was a prudently cautious general, and caution is a military virtue no successful commander can long ignore. Yet the truly successful commander—in warfare like the Civil War, anyway—cannot overemphasize this quality. Such a conclusion helps explain why Meade does not stand in the first echelon of Union generals. Despite all his impressive talk on Saturday about forcing a battle and getting to the plank road; despite his earlier desire to attack when subordinate and superior alike urged restraint; despite his confident expectations as recently as earlier Sunday morning, he failed to live up to his fine words at the moment of decision. When the long-sought opportunity to reach the plank road finally came, its very magnitude confounded him.

He had envisioned getting there by a simple, well-defined, three-piece tactical exercise: (1) The Southerners lay immediately in front of him on Pegram's farm. (2) He would merely advance through the woods and defeat them. (3) Then he would pursue them until he seized the plank road. His entire plan presupposed their immediate proximity to the IX Corps. Their withdrawal changed everything. The scope of the problem now broadened from an exercise in "large-scale minor tactics" to a fundamental question of grand tactics and even minor strategy. Did their redeployment portend a counterattack somewhere east of the Halifax Road? Did it mean that they were waiting near Jones's to ambush whatever troops he moved toward the plank road? If the Pennsylvanian had been a truly first-rate general, he would have answered those questions in his own terms by throwing four or five divisions toward the plank road and forcing Hill to give battle in the open once more. But Meade was not such a commander. Although he was the right officer to conduct the minor tactical operation he had originally planned, he could not rise to the greater opportunity of creating an essentially new grand-tactical maneuver against the plank road. All he saw were the uncertainties posed by the Southern redeployment, and he therefore gave way to his instinctive caution.

At 11:00 A.M., he informed Grant of his decision:

> The inference is [that] the enemy refuse battle outside their works, to which they have retired awaiting attack. Without your orders I shall not attack their intrenchments, but on being satisfied they are not outside of them I will take up the best position I can, connecting with the Weldon railroad and extending as far to the left as practicable, having in view the protection of my left flank, and then intrench. I should be glad to know your views and orders.[10]

Ten minutes later, the lieutenant general replied from Deep Bottom that the Pennsylvanian should "Carry out what you propose in dispatch of 11 a.m.—that is, intrench and hold what you can, but make no attack against defended fortifications."[11] Not long after this, the General-in-Chief returned to City Point. From there he sent Meade another dispatch showing that he not only expected to gain no more but actually did not place top priority on what had been seized on Friday:

> You may shorten the line to the extent you deem necessary to be able to hold it. All you do hold west of the Weldon road be prepared to give up whenever the forces holding it are necessary to defend any other part of the line.[12]

Meade, to be sure, did not actually inform his superior that the Army of the Potomac would not move toward the plank road, yet the overwhelmingly defensive tone of his telegram implied that his forces would not advance. Grant apparently accepted this implication, for his two replies stressed the defensive and made no attempt to urge the junior officer to seize the key supply line.

To a large degree, the lieutenant general's telegrams reflect his approach of deferring to his front-line commander. Yet they also reflect his own strategic assessment. As far as Grant was concerned, the once-bright prospects of capturing Petersburg and even Richmond in these battles had so dimmed as to justify terminating the Fifth Offensive. Sometime the previous day, apparently while on the Northside, he concluded that he could accomplish nothing more of significance during this operation. He thereafter concentrated on solidifying his limited gain and planning entirely new offensives. His subsequent endorsements of attacking were no more than final flickers that almost immediately burned themselves out for lack of fuel. It was not them but Meade's initial enthusiasm to continue advancing that prolonged the battle into Sunday. When the Pennsylvanian, too, abandoned the offensive, Grant was already predisposed to accept his subordinate's decision.

The last officer to favor attacking, Meade, thus could not carry through on his own intentions: He could not rise to the challenge of resolving the problems posed by the Confederate redeployment. And the Illinoisan, who could have urged his wavering subordinate to advance, himself no longer seriously believed that he could achieve another big breakthrough at this time. In his determination to formulate new combinations to bring new victories at some future time, the General-in-Chief overlooked opportunities to exploit his success at this time. Because of such shortcomings, such attitudes, such approaches to generalship, the Union high command did not avail itself of the chance to reach the plank road offered by Hill's redeployment of the previous evening. Instead, the Northern generals took steps to bring the Battle of Poplar Spring Church rapidly to a close.[13]

The first step in concluding operations, of course, was to notify the front-line commanders, who still thought they were to bring on a battle. At 11:15 A.M., possibly even before receiving Grant's approval, Meade informed Parke and Warren of the change of plans. The army commander spelled out his new approach in more detail to his subordinates than he had done to the lieutenant general:

> Appearances indicate that the enemy has withdrawn to his main line of intrenchments. Upon this being ascertained with certainty it is the intention of the commanding general to take up the best line for connecting with the Weldon railroad, and making the left secure, and then to intrench. It is not his intention at present to do more than this. He will neither attack the main intrenchments nor attempt to effect a lodgment on the Boydton plank road. You will be governed in your movements by these considerations.

Even greater indication of the defensive nature of his new plan appears in his subsequent message to Shand's. At 11:45 A.M., he informed Hancock that if the enemy were, indeed, in their main defenses, "I shall take up a position, connect with the Weldon road, guard my left flank, and await attack, unless otherwise directed." "Await attack," he said. Yet he obviously did not expect to be attacked imminently, the way Parke and Warren had feared the previous morning, because he supposed no Graycoats were anywhere near. Rather does the expression sum up his determination to cease advancing and secure his gains. It makes clear how far he had now gone in renouncing the grand-tactical initiative.[14]

This directive was presumably welcomed by the V Corps and IX Corps commanders, who had long been reluctant to advance boldly. Warren, however, had at least considered making a limited probe, only to have it now cut short by the change of plan. At 11:50 A.M., shortly before learning of the change, he told Ayres to capture Fort Cherry if he could keep it. Establishing a forward position there would reveal how the Confederates would respond to its loss. But when the senior officer found out that army headquarters intended to assume a defensive position, he ordered his subordinate not to move so far north of his works "unless it can be done easily."[15]

The aggressive division commander was not so readily dissuaded from attacking. The Butternuts had hovered near him all morning, going no farther back than he forced them. At 11:40, they were in a field just northeast of W. W. Davis', but in the next few minutes they reoccupied the farmyard itself. Ayres was anxious to rid himself of their annoying sharpshooting. Whether he moved against them before or after receiving the second message from corps headquarters is not clear. What is certain is that he wanted to strike if prospects of success seemed reasonable. At first, they appeared questionable. The 157th Pennsylvania, maneuvering through the woods toward the house, sent back word that a battle line appeared to support the Mississippi skirmishers. More adequate reconnaissance, though, discredited this report, so the general went ahead with plans to capture the farmyard. Hazelton continued shelling it, and Grimshaw's four forward regiments again made up the strike force, supported this time by the 5th and 140th New York of the First Brigade. When all was ready, the 157th, covered on its left by skirmishers from the other two Pennsylvania regiments, burst from the woods and spearheaded the rush toward the house. Once more, this powerful force easily outmatched its opponents and handily overran the farmyard, reportedly capturing about twenty prisoners.

There the main Union body stopped. However, part of the combative 190th and 191st, all that was left of the First and Third brigades of the hard-hitting old Pennsylvania Reserves, ignored orders to halt and pressed on up the Squirrel Level Line after the retreating foe. Their resolve and their repeaters could not offset their lack of numbers, though. They, too, halted before long, either of their own volition or because of growing resistance from Confederate sharpshooters who, seeing they were not chased in force, regrouped in their defenses a short way northeast of the house. More than rallying, the Mississippians soon struck back at the two isolated regiments, drove them back on the Third Brigade with some loss, and then swept on to try to outflank and recapture Fort Cherry itself. But Grimshaw's skirmishers—more of the old Reserves, armed with Spencers—readily fended off this counterjab. The Southerners then withdrew to their previous locale.

The repulse of this brief counterattack doubtless bolstered the Federal commanders' assessment that they faced little opposition in this sector. The revised orders from corps headquarters, moreover, ruled out continuing to attack such sharpshooters as remained in the area, let alone pressing up the Squirrel Level Road toward Wilcox's main works. Yet Ayres's forward position did serve a useful purpose. Even though it was too exposed to be held permanently, it could at least be used to keep "the enemy in suspense as to our object."[16] Instead of abandoning it, he, accordingly, regrouped his men around W. W. Davis' house and strengthened his advanced foothold there. Behind this cover, his supply men picked up a whole wagonload of abandoned Confederate rifles, presumably those thrown away by Heth's fleeing men the previous morning. Also back there, some of Grindlay's Regulars may have used the opportunity to continue clearing the field of fire north of Chappell's, not only by chopping trees but also by razing buildings. North of the front line, however, the Yankees were far less active. Only Hazel-

ton kept up the fight, and even the occasional shells he lobbed into
Hill's works drew no more than light counterfire. Just as in the morning, Ayres's second attack up the Squirrel Level Road failed to provoke
a major battle or force the Secessionist commander to reveal his intentions.[17]

Farther west, however, Parke and Mott did at last ascertain what
Hill was doing. Like Warren, the Pennsylvanian had initiated a minor
advance before receiving Meade's orders of 11:15. At 11:00, Hartranft's skirmishers ranged northwest to Dr. Boisseau's, and at about
the same time Potter's light infantry moved north across Pegram's. Advancing there from Peebles's had provoked little opposition, but beyond there the Confederate voltigeurs resisted fiercely, as if confident
of being backed up. Southern artillery, moreover, opened heavy supporting fire. Although the V Corps commander and probably Parke,
also, still felt that they confronted only cavalry, they now halted in the
face of this mounting opposition. Subsequently receiving Meade's order
of 11:15 only confirmed their decision not to challenge the growing resistance. To their left, Mott, too, encountered increased opposition as
he approached the works west of the Harman Road about noon.[18]

Contrary to what the Yankee generals thought, however, more than
just horsemen confronted them in those sectors. During the long delay
of morning the inevitable had happened: Hill had thrown additional
troops athwart the Bluecoats' path. The previous evening he had
seriously weakened the defenses of the plank road, supposedly so he
could reinforce the Northside if necessary and could also meet an advance by the Army of the Potomac on any sector. But on Sunday
morning, he presumably learned that the Yankees were no longer actively threatening north of the James, hence that he need not send
troops to Chaffin's Bluff. This freedom of action he put to use once his
cavalry reported that the Army of the Potomac was groping up the
Church and Harman roads toward the Boydton Plank Road. Mott's
slowness and caution and Meade's unwillingness to act boldly gave the
Virginian time to plug the gap he himself had created the night before.

Initially his front-line commanders tried to meet the threat with their
own men. Joel Griffin sent some troopers from his 4th and 8th regiments (probably from the 7th, too) out to skirmish with the advancing
foe. His main body, however, seemingly remained in place north of
Dr. Boisseau's, strengthening their works. The Butternut infantry,
moreover, apparently made no effort to challenge Meade outside their
trenches but concentrated in their defenses north of the upper fork of
Old Town Creek. Archer likely remained there to block the direct approach up the Church Road. Davis, however, may have shifted westward along the fortifications several times to correspond to the Federal

buildup around Dr. Boisseau's, but he, too, probably did not leave those works. Only Barringer, on the far right, took more active steps. He not only recalled his detached units, including the 2nd North Carolina Cavalry from Perkins' mill, but actually moved out against the Third Division, II Corps. His skirmishers contested the Union advance near C. Smith's, and some of his mounted men are thought to have been the force that demonstrated against Mott's exposed left and left rear. However, neither Barringer's flanking force, his voltigeurs, nor his few reinforcements could stop the powerful Yankee columns. Nor could any help come from Hampton, whose other three brigades were once more confronting Gregg on the Vaughan Road. To save the plank road, Hill had to send more infantry.

He chose for the mission his ready reserve, Heth's men near Battery No. 45. The first signs of the Federal advance evidently led Confederate headquarters to send Cooke down the plank road early in the morning. His Tarheels apparently turned southward along the Church Road and then filed off into the woods and began throwing up works, likely along the incomplete trench line to Archer's right. Increasing indications of danger on the Harman Road soon made clear that simply massing forces north of Jones's house would not contain the Yankees. The last mobile reserve brigade, MacRae's, was, accordingly, hurried off to cover that more westerly highway. To support this concentration, Hill, as usual, called on the services of his favorite artillerist, Willie Pegram. The lieutenant colonel soon had three of his batteries— Crenshaw, Purcell, and Captain Thomas Gregg's C/18th South Carolina Heavy Artillery Battalion—following the infantry down the plank road.

Cooke obviously reached the front in plenty of time. The other reserve brigade did not enjoy such a margin. While it was still en route, couriers galloped up to tell MacRae that Bluecoats were overrunning the country around C. Smith's and driving the cavalry outposts toward Mrs. Hart's. He therefore ordered his men to rush to the threatened sector. He still had a considerable way to go, but with his route safe and his mission compelling, he could make good time. In contrast, Mott, whose surroundings were potentially dangerous and whose objective was increasingly uncertain, continued proceeding slowly. These factors proved decisive. The Tarheels, despite their late start, barely beat the Jerseyman to the works. Just as the blue skirmishers burst into the clearing in front of the trenches about noontime, they spotted the Confederate infantry starting to replace Barringer in those fortifications. At that sight, voltigeurs from the Second and Third brigades (likely also from the First) dashed ahead to try to reach the defenses first. They easily drove in the Secessionist skirmish line, but the main trench line proved more difficult. It now bristled with foot soldiers, who handily beat them off. The Unionists then fell back toward the woods. In their wake, Southern voltigeurs rushed out from the fortifications to resume skirmishing.

Covered by these light infantry, Heth perfected his alignment. MacRae remained responsible for holding the Harman Road. To his right, though perhaps not adjoining him, Barringer likely shifted southwestward to prolong the line at least to Dabney's house, located about five eighths of a mile from Mrs. Hart's. Meantime, from the other direction, Davis, followed by Cooke, had hurried down the incomplete trench line from Jones's toward Mrs. Hart's to help oppose Mott's advance. So much rushing led one soldier of the 55th North Carolina to complain that "we was run nearly to death after the Yankees from one place to another."[19] In actuality, though, their hurrying spared them death, for it created sufficient shows of force as to help forestall a Union attack. Therefore, although they arrived too late to take part in checking the first such probe, they remained in position just left of MacRae to confront the increasingly threatening Northern concentration around Dr. Boisseau's. Joel Griffin, in turn, may have stretched along the gap from the left of Cooke to the right of Archer. Finally, the Marylander presumably stayed in position on the Church Road to block Warren's potential thrust in that sector.

Along this line Willie Pegram's trained eye picked out key locations for his batteries. On the far right, Crenshaw's unlimbered at Dabney's, where it could enfilade MacRae's front. Farther northeast, the Purcell Artillery and the South Carolinians took position beyond MacRae's left to check any advance from Dr. Boisseau's and Oscar Pegram's. Finally, Graham's apparently either served with the latter two companies or else helped cover the Pegram House Road and the Church Road from near Jones's. On taking up these positions, gunners, troopers, and foot soldiers alike labored desperately to convert the incomplete works into a strong line or, where necessary, to dig new trenches.[20]

Although Heth's fortifications were still unfinished, his men were now ready to oppose Mott's main line when it reached the front. The Jerseyman, though, declined to attack. The presence of Confederates here perplexed him as much as had their virtual absence on Route 673. His superiors had told him he could catch them in the open and turn their right. But when he at last located them, they were manning a line of fortifications that extended considerably beyond his own exposed left flank. This drastically new situation, along with his lack of any guns to silence their batteries, caused him to fall back on the defensive along the northern edge of the woods facing the enemy works. DeTrobriand now kept only four regiments on that front line: the 99th and 110th Pennsylvania, the 1st Maine Heavy Artillery, and the 40th New York, right to left. The 40th refused its left, and his four leftmost regiments—the 20th Indiana, 17th Maine, and 124th and either 73rd or 86th New York—dropped back *en potence* to anchor that potentially threatened flank in a dense forest. To provide further protection, his skirmishers, the 2nd U. S. Sharpshooters and one company of the 20th Indiana, stretched all the way around to C. Smith's in the left rear.

The First Brigade in this position and McAllister and Pierce farther right came under brisk enfilading fire from Dabney's. Shifting rightward to try to avoid it proved unavailing. Mott, therefore, allowed his main line to seek protection by lying down. At least the 1st Maine Heavies were initially reluctant to get down on the wet, swampy ground. However, when a shell burst among them with fatal effect, they and the other regiments quickly sought safety on the ground—some men in the excellent cover of ravines and thickets, others sheltered only by gentle undulations of the earth. Mott thus kept his main line inactive. Only his skirmishers, soon reinforced by the 141st Pennsylvania, maintained the battle. Here he would wait until he received new orders.[21]

He would have a considerable wait. His chief, far from issuing new instructions, was himself groping for ways to deal with the recent discovery of strong Confederate forces on his own front. Like the junior officer, Parke found this out as his troops finally neared the Southern works at about 1:00 P.M. A simple desire to expand his perimeter around Pegram's may have led the corps commander to resume advancing then. Or he may have wanted to ascertain what lay behind the increasingly resisting Secessionist skirmishers. Then again, he may have been trying to carry out the implied directive from army headquarters at 11:15 that he determine if any Butternut troops remained outside their principal defenses. But for whatever reason his own two divisions plus Griffin's moved to their left front in early afternoon. Willcox now shifted his axis from north to northwest to confront the enemy trench line running southwest to Mrs. Hart's. His Third Brigade led the way to Dr. Boisseau's. To secure his left and strengthen the connection with the Third Division, Harriman moved up into the gap between McLaughlen and Pierce, apparently on the right bank of Arthur's Swamp. The division commander also covered McLaughlen's other flank by sliding his Second Brigade's front line slightly to the left and then moving it abreast of the Third Brigade's right. Hartranft's second line, on the other hand, probably remained in immediate reserve. Simon Griffin meantime took position to Willcox's right near Boisseau's, also facing northwest but bent back farther eastward than the First Division. Curtin, in turn, advanced far enough to maintain the connection on his left but apparently continued fronting north toward Robert Jones's. Finally, Griffin's division presumably also shifted northwest correspondingly and then moved into line with Potter, facing north.

When the Yankees reached Boisseau's, they discovered that Confederate infantry and artillery occupied the works on both sides of Mrs. Hart's. The very sight of defended fortifications stopped Parke. Two days earlier, he had allowed this line to retard his expressly ordered advance toward the plank road. He was certainly not going to attack these works on Sunday now that army headquarters so strongly suggested that the battle was ending. He instead halted, and as he came under increasingly heavy shelling, he directed his men to throw up works of their own. Curtin and probably Charles Griffin worked to improve what were apparently Hofmann's old outpost pits, abandoned on Saturday morning. Parke's other four brigades began digging new trenches. Only Federal skirmishers ranged ahead to engage their Southern counterparts.[22]

Pegram did not let the Yankees take position unmolested. The combative Virginian opened a heavy fire on them with his two leftmost batteries and presumably Edward Graham. The lieutenant colonel's guns soon enfiladed Curtin's line and even landed a shell right on the 36th Massachusetts, killing two men and wounding three others. Now that the trying flank fire was actually producing casualties, the First Brigade had to fall back out of range about twenty yards and seek shelter in Hofmann's old pits, which it began repairing. From there, too, it soon had to move, this time about 200 yards leftward, where it began erecting new railworks in a wood. Most Federal units, though, found safety behind their initial defenses. For them, the Confederate fire caused only annoyance, not outright losses. Perhaps because casualties remained so low, perhaps because Meade and Parke no longer sought a major battle, their artillery made surprisingly little effort to silence the Butternut cannoneers. Despite all the guns Monroe had back on Peebles's, he used only the 7th Maine Battery for counterfire. The Maine men evidently started for the front about 9:00 A.M. but did not unlimber near Oscar Pegram's house until about noon. Even then, they did not actually open fire until after Willie Pegram did. Their challenge proved ineffectual. Outgunned and outfought, they were severely pummeled and lost a limber to Pegram's telling fire. Monroe, moreover, left them to their fate. Although he moved the 34th New York Battery to the front, he simply allowed it to erect works on a knoll near the farmhouse and did not use it to assist the 7th. Nor do Fitzhugh's batteries seem to have provided much, if any, support. Throughout the afternoon, Pegram enjoyed supremacy of artillery firepower at the immediate tactical front.[23]

This preponderance was more a potential safeguard against a Northern assault than an actual danger to the entrenched Bluecoats. At one point in the afternoon, however, the Southern gunners came within inches of dealing the Union high command a grievous blow. Among the Federal officers examining the Confederate line were Meade and Humphreys themselves. They had initially planned to leave Globe Tavern for the front shortly after 10:45, but the need to correspond with City Point over the radical change of battle plans and to see Crawford evidently delayed them at least an hour. By about 1:00 P.M., though, they and most of their field staff had reached the front at Pegram's. Numerous generals now gathered around them to report. To get an even better idea of what was occurring, the headquarters party rode to various sectors on the line, including Griffin's. The Chief-of-Staff later described to his wife what happened as they were discussing the situation with two V Corps generals just behind the 155th Pennsylvania's line:

> Genl. Meade and myself with some eight or ten aides rode to where Genl. Griffin was in the edge of a wood just inside of a fence, which caused us to crowd together. Genl. Meade's horse & mine were less than a foot apart (we did not dismount). Genl. Griffin & Genl. Bartlett stood up a few feet in front of us less than a foot apart and behind them were several staff officers, the whole party rising from a lunch they had been taking spread on the ground. Our staff officers were crowded around & in rear of us. One of them approached me handing me a dispatch, which I turned a little, involuntarily turning my horse a trifle to the left, to receive & in that position opened & was just beginning to read, when a crashing sound, a "charge," and a volcanic shower of dirt covering all the officers in front of me, a slight movement on the part of my horse, and a considerable one on the part of Genl. Meade's took place. A shell thrown from a battery of the enemy on our flank, not at all in view, had passed between Genl. Meade & myself, had taken off a small part of the tail of my horse (my turning to the left had caused that), grazed heavily Genl. Meade's boot close to the knee, passed between Genl. Griffin & Genl. Bartlett, burying itself in the ground five feet behind them & covered them & their staff with dirt. It did not explode. It is extraordinary, for it is almost impossible to have fired a shot into such a crowd without hitting some one. The shot was accidental. We did not notice that a cannon had been fired.[24]

"A more wonderful escape I never saw," added Meade to his wife; "at first I thought my leg was gone, as I felt and heard the blow plainly, but it only rubbed the leather of my riding boot without even bruising the skin."[25] An aide went on to say that witnesses "all said that the staff could not well have been arranged again so that there would have been room for a three-inch shot to pass without hitting anybody."[26]

After this narrow escape, Meade completed examining the front and then returned to his temporary forward headquarters in Peebles's house. His survey apparently convinced him that Heth's position was too strong to storm, so he allowed his men to continue their defensive preparations. Intelligence reports that may have reached him by now likely only increased his determination not to attack. Routine sightings just after noon of the breakup of two camps in Chesterfield and the movement of wounded were, admittedly, inconsequential. Hancock's report of 10:10 that the Graycoats had removed convalescents and supplies from Petersburg, moreover, contained a significant implication, now outdated to be sure, that eluded Union analysts. More noteworthy were the II Corps commander's report at that time that the Light Division was still on the Southside and Babcock's message of 10:00 that Hoke had returned from Chaffin's to Robert Jones's. The information on the North Carolinian was soon exposed as false, but for a time it may have influenced Meade. All he saw and read, in sum, confirmed his earlier decision that he could gain nothing more and should end the battle.[27]

Meantime, on the Squirrel Level Road, Ayres concluded that his striking force was not going to provoke a battle more serious than the lone gun occasionally firing from the main Confederate line could offer. Therefore, before 2:40, he recalled his men from their exposed position to his principal line on Chappell's farm. No Butternuts challenged his withdrawal, not even the sharpshooters who returned to W. W. Davis' in his wake without firing or receiving a shot. Only shortly after his soldiers reached safety did the Danville Artillery of McIntosh's Battalion sally down the Squirrel Level Road to engage Hazelton. The Virginians' overshots may have been the fire that caused the division commander to move his headquarters to a safer spot east of Talmage's house, but they did little real damage. After only a few shots, the Southern company ceased firing and returned to Battery No. 45. By midafternoon, probably no more than skirmish fire crackled along the Second Division's front.

Ayres, of course, had to take precautions against the temporary Secessionist resurgence issuing in an attack, so he returned the Third Brigade to its works. But the continued relative quiet in his sector, at the same time, enabled him to concentrate on the more important matters of strengthening and rearranging his line. Three of his brigades probably continued entrenching the existing front line. The 15th New York Heavy Artillery and the 146th New York, however, withdrew to

more favorable ground about one-eighth mile south of Fort Bratton
that afternoon and began digging a new east–west line across the Squirrel Level Road, again facing north. They may also have slashed timber
leftward across the middle branch of Arthur's Swamp toward Griffin's
right. The rest of Grindlay's outfit also fell back to form a reserve for
the three front-line brigades. Farther east, Bragg's men, too, labored to
link the Second Division's works to Globe Tavern.[28]

Ayres's advance and withdrawal thus provoked a little skirmishing
and shelling but no serious fighting. His operations, however, seemingly
at least pinned the Light Division in place in the main works between
Battery No. 45 and the Weldon Railroad. Unlike on Friday, Wilcox's
command could not now afford to leave that sector to meet the threat
on the Church and Harman roads. Admittedly, Hill considered shifting
it to the more southwesterly area. He himself apparently galloped past
No. 45 at 2:15 P.M., presumably en route to Jones's and Mrs. Hart's,
and either about then or at 3:00 he alerted the two brigades to be
ready to march. He did not actually set them in motion, though. Concern over what Ayres might do apparently caused him to leave them in
the works.[29]

A comparable stalemate also developed at the opposite end of the
Squirrel Level Road, where Hampton and Gregg once more blocked
each other. The Pennsylvanian went into Sunday braced to defend
McDowell's against an expected resumption of the Confederate onslaught. However, no attack developed. He therefore took steps to
locate the enemy and to screen the infantry's left rear. Either the 1st or
4th Pennsylvania Cavalry or the Ohioans relieved the 13th on the far
left at Reams's Station. At least the 2nd remained on guard at Colonel
Wyatt's, and at least the 10th and probably Battery A continued manning the works at McDowell's. The New Yorkers may also have joined
the divisional pioneers in burying dead Butternuts left on the field from
Saturday's battle. The Maine regiment meantime picketed up the
Vaughan Road to link McDowell's to Poplar Spring Church. To provide a more effective and informative connection, the division commander pushed the Jerseymen west to E. Wilkinson's. One battalion
occupied the abandoned works there, and the other two rode out on
picket. With the lower end of the Squirrel Level Road thus secured, the
1st Massachusetts Cavalry then established a more westerly screen
along that highway from E. Wilkinson's to Clements' to cover Mott's
rear more effectively.

These moves were basically defensive. Gregg also took more active
steps to locate the Secessionists. With his First Brigade exhausted from
the previous day's fight, he now turned to the Second Brigade. It had
been ready to move since shortly after 4:00 A.M. Sometime after sun-

rise, Smith led the 8th, likely the 13th and the battery, and possibly the
4th west along the Wyatt and Vaughan roads. The division commander
himself probably accompanied this reconnaissance. Past McDowell's
they moved, then past the forward outposts at E. Wilkinson's at about
9:00. They were in enemy country now. If Hampton were anywhere
near, he would not allow them to cross Hatcher's Run unchallenged.
The corps commander did not disappoint them. Near the junction of
the Vaughan Road with the crossroad to Armstrong's house, the South
Carolina brigade and most of Young's Brigade (though still minus the
Jeff Davis Legion) barred their path. A whole division was not about
to yield that intersection to a few regiments and soon lashed back.
Union shells took their toll of the advancing force but could not stop
it. Slowly Butler pushed the hard-fighting Yankees back along the
Vaughan Road. However, along the western edge of some woods,
probably those just west of E. Wilkinson's, Smith made his stand and
either repulsed or gave pause to the pursuers. Butler, too, halted just
right of the Vaughan Road in a large open field, presumably Mrs.
Cummings'.

Hampton, as usual, could not be certain whether these moves were
just minor probes or portents of a major attack. Despite the obvious albeit slow-moving danger to Barringer and Joel Griffin, the corps commander decided to use his remaining brigade and battery to help the
First Division. He apparently brought Davis down the Duncan Road
and then over the crossroad to the Vaughan Road. The colonel halted
on the Vaughan Road about thirty minutes and then moved eastward
to the front through the carnage of Butler's fight. There he deployed
just left of the First Division, with McGregor's battery on his center.
The Virginians' arrival did not foretell another heavy counterattack as
on October 1, however. The tenuous situation along the Harmon Road
—and perhaps also the result of Saturday's battle—made Hampton unwilling to become more heavily engaged on the Vaughan Road than
necessary. He therefore contented himself with a simple defensive response to the Yankees' advance. Once they chose to break off action, he
gladly let fighting die down to light skirmishing, punctuated by no more
than minor forays.

Gregg, too, saw little point in continuing the battle. His reconnaissance not only had re-established contact with the Confederates but
also had disclosed that they were not seeking a fight but were in a position to check him if he pressed the attack. He declined to precipitate a
major battle at Hatcher's Run, presumably because either IX Corps or
army headquarters informed him that the whole army was assuming the
defensive. Even before supposedly receiving those instructions, moreover, he was likely restrained by the need to weaken his force to help
the infantry. Word of gray horsemen hovering around J. Smith's during

the capture of Fort MacRae led Parke, at 11:10, to call for cavalry to occupy "Miss Pegram's" and to patrol the left rear in greater strength. The growing threat to the Third Division's left as it moved north intensified the senior officer's desire for a countering force. Gregg presumably complied by using part of the Massachusetts outfit or perhaps part of the regiment on the Vaughan Road north of McDowell's. The 10th took over that more easterly highway from the 1st Maine Cavalry about noon. On being relieved, at least some Maine men returned to Wyatt's to help cover the cavalry's own left rear. Others from that regiment or perhaps some of the New Yorkers, however, may have gone to assist the infantry. With some of his troopers diverted northwestward, others checked in front, and the foe equally restrained, the Vaughan Road sector rapidly quieted down. Like their counterparts to the north and northwest, Gregg and Hampton concentrated on defending what they already had.[30]

This absence of heavy fighting continued across the entire battlefield until midafternoon. Then, however, Parke took it upon himself to order a reconnaissance in force against the works near Mrs. Hart's, presumably to ascertain whether or not they were, indeed, held in strength. He would have done better to have made this move on first nearing the Southern position. His habitual caution—not to say, indecision—as well as the tenor of Meade's orders, however, caused him to desire to complete his rifle pits first. Only when he secured his own position did he resume advancing. He apparently did not realize that the same hours he spent strengthening his line were used by his opponents in bolstering theirs.

His plan called for a two-pronged demonstration by part of Willcox's division from Dr. Boisseau's and by part of Mott's east of Dabney's. His main line, though, apparently made no preparations to exploit any weakness the reconnaissance forces might discover. Nor does the V Corps seem to have taken part. Out of 30,000 men who had assembled west of the Weldon Railroad overnight for the decisive advance on Sunday, only 2,100, supported by 700 more, were actually to participate in the final move toward the Boydton Plank Road. Similar fragmentation on Friday was caused by the loss of tactical cohesion ruining a serious effort. On October 2, though, the tactical integrity from Chappell's to C. Smith's had been preserved. So few men were now used because the effort was no longer serious. The grand onslaught against the supply lines, with all its potential opportunities, had degenerated into a mere reconnaissance by just 7 per cent of the strike force.[31]

Still, such as they were, these reconnaissances managed to provoke the heaviest fighting of the day. Parke's orders to reconnoiter infused

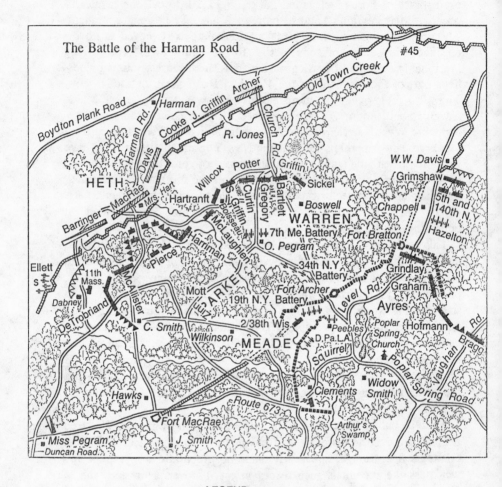

The Battle of the Harman Road

#45

Boydton Plank Road
Old Town Creek
Archer
J. Griffin
Griffin
Harman
Harman Rd.
Cooke
Church Rd.
R. Jones
W.W. Davis
Grimshaw
Davis
Potter
Griffin
Sickel
HETH
Willcox
Bartlett
Boswell
Chappell
5th and
140th N.Y.
Barringer
MacRae
Mrs. Hart
Hartranft
J. Griffin
Curtin
Gregory
WARREN
Fort Bratton
Hazelton
McLaughlen
7th Me. Battery
Boisseau
O. Pegram
Harriman
34th N.Y.
Grindlay
Ellett
Pierce
Battery
Graham
11th Mass.
McAllister
Mott
Fort Archer
Level Rd.
Ayres
Dabney
19th N.Y. Battery
Hofmann
Rd.
DeTrobriand
Peebles
Poplar
Bragg
C. Smith
2/38th Wis.
Spring
Wilkinson
MEADE
D.Pa.LA
Church
Vaughan
Hawks
Squirrel
Poplar Spring Road
Widow
Route 673
Clements
Smith
Fort MacRae
"Miss Pegram"
J. Smith
Arthur's
Duncan Road
Swamp

LEGEND

- Yankee Infantry
- Southern Infantry
- Yankee Cavalry
- Southern Cavalry
- ▲▲▲▲ Yankee Skirmishers
- △△△△ Southern Skirmishers
- Yankee Artillery
- S Southern Artillery
- Yankee Works
- Southern Works
- Abandoned Southern Works

new action into the long stalemated sector west of Arthur's Swamp. On receiving them about 2:00 P.M., Mott began looking first for a target, then for a reconnaissance force. The danger of further exposing his already outflanked left presumably ruled out moving west of Dabney's. In contrast, the desirability of co-operating with Willcox's probe evidently commended a move closer to Mrs. Hart's. The Jerseyman therefore decided to throw forward his right against MacRae's front just southwest of where the main northwestern creek branch flowed out of Heth's line.

Mott entrusted operational control of this mission to his brigadier in the area, Pierce. The junior officer eventually had three brigades at his disposal: McAllister's, his own, and Harriman's, left to right. From among them, the Michigander decided to attack in force with his right center and to create a diversion with his left. He now massed his main striking force in the ravine of a small tributary that flowed eastward into the northwestern branch of Arthur's Swamp. This ravine crossed the Harman Road 300 yards south of the Confederate works; farther northeast it bent to within 200 yards of those defenses. His skirmish line already occupied this depression. The supporting companies of the

COMMENTARY

1. Whether or not Parke left any other infantry on Peebles's farm besides the 2/38th Wisconsin is not known. The location of that battalion is only schematically representational.

2. DeTrobriand's regiment at Clements' house was either the 73rd or the 86th New York.

3. The deployment of Monroe's 18 guns is essentially correct, with those of Heasley's battery being shown advancing toward Pegram's house, where they took position but apparently saw no action. Of Fitzhugh's 12 guns in contrast, only Hazelton's are shown since it is not certain whether Rogers and Mink accompanied Griffin or remained on Peebles's farm. The latter possibility seems more likely.

4. Only Ellett's battery of Pegram's Battalion is shown. The locations of Gregg's, Hollis', and Graham's 12 guns along the works north of Arthur's Swamp are not known.

5. The positions of Archer and Joel Griffin and the relative order of Charles Griffin's three brigades are probable but not certain.

6. For the Main reconnaissance force, Zinn deployed the 1st Massachusetts Heavy Artillery, 141st Pennsylvania, and 84th Pennsylvania, left to right, with the 105th Pennsylvania behind the heavies. The 1st U. S. Sharpshooters and part of the 57th Pennsylvania skirmished on his right and left, respectively. Pierce kept the rest of the 57th on provost duty and the 93rd New York in reserve. The deployment of Mott's other two brigades and of Harriman's and Hartranft's brigades is given in the text.

84th Pennsylvania now joined their voltigeurs to form a regimental battle line there. The 141st Pennsylvania then shifted forward to the 84th's left, and the 1st Massachusetts Heavy Artillery moved over to the 141st's left. Finally, the 105th Pennsylvania deployed fifty yards behind the heavies (whether straight back or echeloned to the left rear is not clear). To command these four regiments, Pierce passed over their senior officer, Lieutenant Colonel Casper Tyler of the 141st, and called upon Lieutenant Colonel George Zinn of the 84th. The other three regiments of the Second Brigade meantime prepared to support Zinn. The 1st U. S. Sharpshooters were to advance as flankers on his right, and the 57th Pennsylvania was to do the same on his left and also to serve as provost guard. Finally, the 93rd New York probably either skirmished for the forces remaining behind or else served as a general reserve.

As the Second Brigade got ready to advance, its commander prepared his other two brigades to support it. From the right, Harriman moved down to plug the gap between the First and Third divisions' main lines, created when Zinn advanced to the ravine. If the Wisconsinite were not already west of the northwestern branch, he clearly moved there at this time. On reconnecting with the II Corps troops, he too reported to Pierce and became a ready reserve for the reconnaissance force. Farther down the line, McAllister received a more active supporting role. Both Pierce and Mott directed him to throw a regiment across DeTrobriand's front to prevent the Crenshaw Battery at Dabney's from enfilading Zinn. For this dangerous mission, the colonel selected one of his better outfits, Major Charles C. Rivers' 11th Massachusetts. The regimental commander, though, somehow misunderstood what was expected of him. Mott, Pierce, and McAllister all planned for him just to distract the Virginia battery. But he thought that he was actually to storm it.

Another error, however, soon canceled this misunderstanding. By 3:00 P.M., Pierce had his own force ready, and he evidently supposed that the supporting units were all set, too. He therefore ordered his demibrigade to charge. This move proved premature, for Rivers was not yet in place to co-operate. When the major saw the four regiments attacking before he was prepared, he concluded that he was too late to join their advance. Therefore, all he did was to move forward slightly, become embroiled with increasingly aggressive Confederate skirmishers (probably MacRae's or Barringer's), and then fire on the Crenshaw cannoneers from a distance. This was all his superiors expected of him. Their principal probe might have fared better, however, had he actually charged the works at Dabney's. Though he would have suffered severely, he would have diverted the Virginians' shelling from Zinn. As matters worked out, the 11th's long-range fire inflicted no casualties on the gunners and failed to draw their fire from the main strike force.

The Southern artillerists enfiladed Zinn's line as it rushed out of the ravine onto the open ground leading up to the works. Its leftmost outfit, the heavies, particularly suffered from such raking. His narrow front, too, withered under the concentrated fire of MacRae's hard-fighting Tarheels. Desperately Zinn and his subordinates urged their line forward. Yet the closer it came to the fortifications, the more the ever-intensifying torrent of lead slowed it down. Seeing its pace slacken made Heth's infantry fire even harder to drive it back. Pegram's artillery, too, continued enfilading the Union line with devastating effect. The battalion commander, in the thick of the fray as usual, had his horse shot from under him (presumably near Dabney's), but he kept on urging his gunners to maintain their fire.

This heavy shelling and musketry stopped Zinn about fifty yards short of the defense line. They also made him realize that the Secessionists held that line in strength. He accordingly decided not to sacrifice any more men by prolonging the reconnaissance in force. About ten minutes after starting, he abandoned the effort and ordered his regiments back to safety. At about this time, he fell grievously wounded in the right leg. His men, however, carried him to safety and managed to withdraw in relatively good order themselves. The 141st rallied on Pierce's skirmish line, and the 105th and probably the 1st and the 84th regrouped on the 57th's provost line a little farther back. Heth continued firing on the retreating regiments but did not counterattack. He therefore did not disrupt their withdrawal but did at least manage to prevent them from recovering their dead and some of their wounded, who were left where they fell—prizes of war to the needy Confederates.

If Zinn's repulse were not enough, Mott now received additional reasons for not renewing his attack. Before this probe got under way, Parke had reported his plans to Meade, only to learn that the army commander did not wish Mott to "run any great risk, but to take up a line and intrench."[32] The IX Corps chief passed these instructions on to Mott, who read them during Zinn's attack. The division commander concluded that precipitating a major battle by throwing his four brigades against Heth's strong position would entail too great a "risk" and, therefore, ordered fighting to cease. His directive came too late to do Zinn any good, but it probably saved his other units from a similar fate.

Although Mott no longer pressed the battle, fighting did not end. Gray sharpshooters, likely from the two rightmost brigades, roamed back over the field to skirmish with his voltigeurs. The Butternuts con-

centrated primarily against Rivers' isolated regiment but also stung the
rest of the Third Brigade and the left of the Second Brigade fairly hard.
The 11th's forward position evidently shielded DeTrobriand's front
from their probes but probably not his refused left. Only Harriman escaped their annoying fire. Even so, the Secessionists did not permit a
serious battle to develop. Heth, either on his own or under Hill's
guidelines, saw his main task as defending the plank road. He declined
to jeopardize his initial success by hurling his weak force against the
powerful Federal line. Since neither he nor Mott desired to renew
fighting, operations near the Harman Road did not again rise above
brisk skirmishing.[33]

Nor did heavy fighting flare up west of Dr. Boisseau's. There
McLaughlen's relatively fresh brigade received the assignment of co-
operating with the troops on the Harman Road. However, it did not
even begin advancing until during or just after the final phase of Zinn's
charge. On once starting, the Massachusetts man headed west along a
road from the doctor's house—either Cutcheon's old route across the
creek toward Mrs. Hart's, or perhaps a trail leading northwest along
the left bank of the main northwestern branch. As the Third Brigade
drove back the Confederate pickets and moved toward MacRae's left,
Heth worried that it might roll up the brigade blocking the Third Division. Fortunately for the Graycoats, though, the colonel was not aware
of the opportunity that Heth feared. Fortunately, too, Davis and probably Cooke by now hurried into place to secure the Tarheels' left and
parry this new threat. As the reinforcements took position, the Secessionist skirmishers apparently dropped to the ground to unmask them.
Over the voltigeurs' heads, the two new brigades opened a brisk fire on
McLaughlen. This vigorous resistance handily checked him. Moreover,
the IX Corps commander, now aware that army headquarters did not
favor pressing the advance, sent word for him to pull back. After advancing a mere 300 yards and enduring no more than nine casualties,
the brigadier fell back to Boisseau's house. Mississippi voltigeurs followed him to the far edge of the doctor's field, where they resumed
skirmishing with Willcox. Behind them, Pegram continued shelling the
Union lines. But as on the Harman Road, this temporary resurgence
portended no Confederate counterattack. Simply winning an easy victory over a feeble Yankee probe sufficed for Harry Heth.[34]

Neither he nor his corps commander, though, knew beforehand how
easy this victory would be. The outbreak of potentially serious fighting
in midafternoon concerned A. P. Hill. Unaware that the Northern high
command had renounced the initiative, he worried that attacks near
Mrs. Hart's portended the long-delayed drive for the Boydton Plank
Road. To meet this threat, he wanted more men. The Light Division
now received marching orders, yet he hesitated actually to move it, lest

its departure tempt Ayres to strike up the Squirrel Level Road again, this time all the way to Battery No. 45.

The lieutenant general instead determined to bolster his far right with troops from his center and far left. No more than skirmishing and shelling had flared up on Mahone's and Johnson's sectors throughout the Fifth Offensive. The projected demonstration against them by Crawford and Hancock on October 2 had not materialized.[35] To the contrary, sniping actually diminished on Sunday as many outposts made informal truces so they could bail out their flooded picket pits and then let them dry in the sun. Before it could do much good, though, the sunshine gave way to cloudiness that portended more rain. Fear of an even greater storm (the wrath of Mahone, who did not tolerate such truces), moreover, caused some outposts to continue firing. Even so, the sectors just east and south of town remained fundamentally quiescent. The lack of danger there was underscored by the report of Union deserters on Saturday night that the II Corps's line was only lightly held now that Grant's main field forces had moved north of the James and west of the Weldon Railroad. Hill, therefore, felt justified in drawing his reinforcements from his center and left. Near 1:00 P.M., he evidently put the troops there on standby, ready to move. Then in midafternoon, he actually ordered Johnson and Mahone each to send a brigade to Heth.

The Ohioan chose his left brigade. Apparently only now, at about 4:30 (not the previous evening or even earlier in the afternoon), did he pull it out of line. To take its place, McAfee stretched down to the lower Appomattox. Covering a double sector spread the North Carolinians' line precariously thin. Calling cooks, extra-duty men, members of courts-martial, and even ambulatory wounded into the trenches still left their sector undermanned. Yet Johnson felt justified in taking that risk. His fellow major general also attenuated his line, but in a much different way. Shortly before dark, Mahone shifted his Alabamians and Virginians rightward and may also have extended his Floridians and Georgians leftward to enable Harris' main body to join the 48th Mississippi in reserve. Using more than one brigade to replace the Mississippians reduced the attenuation of the troops remaining in the works. Even so, King and Weiseger found shifting along the trenches no easy matter. The mud and water greatly impeded movement, and to make matters worse, Bluecoat pickets opened fire on them—apparently only as a matter of course, not as a recognition that a major move was afoot and should be harassed. Despite these difficulties the two colonels got their men into position and relieved Harris.

Once the two brigades were in reserve, they received orders to move westward. Johnson, much to his chagrin, was not allowed to accompany his men but was left behind yet again to command the important but inactive left. Goode instead marched rightward and reported to Mahone, whom corps headquarters evidently desired to have charge of the reinforcements. The latter officer apparently turned command of his own division over to Finegan and then led the two reserve brigades toward the threatened sector on the far right. His makeshift division could have bolstered the threatened sectors by roughly 1,550 men. Hardly had it crossed the Weldon Railroad at about 5:30 to 5:40 P.M., however, before it received word that MacRae's and Pegram's successful stand on the Harman Road made its presence there unnecessary. Hill, nevertheless, kept these reinforcements in the woods behind Battery No. 45 just in case more fighting should flare up farther southwest.[36]

The Federal commanders, though, had no intention of renewing the fighting. They were content with—or at least reconciled to—the outcome. Meade had long since decided against pressing the action. His orders, along with the outcome of the Battle of the Harman Road, effectually dampened Parke's already faint determination to fight. The entire Union high command on the Southside, from army group through army to corps, now regarded the Battle of Poplar Spring Church as over. All that remained was to select the best position for defending their new foothold west of the Halifax Road.

In late afternoon, Parke and Warren presumably conferred with Meade on defensive arrangements. Then they posted their corps along the new line. Their right would stay in place between Flowers' and Chappell's. Their center, too, would virtually retain its present position on Pegram's farm but would fall back slightly to make the line more secure. Their left, on the other hand, would afford too tempting a target if it remained so far northwest. It would have to withdraw all the way to Peebles's farm, where it could cover the army's left rear. When the corps commanders completed their plans, they ordered them carried out.

Mott's redeployment was the most dangerous. He had not merely to fall back but also to break contact with a potentially aggressive foe who already harassed his exposed left flank. Therefore, when orders to withdraw reached him at 5:15, he took every precaution to protect his retreat. A successful disengagement entails a step-by-step, "leapfrogging" movement to the rear, so he first shifted some troops to an intermediate point behind his front to cover the retreat of his other units. He evidently wanted to keep his freshest outfits closest to the foe, so he selected most of his battered Second Brigade to take up this position behind the lines. It turned over its front-line sector to the 93rd New York as skirmishers and to Harriman. Then it moved rearward to occupy the old Confederate works captured in early morning. With Pierce now in position to resist a counterattack, DeTrobriand's brigade pulled back eastward along Route 673 through the Michigander's line and on toward the Clements' house. After the Frenchman withdrew, McAllister skillfully extricated the 11th Massachusetts and then followed him east. When these two brigades had passed his position, Pierce fell in behind them as their mobile rear guard. Finally, Mott's skirmishers and the cavalry brought up the rear. The Third Division had successfully broken contact with Heth. The only men it had left behind were its handful of dead, hastily buried in shallow graves.

On reaching Peebles's farm, Mott's soldiers took up defensive positions along its lower corner, facing south and southwest. His leading brigade filed into Harriman's old fortifications extending westward across the Squirrel Level Road from the main stream of Arthur's Swamp on past Clements'. Most of McAllister's men, too, occupied part of the IX Corps's former works from DeTrobriand's right to Peebles's house. The Second Brigade, on the other hand, did not man any trenches but bivouacked in Peebles's field as the divisional reserve. By 6:30 P.M., Mott had taken up this new defense line.

The other Federal troops also occupied their new positions during the late afternoon and early evening. To connect the new line on Pegram's with the old works on Peebles's, Willcox pulled back from Dr. Boisseau's to a new location facing southwest along the western edge of Pegram's farm. He shifted his Second Brigade from his former right flank to his new left flank, resting on Potter's old works about one-eighth mile west of Fort Archer. A gap of about 400 yards still existed between Hartranft's left and McAllister's right, but their overlapping fields of fire meant that in a military sense, they had connected. Moreover, no gap at all separated the brigades of the First Division. Harriman, no longer needed west of Arthur's Swamp now that Mott had safely withdrawn, fell back to its left bank, then moved down to prolong the Second Brigade's line northwest across Pegram's farm. There the 2/38th Wisconsin came forward to rejoin him. McLaughlen, in turn, presumably remained near Boisseau's to cover the First Brigade's crossing. Then he went into position from Harriman's right nearly to Pegram's house. Potter took up the line around that house. His Second Brigade now withdrew to adjoin the First Division at the truncated northwestern salient that faced Dr. Boisseau's. Finally, Curtin pulled back to occupy the IX Corps's far right, extending to Pegram's farmhouse.

The V Corps took charge of the defenses east of the Pegram House Road. Its First Division continued to cover the Church Road. However, that unit had by now obliqued so far northwest to maintain contact with the IX Corps that it had virtually broken connection with Ayres. To plug this gap, Griffin evidently brought his First Brigade up to the Third Brigade's right sometime during the day. Then in late afternoon, he shifted his Second Brigade to Sickel's right. In the meantime, the 15th New York Heavies and 146th New York stretched leftward from the Squirrel Level Road to slash an abatis and presumably to dig a trench. These moves apparently enabled Gregory and Grindlay to link up again. But instead of the firm bond that existed from Friday night to Sunday morning, their present connection was just a dangerously attenuated line of two regiments. This weak link worried Warren. Technical corrections in the lay of his line he could put off until morning, but strengthening the weak center he wanted done at once. Yet he did not use the main body of the Regular brigade for that purpose, presumably because he desired a mobile reserve for the Second Division's long line. He instead requested Parke to relieve Bartlett's brigade, which would then bolster the weak point. The Pennsylvanian, though, did not get around to this on Sunday evening. The V Corps commander, accordingly, had to rely on the rugged terrain along the headwaters of the central branch of Arthur's Swamp to protect his left center.

His veterans, of course, gave nature a hand. Griffin's soldiers and all other Union troops on the front line fortified their new defense perimeter overnight. They strengthened the works previously begun on Flowers', Chappell's, and Clements' and connected those defenses with new trenches across Pegram's. And right away that evening, Spaulding sent two companies of engineers to help them. His regiment had stood by on the Jerusalem Plank Road all afternoon awaiting their pontoon trains from City Point and awaiting, even more, the big breakthrough that would enable them to bring those pontoons forward to bridge the upper Appomattox. The pontoons finally came, but the opportunity never did. By late afternoon, it seemed clear that they would not be needed, so the engineers bivouacked at Jones's at about 4:30 to 5:00 P.M. Then about dark, marching orders arrived at last—but they were orders to return the recently arrived pontoons to Benham and to bring the main body westward. The bridges duly headed back to Old Court House (not City Point, as directed), and the engineers moved out to camp behind Crawford's left. Harwood bivouacked at Aiken's, which had been selected as Meade's new headquarters, closer to the front than Birchett's. Most of Spaulding's force, meantime, moved on to encamp near the Weldon Railroad for the night. Companies E and F/50th, however, continued to the front and began laying out a new redoubt at the key northwestern salient overnight. The 50th had come forward at last—not to facilitate the offense by bridging the Appomattox but to facilitate the defense by helping to fortify Pegram's farm.

This redoubt was the keystone of the line Meade finally adopted to secure his gains of the past four days. The five divisions around the fort made up the line itself. Mott and Willcox now defended the left rear from Clements' up the left bank of the swamp's northwestern branch nearly to Pegram's house. To their right, Potter and Griffin guarded the left front on Pegram's farm against counterattacks from the new Confederate works on Jones's and the Harman Road. And Ayres and Bragg extended across Chappell's and Flowers' farms to connect Pegram's farm with the Weldon Railroad.[37]

Meade drew his cavalry, too, into this defensive system. Its sector had so quieted down after the initial skirmishing near Mrs. Cummings' that Gregg felt he could safely leave his command in early evening to go confer at Peebles's. He was unable to see Parke, who was still out on Pegram's, but he did meet Meade himself. The army commander explained that the horsemen should continue guarding against a dash up either the Vaughan or Halifax roads into the infantry's left rear. As during the battle, such a mission was best performed by holding the key intersection at McDowell's. Gregg already had some forces there, and he pulled back or moved forward most of his other units to that farm in late afternoon and early evening. At least the Jerseymen, the New Yorkers, the Mainemen, the 2nd, presumably the two batteries, probably the 8th, and perhaps the 13th stood guard there. Two regiments, however, continued to picket the roads that linked the Second Cavalry Division to Mott: the Massachusetts men still on the Squirrel Level Road and either the 4th or the 13th now replacing the 10th on the upper Vaughan Road north of McDowell's. Other troopers comparably patrolled eastward to the Halifax Road and probably still down to Reams's Station to cover the far left flank.[38]

Posting his cavalry and infantry in those positions culminated the army commander's new determination to fall back on the defensive. Since late morning, his orders to his strike force and his recommendations to City Point made clear his intention to terminate the battle. Yet nowhere is his change of attitude better revealed than in the briefing he sent to II Corps headquarters at 5:00 P.M. The previous afternoon, he had assured supreme headquarters that he was "most desirous to attack unless I should not deem it judicious to do so." Events on Sunday, however, had indeed made him think attacking was not "judicious." Now he could write Hancock that "we are all prepared for Lee if he desires to come."[39]

The Virginian probably did "desire to come." Counterattacking and regaining lost ground were two of his favorite principles of generalship. Yet his continuing preoccupation with operations on the Peninsula and his apparent reluctance to counterattack again in this battle after the repulse on Chappell's on Saturday morning limited his response on the Southside on October 2. Throughout the day, he and his local commander, Hill, contented themselves with a restrained defense of the Boydton Plank Road. Simply barring Meade's path and fending off his probes sufficed for the Confederate generals. As the Pennsylvanian's threat diminished in late afternoon and his pullback on the Harman and Squirrel Level roads suggested that he too was going on the defensive, the Southern chieftains presumably realized that their plan had succeeded. They needed to do no more that day than to maintain and strengthen their defenses.

The easy victory at Mrs. Hart's obviated the necessity of bringing Mahone's provisional division to the far right. It accordingly remained in reserve behind Battery No. 45 for the rest of the afternoon, then returned to its parent divisions after dark. The Mississippians probably moved back to the center. Goode definitely marched on to the far left, where he arrived prior to 9:00 P.M. Neither brigade re-entered the trenches, though. Just in case the battle was not over, after all, and they should have to meet a renewed Federal drive for the supply lines on Monday, both stayed in reserve. Harris likely bivouacked on Wilcox's farm, behind Mahone's center, and the Virginians, at Johnson's order, encamped on the Blandford Cemetery hill behind the North Carolinians' right and Gracie's left. Since the colonel did not return to the works, Johnson shifted the South Carolinians and Alabamians northward a little to relieve some of the tension on McAfee's extended line.

Like the Ohioan, Hill redistributed his forces to provide a more balanced defense, should the Yankees continue fighting on October 3. Thus far into the battle, the lieutenant general had secured Petersburg itself. It was no longer in imminent danger. His communications, too, seemed safe, yet the force protecting them was somewhat out of position by late Sunday. The two previous days it had effectively barred the Bluecoats' most direct route to the supply lines, the Church Road. By late on October 2, however, the preponderance of the covering force had shifted farther southwest to the vicinity of the Harman Road. The troops still occupying Heth's left, Archer's Brigade and perhaps Joel Griffin's, had held the Church Road by default on Sunday. They might not suffice, however, to guard it against a determined drive on the third. The corps commander chose not to chance a breakthrough there. After dark, he finally ordered the Light Division to move; it was to occupy in strength the sector adjoining Archer's right. At about 10:00

P.M., Wilcox set off down the plank road to a position northwest of the upper fork of Old Town Creek opposite Jones's house. There he partially overlapped and extended rightward from the sector from which he had attacked on Friday. Lane took position to Cooke's left, and McGowan extended the line northeast to Archer's right. Joel Griffin's men, on being relieved, probably dropped back into reserve, awaiting new orders.

This redeployment effectively covered the Church Road. From Jones's to Dabney's, a formidable line now barred all avenues to the plank road. Establishing that line, however, created a huge gap of over two miles between Archer's left and Mahone's right. Yet Hill was willing to risk such a gap in order to secure Jones's. The threat of the Unionists penetrating it, after all, was much less than the danger of them driving up the Church Road. The unoccupied sector southwest of Battery No. 45 was difficult for them to reach unobserved, and the temporarily denuded works between that redoubt and the Weldon Railroad could be remanned, if necessary, before Ayres could get there. Then too, the III Corps commander probably knew that additional troops would soon fill the gap. The flurry of Yankee activity on the Southside on October 2 and their contrasting quiet north of the James induced Lee to issue orders that day for Scales's Brigade to go back to Petersburg. Although the Tarheels did not actually move until Monday, their prospective return was presumably known to Hill the previous day.

But until those reinforcements arrived, the lieutenant general could rely only on his own troops. To make them doubly strong, he directed his two right divisions to transform their weak and incomplete defenses into a formidable line of fortifications. Wilcox apparently did not begin such work until after daybreak, but Heth, who had been digging in throughout Sunday, presumably continued entrenching overnight.[40]

Beyond Heth's exposed right flank, the gray cavalrymen, too, guarded against another Federal attack. At least the 2nd North Carolina Cavalry remained in the trenches southwest of MacRae, but some of Barringer's other horsemen probably remounted and patrolled the country east of the Duncan Road. South of the Tarheel troopers, most of the First Cavalry Division likely stayed on the Vaughan Road to bar any new attack by Gregg. At least the 9th Virginia Cavalry and probably the rest of the Virginia brigade, on the other hand, left Butler and marched southeast to bivouac on the Military Road about four and a half miles southwest of Malone's Crossing on the Weldon Railroad. From this camp, they sent pickets to the crossing to help guard the approaches to Stony Creek Depot and to aid the Jeff Davis Legion in observing the Unionists at Reams's Station, a mile and a half up the tracks. Davis' move marks a partial return to the troopers' normal

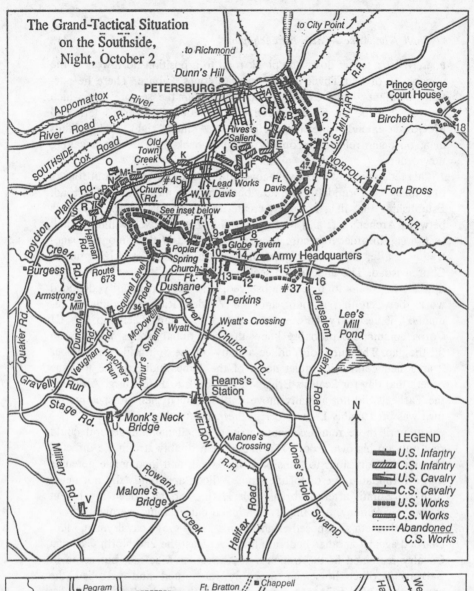

The Grand-Tactical Situation
on the Southside,
Night, October 2

to City Point

to Richmond

Dunn's Hill

PETERSBURG

Prince George
Court House

Appomattox River

Birchett

River Road

R.R.

SOUTHSIDE

Cox Road

Old Town Creek

Rives's Salient

U.S. MILITARY R.R.

18

Boydton Plank Rd.

Church Rd.

#45

Lead Works
W.W. Davis

Ft. Davis

NORFOLK

Fort Bross

17

Harman Rd.

Creek Rd.

See inset below

Ft.

Globe Tavern

Army Headquarters

#37

Burgess

Route 673

Poplar Spring Church

Ft. Dushane

Perkins

Wyatt's Crossing

Lee's Mill Pond

Armstrong's Mill

Squirrel Level Road

McDowell

Arthur's Swamp

Wyatt

Church Rd.

Jerusalem Plank Road

Quaker Rd.

Duncan Rd.

Vaughan Rd.

Hatcher's Run

Reams's Station

WELDON

Gravelly Run

Stage Rd.

Monk's Neck Bridge

Malone's Crossing

Jones's Hole Swamp

Military Rd.

Malone's Bridge

R.R.

Rowanty Creek

Halifax Road

N

LEGEND

U.S. Infantry
C.S. Infantry
U.S. Cavalry
C.S. Cavalry
U.S. Works
C.S. Works
Abandoned
C.S. Works

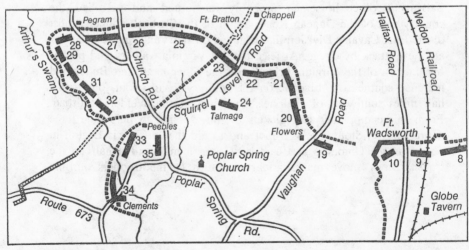

Arthur's Swamp

Pegram

Ft. Bratton

Chappell

Halifax Road

Weldon Railroad

28
29
30
31
32

27

26

25

Church Rd.

Level Road

23

22

21

Squirrel

24

Talmage

20

Flowers

Vaughan Road

Ft. Wadsworth

Peebles

33
35

Poplar Spring Church

19

10

9

8

Route 673

34

Clements

Poplar Spring Rd.

Globe Tavern

Army of the Potomac - MEADE
II Corps - HANCOCK
MILES
- 1 - Glenny
- 2 - McGee
- 3 - Lynch

GIBBON
- 4 - Egan
- 5 - Murphy
- 6 - Smyth

Miscellaneous
- 15 - Pulford
- 16 - Robison
- 17 - Collis
- 18 - Walsh

Globe Tavern - CRAWFORD
FERRERO
- 7 - Russell
- 8 - Stearns

Detachment V Corps

New Troops
- 9 - { 185th N.Y.
       210th Pa.

BAXTER
- 10 - McCoy
- 11 - Coulter
- 12 - 94th N.Y.
- 19 - Bragg

Engineers
- 13 - Spaulding
- 14 - Harwood

V Corps - WARREN
AYRES
- 20 - Hofmann
- 21 - Graham
- 22 - Grimshaw
- 23 - { 15th N.Y. Heavy Artillery
        146th N.Y.
- 24 - Grindlay

GRIFFIN
- 25 - Gregory
- 26 - Sickel
- 27 - Bartlett

IX Corps - PARKE
POTTER
- 28 - Curtin
- 29 - S. Griffin

WILLCOX
- 30 - McLaughlen
- 31 - Harriman
- 32 - Hartranft

MOTT
- 33 - McAllister
- 34 - DeTrobriand
- 35 - Pierce

Cavalry
- 36 - Gregg

Confederate Forces - HILL
III Corps - HILL
MAHONE
- E - Weiseger
- F - King
- G - Harris
- H - Finegan
- J - Gibson
- K - F. Archer

HETH
- L - J. Archer
- P - Cooke
- Q - J.R. Davis
- R - MacRae

WILCOX
- M - McGowan
- N - Lane

JOHNSON
- A - McAfee
- B - Gracie
- C - Goode
- D - Wallace

Cavalry Corps - HAMPTON
Independent
- O - J. Griffin

W.H.F. LEE
- S - Barringer
- V - J.L. Davis

BUTLER
- T - { Young
        Stokes
- U - Waring

COMMENTARY

1. This map reveals the defensive posture of both sides that marked the end of the Battle of Poplar Spring Church. Hill has managed to retain possession of Petersburg and to interpose eight brigades across Meade's path but has failed to recover the lost ground, which the Northerners are now incorporating into their line of works.

2. Of Hampton's corps, only "Rooney" Lee's two brigades are located with certainty.

3. The relative positions of the 210th Pennsylvania and 185th New York are uncertain.

4. The locations of James Archer and Harris are not definite.

5. The length of most brigades' sectors is only approximate.

function of covering the supply line from the depot past Dinwiddie
Court House to Petersburg. As long as the Northerners actively threatened, however, Hampton felt it unwise to resume this duty full scale.
Instead of letting small patrols cover his front while most of his men
rested in camp, he kept his brigades at the front, concentrated and
combat-ready, to take part in any new flare-up of fighting during the
Fifth Offensive.[41]

But that attack never came. The responsible generals in both armies
had already decided against renewing the battle. Hill had, in effect,
renounced the offensive on Saturday after Heth's defeat. During that
day, too, Grant's resolve had wavered, and by Sunday morning, he
firmly opposed additional fighting. Subsequent events on October 2
brought Meade, also, to this line of thinking. Only Lee wished to continue active operations, and he concerned himself almost entirely with
affairs north of the James. Just briefly did he consider renewing fighting
on the Southside. Ever since Saturday night, Johnson had urged a
counterattack against the attenuated II Corps while most Union forces
were away on the far right and far left. Dunn's Hill evidently forwarded this suggestion to the army commander on October 3. The following day Lee encouraged such an attack, in conjunction with a blow
by Hampton against the left flank or rear. The lieutenant general, however, evidently judged such a move impracticable, and his chief, increasingly absorbed in operations on the Peninsula, deferred to his
assessment. Even had such a counterattack occurred on Wednesday or
later, moreover, it would have constituted an entirely new battle, not a
continuation of the current one. By Sunday night, the four ranking participants had concluded that they could gain nothing further from
prolonging present operations. They thus renounced the offensive and
concentrated on consolidating their gains. The Battle of Poplar Spring
Church, accordingly, came to an end.[42]

Operations on October 2 cost the Butternuts about 63 casualties at
the outside and the Federals approximately 142, of which Mott
suffered 89.[43] During all four days of battle, the Yankees had lost 2,898
men in their strike force and perhaps 52 more east of the Weldon
Railroad—a total of 2,950. The over-all Secessionist casualties came to
approximately 1,310, including 1,239 in the field force and 71 right
around the Cockade City.[44]

By paying this price, the Bluecoats destroyed the Squirrel Level
Line, which had threatened to confine them to Globe Tavern. They
also seized the key road junctions at Peebles's farm and forced Lee to
extend his already thin line about five miles farther southwest to
Hatcher's Run. The Virginian could ill afford such losses. Yet he could
take consolation that they had been no worse. The grave danger that

saving his capital might cost him not merely his outer line of works but also his communications and his rail center had not come to pass. Peebles's farm had been lost, true, but the Boydton Plank Road and the Southside Railroad were still safe. Their retention, in turn, gave Petersburg—and, therefore, Richmond—a new lease on life. Grant had gone into the Fifth Offensive hoping to capture one or both of those cities. Whatever his penultimate gains, he had not achieved his broader goals.

CHAPTER XV

Richmond Redeemed

October 2 marked the end of the Battles of Chaffin's Bluff and Poplar Spring Church. For Grant that date also marked the end of the entire Fifth Offensive. He thereafter concentrated on preparing an entirely new offensive against Richmond and Petersburg. Selecting targets, setting a date, most of all obtaining more men from the Shenandoah Valley and Northern recruiting depots were the prerequisites for this new attack. Absorbed with such considerations, he repeatedly rejected Butler's continued entreaties to prolong the Fifth Offensive with renewed attacks against the Confederate capital. Until the lieutenant general was ready to launch his Sixth Offensive, the Massachusetts man and Meade had to remain basically quiescent. Fortifying the recent conquests, firmly linking them to the old works, and redistributing troops to provide a more balanced defense were the two army commanders' principal activities throughout most of October.

The month did not, however, pass without more fighting. Unlike Grant, Lee was unwilling to terminate the Fifth Offensive. The Virginian was, admittedly, reconciled to the stalemate he had achieved around Petersburg. On the Peninsula, though, he still attempted to reduce or eliminate the danger to Richmond. He had checked the Army of the James tactically on September 29 but had signally failed to drive it back the following afternoon. On October 7, he originated another attack against it—the last time he ever took the strategic initiative in quest of positive offensive victory. Again, he was severely defeated in the First Battle of the Darbytown Road. That combat provoked the Second Battle of the Squirrel Level Road south of Petersburg the next day—a little battle that reassured each side that fighting a big battle on the Southside was not then worthwhile. More importantly, the battle of October 7 finally forced Lee to abandon efforts to drive the Bluecoats from the Northside. He thereafter sought to contain them by erecting new defenses northward from Fort Gilmer to the old Exterior Line south of the Charles City Road. Unaware of the extent of these new fortifications, Grant made a limited effort to break them up in the Second Battle of the Darbytown Road, on October 13. The attempt failed, and he was unwilling to commit greater force or to advance the timetable for his Sixth Offensive in order to destroy them.

Thereafter each side completed their works without interruption. The entire Tidewater front became increasingly quiescent. Not until October 27 would a new offensive be launched. By October 16–19, the Fifth Offensive was over.[1]

The Fifth Offensive was, of course, one phase of the over-all Siege of Petersburg. It came close to being the decisive phase—to costing Lee his rail center, even his capital. But as matters worked out, he averted such calamities and won both cities another half year of life. The offensive, therefore, ranks as only one aspect of the siege. It brought the Yankees no great victories, but it did enable them to overrun three forward Confederate lines, to conquer strategic sectors on both sides of the James, and to tighten their grip on both cities.

The Fifth Offensive thus takes its place in the ongoing course of the siege. Yet the operations of September 29–October 19 also represent virtually a distinct campaign of their own. After five weeks of quiescence, they erupted as two massive attacks on both sides of the James. Those first four days of heavy fighting, in turn, generated strategic instability that prolonged the "campaign" into midmonth. Yet by mid-October the progressive restoration of strategic equilibrium caused the opposing sides to become increasingly inactive. Slowly, probably imperceptibly to the participants, the Fifth Offensive blended into another period of quiescence, which lasted until the launching of a new offensive/"campaign" on October 27. Yet what was often unnoticeable to the participants is clear to the historian: Each offensive constitutes a distinct phase, or minicampaign, in the over-all course of the siege. It is thus possible not only to describe but also to analyze each offensive in its own right. This chapter will assess the strategy, tactics, and generalship of the Fifth Offensive, with emphasis on its two opening battles.[2]

The strategic origin and course of the Fifth Offensive reveal the continuing impact of events in the Shenandoah Valley on operations of the main armies in eastern Virginia. In 1861 and 1862, such events had

decisively affected major campaigns east of the Blue Ridge. It is, therefore, understandable that Lee hoped for comparable results in 1864
and that Grant was vigilant against them.

This time, though, operations in the Valley proved only a distraction,
not a fatal blow, to the Federal commander. Their most serious short-
range impact was that they forced him to divert seven veteran divisions
there, four of which were among his best. Consequently, throughout
the Fifth Offensive he had to operate with less strength than desirable.
This was particularly true of his cavalry. He reduced his original numerical superiority in that branch to virtual parity and then placed
himself at an actual disadvantage, especially on the Southside, by drib-
bling many of his remaining troopers out among the infantry. The
Yankee horsemen, to be sure, remained strong enough to hold their
own and to cover the infantry but not to force their way through
Hampton's and Gary's lines. Not until the Northern First and Third
cavalry divisions returned from the Valley in March 1865 would Grant
regain sufficient offensive striking power in his mounted force to deal
the enemy heavy blows. Even among the infantry, moreover, the diversion of the VI Corps and the XIX Corps to the Valley left fewer men
to outflank the Confederate lines. His drives for Richmond and the
Southside Railroad on September 29–30 might have fared better, had
some of those absent troops taken part.[8]

In the long run, however, sending strong forces to the Valley served
the Union well. They eventually achieved major victories there that not
only crippled the Confederate army and destroyed valuable Southern
supplies and supply lines but also inspirited the Northern people. The
first two such successes were won in late September. They had a direct
bearing on the Fifth Offensive. They initially made Grant consider that
the Butternuts might abandon the Shenandoah and concentrate against
him. But within a matter of days, they caused him to launch his own
attack one week ahead of schedule in order to prevent the detachment
of more Secessionists to the Valley or else to take advantage of their
absence. Earlier in the war, battles beyond the Blue Ridge had forced
the main Union army in the East to retreat. Now they prompted it to
attack.

Clearly the old Confederate strategy was no longer working. Simply
diverting enemy forces to the Valley could be helpful only in the short
run. For the strategy really to succeed, such diversion would have to
result in Southern victory somewhere: victory in the Shenandoah, victory in the Tidewater, at the very least the assurance of being able to
beat off each new Yankee onslaught on both fronts. Yet nowhere were
such victories gained. Early proved unable to achieve them in the Valley once the Federal divisions from the Tidewater bolstered the local

forces there. Sending him additional troops from Petersburg, moreover, still did not produce success. As late as September 27, on the eve of the Fifth Offensive, the Laurel Brigade rode off to the Shenandoah—to Tom's Brook and Cedar Creek. Had it remained with Hampton, it might have increased his success on September 29 and diminished his defeat two days later or made it no defeat at all.

Far more serious than the troopers' departure was the absence of Kershaw. His transfer from the Peninsula to the piedmont in mid-August had strengthened the Army of the Valley but had not resulted in the major victory for which Lee had hoped. The Virginian, there-fore, ordered him back to the Tidewater, apparently to participate in an attack directly against Grant. Hardly had the division left Early, though, before Sheridan capitalized on its absence to win two major battles and overrun much of the Valley. These reverses, in turn, caused Kershaw to be diverted back to the Shenandoah. He thus left the Val-ley too soon to help Early but went back there too soon to aid Lee.

Lee consequently went into the Fifth Offensive desperately short of manpower. Kershaw's Division could have significantly reduced this handicap. Even had its projected attack against Grant never occurred, its mere defensive presence in its old sector would have rendered the Northside far less vulnerable on September 29. Starting out with eight brigades there instead of four, moreover, would have necessitated send-ing far fewer reinforcements from Petersburg. The supply lines would thus have been much better guarded than they actually were on Sep-tember 30. By the same token, Kershaw's absence nearly resulted in disaster on both sides of the James. Only through incredible bravery, bold generalship, skillful tactics, and repeated Yankee failure to capi-talize on great opportunities did the Confederates escape such disaster in the Fifth Offensive.

Thus, whereas the diversion of Northern troops to the Valley was a hindrance to Grant, the diversion of Butternut forces to there was an almost fatal loss to Lee. Ironically, it was a loss of his own making, for it was he who kept diverting Kershaw's Division from where it was needed. Earlier in the war, initiating bold, risky maneuvers had pro-duced great results. Now they came close to producing disaster. Less spectacular maneuvers were called for in the late summer and autumn of 1864. For Lee to hold his own, to repulse bloodily each Union probe, and to demonstrate convincingly the futility of the enemy war effort might have so increased Yankee war weariness as to produce peace. Maintaining the tactical equilibrium in the Tidewater was the key to this restrained but promising approach. Yet Lee jeopardized that equilibrium in order to conduct his old plan of grand strategy along the Blue Ridge. Misusing Kershaw that way gained him nothing and came close to costing him his rail center and his capital. It was one of the worst miscalculations he ever made.

Criticizing Lee's approach is not to criticize his basic strategy of holding on to Richmond and Petersburg. Recent indictments of him for not abandoning the capital and all of Virginia in order to retire far into the hinterland—say, North Carolina or even Alabama—are unfair and unrealistic. Defending the Old Dominion reflects not the folly of a Virginian's parochialism but the wisdom of a Confederate's sound strategy. The commonwealth was a major source for men, horses, food, and salt, and its capital was a center of war industry. By 1864, furthermore, Richmond had become an important symbol at home and abroad of Southern claims to independence. Lee was right in continuing to defend these valuable tangible and symbolic assets. He encountered difficulty only in his choice of methods: in seeking another great victory through bold grand-strategic maneuver rather than in letting the Bluecoats defeat themselves if he could just maintain the tactical equilibrium.

The army commander, of course, undertook these risky operations in hopes of wresting the strategic initiative from the Northerners and then translating that accomplishment into major victories. Yet he not only failed to win the desired triumphs on the battlefield but, except for a few weeks in July, did not even succeed in holding the strategic initiative. At the end of September—indeed, almost without interruption from the crossing of the Rapidan to the arrival at Appomattox Court House—Grant retained that valuable asset. It was not Lee but the Illinoisan who decided the fundamental questions of when, where, why, and how to attack.

In choosing the time and the place of attack, the lieutenant general displayed considerable flexibility during the Fifth Offensive. He readily advanced the date of attack from October 5 to September 29 in response to operations in the Valley. Then too, he unhesitatingly postponed the expedition to Cape Fear in favor of a drive on the Peninsula, once Butler convinced him of the promising prospects there. Yet in varying the sites for advancing, the General-in-Chief did not alter his fundamental designation of targets. Despite what he told Washington, he did not strike on September 29 principally to influence events in the Valley but to continue pursuing his own objectives in the Tidewater. On opening his operations in the East nearly five months earlier, he had marked the destruction of the Army of Northern Virginia as his main goal. By the fall of 1864, however, Richmond and Petersburg had supplanted that army as his principal immediate objectives. During the Fifth Offensive, as earlier in the siege, he directed his operations toward capturing those two centers of government, industry, and communications. Taking them would deal the Confederacy a serious, if not mortal, blow. Their fall might also net him the Southern army. At the least, seizing the capital and its rail center would force that army out of its works into the open field, where he could resume his efforts to destroy it.

The Illinoisan did not expect to achieve such success against the cities and their defenders through one great battle. He rather sought victory that summer and autumn through a strategy of attrition. That strategy is often misunderstood. In practicing it, he is mistakenly regarded as the modern Xerxes, who unthinkingly hurled his men to their deaths by thousands in the knowledge that every few hundred enemy soldiers he killed in the process weakened the foe by that much.

This "Grant the Butcher" is a mythical character out of folklore, not history. His conduct of operations from the Wilderness through First Petersburg is not self-evident folly but the understandable consequence of his experience in the West. From Fort Donelson through the second day at Shiloh and on through Vicksburg to Missionary Ridge, he gained major triumphs and made his reputation by carrying the war to the enemy strategically and tactically. It is hardly surprising that he initially continued in Virginia the approach that had earned him promotion and the opportunity to confront Robert E. Lee. Six weeks of bloody campaigning, however, convinced the lieutenant general that such tactics were not efficacious in this theater. Therefore, once he beleaguered the Cockade City, he abandoned them in favor of turning the Secessionists' flanks or attacking their weak points but avoiding frontally assaulting defenses well prepared and well manned. The Fifth Offensive burst forth in just such combined turning-attacking operations against vulnerable Confederate sectors on the Northside and at Peebles's farm. It continued as long as there appeared some prospect of fighting the enemy out in the open and then died down, so far as Union commanders were concerned, when there seemed no alternative to charging strong, well-defended fortifications. "Grant the Butcher" was too protective of the lives of his men to throw them away in attacks on such formidable works as loomed across his path by October 1–2.

His war of attrition is not to be found in the nonexistent tactics of the slaughterpen but in the nonrelaxing tenacity of strategic pressure. He fixed the Southerners in place—not on the battlefield but in the strategic arena—and then wore them down in that context. The daily toll from sniping and shelling was part of this process. The intermittent battles, with their resulting losses of Confederate men and territory— far from representing the totality of the strategy of attrition—were but another of its weapons. And the very loss of strategic mobility resulting from being pinned in place was itself a major contributing factor to the decline of the Army of Northern Virginia. The entire siege and the

Fifth Offensive make clear that the war of attrition was no more mind-less butchery than it was brilliant genius. Rather was the war of attri-tion a process for defeating the foe and winning the war—a process that, like Grant himself, was intelligent, careful, unrelenting, effective, and sure.

Yet City Point did not see victory coming only at some distant date when the last Confederate regiment had been pared down to impo-tence. Attrition sought rather to weaken the Graycoats to some inter-mediate degree between power and nullity where battle would cease to be a mere tool in a process and become, instead, the instrument of vic-tory. The bold goals Grant first set for the Fifth Offensive—taking Petersburg or Richmond or both—show that he thought such a crucial stage had been reached.

The particular strategy he devised for achieving those major objec-tives in the Fifth Offensive, moreover, marks a key phase in the evolu-tion of his conduct of operations within the basic framework of the war of attrition. From the time he settled down before Petersburg following the First Battle of the Weldon Railroad, his strategy for taking the two cities slowly but progressively evolved in search of an approach that would bring strategic victory. Initially that summer and on through the autumn, he strove for such victory through a two-pronged attack north and south of the James, aimed at throwing the Butternuts off guard in one quarter or the other, more likely in the Petersburg sector, where he always hoped to make his greater gains.

Critics then and since have complained that such diffusion of power among two wings and an inactive center left each Federal strike force too weak to achieve more than limited victories, if even those. These critics have contended that a concentration of force for a first-strike grand victory, rather than a second-strike more uncertain success, offered greater promise. Some have even suggested that this first strike should have cut loose its clutch on Petersburg and used virtually the entire army for a bold turning operation around the Confederate right. The latter criticism, however, neglects the positive contribution that the Union "entrenched camp" east of Petersburg made to an offensive strategy. That complaint also overrates the ability of the Army of the Potomac to continue making grand-strategic sweeps. The need to rest and recoup from the ordeal of spring forced upon the Northerners a more restrained offensive strategy. Even so, such a strategy could still have been first-strike, rather than two-pronged. Along that line, it is, indeed, tempting to speculate how the Fifth Offensive would have worked out if Griffin, Ayres, and Smith had joined in Butler's attack while Meade initially remained on the defensive. It is also appealing to conjecture about Grant's originally projected drive of October 5 against the Southside Railroad, though that operation, facing more and immediately available reserves, seems less promising than a massive drive on the Peninsula.[4]

But, of course, the offensive of September 29–October 2 did not work out according to either of those patterns. It is, therefore, more pertinent to examine its place in the evolution of Grant's conduct of operations. His initial two-pronged attack at the end of July involved a first strike from Deep Bottom that began and ended before his left wing even started attacking. By the time he launched his Fourth Offensive from that bridgehead in mid-August, he again held back his left wing until heavy fighting on the Northside was over. That time, though, he kept most of his right wing on the Peninsula, at least to continue threatening Field and at one point almost to resume attacking him. The timing of the two blows came even closer together by September 29. The General-in-Chief, to be sure, did no more than contemplate unleashing the Army of the Potomac that day, but he at least held it ready. Then he sent it into action on the thirtieth, soon enough, it seemed, to take advantage of the departure of so many defenders to counter Butler's breakthrough of the previous day. By the time of his next onslaught, on October 27, he at last sent his two wings forward simultaneously. That zenith of the dual approach surely represents the deliberate culmination of the past four months' experience. Its total failure, one should add, reoriented his planning toward the one-pronged, grand onslaught. Together, Chaffin's Bluff and Poplar Spring Church were thus an important step in the progression toward the new approach that ultimately led to the capture of the two cities.

Beyond its place in the development of Grant's generalship, his handling of his two wings during the Fifth Offensive itself invites examination. He opened the operation with wings of virtually equal strength but soon considered many options for varying their weighting. On Thursday night, he promised Butler to reinforce the Army of the James with two corps should Meade carry Petersburg the next day. Just half an hour later, City Point instructed the Pennsylvanian not to try for even the Southside Railroad, let alone the Cockade City, on Friday unless a great opportunity developed or until the Army of the James could reinforce him. Then the following evening, the General-in-Chief supposedly hinted to Meade that the Army of the Potomac should continue attacking on Saturday, yet at the same time he promised the Massachusetts man another corps on the first or second, if conditions at Petersburg remained unchanged. The proposals, though widely varying, are not contradictory. Neither unclear thinking nor infixity of purpose explain them. Throughout the Fifth Offensive, the Illinoisan consistently gave priority to blows on the Southside. He thought of bolstering the Army of the James only when greater goals elsewhere were attained or unattainable. His varying proposals to alter the weighting of the wings thus reflect creditably upon him: They show flexibility in considering numerous strategic approaches that might bring victory.

His two army commanders also faced problems of weighting in the domain of grand tactics. Meade had to decide how many brigades to commit to the strike force and how many to keep in the fortifications. With hindsight, one can say that he at first left too many units in his works, even within the requirements of the "entrenched camp" strategy. By Saturday, he managed to send four more brigades into the field. Surely at least two of them could have accompanied the initial advance on September 30, while the other two remained east of the Weldon Railroad but in reserve. Even having two more brigades with the field force would probably not have averted the debacle on Jones's farm, which was caused by fragmentation of force, not lack of force. Those extra troops, however, would have made the margin of security on Pegram's farm in late afternoon less precarious. They and the two reserve brigades, moreover, would probably have enabled Meade to carry out his hope to advance on October 1. He would not have had to wait all day for reinforcements, since half of them would already have been at the front and the others would not have needed as much time to get there. He thus seriously handicapped his offensive operations both days by not originally assigning enough troops to the strike force.[5]

Such a mistake did not mar Butler's grand tactics. He used virtually the entire Army of the James for his initial onslaught. The handful of veteran regiments left behind could hardly have affected the outcome, and the big Provisional Brigade was too inexperienced to take the field. He nevertheless made an even more serious error in weighting than Meade. The Massachusetts man made his right wing almost twice as strong as his left, even though the latter force would have greater opportunities to put manpower to good use. He of course could not have known beforehand that the right wing would delay so long at New Market Heights. Yet he should have understood that once the outer lines were carried, the left wing would reach the common second objective (Fort Maury-Fort Gilmer) long before the more easterly right wing could get there. His intelligence system, moreover, should have made him realize that Ord had much greater prospects for breaking through a weak sector than Birney did on a relatively strong one. Both logistical and tactical considerations thus suggested that the left wing should have been stronger.

Had the X Corps reached Bermuda Hundred on September 27, it could have constituted the left wing while the weaker XVIII Corps moved up to Deep Bottom. Having the two corps cross each other's line of march on Wednesday night, however, was out of the question.

Even so, Holman and Duncan could have rejoined Ord, leaving only the garrison of Deep Bottom to serve with the right wing. Their five regiments could well have made the difference on Chaffin's farm. They could have done what Heckman should have done: follow Stannard into the entrenched camp and then immediately spearhead a drive toward the second-stage objectives. But Paine's Negroes were not available for that promising task. They were tied down in the huge, largely inactive right wing, only two of whose eleven brigades were heavily engaged in early morning. Misallocating his forces this way was a serious blunder by Butler.

However weighted, Butler's wings initially sought victory through penetrating the enemy position. Such advances repeatedly succeeded: grand tactically up the Varina Road, tactically at Fort Harrison, derivatively at New Market Heights. The Yankees, though, consistently failed to exploit the advantages such breakthroughs offered. Instead of moving through the breach, fanning out over the rear, and rolling up the interior flanks, they reverted to frontal attacks. From Forts Hoke and Maury, through Forts Gregg and Johnson, to Fort Gilmer, such assaults failed.

Lee, too, met defeat in the frontal attacks he launched against Forts Harrison and Bratton and against Pegram's farmyard. For him, though, such charges were aberrations. His favorite offensive tactic was the flank attack. Again and again during the Fifth Offensive, as earlier in the siege, such flanking movements brought him victory. The overthrow of Simon Griffin, both of Curtin's demibrigades, Hartranft, and Hofmann was due to flank attacks or double envelopments. Even the attacks against Pegram's and Chappell's farms were projected as flank attacks. They failed only because the interposition of Federal troops athwart the flankers' line of advance reduced the charges to frontal assaults.

The woods and ravines of Dinwiddie County were well suited for concealing such flanking movements. The heavily fortified field of Chaffin's Bluff, together with the relative paucity of Graycoats there, afforded far fewer such opportunities. Moore's blow against Fairchild in midmorning and Montague's counterattack against Stannard in late afternoon on September 29 were the only flank attacks the Confederates made that day. Though successful, they were too limited in force and field to produce results like those gained on the Southside. On the following day, moreover, Lee apparently felt that seeking out either enemy flank was too risky, with the fate of Richmond still at stake. He instead chose to counterattack frontally in hopes of penetrating the Union center. Like most frontal charges the preceding day, his attack was bloodily repulsed.

The flank attacks by Lee and head-on charges by Butler were synthesized in the tactics of Meade. The Pennsylvanian repeatedly projected a direct advance to pin and defeat the Secessionists on the field while a mobile column moved through the unfortified country farther south to turn and envelop their right. Each day he planned such moves, yet each day the exigencies of battle forestalled them. At Peebles's farm, the frontal force carried the position before the flanking column could get into place. At Jones's farm, the frontal force disintegrated due to poor handling and enemy counterattack long before Davies could ride up from the south. On Saturday the flanking cavalry got into position on Route 673, but the frontal force refused to budge. At Pegram's the next day, no enemy remained to fall victim to such tactics. And when the Butternuts were finally located on the Harman Road on Sunday, they appeared able to outflank the flankers. Such a threat, together with the obvious winding down of the entire battle, caused the projected frontal-flanking attack to degenerate into a feeble reconnaissance in force.

The differing degrees of success each general achieved with his chosen tactical method suggest several conclusions as to the efficacy of various kinds of attacks—indeed, of the whole matter of offense versus defense. Clearly, no one tactical approach gave assurance of victory. Frontal charges were the most likely to fail yet offered the greatest prospects when they succeeded. Flank attacks were the most promising yet were often impracticable to carry through or even attempt. Surprise obviously aided attackers but was usually difficult to achieve, particularly after the first day of battle and especially for attackers, as opposed to counterattackers.

Tactical formation, too, offered little guarantee of victory. Columnar formation succeeded for Stannard but not for Draper. Lines of battle did Foster, William Birney, Dick Anderson, Potter, and Heth no good. Griffin and Wilcox, however, repeatedly succeeded with linear formations. Even the two great Northern charges that broke the enemy outer lines suggest differing lessons. Roberts was sure that he carried Fort Harrison because he advanced so slowly under Confederate fire as not to tire his men. An officer at Meade's headquarters, in contrast, attributed the storming of Fort Archer to Griffin's surging forward as fast as possible, sacrificing tactical formation in order to minimize his exposure to Southern fire.[6]

Even the relative state of attack versus defense did not assure the outcome. Defenders, of course, enjoyed many advantages by this period of the war, especially if they were fortified and had good fields of fire. Tactical stability of defense was also a key element. Weitzel on September 30 and Ayres the next day enjoyed such stability. Their forces were adequate; their fronts were protected; their flanks were secure. All they had to do was keep their men in place and mow down every head-on charge made against them.

Lack of stability comparably handicapped the Butternuts in resisting the initial attacks by the Army of the James. Divided command, misallocation of weak manpower, and poorly designed and equipped works caused them to have to defend Fort Harrison at a terrible disadvantage.[7] Yet even such instability did not prevent them from holding their inner works for the rest of that day. By shifting their handful of men from one sector to another and creating an impromptu defense line wherever the danger was greatest, they secured the position from Fort Maury to Fort Gilmer. Comparable instability marked the seesaw fighting up and down the Church Road the following afternoon. There, however, the instability was not that of a fluctuating defense but of clashing offenses. Once Peebles's farm had been overrun, both sides meant to attack. Defensive tactics then became mere responses of the moment as one army or the other temporarily relinquished the initiative. Yet even in such aggressive operations, the defensive played a key role at two crucial times. The defense line beyond Jones's helped dissuade Parke from driving for the plank road and thus gave Wilcox time to counterattack. What finally stopped that counterattack, moreover, was the defense line the Federals finally put together through the middle of Pegram's farm just before dark.

Yet it was not whether an army was in an offensive or a defensive posture that ultimately determined the outcome—any more than did deployment or tactics. The determining factor was not availability of force but co-ordination of force. The attacks that succeeded—whatever their deployment or tactics—did so because they were well co-ordinated. Stannard's thorough planning and Roberts' skillful execution caused virtually all the First Division of the XVIII Corps to be concentrated against Fort Harrison on Thursday morning. Griffin comparably massed his entire command against Fort Archer the following afternoon. And Wilcox similarly used his whole force to hurl back the Union advance toward the Boydton Plank Road later on September 30. The North Carolinian succeeded as long as he kept his command together, and he was finally checked only when his command became exhausted and fragmented just as the Bluecoats were at last uniting their efforts to stop him.

By the same token, the tactical failures are invariably marked by lack of co-ordination of force. The Graycoats were initially afflicted with this problem in trying to defend Fort Harrison. Most of their few available forces were misallocated to the extreme flanks, and not enough remained to guard the center at the fort. The Yankees, however, were the ones who repeatedly suffered on September 29 from such lack of co-ordination. Birney at New Market Heights and again before Fort Gilmer, Ord in initially trying to exploit the first break-through on Chaffin's farm, and Heckman as both division and corps commander made this mistake. Stannard along the Diagonal Line and Foster north of Fort Gilmer endured a variant of this same short-coming. Instead of failing to use all their men still at the front, they were handicapped by having lost too many soldiers behind the front for their attacks to remain effective. The Vermonter had at least lost his men to good cause in Childrey's field and Fort Harrison. The Indianian had no such excuse; shameful straggling was what caused his division to melt away. William Birney similarly lacked any justification for his gross misuse of forces: trying to carry with battalions, committed one at a time, works that had repulsed divisions. The Confederates suffered the same problem the next day. Their promising prospects of recaptur-ing Fort Harrison were lost as Anderson's corps and both of its divi-sions fell apart in trying to charge. Well might Lee's Chief-of-Staff write with disgust: "Our effort to retake it was not an energetic nor sys-tematic one. We could & should have retaken it, but matters were not executed as well as they were planned."[8]

The story on the Southside was the same. Joel Griffin, heavily out-numbered at best, apparently left one of his three regiments too far left to help defend Peebles's farm. Wilcox, trying to retake Pegram's farm on Friday, and Heth, attempting to overrun Chappell's the next day, were comparably handicapped by unavailability of or failure to use all their troops. The most egregious case of all was the whole Northern effort to reach the Boydton Plank Road on September 30. The 24,000-man strike force fragmented so badly that just one demibrigade, a mere 1,200 to 1,300 soldiers, actually attempted to get to that highway. Such failure to co-ordinate forces not only doomed that effort but also ena-bled the Secessionists to defeat brigade after brigade in detail and nearly to regain all they had lost since early afternoon.

Such lack of co-ordination was a sure way to doom an attack or to nullify the many advantages of the defense. Co-ordination of force, on the other hand, was the best means for utilizing all the inherent strengths of being on the defense. Virtually the only chance for over-coming all these defensive advantages was for attackers to co-ordinate potential power into actual force simultaneously applied. That princi-ple of co-ordination, more than any other, explains the outcome of vir-tually all the fighting during the Fifth Offensive.

Such co-ordination or lack thereof centers on infantry operations. The foot soldier was still the Queen of Battles, particularly in the at-tack. During the Civil War, artillery played only a minor role on the offensive, and that usually of negligible effect. This pattern persisted

51. Gouverneur K. Warren

52. Charles S. Wainwright

THE V ARMY CORPS

53. Charles Griffin

54. Romeyn B. Ayres

55. John G. Parke

56. John Albert Monroe

THE IX ARMY CORPS

57. Orlando Bolivar Willcox

58. Robert B. Potter

59. David M. Gregg

60. Gershom Mott

REINFORCERS OF THE FIELD FORCE

DEFENDERS OF THE UNION CENTER

61. Samuel W. Crawford

62. Edward Ferrero

63. Winfield Scott Hancock

64. John G. Hazard

THE II ARMY CORPS

65. Nelson A. Miles

66. John Gibbon

MHRC

67. Andrew A. Humphreys

MHRC

68. Henry J. Hunt

ARMY OF THE POTOMAC STAFF

69. Seth Williams

MHRC

70. Henry W. Benham

MHRC

71. Wade Hampton

72. W. H. F. ("Rooney") Lee

THE SOUTHERN CAVALRY CORPS

73. Matthew C. Butler

74. Pierce M. B. Young

VHS

75. Henry Heth

LC

76. Cadmus Marcellus Wilcox

DEFENDERS OF THE BOYDTON PLANK ROAD

77. James J. Archer

MHRC

78. William J. Pegram

CM

79. William Mahone

80. Bushrod R. Johnson

DEFENDERS OF PETERSBURG

81. Henry A. Wise

82. Reuben Lindsay Walker

through the Fifth Offensive. The Army of the James used its artillery offensively only twice, before Jourdan's second charge on Thursday and during Terry's reconnaissance on Saturday. Federal cannoneers on the Southside were similarly restrained. Out of several projected attacks, Sunday's fight at W. W. Davis' was the only one in which they actually participated. Alexander, Pegram, and Chew, in contrast, did use their guns more aggressively. The lieutenant colonel's guns may even have played a role in breaking up the Second Division of the IX Corps on Friday. None of those officers, though, succeeded in softening up the main Yankee positions on Chaffin's, Pegram's, Chappell's, Wyatt's, or McDowell's. Despite the bombardments those positions remained strong enough to repulse charges by the Butternut infantry and cavalry.

It was on the defensive that artillery was so effective. It lent weight to defense lines at New Market Heights, Pegram's farm, Fort Bratton, and McDowell's. It helped bluff down threats to Richmond on Thursday and Saturday and to the Boydton Plank Road on Friday and Sunday. Through mutually defensive shellings it played a major role in assuring the tactical quiescence of the sector east of Petersburg. Even where ultimately unsuccessful in stopping attacks, it so crippled the captors of Fort Harrison that they could not exploit their victory. But its greatest service was in containing the Bluecoats' breakthrough on Chaffin's farm. Virtually unaided, artillerists anchored the Confederate right until Snowden could arrive. Together with DuBose and Bass, cannoneers beat off every thrust at Forts Johnson, Gregg, and Gilmer. Rarely has the long arm rendered such a contribution to its cause as in saving Richmond on September 29.

The artillery was thus relegated to a largely defensive role. Mounted troops were shunted even farther aside—except in dire emergencies, almost entirely off the field of battle. Kautz, indeed, was twice detached from the main army, first for a raid, then for a reconnaissance against Richmond. His absence did his army no harm, for the lack of danger to its flanks during the Battle of Chaffin's Bluff obviated the need to screen those areas. He might have done some good, had he boldly pressed the attack and overrun the Intermediate Line on the Darbytown Road on Thursday morning. But his literal reading of orders and his hesitant, inept leadership caused him to overlook these opportunities and to accomplish nothing. No loss, no gain—it was the same old story for Kautz.

David Gregg also spent September 29 on detached raiding. Thereafter, though, he worked in close and effective conjunction with the main army. Defensively, he screened and protected its left rear. Offensively, he prepared to join its advance toward the plank road on each of the next three days. Yet except for the First Brigade's reconnaissance out

Route 673 on Saturday morning, he was never able to carry out his offensive role. The defeat of the infantry, the unwillingness of their commanders to advance, and the need to meet Hampton's superior numbers farther south kept thwarting Gregg's efforts to take part in the grand drive for the supply lines. Few of these factors were the Pennsylvanian's fault. And as his mission became increasingly defensive—whatever the over-all posture of the army—he became increasingly effective in securing the left rear.

Like the Second Cavalry Division, Hampton worked in close cooperation with the main army. Guarding the supply lines, helping block the Union infantry, and defeating the Northern troopers were his responsibilities. His numerical superiority enabled him to secure the communications and to fight both the enemy infantry and cavalry. He did not, however, sufficiently outnumber Gregg that he could succeed against both. The South Carolinian could block the blue horsemen, push them back, even pummel them at Wyatt's, but he could not crush them and force his way into the infantry's left rear. His greatest service against the Federal foot soldiers was directed toward their front and flank, not their rear. On Friday and Sunday he nearly paralyzed their move toward the Boydton Plank Road by threatening their exposed left flank. Also on both days he helped man the works blocking their front. And on the thirtieth he even delivered the *coup de grâce* to Curtin's three forward regiments. Superiority of numbers and mobility enabled him to achieve all these against the infantry while still blocking the cavalry.

Gary, too, made use of his mobility to hasten from one sector to another in an effort to block the Union threats on the Peninsula. He served in the trenches at New Market Heights and Chaffin's farm, conducted an effective rear-guard action from the Exterior Line to Laurel Hill Church, and helped secure the Intermediate Line against Kautz's and Terry's supposed threats. The drastic emergency placed such unorthodox demands on cavalry. Their mobility and Gary's competence enabled them to meet such requirements.

Handling cavalry, artillery, and infantry; deploying forces; and conducting tactics and strategy are all functions of generalship. Generalship is exercised by "army group," army, and corps commanders. At the divisional level, generalship blends with leadership, and from brigade level down, leadership is the principal responsibility of command. The generalship of the Fifth Offensive must thus be examined from the divisional level up.

Many division commanders on the Southside performed well in these operations. Charles Griffin and Romeyn Ayres once more proved themselves master tacticians, able both to co-ordinate and to inspire their forces offensively and defensively. David Gregg performed with accustomed competence his varied missions of raiding, scouting, screening, and fighting. His hallmark continued to be not boldness but reliability. Everything that Birchett's expected he accomplished. Cadmus Wilcox went beyond expectations. He displayed perception, initiative, and skillful execution in responding to both danger and opportunity. Poplar Spring Church was the finest battle he ever fought.

His opposing division commander of similar name, Orlando Willcox, came through the Fifth Offensive with a more mixed record. Severely criticized for his generalship on July 30 but redeemed by his service on August 19, he showed elements of both such days on September 30. His division did not operate as a unit (largely through Parke's fault), and two of its brigades were badly beaten. Still, its Third Brigade opportunely helped turn the tide of the Confederate onrush, and the Michigander himself played a major role in establishing and holding together the successful defense of Pegram's yard. His fellow general of division in the IX Corps did not fare so well, though. Peremptory orders from corps headquarters excuse Potter's advance onto Jones's farm with both flanks in air, but he must take the blame for allowing his division to fragment there. The ensuing debacle marred his fine reputation. Heth had less of a reputation to mar, but his generalship on October 1 hardly enhanced it. His feeble, disjointed effort to overrun Chappell's speaks ill for him as a commander. His characteristic effort to pretend nothing untoward happened speaks ill for him as a man. Only on Sunday did he perform creditably in rushing troops to threatened sectors in time.

The division commanders on the Peninsula proved far less skillful than those at Petersburg. The debut of two such officers, Heckman and Foster, was disastrous. William Birney, with slightly more experience at their level, performed as poorly. They allowed their strength to wither away before they could bring it to bear. Such forces as did remain, moreover, they sent with ineffective formations against inappropriate targets. Paine squandered his strength almost as unwisely on September 29 but finally managed to occupy his goal by default. On Friday, though, the latter general handled his forces adequately in defending the curtains just right of Fort Harrison. Prime credit for holding those works, however, belongs to Stannard. He also deserves much of the praise for capturing them. He selected the massed formation and persuaded his wavering superior to charge on September 29. Once the First Division attacked, though, not he but his brigadiers (chiefly Roberts) were responsible for the minor tactics and leadership that produced victory. When the Vermonter himself had an opportunity to direct attacks along the lower Diagonal Line, he displayed hesitancy and lack of initiative in capitalizing on the great opportunity he had helped create.

The ablest tactician of the Army of the James, Terry, had minimal opportunity to participate tactically in the Battle of Chaffin's Bluff. His assignments were usually grand tactical. Being off on semi-independent missions was an unaccustomed and probably uncomfortable role. Bearing direct responsibility himself not just for minor tactics but also for the safety, conduct, and use of a detached column evidently made him hesitant. On Thursday afternoon he did not attack at all. Two days later he contented himself with skirmishing. Not until early 1865 would he be able to use such a force well. Kautz never would have that ability. He once more revealed lack of initiative and an inability even to recognize opportunity, let alone to exploit it. The Badener, as usual, did the Federals no good.[9]

Nor was the Southern side much brighter. Hoke, too, performed particularly ineptly. He once more failed to co-operate in a combined attack. He refused to budge before the prescribed time even though the attack was obviously beginning ahead of schedule. And he committed less than half his force when he finally did move forward. Field, also, hardly added to his reputation on September 30. He was, of course, not directly to blame that the Georgians advanced prematurely, thus disrupting his dispositions. Yet he must share the fault for expecting increasingly ineffective units to execute such complicated maneuvers while charging. Only his senior subordinate and acting demidivision commander, Gregg, came through the battle with reputation enhanced. Even the Texan made errors: not so much his decision to defend New Market Heights, a miscalculation inherent in the divided command structure on the Northside, but his constant shifting of DuBose's men back and forth along the New Market Line, thus keeping them out of action everywhere there. Gregg more than redeemed that mistake, though, by his brilliant, inspired, unyielding defense of the Fort Johnson–Fort Gilmer Line.

The absence of an over-all commander when fighting erupted on Thursday and the lack of co-ordination in the counterattack the next day reflect on the corps commander on the Peninsula, Anderson. He had gotten back from the Valley two days earlier yet had still not assumed command of the forward defenses when the battle began. Once he arrived in late morning, moreover, he apparently did not make such spectacular contributions to containing the Yankee breakthrough as Ewell and Gregg did. Then on September 30 Anderson allowed the grand counterattack to degenerate into disjointed charges that were defeated in detail. Once more, he failed to fulfill the responsibilities of his high office.[10]

His fellow South Carolinian Hampton, in contrast, continued proving the wisdom of his relatively recent elevation to corps command. He showed commendable initiative in retaining his Third Division in Dinwiddie County, in forging a new line to defend the Boydton Plank Road, and in overrunning Curtin's front line. He also displayed his capacity for breadth of command by fighting, usually successfully, on two widely separated sectors: against cavalry on the Vaughan and Duncan roads and against infantry on the Church and Harman roads. As often as he could, moreover, he waged such fighting offensively to keep potential attackers off balance and to drive them back. Such aggressiveness occasionally caused him to attack prematurely before his far-flung outfits could be massed against the foe. Nevertheless, his setbacks were only checks to his own advance, not ruptures of his defense. In his principal mission—stopping the Bluecoats short of the supply lines —he succeeded admirably.

No Union corps commander performed nearly as well as Hampton. Weitzel came closest, relatively speaking, in that he succeeded in his one task: defending Fort Harrison. Conducting a stabilized defense against disjointed frontal attacks upon a sector mostly fortified was, however, an almost elementary tactical exercise. It provided little opportunity to display the higher arts of generalship. When such opportunity came the Bavarian's way a month later, he would be found severely wanting.

The other corps commanders in the Army of the James, faced with greater challenges in the Battle of Chaffin's Bluff, did not need another month to fall short. The most conspicuous failure, of course, was Heckman. His inability to keep his division together was magnified when he took over the XVIII Corps. He scattered his troops, hurled them piecemeal against inappropriate targets, failed to seek out opportunities to pierce the Secessionist center, and personally behaved with reckless irresponsibility. Nor was Ord's generalship free from some of those weaknesses. He lost control of his Second Division in attacking Fort Harrison, and he took a terrible chance—foolhardy in retrospect —in personally leading the pursuit toward Fort Hoke. He also briefly displayed hesitancy and disobedience of orders in initially delaying in Cox's woods before charging the entrenched camp. For all that, though, he did succeed in grand-tactically penetrating the Butternuts' center, and he correctly understood how to exploit that breakthrough. Had he not rashly exposed himself to enemy fire, he might have carried out his plans to overrun the camp. Birney, too, exposed himself to Confederate fire, but with nothing to show for it. He started late from Petersburg, lost thousands of stragglers before reaching the battle zones, and then committed his surviving forces to battle disjointedly.

He remained an able division commander who was not rising to the greater demands of his higher office. By the end of September, it was becoming increasingly apparent that he was not maturing in corps command.

By then, considerable shortcomings were also evident in Parke's generalship. Although he had led a corps in battle only infrequently prior to Poplar Spring Church, his extensive service at senior headquarters should have fitted him for corps command. Yet his conduct of operations in early autumn left much to be desired. No gleam of tactical expertise brightened his record. He was overcautious when boldness was desirable, and rash when restraint was in order. His ill-co-ordinated mishandling of his corps on Friday afternoon was a major factor in dooming the Union advance toward the Boydton Plank Road. His reluctance to leave the safety of his works the next day similarly helped thwart his superiors' desire to renew the attack. Warren, willful as usual, shared the Pennsylvanian's reluctance to budge on October 1. The V Corps commander also displayed once more his extreme caution, hesitancy, and reluctance to accept responsibility for precipitating battle and exploiting initial successes. Below the grand-tactical level, though, the New Yorker again performed well, especially when the Butternuts forced battle upon him. Except for his decision to leave Hofmann's brigade on Pegram's farm until Saturday, his tactics were flawless. Few corps commanders then in Virginia could handle combat as well as Gouverneur Warren—if only a senior officer was around to free him from grand-tactical responsibility.

That officer might have been Meade. Yet army command in the Civil War did not entail direct control of the battle line. The army commander rather devised the basic plans, launched the operation, decided how to change and when to terminate it, and then allowed his senior subordinates to carry it out. Meade's conduct during the Fifth Offensive followed this pattern. He was nowhere near the front when fighting broke out on each day of the battle. On Friday and Saturday he did not reach the combat zone until well into the afternoon. Prior to that, he had to rely on messages from afar to urge his reluctant corps commanders to attack—admittedly, a more active role than City Point played but hardly an efficacious one. Even after he joined the troops, moreover, he left much of the conduct of operations to his subordinates without personally checking how well they were doing. His relations with them were not as abrasive as earlier in the year, though he was clearly displeased with Warren's delay on October 1 and probably with Ferrero's supposed lack of vigilance the next day. More to the point, the senior officer's relations with the corps commanders were less extensive, simply because he left them more on their own.

He instead concentrated on the broader questions of opening, pressing, and concluding the operation. There his strengths and weaknesses as a general became apparent. Soundness, not brilliance; trustworthiness, not audacity; steadfastness, not dash were his principal characteristics. His basic plan for striking west from Globe Tavern was a competent effort to overrun the Squirrel Level Line, not a brilliant massing of overwhelming force to conquer its way to the upper Appomattox. Troop capabilities, of course, limited the scope of his plans. So did logistics. But the biggest limitation was his own outlook. Meade was not as hopeful as Grant about the rich prizes that awaited plucking in early autumn. The Pennsylvanian probably instead agreed with Humphreys that the army was not ready to advance, hence should not advance. And the army commander definitely felt there was little point in continually extending the left flank westward. In consequence, he did not perceive the great opportunity for taking Petersburg on September 30. Instead, he would have fallen for Lee's bluff, had not supreme headquarters ordered an attack. Events at the end of September underscored what had been apparent for the preceding fifteen months: Prudent and competent, Meade would never have lost the war in Virginia, but, unaided, he would never have won it, either.

He thought small; therefore he acted small. He made limited efforts for limited gains. But where he did act, he displayed considerable ability as a tactical administrator. Once prompted into action, moreover, he entered into the spirit of the thing and by October 1–2 was even more desirous than his superior of forcing a battle. Meade, admittedly never shared City Point's optimism. Nor did he display Butler's mercurial flights of enthusiasm. The Pennsylvanian instead pursued a rational, straightforward belief that he had an opportunity to strike the Southerners outside their works. This assessment led him to prolong the battle even after supreme headquarters wanted to end it. Discovery that his premise was wrong, however, proved too strong for his resolve, limited in nature and depth as it was. He neither attacked the foe where found nor created a new grand-tactical situation by advancing to the Boydton Plank Road. He rather allowed himself to be bluffed down again, a deception for which the General-in-Chief, too, fell this time. In consequence, Meade's generalship had brought him only what he had originally expected: the conquest of Peebles's and Pegram's farms. He had written of greater goals but had not effectively acted for them, and he did not gain them.[11]

His counterpart in the Army of the James did not lack grandeur of vision. Vast opportunities, grand conquests, probably himself as the next President were all within Butler's expectations. Yet he was not just an impractical dreamer. He could spot real openings and could conceptualize over-all approaches for penetrating them. He also showed far more persistence than Grant—even than Meade—in urging that the opening battle and the entire Fifth Offensive be prolonged until Richmond was captured. Butler's very lack of professional under-standing of what army commanders should do, moreover, apparently caused him to play a useful direct role in the fighting by peremptorily ordering an attack on Fort Gilmer. He was hardly to blame that Birney executed it so poorly. If Meade had comparably interceded to hasten the IX Corps's movements on Friday, it might have achieved a major breakthrough on Jones's farm.

Lack of both professional military education and experience, how-ever, hurt the Massachusetts man far more than it helped him. His in-sight enabled him to perceive openings on the Northside, even avenues of attack. His lack of professionalism, however, severely undercut his ability to translate his perceptions into results. Even in planning, he misallocated the preponderance of force to the right wing, instead of to the left wing. Then the closer his generalship got from headquarters to battlefield, the more it suffered from his inexperience. His insistence on spearheading the attack with relatively inexperienced Negroes and his subsequent mooning over their corpses handicapped his attack and his perception of its results. He was so sure the blacks had sacrificed them-selves at New Market Heights for a great victory and a noble cause that he neglected the real opportunities at Chaffin's farm. Indeed, he virtually ignored the left wing for most of the day, yet there was where opportunity was greatest and where generalship was most needed.

Worst of all were his mercurial changes of outlook. His confidence of Thursday gave way to growing doubts the next morning. His victory on Friday afternoon made his spirits soar, but by night he was horrified of being overwhelmed. Then the following evening he again saw great opportunities for his advance. Such fluctuations represent more than rational analyses of a changing situation. Butler adopted each view with an emotional commitment that blinded him to strategic and tacti-cal realities and that often rendered him willful, even insubordinate, in dealing with City Point. His idea that the Graycoats would try to hold Petersburg with only two divisions while four others massed against him was not only unsubstantiated but also absurd. Yet he firmly believed it simply because Confederate prisoners fed him such a line. Therein lay one of his greatest weaknesses. Lacking military education and experience, he relied almost entirely on military intelligence. His legal background gave him particular confidence in his ability to cross-examine such intelligence out of captives and deserters. The resulting intelligence guided him in planning and operating. When it was correct, his plans could be promising. But when it was in error, he was readily led astray. His infixity of purpose and lack of resolve caused him to be buffeted by each new piece of intelligence. Such instability at army headquarters created needless alarm and dissension in dealings with City Point. It had less direct impact on the conduct of the Battle of Chaffin's Bluff, where other Union shortcomings and Southern strengths were more important in halting his advance. In his next battle, on October 7, though, his mental oscillations would virtually immobilize his army.

Butler thus revealed serious shortcomings during the battle of September 29–October 2. He thought big, planned big, worried big. But he could not act on a scale commensurate with his thoughts. He, of course, deserves credit for what he did accomplish. Chaffin's Bluff, after all, was the greatest victory he ever achieved. Yet it would have been far greater had his generalship been equal to his visions.

His opposing commander the first day also fought his finest battle on September 29. Dick Ewell had no time for the doubts, lost opportunities, and ill health that had marred his generalship since July 1863. The need to save his capital and his country sparked again the smoldering fire in the old warrior. True, his conduct was not perfect. He evidently neglected sectors north of the New Market Road, where Bragg and Kemper had to take over his responsibilities by default. The lieutenant general also misinterpreted the XVIII Corps's initial target, hence misdistributed his forces too far right. For that matter, he must share with Pemberton responsibility for the ill preparedness of the works and armament that proved so vulnerable on Thursday morning. All these shortcomings, though, were offset by what Ewell achieved. From Fort Gilmer to the James, his generalship, leadership, and personal inspiration forged the line that contained the most threatening attack ever launched against Richmond. More than any other commander, he deserves credit for stopping the breakthrough that day. It was the greatest contribution he ever rendered to the Confederate cause.

The corresponding Southern commander at Petersburg cannot be comparably assessed. The dearth of extant sources precludes differentiating Hill's generalship there from Lee's guidance from across the river. Nor can the lieutenant general's precise impact on the conduct of operations be discerned. The Confederate high command on the Southside must, therefore, be treated collectively, with the assumption that most of the far-reaching decisions were made by the army commander.

For that matter, the degree to which Lee accorded initiative to Dick Anderson is not documented, either. Only with Bragg and Ewell can the Virginian's exercise of command be delineated. He treated the nominal General-in-Chief as a subordinate, to whom he issued direct orders. He also felt the need to send frequent, specific instructions to "Old Bald Head" on September 29. The urgency of the crisis that day and Ewell's failures in earlier battles doubtless accounted for Lee's direct involvement. The department commander needed no such orders, though. He not only handled the situation superbly himself but also, as front-line commander, had a more realistic appraisal of it than did his chief, still at Dunn's Hill.

In his orders to Ewell, as throughout the Battles of Chaffin's Bluff and Poplar Spring Church, Lee's generalship was still marked by audacity and aggressiveness. They had always been his hallmarks. The military necessity of offsetting his numerical weakness dictated such an approach. His personal preferences commended such a style of generalship. Much of his success in those halcyon days of 1862 and 1863 was due to such qualities. They continued to serve him well in the fall of 1864.

His bold grand-strategic maneuvers with Kershaw's Division just prior to the Fifth Offensive had, admittedly, done the Confederates more harm than good. Strategically and tactically, though, Lee's audacity and aggressiveness were what saved his capital and rail center in early autumn. Confronted with a dire threat to Richmond, he rushed so many troops to the Peninsula as to imperil his communications on the Southside. Yet he did not simply abandon Petersburg. As during the Seven Days, Antietam, and Chancellorsville, he kept up a bold front on a weaker sector while his main strike force sought victory elsewhere. And as during those battles, his strategy basically succeeded. He stopped the Bluecoats short of their goals and saved both cities. However out of place audacious strategic maneuvers may have been theaterwide in Virginia in late 1864, they were still the best approach for securing the vital position then occupied in the Tidewater.

Lee's bold strategy, moreover, was still carried out through bold grand tactics and tactics. He shifted troops to Chaffin's not just to stop the Army of the James but also to hurl it back. He defended his supply lines not just by manning fortifications and creating illusions of strength but also by smiting whatever force ventured out against his communications. He knew that to remain on the tactical defensive was to forfeit the initiative to the foe and to leave them free to mass their forces at a place of their choosing to call his bluff and penetrate or turn his defenses. The way to stop them was to wrest the initiative from them, capitalize on their disjointed efforts, and use superior knowledge of the local countryside to ambush them and seek out their vulnerable flanks. The way, in sum, was to counterattack. Limited counterattacks on Thursday afternoon helped force the Northerners to recoil to their main line on Chaffin's farm. Wilcox's major counterattack on September 30 overthrew the IX Corps's drive toward the Boydton Plank Road. Subsequent counterattacks against Fort Harrison, Pegram's farm, and Chappell's farms were projected as the means for regaining all that had been lost. Aggressively pressing the tactical initiative was the best means to thwart the Yankees' strategic initiative. As earlier in the war, attacking brought Lee a considerable measure of success. Far from a shortcoming, his aggressiveness was one of his most valuable attributes in producing victory.

This late in the war, though, limitations on this approach were becoming apparent. Sometimes—as on Thursday morning—his exhortations to counterattack were clearly impracticable. Simply maintaining the defensive on the Peninsula was sufficiently trying and all that could be expected then. Even when counterattacks became possible, they no longer produced spectacular results comparable to Second Manassas and Chancellorsville. The victory on Jones's farm, after all, could not even be carried on to Pegram's on September 30, let alone to Chappell's the next day. And the limited success in counterattacking on Chaffin's on Thursday led on to total failure the following afternoon. In retrospect, it is clear that Lee ran into trouble not by attacking but by continuing to attack. Had he attacked once by surprise and then stopped, he would have halted the Bluecoats, dealt them a serious blow, and incurred few casualties. By attempting to exploit this first success, though, especially after they had a night to dig in and stabilize their defense, he only increased his own loss with nothing to show for it. The differential of casualties and of success would have been far more in his favor had he not prolonged his attacks. Over many months, such an obvious disparity in his favor could have suggested the futility of the war effort and increased war weariness in the Union. But he overlooked this opportunity in his quest for the spectacular victories of old. He did not realize that the declining quality of manpower and subordinate leadership made such grand successes no longer attainable. His counterattacks no longer swept the Federal army from the field. Despite his predilections, they were now just tools of minor tactics for slowing down the Northern juggernaut and stopping it somewhere short of its goal. Restoring defensive stability—tactically on the battlefield, strategically within the time period of the particular offensive—was all he could now achieve. His approach remained constant, but his achievable goals had been drastically reduced.

The diversion of eighteen brigades to the Valley and the declining effectiveness of the senior commanders and troops remaining in the Tidewater thus proved fatal constraints to Lee. Such diversion and decline also affected the Union army, yet for Grant they were only temporary inconveniences. In the long run, they would be eliminated by

Sheridan's return to Dinwiddie County. Even before then, the General-in-Chief sought to offset them by a constantly evolving strategic approach, within the over-all context of his war of attrition, in quest of victory at Petersburg.

The evolution of his strategy from June to October has already been traced. His strategic flexibility in considering shifting the weighting of each wing during the Fifth Offensive itself has also been recounted. Yet, it must be added, he did not actually carry out any of the latter options, and he evolved his over-all strategy only over a period of weeks and months. This was because he was not a military genius who could comprehend the situation at a glance, discern the optimum course of action, and immediately carry it through to victory. Rather was he a sound, solid, competent soldier, confident in himself, confident in his cause, confident in the ultimate success of his arms. Because he had confidence in himself, he was willing to learn, and he learned best from experience. Thus, over the long run, through a series of limited gains and outright setbacks, his generalship matured to the point that it ultimately produced victory. Hence his approach was better in September than it had been in August, far better than in July. It would be better still in late October, even more successful in February, and totally victorious in April. Yet because he needed time to derive and apply the lessons of experience, he was not prepared to act promptly on the various strategic options that he formulated during the Fifth Offensive. He could consider them but could not carry them out.

More than that, he was downright inflexible in declining to exploit many tactical opportunities. Here, too, his confidence in ultimate victory—so often one of his most beneficial qualities—handicapped his generalship. With characteristic self-confidence, he went into the autumn operations sanguine of achieving great results on the Southside, perhaps on the Peninsula, too, though he did not share Butler's original expectation that Richmond itself could be captured. The lieutenant general refused to be bluffed down by the Secessionists or dissuaded from attacking by his subordinates. He even hoped to take advantage of the first breakthroughs on each sector. But once his optimism came up against the stern reality of having to charge formidable fortifications, it was diverted elsewhere.

Grant, to be sure, was not mercurial like his senior army commander. Encountering opposition did not plunge the General-in-Chief into despair. Nor did he suffer from Meade's lack of initiative in formulating new combinations to overcome resistance. Rather was the Illinoisan almost too eager to devise new plans. Sure that victory would come eventually, he was easily reconciled to any one reverse and promptly sought success by some other means. But those means were

strategic, not tactical, for to him the offensives themselves were basically strategic, not tactical, exercises. He did not seek to capitalize on
all the opportunities of any given battle to their fullest extent. To the
contrary, he promptly abandoned an offensive at the first sign that he
might have to attack well-defended earthworks and sought his victory
through an entirely new offensive. More than that, he actually restrained his army commanders, who wanted to follow through on the
openings of the current offensive. The tactical inflexibility of his
generalship thus caused him to overlook opportunities below Petersburg on Sunday and on the Northside on Monday.

Yet missing these chances hardly brands Grant as inept. He overlooked them not out of incompetence, not out of unreasoning fear of
the foe, not out of a desire to become inactive or even to retreat.
Rather did he neglect them in his eagerness to get on with prosecuting
the attack at the strategic level. Precisely how he would weight and
time his wings for the next onslaught he probably did not know when
he called off the Fifth Offensive the second weekend in autumn. How
he would obtain reinforcements he definitely did not know that early.
But that he would strike again was beyond question. The man who
never turned back never looked back. He did not have time to dwell on
lost opportunities of the Fifth Offensive, for by early October he was
already contemplating launching the Sixth Offensive. Tactically rigid,
strategically flexible, grand-strategically unrelenting—such was the generalship of U. S. Grant.

His concept of generalship understandably governed his technique of
command. Since his view of offensives was strategic, he confined himself to setting over-all objectives, to initiating the operation and the first
onslaught by each army, to co-ordinating both prongs of his attack,
and to seeing that his subordinates acted consistently with his intentions. He did not, however, exercise direct grand-tactical or tactical
control of the battles themselves. Even army commanders remained
above the tactical level, so it is not surprising that the General-in-Chief
did so, too. He also generally avoided grand-tactical involvement. Unwilling even to concern himself with pursuing tactical opportunities, he
would hardly take part in more routine tactical control.

Once he initiated the battles, he relied on his army commanders to
carry them through to victory. All that he asked was to be kept informed, so that he could continue making the necessary strategic decisions. Much of this information could be telegraphed to him at City
Point or Deep Bottom. Occasionally he felt it necessary to ride out to
one prong or the other to confer directly with his senior subordinate
there. And sometimes that trip would include a visit to the front. But
such a visit was made so he could see, firsthand, what was occurring,

not so he could assume immediate control of the battle line. The information that he gathered from such visits, conferences, and telegrams he used to formulate his strategic decisions. He then relayed these decisions through the chain of command to his subordinates to implement. He did not issue direct tactical instructions to combat troops on the firing line.

During the Battles of Chaffin's Bluff and Poplar Spring Church, he visited the Peninsula on all four days but did not once go to the Southside. These travels do not denote his primary area of interest, though, for he felt the opportunity was greater below Petersburg. They may instead reflect his concern over how Butler would perform as a field commander. This was, after all, the first time that the major general had actually functioned as an army commander directly under the Illinoisan. Butler's earlier army command in the Bermuda Hundred Campaign, moreover, was hardly encouraging. The senior officer may, therefore, have wanted to keep a close eye on how the Massachusetts man would do.

The achievements of the Army of the James, especially on the first two days, could not help but impress the lieutenant general. The initial breakthrough, for that matter, may even have misled him as to the progress of the battle. It may be questioned, though, that he was equally impressed with Butler's own conduct. He found the junior officer mercurial on the weekend, panicky and willfully insistent on Friday night, negligent in relaying information about Kautz and Terry on Friday and Saturday, and inattentive to his responsibilities on Thursday morning. Grant, indeed, was so concerned about Butler's neglect of his front-line forces, especially his left wing, in midmorning on September 29 that the Illinoisan took the unusual step of directly ordering the two corps commanders to press the attack. Even then, the General-in-Chief did not take direct control of the battle line. Indeed, he probably did not grasp the tactical opportunities awaiting the Bluecoats on Chaffin's farm. His broad grand-tactical guidelines are notable principally as an aberration caused by his concern over Butler's failure to exercise such tactical control himself.

The lieutenant general suffered no such problems with his other army commander. Five months of working together made him confident that the left prong would do well in Meade's hands. Grant trusted Meade. Grant permitted the subordinate to choose the means and the place for carrying out the mission; Grant repeatedly deferred to the junior officer's recommendations about restricting or expanding the scope of operations; and Grant even allowed the Pennsylvanian to prolong the battle an extra day—the last discretion one that he repeatedly denied to Butler. The supreme commander, moreover, knew that

Birchett's would keep him fully informed by telegraph. Much as he would probably have liked to visit Peebles's farm, he realized that such a trip was unnecessary and that his travels were better directed to Henrico County.

Only when the major general transcended the proper bounds of discretion by urging that the operation be aborted (Thursday night) or terminated (Friday night) did the Illinoisan overrule him. Even then, the General-in-Chief adopted many of the subordinate's suggestions while rejecting the basic concept. The two officers thus formed a harmonious and effective combination. Grant, the strategic innovator, devised, launched, and pressed the strategic initiative. Meade, the competent tactical administrator, executed that initiative not only with ability but also eventually with a determination that exceeded his chief's.

Such, then, was the generalship of Grant, Lee, and their subordinates. Before turning from such analyses, one must also say a word about the men in the ranks. Most crack units sustained their reputations in these battles: the Light Division, the Texas Brigade, Griffin's division, the Regular brigade. Some outfits, moreover, made their reputations in these operations. Storming Fort Harrison was the greatest victory ever won by the First Division, XVIII Corps. However, other renowned units, such as Cooke's Brigade, Mahone's Division, Terry's division, and Hancock's corps, had little or no opportunity to become engaged. Only MacRae's Brigade emerged from the fighting with its bright record somewhat tarnished by its breakup and defeat on Saturday. Even then, it partially offset that reverse by its handsome victories on Friday and Sunday.

Generally, though, it was the forces of less repute that continued to perform marginally. Archer's, Davis', and Clingman's brigades once more proved themselves incapable of storming a position. The 22nd Virginia Battalion, in particular, again shamed itself with its poltroonery. Foster's division also repeated its old vice of excessive straggling, this time in unprecedented proportions. Then, too, Heckman's division, virtually re-created on the eve of the battle, inevitably lacked tactical cohesion in its first fight, a weakness that its commander compounded through misuse. Potter's division, too, suffered the understandable consequences of a dangerous practice: pouring hundreds of raw recruits into old units so late in the war that not enough veterans remained to absorb them. These unassimilated recruits vitiated that division. Once it was defeated on Jones's farm, their panicky flight caused it to go to pieces. Even the bravest men will run from a flank attack, but brave veterans will soon rally if not swept away by their fleeing comrades. It was the latter problem that caused the Second Division of the IX Corps to disintegrate as a functioning unit late Friday afternoon. And if inexperienced men of martial age panicked, it is hardly surprising that the old men and young boys of the 1st and 2nd Virginia Reserve battalions did the same on Thursday morning.

Yet on balance the troops performed creditably. Most who failed did so only after heroic efforts: the Negroes at New Market Heights, the Unionists charging the Intermediate Line, the Butternuts counterattacking Forts Harrison and Bratton, the blue cavalry at Wyatt's, and the gray troopers at McDowell's. And those who succeeded did so handsomely: the Northerners who stormed and held the outer lines east of Richmond and south of Petersburg, the Secessionists who hurled back the IX Corps from Jones's yard to Pegram's, the horsemen of each side who achieved their basic mission of securing the far southern flank. But most of all, tribute is owed to that unshakable handful of Confederates —infantry, cavalry, and artillery—who held fast the line that Ewell and Gregg put together: brave men who resisted an army and rescued their capital.

To what does all this storming of works and holding of lines, attacking and counterattacking amount? What did all these combat units, used by all these generals in all these strategic and tactical ways, accomplish? Which side, in sum, won the battles and the offensive? The answer is not clear-cut. Unlike many Civil War battles, Chaffin's Bluff and Poplar Spring Church did not produce decisive victory for either side. Various standards must, therefore, be used to try to measure success.

Possession of the field is least revealing. Each battle ended with both sides holding part of the battlefield. Casualties are little more instructive. The Yankees, admittedly, lost twice as many men as the Graycoats: 6,300 to 3,000 in the first two battles, 7,300 to 3,700 in the entire Fifth Offensive. Yet in other battles of the war, the victors often endured more casualties than the vanquished. The Federals suffered a comparable disparity of losses at Cedar Creek, for instance, yet won there one of the greatest tactical and strategic victories of the war. In proportionate terms, moreover, the difference is so much less as to be insignificant. Chaffin's Bluff cost Butler 9 per cent of his army, 13 per cent of his strike force. That same battle cut down only 6 per cent of the Secessionists north of the Appomattox, but 10 per cent of the troops engaged against the Union attack. At Poplar Spring Church, the proportions were even closer. Four per cent of each army and twice as large a fraction of the main field forces fell there. Over-all on September 29–October 2, Grant lost 6 per cent of his command and 10 per cent of his attack force, and Lee lost 5.5 per cent of his troops and 9 per cent of the men he sent into the field. Such virtually equal proportionate casualties thus offer little clue as to who won.[12]

A better index is to compare aspirations with attainments. Grant launched the operation to achieve three objectives: to prevent reinforcements from leaving the Tidewater for the Valley, to capture Richmond, and to cut at least the Boydton Plank Road, with the Southside Railroad a promising second target and Petersburg itself a possible prize. Not one of these did he gain. The Laurel Brigade left for the Valley two days before he struck and did not return until March 1865. The Butternuts who remained behind, moreover, denied him all his objectives in his own war zone. Such measurement clearly marks Lee as the victor in the two opening battles and in the Fifth Offensive.

Yet that standard may be too rigorous. The war, after all, is replete with examples of commanders who fell far short of their goals in a given battle yet who still achieved major victories there. Not just fulfilled objectives but actual attainments must be measured to determine success. Doing so markedly tempers Confederate claims to decisive victory.

Butler, to be sure, failed to capture Richmond. He did, however, take the New Market Line, the lower Exterior Line, part of the entrenched camp on Chaffin's Bluff, and Signal Hill. He thereby relieved the pressure on Dutch Gap and Deep Bottom and established a significant Northern presence on the Peninsula. That presence had major strategic consequences far beyond the mere capture of territory. Because it confronted the Graycoats south of the New Market Road and had access to all the highways leading to Richmond farther north, it forced Lee to keep a strong force there to contain it. No longer could he leave a token guard on the Northside while his main body protected Petersburg and the supply lines. He could not afford to divert his precious manpower to Henrico, yet he could not afford not to do so. Confronting him with this dilemma was the major long-range benefit to the Federals of the breakout at Chaffin's Bluff. It was a dilemma, moreover, on which they eventually capitalized. In the final, decisive offensive the following spring, they would transfer most of the Army of the James back to Petersburg before Lee could correspondingly shift his forces there. They thus feinted him out of place after all, not in the Fifth Offensive but in the long haul.

Comparable advantages also resulted from Meade's operations, even though he too did not reach any of his objectives. Yet he did breach and render virtually untenable the Squirrel Level Line. Doing so thwarted Butternut efforts to confine him to Globe Tavern and gave him safe access to numerous avenues toward their supply lines. Along the three roads radiating out from Peebles's farm plus the Vaughan and Stage roads farther south, the Yankees would conduct future offensives to cut the Confederate communications. To try to counter such future attacks, Lee could no longer rely on a short, forward line along the Squirrel Level Road. He now had to take up and man in strength the much longer line near the Boydton Plank Road all the way to Hatcher's Run. Such precautions, though, were in vain. Six months to the day after capturing Pegram's farm, the Federals used it as the staging area for their grand assault that finally overran the Southern works and doomed Petersburg and Richmond.

Lee could not, of course, have known in early autumn the disasters that his losses then would cause him the following spring. He did realize, though, that strong Northern forces at Chaffin's and Peebles's would seriously tie down his own countering forces in ways that he could ill afford. He therefore counterattacked those positions with great violence on Friday and Saturday, not just because counterattacks were his favorite tactic but also because the Union presence there was so dangerous. Yet his counterattacks failed, and the enemy retained possession of those threatening sectors. The Virginian himself thus fell far short of achieving all his goals. Hence the very reasoning on which rests the strongest Secessionist claims to victory—denying the enemy his objectives—can be used to undercut those pretensions.

Determining actual accomplishments seriously complicates efforts to decide who won. The Bluecoats unquestionably achieved a great deal, and the Southerners did not accomplish much of what they had intended. Still, the original stakes—Richmond and Petersburg—were so high, their capture was so possible, and their retention was so momentous that their fate must be the standard for evaluating the outcome. By that measure, the Graycoats won the Battles of Chaffin's Bluff and Poplar Spring Church.

Lee's success in three of the five battles of the Fifth Offensive, with one other being a draw and only one going to the Yankees, does not, however, mean that he won the offensive. The whole, in this case, was considerably different from the sum of its parts. His victories, after all, were only tactical. He blunted the enemy onslaught and re-established stability, first tactical, then strategic. But he signally failed to hurl the Federals back, even tactically, let alone strategically. He had been forced back closer to his capital and its communications, now become more vulnerable. Grant, for all his setbacks, succeeded in holding his initial conquests. They in turn became staging areas for future attacks. His advance had been retarded, but only in the most narrow and temporary sense had it been stopped. In the broader view, his gains in early autumn formed another tightening of the grip in the stranglehold he was fixing on the Army of Northern Virginia. In that sense, he lost most of its battles and still won his Fifth Offensive at Petersburg.

Lee understood this. It was clear to those who saw his great worry at the failure to retake Fort Harrison. It was clear in the letter he wrote to Hampton just two days after the Battle of Poplar Spring Church: "The failure of Dearing's Brigade to hold the position assigned to it [Peebles's farm], I fear, will entail upon us great loss. If the enemy cannot be prevented from extending his left, he will eventually reach the Appomattox and cut us off from the south side altogether." That same day, Grant underscored the danger. Supremely confident as ever, he informed a friend, "Another equal surprise on the North side of James River will carry us into Richmond. I believe the enemy look upon the city as doomed."[13]

Yet "doomed" was too strong a word. The Fifth Offensive had shown once more that Lee sought to make his own fate. No matter how dire the threat, he fought bravely, skillfully, and unyieldingly to hold on to his capital and its rail center. Hold them he did. His concern and Northern expectations of future conquests all pertained to later offensives. They could be entertained only because he had thwarted Yankee efforts to achieve them during the Fifth Offensive. His success in that offensive meant that for the fall of 1864—indeed, for another half year —Richmond had been redeemed.

Appendix A

ORDER OF BATTLE

Federal Forces[1]

———◆———

HEADQUARTERS, ARMIES IN THE FIELD—
Lt. Gen. Ulysses S. Grant
B-F-K/5th U. S. Cavalry
4th U.S.

ARMY OF THE POTOMAC—Maj. Gen. George Gordon Meade
Oneida Cavalry Company

Second Cavalry Division,[2]
Brig. Gen. David M. Gregg

1. First Brigade,
   Brig. Gen. Henry E. Davies
   1st Massachusetts Cavalry
   1st New Jersey Cavalry
   10th New York Cavalry
   6th Ohio Cavalry
   1st Pennsylvania Cavalry
   A/2nd U. S. Artillery

2. Second Brigade,
   Col. Charles H. Smith
   1st Maine Cavalry
   2nd Pennsylvania Cavalry
   4th Pennsylvania Cavalry
   8th Pennsylvania Cavalry
   13th Pennsylvania Cavalry
   16th Pennsylvania Cavalry
   H-I/1st U. S. Artillery

3. Remount Camp,
   Capt. Andrew H. Bibber

Artillery Reserve,[3]
Brig. Gen. Henry J. Hunt

1. Artillery Park,
   Capt. Calvin Shaffer
   2nd Maine Battery
   3rd Maine Battery
   14th Massachusetts Battery
   F/15th New York Heavy Artillery
   3rd Vermont Battery

2. Detachment, VI Corps,
   Capt. William Harn
   4th Maine Battery
   A/1st New Jersey Light Artillery
   3rd New York Battery
   H/1st Ohio Light Artillery
   E/1st Rhode Island Light Artillery
   E/5th U. S. Artillery

Benham's Command,[4] Brig. Gen. Henry W. Benham

1. Engineer Brigade
     15th New York Engineers
     50th New York Engineers

2. Independent forces
     Two New York provisional companies of recruits
     Van Raden's provisional battery

     Regular Engineers, Capt. Franklin Harwood
     1st U. S. Engineer Battalion

     Provost Brigade,[5] Brig. Gen. Marsena R. Patrick
          K/1st   Indiana Cavalry
       C-D/1st   Massachusetts Cavalry
         80th   New York
          3rd   Pennsylvania Cavalry
         68th   Pennsylvania
        114th   Pennsylvania

Signal Corps Detachment, Maj. Benjamin F. Fisher

II ARMY CORPS — Maj. Gen. Winfield Scott Hancock[6]
M/1st Vermont Cavalry

First Division, Brig. Gen. Nelson A. Miles

1. First Brigade,
   Col. James Lynch
   - 28th Massachusetts
   - 26th Michigan
   - 5th New Hampshire
   - 2nd New York Heavy Artillery
   - 4th New York Heavy Artillery
   - 61st New York
   - 81st Pennsylvania
   - 140th Pennsylvania
   - 183rd Pennsylvania

2. Consolidated Brigade,
   Lt. Col. James McGee
   - 7th New York
   - 39th New York
   - 52nd New York
   - 57th New York
   - 63rd New York
   - 69th New York
   - 88th New York
   - 111th New York
   - 125th New York
   - 126th New York

3. Fourth Brigade,
   Lt. Col. William Glenny
   - 7th New York Heavy Artillery
   - 64th New York
   - 66th New York
   - 53rd Pennsylvania
   - 116th Pennsylvania
   - 145th Pennsylvania
   - 148th Pennsylvania

Second Division, Maj. Gen. John Gibbon

1. First Brigade,
   Brig. Gen. Thomas W. Egan
   - 19th Maine
   - 19th Massachusetts
   - 20th Massachusetts
   - Andrew Sharpshooter Company
   - 7th Michigan
   - 1st Minnesota
   - 59th New York
   - 152nd New York
   - 184th Pennsylvania
   - 36th Wisconsin

2. Second Brigade,
   Col. Mathew Murphy
   - 8th New York Heavy Artillery
   - 155th New York
   - 164th New York
   - 170th New York
   - 182nd New York

3. Third Brigade,
   Col. Thomas A. Smyth
   - 14th Connecticut
   - 1st Delaware
   - 2nd Delaware
   - 12th New Jersey
   - 10th New York
   - 108th New York
   - 4th Ohio
   - 69th Pennsylvania
   - 106th Pennsylvania
   - 7th West Virginia

Third Division, Brig. Gen. Gershom Mott

1. First Brigade,
   Brig. Gen. P. Regis DeTrobriand
   - 20th Indiana
   - 1st Maine Heavy Artillery
   - 17th Maine
   - 40th New York
   - 73rd New York
   - 86th New York
   - 124th New York
   - 99th Pennsylvania
   - 110th Pennsylvania
   - 2nd U. S. Sharpshooters

2. Second Brigade,
   Brig. Gen. Byron R. Pierce
   - 1st Massachusetts Heavy
        Artillery
   - 5th Michigan
   - 93rd New York
   - 57th Pennsylvania
   - 84th Pennsylvania
   - 105th Pennsylvania
   - 141st Pennsylvania
   - 1st U. S. Sharpshooters

3. Third Brigade,
   Col. Robert McAllister
   - 11th Massachusetts
   - 5th New Jersey
   - 6th New Jersey
   - 7th New Jersey
   - 8th New Jersey
   - 11th New Jersey
   - 72nd New York
   - 120th New York

Artillery Brigade,[7] Maj. John Hazard
   - 6th Maine Battery
   - 10th Massachusetts Battery
   - 1st New Hampshire Battery
   - B/1st New Jersey Light Artillery
   - 3rd New Jersey Battery
   - G/1st New York Light Artillery
   - C/4th New York Heavy Artillery
   - D/4th New York Heavy Artillery
   - L/4th New York Heavy Artillery
   - 11th New York Battery
   - 12th New York Battery
   - F/1st Pennsylvania Light Artillery
   - A-B/1st Rhode Island Light Artillery
   - K/4th U. S. Artillery
   - C-I/5th U. S. Artillery

V ARMY CORPS — Maj. Gen. Gouverneur K. Warren[8]

E-F/5th New York
Detail/4th Pennsylvania Cavalry

First Division, Brig. Gen. Charles Griffin

1. First Brigade,
   Col. Horatio G. Sickel

   21st Pennsylvania Cavalry
   198th Pennsylvania

2. Second Brigade,
   Col. Edgar Gregory

   22nd Massachusetts
   32nd Massachusetts
   91st Pennsylvania
   155th Pennsylvania

3. Third Brigade,
   Col. James Gwyn

   20th Maine
   18th Massachusetts
   1st Michigan
   16th Michigan
   44th New York
   83rd Pennsylvania
   118th Pennsylvania

Second Division, Brig. Gen. Romeyn B. Ayres

1. First Brigade,
   Lt. Col. Elwell S. Otis

   15th New York Heavy Artillery
   5th New York
   140th New York
   146th New York
   10th U.S.
   11th U.S.
   12th U.S.
   14th U.S.
   17th U.S.

2. Second Brigade,
   Col. Samuel Graham

   1st Maryland
   4th Maryland
   7th Maryland
   8th Maryland
   Purnell Legion

3. Third Brigade,
   Col. Arthur Grimshaw

   3rd Delaware
   4th Delaware
   157th Pennsylvania
   190th Pennsylvania
   191st Pennsylvania

4. Provost Guard
   C/2nd U.S.

Third Division,[9] Brig. Gen. Samuel W. Crawford

1. First Brigade,
   Brig. Gen. Edward S. Bragg
   19th Indiana
   24th Michigan
   1st New York Sharpshooter
        Battalion
   143rd Pennsylvania
   149th Pennsylvania
   150th Pennsylvania
   2nd Wisconsin Battalion
   6th Wisconsin
   7th Wisconsin

2. Second Brigade,
   Brig. Gen. Henry Baxter
   16th Maine
   39th Massachusetts
   94th New York
   97th New York
   104th New York
   11th Pennsylvania
   88th Pennsylvania
   90th Pennsylvania
   107th Pennsylvania

3. Third Brigade,
   Col. John William Hofmann
   76th New York
   95th New York
   147th New York
   56th Pennsylvania
   121st Pennsylvania
   142nd Pennsylvania

Independent infantry commands
185th New York
210th Pennsylvania

Artillery Brigade, Col. Charles S. Wainwright
   5th Massachusetts Battery
   9th Massachusetts Battery
   B/1st New York Light Artillery
   C-E/1st New York Light Artillery
   D/1st New York Light Artillery
   H/1st New York Light Artillery
   L/1st New York Light Artillery
   15th New York Battery
   B/1st Pennsylvania Light Artillery
   B/4th U. S. Artillery
   D-G/5th U. S. Artillery

IX ARMY CORPS — Maj. Gen. John G. Parke[10]
Detail/3rd New Jersey Cavalry
8th U.S.

First Division, Brig. Gen. Orlando B. Willcox

1. First Brigade,
   Col. Samuel Harriman
   8th Michigan
   27th Michigan
   79th New York
   109th New York
   13th Ohio Cavalry
   51st Pennsylvania
   37th Wisconsin
   38th Wisconsin

2. Second Brigade,
   Brig. Gen. John F. Hartranft
   1st Michigan Sharpshooters
   2nd Michigan
   20th Michigan
   24th New York Cavalry
   46th New York
   60th Ohio
   50th Pennsylvania

3. Third Brigade,
   Col. Napoleon B. McLaughlen
   3rd Maryland
   29th Massachusetts
   57th Massachusetts
   59th Massachusetts
   14th New York Heavy Artillery
   100th Pennsylvania

4. Engineers
   17th Michigan

Second Division, Brig. Gen. Robert B. Potter

1. First Brigade,
   Col. John I. Curtin
   21st Massachusetts
   35th Massachusetts
   36th Massachusetts
   58th Massachusetts
   51st New York
   45th Pennsylvania
   48th Pennsylvania
   4th Rhode Island
   7th Rhode Island

2. Second Brigade,
   Brig. Gen. Simon G. Griffin
   31st Maine
   32nd Maine
   2nd Maryland
   56th Massachusetts
   6th New Hampshire
   9th New Hampshire
   11th New Hampshire
   2nd New York Mounted Rifles
   179th New York
   17th Vermont

Third Division, Brig. Gen. Edward Ferrero

1. First Brigade,
   Col. Ozora P. Stearns
   - 27th USCT
   - 30th USCT
   - 39th USCT
   - 43rd USCT

2. Second Brigade,
   Col. Charles S. Russell
   - 19th USCT
   - 23rd USCT
   - 28th USCT
   - 29th USCT
   - 31st USCT

Artillery Brigade, Lt. Col. John Albert Monroe
- 7th Maine Battery
- 11th Massachusetts Battery
- 19th New York Battery
- 27th New York Battery
- 34th New York Battery
- D Pennsylvania Light Artillery

ARMY OF THE JAMES — Maj. Gen. Benjamin F. Butler
I/3rd Pennsylvania Heavy Artillery

Cavalry Division, Brig. Gen. August V. Kautz

1. First Brigade,
   Col. Robert M. West
   3rd New York Cavalry
   5th Pennsylvania Cavalry
   4th Wisconsin Battery

2. Second Brigade,
   Col. Samuel P. Spear
   1st District of Columbia Cavalry
   11th Pennsylvania Cavalry
   B/1st U. S. Artillery

3. Independent regiment
   1st New York Mounted Rifles

Separate Brigade,[11] Brig. Gen. Gilman Marston
M/4th Massachusetts Cavalry
1/38th New Jersey
E-H/16th New York Heavy Artillery
33rd New York Battery
2/184th New York
Detail/3rd Pennsylvania Heavy Artillery
E-I/1st USCT Cavalry

Naval Brigade, Brig. Gen. Charles K. Graham
I/13th New York Heavy Artillery
L/13th New York Heavy Artillery
Battalion/3rd Pennsylvania Heavy Artillery
Detail/3rd Pennsylvania Heavy Artillery[12]

Siege Train, Col. Henry L. Abbot
1st Connecticut Heavy Artillery:[13]
   Batteries B, C, D, F, G, H
   Batteries A, E, I, K, L, M
A-H/13th New York Heavy Artillery
Detail/16th New York Heavy Artillery
M/3rd Pennsylvania Heavy Artillery

Engineers, Col. Edward W. Serrell
1st New York Engineers[14]

Pontoneers,[15] Capt. John Pickering
13th Massachusetts Heavy Artillery Company

Signal Corps Detachment, Capt. Henry R. Clum

X ARMY CORPS — Maj. Gen. David B. Birney[16]
Detail/4th Massachusetts Cavalry

First Division,
Brig. Gen. Alfred H. Terry

1. First Brigade,
   Col. Francis B. Pond
   39th Illinois
   62nd Ohio
   67th Ohio
   85th Pennsylvania

2. Second Brigade,
   Col. Joseph C. Abbott
   6th Connecticut
   7th Connecticut
   3rd New Hampshire
   7th New Hampshire
   16th New York Heavy Artillery
      (seven companies)

3. Third Brigade,
   Col. Harris M. Plaisted
   10th Connecticut
   11th Maine
   1st Maryland Cavalry
   24th Massachusetts
   100th New York

Second Division,[17]
Brig. Gen. Robert S. Foster

1. First Brigade,
   Col. Rufus Daggett
   3rd New York
   112th New York
   117th New York
   142nd New York

2. Second Brigade,
   Col. Galusha Pennypacker
   47th New York
   48th New York
   76th Pennsylvania
   97th Pennsylvania
   203rd Pennsylvania

3. Third Brigade,
   Col. Louis Bell
   13th Indiana
   9th Maine
   4th New Hampshire
   115th New York
   169th New York

First Brigade, Third Division, Brig. Gen. William Birney
29th Connecticut
7th USCT
8th USCT
9th USCT
2/45th USCT

Artillery Brigade,[18] Lt. Col. Richard H. Jackson
1st Connecticut Battery
4th New Jersey Battery
5th New Jersey Battery
Section/16th New York Heavy Artillery
E/1st Pennsylvania Light Artillery
C/3rd Rhode Island Heavy Artillery
C-D/1st U. S. Artillery
M/1st U. S. Artillery
E/3rd U. S. Artillery
D/4th U. S. Artillery

XVIII ARMY CORPS — Maj. Gen. Edward O. C. Ord[19]

Detail/11th Connecticut
E-H/4th Massachusetts Cavalry

First Division,[20] Brig. Gen. George J. Stannard

1. First Brigade,
   Col. Aaron F. Stevens
   13th New Hampshire
   81st New York
   98th New York
   139th New York

2. Second Brigade,
   Brig. Gen. Hiram Burnham
   8th Connecticut
   10th New Hampshire
   96th New York
   118th New York

3. Third Brigade,
   Col. Samuel H. Roberts
   21st Connecticut
   92nd New York
   58th Pennsylvania
   188th Pennsylvania

Second Division,[21] Brig. Gen. Charles A. Heckman

1. First Brigade,
   Col. James Jourdan
   148th New York
   158th New York
   55th Pennsylvania

2. Second Brigade,
   Col. Edward H. Ripley
   8th Maine
   9th Vermont

3. Third Brigade,
   Col. Harrison Fairchild
   89th New York
   2nd Pennsylvania Heavy Artillery

Third Division,[22] Brig. Gen. Charles J. Paine

1. First Brigade,
   Col. John H. Holman
   1st USCT
   22nd USCT
   37th USCT

2. Second Brigade,
   Col. Alonzo G. Draper
   5th USCT
   36th USCT
   38th USCT

3. Third Brigade,
   Col. Samuel A. Duncan
   4th USCT
   6th USCT
   10th USCT

4. Independent regiment
   2nd USCT Cavalry

Temporary brigade,[23] Maj. David B. White

    5th Maryland
    2nd New Hampshire
  12th New Hampshire

Artillery Brigade,[24] Maj. George B. Cook

  E/3rd New York Light Artillery
  H/3rd New York Light Artillery
  K/3rd New York Light Artillery
  M/3rd New York Light Artillery
    7th New York Battery
  16th New York Battery
  17th New York Battery
  A/1st Pennsylvania Light Artillery
  F/1st Rhode Island Light Artillery
  L/4th U. S. Artillery
  A/5th U. S. Artillery
  F/5th U. S. Artillery

Provisional Brigade,[25] Col. Joseph Potter

  11th Connecticut
  40th Massachusetts
 200th Pennsylvania
 205th Pennsylvania
 206th Pennsylvania
 207th Pennsylvania
 208th Pennsylvania
 209th Pennsylvania
 211th Pennsylvania

Confederate Forces[26]

———◆———

ARMY OF NORTHERN VIRGINIA — Gen. Robert E. Lee

Engineers,
Col. T. M. R. Talcott
      1st Confederate Engineers
C-G-H-K/2nd Confederate Engineers

Provost Guard,
Maj. D. B. Bridgford
39th Virginia Cavalry Battalion
1st Virginia Regular Battalion

Cavalry Corps — Maj. Gen. Wade Hampton[27]

First Division, Brig. Gen. Matthew C. Butler

1. Dunovant's Brigade,
   Brig. Gen. John Dunovant
   4th South Carolina Cavalry
   5th South Carolina Cavalry
   6th South Carolina Cavalry

2. Young's Brigade,
   Brig. Gen. Pierce M. B. Young
   4th Alabama Cavalry Battalion
   7th Georgia Cavalry
   20th Georgia Cavalry Battalion
   Cobb's Legion (Cavalry Regiment)
   Phillips' Legion (Cavalry Battalion)
   Jeff Davis Legion

Third Division, Maj. Gen. W. H. F. Lee

1. Chambliss' Brigade,
   Col. J. Lucius Davis
   9th Virginia Cavalry
   10th Virginia Cavalry
   13th Virginia Cavalry

2. Barringer's Brigade,
   Brig. Gen. Rufus Barringer
   1st North Carolina Cavalry
   2nd North Carolina Cavalry
   3rd North Carolina Cavalry
   5th North Carolina Cavalry

Dearing's Brigade, Col. Joel R. Griffin
    7th Confederate Cavalry
    8th Georgia Cavalry
    4th North Carolina Cavalry

Horse Artillery Battalion, Maj. R. Preston Chew
    Washington Artillery Battery
    2nd Jeb Stuart Horse Artillery
    Petersburg Light Artillery

Foot Dragoons, Maj. Henry Farley

I ARMY CORPS — Lt. Gen. Richard H. Anderson[28]

Field's Division, Maj. Gen. Charles W. Field

1. Gregg's Brigade,
   Brig. Gen. John Gregg

   3rd Arkansas
   1st Texas
   4th Texas
   5th Texas

2. Benning's Brigade,
   Col. Dudley M. DuBose

   2nd Georgia
   15th Georgia
   17th Georgia
   20th Georgia

3. Anderson's Brigade,
   Brig. Gen. George T. Anderson

   7th Georgia
   8th Georgia
   9th Georgia
   11th Georgia
   59th Georgia

4. Law's Brigade,
   Col. Pinckney D. Bowles

   4th Alabama
   15th Alabama
   44th Alabama
   47th Alabama
   48th Alabama

5. Bratton's Brigade,
   Brig. Gen. John Bratton

   1st South Carolina Volunteers
   2nd South Carolina Rifles
   5th South Carolina
   6th South Carolina
   Palmetto Sharpshooters

Pickett's Division, Maj. Gen. George E. Pickett

1. Terry's Brigade,
   Brig. Gen. William R. Terry

   1st Virginia
   3rd Virginia
   7th Virginia
   11th Virginia

2. Hunton's Brigade,
   Brig. Gen. Eppa Hunton

   8th Virginia
   18th Virginia
   19th Virginia
   28th Virginia

3. Steuart's Brigade,
   Brig. Gen. George H. Steuart

   9th Virginia
   14th Virginia
   38th Virginia
   57th Virginia

4. Corse's Brigade,
   Brig. Gen. Montgomery D. Corse

   15th Virginia
   17th Virginia
   29th Virginia
   30th Virginia

5. Provisional brigade,
   Col. Edgar B. Montague

   24th Virginia
   32nd Virginia
   53rd Virginia
   56th Virginia

Artillery Brigade, Brig. Gen. Edward Porter Alexander[29]

1. Cabell's Battalion, Col. Henry Coalter Cabell
   Pulaski Artillery
   Troup Artillery
   A/1st North Carolina Artillery
   First Richmond Howitzers

2. Huger's Battalion, Maj. Frank Huger
   Madison Artillery
   Brooks Artillery
   Ashland Artillery
   Bedford Artillery
   Parker Battery
   Taylor Battery

3. Haskell's Battalion, Maj. John Cheves Haskell
   D/1st North Carolina Artillery
   F/13th North Carolina Light Artillery Battalion
   Second Palmetto Artillery
   Nelson Battery

4. 13th Virginia Light Artillery Battalion, Maj. William Miller Owen
   A Battery
   B Battery
   C Battery

5. 1st Virginia Light Artillery Battalion, Lt. Col. Robert Archelaus Hardaway
   Third Richmond Howitzers
   First Rockbridge Artillery
   Powhatan Artillery
   Salem Flying Artillery

6. Johnson's Battalion, Maj. Marmaduke Johnson
   Marye Battery
   Clutter Battery

7. Independent companies
   E/1st North Carolina Artillery
   B/38th Virginia Light Artillery Battalion

III ARMY CORPS — Lt. Gen. Ambrose Powell Hill[30]
5th Alabama Battalion

Heth's Division, Maj. Gen. Henry Heth

1. MacRae's Brigade,
   Brig. Gen. William MacRae
   - 11th North Carolina
   - 26th North Carolina
   - 44th North Carolina
   - 47th North Carolina
   - 52nd North Carolina

2. Cooke's Brigade,
   Brig. Gen. John R. Cooke
   - 15th North Carolina
   - 27th North Carolina
   - 46th North Carolina
   - 48th North Carolina

3. Davis' Brigade,
   Brig. Gen. Joseph R. Davis
   - 1st Confederate Battalion
   - 2nd Mississippi
   - 11th Mississippi
   - 26th Mississippi
   - 42nd Mississippi
   - 55th North Carolina

4. Archer's Brigade,
   Brig. Gen. James J. Archer
   - 13th Alabama
   - 2nd Maryland Battalion
   - 1st Tennessee Provisional Army
   - 7th Tennessee
   - 14th Tennessee
   - 22nd Virginia Battalion
   - 40th Virginia
   - 47th Virginia
   - 55th Virginia

Light Division, Maj. Gen. Cadmus M. Wilcox

1. Lane's Brigade,
   Brig. Gen. James H. Lane
   - 7th North Carolina
   - 18th North Carolina
   - 28th North Carolina
   - 33rd North Carolina
   - 37th North Carolina

2. McGowan's Brigade,
   Brig. Gen. Samuel McGowan
   - 1st South Carolina Provisional Army
   - 1st South Carolina Rifles
   - 12th South Carolina
   - 13th South Carolina
   - 14th South Carolina

3. Scales's Brigade,
   Brig. Gen. Alfred M. Scales
   - 13th North Carolina
   - 16th North Carolina
   - 22nd North Carolina
   - 34th North Carolina
   - 38th North Carolina

4. Thomas' Brigade,
   Brig. Gen. Edward L. Thomas
   - 14th Georgia
   - 35th Georgia
   - 45th Georgia
   - 49th Georgia

Mahone's Division, Maj. Gen. William Mahone

1. Mahone's Brigade,
   Col. David A. Weiseger

   6th Virginia
   12th Virginia
   16th Virginia
   41st Virginia
   61st Virginia

2. Harris' Brigade,
   Brig. Gen. Nathaniel H. Harris

   12th Mississippi
   16th Mississippi
   19th Mississippi
   48th Mississippi

3. Finegan's Brigade,
   Brig. Gen. Joseph Finegan

   2nd Florida
   5th Florida
   8th Florida
   9th Florida
   10th Florida
   11th Florida

4. Sanders' Brigade,
   Col. J. Horace King

   8th Alabama
   9th Alabama
   10th Alabama
   11th Alabama
   14th Alabama

5. Girardey's Brigade,
   Col. William Gibson

   2nd Georgia Battalion
   10th Georgia Battalion
   3rd Georgia
   22nd Georgia
   48th Georgia
   64th Georgia

Artillery Brigade,[31] Col. Reuben Lindsay Walker

1. Pegram's Battalion,
   Lt. Col. William J. Pegram

   C/18th South Carolina Heavy
       Artillery Battalion
   Crenshaw Artillery
   Letcher Artillery
   Purcell Artillery

2. McIntosh's Battalion,
   Lt. Col. David G. McIntosh

   Hurt Artillery
   1st Maryland Battery
   4th Maryland Battery
   Danville Artillery
   Second Rockbridge Artillery

3. Richardson's Battalion,
   Lt. Col. Charles Richardson

   Landry Artillery
   Norfolk Artillery
   Huger Artillery

4. 11th Georgia Light Artillery
   Battalion,
   Maj. John Lane

   A Company
   B Company
   C Company

5. Poague's Battalion,
   Lt. Col. William Poague

   Madison Light Artillery
   C/1st North Carolina Artillery
   Albemarle Artillery
   Brooke Artillery
   Lewis Artillery

6. Washington Artillery Battalion,
   Lt. Col. Benjamin Eshelman

   First Company
   Second Company
   Third Company
   Fourth Company

DEPARTMENT OF NORTH CAROLINA AND SOUTHERN VIRGINIA[32]

Hoke's Division, Maj. Gen. Robert F. Hoke

1. Clingman's Brigade,
   Col. Hector M. McKethan

   8th North Carolina
   31st North Carolina
   51st North Carolina
   61st North Carolina

2. Colquitt's Brigade,
   Brig. Gen. Alfred H. Colquitt

   6th Georgia
   19th Georgia
   23rd Georgia
   27th Georgia
   28th Georgia

3. Hagood's Brigade,
   Brig. Gen. Johnson Hagood

   7th South Carolina Battalion
   11th South Carolina
   21st South Carolina
   25th South Carolina
   27th South Carolina

4. Kirkland's Brigade,
   Brig. Gen. William W. Kirkland

   17th North Carolina
   42nd North Carolina
   66th North Carolina

Johnson's Division, Maj. Gen. Bushrod R. Johnson

1. Wise's Brigade,
   Col. John Thomas Goode

   26th Virginia
   34th Virginia
   46th Virginia
   59th Virginia

2. Ransom's Brigade,
   Col. Lee McAfee

   24th North Carolina
   25th North Carolina
   35th North Carolina
   49th North Carolina
   56th North Carolina

3. Gracie's Brigade,
   Brig. Gen. Archibald Gracie

   23rd Alabama Sharpshooter Battalion
   41st Alabama
   43rd Alabama
   59th Alabama
   60th Alabama

4. Wallace's Brigade,
   Brig. Gen. William H. Wallace

   17th South Carolina
   18th South Carolina
   22nd South Carolina
   23rd South Carolina
   26th South Carolina

First Military District,[33] Brig. Gen. Henry A. Wise

1. Walker's Brigade,
   Brig. Gen. James A. Walker

   18th Georgia Battalion
   1st Virginia Reserves
   3rd Virginia Reserves
   5th Virginia Reserve Battalion
   Withers' Virginia Reserve Battalion
   Maurin's Artillery

2. Garnett's Brigade,
   Lt. Col. John J. Garnett

   1st Confederate Zouave Battalion
   H/8th Georgia Cavalry
   Section Confederate Guards Artillery
   4th Virginia Reserve Battalion

3. Post of Petersburg,
   Maj. William Ker

   3rd Virginia Reserve Battalion (Archer's)
   44th Virginia Battalion
   Hood's Virginia Reserve Battalion
   Hobson's Virginia Militia Company

4. Fort Clifton,
   Lt. Col. Henry Guion

   Detail/1st North Carolina Artillery
   Detail/34th Virginia

5. Independent regiment
   Holcombe Legion

Artillery Brigade,[34] Col. Hilary P. Jones

1. 12th Virginia Light Artillery Battalion,
   Maj. Francis Boggs

   A Battery
   B Battery

2. 38th Virginia Light Artillery Battalion,
   Lt. Col. John Read

   A Battery
   C Battery
   D Battery

3. Coit's Battalion,
   Maj. James Coit

   Section Confederate Guards Artillery
   Section Chesterfield Artillery
   Pegram Battery
   Wright Battery

4. Moseley's Battalion,
   Lt. Col. Edgar Moseley

   Slaten Battery
   C/13th North Carolina Light Artillery Battalion
   Young Battery

Drewry's Bluff, Lt. Col. George H. Terrett

   Battalion Confederate Marines
   Neblett Artillery
   South Side Artillery

Smith's Artillery Battalion, Maj. Francis Smith

   Johnston Artillery
   United Artillery

DEPARTMENT OF RICHMOND — Lt. Gen. Richard S. Ewell

Front-line Infantry[35]

1. Johnson's Brigade,
   Col. John M. Hughs
   17th Tennessee
   23rd Tennessee
   25th Tennessee
   44th Tennessee
   63rd Tennessee

2. 1st Virginia Reserve Battalion,
   Maj. James Strange

3. 2nd Virginia Reserve Battalion,
   Lt. Col. John H. Guy

4. 25th Virginia Battalion,
   Maj. Wyatt Elliott

Front-line Cavalry

1. Gary's Brigade,
   Brig. Gen. Martin W. Gary
   Hampton Legion
     7th South Carolina Cavalry
   24th Virginia Cavalry

Richmond Forces,[36] Maj. Gen. James L. Kemper

Barton's Division, Brig. Gen. Seth M. Barton

1. Local Defense Brigade,
   Brig. Gen. Patrick T. Moore
   1st Virginia LDF Battalion
   2nd Virginia LDF
   3rd Virginia LDF
   4th Virginia LDF Battalion
   5th Virginia LDF Battalion
   Company VMI Cadet Battalion
   Richmond Ambulance Company
   Detail Maryland Line

2. Barton's City Brigade,
   Col. Meriwether Lewis Clark
   1st City Regiment
   2nd City Regiment
   3rd City Regiment
   4th City Regiment
   Castle Thunder Company

Independent Richmond Infantry
   1st Virginia Militia
   19th Virginia Militia
   3rd Virginia Reserve Battalion (Chrisman's)
   Provost Guard

Independent Richmond Cavalry
   1st Virginia LDF Cavalry Battalion
   Owen's City Cavalry Regiment

Artillery Defenses,[37] Lt. Col. John C. Pemberton

1. First Division,
   Lt. Col. John W. Atkinson
   10th Virginia Heavy Artillery Battalion
   19th Virginia Heavy Artillery Battalion

2. Second Division,
   Lt. Col. James M. Howard
   18th Virginia Heavy Artillery Battalion
   20th Virginia Heavy Artillery Battalion

3. Lightfoot's Battalion,
   Lt. Col. Charles E. Lightfoot
   Caroline Artillery
   Second Nelson Artillery
   Surry Light Artillery

4. Stark's Battalion,
   Maj. Alexander W. Stark
   Louisiana Guard Artillery
   Mathews Artillery
   McComas Artillery

5. Chaffin's Bluff Battalion,
   Lt. Col. John Minor Maury
   Goochland Artillery
   James City Artillery
   Lunenburg Artillery
   Norfolk Howitzers
   Pamunkey Artillery

James River Naval Squadron — Commander John K. Mitchell[38]

Ironclads

1. C.S.S. *Virginia II*,
   Lt. Francis Shepperd

2. C.S.S. *Richmond*,
   Lt. John S. Maury

3. C.S.S. *Fredericksburg*,
   Commander Thomas R. Rootes

Battery Semmes,
Lt. Michael Goodwyn

Gunboats

1. C.S.S. *Beaufort*,
   Lt. William Mason

2. C.S.S. *Drewry*,
   Lt. William Wall

3. C.S.S. *Hampton*,
   Lt. John W. Murdaugh

4. C.S.S. *Nansemond*,
   Lt. Charles Hays

5. C.S.S. *Roanoke*,
   Acting Master W. Frank Shippey

6. C.S.S. *Patrick Henry*,
   Lt. William H. Parker

Appendix B

CASUALTIES

Northern Forces

———◆———

ARMY OF THE POTOMAC[1]

CAVALRY DIVISION

	Killed	Wounded	Missing	Total
Gregg				
Div. Headquarters	0	1	0	1
Davies				
Brig. Headquarters	0	0	0	0
1st Massachusetts Cavalry	2	2	0	4
1st New Jersey Cavalry	4	8	3	15
10th New York Cavalry	4	11	0	15
6th Ohio Cavalry	3	11	51	65
1st Pennsylvania Cavalry	0	10	0	10
A/2nd U. S. Artillery	0	3	0	3
Subtotal (DAVIES)	13	45	54	112

	Killed	Wounded	Missing	Total
Smith				
Brig. Headquarters	0	0	0	0
1st Maine Cavalry	2	3	1	6
2nd Pennsylvania Cavalry	0	1	0	1
4th Pennsylvania Cavalry	1	3	7	11
8th Pennsylvania Cavalry	0	1	3	4
13th Pennsylvania Cavalry	0	9	17	26
H-I/1st U. S. Artillery	1	2	0	3
Subtotal (SMITH)	4	19	28	51
Total (GREGG)	17	65	82	164

V ARMY CORPS

	Killed	Wounded	Missing	Total
Warren				
Corps Headquarters	0	0	0	0
E-F/5th New York	0	0	0	0
Detail/4th Pennsylvania Cavalry	0	0	0	0
Subtotal (CORPS HEADQUARTERS)	0	0	0	0
Bragg				
Brig. Headquarters	0	0	0	0
19th Indiana	0	0	0	0
24th Michigan	0	0	0	0
1st New York Sharpshooter Battalion	0	0	0	0
143rd Pennsylvania	0	0	0	0
149th Pennsylvania	0	0	0	0
150th Pennsylvania	0	0	0	0
2nd Wisconsin	0	0	0	0
6th Wisconsin	0	0	0	0
7th Wisconsin	0	0	0	0
Subtotal (BRAGG)	0	0	0	0

	Killed	*Wounded*	*Missing*	*Total*
Griffin				
Div. Headquarters	0	0	0	0
Sickel				
Brig. Headquarters	0	0	0	0
21st Pennsylvania				
Cavalry	1	9	1	11
198th Pennsylvania	1	9	0	10
Subtotal (SICKEL)	2	18	1	21
Gregory				
Brig. Headquarters	0	0	0	0
32nd Massachusetts	2	15	19	36
91st Pennsylvania	1	2	8	11
155th Pennsylvania	5	15	3	23
Subtotal (GREGORY)	8	32	30	70
Gwyn				
Brig. Headquarters	0	1	0	1
20th Maine	6	52	0	58
18th Massachusetts	0	3	10	13
1st Michigan	3	20	4	27
16th Michigan	7	41	0	48
44th New York	1	22	4	27
83rd Pennsylvania	6	28	0	34
118th Pennsylvania	8	36	3	47
Subtotal (GWYN)	31	203	21	255
Subtotal (GRIFFIN)	41	253	52	346
Ayres				
Div. Headquarters	0	0	0	0
C/2nd U.S.	0	0	0	0
Otis				
Brig. Headquarters	0	1	0	1
15th New York Heavy				
Artillery	2	5	0	7
5th New York	3	5	0	8
140th New York	0	5	7	12
146th New York	0	3	0	3
10th U.S.	3	6	18	27
11th U.S.	5	12	0	17
12th U.S.	3	0	1	4
14th U.S.	2	3	0	5
17th U.S.	0	7	16	23
Subtotal (OTIS)	18	47	42	107

	Killed	*Wounded*	*Missing*	*Total*
Graham				
Brig. Headquarters	0	0	0	0
1st Maryland	3	9	0	12
4th Maryland	0	1	0	1
7th Maryland	0	0	0	0
8th Maryland	0	3	0	3
Purnell Legion	0	0	0	0
Subtotal (GRAHAM)	3	13	0	16
Grimshaw				
Brig. Headquarters	0	0	0	0
3rd Delaware	2	3	0	5
4th Delaware	1	4	0	5
157th Pennsylvania	2	10	0	12
190th Pennsylvania	3	8	3	14
191st Pennsylvania	0	0	1	1
Subtotal (GRIMSHAW)	8	25	4	37
Hofmann				
Brig. Headquarters	0	0	0	0
76th New York	0	3	24	27
95th New York	1	1	30	32
147th New York	0	0	11	11
56th Pennsylvania	0	0	6	6
121st Pennsylvania	0	0	45	45
142nd Pennsylvania	0	1	0	1
Subtotal (HOFMANN)	1	5	116	122
Subtotal (AYRES)	30	90	162	282
Wainwright				
Brig. Headquarters	0	0	0	0
B/1st New York Light Artillery	0	0	0	0
D/1st New York Light Artillery	0	4	0	4
H/1st New York Light Artillery	0	4	0	4
L/1st New York Light Artillery	0	0	0	0
15th New York Battery	0	0	0	0
B/1st Pennsylvania Light Artillery	0	0	0	0
Subtotal (WAINWRIGHT)	0	8	0	8
Total (WARREN)	71	351	214	636

IX ARMY CORPS

	Killed	Wounded	Missing	Total
Parke				
Corps Headquarters	0	0	0	0
Detail/3rd New Jersey				
Cavalry	0	0	0	0
8th U.S.	0	0	0	0
Subtotal (CORPS				
HEADQUARTERS)	0	0	0	0
Monroe				
Brig. Headquarters	0	0	0	0
7th Maine Battery	0	0	0	0
19th New York Battery	0	0	0	0
34th New York Battery	3	3	0	6
D Pennsylvania Light				
Artillery	0	0	0	0
Subtotal (MONROE)	3	3	0	6
Willcox				
Div. Headquarters	1	1	0	2
17th Michigan	0	0	0	0
Harriman				
Brig. Headquarters	0	0	0	0
8th Michigan	0	4	3	7
27th Michigan	0	7	1	8
109th New York	0	0	0	0
13th Ohio Cavalry	10	17	4	31
37th Wisconsin	0	9	0	9
38th Wisconsin	0	4	0	4
Subtotal (HARRIMAN)	10	41	8	59
Hartranft				
Brig. Headquarters	0	0	0	0
1st Michigan				
Sharpshooters	0	3	18	21
2nd Michigan	0	7	11	18
20th Michigan	2	3	19	24
24th New York Cavalry	3	12	45	60
46th New York	2	17	38	57
60th Ohio	0	7	20	27
50th Pennsylvania	2	5	9	16
Subtotal (HARTRANFT)	9	54	160	223

	Killed	Wounded	Missing	Total
McLaughlen				
Brig. Headquarters	0	0	0	0
3rd Maryland	1	6	0	7
57th Massachusetts	1	7	0	8
59th Massachusetts	1	9	2	12
14th New York Heavy				
Artillery	4	20	4	28
100th Pennsylvania	2	8	4	14
Subtotal (MᴄLᴀᴜɢʜʟᴇɴ)	9	50	10	69
Subtotal (Wɪʟʟᴄᴏx)	29	146	178	353
Potter				
Div. Headquarters	0	1	0	1
Curtin				
Brig. Headquarters	0	0	0	0
21st Massachusetts	2	8	15	25
35th Massachusetts	6	19	156	181
36th Massachusetts	2	9	13	24
58th Massachusetts	1	2	90	93
51st New York	2	10	332	344
45th Pennsylvania	4	15	185	204
48th Pennsylvania	2	8	44	54
4th Rhode Island	2	3	0	5
7th Rhode Island	2	7	0	9
Subtotal (Cᴜʀᴛɪɴ)	23	81	835	939
Simon Griffin				
Brig. Headquarters	0	0	0	0
31st Maine	7	12	18	37
32nd Maine	0	9	34	43
2nd Maryland	2	16	57	75
56th Massachusetts	1	10	28	39
6th New Hampshire	5	30	77	112
9th New Hampshire	3	22	95	120
11th New Hampshire	5	30	35	70
2nd New York Mounted				
Rifles	3	10	63	76
179th New York	1	24	33	58
17th Vermont	7	30	43	80
Subtotal (Sɪᴍᴏɴ Gʀɪꜰꜰɪɴ)	34	193	483	710
Subtotal (Pᴏᴛᴛᴇʀ)	57	275	1,318	1,650

	Killed	Wounded	Missing	Total
Mott				
Div. Headquarters	0	0	0	0
DeTrobriand				
Brig. Headquarters	0	0	0	0
20th Indiana	0	0	0	0
1st Maine Heavy Artillery	2	5	1	8
17th Maine	1	2	0	3
40th New York	0	1	0	1
73rd New York	0	0	0	0
86th New York	0	0	0	0
124th New York	0	0	0	0
99th Pennsylvania	0	2	0	2
110th Pennsylvania	1	2	0	3
2nd U. S. Sharpshooters	0	3	0	3
Subtotal (DeTrobriand)	4	15	1	20
Pierce				
Brig. Headquarters	0	0	0	0
1st Massachusetts Heavy Artillery	2	11	8	21
93rd New York	0	3	0	3
57th Pennsylvania	0	3	0	3
84th Pennsylvania	0	8	0	8
105th Pennsylvania	1	5	0	6
141st Pennsylvania	1	6	0	7
1st U. S. Sharpshooters	0	3	3	6
Subtotal (Pierce)	4	39	11	54
McAllister				
Brig. Headquarters	0	0	0	0
11th Massachusetts	2	1	0	3
5th New Jersey	1	0	0	1
6th New Jersey	0	0	0	0
7th New Jersey	0	1	0	1
8th New Jersey	0	1	0	1
11th New Jersey	0	0	0	0
72nd New York	0	0	0	0
120th New York	1	8	0	9
Subtotal (McAllister)	4	11	0	15
Subtotal (Mott)	12	65	12	89
Total (Parke)	101	489	1,508	2,098

Summary for the Army of the Potomac[2]

	Killed	Wounded	Missing	Total
Meade				
Army Headquarters	0	0	0	0
Hancock	–	–	–	32
Crawford	–	–	–	20
Warren	71	351	214	636
Gregg	17	65	82	164
Parke	101	489	1,508	2,098
Total (MEADE)[3]	189	905	1,804	2,950

ARMY OF THE JAMES[4]

CAVALRY DIVISION

	Killed	Wounded	Missing	Total
Kautz				
Div. Headquarters	0	0	0	0
West				
Brig. Headquarters	0	0	0	0
3rd New York Cavalry	0	3	2	5
5th Pennsylvania Cavalry	1	14	5	20
4th Wisconsin Battery	1	2	0	3
Subtotal (WEST)	2	19	7	28
Spear				
Brig. Headquarters	0	0	0	0
1st District of Columbia Cavalry	0	2	1	3
11th Pennsylvania Cavalry	0	3	2	5
B/1st U. S. Artillery	0	1	0	1
Subtotal (SPEAR)	0	6	3	9
1st New York Mounted Rifles	0	0	0	0
Total (KAUTZ)	2	25	10	37

X ARMY CORPS

	Killed	Wounded	Missing	Total
Birney				
Corps Headquarters	0	0	0	0
1–3/4th Massachusetts Cavalry	0	0	0	0
Subtotal (HEADQUARTERS)	0	0	0	0
Terry				
Div. Headquarters	0	0	0	0
Pond				
Brig. Headquarters	0	0	0	0
39th Illinois	0	0	1	0
62nd Ohio	0	0	0	0
67th Ohio	1	1	0	2
85th Pennsylvania	0	0	1	1
Subtotal (POND)	1	1	2	4
Abbott				
Brig. Headquarters	0	0	0	0
6th Connecticut	0	3	6	9
7th Connecticut	2	11	11	24
3rd New Hampshire	0	4	1	5
7th New Hampshire	0	7	11	18
16th New York Heavy Artillery	0	4	0	4
Subtotal (ABBOTT)	2	29	29	60
Plaisted				
Brig. Headquarters	0	0	0	0
10th Connecticut	2	4	0	6
11th Maine	0	0	0	0
1st Maryland Cavalry	0	0	0	0
24th Massachusetts	0	0	0	0
100th New York	0	1	1	2
Subtotal (PLAISTED)	2	5	1	8
Subtotal (TERRY)	5	35	32	72

	Killed	Wounded	Missing	Total
Foster[5]				
Div. Headquarters	0	0	0	0
Daggett				
Brig. Headquarters	0	1	0	1
3rd New York	5	16	4	25
112th New York	2	38	20	60
117th New York	15	75	33	123
142nd New York	2	51	14	67
Subtotal (DAGGETT)	24	183	71	278
Pennypacker				
Brig. Headquarters	0	0	0	0
47th New York	1	10	3	14
48th New York	0	3	2	5
76th Pennsylvania	0	8	2	10
97th Pennsylvania	0	9	2	11
Subtotal (PENNYPACKER)	1	30	9	40
Bell				
Brig. Headquarters	0	0	0	0
13th Indiana	0	11	5	16
9th Maine	5	22	18	45
4th New Hampshire	2	16	4	22
115th New York	1	26	6	33
169th New York	2	23	6	31
Subtotal (BELL)	10	102	39	151
Subtotal (FOSTER)	35	315	119	469
W. Birney				
Brig. Headquarters	0	0	0	0
29th Connecticut	5	20	0	25
7th USCT	20	80	136	236
8th USCT	7	60	1	68
9th USCT	7	79	18	104
2/45th USCT	0	4	0	4
Subtotal (W. BIRNEY)	39	243	155	437
Jackson				
Brig. Headquarters	0	0	0	0
1st Connecticut Battery	0	0	0	0
4th New Jersey Battery	0	2	0	2
5th New Jersey Battery	0	0	0	0

	Killed	Wounded	Missing	Total
16th New York Heavy Artillery (Sctn.)	0	0	0	0
E/1st Pennsylvania Light Artillery	0	0	0	0
C/3rd Rhode Island Heavy Artillery	0	0	0	0
C-D/1st U. S. Artillery	0	0	0	0
M/1st U. S. Artillery	0	0	0	0
E/3rd U. S. Artillery	0	0	0	0
D/4th U. S. Artillery	0	0	0	0
Subtotal (JACKSON)	0	2	0	2
Total (BIRNEY)[6]	79	595	306	989

XVIII ARMY CORPS

	Killed	Wounded	Missing	Total
Ord				
Corps Headquarters	0	1	0	1
Battalion/11th Connecticut	0	0	0	0
Subtotal (HEADQUARTERS)	0	1	0	1
Stannard				
Div. Headquarters[7]	3	16	2	21
Stevens				
Brig. Headquarters	0	1	0	1
13th New Hampshire	14	62	1	77
81st New York	9	50	0	59
98th New York	8	54	1	63
139th New York	12	29	0	41
Subtotal (STEVENS)	43	196	2	241
Burnham				
Brig. Headquarters	1	0	0	1
8th Connecticut	7	42	13	62
10th New Hampshire	8	24	0	32
96th New York	8	66	29	103
118th New York	3	64	0	67
Subtotal (BURNHAM)	27	196	42	265

	Killed	*Wounded*	*Missing*	*Total*
Roberts				
Brig. Headquarters	1	0	0	1
21st Connecticut	1	23	4	28
92nd New York	7	19	9	35
58th Pennsylvania	15	85	5	105
188th Pennsylvania	10	45	9	64
Subtotal (Roberts)	34	172	27	233
Subtotal (Stannard)	107	580	73	760
Heckman				
Div. Headquarters	0	0	0	0
Jourdan				
Brig. Headquarters	0	0	0	0
148th New York	4	20	0	24
158th New York	14	54	10	78
55th Pennsylvania	2	39	41	82
Subtotal (Jourdan)	20	113	51	184
Ripley				
Brig. Headquarters	0	0	0	0
8th Maine	0	9	0	9
9th Vermont	7	34	0	41
Subtotal (Ripley)	7	43	0	50
Fairchild				
Brig. Headquarters	0	1	0	1
89th New York	3	19	20	42
2nd Pennsylvania Heavy Artillery	14	84	138	236
Subtotal (Fairchild)	17	104	158	279
Subtotal (Heckman)	44	260	209	513
Paine				
Div. Headquarters[8]	3	22	0	25
2nd USCT Cavalry	5	33	2	40
Subtotal (Div. Headquarters)	8	55	2	65

	Killed	Wounded	Missing	Total
Holman				
Brig. Headquarters	0	0	0	0
1st USCT	3	18	0	21
22nd USCT	6	68	4	78
37th USCT	4	16	0	20
Subtotal (HOLMAN)	13	102	4	119
Draper				
Brig. Headquarters	0	1	0	1
5th USCT	28	185	23	236
36th USCT	21	87	0	108
38th USCT	17	94	0	111
Subtotal (DRAPER)	66	367	23	456
Duncan				
Brig. Headquarters	0	1	0	1
4th USCT	27	136	14	177
6th USCT	41	160	8	209
Subtotal (DUNCAN)	68	297	22	387
Subtotal (PAINE)	155	821	51	1,027
White				
Brig. Headquarters	0	0	0	0
5th Maryland	0	0	0	0
2nd New Hampshire	0	0	0	0
12th New Hampshire	0	0	0	0
Subtotal (WHITE)	0	0	0	0
Cook				
Brig. Headquarters	0	0	0	0
H/3rd New York Light Artillery	0	0	0	0
K/3rd New York Light Artillery	0	3	0	3
16th New York Battery	0	4	0	4
A/1st Pennsylvania Light Artillery	0	3	0	3
F/1st Rhode Island Light Artillery	0	6	0	6
F/5th U. S. Artillery	1	3	0	4
Subtotal (COOK)	1	19	0	20
Serrell	0	0	0	0
Total (ORD)[9]	307	1,681	333	2,327

BERMUDA HUNDRED[10]

	Killed	Wounded	Missing	Total
Potter				
Brig. Headquarters	0	0	0	0
11th Connecticut	0	0	0	0
40th Massachusetts	0	0	0	0
12th New Hampshire	0	1	0	1
206th Pennsylvania	0	0	0	0
207th Pennsylvania	0	0	0	0
208th Pennsylvania	1	0	0	1
209th Pennsylvania	0	0	0	0
211th Pennsylvania	2	7	0	9
E/3rd New York Light Artillery	0	8	0	8
M/3rd New York Light Artillery	0	0	0	0
7th New York Battery	0	0	0	0
L/4th U. S. Artillery	0	0	0	0
A/5th U. S. Artillery	0	0	0	0
Total (POTTER)	3	16	0	19

DEEP BOTTOM

	Killed	Wounded	Missing	Total
Moore				
Post Headquarters	0	0	0	0
17th New York Battery	0	0	0	0
203rd Pennsylvania	0	0	0	0
Total (MOORE)	0	0	0	0

Summary for the Army of the James

Butler	Killed	Wounded	Missing	Total
Army Headquarters	0	0	0	0
Kautz	2	25	10	37
Moore	0	0	0	0
Birney	79	595	306	989
Potter	3	16	0	19
Ord	307	1,681	333	2,327
Abbot	0	0	0	0
Graham	0	0	0	0
Strong	0	0	0	0
Total (BUTLER)[11]	391	2,317	649	3,372

Summary for the Northern Forces

Grant	Killed	Wounded	Missing	Total
Grant's Headquarters	0	0	0	0
Butler	391	2,317	649	3,372
Meade	189	905	1,804	2,950
Grand Total (GRANT)[12]	580	3,222	2,453	6,322

Southern Forces

———◆———

Presenting a table of Secessionist losses is no easy matter. Unlike for Grant's command, no detailed and comprehensive table of Confederate casualties already exists. One must, accordingly, be constructed from highly fragmentary sources. Only for Field, Bushrod Johnson, McKethan, McGowan, Lane, King, Guy, Elliott, Hardaway, Minor Maury, Haskell, and Chew have full statistics been found. Colquitt, Gary, MacRae, Archer, Joseph Davis, Dunovant, and Pegram are partially documented. For the other forces, data are more marginal or even lacking altogether. Federal provost rolls reveal how many prisoners were captured but shed no light on numbers of killed and wounded. To produce some idea of casualties, losses of a single regiment are sometimes extrapolated for an entire brigade. Reasonable estimates are also occasionally made concerning a brigade's total loss and especially its loss on the Peninsula over the weekend. In such cases, it is often impossible to break casualties down by regiments or to specify killed and wounded. Numerous blanks thus appear in the resulting table. Where nothing but blanks can be offered, no listing of regiments is made under entries for brigades. Even where numbers do appear, many are not precise. Readers should, therefore, not be misled by the appearance of specificity. The ensuing table is basically a reasonable approximation, not a confirmed body count.[13]

FORCES NORTH OF THE APPOMATTOX RIVER

DEPARTMENT OF RICHMOND

	Killed	Wounded	Missing	Total
Ewell				
Dept. Headquarters	0	0	0	0
INFANTRY[14]				
Elliott	1	11	8	20
Strange	–	–	4	12
Guy	0	8	6	14
Second-class Troops	0	0	8	8
Moore				
Brig. Headquarters	–	–	0	–
1st Virginia LDF Bat.	–	–	0	–
2nd Virginia LDF	–	–	1	–
3rd Virginia LDF	–	–	0	–
4th Virginia LDF Bat.	–	–	1	–
5th Virginia LDF Bat.	–	–	2	–
Company VMI Cadet Bat.	–	–	0	–
Richmond Ambulance Co.	–	–	0	–
3rd Virginia Reserve Bat.	–	–	0	–
Subtotal (MOORE)	–	–	4	11
Hughs				
Brig. Headquarters	–	1	0	–
17th Tennessee	–	–	17	–
23rd Tennessee	–	–	8	–
25th Tennessee	–	–	0	–
44th Tennessee	–	–	0	–
63rd Tennessee	–	–	2	–
Subtotal (HUGHS)	–	–	27	50
Subtotal (INFANTRY)	–	–	57	115

	Killed	Wounded	Missing	Total
CAVALRY[15]				
Gary				
Brig. Headquarters	0	0	0	0
Hampton Legion	–	–	5	14
7th South Carolina Cavalry	–	–	1	26
24th Virginia Cavalry	–	–	3	10
Subtotal (GARY)	–	–	9	50
Owen	0	0	0	0
Subtotal (CAVALRY)	–	–	9	50
ARTILLERY[16]				
Hardaway				
Batn. Headquarters	0	0	0	0
Third / Richmond Howitzers	0	0	0	0
First Rockbridge Artillery	0	0	0	0
Powhatan Artillery	4	18	0	22
Salem Flying Artillery	1	1	0	2
Subtotal (HARDAWAY)	5	19	0	24
Maury				
Batn. Headquarters	0	1	3	4
Goochland Artillery	2	1	5	8
James City Artillery	1	1	0	2
Lunenburg Artillery	0	1	0	1
Norfolk Howitzers	0	2	0	2
Pamunkey Artillery	0	0	0	0
Subtotal (MAURY)	3	6	8	17
Stark	–	–	0	9
Hardin	–	–	6	12
Pemberton	0	0	0	0
Subtotal (ARTILLERY)	–	–	14	62
Total (EWELL)	–	–	80	227

I ARMY CORPS

	Killed	Wounded	Missing	Total
Anderson				
Corps Headquarters	0	0	0	0
Montague[17]				
Brig. Headquarters	–	–	–	–
24th Virginia	–	–	–	–
32nd Virginia	–	–	–	–
53rd Virginia	–	–	–	–
56th Virginia	3	7	0	10
Subtotal (MONTAGUE)	–	–	17	61
Field[18]				
Div. Headquarters	0	0	0	0
Gregg				
Brig. Headquarters	0	0	0	0
3rd Arkansas	1	3	4	8
1st Texas	7	5	3	15
4th Texas	2	10	2	14
5th Texas	1	15	0	16
Subtotal (GREGG)	11	33	9	53
DuBose				
Brig. Headquarters	0	0	0	0
2nd Georgia	1	8	11	20
15th Georgia	9	13	12	34
17th Georgia	2	10	7	19
20th Georgia	5	5	30	40
Subtotal (DUBOSE)	17	36	60	113
G. T. Anderson				
Brig. Headquarters	0	0	0	0
7th Georgia	2	13	0	15
8th Georgia	6	14	0	20
9th Georgia	5	12	0	17
11th Georgia	2	8	0	10
59th Georgia	6	14	0	20
Subtotal (G. T. ANDERSON)	21	61	0	82

	Killed	Wounded	Missing	Total
Bratton				
Brig. Headquarters	0	0	0	0
1st South Carolina				
Volunteers	10	64	2	76
2nd South Carolina				
Rifles	10	39	0	49
5th South Carolina	6	50	0	56
6th South Carolina	22	114	4	140
Palmetto Sharpshooters	10	46	0	56
Subtotal (BRATTON)	58	313	6	377
Bowles				
Brig. Headquarters	0	0	0	0
4th Alabama	0	4	0	4
15th Alabama	4	9	0	13
44th Alabama	2	4	1	7
47th Alabama	2	0	0	2
48th Alabama	0	0	0	0
Subtotal (BOWLES)	8	17	1	26
Subtotal (FIELD)	115	460	76	651
Hoke[19]				
Div. Headquarters	0	0	0	0
McKethan				
Brig. Headquarters	0	1	1	2
8th North Carolina	36	41	70	147
31st North Carolina	30	67	47	144
51st North Carolina	32	45	27	104
61st North Carolina	24	50	58	132
Subtotal (McKETHAN)	122	204	203	529
Colquitt				
Brig. Headquarters	–	–	–	–
6th Georgia	–	–	2	–
19th Georgia	–	–	3	–
23rd Georgia	–	–	5	–
27th Georgia	–	–	0	–
28th Georgia	–	–	3	–
Subtotal (COLQUITT)	–	–	13	223
Kirkland	–	–	7	15
Hagood	–	–	0	19
Scales	–	–	0	5
Subtotal (HOKE)	–	–	223	791

	Killed	Wounded	Missing	Total
Alexander[20]				
Brig. Headquarters	0	0	0	0
Haskell				
Batn. Headquarters	0	0	0	0
Flanner	0	0	0	0
Garden	0	0	0	0
Lamkin	0	0	0	0
Subtotal (HASKELL)	0	0	0	0
Johnson				
Batn. Headquarters	–	–	0	–
Clutter	–	–	0	–
Pollock	–	–	0	–
Subtotal (JOHNSON)	–	–	0	–
Independent				
Clopton	–	–	0	–
Miller	–	–	0	–
Subtotal (INDEPENDENT)	–	–	0	–
Subtotal (ALEXANDER)	–	–	0	3
Total (ANDERSON)	–	–	316	1,506

Summary for the Forces North of the Appomattox[21]

	Killed	Wounded	Missing	Total
Lee				
Army Headquarters	0	0	0	0
Ewell	–	–	80	227
Anderson	–	–	316	1,506
Pickett	–	–	0	4
Mitchell	0	0	0	0
Total (NORTH OF THE APPOMATTOX)[22]	–	–	396	1,737

FORCES SOUTH OF THE APPOMATTOX

III ARMY CORPS

	Killed	Wounded	Missing	Total
Hill				
Corps Headquarters	0	0	0	0
5th Alabama Battalion	0	0	0	0
Subtotal (CORPS HEADQUARTERS)		0	0	0	0
Wilcox[23]				
Div. Headquarters	0	0	0	0
McGowan				
Brig. Headquarters	0	0	0	0
1st South Carolina Provisional Army	2	20	1	23
1st South Carolina Rifles	9	37	1	47
12th South Carolina	5	18	0	23
13th South Carolina	10	24	0	34
14th South Carolina	5	30	0	35
Subtotal (McGOWAN)	31	129	2	162
Lane				
Brig. Headquarters	0	0	0	0
7th North Carolina	3	34	0	37
18th North Carolina	3	20	0	23
28th North Carolina	3	29	0	32
33rd North Carolina	2	5	0	7
37th North Carolina	7	16	1	24
Subtotal (LANE)	18	104	1	123
Subtotal (WILCOX)	49	233	3	285
Heth[24]				
Div. Headquarters	–	–	20	30
Archer				
Brig. Headquarters	–	–	0	–
13th Alabama	–	–	0	–
2nd Maryland Battalion	13	34	4	51
1st Tennessee Provisional Army	–	–	2	–
7th Tennessee	–	–	0	–
14th Tennessee	–	–	2	–
22nd Virginia Battalion	3	11	1	15

	Killed	Wounded	Missing	Total
40th Virginia	3	30	2	35
47th Virginia	1	8	1	10
55th Virginia	4	18	4	26
Subtotal (ARCHER)	–	–	16	215

Davis

Brig. Headquarters	0	0	0	0
1st Confederate Battalion	0	5	1	6
2nd Mississippi	3	19	1	23
11th Mississippi	1	3	2	6
26th Mississippi	4	12	3	19
42nd Mississippi	0	6	2	8
55th North Carolina	–	–	3	39
Subtotal (DAVIS)	–	–	12	101

Cooke

Brig. Headquarters	–	–	0	–
15th North Carolina	–	–	4	–
27th North Carolina	–	–	3	–
46th North Carolina	–	–	3	–
48th North Carolina	–	–	6	–
Subtotal (COOKE)	–	–	16	53

MacRae

Brig. Headquarters	–	–	0	–
11th North Carolina	–	–	0	–
26th North Carolina	–	–	1	–
44th North Carolina	11	78	2	91
47th North Carolina	1	25	1	27
52nd North Carolina	–	–	0	–
Subtotal (MACRAE)	–	–	4	243
Subtotal (HETH)	–	–	68	642

Mahone[25]

Div. Headquarters	–	–	0	–

King

Brig. Headquarters	0	0	0	0
8th Alabama	0	1	0	1
9th Alabama	0	0	0	0
10th Alabama	0	0	0	0
11th Alabama	1	1	0	2
14th Alabama	0	2	0	2
Subtotal (KING)	1	4	0	5

	Killed	*Wounded*	*Missing*	*Total*
Gibson				
Brig. Headquarters	–	–	0	–
2nd Georgia Battalion	–	–	0	–
10th Georgia Battalion	–	–	1	–
3rd Georgia	–	–	0	–
22nd Georgia	–	–	0	–
48th Georgia	–	–	1	–
64th Georgia	–	–	0	–
Subtotal (GIBSON)	–	–	2	5
Harris				
Brig. Headquarters	–	–	0	–
12th Mississippi	–	–	0	–
16th Mississippi	–	–	0	–
19th Mississippi	–	–	0	–
48th Mississippi	–	–	2	–
Subtotal (HARRIS)	–	–	2	10
Weiseger	–	–	0	7
Finegan	–	–	0	5
F. Archer	0	0	0	0
Subtotal (MAHONE)	–	–	4	32
Walker[26]				
Brig. Headquarters	–	–	0	–
Pegram				
Batn. Headquarters	0	1	0	1
Gregg	–	–	0	–
Brander	–	–	0	–
Crenshaw	0	0	0	0
Purcell	2	6	0	8
Subtotal (PEGRAM)	–	–	0	13
Eshelman	–	–	0	–
Lane	–	–	0	–
McIntosh	–	–	0	–
Richardson	–	–	0	–
Subtotal (WALKER)	–	–	0	13
Total (HILL)	–	–	75	980

CAVALRY CORPS

	Killed	Wounded	Missing	Total
Hampton				
Corps Headquarters	0	0	0	0
Butler[27]				
Div. Headquarters	0	0	0	0
Dunovant				
Brig. Headquarters	1	0	1	2
4th South Carolina Cavalry	1	7	0	8
5th South Carolina Cavalry	3	12	1	16
6th South Carolina Cavalry	–	–	1	12
Subtotal (DUNOVANT)	–	–	3	38
Young	–	–	10	47
Subtotal (BUTLER)	–	–	13	85
W. Lee[28]				
Div. Headquarters	–	–	0	–
Davis				
Brig. Headquarters	–	–	0	–
9th Virginia Cavalry	2	9	0	11
10th Virginia Cavalry	–	–	0	7
13th Virginia Cavalry	–	–	55	62
Subtotal (DAVIS)	–	–	55	80
Barringer				
Brig. Headquarters	–	–	0	–
1st North Carolina Cavalry	–	–	4	–
2nd North Carolina Cavalry	–	–	0	–
3rd North Carolina Cavalry	–	–	0	–
5th North Carolina Cavalry	–	–	0	–
Subtotal (BARRINGER)	–	–	4	14
Subtotal (W. LEE)	–	–	59	94

	Killed	Wounded	Missing	Total
J. Griffin[29]				
Brig. Headquarters	–	–	0	–
7th Confederate Cavalry	–	–	51	–
8th Georgia Cavalry	–	–	3	–
4th North Carolina				
Cavalry	–	–	2	–
Subtotal (J. GRIFFIN)	–	–	56	83
Farley[30]	–	–	6	18
Chew[31]				
Batn. Headquarters	0	0	0	0
Hart	0	2	0	2
McGregor	0	0	0	0
Graham	3	3	5	11
Subtotal (CHEW)	3	5	5	13
Total (HAMPTON)	–	–	139	293

DEPARTMENT OF NORTH CAROLINA AND SOUTHERN VIRGINIA[32]

	Killed	Wounded	Missing	Total
"Otey"				
Department Headquarters	0	0	0	0
Jones	–	–	0	8
Johnson				
Div. Headquarters	0	0	0	0
Goode	0	0	0	0
Gracie	1	4	0	5
McAfee	2	9	0	11
Wallace	4	3	0	7
Subtotal (JOHNSON)	7	16	0	23
Total ("OTEY")	–	–	0	31

Summary for Forces South of the Appomattox[33]

Hill	Killed	Wounded	Missing[34]	Total
III Corps	–	–	75	980
Cavalry Corps	–	–	139	293
Dept. of N. Carolina and S. Virginia	–	–	0	31
Engineers	0	0	0	0
Provost Guard	0	0	0	0
Signal Corps	0	0	0	0
Total (HILL)[35]	–	–	214	1,304

Summary for the Southern Forces

Lee	Killed	Wounded	Missing[36]	Total
Army Headquarters	0	0	0	0
Ewell-Anderson	–	–	396	1,737
Hill	–	–	214	1,304
Grand Total (LEE)	–	–	610	3,041

Comparative Summary by Sectors

Sector	Killed		Wounded		Missing[37]		Total	
	U.S.	C.S.	U.S.	C.S.	U.S.	C.S.	U.S.	C.S.
North of the Appomattox	391	–	2,317	–	649	396	3,372	1,737
South of the Appomattox	189	–	905	–	1,804	214	2,950	1,304
Total	580	–	3,222	–	2,453	610	6,322	3,041

NOTES

Note: For complete names of sources
and repositories, refer to Bibliography.

CHAPTER I

1. J. William Jones, *Life and Letters of Lee*, p. 40.

2. U. S. Grant, *Personal Memoirs*, v. II, pp. 127–32, 146; Ely Parker to C. J. Faulkner, Sept. 23, 1864, VSL; George Leet to William R. Rowley, Sept. 23, 1864, Rowley Papers, ISHL; Frederick H. Dyer, *Compendium*, pp. 1,366, 1,470, 1,624–25; *OR*, v. XLII, pt. 2, pp. 832–33, 881–82, 912, 1,010, 1,050, 1,062–63, 1,119, and v. XXXIX, pt. 2, pp. 363–65; *ORN*, v. X, pp. 430–31; Richard Sommers, "Grant's Fifth Offensive at Petersburg," Ph.D. dissertation at Rice University (1970), v. I, pp. 13–14, 41.

3. At least the IX Corps high command shared Grant's confidence in winning big in early fall. *OR*, v. XLII, pt. 1, p. 874, and pt. 2, pp. 766–67, 770–71, 856, 893, 914, 959–60, 963–64, 977, 989, 1,008–10, 1,025, 1,046–47, 1,050, 1,058–59, 1,082–88, 1,090–91, 1,257–58, and pt. 3, p. 48, and v. XLIII, pt. 2, pp. 110, 118, 119, 142, 152; William McDonald, *Laurel Brigade*, pp. 299–300; Andrew A. Humphreys to his wife, Oct. 28, 1864, AAH Papers, HSP; Ely Parker to C. J. Faulkner, Sept. 23, 1864, VSL; Cyrus Comstock, *Diary*, Sept. 26, 1864, LC; RG 94, entry 159, W. S. Hancock file, and entry 731, box 63, Grant to Meade, letter received 1:00 P.M., Sept. 25, 1864, NA; RG 393, AP, v. VI, bk. 6, pp. 463, 466, 473, NA; RG 108, entry 1, v. XXI, p. 428, and entry 11, box 86, No. V233, NA; RG 393, DVNC, v. LV, bk. 79, pp. 238–39, and letter box 6, No. R138, and telegram box 10, Comstock to Butler, Sept. 26, 1864, NA; Charles J. Mills to his mother, Sept. 26, 1864, Gregory Coco mss.; "Fort Fisher Testimony," *Report of the Joint Committee on the Conduct of the War, at the Second Session, 38th Congress*, v. II, pp. 3, 67–68; David Dixon Porter, *Journal*, box 23, v. I, pp. 807–10, LC; J. W. Jones, op. cit., p. 40; Benjamin F. Butler, *Butler's Book*, pp. 718–30; Samuel Pollack, *Diary*, Aug. 24 and Sept. 26, 1864, ISHL; Jessie Ames Marshall, ed., *Correspondence of Benjamin F. Butler*, v. V, pp. 154, 218; *ORN*, v. X, pp. 326, 363, 515; Sommers, op. cit., v. I, pp. 40–43, 52–56.

4. "Returns of the 18th, 2nd, 5th, Artillery Brigade/6th, 9th, and 10th Corps and Second Division/Cavalry Corps/Army of the Potomac, and of the Army of the Potomac and Army of the James, Sept. 20 and 30, 1864," RG 94, entries 65 and 62, respectively, NA; RG 391, 5AC, v. XXXIX, bk. 205, Sept. 30, 1864, and v. LIV, bk. 260, Sept. 30, 1864, and v. XI, bk. 39, pp. 100–3, NA; RG 391, CC, v. XXVI, bk. 51, pp. 84–85, NA; RG 391, 24AC, v. XXX, bk. 63, Sept. 27, 1864, NA; "Returns of the 15th New York Engineers, 10th USCT, 4th U. S. Infantry, and 5th U. S. Cavalry, Sept., 1864," RG 94, entries 57 and 66, respectively, NA; Sommers, op. cit., pp. 44–45, 47, 51–52, 56–58, 64–68, 91–92, 143–44, 183–85, 390, 648–49, 734–41; *Ripley Ms.*, p. 1, DSF Coll., UV; "Returns of A/55th Pennsylvania, A-K/9th Vermont, Staff/184th New York, Staff/1st New York Engineers, C-G-K/4th USCT, Staff-A-K/6th USCT, and B/1st U. S. Artillery, S-O, 1864," RG 94, M594 and entry 53, respectively, NA; George Ward, *2nd Pennsylvania Heavy Artillery*, pp. 104–5; RG 94, entry 731, box 57, Smyth to Wilson, Sept. 25, 1864, and box 59, Howard to Birney, received 7:13 P.M., Sept. 24, 1864, and box 63, Meade to Grant, noon, Sept. 25, 1864, and Ord to Kensel, received 8:30 P.M., Sept. 27, 1864, NA; RG 393, DVNC, v. CV, bk. 216, pp. 24–25, and v. CLXXXVIII, bk. 455, p. 47, and v. CVI, bk. 217, p. 9, and bk. 219, p. 258, and v. LV, bk. 79, pp. 254–57, and v. DXXXIX, bk. 117, pp. 159–63, and v. CCLXXXII, bk. 725, No. H117, and telegram box 10, Marston to Butler, Sept. 28, 1864, and telegram box 12, Birney to Davis, Sept. 24, 1864, NA; Martin Haynes, *2nd New Hampshire*, pp. 251–52; Wardwell Robinson, *184th New York*, pp. 18–20; George Bailey to his parents, Oct. 1, 1864, Bailey Papers, Stanford University; "Return of H/22nd USCT, S-O, 1864," Luther Osborn Papers, HHL; John McMurray, *Recollections*, p. 50; Horace Montgomery, "A Union Officer's Recollections," *Pennsylvania History*, v. XXVIII, p. 175; Christian Fleetwood, *Diary*, Sept. 27–28, 1864, LC; *OR*, v. XLII, pt. 1, pp. 42, 44, 48, 99, 100, 105, 109–10, and pt. 2, pp. 692, 712, 714, 730, 755, 849, 895, 955, 991–98, 1,002–4, 1,008–10, 1,014–19, 1,025–26, 1,029–30, 1,040, 1,043–47, 1,057–58, 1,060, 1,062–64, 1,079–81, 1,088–90, and pt. 3, p. 10; August V. Kautz, *Reminiscences*, p. 87, Kautz Papers, LC; Asch to Spear, Sept. 27, 1864, RG 94, entry 731, box 51, NA; Butler to Ord, 11:45, Sept. 27, 1864, RG 94, entry 159, Butler file, v. LIX-A, No. D, NA; RG 94, entry 12, 1864 file, No. B1379, NA; William Haskin, *1st U. S. Artillery*, p. 209; RG 108, entry 1, v. XXI, p. 433, NA; Robert Faulkner, *Diary*, Sept. 25, 1864, HHL; RG 391, 2AC, v. LXVIII, bk. 347, pp. 36–37, and v. LXIX, bk. 348, p. 201, and box 1, Miles to Bingham, Sept. 25, 1864, and box 21, Hunt to Edgell, Sept. 24, 1864, NA; RG 391, 6AC, v. XC, bk. 199, pp. 49–50, NA; Henry J. Hunt, *Journal, 1864–1865*, p. 129, HJH Papers, LC; RG 391, 25AC, v. XXXIII, bk. 66½, pp. 292–95, 299–300, 310, and v. XLIX, bk. 123, p. 46, and box 4, James to Dewey, Sept. 25, 1864, and Butler, order of Sept. 25, 1864, NA; Deployment of Cook's brigade, Sept. 27, 1864, RG 391, 18AC, box 1, NA; RG 391, 10AC, v. XV, bk. 50, p. 121, NA; Alfred H. Terry to Harry, Sept. 26, 1864, Terry Family Papers, Yale University; Edward L. Cook to Laura, Sept. 27, 1864, Cook Papers, UCSB.

5. *OR,* v. XLII, pt. 1, pp. 48, 65, 74–79, 82–96, 132–44, 193, 599–605, and pt. 2, pp. 405–6, 494, 533, 638, 689, 707, 740–41, 826, 845–46, 867, 1,001, 1,014–22, 1,032, 1,037–41, 1,056, 1,069, 1,075, and v. XXXVI, pt. 1, pp. 123–87, and pt. 2, pp. 15–19, and v. XL, pt. 1, pp. 222–67, 655–74; RG 391, 2AC, letter box 1, Miles to Bingham, Sept. 25, 1864, and First Division box 4, Bingham to Miles, Sept. 25, 1864, and v. XX, bk. 83, pp. 327–32, and v. I, bk. 8, pp. 433–34, 443–44, and v. XLVII, bk. 216, p. 33, and v. LXIX, bk. 344, p. 31, and bk. 348, p. 201, and v. LXVIII, bk. 347, pp. 35–36, NA; Charles S. Wainwright, *Diary,* Sept. 25, 1864, HHL; RG 391, 9AC, v. LXVI, bk. 232, Sept. 26–27, 1864, NA; Hunt, *Journal,* p. 129, HJH Papers, LC; "Return of the Siege Train, Oct. 10 and Nov. 3, 1864," RG 94, entry 62, DVNC, NA; RG 94, entry 113, 1st Connecticut Heavy Artillery order book for 1864, p. 148, NA; RG 391, 6AC, v. XC, bk. 201, pp. 133, 142–44, NA; Sommers, op. cit., v. I, pp. 56, 58–64.

6. These figures include the following estimates: Cooke—1,200, King —900, Talcott—500, Bridgford—250, artillery in Chesterfield (excluding Poague)—1,550, Guy—200. *OR,* v. XLII, pt. 1, p. 880, and pt. 2, pp. 979, 1,214, 1,221, 1,243, 1,266–68, 1,306–11, and v. XLVI, pt. 2, p. 1,169; RG 109, entry 15, Nos. C-16, G-9, K-5, P-15, 20-P-24, 22-P-31, 22-P-33, NA; R. S. Ewell to Taylor, Nov. 8, 1864, Ewell Papers, DU; Walter Harrison, *Record Book,* SHC; "Return of Moseley's artillery brigade, Sept. 10, 1864," RG 109, entry 65, box 13, NA; Hector McKethan to Thomas L. Clingman, Oct. 3, 1864, William Burgwyn Papers, NCDAH; Sommers, op. cit., v. I, pp. 44–51.

7. Clifford Dowdey and Louis Manarin, eds., *The Wartime Papers of R. E. Lee,* pp. 847–58; Taylor to Pendleton, letter and order, Sept. 28, 1864, and D. D. Pendleton to W. N. Pendleton, Oct. 2, 1864, WNP Coll., and John Ramsay to Maggie, Aug. 26 and Sept. 26, 1864, Ramsay Papers, and J. Fred Waring, *Diary,* Sept. 22, 1864, and Thomas Norman to William H. Wills, Sept. 24, 1864, Wills Papers, and William Reinhardt to his aunt, Sept. 22, 1864, Mary Kennedy Papers, and E. J. Williams to his sister, Sept. 20, 1864, Williams Papers, SHC; John Hartman, letter of Sept. 21, 1864, Hartman Papers, and J. F. Maides to his mother, Sept. 23, 1864, Maides Papers, and John Couch to Julia Shields, Sept. 25, 1864, Couch Papers, and J. D. McGeachy to his sister, Sept. 27, 1864, Catherine Buie Papers, and William Russell, *Diary,* Sept. 29, 1864, and William Andrews, letter of Sept. 13, 1864, William Andrews Papers, DU; Robert Mabry to his wife, Sept. 5 and Oct. 11, 1864, Mabry Papers, and Henry Talley to his mother, Sept. 25, 1864, Henry C. Brown Papers, and William Burgwyn, *Diary,* Sept. 26, 1864, NCDAH; William H. Smith, *Diary,* Sept. 26–27, 1864, and David Pope to his wife, Sept. 9, 1864, Pope Papers, and J. W. Shank to J. B. Smith, Sept. 21, 1864, Shank Family Papers, and UDC Coll., v. II, E. D. Graham to Lamar Mann, Sept. 14, 1864, and v. V, Washington Dunn, "Diary," p. 145, and Floyd County UDC Coll., Donald Fleming, *Diary,* Sept. 28, 1864, and microfilm, William Mosely to his parents, Sept. 16, 1864, Mosely Papers, GDAH; W. G. Coyle to Clementine England, Sept.

16, 1864, Lucas Family Papers, and John F. Sale, *Diary,* Sept. 22, 1864, VSL; Rosser Rock to his sister, Sept. 19, 1864, Rock Papers, CM; Alfred Simons, *Diary,* Sept. 18–28, 1864, SCHS; John Shotwell to his cousin, Sept. 19, 1864, Shotwell Papers, Texas State Library; J. A. F. Coleman, *Diary,* p. 7, CMC-Ib, and John Everett to Ma, Sept. 23, 1864, Everett Papers, EU; William J. Pegram to his sister, Sept. — and 24 and Oct. 5, 1864, PJM Coll., VHS; Henry Greer to his mother, Sept. 26, 1864, Greer Papers, LC; Johnson Hagood, *Memoirs,* pp. 301–4; William Izlar, *Edisto Rifles,* pp. 101–2; *OR,* v. XLII, pt. 1, p. 896; Sommers, op. cit., v. I, pp. 68–70.

8. Robert Stiles, *Four Years,* pp. 312–14; James McHenry Howard, "Closing Scenes," *SHSP,* v. XXXI, p. 134; Nathaniel Burwell Johnston, *Military Record,* p. 6, Johnston mss.; D. S. Burwell to E. S. Burwell, Oct. 5, 1864, Burwell Papers, SHC; Columbus *Daily Enquirer,* Oct. 1, 1864; *McCarty Ms.,* p. 1, TXU; Angelina Winkler, *Confederate Capital,* pp. 191–95; Joe Joskins, *Ms. Sketch of Hood's Texas Brigade,* p. 83, and Watson D. Williams to Curls, Sept. 18, 1864, Williams Papers, and Rufus K. Felder to his sister, Sept. 18, 1864, Felder Papers, HJC; J. B. Polley, *Charming Nellie,* pp. 249, 259; Sommers, op. cit., v. I, p. 70.

9. *OR,* v. XL, pt. 1, pp. 665–66, and v. XLII, pt. 1, pp. 653, 659–60, and pt. 2, pp. 588–89, 754, 764–65, 780, 790, 828–29, 847–48, 961, 985, 1,025–28, 1,044, 1,060–61, 1,083; John Taylor and Samuel Hatfield, *1st Connecticut Heavy Artillery,* pp. 110–11; C. H. Osgood, "A Sutler's Clerk," *NT,* Oct. 8, 1891; *ORN,* ser. 2, v. I, pp. 130–31; Linden Kent to Ma, Sept. 27, 1864, Kent-Hunter Papers, UV; William D. Reinhardt to his aunt, Sept. 22, 1864, Kennedy Papers, SHC; Charles and Pinckney Anthony to Ma, Oct. 3 and 24, 1864, Anthony Family Papers, VSL; George Breckinridge, "Boy Captain," *CV,* v. XIII, p. 415; Thomas McCarty, *Diary,* Sept. 17, 1864, TXU; James Moore, "Fort Harrison," *CV,* v. XIII, p. 418; D. D. Pendleton to W. N. Pendleton, Oct. 2, 1864, WNP Coll., SHC; Rosser Rock to his sister, Sept. 19, 1864, Rock Papers, CM; RG 109, ch. 6, v. CCCLXIV, p. 217, NA; *Artillery Defenses,* pp. 164, 192, CHHS; Richard S. Ewell, *Letterbook,* p. 15, DU; Sommers, op. cit., v. I, pp. 118–20.

CHAPTER II

1. *McCarty Ms.,* p. 1, TXU; *Alexander Ms.,* v. LI, p. 258, EPA Coll., SHC; Ewell, *Letterbook,* p. 15, DU; Sommers, op. cit., v. I, pp. 118, 150.

2. In figuring Confederate strength, the following estimates are used: Guy—200, Maury—375, Stark—225, Richmond militia—500, Richmond reserves—500. The 11th Virginia Reserve Battalion is not counted since it apparently did not reach the Tidewater until mid-October. Lewellyn Shaver, *60th Alabama,* pp. 72–73, 77; Ewell, *Letterbook,* pp. 15–16, 19, and Ewell to Taylor, Nov. 8, 1864, Ewell Papers, DU; *OR,* v. XXXVI, pt. 3, pp. 810–11, and v. XLII, pt. 1, pp. 875, 935, and pt. 2, pp. 1,083, 1,243, 1,266, 1,285–87, 1,298–99, 1,305, and pt. 3, pp. 1,131–33, 1,203, and v. XLIII, pt. 2, pp. 898–99, and v. XLVI, pt. 2, pp. 1,169, 1,196–98, and v.

LI, pt. 2, pp. 507–10, 1,040; Lee Wallace, *Virginia Military Organizations,*
pp. 247–52; RG 109, entry 12, 1864 file, No. B3214, NA; Braxton Bragg,
Endorsement Book, 1864–65, p. 123, TU; Dowdey and Manarin, op. cit., p.
265; *Artillery Defenses,* p. 152, CHHS; Richmond *Sentinel,* Oct. 13, 1864;
Stiles, op. cit., pp. 312–14; Howard, loc. cit., v. XXXI, p. 134; R. C.
Taylor, *Personal Experiences,* quoted in Charles Calrow, *Chaffin's Farm,* p.
27, RNBP; RG 109, ch. 2, entry 112, box 12, Nos. 84, 85, 102, 144, and
box 13, Brown to Ewell, Sept. 21, 1864, NA; Benjamin Jones, *Under the
Stars and Bars,* pp. 210, 215; Richmond *Enquirer,* Nov. 22, 1864; Herman
H. Perry, "Fort Gilmer," *CV,* v. XIII, p. 414; J. H. Martin, "Fort Gilmer,"
CV, v. XIII, p. 269; J. D. Pickens, "Fort Harrison," *CV,* v. XXI, p. 484;
McCarty Ms., p. 1, TXU; "Return of Staff/25th Virginia Battalion, S-O,
1864," RG 109, ch. 1, entry 18, NA; Breckinridge, loc. cit., v. XIII, p. 415;
Joseph Waring, ed., "The Diary of William G. Hinson," *The South Carolina
Historical Magazine,* v. LXXV, p. 111; William White, "Diary," *History of
the Richmond Howitzer Battalion,* No. 2, p. 273; RG 109, entry 15, Nos.
1-B-33, K-5, P-15, NA; R. H. Anderson, *Report, 1864,* p. 24, LHQ Coll.,
VHS; Sommers, op. cit., v. I, pp. 111–18.

3. Ord to Kensel, 8:15, Sept. 28, 1864, RG 393, DVNC, telegram box
10, NA; Comstock, *Diary,* Sept. 28, 1864, LC; Butler to Birney, Sept. 27,
1864, RG 391, 10AC, v. III, bk. 34, NA; Kautz, *Reminiscences,* p. 88, and
Journal, Sept. 28, 1864, Kautz Papers, LC; Ord to Stanton, Dec. 14, 1864,
Simon Gratz Coll., HSP; *OR,* v. XLII, pt. 2, pp. 1,058–59, 1,082–88; RG
108, entry 11, box 82, No. E21, NA; Sommers, op. cit., pp. 54–55, 88–89,
119, 1,361–73.

4. Besides the six batteries in Ord's field force, the 7th and M contributed 40 and 20 mounted men, respectively, to accompany the vanguard and
help operate any guns that might be captured. All these forces made Ord's
column approximately twice as strong as he alleged when he wrote his report 9 months later. His error presumably derived from his failure to count
engineers, artillery, and the 2,600 infantry who rejoined him, September
27–28. *Ripley Ms.,* p. 1, DSF Coll., UV; Kautz, *Journal,* Sept. 28–29, 1864,
LC; Ord to Kensel, 8:30 P.M., Sept. 27, 1864, RG 94, entry 731, box 63,
NA; Walter Harrison, *Pickett's Men,* pp. 129–31; "Return of Staff/35th
Georgia, S-O, 1864," RG 109, ch. 1, entry 18, NA; "Returns of 9th Vermont, F/89th and D-H/158th New York, F/1st New York Engineers, 7th
New York Battery, F/1st Rhode Island Light Artillery, and Staff/2nd and
I/3rd Pennsylvania Heavy Artillery, and of L/4th and A/5th U. S. Artil-
lery, S-O, 1864," RG 94, M594 and entry 53, respectively, NA; RG 94,
entry 12, 1864 file, Nos. D664 and H1197, NA; Henry and James Hall,
Cayuga in the Field, pp. 257–60; *OR,* v. XLII, pt. 1, pp. 134–35, 660–62,
674–75, 793, 798–99, 805, 811, and pt. 2, pp. 929, 1,088; John B. Raulston, *Ms. History of 81st New York,* p. 18, HHL; *AG-Mass-1864,* p. 866;
Charles Currier, *Recollections,* p. 125, MOLLUS-Mass. Coll., MHRC; Milton Embick, ed., *Third Division, Ninth Corps,* pp. 1–3; S. Millett Thompson, *13th New Hampshire,* pp. 458–59; "Returns of Army of the James,
Provisional Brigade, Naval Brigade, and Siege Train, and of the 18th Corps,

S-O, 1864," RG 94, entries 62 and 65, DVNC and 18AC, respectively, NA; RG 391, 24AC, v. XL, bk. 99, S-O, 1864, NA; RG 393, DVNC, v. LV, bk. 79, pp. 333–34, and v. CVI, bk. 217, p. 10, and two-name box 5, No. W273–9, and v. XXXVII, bk. 82, Cook to McIntyre and Howell, Sept. 28, 1864, NA; RG 391, 18AC, v. VI, bk. 15, Sept. 28–Oct. 31, 1864, and v. VII, bk. 12, p. 108, and box 1, Deployment of Cook's brigade, Sept. 27, 1864, and Strength of Ripley's command, Sept. 27, 1864, NA; Sommers, op. cit., v. I, pp. 89–94, 183–85; Cecil Clay, "Col. Clay's Account," *NT*, Sept. 29, 1904; *CWR*, p. 330; Merlin Harris, "Fort Harrison," *NT*, May 12, 1887; W. S. Hubbell et al., *21st Connecticut*, pp. 288–91; E. Ware, "Battery Harrison," *NT*, Jan. 20, 1887; Otto Eisenschiml, ed., *Vermont General*, p. 247; *Bangor Daily Whig and Courier*, Oct. 25, 1864; *Rutland Weekly Herald*, Oct. 13, 1864; Andrew Robeson, letter of Oct. 5, 1864, Robeson Papers, MSHS; David Dobie to Hattie, Oct. 3, 1864, Dobie Papers, UV; William Kreutzer, *Notes and Observations*, p. 233; Joseph Alexander, "Army of the James," *NT*, July 31, 1890; "Morning report of M/3rd New York Light Artillery, Sept. 29, 1864," RG 94, entry 115, NA.

5. George Bailey to his parents, Oct. 1, 1864, Bailey Papers, Stanford; G. W. Shurtleff to Edward Merrell, Oct. 22, 1864, Merrell Papers, WHS; RG 391, 25AC, v. XXXIII, bk. 66½, pp. 292–97, NA; RG 393, DVNC, v. CLX, bk. 377, pp. 181–82, and v. CLXXIII, bk. 408, pp. 65–66, NA; Sommers, op. cit., v. I, p. 95.

6. RG 391, 10AC, v. III, bk. 34, Puffer to Birney, Sept. 25, 1864, and Birney to Butler, Sept. 27, 1864, and v. XXVII, bk. 52, Sept. 28, 1864, NA; Dodge to Kensel, Sept. 28, 1864, RG 393, DVNC, telegram box 10, NA; Andrew Robeson, letter of Oct. 5, 1864, Robeson Papers, MSHS; Herbert Beecher, *1st Connecticut Battery*, v. II, pp. 578–79; *OR*, v. XLII, pt. 1, pp. 105, 133–36, 702, 708, 712, 715, 726, 760–62, 764, 767, 769, 772, 778, 780, 820, and pt. 2, pp. 1,058, 1,080–82; Harry Jackson and Thomas O'Donnell, eds., *Back Home in Oneida*, p. 164; John Foote to his sister and father, Sept. 28 and Oct. 2, 1864, Foote Papers, DU; Benjamin Wright to his wife, Oct. 2, 1864, Wright Papers, WHS; Hartford *Courant*, Oct. 10, 1864; Edward Cook to Laura, Oct. 6, 1864, Cook Papers, UCSB; J. A. Mowris, *117th New York*, pp. 133–34; Henry Marshall, letter of Oct. 2, 1864, Marshall Papers, WCL, UM; Edgar Nickels to Lewis Newcomb, Sept. 26, 1864, Newcomb Papers, Stanford; *AG-Conn-1865*, p. 207; Buffalo *Morning Express*, Oct. 13, 1864; New York *Times*, Oct. 23, 1864; Henry Clay Trumbull, *The Knightly Soldier*, p. 296; Adrian Terry to Isadore, Oct. 3, 1864, quoted in Carl Marino, "General Alfred Howe Terry," Ph.D. dissertation at New York University (1968), p. 351; "Returns of the Army of the James, 10th Corps, and Third Division, 18th Corps, Sept. 1864," RG 94, entries 62 and 65, DVNC and 10AC and 18AC, respectively, NA; RG 391, 25AC, v. XXXIII, bk. 66½, pp. 292–95, 299–300, 310, 318, NA; RG 391, 24AC, v. XXII, bk. 42, pp. 1–2, and Plaisted to Terry, Oct. 1, 1864, NA; Philadelphia *Public Ledger*, July 4, 1908; William W. Brown, *The Negro in the American Revolution*, p. 378; "Returns of Staff/7th New Hampshire, 4th New Jersey Battery, Staff-A-B-C/16th New York Heavy Artillery, Staff/

11th Maine, B-G-K/100th and D/115th New York, B-F-K/76th and I/97th and Staff/203rd Pennsylvania, and 1st New York Engineers, S-O, 1864," RG 94, M594, NA; RG 94, entry 12, 1864 file, Nos. H1124 and P1213, NA; William H. Hyde, *112th New York*, pp. 101–2; Henry Brown, letter of Oct. 5, 1864, Brown Papers, CNHS; Nicholas DeGraff, *Memoirs*, p. 308, CWTI Coll., MHRC; Sommers, op. cit., v. I, pp. 96–98, 140–42.

7. B. A. Oehming, "Johnson's Brigade," *CV*, v. IX, p. 560; Marcus J. Wright, "Johnson's Men," *CV*, v. XIV, p. 545; J. A. H. Granberry, "Fort Gilmer," *CV*, v. XIII, p. 413; Martin, loc. cit., v. XIII, pp. 269–70; Pickens, loc. cit., v. XXI, p. 484; J. B. Lott, "Two Boys," *CV*, v. XIII, p. 416; Edward Moore, *Cannoneer Under Stonewall Jackson*, p. 263; Polley, *Charming Nellie*, pp. 259–60; *McCarty Ms.*, p. 1, and McCarty, *Diary*, Sept. 29, 1864, TXU; Edward Crockett, *Diary*, Sept. 29, 1864, Martin L. Crimmins Coll., TXU; O. T. Hanks, *Ms. History of Benton's Company*, pp. 47–48, HJC; Richmond *Enquirer*, Nov. 22, 1864; *OR*, v. XLII, pt. 2, pp. 1,304–5; R. E. Lee, *Telegram Book, 1862–64*, pp. 294–95, LHQ Coll., VHS; Charles W. Field, "The Campaign of 1864 and 1865," *SHSP*, v. XIV, p. 555; Ewell, *Letterbook*, p. 16, DU; J. Marshall, op. cit., v. V, p. 193; D. S. Burwell to E. S. Burwell, Oct. 5, 1864, Burwell Papers, SHC; *Johnston Ms.*, p. 4, box 179, DSF Coll., LC; Richmond *Sentinel*, Oct. 5, 12, 13, 1864; Taylor quoted in Calrow, op. cit., p. 27, RNBP; Waring, loc. cit., v. LXXV, p. 111; Perry, loc. cit., v. XIII, p. 414; Breckinridge, loc. cit., v. XIII, p. 415; Sommers, op. cit., v. I, pp. 119–23.

8. The X Corps commander will henceforth be called "Birney," and his older brother will be called "William Birney." *OR*, v. XLII, pt. 1, pp. 702, 708, 713, 715, 719, 726, 760, 764, 767, 769, 772, 778, 780, 817–20, and pt. 2, pp. 325, 766, 1,082, 1,084, 1,087–88, 1,109, and pt. 3, pp. 100–1; RG 393, DVNC, v. CLXXIII, bk. 408, p. 66, NA; RG 391, 24AC, v. II, bk. 5, p. 187, and v. XXII, bk. 42, p. 2, NA; Luther Dickey, *85th Pennsylvania*, p. 407; Daniel Eldridge, *3rd New Hampshire*, p. 336; Mowris, op. cit., p. 133; New York *Times*, Oct. 23, 1864; Hartford *Courant*, Oct. 10, 1864; Hyde, op. cit., p. 102; "Returns of E/4th Massachusetts Cavalry, D/24th Massachusetts, Staff/7th New Hampshire, K/100th New York, B-D-F-G/62nd and Staff/67th Ohio, and I/97th and Staff/203rd Pennsylvania, S-O, 1864," RG 94, M594, NA; John Spear, *Army Life*, p. 266, MSHS; RG 94, entry 12, 1864 file, Nos. H1124 and P1213, NA; Buffalo *Morning Express*, Oct. 13, 1864; Henry Brown, letter of Oct. 5, 1864, and *Diary*, Sept. 29, 1864, Brown Papers, CNHS; Benjamin Wright to his wife, Oct. 2, 1864, Wright Papers, WHS; Joseph Scroggs, *Diary*, Sept. 29, 1864, CWTI Coll., MHRC; Langdon to Butler, Feb. 15, 1865, BFB Coll., LC; Haskin, op. cit., pp. 209, 445; Deployment of Cook's brigade, Sept. 27, 1864, RG 391, 18AC, box 1, NA; Robert Brady, *11th Maine*, p. 271; George Stowits, *100th New York*, pp. 306–7; Trumbull, op. cit., p. 297; Henry Marshall, letter of Oct. 2, 1864, Marshall Papers, WCL, UM; Joseph Califf, *7th USCT*, p. 41; Kautz, *Journal*, Sept. 29, 1864, Kautz Papers, LC; New York *Herald*, Oct. 2, 1864; Beecher, op. cit., v. II, p. 578; Ford to Foster, Sept. 28, 1864, RG 391, 10AC, v. III, bk. 26, NA; RG 94, entry 159,

Charles J. Paine file, NA; Butler, op. cit., pp. 731, 742; Pickens, loc. cit., v. XXI, p. 484; Richmond *Enquirer*, Nov. 22, 1864; Joseph B. Polley, *Hood's Texas Brigade*, pp. 252–53; Solon Carter, "Service with Colored Troops," *MOLLUS-Mass*, v. I, p. 170; Robert Dollard, *Recollections*, pp. 132–33; Montgomery, loc. cit., v. XXVIII, p. 176; St. Clair Mulholland, *The American Volunteer*, pp. 59–60; James H. Hincks, letters of Oct. 2 and 7, 1864, Bond-McCulloch Family Papers, MDHS; McMurray, op. cit., p. 53; RG 391, 25AC, v. XXXIII, bk. 66½, pp. 292–93, 305, NA; Philadelphia *Public Ledger*, July 4, 1908; Sommers, op. cit., v. I, pp. 140–49.

9. Butler, op. cit., p. 731; Carter, loc. cit., v. I, pp. 170–71; *OR*, v. XLII, pt. 1, pp. 702, 719, 817–20, and pt. 2, pp. 766, 1,083; James Hincks to his father, Oct. 2, 1864, Bond-McCulloch Family Papers, MDHS; Scroggs, *Diary*, Sept. 29, 1864, CWTI Coll., MHRC; *McCarty Ms.*, pp. 1–2, TXU; Polley, *Texas Brigade*, pp. 252–54, and *Charming Nellie*, p. 259; A. C. Jones, "Fort Harrison," *CV*, v. XXV, p. 24; Moore, op. cit., p. 263; "Returns of C/15th Georgia, Hampton Legion of South Carolina, and Staff/25th Virginia Battalion, S-O, 1864," RG 109, ch. 1, entry 18, NA; Waring, loc. cit., v. LXXV, p. 111; Boyd, loc. cit., p. 21, VHS; Crockett, *Diary*, Sept. 29, 1864, Crimmins Coll., TXU; T. J. May, "Fort Gilmer," *CV*, v. XII, p. 588; Pickens, loc. cit., v. XXI, p. 484; Richmond *Enquirer*, Nov. 22, 1864; Richmond *Whig*, Sept. 30, 1864; Martin, loc. cit., v. XIII, pp. 269–70; Perry, loc. cit., v. XIII, p. 414; Breckinridge, loc. cit., v. XIII, p. 415; D. S. Burwell to E. S. Burwell, Oct. 5, 1864, Burwell Papers, SHC; *Johnston Ms.*, p. 4, box 179, DSF Coll., LC; White, loc. cit., No. 2, p. 273; Winkler, op. cit., pp. 192–95; RG 109, ch. 3, v. VII, p. 66, NA; Linden Kent to his mother, Oct. 3, 1864, CM; W. A. Nabours, "Active Service," *CV*, v. XXIV, p. 69; Hanks, *History*, pp. 47–48, HJC; Sommers, op. cit., v. I, pp. 140–53, and v. V, pp. 1,374–76; Dollard, op. cit., p. 132; Montgomery, loc. cit., v. XXVIII, p. 176; Mulholland, op. cit., pp. 59–60; RG 109, entry 15, box 1, No. K-5, NA.

10. Joskins, *Sketch*, p. 84, and Hanks, *History*, pp. 47–48, HJC; Boyd, loc. cit., p. 21, VHS; Crockett, *Diary*, Sept. 29, 1864, Crimmins Coll., and *McCarty Ms.*, pp. 1–3, TXU; May, loc. cit., v. XII, p. 588; Pickens, loc. cit., v. XXI, p. 484; Polley, *Texas Brigade*, pp. 252–53, and *Charming Nellie*, pp. 259–60; Richmond *Enquirer*, Nov. 22, 1864; Mamie Yeary, comp., *Boys in Gray*, p. 62; Butler, op. cit., p. 731; Carter, loc. cit., v. I, p. 170; Dollard, op. cit., p. 132; Samuel Duncan to Julia Jones, Oct. 22, 1864, Duncan-Jones Papers, NHHS; "CSR of Samuel Duncan, 4th USCT," RG 94, CSR, NA; Christian Fleetwood, *The Negro as a Soldier*, p. 15; James Hincks, letters of Oct. 2 and 7, 1864, Bond-McCulloch Family Papers, MDHS; McMurray, op. cit., p. 53; Montgomery, loc. cit., v. XXVIII, pp. 176–80; Mulholland, op. cit., pp. 59–60; *ORA*, pl. LXVIII, No. 4; Pollack, *Diary*, Oct. 2, 1864, ISHL; *OR*, v. XLII, pt. 1, pp. 133, 702, 708, 713, 715, 719, 726, 760, 817–19, and pt. 3, pp. 100–1; Adrian Terry to Isadore, Oct. 3, 1864, quoted in Marino, op. cit., pp. 351–52; Hartford *Courant*, Oct. 10, 1864; E. L. Cook to Laura, Oct. 6, 1864, Cook Papers, UCSB; Buffalo *Morning Express*, Oct. 13, 1864; "Return of D/24th Massachusetts, S-O,

1864," RG 94, M594, NA; Waring, loc. cit., v. LXXV, p. 111; Sommers, op. cit., v. I, pp. 153–58.

11. Adrian Terry to Isadore, Oct. 3, 1864, quoted in Marino, op. cit., pp. 351–52; Butler, op. cit., pp. 731–33; Carter, loc. cit., v. I, p. 170; RG 94, entry 160, v. X, p. 503, NA; Scroggs, *Diary*, Sept. 29, 1864, CWTI Coll., MHRC; Joseph Wilson, *The Black Phalanx*, pp. 435–36; *McCarty Ms.*, pp. 1–3, TXU; Richmond *Enquirer*, Nov. 22, 1864; *OR*, v. XLII, pt. 1, pp. 702, 713, 715–16, 719, 726, 817–20, and pt. 2, p. 1,086, and pt. 3, pp. 100–1; Granberry, loc. cit., v. XIII, p. 413; Martin, loc. cit., v. XIII, p. 269; Moore, loc. cit., v. XIII, p. 419; Perry, loc. cit., v. XIII, pp. 413–14; White, loc. cit., No. 2, p. 273; "Returns of D/24th Massachusetts and 62nd and 67th Ohio, S-O, 1864," RG 94, M594, NA; Hartford *Courant*, Oct. 10, 1864; Buffalo *Morning Express*, Oct. 13, 1864; RG 393, DVNC, v. CLXXXVII, bk. 455, pp. 147–48, NA; RG 109, entry 385, pt. 1, p. 173, NA; Boston *Evening Transcript*, Oct. 14, 1864; Sommers, op. cit., v. I, pp. 158–62.

12. G. W. Shurtleff to Edward Merrell, Oct. 22, 1864, Merrell Papers, WHS; Stowits, op. cit., p. 306; Pickens, loc. cit., v. XXI, p. 484; Butler, op. cit., pp. 731–33, 742; George Williams, *Negro Troops*, pp. 251–56; Wilson, op. cit., pp. 435–36; Dudley Cornish, *The Sable Arm*, pp. 279–80; Benjamin Quarles, *The Negro in the Civil War*, p. 305; Crockett, *Diary*, Sept. 29, 1864, Crimmins Coll., TXU; Hanks, *History*, p. 49, and Joskins, *Sketch*, p. 84, HJC; Jones, loc. cit., v. XXV, p. 24; Martin, loc. cit., v. XIII, p. 269; May, loc. cit., v. XII, p. 588; *OR*, v. XLII, pt. 1, pp. 702, 719, 817–20, and pt. 2, p. 1,091; RG 393, DVNC, two-name box 5, No. W273-18, NA; Polley, *Charming Nellie*, pp. 259–60, and *Texas Brigade*, p. 254; Richmond *Enquirer*, Nov. 22, 1864; Waring, loc. cit., v. LXXV, p. 111; Sommers, op. cit., v. I, pp. 162–63.

13. *OR*, v. XLII, pt. 1, pp. 793, 798; Thompson, op. cit., p. 476; John Cunningham, *118th New York*, p. 148; David Dobie to Hattie, Oct. 3, 1864, Dobie Papers, UV; Ware, loc. cit., Jan. 20, 1887; Harris, loc. cit., May 12, 1887; *AG-Conn-1865*, pp. 401–2; RG 391, 24AC, v. XXXIX, bk. 101, Sept. 30, 1864, and v. VII, bk. 16A, p. 144, NA; "Returns of B-D/23rd and C-F-I/63rd Tennessee, S-O, 1864," RG 109, ch. 1, entry 18, NA; Silas B. O'Mohundro to Cecil Clay, Feb. 14, 1887, Curtis Clay Papers, HSP; Richmond *Sentinel*, Oct. 5, 1864; Ewell, *Letterbook*, p. 16, DU; George A. Bruce, "Petersburg," *Military Historical Society of Massachusetts Papers*, v. XIV, p. 91; Sommers, op. cit., v. I, pp. 185–86.

14. Most names of these defenses are those used during the battle. "Fort Hoke," however, received its name later in 1864, and "Battery x" is the designation applied by postwar Federal cartographers. The terms "Diagonal Line" and "Jones's Salient," moreover, were coined by this historian in the absence of known names. Contrary to common belief, Fort Harrison was not named for the famous Harrisons of Berkeley but for Lieutenant William Elzey Harrison, the engineer who supervised its construction by Hunton's Brigade early in 1864. Bruce, loc. cit., v. XIV, p. 92; *Ripley Ms.*, p. 4, DSF Coll., UV; *OR*, v. XLII, pt. 1, pp. 663, 675, 793–94, 798, 805,

812; Cecil Clay, "Fort Harrison," *MOLLUS-DC*, v. I, No. 7, p. 5; Cunningham, op. cit., pp. 148–50; Harris, loc. cit., May 12, 1887; Hubbell et al., op. cit., pp. 291–300; Kreutzer, op. cit., p. 233; Moore, loc. cit., v. XIII, p. 419; Thompson, op. cit., pp. 461–64, 467–71, 476–78; *AG-Conn-1865*, p. 402; Mason Graham Ellzey, *The Cause We Lost and the Land We Love*, pp. 45, 73–74, ms. made available through the courtesy of Mr. J. Ambler Johnston, Sr., and Mr. Eppa Hunton III; RG 109, ch. 3, v. VII, p. 80, No. H423, NA; Map No. Ga-29-3, CM; *ORA*, pls. LXVIII, Nos. 1–2, and XCII, No. 1, and C, No. 2, and CXXXV, No. 3; D. E. Henderson, *Map of Lines from Drewry's Bluff to Dutch Gap*, Charles Tayloe Mason Papers, VHS; John G. Barnard, *Map of Chaffin's Bluff*, RG 77, No. 2391, NA; RG 77, entry 161, box 244, No. 35-4-18-1, NA; Department of the Interior, National Park Service, Richmond National Battlefield Park, *Self-guide Tour of Fort Harrison*, No. OF-620229; Richmond *Sentinel*, Oct. 12 and 13, 1864; Taylor quoted in Calrow, op. cit., p. 27, RNBP; Sommers, op. cit., v. I, pp. 186–90.

15. Richmond *Sentinel*, Oct. 5, 12, 13, 1864; Taylor quoted in Calrow, op. cit., p. 27, RNBP; Ewell, *Letterbook*, p. 16, DU; C. T. Allen, "Chaffin's Farm," *CV*, v. XIII, p. 418; Richmond *Enquirer*, Oct. 10, 15, 21, 1864; *ANJ*, v. II, pp. 97, 122; New York *Tribune*, Oct. 4, 1864; Samuel P. Bates, *Pennsylvania Volunteers*, v. II, pp. 290–91; Rosser Rock to his sister, Sept. 19 and Nov. 25, 1864, Rock Papers, CM; *Ripley Ms.*, p. 4, DSF Coll., UV; RG 94, entry 160, v. VIII, p. 609, NA; Richard C. Taylor, Silas B. O'Mohundro, Joseph E. Johnson, and H. H. Hoyer to Cecil Clay, Feb. 14, July 8 and 14 and 24, Aug. 12, 1887, and March 26, 1888, and O'Mohundro, *Map . . . Vicinity of Richmond*, Clay Papers, HSP; Bruce, loc. cit., v. XIV, pp. 91–93; Royal B. Prescott, "Capture of Richmond," *MOLLUS-Mass*, v. I, p. 51; Thompson, op. cit., pp. 460–79; *OR*, v. XLII, pt. 1, p. 875, and pt. 2, pp. 1,010–11, 1,092, 1,113–14, and pt. 3, pp. 512, 1,131–33, and v. XL, pt. 1, pp. 661, 666; B. G. Baldwin to John Minor Maury and W. Leroy Brown, Sept. 13 and 28, 1864, respectively, Harrison Coll., CM; Eisenschiml, op. cit., p. 245; *AG-Conn-1865*, p. 58; Cunningham, op. cit., p. 150; Comstock, *Diary*, Sept. 29, 1864, LC; Moore, loc. cit., v. XIII, p. 419; Butler, op. cit., pp. 735–36; Taylor and Hatfield, op. cit., pp. 93–94, 188; Harris, loc. cit., May 12, 1887; *CWR*, p. 330; Cecil Clay, "Fort Harrison," *NT*, Nov. 26, 1881; Richard Duke, "Confederate Reserves," *CV*, v. XXVI, pp. 486–87; Polley, *Texas Brigade*, p. 254; Martin, loc. cit., v. XIII, p. 269; Linden Kent to his mother, Oct. 3, 1864, CM; Sommers, op. cit., v. I, pp. 191–97.

16. *OR*, v. XLII, pt. 1, pp. 675, 793–94, 797–98, 805, and pt. 2, pp. 1,058–59, 1,084–85; Bruce, loc. cit., v. XIV, pp. 91–93; Comstock, *Diary*, Sept. 29, 1864, LC; Hubbell et al., op. cit., pp. 291, 299–300; Thompson, op. cit., pp. 460, 477–78; *Ripley Ms.*, pp. 12–13, DSF Coll., UV; Harris, loc. cit., May 12, 1887; H. A. Camp, "Fort Harrison," *NT*, June 14, 1888; *CWR*, p. 363; *AG-Conn-1865*, pp. 175, 401; Clay, loc. cit., v. I, No. 7, p. 4; Cecil Clay, "Fort Harrison," *NT*, March 22, 1888; T. J. Leiper and Joseph E. Johnson to Cecil Clay, Dec. 6 and 10, 1883, respectively, Clay Papers,

HSP; Bates, *Pennsylvania Volunteers,* v. II, p. 290; "Return of D/188th Pennsylvania, S-O, 1864," RG 94, M594, NA; Sommers, op. cit., v. V, pp. 1,374–87, and v. I, pp. 197–200.

17. Thompson, op. cit., p. 477; Clay, loc. cit., v. I, No. 7, p. 7.

18. Richard C. Taylor to Cecil Clay, July 24, 1887, Clay Papers, HSP.

19. No evidence has been found to support the claim that Lieutenant Colonel Thomas B. Mulcahy of the 139th temporarily succeeded Stevens before Raulston took charge. Bruce, loc. cit., v. XIV, pp. 92–95; Camp, loc. cit., June 14, 1888; Cunningham, op. cit., pp. 148–49; *CWR,* p. 330; Harris, loc. cit., May 12, 1887; Hubbell et al., op. cit., pp. 292–94, 299–301; *OR,* v. XLII, pt. 1, pp. 794, 798–99, 805, and pt. 3, pp. 164–65; Prescott, loc. cit., v. I, p. 51; Taylor quoted in Calrow, op. cit., p. 27, also p. 9, RNBP; Ware, loc. cit., Jan. 20, 1887; Richmond *Sentinel,* Oct. 13, 1864; *ORN,* v. X, pp. 753–62; *AG-Conn-1865,* pp. 401–2; Martin, loc. cit., v. XIII, p. 269; Linden Kent to his mother, Oct. 3, 1864; CM; Samuel Roberts, Richard C. Taylor, Silas B. O'Mohundro, and H. H. Hoyer to Cecil Clay, Jan. 31, 1884, and July 8 and 24 and Aug. 12 and Feb. 14 and May 23, 1887, and March 26, 1888, respectively, and O'Mohundro, *Map . . . Vicinity of Richmond,* Clay Papers, HSP; Thompson, op. cit., pp. 460, 463, 475–79, 532; *Aaron Fletcher Stevens,* pp. 59–60, 70–72; Dyer, op. cit., p. 397; Moore, loc. cit., v. XIII, p. 419; Henry Snow, letter of Oct. 3, 1864, Snow Papers, CNHS; Richmond *Enquirer,* Oct. 21, 1864; Rosser Rock to his sister, Nov. 25, 1864, Rock Papers, CM; William W. Anderson to Peter Guerrant, Oct. 13, 1864, Guerrant Family Papers, VHS; John Berrien Lindsley, *Military Annals,* p. 408; Clay, loc. cit., v. I, No. 7, pp. 7–11; Joseph E. Johnson to J. Fisher Leaming, Sept. 30, 1864, enclosed in Leaming to William Meredith, Oct. 24, 1864, Meredith Papers, HSP; Raulston, *History,* p. 18, HHL; Sommers, op. cit., v. I, pp. 200–06.

20. *OR,* v. XLII, pt. 1, pp. 795, 798–99, and pt. 2, pp. 1,058–59, 1,303; RG 391, 24AC, v. XXXIX, bk. 101, Sept. 29, 1864, NA; RG 393, DVNC, v. CXCI, bk. 466, pp. 93–98, and v. CLXXXVII, bk. 455, p. 89, NA; Richmond *Sentinel,* Oct. 12, 1864; Cunningham, op. cit., p. 150; *ORN,* v. X, pp. 753, 755, 761; Sommers, op. cit., v. I, pp. 206–7, and v. V, pp. 1,374–87.

CHAPTER III

1. *OR,* v. XLII, pt. 1, p. 935, and pt. 2, pp. 1,084, 1,302–5; *ORN,* v. X, pp. 752–53; R. E. Lee to J. K. Mitchell, 7:45 A.M., Sept. 29, 1864, CM; D. D. Pendleton to W. N. Pendleton, Oct. 2, 1864, and Alexander to Pendleton, March 24, 1865, WNP Coll., SHC; Charles Mason to D. B. Harris, June 14, 1864, and Henderson, *Map,* Mason Papers, VHS; *Johnston Ms.,* p. 4, box 179, DSF Coll., LC; Johnston, *Record,* p. 6, and R. A. Hardaway to N. B. Johnston, June 25, 1894, Johnston mss.; D. S. Burwell to E. S. Burwell, Oct. 5, 1864, Burwell Papers, SHC; White, loc. cit., No. 2, p. 273; "CSR of Willis J. Dance, Dance's Virginia Battery, and return of

Green's Louisiana Battery, S-O, 1864," RG 109, ch. 1, entry 18, NA; Charles Johnston, "Fort Harrison," *SHSP*, v. I, p. 441; Ewell, *Letterbook*, p. 17, DU; Comstock, *Diary*, Sept. 29, 1864, LC; Sommers, op. cit., v. I, pp. 253–56; Charles Baughman to his mother, Oct. 14, 1864, Baughman Papers, CM.

2. *OR*, v. XLII, pt. 1, pp. 794–95, 798–99, 805; David Dobie to Hattie, Oct. 3 and 24, 1864, Dobie Papers, UV; Silas B. O'Mohundro, Joseph E. Johnson, and W. S. Hubbell to Cecil Clay, July 29, 1887, Dec. 10, 1883, and Mar. 29, 1884, respectively, Clay Papers, HSP; Comstock, *Diary*, Sept. 29, 1864, LC; Harris, loc. cit., May 12, 1887; Bruce, loc. cit., v. XIV, p. 95; Cunningham, op. cit., p. 149; Ord to Stanton, Dec. 14, 1864, Gratz Coll., HSP; Hall and Hall, op. cit., p. 258; *AG-Maine-1864/65*, v. I, p. 328; Philadelphia *Evening Bulletin*, Oct. 3, 1864; Otis Waite, *New Hampshire in the Great Rebellion*, p. 441; E. J. Copp, *Reminiscences*, pp. 480–82; *AG-Conn-1865*, p. 175; Clay, loc. cit., Nov. 26, 1881; Clay, loc. cit., v. I, No. 7, pp. 8–10; *CWR*, p. 330; Thompson, op. cit., p. 462; Ware, loc. cit., Jan. 20, 1887; Linden Kent to his mother, Oct. 3, 1864, CM; Breckinridge, loc. cit., v. XIII, pp. 415–16; Granberry, loc. cit., v. XIII, p. 413; RG 391, 24AC, v. XXXIX, bk. 101, Sept. 29, 1864, NA; RG 393, DVNC, v. CXCI, bk. 466, pp. 93–98, NA; Dudley DuBose to E. P. Alexander, Aug. 23, 1866, EPA Coll., SHC; Moore, loc. cit., v. XIII, p. 419; Herman Perry to Henry L. Benning, July 22, 1864, Benning Papers, SHC; Columbus *Daily Enquirer*, Nov. 16, 1864; "Returns of C-I/15th Georgia, S-O, 1864," RG 109, ch. 1, entry 18, NA; W. A. Flanigan, "Fort Gilmer," *CV*, v. XIII, p. 123; Bates, *Pennsylvania Volunteers*, v. V, p. 254; Jones, loc. cit., v. XXV, p. 24; John W. Lokey, *My Experiences*, p. 22, GDAH; Martin, loc. cit., v. XIII, pp. 269–70; Perry, loc. cit., v. XIII, pp. 414–15; Sommers, op. cit., v. I, pp. 256–60; "Morning report of M/3rd New York Light Artillery, Sept. 29, 1864," RG 94, entry 115, NA.

3. Bangor *Daily Whig and Courier*, Oct. 11 and 25, 1864; Rutland *Weekly Herald*, Oct. 13, 1864; Bruce, loc. cit., v. XIV, p. 93; Philip S. Chase, *F/1st Rhode Island Light Artillery*, p. 224; *Ripley Ms.*, pp. 3–6, DSF Coll., UV; *OR*, v. XLII, pt. 1, pp. 794, 811–12, and pt. 2, pp. 1,087, 1,116, and pt. 3, pp. 166–67; Ward, op. cit., pp. 106–10; Bates, *Pennsylvania Volunteers*, v. II, p. 179; Pottsville *Miners' Journal*, Nov. 12, 1864; RG 393, DVNC, two-name box 5, Nos. W273-11, -12, -14, NA; RG 94, entry 12, 1864 file, No. H1197, NA; "Return of Staff/2nd Pennsylvania Heavy Artillery, S-O, 1864," RG 94, M594, NA; Alexander, loc. cit., July 31, 1890; Richmond *Sentinel*, Oct. 13, 1864; RG 391, 24AC, v. XXXIX, bk. 101, Sept. 29, 1864, NA; Perry, loc. cit., v. XIII, pp. 414–15; RG 94, entry 160, v. VIII, pp. 609–11, NA; Granberry, loc. cit., v. XIII, p. 413; Martin, loc. cit., v. XIII, p. 269; Linden Kent to his mother, Oct. 3, 1864, CM; J. Marshall, op. cit., v. V, p. 260; New York *Herald*, Oct. 23, 1864; John Bowden, "Reminiscences," UDC Coll., v. VII, pp. 42–44, GDAH; Sommers, op. cit., v. I, pp. 260–65.

4. Like Hardaway, the units on the outer line left behind valuable supplies in the camps they abandoned too hastily to break up. *OR*, v. XLII,

pt. 1, pp. 760, 764, and pt. 2, pp. 1,302–3; White, loc. cit., No. 2, pp. 273–74; Moore, op. cit., pp. 263–64; Martin, loc. cit., v. XIII, p. 269; Polley, *Charming Nellie,* pp. 260–62, and *Texas Brigade,* p. 254; RG 109, entry 112, box 12, No. 111, NA; Joskins, *Sketch,* p. 89, HJC; Jones, loc. cit., v. XXV, p. 24; Linden Kent to his mother, Oct. 3, 1864, CM; Ward, op. cit., p. 109; Alexander, loc. cit., July 31, 1890; *McCarty Ms.,* p. 3, TXU; Lott, loc. cit., v. XIII, pp. 416–17; Johnston, loc. cit., v. I, p. 440; Ewell, *Letterbook,* p. 17, DU; RG 94, entry 160, v. VIII, pp. 609–11, NA; *Ripley Ms.,* pp. 4–5, DSF Coll., UV; Sommers, op. cit., v. I, pp. 265–67.

5. *Ripley Ms.,* p. 5, DSF Coll., UV; Ord to Stanton, Dec. 14, 1864, Gratz Coll., HSP; *OR,* v. XLII, pt. 1, pp. 794, 799, 805, and pt. 2, pp. 1,266, 1,303, and pt. 3, p. 164; RG 393, DVNC, two-name box 5, No. W273-3, NA; Cunningham, op. cit., p. 150; Hubbell et al., op. cit., p. 303; Thompson, op. cit., p. 480; Allen, loc. cit., v. XIII, p. 418; Richmond *Enquirer,* Oct. 10 and 21, 1864; Richmond *Sentinel,* Oct. 5, 12, and 13, 1864; *ANJ,* v. II, p. 97; Bates, *Pennsylvania Volunteers,* v. II, pp. 290–91; O'Mohundro, *Map,* Clay Papers, HSP; Ewell, *Letterbook,* p. 17, DU; R. A. Hardaway to N. B. Johnston, June 25, 1894, Johnston mss.; D. E. Johnston, *Confederate Boy,* p. 277; Wright, loc. cit., v. XIV, p. 545; Sommers, op. cit., v. I, pp. 267–70.

6. The relative order of the two passages in the quotation has been reversed for literary effect without altering their author's meaning. Ewell, *Letterbook,* p. 17, DU; Silas B. O'Mohundro to Cecil Clay, Feb. 14 and May 23, 1887, and *Map,* Clay Papers, HSP; Moore, loc. cit., v. XIII, p. 419; Johnston, loc. cit., v. I, pp. 439–41; *OR,* v. XLII, pt. 1, p. 799, and pt. 2, p. 1,303; War Department, *List of Official Communications,* p. 208, C.S.A. Coll., LC; Sommers, op. cit., v. I, pp. 270–72.

7. If Fairchild nominally took over the division, his own unit presumably passed to the ranking regimental commander in either the division, Colonel George Guion of the 148th New York, or the Third Brigade, Major James L. Anderson of the 2nd Pennsylvania Heavy Artillery. Dudley DuBose to E. P. Alexander, Aug. 23, 1866, EPA Coll., SHC; Ewell to Bragg, 9:50 A.M. and 10:00 A.M. and untimed, Sept. 29, 1864, Jefferson Davis Coll., TU; Braxton Bragg, *Letters Sent, 1864–65,* p. 266, TU; *OR,* v. XLII, pt. 1, pp. 793–94, 799, and pt. 2, p. 1,115; Cunningham, op. cit., pp. 146, 150; Butler, op. cit., p. 734; *Ripley Ms.,* pp. 5–6, DSF Coll., UV; Comstock, *Diary,* Sept. 29, 1864, LC; Bruce, loc. cit., v. XIV, p. 89; Eisenschiml, op. cit., p. 244; Sommers, op. cit., v. I, p. 272.

8. Bates, *Pennsylvania Volunteers,* v. II, p. 179; Pottsville *Miners' Journal,* Nov. 12, 1864; *OR,* v. XLII, pt. 3, p. 166; RG 393, DVNC, two-name box 5, Nos. W273-11 and -14, NA; *Ripley Ms.,* pp. 6–7, DSF Coll., UV; William Anderson to Peter Guerrant, Oct. 7, 1864, Guerrant Papers, VHS; Richmond *Sentinel,* Oct. 13, 1864; Sommers, op. cit., v. I, pp. 272–73.

9. If Anderson temporarily commanded the brigade when he fell, his successor as brigadier was presumably Major Wellington M. Lewis of the 89th New York. Ward, op. cit., pp. 106–10; RG 94, entry 12, 1864 file, No. H1197, NA; Alexander, loc. cit., July 31, 1890; RG 94, entry 160, v. VIII,

p. 611, NA; "Returns of B-K/89th New York and Staff/2nd Pennsylvania Heavy Artillery, S-O, 1864," RG 94, M594, NA; Stephen F. Wells, "Forts Harrison and Gilmer," *National Tribune Scrapbook*, No. 3, p. 32; *Ripley Ms.*, pp. 6–7, DSF Coll., UV; Moore, loc. cit., v. XIII, pp. 419–20; Dudley DuBose to E. P. Alexander, Aug. 23, 1866, EPA Coll., SHC; "CSR of Willis J. Dance, Dance's Virginia Battery," RG 94, CSR, NA; R. A. Hardaway to N. B. Johnston, June 25, 1894, Johnston mss.; RG 109, entry 15, No. P-15, NA; Richmond *Enquirer*, Nov. 22, 1864; Bates, *Pennsylvania Volunteers*, v. II, p. 1,061; T. Henry Pippitt, "Before Richmond," *NT*, Oct. 10, 1918; RG 393, DVNC, two-name box 5, No. W273-12, NA; John C. Reed, *Journal*, p. 132, ADAH; RG 109, entry 22, box 4, No. 194, NA; Columbus *Daily Enquirer*, Oct. 28, 1864; Richmond *Sentinel*, Oct. 3, 1864; Johnston, loc. cit., v. I, p. 440; Flanigan, loc. cit., v. XIII, p. 123; Perry, loc. cit., v. XIII, p. 415; *OR*, v. XLII, pt. 1, pp. 135, 794, and pt. 2, pp. 1,114–15; Comstock, *Diary*, Sept. 29, 1864, LC; Ewell, *Letterbook*, pp. 17–18, DU; Joskins, *Sketch*, pp. 85–88, HJC; Sommers, op. cit., v. I, pp. 273–77.

10. Lee's order that Montague report to Ewell superseded Pickett's directive that the colonel keep reporting to division headquarters. Embick, op. cit., p. 3; Andrew Mensch, *Memoirs*, p. 17, MHRC; *OR*, v. XLII, pt. 1, pp. 136, 794, 799, 876, and pt. 2, pp. 1,113, 1,115–16, 1,271, 1,303–4; Launcelot Minor Blackford to Mrs. W. M. Blackford, Oct. 16, 1864, Blackford Papers, UV; Eppa Hunton, *Autobiography*, p. 104; 56th Virginia file, data gathered for a history of Longstreet's Corps, EPA Coll., SHC; "Brunswick Guard," *SHSP*, v. XXVIII, p. 13; Steuart to Edmundson, Sept. 29, 1864, Steuart's Brigade, *Book of Letters Sent*, CM; George Waller to Sallie, Oct. 7, 1864, Waller Papers, SHC; D. Johnston, op. cit., p. 277; Allen, loc. cit., v. XIII, p. 418; Anderson, *Report, 1864*, p. 24, LHQ Coll., VHS; Francis Dawson, *Reminiscences*, p. 125; Richmond *Sentinel*, Oct. 5, 12, and 13, 1864; Daniel Baldridge to his parents, Sept. 30, 1864, Baldridge Papers, PSU; Richmond *Enquirer*, Dec. 1, 1864; Cunningham, op. cit., p. 150; Monroe Cockrell, ed., *Gunner with Stonewall*, p. 107; "CSR of Mark B. Hardin, 18th Virginia Heavy Artillery Battalion," RG 109, CSR, NA; RG 391, 24AC, v. XL, bk. 99, Oct. 1, 1864, NA; D. D. Pendleton to W. N. Pendleton, Oct. 2, 1864, WNP Coll., SHC; *ORN*, v. X, pp. 752–62, 765–67; Edward Crenshaw, *Diary*, Sept. 29, 1864, ADAH; RG 393, DVNC, v. CV, bk. 219, p. 15, NA; Ruffin Thomson to Pa, Oct. 2, 1864, Thomson Papers, SHC; *Ripley Ms.*, p. 9, DSF Coll., UV; Marion Fitzpatrick to Amanda, Oct. 4, 1864, Marion Fitzpatrick Papers, MHRC; Sommers, op. cit., v. I, pp. 277–81.

11. Whether the 16th New York Battery remained in reserve or saw action at this time is not known. Allen, loc. cit., v. XIII, p. 418; *AG-Conn-1865*, p. 402; Richmond *Enquirer*, Oct. 21, 1864; Richmond *Sentinel*, Oct. 12, 1864; Alexander, loc. cit., July 31, 1890; Ward, op. cit., pp. 108–10; RG 94, entry 160, v. VIII, p. 611, NA; Moore, loc. cit., v. XIII, pp. 419–20; *Ripley Ms.*, p. 3, DSF Coll., UV; Chase, op. cit., p. 224; Hall and Hall, op. cit., pp. 257–58; *Johnston Ms.*, p. 5, box 179, DSF Coll., LC;

"Returns of H/3rd New York Light Artillery, 16th New York Battery, and A/1st Pennsylvania Light Artillery, and of F/5th U. S. Artillery, S-O, 1864," RG 94, M594 and entry 53, respectively, NA; *OR*, v. XLII, pt. 1, pp. 136, 794–95, 799, 935; Philadelphia *Evening Bulletin*, Oct. 3, 1864; Thompson, op. cit., p. 463; "Returns of Dance's and Griffin's Virginia Batteries, S-O, 1864," RG 109, ch. 1, entry 18, NA; Sommers, op. cit., v. I, pp. 281–83.

12. *OR*, v. XLII, pt. 2, pp. 1,303–4.

13. *Ibid.*, pp. 1,114–15, and pt. 1, pp. 794–95, 799; RG 108, entry 11, box 83, Nos. E36 and E37, and entry 1, v. XXI, p. 448, NA; Sommers, op. cit., v. I, p. 283.

14. Henry Brown, letter of Oct. 5, 1864, Brown Papers, CNHS.

15. *OR*, v. XLII, pt. 2, pp. 1,115–16.

16. New York *Times*, Oct. 23, 1864.

17. Adam Badeau, *Military History of Grant*, v. III, p. 71; Horace Porter, *Campaigning with Grant*, pp. 301–2; Frank Burr, *Life and Deeds of Grant*, pp. 659–62; Thompson, op. cit., p. 471.

18. *OR*, v. XLII, pt. 2, p. 1,114.

19. Grant put Parker, a military secretary, in charge at City Point because his Chief-of-Staff, Brigadier General John A. Rawlins, was on sick leave. Ibid., pp. 1,046–47, 1,090–92, 1,109–10, 1,114–16, and pt. 1, pp. 100–1, 653, 713, 720, 760, 764, 767, 769, 778, 794–95, 818, 820, 935; RG 393, DVNC, v. DXLII, bk. 128, pp. 71–72, NA; Beecher, op. cit., v. II, p. 578; "Returns of the 4th and 5th New Jersey Batteries and E/1st Pennsylvania Light Artillery, and of C-D-M/1st and E/3rd and D/4th U. S. Artillery, S-O, 1864," RG 94, M594 and entry 53, respectively, NA; Frederic Denison, *Shot and Shell*, p. 311; Brown to Bragg, Sept. 29, 1864, RG 109, entry 450, box 3, NA; Pollack, *Diary*, Sept. 29, 1864, ISHL; RG 108, entry 1, v. XXI, p. 448, NA; New York *Herald*, Oct. 2, 1864; Kautz, *Journal*, Sept. 29, 1864, LC; RG 94, entry 12, 1864 file, No. H1124, NA; Butler, op. cit., pp. 730–36, 741–42; J. Marshall, op. cit., v. V, p. 192; New York *Tribune*, Oct. 13, 1864; Wilson, op. cit., pp. 435–36; Valentine Moulder, "The 16th N. Y. H. A.," *NT*, Aug. 22, 1901; Milton Holland, quoted in Joseph Mitchell, *The Badge of Gallantry*, p. 142; New York *Times*, Oct. 3 and 23, 1864; Henry Brown, letter of Oct. 5, 1864, Brown Papers, CNHS; Hartford *Courant*, Oct. 10, 1864; Porter, op. cit., pp. 300–2; D. S. Burwell to E. S. Burwell, Oct. 5, 1864, Burwell Papers, SHC; White, loc. cit., No. 2, pp. 273–74; Foster to Shreve, report of Oct. 5, 1864, RG 391, 10AC, v. XV, bk. 51, NA; Oliver Davis, *David Bell Birney*, p. 259; Eisenschiml, op. cit., p. 255; RG 94, entry 160, v. VIII, p. 611, NA; Badeau, op. cit., v. III, p. 71; Burr, op. cit., p. 661; Sommers, op. cit., v. I, pp. 283–86, and v. II, pp. 326–30.

20. Lieutenant Colonel C. R. MacDonald, commanding the 47th New York of the Second Brigade, who was shot sometime that day, may have been wounded by Gathright's shelling. White, loc. cit., No. 2, pp. 273–74; Brown to Bragg, Sept. 29, 1864, RG 109, entry 450, box 3, NA; Ewell to Bragg, 10:00 A.M., Sept. 29, 1864, Davis Coll., TU; D. S. Burwell to E. S.

Burwell, Oct. 5, 1864, Burwell Papers, SHC; John Foote to his father, Oct. 2, 1864, Foote Papers, DU; *OR,* v. XLII, pt. 1, pp. 105, 760, 764–65, 767, 769, 935, and pt. 2, p. 1,303; New York *Times,* Oct. 23, 1864; RG 391, 10AC, v. XXVII, bk. 81, Pennypacker to Davis, Oct. 9, 1864, and v. XV, bk. 51, Foster to Shreve, Oct. 5, 1864, NA; DeGraff, *Memoirs,* p. 308, CWTI Coll., MHRC; "Return of D/115th New York, S-O, 1864," RG 94, M594, NA; Boyd, loc. cit., p. 22, VHS; Sommers, op. cit., v. II, pp. 330–32.

21. White, loc. cit., No. 2, pp. 274–75; D. S. Burwell to E. S. Burwell, Oct. 5, 1864, Burwell Papers, SHC; New York *Times,* Oct. 23, 1864; John Foote to his father, Oct. 2, 1864, Foote Papers, DU; Jackson and O'Donnell, op. cit., pp. 164–65; Bangor *Daily Whig and Courier,* Oct. 21, 1864; Hartford *Courant,* Oct. 10, 1864; "Returns of Staff (Detachment)/16th New York Heavy Artillery, D-K/24th Massachusetts, and K/100th and D/115th New York, S-O, 1864," RG 94, M594, NA; Buffalo *Morning Express,* Oct. 13, 1864; Henry Marshall, letter of Oct. 2, 1864, Marshall Papers, WCL, UM; Scroggs, *Diary,* Sept. 29, 1864, CWTI Coll., MHRC; RG 393, DVNC, two-name box 5, Nos. F96-2 and -6, and v. L, bk. 74, pp. 109–12, NA; "CSR of Isaac Hobbs, 4th New Hampshire," RG 94, CSR, NA; RG 391, 10AC, box 1, Pennypacker, letter of S-O, 1864, Sept. 1864 file, and v. XXVII, bk. 52, G.O. No. 29, Oct. 6, 1864, and v. I, bk. 8, No. 718, NA; *AG-Maine-1864/65,* v. I, p. 258; New York *Herald,* Oct. 2, 1864; *OR,* v. XLII, pt. 1, pp. 110, 653–55, 703, 708, 713, 716, 726, 760–62, 765, 767, 769, 772, 774, 778, 935, and pt. 2, pp. 1,109–10, 1,303–4, and pt. 3, pp. 65, 78–79; Perry, loc. cit., v. XIII, pp. 414–15; Sommers, op. cit., v. II, pp. 332–36.

22. Granberry, loc. cit., v. XIII, p. 413; Flanigan, loc. cit., v. XIII, p. 123; Moore, loc. cit., v. XIII, p. 420; Dudley DuBose to E. P. Alexander, Aug. 23, 1866, and *Alexander Ms.,* v. LI, p. 264, EPA Coll., SHC; *OR,* v. XLII, pt. 1, pp. 761, 764–65; Lokey, op. cit., p. 22, GDAH; Richmond *Sentinel,* Oct. 13, 1864; Hanks, *History,* p. 50, HJC; May, loc. cit., v. XII, pp. 587–88; R. A. Hardaway to N. B. Johnston, June 25, 1894, Johnston mss.; *ORA,* pls. LXXVII, No. 1, and XCII, No. 1; Moore, op. cit., p. 264; New York *Times,* Oct. 23, 1864; Martin, loc. cit., v. XIII, pp. 269–70; Richmond *Dispatch,* Oct. 22, 1864; "Returns of C/15th Georgia, Green's Louisiana Battery, Griffin's Virginia Battery, and Staff/25th Virginia Battalion, S-O, 1864, and Staff/2nd Virginia Reserve Battalion, July–Oct., 1864," RG 109, ch. 1, entry 18, NA; Lott, loc. cit., v. XIII, p. 417; Breckinridge, loc. cit., v. XIII, pp. 415–16; W. J. Thomas to his cousin, Nov. 4, 1864, Confederate Soldiers' Letters No. 24238, VSL; Richmond *Whig,* Sept. 30, 1864; Richmond *Enquirer,* Nov. 22, 1864; Johnston, loc. cit., v. I, p. 441; Jackson and O'Donnell, op. cit., p. 165; "Return of K/7th USCT, S-O, 1864," RG 94, M594, NA; *McCarty Ms.,* p. 4, TXU; D. D. Pendleton to W. N. Pendleton, Oct. 2, 1864, WNP Coll., SHC; Edward Younger, ed., *Inside the Confederate Government,* p. 176; Walter Stevens, *Map of Confederate Lines from Fort Gregg to Mrs. Price's,* LC Maps; RG 77, Map G204, No. 49, NA; George Reese, "Five Confederates," *CV,* v. XII, p. 286; Moore,

loc. cit., v. XIII, p. 420; Jones, loc. cit., v. XXV, p. 24; Pickens, loc. cit., v. XXI, p. 484; Winkler, op. cit., p. 194; W. A. McClendon, *Recollections,* p. 213; Polley, *Texas Brigade,* pp. 254–55; Sommers, op. cit., v. II, pp. 336–39.

23. New York *Times,* Oct. 23, 1864.

24. Ibid.

25. Scroggs, *Diary,* Sept. 29, 1864, CWTI Coll., MHRC.

26. Besides Pennypacker on the far right, one company of the 112th New York, detailed leftward as skirmishers, managed to escape the heavy casualties that befell its regiment and other troops on Foster's center. Ibid.; Jackson and O'Donnell, op. cit., p. 165; Isaiah Price, *97th Pennsylvania,* pp. 323–24, 418; New York *Times,* Oct. 15 and 23, 1864; Bangor *Daily Whig and Courier,* Oct. 21, 1864; RG 94, entry 160, v. VI, "G. Pennypacker," and v. X, p. 504, NA; RG 391, 10AC, v. II, bk. 75, p. 59, and box 3, casualty report of Foster's division, Sept. 29–Oct. 1, 1864, and box 4, Granger to Dyer, Oct. 1864, NA; RG 393, DVNC, two-name box 5, No. F96-2, NA; Johnston, loc. cit., v. I, p. 441; R. A. Hardaway to N. B. Johnston, June 25, 1894, Johnston mss.; John Foote to his father, Oct. 2, 1864, Foote Papers, DU; Granberry, loc. cit., v. XIII, p. 413; Jones, loc. cit., v. XXV, p. 24; Richmond *Enquirer,* Nov. 22, 1864; DeGraff, *Memoirs,* pp. 308–9, CWTI Coll., and Theodore W. Skinner to friends, Oct. 3, 1864, Skinner Papers, Civil War Misc. Coll., MHRC; *OR,* v. XLII, pt. 1, pp. 109–10, 133–35, 761–62, 765, 767, 769, 818, 820, 934–35, and pt. 3, pp. 100–1; New York *Herald,* Oct. 15, 1864; "Returns of A-F/5th and Staff/36th USCT, S-O, 1864," RG 94, M594, NA; Pickens, loc. cit., v. XXI, p. 484; John Bell Bouton, *Louis Bell,* pp. 23–24; Winkler, op. cit., p. 194; RG 94, entry 12, 1864 file, No. H1124, NA; RG 94, entry 178, No. 411, NA; Sommers, op. cit., v. II, pp. 339–43.

27. William Anderson to Peter Guerrant, Oct. 7, 1864, Guerrant Papers, VHS; Jones, loc. cit., v. XXV, p. 24; *OR,* v. XLII, pt. 2, p. 1,303; New York *Times,* Oct. 23, 1864; R. T. Coles, *Ms. History of 4th Alabama,* ch. XX, p. 11, and Rufus Hollis, *Confederate Veteran,* pp. 20–21, 4th Alabama Coll., ADAH; Pinckney D. Bowles, letter of Oct. 5, 1886, William Palmer Coll., WRHS; Richmond *Enquirer,* Nov. 22, 1864; Field, loc. cit., v. XIV, p. 555; Granberry, loc. cit., v. XIII, p. 413; Reese, loc. cit., v. XII, p. 286; McClendon, op. cit., p. 213; Sommers, op. cit., v. II, pp. 343–45.

28. *OR,* v. XLII, pt. 1, p. 772, and pt. 3, p. 253.

29. Ibid., pt. 1, p. 772; Shaw to Bailey, Oct. 16, 1864, RG 391, 10AC, box 2, NA; Joseph Califf, *Ex-Members,* pp. 5–6, and *7th USCT,* p. 42; George Sherman, "Fort Gilmer," *RISSHS,* s. 5, v. VIII, No. 7, pp. 6–7, 15.

30. Polley, *Texas Brigade,* p. 256.

31. Only one of Weiss's men was neither shot nor captured. Forty-seven more, wounded in the cornfield, were rescued later in the day. Most of those wounded were hailed as heroes. Lieutenant Joseph Prime, however, was regarded by many of his brother regimental officers as a skulker, though his brigadier upheld him. Ibid., pp. 255–56, and *Charming Nellie,* pp. 261–62; William Birney, *Answer to Libels,* pp. 15–21; Breckinridge, loc.

cit., v. XIII, p. 416; Coles, op. cit., ch. XX, p. 11, and Hollis, op. cit., p. 20, 4th Alabama Coll., ADAH; Ewell, *Letterbook,* p. 17, DU; Granberry, loc. cit., v. XIII, p. 413; McClendon, op. cit., p. 213; Reese, loc. cit., v. XII, p. 286; Jones, loc. cit., v. XXV, p. 24; Haskin, op. cit., pp. 209, 445; Denison, op. cit., p. 311; Henry Brown, letter of Oct. 5, 1864, and *Diary,* Sept. 29, 1864, Brown Papers, CNHS; *OR,* v. XLII, pt. 1, pp. 134–37, 760–61, 772–75, 778, 780–81, 870–71, 875–76, 935, and pt. 2, pp. 1,026, 1,044, 1,304, and pt. 3, p. 253; Henry Marshall, letter of Oct. 5, 1864, Marshall Papers, WCL, UM; *AG-Maine-1864/65,* v. I, p. 258; "Returns of D-K/24th Massachusetts and K/7th USCT, S-O, 1864," RG 94, M594, NA; George Dennett, *9th USCT,* p. 65; Bates, *Pennsylvania Volunteers,* v. V, p. 967; Califf, *7th USCT,* pp. 41–46, 51–56, 98–132, and *Ex-Members,* pp. 5–6; Sherman, loc. cit., s. 5, v. VIII, No. 7, pp. 1–79; Joseph R. Hawley to his wife, Oct. 25, 1864, Hawley Papers, LC; RG 391, 10AC, box 2, Shaw to Bailey, Oct. 16, 1864, and box 3, casualty report of Birney's brigade, Sept. 29–30, 1864, NA; Lokey, op. cit., pp. 22–23, GDAH; Richmond *Dispatch,* Oct. 22, 1864; Field, loc. cit., v. XIV, pp. 555–56; Montgomery, loc. cit., v. XXVIII, p. 178; RG 391, 25AC, v. XXI, bk. 45, p. 167, and v. XXIV, bk. 46, pp. 64–65, NA; "CSR of Joseph Prime, 7th USCT," RG 94, CSR, NA; George Sherman, "The Negro as a Soldier," *RISSHS,* s. 7, No. 7, p. 22; Johnston, loc. cit., v. I, p. 441; Anderson, *Report, 1864,* p. 25, LHQ Coll., VHS; Lott, loc. cit., v. XIII, p. 417; Martin, loc. cit., v. XIII, pp. 269–70; May, loc. cit., v. XII, p. 588; Perry, loc. cit., v. XIII, p. 415; Richmond *Enquirer,* Nov. 22, 1864; W. J. Thomas to his cousin, Nov. 4, 1864, Confederate Soldiers' Letters No. 24238, VSL; Moore, op. cit., p. 264; *Alexander Ms.,* v. LI, pp. 264, 269, and Dudley DuBose to E. P. Alexander, Aug. 23, 1866, EPA Coll., SHC; Hanks, *History,* pp. 49–50, HJC; *McCarty Ms.,* p. 4, TXU; Silas B. O'Mohundro, *Map,* Clay Papers, HSP; Reed, *Journal,* p. 132, ADAH; J. R. Winder, "Judge Martin's Report Approved," *CV,* v. XIII, p. 417; Richmond *Sentinel,* Oct. 13, 1864; Samuel McKinney to his wife, Oct. 2, 1864, McKinney Papers, EU; Sommers, op. cit., v. II, pp. 308, 345–56.

32. Pottsville *Miners' Journal,* Nov. 12, 1864; Jones, loc. cit., v. XXV, p. 24; "Return of Griffin's Virginia Battery, S-O, 1864," RG 109, ch. 1, entry 18, NA; Moore, loc. cit., v. XIII, p. 420; *Johnston Ms.,* pp. 7–8, box 179, DSF Coll., LC; R. A. Hardaway to N. B. Johnston, June 25, 1894, Johnston mss.; Bates, *Pennsylvania Volunteers,* v. II, p. 179; RG 393, DVNC, two-name box 5, No. W273-11, NA; *OR,* v. XLII, pt. 1, p. 135, and pt. 2, p. 1,116, and pt. 3, pp. 166–67; New York *Herald,* Oct. 23, 1864; Comstock, *Diary,* Sept. 29, 1864, LC; Moore, loc. cit., v. XIII, p. 420; Sommers, op. cit., v. II, pp. 356–57.

33. *OR,* v. XLII, pt. 2, p. 1,110.

34. Ibid., pp. 1,109–10.

35. Ibid., pp. 1,084–85, 1,092, 1,109–11, 1,303–4, and pt. 1, pp. 99–100, 662, 703, 708, 713, 715–16, 720, 726, 773, 775, 781, and pt. 3, p. 166; RG 393, DVNC, two-name box 5, No. W273-11, and v. CXCI, bk. 466, pp. 97–101, NA; Birney, op. cit., pp. 17–18; Hanks, *History,* p. 50,

HJC; Haskin, op. cit., pp. 209, 445; Langdon to Butler, Feb. 15, 1865, BFB Coll., LC; Moore, op. cit., p. 264; White, loc. cit., No. 2, p. 274; D. S. Burwell to E. S. Burwell, Oct. 5, 1864, Burwell Papers, SHC; R. A. Hardaway to N. B. Johnston, June 25, 1894, Johnston mss.; *Johnston Ms.*, pp. 7–8, box 179, DSF Coll., LC; Pottsville *Miners' Journal*, Nov. 12, 1864; "Returns of B-H/6th Connecticut, B/39th Illinois, D-K/24th Massachusetts, K/100th New York, and B/62nd Ohio, S-O, 1864," RG 94, M594, NA; Hartford *Courant*, Oct. 10, 1864; *ANJ*, v. II, p. 98; 3rd New Hampshire, *Notebook*, Sept. 29, 1864, MOLLUS-Mass Coll., box 7, Harvard; Dickey, op. cit., p. 407; *AG-Maine-1864/65*, v. I, p. 258; Alfred Roe et al., *24th Massachusetts*, p. 360; RG 391, 25AC, v. XI, bk. 17, Sept. 29, 1864, NA; Ferdinand Davis, *Recollections*, p. 133, MHC, UM; Adrian Terry to Isadore, Oct. 3, 1864, quoted in Marino, op. cit., p. 354; J. Marshall, op. cit., v. V, pp. 95–96, 228; Sommers, op. cit., v. II, pp. 357–61.

36. Ewell dispatched this promise to Richmond at 3:00 P.M.; he presumably sent comparable tidings to Lee. Bragg, *Book of Letters Sent*, p. 267, TU; *OR*, v. XLII, pt. 1, pp. 773, 775, 778, 781, 875, 879, and pt. 2, pp. 1,301, 1,303–4; Anderson, *Report, 1864*, p. 25, LHQ Coll., VHS; D. D. Pendleton to W. N. Pendleton, Oct. 2, 1864, WNP Coll., SHC; Crockett, *Diary*, Sept. 29, 1864, Crimmins Coll., TXU; Polley, *Charming Nellie*, p. 264; Sherman, loc. cit., s. 5, v. VIII, No. 7, pp. 62–63; RG 391, 25AC, v. XXVII, bk. 55A, pp. 29–30, NA; Bates, *Pennsylvania Volunteers*, v. V, p. 967; Califf, *7th USCT*, p. 45; Henry Brown, letter of Oct. 5, 1864, Brown Papers, CNHS; Sommers, op. cit., v. II, pp. 361–63.

37. *OR*, v. XLII, pt. 1, pp. 99–100, 102, 105, 703, 708, 713, 715–16, 720, 726, 761, 765, 767, 769, 773, 775, 778, 781, 818, 877, and pt. 2 pp. 1,114, 1,304; Henry Brown, letter of Oct. 5, 1864, Brown Papers, CNHS; Haskin, op. cit., p. 445; RG 94, entry 12, 1864 file, No. H1124, NA; New York *Herald*, Oct. 15, 1864; Polley, *Charming Nellie*, p. 264; William McFall to his sister, Sept. 30, 1864, McFall Papers, EU; "Returns of B/39th Illinois, D-K/24th Massachusetts, Staff/7th New Hampshire, K/100th New York, and A/1st Pennsylvania Light Artillery, and of F/5th U. S. Artillery, S-O, 1864," RG 94, M594 and entry 53, respectively, NA; Davis, op. cit., p. 133, MHC, UM; Hartford *Courant*, Oct. 10, 1864; *Ripley Ms.*, p. 9, DSF Coll., UV; Adrian Terry to Isadore, Oct. 3, 1864, quoted in Marino, op. cit., p. 354; Alexander, loc. cit., July 31, 1890; Benjamin Wright to his wife, Oct. 2, 1864, Wright Papers, WHS; *ORN*, v. X, pp. 752–63, 778; Butler, op. cit., pp. 734–35; Philadelphia *Evening Bulletin*, Oct. 3, 1864; Chase, op. cit., p. 224; Ward, op. cit., p. 110; Hall and Hall, op. cit., p. 257; Sommers, op. cit., v. II, pp. 363–66.

38. Alexander's Chief-of-Staff, who did not witness the counterattack but who may have been privy to the assessment of senior officers who did see it, described Montague's effort in this way:

They [the Bluecoats] at one time held the Ft. just this side of Ft. H. but were driven from it and all before we came except Ft. H. itself. . . . Had the thing been properly managed Ft. H. wd. have been taken at the time the others were but it was not.

Whether the staff officer referred to the failure to use more men in the operation or to some unspecified tactical error by Montague or his seniors or subordinates is not known. *OR*, v. XLII, pt. 1, pp. 135, 799, 805, 876, and pt. 2, p. 1,303, and pt. 3, p. 165; *ANJ*, v. II, p. 97; New York *Tribune*, Oct. 4, 1864; Bates, *Pennsylvania Volunteers*, v. II, pp. 290–91; Allen, loc. cit., v. XIII, p. 418; Richmond *Enquirer*, Oct. 10, 1864; C. L. and Pinckney Anthony to their mother, Oct. 3 and 24, 1864, Anthony Family Papers, VSL; RG 391, 24AC, v. XXXIX, bk. 101, Sept. 29, 1864, NA; RG 393, DVNC, v. CXCI, bk. 466, p. 107, NA; *ORN*, v. X, pp. 754–55, 758; D. D. Pendleton to W. N. Pendleton, Oct. 2, 1864, WNP Coll., SHC; RG 94, entry 160, v. VIII, p. 611, NA; Thompson, op. cit., p. 480; Field, loc. cit., v. XIV, p. 556; Eisenschiml, op. cit., p. 245; Sommers, op. cit., v. II, pp. 366–71; Bragg, *Book of Letters Sent*, p. 266, TU; Wright, loc. cit., v. XIV, p. 545; Coles, op. cit., ch. XX, pp. 13–14, 4th Alabama Coll., ADAH; Samuel McKinney to his wife, Oct. 2, 1864, McKinney Papers, EU; "Return of F/63rd Tennessee, S-O, 1864," RG 109, ch. 1, entry 18, NA; Anderson, *Report, 1864*, p. 25, LHQ Coll., VHS; Silas B. O'Mohundro to Cecil Clay, Feb. 14 and May 23, 1887, Clay Papers, HSP; Hubbell et al., op. cit., p. 303; Richmond *Sentinel*, Oct. 5 and 13, 1864; *CWR*, p. 363; Lindsley, op. cit., p. 408; Ewell, *Letterbook*, p. 17, DU; Osman Latrobe, *Diary*, Sept. 29, 1864, VHS.

CHAPTER IV

1. RG 393, DVNC, v. CXXVIII, bk. 298, Sept. 30 and Oct. 10, 1864, NA; "Monthly Returns of Artillery Brigade/18th Corps and of Kautz's Division and Monthly and Trimonthly Returns of the Army of the James, Sept. 30, 1864," RG 94, entries 65 and 62, 18AC and DVNC, respectively, NA; *OR*, v. XXXVI, pt. 3, pp. 809–11, and v. XLII, pt. 1, pp. 137, 760, 764, 767, 769, 847, and pt. 2, pp. 1,084–85, 1,109, 1,237–38, 1,304, and v. XLVI, pt. 2, p. 1,196; Haskin, op. cit., pp. 209–10; Seth Eyland, *The Evolution of a Life*, p. 236; Kautz, *Reminiscences*, pp. 89–90, and *Journal*, Sept. 29, 1864, Kautz Papers, LC; *ORA*, pls. XCII, No. 1, and LXXVII, No. 1, and C, No. 2, and LXVIII, No. 4; W. E. Doyle, "A Ride with Kautz," *NT*, July 6, 1899, and "A Confederate Prisoner," *CV*, v. XXXIV, p. 51; New York *Herald*, Oct. 2, 1864; Brown to Bragg, Sept. 29, 1864, RG 109, entry 450, box 3, NA; Sommers, op. cit., v. II, pp. 390–94, 406–7; Charles and Pinckney Anthony to their mother, Oct. 3 and 24, 1864, Anthony Family Papers, VSL; "Returns of the 10th, 20th, and 19th Virginia Heavy Artillery Battalions, July–Aug., S-O, and Nov.–Dec. 1864, respectively," RG 109, ch. 1, entry 18, NA; *Artillery Defenses*, p. 162, CHHS; Kemper to Bragg, Sept. 29, 1864, Frederick M. Dearborn Coll., Harvard; Richmond *Whig*, Sept. 30, 1864, John B. Jones, *A Rebel War Clerk's Diary*, v. II, pp. 295–96.

2. Kemper to Moore, Sept. 29, 1864, CMC-Ic, EU; Confederate War Department, *List of Official Communications*, pp. 208–9, box 110, C.S.A. Coll., LC; White, loc. cit., No. 2, p. 274; John Hatton, *Memoirs*, pp. 649,

652, LC; Louise Haskell Daly, *Alexander Cheves Haskell,* pp. 141–43; Sommers, op. cit., v. II, pp. 406–9; *OR,* v. XXXVI, pt. 3, pp. 809–11, and v. XLII, pt. 2, pp. 1,303–4; "Returns of the 10th and 19th Virginia Heavy Artillery Battalions, July–Aug. and Nov.–Dec. 1864, respectively," RG 109, ch. 1, entry 18, NA; Pemberton to Seddon, 4:30 P.M., Sept. 29, 1864, RG 109, entry 6, No. 3520, NA; Younger, op. cit., p. 176; Kemper to Bragg, Sept. 29, 1864, Dearborn Coll., Harvard; John Danforth, *Copybook,* p. 196, DU; Wallace, op. cit., pp. 283–85; D. D. Pendleton to Bob, Oct. 9, 1864, Pendleton Papers, DU.

3. "Returns of C-D/5th and G-M/11th Pennsylvania Cavalry, Staff/1st District of Columbia Cavalry, and 4th Wisconsin Battery, S-O, 1864," RG 94, M594, NA; Kautz, *Reminiscences,* pp. 89–90, Kautz Papers, LC; Eyland, op. cit., p. 239; *OR,* v. XXXVI, pt. 3, pp. 809–11, and v. XLII, pt. 1, p. 847, and pt. 2, pp. 1,084–85, 1,304, and v. XLVI, pt. 2, p. 1,196; Daly, op. cit., pp. 141–44; Richmond *Dispatch,* Oct. 1, 1864; Doyle, loc. cit., v. XXXIV, p. 52; Richmond *Whig,* Sept. 30, 1864; Haskin, op. cit., pp. 209–10; J. B. Jones, op. cit., v. II, pp. 295–96; Pemberton to Seddon, 4:30 P.M., Sept. 29, 1864, RG 109, entry 6, No. 3520, NA; Sommers, op. cit., v. II, pp. 409–11.

4. "Return of Staff/10th Virginia Heavy Artillery Battalion, S-O, 1864," RG 109, ch. 1, entry 18, NA; Richmond *Whig,* Sept. 30, 1864; Kautz, *Journal,* Sept. 29, 1864, and *Reminiscences,* pp. 89–90, and *Report of Military Services,* p. 15, Kautz Papers, LC; *OR,* v. XLII, pt. 2, p. 1,149, and v. XLVI, pt. 2, p. 364; Emma Mordecai, *Diary,* Oct. 8, 1864, SHC; Danforth, *Copybook,* p. 196, DU; Eyland, op. cit., pp. 239–40; August Kautz to Mrs. Savage, Oct. 5, 1864, Kautz Papers, ISHL; Sommers, op. cit., v. II, pp. 411–12.

5. Butler notified City Point at 9:10 P.M., September 29, that Kautz had "flanked to the right and cut his connections, and we have not heard from him." As the hours ticked into Friday afternoon with no further word of the horsemen's fate, the lieutenant general felt "some uneasiness" for them and inquired about them. Only at 3:00 P.M., over seven hours after Kautz reported back, did the Massachusetts man finally notify Grant of his return. Kautz, *Journal,* Sept. 29–30, 1864, and *Reminiscences,* p. 90, Kautz Papers, LC; *OR,* v. XLII, pt. 1, pp. 137, 847, and pt. 2, pp. 1,111, 1,142, 1,149–50; Doyle, loc. cit., v. XXXIV, p. 52; "Return of B/1st U. S. Artillery, S-O, 1864," RG 94, entry 53, NA; Sommers, op. cit., v. II, pp. 412–13.

6. Mordecai, *Diary,* Oct. 8, 1864, SHC; *OR,* v. XLII, pt. 1, p. 137, and pt. 2, pp. 1,149–50, and pt. 3, p. 35; Charles Anthony to his mother, Oct. 3, 1864, Anthony Family Papers, VSL; Haskin, op. cit., p. 577; "Return of B/1st U. S. Artillery, S-O, 1864," RG 94, entry 53, NA; RG 391, 25AC, v. XI, bk. 17, Sept. 29, 1864, NA; RG 393, DVNC, v. CXCI, bk. 466, pp. 97–101, NA; Sommers, op. cit., v. II, pp. 413–14.

7. Samuel Cooper to his wife, Oct. 3, 1864, VHS.

8. *OR,* v. XLII, pt. 2, p. 1,302.

9. Hatton, *Memoirs,* p. 661, LC.

10. Two regiments and three battalions of infantry made up the Local Defense Brigade. The 1st Virginia LDF Cavalry Battalion was also available. One of its officers, indeed, was scouting on Curl's Neck, just east across the James from Jones's Neck, as early as 6:30 A.M., so the possibility cannot be excluded that the whole cavalry battalion was on duty with Gary from the outset. Ibid., pp. 648–51, 661, LC; Lee, *Telegram Book,* pp. 294–95, LHQ Coll., VHS; *OR,* v. XLII, pt. 2, pp. 1,237–40, 1,301–4; Wallace, op. cit., pp. 210–16, 225, 283–85; Samuel Cooper to his wife, Oct. 3, 1864, VHS; Charleston *Mercury,* Oct. 5, 1864; Confederate War Department, *List of Official Communications,* pp. 209–10, box 110, C.S.A. Coll., LC; Bragg, *Endorsement Book, 1864–65,* p. 123, TU; William Couper, *One Hundred Years at V.M.I.,* v. III, pp. 62–63; J. B. Jones, op. cit., v. II, pp. 295–96, 302; Sally Brock, *Richmond During the War,* p. 330; Sarah to A. L. Alexander, Sept. 29–Oct. 3, 1864, Alexander-Hillhouse Papers, SHC; Kate Sperry, *Diary,* Sept. 29, 1864, VSL; Richard Ewell to Walter Taylor, Nov. 8, 1864, and Ewell, *Letterbook,* p. 16, Ewell Papers, DU; R. S. Bevier, *Missouri Confederate Brigades,* p. 452; T. S. Ruffin to his cousin, Oct. 15, 1864, Harrison Cocke Papers, SHC; Jasper Davis to his wife, Oct. 4, 1864, Jasper Davis Papers, DU; Joseph Graves, *The Bedford Light Artillery,* (Oct. 3, 1864); Joseph Hilton to Coz, Oct. 14, 1864, Hilton Papers, CMC-Ib, EU; Samuel S. Biddle to his father, Oct. 3, 1864, Biddle Papers, DU; Peter McMichael, *Diary,* Sept. 29, 1864, SCHS; Columbus *Daily Enquirer,* Sept. 30, 1864; Charles Andrews, letter of Oct. 23, 1864, Charles Andrews Papers, DU; Richmond *Sentinel,* Oct. 3, 1864; RG 109, entry 5, 1864 file, Nos. G230 and M503, and entry 12, 1864 file, Nos. B3214, C2449, P1710, S2576, W2564½, and W2565½, and entry 450, box 3, Brown to Bragg, Sept. 29, 1864, and ch. 1, v. CCX, p. 375, and ch. 6, v. CCCLXIV, pp. 217–18, 251, 639, NA; Richmond *Whig,* Sept. 30 and Oct. 3, 1864; Richmond *Dispatch,* Oct. 3, 1864; Richmond *Examiner,* Nov. 7, 1864; White, loc. cit., No. 2, p. 274; Buffalo *Morning Express,* Oct. 13, 1864; Frank E. Vandiver, ed., *Diary of Gorgas,* p. 143; Alfred Grima to his mother, Sept. 29, 1864, Grima Papers, Louisiana State University; Mordecai, *Diary,* Sept. 29, 1864, SHC; Abner Small, "Personal Observations," *MOLLUS-Maine,* v. I, pp. 301–4; Harold Small, ed., *The Road to Richmond,* pp. 161–62, 257; Sommers, op. cit., v. II, pp. 394–99.

11. Although twice as many stray soldiers as impressed civilians made up the City Brigade by October 8, the ratio was probably less imbalanced ten days earlier. Besides the four regimental commanders named, a Captain D. C. Cohn (Cohen?, Cone?), a Major Huffman, and Lieutenant Colonel Peter McMichael led provisional battalions in early October. At least McMichael's force, though, was not created until October 6; it is not known when the other two were raised. Nor has the commander of the 2nd City Regiment been identified. Owen's cavalry regiment may have included not only such impressed provisionals but also the three mounted militia troops and the LDF Cavalry Battalion in the city. RG 109, entry 5, 1864 file, Nos. G230 and J173, and entry 12, 1864 file, Nos. C2449, G1459, R2882, R2887½, W2564½, and W2565½, and 1865 file, No. E544, and entry

450, box 3, Brown to Bragg, Sept. 29, 1864, and ch. 1, v. CCX, pp. 358, 380–81, and ch. 2, entry 112, box 12, No. 144, and box 13, No. 299, and ch. 6, v. CCCLXV, p. 309, and ch. 9, v. CCXLVIII, p. 31, NA; Hatton, *Memoirs,* pp. 650–51, LC; Joseph Hilton to Coz, Oct. 14, 1864, Hilton Papers, CMC-Ib, EU; New York *Times,* Oct. 17, 1864; Bevier, op. cit., pp. 452–58; Jasper Davis to his wife, Oct. 4, 1864, Jasper Davis Papers, DU; Richmond *Examiner,* Oct. 21 and 24, 1864; Richmond *Enquirer,* Oct. 21, 1864; Charleston *Mercury,* Oct. 5, 1864; McMichael, *Diary,* Oct. 6–7, 1864, SCHS; Kemper to Bragg, Sept. 29, 1864, Dearborn Coll., Harvard; Wallace, op. cit., pp. 210, 283–86; Isaac Hammond, Correspondence, VSL; Sommers, op. cit., v. II, pp. 399–405; Kemper to Moore, Sept. 29, 1864, CMC-Ic, EU; "CSR of M. L. Clark, Confederate Staff," RG 109, CSR, NA; Columbus *Daily Enquirer,* Oct. 26, 1864; Augusta *Chronicle,* Oct. 28, 1864; Confederate War Department, *List of Official Communications,* pp. 201, 209, box 110, C.S.A. Coll., LC; *OR,* v. XLII, pt. 2, pp. 1,296, 1,301–3, and pt. 3, p. 1,218, and v. XLIII, pt. 2, pp. 879–80, and v. XLVI, pt. 2, p. 1,169, and s. 2, v. VII, pp. 870, 963–64; Bragg, *Book of Letters Sent,* pp. 266–67, TU; Sperry, *Diary,* Sept. 29, 1864, VSL.

12. Jasper Davis to his wife, Oct. 4, 1864, Jasper Davis Papers, DU; Hatton, *Memoirs,* p. 650, LC; Joseph Hilton to Coz, Oct. 14, 1864, Hilton Papers, CMC-Ib, EU; Charleston *Mercury,* Oct. 5, 1864; *OR,* v. XLII, pt. 1, p. 879, and pt. 2, pp. 1,143, 1,302–3, and pt. 3, p. 34; Bragg, *Book of Letters Sent,* p. 266, TU; Samuel McKinney to his wife, Oct. 2, 1864, McKinney Papers, EU; RG 393, DVNC, v. CXCI, bk. 466, p. 107, NA; Wright, loc. cit., v. XIV, p. 545; Coles, op. cit., ch. XX, pp. 13–14, 4th Alabama Coll., ADAH; Richmond *Sentinel,* Oct. 4, 1864; Linden Kent to his mother, Oct. 3, 1864, CM; Field, loc. cit., v. XIV, p. 556; Sommers, op. cit., v. II, pp. 405–6, 481–82; Sperry, *Diary,* Sept. 29, 1864, VSL.

13. *OR,* v. XLII, pt. 1, pp. 875–76, 879, 947, and pt. 2, p. 1,302; Lee, *Telegram Book,* p. 294, LHQ Coll., VHS; John Ramsay to Maggie, Oct. 5, 1864, Ramsay Papers, SHC; Sommers, op. cit., v. II, p. 472.

14. The brigadier will be referred to as " 'Tige' Anderson," and his corps commander will be called simply "Anderson." *OR,* v. XLII, pt. 1, pp. 654, 879, and pt. 2, pp. 1,092, 1,112; Lee, *Telegram Book,* p. 294, LHQ Coll., VHS; Robert F. Davis, *Diary,* Sept. 29, 1864, CMC-Ib, EU; Hollis, op. cit., p. 20, 4th Alabama Coll., ADAH; Joseph B. Lyle, *Diary,* Sept. 29, 1864, made available through the generosity of Mr. Elmer O. Parker; Sommers, op. cit., v. II, pp. 470–72.

15. Inconclusive evidence indicates that the Southerners built a second bridge over the James to facilitate Hoke's crossing. One doubts that such construction, if it occurred, accounts for his main body's delay in leaving Dunlop's. Burgwyn, *Diary,* Sept. 29–30, 1864, NCDAH; Dunn, loc. cit., v. V, p. 146, GDAH; Smith, *Diary,* Sept. 29, 1864, GDAH; David Hampton to Caleb Hampton, Oct. 4, 1864, Hampton Papers, DU; Henry Greer to his mother, Oct. 3, 1864, Greer Papers, LC; J. H. Pegram, letter of Oct. 6, 1864, CMC, DU; James D. Morgan, *Rebel Reefer,* p. 205; *OR,* v. XLII, pt. 1, pp. 210, 875–76, 897, and pt. 2, pp. 1,092, 1,094, 1,096–97, 1,100–1,

1,302, and pt. 3, p. 9; Russell, *Diary,* Sept. 30, 1864, DU; Hagood, op. cit., p. 305; "Returns of B/66th North Carolina and K/25th South Carolina, S-O, 1864," RG 109, ch. 1, entry 18, NA; J. F. J. Caldwell, *McGowan's Brigade,* p. 162; William D. Alexander, *Diary,* Sept. 29, 1864, SHC; P. G. T. Beauregard, *Letterbook,* v. XXXIII, pp.—(6–8), LC (this citation refers to pp. 6–8 from the back of this unpaginated volume); Sommers, op. cit., v. II, pp. 472–77.

16. W. D. Alexander, *Diary,* Sept. 29–30, 1864, SHC; Beauregard, *Letterbook,* v. XXXIII, pp.—(3–7), LC; James H. Lane, "Glimpses," *SHSP,* v. XVIII, p. 411; *OR,* v. XLII, pt. 1, pp. 210, 947, and pt. 2, pp. 1,092, 1,094, 1,097, 1,103, 1,112, 1,123–24; S. G. Welch, *Confederate Surgeon,* p. 106; W. S. Dunlop, *Lee's Sharpshooters,* p. 209; Caldwell, op. cit., p. 182; Clifford Dowdey, *Lee,* p. 507; Sommers, op. cit., v. II, pp. 477–78.

17. Haskell did not take his remaining battery, D/1st North Carolina Artillery, which had long been detached to the Howlett Line. Whether Jones's two batteries were attached to Haskell's or some other battalion or whether they formed a provisional battalion of their own is not known. D. D. Pendleton to W. N. Pendleton, Oct. 2, 1864, and Morgan to Haskell, Dec. 28, 1864, and Alexander to Pendleton, Dec. 29, 1864, WNP Coll., SHC; Richmond *Sentinel,* Oct. 12, 1864; "Returns of Griffin's, Pollack's, and Price's Virginia Batteries, S-O, 1864," RG 109, ch. 1, entry 18, NA; *OR,* v. XLII, pt. 1, pp. 859–60, and pt. 2, pp. 1,096–97, and pt. 3, pp. 1,340–41; John Ramsay to Maggie, Aug. 26–Dec. 12, 1864, Ramsay Papers, SHC; E. P. Alexander to his wife, Oct. 3, 1864, EPA Coll., SHC; Merrick Reid to his parents, Oct. 2, 1864, W. M. Reid Papers, SCL; Brown to Davenport, Oct. 15, 1864, RG 109, entry 199, misc. rolls, box 7, NA; D. K. Newsom to Sarah, Nov. 28, 1864, Mercer Family Papers, SHC; Edwin Chamberlayne, *Richmond Fayette Artillery,* pp. 6, 9, 23; Graves, op. cit., (Oct. 1864); William Clopton to his mother, Oct. 28, 1864, Clopton Papers, DU; Jedediah Hotchkiss, *Confederate Military History: Virginia,* v. III, pp. 795, 807; Sommers, op. cit., v. II, pp. 478–81; D. S. Burwell to E. S. Burwell, Oct. 5, 1864, Burwell Papers, SHC; Moore, op. cit., p. 265; *Johnston Ms.,* pp. 7–8, box 179, DSF Coll., LC; James Howard, Nov. 14, 1864, in "CSR of Robert N. Stiles, Confederate Staff," RG 109, CSR, NA.

18. Butler's strength does not include his forces at Deep Bottom, Dutch Gap, and Bermuda Hundred. A breakdown of these figures is in Sommers, op. cit., v. II, pp. 482–85. They, however, require slight revision to show that Maury lost seventeen, rather than an estimated fifteen, and that Bass may have had forty-nine instead of forty casualties. Sources for the two changes are Richmond *Enquirer,* Dec. 1, 1864, and Morgan M. Reese, "John Bell Hood and the Texas Brigade," master's thesis at Southwest Texas State Teachers College (1941), pp. 73–76.

19. Alexander to Pendleton, Feb. 25 and March 24, 1865, WNP Coll., SHC; Richmond *Whig,* Nov. 7, 1864.

20. The great historian of the Army of Northern Virginia implies that Hoke's quest for the glory of another impressive victory of his own underlay his repeated failure to co-operate. Douglas Southall Freeman, *Lee's*

Lieutenants, v. III, p. 593; Charles Elliott, "Martin's Brigade," *SHSP,* v. XXIII, pp. 196–97; Moxley Sorrel, *Recollections,* pp. 247–49; Sommers, op. cit., v. II, pp. 485–86.

21. Since the Yankees did not try to cross into Pickett's left rear overnight, Rootes's two ships left Bishop's at 5:00 A.M. to participate in Friday's battle. *ORN,* v. X, pp. 748–49, 758–59, 768, 809; Sommers, op. cit., v. II, pp. 486–87.

22. Field, loc. cit., v. XIV, p. 556; Hollis, op. cit., pp. 21–22, and Coles, op. cit., ch. XX, pp. 13–14, 4th Alabama Coll., ADAH; *OR,* v. XLII, pt. 1, pp. 879–80; Sarah to A. L. Alexander, Sept. 29–Oct. 3, 1864, Alexander-Hillhouse Papers, SHC; J. L. Coker, *E/6th South Carolina,* p. 158; Lyle, *Diary,* Sept. 30, 1864, Parker mss.; Wright, loc. cit., v. XIV, p. 545; Samuel McKinney to his wife, Oct. 2, 1864, McKinney Papers, EU; "Return of F/63rd Tennessee, S-O, 1864," RG 109, ch. 1, entry 18, NA; Sommers, op. cit., v. II, pp. 488–89.

23. *OR,* v. XLII, pt. 1, pp. 655, 663, 666, 703, 708, 713, 716, 726, 761, 765, 769, 775, 800, and pt. 2, pp. 1,114, 1,142, 1,148–50, and pt. 3, pp. 78–79; RG 391, 10AC, v. III, bk. 26, Ford, circular of Sept. 29, 1864, and Ford to Lentz, Sept. 30, 1864, and box 4, W. Birney to Ford, Sept. 30, 1864, NA; "Returns of Staff/7th New Hampshire and K/100th New York, S-O, 1864," RG 94, M594, NA; Hartford *Courant,* Oct. 10, 1864; Philadelphia *Public Ledger,* Oct. 12, 1864; RG 94, entry 12, 1864 file, No. H1124, NA; DeGraff, *Memoirs,* p. 309, CWTI Coll., MHRC; Kautz, *Journal,* Sept. 30, 1864, Kautz Papers, LC; Jackson to Rand, Sept. —, 1864, Arnold A. Rand, *Personal Records,* p. 24, MOLLUS-Mass. Coll., MHRC; Sommers, op. cit., v. II, pp. 435–36.

24. Stannard's Second Brigade apparently held the right of his new line just south of Fort Harrison. How far south the corps's left reached is not clear. Its battle line probably did not extend to Signal Hill, though Pennypacker's pickets likely prolonged the line that far. Kreutzer, op. cit., p. 234; New York *Times,* Oct. 4, 1864; RG 94, entry 160, v. VIII, p. 611, NA; Philadelphia *Evening Bulletin,* Oct. 3, 1864; Eisenschiml, op. cit., p. 245; *AG-Conn-1865,* p. 58; 1st Connecticut Heavy Artillery, *Book of Letters Received and Endorsements,* pp. 208–9, RG 94, entry 112, NA; Taylor and Hatfield, op. cit., pp. 93–94, 188; Butler, op. cit., pp. 735–36; Comstock, *Diary,* Sept. 29, 1864, LC; *Ripley Ms.,* pp. 10–11, DSF Coll., UV; "Returns of E/89th and K/100th and B/158th New York, and of F/5th U. S. Artillery, S-O, 1864," RG 94, M594, and entry 53, respectively, NA; Ward, op. cit., p. 111; Harris, loc. cit., May 12, 1887; Ware, loc. cit., Jan. 20, 1887; Fleetwood, *Diary,* Sept. 29, 1864, LC; Prescott, loc. cit., v. I, p. 54; *OR,* v. XLII, pt. 1, pp. 109, 675–76, 708, 713, 761, 765, 767, 769, 773, 775, 781, 798–801, 805, and pt. 2, pp. 1,111–15, 1,146–47, and pt. 3, p. 512, and v. XL, pt. 1, pp. 661, 666; Henry Brown, letter of Oct. 5, 1864, Brown Papers, CNHS; Thompson, op. cit., pp. 480, 484, 486; Hubbell et al., op. cit., p. 307; James R. Hagood, *Memoirs,* pp. 181, 185–86, SCL; Sommers, op. cit., v. II, pp. 436–41.

25. Marston did send most of the 2/184th New York upriver, Thurs-

day afternoon, but only as far as Harrison's Landing, not to the front. Fleet-wood, *Diary*, Sept. 30, 1864, LC; J. D. Richardson, "The Colored Troops," *NT*, Nov. 1, 1906; Plaisted to Terry, Oct. 1, 1864, RG 391, 24AC, v. XXII, bk. 42, NA; RG 391, 10AC, v. III, bk. 26, No. 37, NA; Robinson, op. cit., pp. 19–20; Sommers, op. cit., v. II, pp. 432–33, 484–85.

26. Butler exceeded his authority in assigning Weitzel to command ac-cording to his brevet rank, but President Lincoln subsequently upheld the appointment. The junior officer had command of the corps by 9:55 A.M. on Friday. "Fort Fisher," *Joint Committee-1865*, y. II, pp. 67–68; RG 393, DVNC, v. XC, bk. 179, Hoffman to Carey, Sept. 28, 1864, and v. LIX-A, bk. 184, Sealy to Dodge, Sept. 29, 1864, NA; Carey to Hoffman, and Shaffer to Butler and to Shepley, Sept. 28, 1864, RG 94, entry 159, Weitzel Papers, NA; RG 94, entry 731, box 59, Butler to Blunt, 2:40 P.M., Sept. 29, 1864, and box 51, Leet, S. O. No. 100, Sept. 30, 1864, NA; RG 108, entry 11, box 83, No. E38, NA; *OR*, v. XLII, pt. 1, pp. 675, 800, and pt. 2, pp. 1,112, 1,146, 1,148, and pt. 3, p. 100; New York *Tribune*, Oct. 3, 1864; Philadelphia *Evening Bulletin*, Oct. 4, 1864; Porter, op. cit., p. 303; Isaac J. Wistar, *Autobiography*, pp. 447–48; J. Marshall, op. cit., v. V, pp. 298–99; the author is indebted to Dr. Louis H. Manarin for pointing out that Weit-zel was born in Bavaria, not Cincinnati.

27. Moffitt may have temporarily led the Second Brigade after Dono-hoe fell and before Cullen returned to it. "CSR of Stephen Moffitt, 96th New York, and Michael Donohoe, 10th New Hampshire," RG 94, CSR, NA, *OR*, v. XLII, pt. 1, pp. 762, 766–67, 799; "Returns of the Second and Third Brigades, First Division, 18th Corps, Sept. 1864," RG 94, entry 65, 18AC, NA; RG 391, 24AC, v. XXXIV, bk. 79, p. 469, and v. XVIII, bk. 25, p. 19, NA; RG 393, DVNC, two-name box 5, No. W273-6, NA; RG 94, entry 160, v. VI, Jan. 31, 1873, and v. VIII, p. 611, NA; Price, op. cit., pp. 324, 418; Samuel P. Bates, *Martial Deeds*, pp. 899–901; Sommers, op. cit., v. II, p. 435.

28. Butler received the reports of Potter's lookouts at 2:00 and 2:20 P.M.; whether Grant saw them, too, before writing his order of 3:50 is not known. Potter's observers, by the way, particularly concerned the Seces-sionists, who vainly tried to shoot down his James River tower with concen-trated artillery fire. *OR*, v. XLI, pt. 3, pp. 468–69, and v. XLII, pt. 1, pp. 652–54, and pt. 2, pp. 1,092–94, 1,110–16, 1,123, 1,142–45, and pt. 3, p. 17; Asa Bartlett, *12th New Hampshire*, p. 383; J. Marshall, op. cit., v. V, pp. 195–96, 228; RG 393, DVNC, v. CV, bk. 219, p. 15, NA; Hall and Hall, op. cit., pp. 257–59; Taylor and Hatfield, op. cit., pp. 93, 188; Sommers, op. cit., v. II, pp. 441–44.

CHAPTER V

1. Porter, op. cit., p. 303; *OR*, v. XLII, pt. 2, pp. 1,094, 1,117–18, 1,142; Sommers, op. cit., v. II, pp. 444–45.

2. Where the Requa gun section of the X Corps was on Friday morn-ing is not clear. *OR*, v. XLII, pt. 1, pp. 102, 108, 110, 134, 675, 702, 708,

726, 761, 765, 767, 769, 775, 781, 799–800, 805, 818, 880, 938, and pt. 2, pp. 1,146–49; "Returns of 4th and 5th New Jersey Batteries, H/3rd New York Light Artillery, 16th New York Battery, B/158th New York, A-E/1st Pennsylvania Light Artillery, F/1st Rhode Island Light Artillery, and Staff/36th and A/37th USCT, and of E/3rd, D/4th, and F/5th U. S. Artillery, S-O, 1864," RG 94, M594 and entry 53, respectively, NA; Chase, op. cit., p. 225; Hall and Hall, op. cit., p. 258; Denison, op. cit., p. 311; RG 391, 25AC, v. XLIX, bk. 123, pp. 48, 50–53, NA; Bell, *Map,* RG 77, entry 161, box 244, No. 35-4-18-1, NA; RG 94, entry 160, v. X, p. 504, NA; Montgomery, loc. cit., v. XXVIII, p. 179; Fleetwood, *Diary,* Sept. 30, 1864, LC; *Ripley Ms.,* pp. 10–11, DSF Coll., UV; Evan Brimble, *Diary,* Sept. 30, 1864, WHGS; RG 391, 10AC, v. III, bk. 26, Ford to Moore, Oct. 1, 1864, and box 3, Butler to West, [Sept. 30, 1864], NA; Kautz, *Journal,* Sept. 30, 1864, LC; Haskin, op. cit., pp. 210, 445; W. A. Croffut and John M. Morris, *The Military and Civil History of Connecticut,* p. 668; Sommers, op. cit., v. II, pp. 445–50; Prescott, loc. cit., v. I, pp. 54–56.

3. Sorrel, op. cit., p. 268; Sperry, *Diary,* Sept. 30, 1864, VSL.

4. The First Rockbridge Artillery and Third Richmond Howitzers were not among the batteries Alexander concentrated against Fort Harrison. Waring, loc. cit., v. LXXV, p. 111; *OR,* v. XLII, pt. 1, pp. 800, 859, 880; Hollis, op. cit., pp. 21–22, 4th Alabama Coll., ADAH; Field, loc. cit., v. XIV, pp. 556–57; Frank Mixson, *Reminiscences,* pp. 102–3; Burgwyn, *Diary,* Sept. 30, 1864, NCDAH; "Returns of B/51st and B/66th North Carolina and Griffin's Virginia and Green's Louisiana Batteries, S-O, 1864," RG 109, ch. 1, entry 18, NA; Davie Hampton to Caleb Hampton, Oct. 4, 1864, Hampton Papers, DU; John K. Coleman, *Diary,* Sept. 30, 1864, CWTI Coll., MHRC; Hagood, op. cit., p. 305; Dunn, loc. cit., v. V, p. 146, GDAH; E. P. Alexander to his wife, Oct. 3, 1864, EPA Coll., SHC; Moultrie Reid to his sister, Oct. 3, 1864, Reid Papers, SCL; D. D. Pendleton to W. N. Pendleton, Oct. 2, 1864, WNP Coll., SHC; Moore, op. cit., p. 265; D. S. Burwell to E. S. Burwell, Oct. 5, 1864, Burwell Papers, SHC; *ORN,* v. X, pp. 754–55; Sommers, op. cit., v. II, pp. 510–12.

5. Most Confederate vessels shot much less vigorously than on September 29. Wall and Shepperd fired only sixteen and twelve times, respectively. Rootes was probably comparably restrained. Only Maury played a big part, shooting ninety-three times. The ships, of course, were below Chaffin's Bluff. Less is known about where the artillery deployed. All that is certain is that the South Carolina battery was on a hill of red clay, perhaps the one about five hundred yards south of Fort Johnson. *ORN,* v. X, pp. 754–64; D. D. Pendleton to W. N. Pendleton, Oct. 2, 1864, WNP Coll., SHC; E. P. Alexander to his wife, Oct. 3, 1864, EPA Coll., SHC; summary of military service of Robert Hunter Fitzhugh, in Lucy Stuart Fitzhugh, *Scrapbook,* Filson Club; J. M. Alexander, loc. cit., July 31, 1890; Andrew Robeson, letter of Oct. 5, 1864, Robeson Papers, MSHS; Moultrie Reid to his sister, Oct. 3, 1864, Reid Papers, SCL; *OR,* v. XLII, pt. 1, pp. 800, 818, 859; Hagood, *Memoirs,* p. 181, SCL; Morgan, op. cit., pp. 205–6; Hall and Hall, op. cit., p. 258; Chase, op. cit., p. 225; "Returns of 16th New York Battery, H-K/3rd New York Light Artillery, A/1st Pennsylvania Light Artillery,

and F/1st Rhode Island Light Artillery, and of F/5th U. S. Artillery, S-O, 1864," RG 94, M594 and entry 53, respectively, NA; Field, loc. cit., v. XIV, p. 556; Brown to Davenport, Oct. 15, 1864, RG 109, entry 199, misc. rolls, box 7, NA; Sommers, op. cit., v. II, pp. 512–14.

6. Hollis, op. cit., p. 22, 4th Alabama Coll., ADAH; Richmond *Enquirer,* Nov. 22, 1864; Hector McKethan to Thomas L. Clingman, Oct. 3, 1864, and Burgwyn, *Diary,* Sept. 30, 1864, Burgwyn Papers, NCDAH; John Higgins, "A Georgia Command," *CV,* v. XXV, p. 79; George Warthen to James Thomas, Oct. 6, 1864, Warthen Papers, DU; Simons, *Diary,* Sept. 30, 1864, SCHS; Davie Hampton to Caleb Hampton, Oct. 4, 1864, Hampton Papers, DU; "Returns of D/17th and B-I/66th North Carolina, G/7th South Carolina Battalion, D-E-G/21st South Carolina, and B/63rd Tennessee, S-O, 1864," RG 109, ch. 1, entry 18, NA; Daniel Abernathy to his wife, Oct. 6, 1864, Abernathy Papers, DU; Polley, *Texas Brigade,* p. 257; Field, loc. cit., v. XIV, pp. 556–57; Barnard, *Defenses of Chaffin's Bluff,* RG 77, map No. 2391, NA; Clay, loc. cit., Nov. 26, 1881; E. P. Alexander to his wife, Oct. 3, 1864, EPA Coll., SHC; Moore, op. cit., p. 265; Morgan, op. cit., pp. 206–7; Silas B. O'Mohundro to Cecil Clay, Feb. 14, 1887, Clay Papers, HSP; Hagood, *Memoirs,* pp. 180–81, SCL; *OR,* v. XLII, pt. 1, pp. 775, 800, 818, 876, 880, 938; RG 94, entry 160, v. VIII, p. 611, NA; Kreutzer, op. cit., pp. 234–35; Dunn, loc. cit., v. V, p. 146, GDAH; "Return of A/37th USCT, S-O, 1864," RG 94, M594, NA; Thompson, op. cit., p. 481; Sommers, op. cit., v. II, pp. 515–19.

7. The 13th New Hampshire held Stannard's far right, and the 118th New York manned a flèche on his center. Weitzel to Smith, Sept. 30, 1864, RG 393, DVNC, telegram box 10, NA; *OR,* v. XLII, pt. 1, pp. 773, 775, 800, 805; Henry Brown, letter of Oct. 5, 1864, and *Diary,* Sept. 30, 1864, Brown Papers, CNHS; Califf, *Ex-Members,* p. 5; Thompson, op. cit., pp. 480–81, 486, 488; Ware, loc. cit., Jan. 20, 1887; Cunningham, op. cit., pp. 151–52; Hubbell et al., op. cit., pp. 308–9; *CWR,* pp. 396–97; Kreutzer, op. cit., pp. 234, 238; *Ripley Ms.,* p. 11, DSF Coll., UV; Clay, loc. cit., Nov. 26, 1881; Burgwyn, *Diary,* Sept. 30, 1864, NCDAH; Sommers, op. cit., v. II, pp. 519–21.

8. Thompson, op. cit., p. 481; Bruce, loc. cit., v. XIV, p. 97.

9. Hagood, *Memoirs,* p. 181, SCL.

10. Where the 29th Connecticut took position is not clear; it may still have held the far right. Little credence should be given an extremely dubious allegation that it actually entered the trenches between Ames and Raulston to help battle Field. Ibid., pp. 180–86, SCL; Field, loc. cit., v. XIV, p. 557; Richmond *Enquirer,* Nov. 22, 1864; Hollis, op. cit., pp. 22–24, 4th Alabama Coll., ADAH; RG 391, 25AC, v. XXXIV, bk. 66¼, p. 401, NA; Morgan, op. cit., p. 206; Thompson, op. cit., p. 481; Clay, loc. cit., Nov. 26, 1881; Cunningham, op. cit., p. 151; Fleetwood, *Diary,* Sept. 30, 1864, LC; Montgomery, loc. cit., v. XXVIII, p. 179; *CWR,* p. 396; M. O. Young, *History of the First Brigade,* p. 120, microfilm, GDAH; Joskins, *Sketch,* p. 88, HJC; *OR,* v. XLII, pt. 1, pp. 110, 773, 775, 778, 781, 800–1, 818, 880–81, 938, and pt. 3, p. 254; Hall and Hall, op. cit., p. 258; Coleman, *Diary,* Oct.

1, 1864, CWTI Coll., MHRC; Mixson, op. cit., pp. 103–6; Hubbell et al., op. cit., p. 308; Ware, loc. cit., Jan. 20, 1887; Califf, *Ex-Members,* p. 5; Brown, *Diary,* Sept. 30, 1864, and letter of Oct. 5, 1864, Brown Papers, CNHS; "Returns of K/3rd New York Light Artillery, A-I/29th Connecticut, and Staff/36th and A/37th and E/45th USCT, S-O, 1864," RG 94, M594, NA; Croffut and Morris, op. cit., p. 668; Asbury Coward, *Memoirs,* pp. 90–91, SCL; Coker, op. cit., p. 158; RG 109, entry 22, bcx 4, No. 194, NA; [O. A. Wylie], *"Rebel Diary,"* Sept. 28–Oct. 11, 1864, BU; Sommers, op. cit., v. II, pp. 521–26.

11. A Union claim that some Graycoats actually penetrated Paine's line, only to be driven out, may relate to the temporary loss of the lunette but seems unlikely to refer to his main position. *OR,* v. XLII, pt. 1, pp. 818, 880, 938; Richmond *Enquirer,* Nov. 22, 1864; "Return of A/37th USCT, S-O, 1864," RG 94, M594, NA; Prescott, loc. cit., v. I, p. 54; Hollis, op. cit., pp. 22–23, 4th Alabama Coll., ADAH; *Memorandum from the 4th Alabama History,* p. 2, EPA Coll., SHC; Thompson, op. cit., p. 484; Hagood, *Memoirs,* p. 186, SCL; Field, loc. cit., v. XIV, p. 557; Hubbell et al., op. cit., p. 308; Sommers, op. cit., v. II, pp. 526–27.

12. Highly circumstantial evidence hints that Major Francis Reichard of the 188th Pennsylvania, also, may have briefly led the Third Brigade sometime on Friday. Cullen, it should be added, had been in major combat prior to June 1864, but far below the regimental level, as a lieutenant in the 1st U. S. defending Battery Robinett on October 4, 1862. *Ripley Ms.,* p. 11, DSF Coll., UV; Ezra J. Warner, *Generals in Blue,* p. 471; Cunningham, op. cit., pp. 152, 155; Kreutzer, op. cit., pp. 198–99; Clay, loc. cit., Nov. 26, 1881; "Return of B/158th New York, S-O, 1864," RG 94, M594, NA; New York *Tribune,* Oct. 4 and 7, 1864; Jourdan to Marston, Oct. 13, 1864, RG 391, 18AC, v. IV, bk. 5, NA; "Returns of the First and Third Brigades, First Division, 18th Corps, Sept. 1864," RG 94, entry 65, 18AC, NA; RG 393, DVNC, two-name box 5, Nos. W273-3, -5, and -6, NA; "Returns of 96th New York, 8th Connecticut, and 188th Pennsylvania, Sept. and Oct. 1864," RG 94, entry 57, NA; "CSR of John E. Ward, 8th Connecticut," RG 94, CSR, NA; *AG-Conn-1865,* p. 175; *OR,* v. XLII, pt. 1, pp. 793–95, 797–801; RG 391, 24AC, v. XVIII, bk. 25, p. 19, and v. XXIII, bk. 31A, p. 107, and v. XXXIV, bk. 79, p. 469, NA; Samuel Givin to A. L. Russell, Oct. 18, 1864, RG 19, v. XXII, Pennsylvania History Commission; *CWR,* pp. 330, 397; Sommers, op. cit., v. II, pp. 527–29 (this last source misasserts that Ward was not present, September 29, but correctly states that he was not on the field to take over a brigade the next day; he was, in fact, wounded during the initial charge on Thursday).

13. Davie Hampton to Caleb Hampton, Oct. 4, 1864, Hampton Papers, DU; Henry Greer to his mother, Oct. 3, 1864, Greer Papers, LC; see also Alfred Scales to his wife, Oct. 9, 1864, Alfred Scales Papers, East Carolina University.

14. Hector McKethan to Thomas L. Clingman, Oct. 3, 1864, Burgwyn Papers, NCDAH.

15. John Cunningham to Derby, Oct. 1, 1864, Cunningham Papers, NYHS; Burgwyn, *Diary,* Sept. 30, 1864, NCDAH.

16. The 31st North Carolina held the right of McKethan's battle line. *OR,* v. XLII, pt. 1, pp. 880, 938, and pt. 2, pp. 1,244, 1,307; Davie Hampton to Caleb Hampton, Oct. 4, 1864, Hampton Papers, DU; Henry Greer to his mother, Oct. 3, 1864, Greer Papers, LC; Simons, *Diary,* Sept. 30, 1864, SCHS; Hagood, *Memoirs,* pp. 185–86, SCL; Hagood, op. cit., p. 307; Daniel Abernathy to his wife, Oct. 6, 1864, Abernathy Papers, DU; "Returns of A-D/17th North Carolina and Staff/7th South Carolina Battalion, S-O, 1864," RG 109, ch. 1, entry 18, NA; Hector McKethan to Thomas L. Clingman, Oct. 3, 1864, and Burgwyn, *Diary,* Sept. 30, 1864, NCDAH; E. J. Williams to his mother, Oct. 2, 1864, Williams Papers, SHC; Dunn, loc. cit., v. V, p. 146, GDAH; Hotchkiss, op. cit., v. III, p. 719; Raleigh *Daily Confederate,* Oct. 11–12, 1864; Clay, loc. cit., Nov. 26, 1881; Clark, *NC,* v. I, p. 408, and v. III, pp. 213–15, and v. IV, pp. 495–96; John Cunningham to Derby, Oct. 1, 1864, Cunningham Papers, NYHS; Joseph Haynes to his father, Oct. 1, 1864, Haynes Papers, DU; Hubbell et al., op. cit., p. 308; Cunningham, op. cit., p. 152; Thompson, op. cit., pp. 484–85; *CWR,* p. 397; Augustus Avant, *Sandersville Volunteers,* p. 17, CMC, GDAH; Wendell Croom, *C/6th Georgia,* p. 26; Higgins, loc. cit., v. XXV, p. 79; George Warthen to James Thomas, Oct. 6, 1864, Warthen Papers, DU; Sommers, op. cit., v. II, pp. 530–33.

17. Wright, loc. cit., v. XIV, p. 545; Sommers, op. cit., v. II, pp. 533–34, and v. V, pp. 1,332–44; *OR,* v. XLII, pt. 2, pp. 1,112–13; Hector McKethan to Thomas L. Clingman, Oct. 3, 1864, Burgwyn Papers, NCDAH.

18. Morgan, op. cit., pp. 207–8; Douglas Southall Freeman, *R. E. Lee,* v. III, pp. 503–4; Silas B. O'Mohundro to Cecil Clay, Feb. 14, 1887, Clay Papers, HSP; Burgwyn, *Diary,* Sept. 30, 1864, and Hector McKethan to Thomas L. Clingman, Oct. 3, 1864, Burgwyn Papers, NCDAH; Simons, *Diary,* Sept. 30, 1864, SCHS; Thompson, op. cit., p. 484; *ORN,* v. X, pp. 754–60, 773; *OR,* v. XLII, pt. 1, pp. 880, 938; Sommers, op. cit., v. II, p. 534.

19. Thompson, op. cit., pp. 484–85; Bates, *Pennsylvania Volunteers,* v. V, p. 255; *OR,* v. XLII, pt. 1, pp. 818, 880, 938; Hagood, *Memoirs,* p. 186, SCL; Hollis, op. cit., pp. 23–24, 4th Alabama Coll., ADAH; Sommers, op. cit., v. II, pp. 535–36.

20. Besides the 203 prisoners from Clingman's Brigade, about 21 more Butternuts were captured. Cunningham, op. cit., p. 152; Hubbell et al., op. cit., pp. 308–9; Thompson, op. cit., pp. 482–85; *CWR,* p. 397; *Ripley Ms.,* pp. 11–12, DSF Coll., UV; Pottsville *Miners' Journal,* Nov. 12, 1864; Burgwyn, *Diary,* Sept. 30, 1864, and Hector McKethan to Thomas L. Clingman, Oct. 3, 1864, Burgwyn Papers, NCDAH; Hollis, op. cit., p. 24, 4th Alabama Coll., ADAH; Clay, loc. cit., Nov. 26, 1881; Morgan, op. cit., p. 206; New York *Times,* Oct. 4, 1864; Clark, *NC,* v. I, p. 408, and v. IV, p. 496; *OR,* v. XLII, pt. 1, pp. 805–6, and pt. 2, p. 1,145, and pt. 3, pp. 50, 89, 164–65; H. H. Hoyer to Cecil Clay, March 26, 1888, Clay Papers, HSP; RG 393, DVNC, v. CXCI, bk. 466, pp. 93–105, and two-name box 5, No. W273-5, NA; RG 109, entry 199, box 282, and entry 385, pts. 1–2, NA; J. D. McGeachey to his sister, Oct. 14, 1864, Buie Papers, DU; Coker, op.

cit., p. 158; RG 94, entry 12, 1864 file, No. V181, NA; New York *Herald*, Oct. 23, 1864; "Return of Staff/98th New York, S-O, 1864," RG 94, M594, NA; Raulston, op. cit., p. 19, HHL; Hotchkiss, op. cit., v. III, p. 720; Raleigh *Daily Confederate*, Oct. 11–12, 1864; Richmond *Examiner*, Nov. 15, 1864; E. J. Williams to his mother, Oct. 2, 1864, Williams Papers, SHC; Sommers, op. cit., v. II, pp. 533, 536–39.

21. Thompson, op. cit., p. 482; Walter Taylor to Bettie, Oct. 6, 1864, Taylor Papers, VSL; Henry Snow, letter of Oct. 3, 1864, Snow Papers, CNHS; E. P. Alexander to his wife, Oct. 3, 1864, EPA Coll., SHC; *OR*, v. XLII, pt. I, pp. 859, 880.

CHAPTER VI

1. *OR*, v. XLII, pt. 1, pp. 716, 880, 938; Hollis, op. cit., pp. 23–24, 4th Alabama Coll., ADAH; Simons, *Diary*, Oct. 1–2, 1864, SCHS; "Returns of A/17th and B/51st North Carolina and C/63rd Tennessee, S-O, 1864," RG 109, ch. 1, entry 18, NA; Dunn, loc. cit., v. V, p. 146, GDAH; New York *Times*, Oct. 4, 1864; Burgwyn, *Diary*, Sept. 30, 1864, and Hector McKethan to Thomas L. Clingman, Oct. 3, 1864, Burgwyn Papers, NCDAH; Kreutzer, op. cit., p. 235; D. D. Pendleton to W. N. Pendleton, Oct. 2, 1864, WNP Coll., SHC; Cunningham, op. cit., p. 152; Clark, *NC*, v. IV, p. 496; Hotchkiss, op. cit., v. III, p. 720; Sommers, op. cit., v. II, pp. 568–69.

2. Trumbull, op. cit., p. 298.

3. Birney to Smith, 11:15 A.M., Oct. 1, 1864, BFB Coll., LC.

4. Ibid.; Harris, loc. cit., May 12, 1887; Denison, op. cit., p. 311; Birney, order of Sept. 30, 1864, RG 391, 10AC, box 4, NA; RG 391, 25AC, v. XXXIII, bk. 66½, pp. 292–93, 299–300, 311, NA; RG 393, DVNC, v. CLX, bk. 377, pp. 82–83, and v. CLXXIII, bk. 408, pp. 67–68, NA; Montgomery, loc. cit., v. XXVIII, p. 179; "Returns of E/4th Massachusetts Cavalry and C-D-E-F-G-K/4th USCT, and of C-D/1st U. S. Artillery, S-O, 1864," RG 94, M594 and entry 53, respectively, NA; "Trimonthly returns of the 18th Corps, Sept. 30 and Oct. 10, 1864," RG 94, entry 65, 18AC, NA; *OR*, v. XLII, pt. 1, pp. 108, 110, 654, 664, 675–76, 761, 767, 773, 775, 781, 819–20, and pt. 2, pp. 1,146–49, and pt. 3, pp. 117, 254; Henry Marshall, letter of Oct. 2, 1864, Marshall Papers, MHC, UM; Califf, *Ex-Members*, p. 5; Croffut and Morris, op. cit., p. 668; Fleetwood, *Diary*, Sept. 30 and Oct. 7, 1864, LC; Alexander, loc. cit., July 31, 1890; Sommers, op. cit., v. II, pp. 569–73.

5. *OR*, v. XLII, pt. 2, pp. 1,143–44.

6. Ibid., pp. 1,121, 1,144.

7. Ibid., pp. 1,144–45.

8. Although telegraph wires were laid to within half a mile of Butler's headquarters by 7:50 P.M., September 30, they were not actually extended to his camp until the following morning. Ibid., pp. 1,117, 1,119, 1,121–22, 1,142–45, 1,149, and pt. 3, p. 30; New York *Times*, Oct. 4, 1864; RG 393,

DVNC, v. L, bk. 74, p. 96, and v. LIX-A, bk. 184, Sealy to Dodge, Sept. 30, 1864, and Butler to O'Brien, 7:20 A.M., Oct. 1, 1864, NA; "Return of I/3rd Pennsylvania Heavy Artillery, S-O, 1864," RG 94, M594, NA; Doyle, loc. cit., July 6, 1899; Burgwyn, *Diary,* Sept. 30–Oct. 1, 1864, NCDAH; RG 391, 10AC, v. III, bk. 26, Ford to Terry, Sept. 30, 1864, and v. XXIII, bk. 54, No. 102.5, and box 4, Butler to Birney, Sept. 30, 1864, NA; Benjamin Wright to his wife, Oct. 2, 1864, Wright Papers, WHS; Tom Welles to Gideon Welles, 2:00 A.M., Oct. 1, 1864, v. LVII, Gideon Welles Papers, LC; J. Marshall, op. cit., v. V, pp. 191–92, 202; RG 108, entry 11, box 86, Nos. V230 and V235, NA; Sommers, op. cit., v. II, pp. 573–77.

9. The ill Marston temporarily turned over the First Separate Brigade to his most experienced subordinate, the commander of the 2nd New Hampshire, Lieutenant Colonel Joab Patterson, on October 3. The junior officer did not actually assume command until Thursday. *OR,* v. XLII, pt. 1, p. 75, and pt. 2, pp. 1,143, 1,145, and pt. 3, pp. 30, 68, 114–15, 308, 314, and v. LI, pt. 1, p. 1,186; Rice to Smith, Oct. 1, 1864, RG 94, entry 159, Gilman Marston Papers, NA; RG 391, 9AC, v. XVIII, bk. 34, p. 133, NA; "CSR of William Schley, 5th Maryland, and David White, 81st New York, and Joab Patterson, 2nd New Hampshire," RG 94, CSR, NA; Robinson, op. cit., p. 21; Haynes, op. cit., pp. 253–54; Willis Parker to Peter Guerrant, Oct. 3, 1864, Guerrant Papers, VHS; RG 391, 24AC, v. VII, bk. 16-A, p. 148, and v. VIII, bk. 16-B, pp. 235–36, and v. XXII, bk. 42, Plaisted to Terry, Oct. 1, 1864, and v. XL, bk. 99, Sept. 30–Oct. 1–3, 1864, NA; RG 393, DVNC, v. XLVIII, bk. 66, p. 439, and v. LIX-A, bk. 184, Sealy to Kensel, received 4:30 P.M., Oct. 2, 1864, and telegram box 10, Weitzel to Smith, Sept. 30, 1864, and v. LV, bk. 59, pp. 254–55, and v. VII, bk. 90, p. 185, and v. CCLXXXIII, bk. 726, pp. 538–39, and v. CVI, bk. 217, pp. 14, 28–29, and bk. 219, pp. 24–26, 265, 270, 277–79, and v. CV, bk. 216, pp. 52, 58, 66, 70–71, 76–78, NA; "Return of Staff/12th New Hampshire, S-O, 1864," RG 94, M594, NA; RG 94, entry 12, 1864 file, No. D664, NA; 11th Connecticut, *Special Order Book,* p. 145, and *Morning Report Book,* Oct. 1864, and 2nd New Hampshire, *Letter Book,* Cooper to Nixon, Oct. 6, 1864, RG 94, entries 112, 113, and 115, respectively, NA; Joseph Haynes to his father, Oct. 1 and 8, 1864, Haynes Papers, DU; Bartlett, op. cit., p. 241; "Returns of Potter's and Marston's brigades, Sept. and Oct. 1864," RG 94, entry 62, DVNC, NA; Sommers, op. cit., v. II, pp. 577–79.

10. Sorrel, op. cit., p. 256; cf. Freeman, *Lee,* v. III, p. 504.

11. Mordecai, *Diary,* Oct. 1, 1864, SHC.

12. Why Weitzel anticipated an attack against Birney's right about 8:30 A.M. is not clear. More certain is the fact that once the Signal Corps established two stations on his line, it closed the old, now unnecessary tower in Dutch Gap. E. P. Alexander to his wife, Oct. 3, 1864, EPA Coll., SHC; Butler to Weitzel, 7:00 A.M., Oct. 1, 1864, RG 94, entry 159, Butler Papers, v. LIX-A, No. D, NA; J. Marshall, op. cit., v. V, pp. 191–92; New York *Herald,* Oct. 4, 1864; *ORN,* v. X, pp. 754, 756–57, 762–65; Hector McKethan to Thomas L. Clingman, Oct. 3, 1864, Burgwyn Papers, NCDAH; Hagood, *Memoirs,* p. 187, SCL; Dunn, loc. cit., v. V, p. 146,

GDAH; Hall and Hall, op. cit., p. 259; Chase, op. cit., p. 225; *OR,* v. XLII, pt. 1, pp. 653–57, 662–63, 675–76, 778, 859, 880, 938, and pt. 3, pp. 30–35; Dearborn to Weitzel, 5:00 P.M., Oct. 1, 1864, RG 391, 18AC, box 1, NA; Ford, circular of Oct. 1, 1864, RG 391, 10AC, v. III, bk. 26, NA; Harris, loc. cit., May 12, 1887; DeGraff, *Memoirs,* p. 310, CWTI Coll., MHRC; Thompson, op. cit., pp. 491–92; Jimmie Rawlings to Nannie, Oct. 10, 1864, Rawlings Family Papers, UV; "Returns of B-K/1st New York Engineers and K/3rd New York Light Artillery, S-O, 1864," RG 94, M594, NA; Reed, *Journal,* pp. 132–33, ADAH; Sommers, op. cit., v. II, pp. 579–82.

13. *OR,* v. XLII, pt. 1, pp. 101–2, 662, 703, 713, 716, 720, 761, 767, 876, and pt. 2, p. 1,144, and pt. 3, pp. 32–35; J. Marshall, op. cit., v. V, p. 207; Birney to Smith, 11:15 A.M., Oct. 1, 1864, BFB Coll., LC; Davis, op. cit., p. 134, MHC, UM; New York *Herald,* Oct. 4, 1864; Haskin, op. cit., p. 210; "Return of the 4th Wisconsin Battery, S-O, 1864," RG 94, M594, NA; New York *Times,* Oct. 4, 1864; Eldredge, op. cit., p. 542; Henry Little, *7th New Hampshire,* p. 308; Richmond *Whig,* Oct. 2, 1864; Richmond *Sentinel,* Oct. 4, 1864; Sommers, op. cit., v. II, pp. 582–84.

14. Hatton, *Memoirs,* pp. 650–54, LC; J. B. Jones, op. cit., v. II, p. 296; Joseph Hilton to Coz, Oct. 14, 1864, Hilton Papers, CMC-Ib, EU; Jasper Davis to his wife, Oct. 4, 1864, Jasper Davis Papers, DU; Bevier, op. cit., p. 452; Sarah to A. L. Alexander, Sept. 29–Oct. 3, 1864, Alexander-Hillhouse Papers, SHC; Richmond *Dispatch,* Richmond *Enquirer,* Richmond *Whig,* all of Oct. 1, 1864; Mordecai, *Diary,* Oct. 3, 1864, SHC; Danforth, *Copybook,* p. 196, DU; Mrs. William Gray to William Gray, Sept. 30–Oct. 6, 1864, Gray Family Papers, Valentine Museum; John Latane Waring to Robert Lancaster, Oct. 2, 1864, Lancaster Family Papers, VHS; *OR,* v. XLII, pt. 1, pp. 662, 716, and pt. 3, p. 33; RG 109, ch. 6, v. CCCLXIV, p. 218, and v. CXXXII, p. 65, and entry 12, 1864 file, No. C2449, NA; Mobile *Advertiser,* Oct. 11, 1864, quoted in Detroit *Advertiser and Tribune,* Oct. 29, 1864; Second Regiment of Virginia Reserve Forces, Paper, Oct. 1, 1864, VSL; Richmond *Examiner,* Oct. 1 and 3, 1864; Linden Kent to his mother, Oct. 3, 1864, CM; Richmond *Sentinel,* Oct. 1 and 4, 1864; Charles Anthony to his mother, Oct. 3, 1864, Anthony Family Papers, VSL; B. Jones, op. cit., pp. 215–16; Couper, op. cit., v. III, pp. 62–63; Waring, loc. cit., v. LXXV, p. 111; Sommers, op. cit., v. II, pp. 584–87.

15. *OR,* v. XLII, pt. 1, pp. 101, 662, 703, 708, 713, 716, 720, 726–27, and pt. 3, pp. 33–34, and v. XLVI, pt. 2, p. 1,196; Charles Anthony to his mother, Oct. 3, 1864, Anthony Family Papers, VSL; Haskin, op. cit., pp. 210, 557; "Return of Staff/10th Virginia Heavy Artillery Battalion, S-O, 1864," RG 109, ch. 1, entry 18, NA; B. Jones, op. cit., pp. 215–16; *ANJ,* v. II, p. 133; Sommers, op. cit., v. II, pp. 587–91; "Returns of Staff/39th Illinois and C/62nd Ohio, and of B/1st U. S. Artillery, S-O, 1864," RG 94, M594 and entry 53, respectively, NA; New York *Herald,* Oct. 4, 1864; Davis, op. cit., p. 136, MHC, UM; Joseph C. Abbott to Joseph R. Hawley, Oct. 5, 1864, Hawley Papers, LC; Stevens, *Map,* LC Maps; Cohasco Manu-

script Catalogue 9, entry 95; Richmond *Sentinel,* Oct. 4, 1864; Adrian Terry to Isadore, Oct. 3, 1864, quoted in Marino, op. cit., p. 356.

16. *OR,* v. XLII, pt. 1, p. 847, and pt. 3, pp. 33–35; Kautz, *Journal,* Oct. 1, 1864, LC; John L. Roper et al., *11th Pennsylvania Cavalry,* p. 142; "Returns of Staff/1st District of Columbia Cavalry and of the 4th Wisconsin Battery, S-O, 1864," RG 94, M594, NA; Waring, loc. cit., v. LXXV, p. 111; Sommers, op. cit., v. II, p. 591.

17. Davis, op. cit., p. 140, MHC, UM; Adrian Terry to Isadore, Oct. 3, 1864, quoted in Marino, op. cit., p. 356; *OR,* v. XLII, pt. 1, pp. 703, 708, 713, 715–16, 720, 727, 847, and pt. 3, pp. 33–34; 3rd New Hampshire, *Notebook,* Oct. 1, 1864, MOLLUS-Mass. Coll., box 7, Harvard; Charles Anthony to his mother, Oct. 3, 1864, Anthony Family Papers, VSL; Eldredge, op. cit., p. 542; "Return of Staff/10th Virginia Heavy Artillery Battalion, S-O, 1864," RG 109, ch. 1, entry 18, NA; "Return of the 4th Wisconsin Battery, S-O, 1864," RG 94, M594, NA; Joseph Hilton to Coz, Oct. 14, 1864, Hilton Papers, CMC-Ib, EU; Sommers, op. cit., v. II, pp. 591–93.

18. Bevier, op. cit., pp. 452–53; Joseph Hilton to Coz, Oct. 14, 1864, Hilton Papers, CMC-Ib, EU.

19. Hensley took over the First Artillery Division during Atkinson's absence. *OR,* v. XLII, pt. 1, pp. 713, 876, and pt. 3, pp. 34–35, 1,131–33; Richmond *Whig,* Oct. 3, 1864; John Latane Waring to Robert Lancaster, Oct. 2, 1864, Lancaster Family Papers, VHS; *Artillery Defenses,* pp. 164–70, CHHS; Hatton, *Memoirs,* pp. 653–54, LC; Bevier, op. cit., pp. 452–53; Jasper Davis to his wife, Oct. 4, 1864, Jasper Davis Papers, DU; Joseph Hilton to Coz, Oct. 14, 1864, Hilton Papers, CMC-Ib, EU; "Return of Staff/10th Virginia Heavy Artillery Battalion, S-O, 1864," RG 109, ch. 1, entry 18, NA; Richard Ewell to Walter Taylor, Nov. 8, 1864, Ewell Papers, DU; Couper, op. cit., v. III, pp. 62–63; Sommers, op. cit., v. II, pp. 593–97; Anderson, *Report, 1864,* p. 25, LHQ Coll., VHS; Latrobe, *Diary,* Oct. 1, 1864, VHS; Richmond *Examiner,* Oct. 3, 1864; Sperry, *Diary,* Oct. 1, 1864, VSL.

20. While in the woods the Yankees took time to provide rations to a woman, perhaps Mrs. Throgmorton, who had remained in her home, isolated between the two battling armies, for three days. Sarah to A. L. Alexander, Sept. 29–Oct. 3, 1864, Alexander-Hillhouse Papers, SHC; *OR,* v. XLII, pt. 3, pp. 33–34, and pt. 1, p. 730; *AG-Conn-1865,* pp. 207–8; RG 391, 24AC, v. XXII, bk. 42, pp. 1–2, NA; Trumbull, op. cit., pp. 298–301; Hartford *Courant,* Oct. 10, 1864; McCarty, *Diary,* Oct. 1, 1864, TXU; Samuel McKinney to his wife, Oct. 2, 1864, McKinney Papers, EU; Benjamin Wright to his wife, Oct. 2, 1864, Wright Papers, WHS; Sommers, op. cit., v. II, pp. 597–99.

21. *OR,* v. XLII, pt. 1, pp. 99, 103, 703, 709, 713, 716, 720, 727, 731, 792, and pt. 3, pp. 31–35; Little, op. cit., p. 308; Davis, op. cit., p. 144, MHC, UM; J. Marshall, op. cit., v. V, p. 208; Bates, *Pennsylvania Volunteers,* v. III, p. 6; "Return of Staff/7th New Hampshire, S-O, 1864," RG 94, M594, NA; Haskin, op. cit., p. 210; Birney to Smith, 11:15 A.M., Oct. 1, 1864, BFB Coll., LC; Grant to Butler, 8:30 P.M., Oct. 1, 1864, Head-

quarters Papers, U. S. Grant Coll., LC; Sommers, op. cit., v. II, pp. 599–600.

22. *OR*, v. XLII, pt. 3, p. 48.

23. The General-in-Chief was on the Peninsula by 11:10 A.M., October 2, and was back at his own headquarters by 12:35 P.M. Ibid., pp. 4–6, 31–34, 36, 48–51, 65–67, 77–78, and pt. 1, p. 662, and pt. 2, pp. 1,121, 1,144–45; Comstock, *Diary,* Oct. 1, 1864, LC; Grant to Butler, 11:00 P.M., Oct. 1, and Oct. 2, 1864, BFB Coll., LC; J. Marshall, op. cit., v. V, pp. 208, 221; Sommers, op. cit., v. II, pp. 601–2.

24. J. Marshall, op. cit., v. V, p. 221; Thompson, op. cit., pp. 491–92; "Returns of E/3rd and F/5th U. S. Artillery, and of A-E/1st Pennsylvania Light Artillery, 5th New Jersey Battery, B-K/1st New York Engineers, and Staff-E-H-K/127th USCT, S-O, 1864," RG 94, entry 53 and M594, respectively, NA; *AG-Conn-1865,* p. 442; Beecher, op. cit., v. II, pp. 578–83; Pollack, *Diary,* Oct. 2, 1864, ISHL; RG 94, entry 352, v. III, p. 145, and entry 361, v. III, pp. 1,921–22, NA; RG 393, DVNC, v. LV, bk. 79, pp. 261–62, and v. LIX-A, bk. 184, Sealy to Kensel, received 5:18 P.M., Oct. 2, 1864, and telegram box 10, Moore to Smith, 6:15 P.M., Oct. 1, 1864, and Birney to Smith, Oct. 2, 1864, NA; Ford to Foster, to Moore, and to William Birney, Oct. 2, 1864, RG 391, 10AC, v. III, bk. 26, NA; *OR*, v. XLII, pt. 1, pp. 662, 665, 675–76, and pt. 3, pp. 31–32, 48, 50, 68; Joseph Haynes to his father, Oct. 8, 1864, Haynes Papers, DU; DeGraff, *Memoirs,* p. 310, CWTI Coll., MHRC.

25. The three ironclads were out of proper munitions on Sunday but received a fresh supply in the evening. Even the Richmond depots ran out by October 5. D. D. Pendleton to W. N. Pendleton, Oct. 2, 1864, WNP Coll., SHC; Simons, *Diary,* Oct. 2–3, 1864, SCHS; *OR,* v. XLII, pt. 1, pp. 859, 880; "Returns of F/63rd Tennessee and B/51st North Carolina, S-O, 1864," RG 109, ch. 1, entry 18, NA; W. L. Timberlake, "Last Days in Front of Richmond," *CV,* v. XX, p. 119; New York *Herald,* Oct. 6, 1864; RG 393, DVNC, v. CXCI, bk. 466, p. 107, NA; Hector McKethan to Thomas L. Clingman, Oct. 3, 1864, Burgwyn Papers, NCDAH; Latrobe, *Diary,* Oct. 3, 1864, VHS; Moultrie Reid to his sister, Oct. 3, 1864, Reid Papers, SCL; Sarah to A. L. Alexander, Sept. 29–Oct. 3, 1864, Alexander-Hillhouse Papers, SHC; McCarty, *Diary,* Oct. 1, 1864, TXU; Hagood, op. cit., p. 307; Hagood, *Memoirs,* p. 187, SCL; George H. Moffett to Liz, Oct. 3 and 5, 1864, and *Diary,* Sept. 30–Oct. 6, 1864, Moffett Papers, SCHS; Robert F. Graham to his wife, Oct. 4, 1864, William C. Harllee Papers, SHC; Smith, *Diary,* Oct. 1, 1864, GDAH; Tuckerman to Clum, received 2:00 P.M., Oct. 2, 1864, RG 391, 10AC, box 3, NA; Sommers, op. cit., v. II, pp. 603–4; Chase, op. cit., pp. 225–26; Charleston *Mercury,* Oct. 4, 1864; *ORN,* v. X, pp. 753–54, 761, 763–64, 773; Fleetwood, *Diary,* Oct. 1, 1864, LC.

26. Hatton, *Memoirs,* p. 654, LC; RG 109, ch. 1, v. XLIII, pp. 87, S524, NA; Mordecai, *Diary,* Oct. 3, 1864, SHC; Sarah to A. L. Alexander, Sept. 29–Oct. 3, 1864, Alexander-Hillhouse Papers, SHC; Sperry, *Diary,* Oct. 2, 1864, VSL.

27. Federal units known to have fought Field include the 39th Illinois,

62nd Ohio, and 85th Pennsylvania of Pond's brigade and Plaisted's own 11th Maine. Whether or not Bowles joined Montague in the probing is not known. Though placed on standby on Sunday, Scales did not leave for Petersburg until October 3. *OR,* v. XLII, pt. 1, p. 876, and pt. 3, pp. 36, 49, 65; Waring, loc. cit., v. LXXV, p. 111; Alfred Scales to his wife, Oct. 7, 1864, Scales Papers, East Carolina University; Latrobe, *Diary,* Oct. 2–3, 1864, VHS; New York *Herald,* Oct. 5, 1864; Kautz, *Journal,* Oct. 2, 1864, LC; "Returns of I/5th Pennsylvania Cavalry and Staff/39th Illinois, S-O, 1864," RG 94, M594, NA; Roper et al., op. cit., p. 142; RG 393, DVNC, v. CXCI, bk. 466, p. 107, and v. CLXXXVII, bk. 455, p. 105, and two-name box 5, No. B272, NA; Dickey, op. cit., p. 407; Hartford *Courant,* Oct. 10, 1864; *AG-Maine-1864/65,* v. I, p. 259; Benjamin Wright to his wife, Oct. 2, 1864, Wright Papers, WHS; Pollack, *Diary,* Oct. 2, 1864, ISHL; *ANJ,* v. II, pp. 99, 113; Birney to Butler, 11:35 A.M., Oct. 2, 1864, BFB Coll., LC; J. Marshall, op. cit., v. V, p. 211.

28. Terry lost fifty-six men on Saturday, and Otis only three; other Union casualties that day are estimated at twenty-five. Perhaps sixteen more Bluecoat foot soldiers fell the next day; Kautz passed the second day unscathed. Lee's losses may have been around forty men on October 1, and thirty more on Sunday. *OR,* v. XLII, pt. 1, pp. 101, 133, 137, 703, 708, 713, 715–16, 720, 727, 730, and pt. 3, pp. 34, 65; casualties of Foster's division, Sept. 29–Oct. 1, 1864, RG 391, 10AC, box 3, NA; *ANJ,* v. II, p. 113; Sommers, op. cit., v. II, p. 602.

29. Two events in Chesterfield County, October 1–2, indicate Lee's awareness that the emergency was subsiding. For one thing, on Saturday night he actually established a truce on Bermuda Hundred to send Grant a proposal to exchange prisoners. The lieutenant general relaxed his opposition to such exchanges sufficiently to offer to trade those captives taken over the weekend, provided that ex-Confederate slaves, now USCTs, were included. This counterproposal of October 2 Lee rejected on Monday. The second measure of the return of relative quiet was the resumption of passenger service on the Richmond and Petersburg Railroad on Sunday. RG 393, DVNC, v. CVI, bk. 217, pp. 14, 18, and v. LIX-A, bk. 184, Sealy to Kensel and to Smith, received 6:35 P.M. and 7:30 P.M., respectively, on Oct. 2, 1864, NA; RG 108, entry 1, v. XXI, p. 461, NA; *OR,* s. 2, v. VII, pp. 906, 909, 914.

30. *OR,* v. XLII, pt. 1, pp. 133–37; Sommers, op. cit., v. V, pp. 1,320–25, 1,332–44.

CHAPTER VII

1. *Map,* Sept. 21, 1864, box 10, HJH Papers, LC; Clark, *NC,* v. III, p. 249; Hagood, *Memoirs,* p. 177, SCL; Lyle, *Diary,* Sept. 23–28, 1864, Parker mss.; Waring, *Diary,* pp. 117, 131, 135, SHC; *OR,* v. XLII, pt. 1, pp. 230–31, 619, 621, 879, 947–48, and pt. 2, pp. 914, 952–53, 965, 979, 990, 1,011–12, 1,031, 1,051–52, 1,066, 1,266–68, and pt. 3, pp. 27–28,

358, 1,191; John Bratton, *Letters of J. Bratton to His Wife*, p. 181; Henry Heth, *Report*, Dec. 7, 1864, Heth Papers, CM; Cadmus Wilcox, *Report*, 1864, p. 62, LHQ Coll., VHS.

2. *OR*, v. XLII, pt. 1, p. 586, and pt. 2, pp. 1,046–48, 1,064, 1,076, 1,105; RG 108, entry 1, v. XXI, p. 442, and entry 11, box 82, No. E21, NA; Grant to Meade, 9:00 P.M., Sept. 27, 1864, U. S. Grant Papers, HHL; Grant to Meade, received 11:15 P.M., Sept. 27, 1864, RG 94, entry 731, box 63, NA; RG 391, 9AC, v. XV, bk. 17, p. 84, NA; Stephen Rogers to his parents, Oct. 3, 1864, Rogers Papers, ISHL; *AG-Mass-1865*, p. 479; Peleg Jones and Albert Pope, *Diaries*, Sept. 28, 1864, CWTI Coll., MHRC.

3. The engineers reached City Point at 3:00 A.M. *OR*, v. XLII, pt. 1, pp. 32, 75, 166–67, and pt. 2, pp. 1,009, 1,046–47, 1,064, 1,069–70, 1,075, 1,128; RG 393, AP, v. VI, bk. 6, p. 492, NA; Williams, order received 8:30 P.M., Sept. 28, 1864, RG 94, entry 730, box 3, NA; Sullivan Green, *Diary*, Sept. 28, 1864, WHS; "Returns of the 50th New York Engineers, S-O, 1864," RG 94, M594, NA; "Return of Benham's Brigade, Sept., 1864," RG 94, entry 62, AP, NA; William Folwell, *Diary*, Sept. 29, 1864, MNHS; Hamilton Dunlap, *Diary*, Sept. 28–29, 1864, McDowell Coll., PSU; Pope, *Diary*, Sept. 28, 1864, CWTI Coll., MHRC; Regis DeTrobriand, *Diary*, Sept. 28, 1864, WP.

4. *OR*, v. XLII, pt. 2, pp. 1,065, 1,072–78, 1,100, 1,102, 1,105; W. D. Alexander, *Diary*, Sept. 28, 1864, SHC; Frank Lobrano, *Diary*, Sept. 28, 1864, TU; RG 391, 9AC, v. XVIII, bk. 34, p. 25, NA; RG 108, entry 11, box 83, No. P392, NA; James Eldridge, *Diary*, Sept. 28, 1864, CNHS; Rivers to Finklemeier, Sept. 29, 1864, RG 391, 2AC, misc. box 6, NA; John Council, *Diary*, Sept. 28, 1864, NCDAH; Russell, *Diary*, Sept. 28, 1864, DU; James Aubery, *36th Wisconsin*, p. 163; David Sparks, ed., *Inside Lincoln's Army*, p. 425; Pope, *Diary*, Sept. 28, 1864, CWTI Coll., MHRC; Henry Metzger to his father, Oct. 5, 1864, Metzger Papers, Harrisburg CWRT Coll., MHRC; DeTrobriand, *Diary*, Sept. 28, 1864, WP.

5. James Perry, *Diary*, Sept. 29–30, 1864, WHS; Amos Rood, *Memoir*, p. 170, UCSB; Charles Cuffel, *Durell's Battery*, p. 215; RG 391, 5AC, v. XXXIX, bk. 205, Sept. 28, 1864, NA; Allen Albert, *45th Pennsylvania*, p. 163; William Paine, *Diary*, Sept. 29, 1864, J. W. dePeyster Papers, ISHL; Robert McAllister to his wife, Sept. 29, 1864, McAllister Papers, Palmer Coll., WRHS; Marsena Patrick, *Diary*, Sept. 28, 1864, LC; George Agassiz, ed., *Meade's Headquarters*, p. 233; Dunlap, *Diary*, Sept. 28, 1864, McDowell Coll., PSU.

6. Henry S. Burrage, *36th Massachusetts*, p. 258; Edward S. Bragg to his wife, Sept. 27, 1864, Bragg Papers, WHS; Jones, *Diary*, Sept. 29, 1864, CWTI Coll., MHRC; *OR*, v. XLII, pt. 1, pp. 58, 75, 619, and pt. 2, pp. 1,056, 1,069, 1,073–75, 1,100–5; Hancock to Humphreys, 7:45 P.M., and Humphreys to Hancock, 8:20 P.M., Sept. 28, 1864, RG 94, entry 731, box 51, NA; Cowdrey to Bragg, Sept. 29, 1864, RG 391, 5AC, v. XXVI, bk. 87, NA; Monteith to Sickel, Sept. 29, 1864, RG 391, 5AC, box 8, NA; "Returns of B-F/11th U.S., S-O, 1864," RG 94, entry 53, NA; Wainwright, *Diary*, Sept. 30, 1864, HHL; DeTrobriand, *Diary*, Sept. 29, 1864, WP;

Dunlap, *Diary,* Sept. 29, 1864, McDowell Coll., PSU; Sommers, op. cit., v. III, pp. 620–21.

7. Russell, *Diary,* Sept. 30–Oct. 1, 1864, DU; Beauregard, *Letterbook,* v. XXXIII, pp.—(6–8), LC; Nathaniel Watkins to his wife, Oct. 1, 1864, Watkins Papers, College of William and Mary; Coleman, *Diary,* Sept. 29–Oct. 2, 1864, CMC-Ib, EU; Fleming, *Diary,* Sept. 29, 1864, Floyd County UDC Coll., GDAH; Eugene Cox, *Diary,* Sept. 29, 1864, UV; Dunn, loc. cit., v. V, p. 144, GDAH; *OR,* v. XLII, pt. 1, pp. 875–76, 897; "Returns of B-I/66th North Carolina and K/25th South Carolina, S-O, 1864," RG 109, ch. 1, entry 18, NA; Simons, *Diary,* Sept. 29, 1864, SCHS.

8. Johnson's cooks and the 1st Confederate Engineers, however, did not enter the trenches, Thursday. W. D. Alexander, *Diary,* Sept. 29, 1864, SHC; Lane, *Glimpses,* v. XVIII, p. 411; James S. Harris, *Historical Sketches,* p. 56; *OR,* v. XLII, pt. 1, p. 876, and pt. 2, pp. 1,095, 1,103, 1,118, 1,123, and pt. 3, p. 38; William Mosely to his parents, Sept. 30, 1864, Mosely Papers, microfilm, GDAH; Henry Chambers, *Diary,* Oct. 2, 1864, NCDAH; Alfred Scales to his wife, Oct. 7, 1864, Scales Papers, East Carolina University; Coleman, *Diary,* Oct. 2, 1864, CMC-Ib, EU; Petersburg *Daily Express,* Sept. 30, 1864; Beauregard, *Letterbook,* v. XXXIII, pp.—(4–5), LC; RG 109, ch. 6, v. DLIV, pp. 18–19, NA; John Vincent, *Diary,* Aug. 22, Sept. 29, Oct. 10, 1864, VHS; "Returns of 1st Confederate Engineers and E/1st Virginia Battalion, S-O, 1864," RG 109, ch. 1, entry 18, NA; Sommers, op. cit., v. III, pp. 690–92.

9. Lane, *Glimpses,* v. XVIII, p. 411; Caldwell, op. cit., p. 182; Beauregard, *Letterbook,* v. XXXIII, pp.—(3–7), LC; *OR,* v. XLII, pt. 2, pp. 833–34, 1,049, 1,103, 1,123, 1,305, and pt. 3, p. 1,140; Fleming, *Diary,* Sept. 29, 1864, Floyd County UDC Coll., GDAH; Joseph Mullen, *Diary,* Sept. 29, 1864, CM; I. F. Cavaness, *Diary,* Sept. 29, 1864, TXU; "Returns of B/2nd Mississippi, H/48th North Carolina, and Price's Virginia Battery, S-O, 1864," RG 109, ch. 1, entry 18, NA; Lobrano, *Diary,* Sept. 29, 1864, TU; RG 109, entry 15, No. 12-P-24, NA; RG 393, AP, v. LXXIII, bk. 194, Sept. 15, 1864, NA; *Map,* Civil War Papers, box 13, folder 8, TU; Sale, *Diary,* Sept. 29, 1864, VSL; Sommers, op. cit., v. III, pp. 692–95.

10. The troops sighted maneuvering toward the lower Appomattox from Chesterfield were unquestionably demonstrating. *OR,* v. XLII, pt. 1, pp. 210, 947, and pt. 2, pp. 1,092–1,108; D. D. Pendleton to W. N. Pendleton, Oct. 2, 1864, WNP Coll., SHC; Jordan to Fisher, 9:00 A.M., Sept. 29, 1864, RG 94, entry 731, box 51, NA; RG 111, entry 13, v. XLIV, p. 170, NA; Samuel Cormany, *Diary,* Sept. 29, 1864, Mohr mss.; Sommers, op. cit., v. III, pp. 622–24.

11. *OR,* v. XLII, pt. 2, pp. 1,048–50, 1,065–66, 1,079, 1,091–94, 1,104–6; Theodore Lyman, *Diary,* Sept. 29, 1864, MSHS; Agassiz, op. cit., p. 233; Williams to Meade, noon, Sept. 29, 1864, RG 94, entry 731, box 51, NA.

12. *OR,* v. XLII, pt. 1, pp. 65–66, 73, 511–13, 599, 601–5, 645, and pt. 2, pp. 839–46, 1,011, 1,065, 1,093, 1,098, 1,104, 1,108; Locke to Griffin, 1:45–2:00 P.M., Sept. 29, 1864, RG 94, entry 730, box 3, NA; RG

391, 9AC, v. LII, bk. 226, p. 89, NA; RG 94, entry 729, box 93, Nos. 222, 224, NA; Dunlap, *Diary,* Sept. 29, 1864, McDowell Coll., PSU; Byron Mac Cutcheon, *20th Michigan,* p. 152; Lyman, *Diary,* Sept. 29, 1864, MSHS; *AG-Mass-1864,* p. 852; John Dusseault, *E/39th Massachusetts,* p. 35; Pope, *Diary,* Sept. 29, 1864, CWTI Coll., MHRC; Monteith to Sickel, Sept. 29, 1864, RG 391, 5AC, box 8, NA; A. S. Webb to his mother and sister, Sept. 29 and Oct. 3, 1864, Webb-Moore Papers, SHC; Clark, *NC,* v. III, p. 249; Charles McKnight, *Diary,* Sept. 29, 1864, HSP; Charles W. Reed, letter of Oct. 5, 1864, Reed Papers, Princeton.

13. Just before midnight Humphreys ordered Benham to begin picketing the approaches to City Point now that the First Cavalry Brigade was pulling out. These infantry outposts were too far north to connect with Robison. *OR,* v. XLII, pt. 1, pp. 39, 87–88, 90–96, 619, 634, and pt. 2, pp. 1,043–44, 1,057, 1,069–71, 1,078–79, 1,099, 1,106, 1,150; RG 77, entry 161, box 135, No. 13-4-45-1, p. 11, NA; W. A. Bushnell, *Ms. 6th Ohio Cavalry,* pp. 310–11, Palmer Coll., WRHS; "Monthly and Trimonthly Returns of the Second Division and Second Brigade, Second Division, Cavalry Corps, Army of the Potomac, Sept. 30, 1864," RG 94, entry 62, AP, NA; RG 391, 24AC, v. XXX, bk. 63, Sept. 27, 1864, NA; RG 391, CC, v. X, bk. 62, p. 26, and v. XLV, bk. 67, Sept. 28, 1864, NA; "Returns of Staff/1st Massachusetts Cavalry and A/2nd U. S. Artillery, S-O, 1864," RG 94, M594 and entry 53, respectively, NA; Lewis Rappalyea, *Diary,* Sept. 27–28, 1864, NJHS; RG 94, entry 12, 1864 file, No. B1379, NA; Lillian Rea, ed., *Walter Robbins,* pp. 97–98; Noble Preston, *10th New York Cavalry,* p. 227; RG 393, AP, v. XLV, bk. 93, p. 168, and v. XLVII, bk. 96, pp. 99–100, NA; Pitkin-Williams, correspondence, Sept. 29, 1864, RG 94, entry 731, box 51, NA; Levi Baker, *9th Massachusetts Battery,* p. 145; Charles W. Reed, letter of Oct. 5, 1864, Reed Papers, Princeton; Albion Clark, *Diary,* Sept. 28–29, 1864, NYPL; Sommers, op. cit., v. III, pp. 648–50.

14. *OR,* v. XLII, pt. 2, pp. 1,008–9; Hancock to Thomas, Jan. 21, 1866, and Gregg to Thomas, Jan. 26, 1865, RG 94, CB file, Gregg Papers, NA; Russell Weigley, "David McMurtrie Gregg," *Civil War Times Illustrated,* v. I, no. 7, pp. 10–13, 26–30.

15. *OR,* v. XLII, pt. 2, pp. 698, 1,171, 1,309, and pt. 3, pp. 1,159–62; RG 109, entry 15, Nos. 35-, 36-, 3-, 4-, 39-, 40-, and 37-P-24, NA; "Return of Hampton's Corps, Sept. 1864," LHQ Coll., VHS; N. J. Brooks, *Diary,* Sept. 18–19, 1864, SHC; Zimmerman Davis and Thomas L. Rosser to Edward L. Wells, May 24 and 25, 1898, respectively, Wells Papers, Charleston Library Society; Cole to Johnson, Nov. 18, 1864, RG 109, ch. 5, entry 43, box 1, NA; U. R. Brooks, *Butler and His Cavalry,* pp. 380–82; Sommers, op. cit., v. III, pp. 651–56.

16. Griffin's own regiment will be called the "8th Georgia Cavalry," as was common practice by that late in the war, even though it was still officially styled the 62nd Georgia Cavalry. Fred Foard, *Reminiscences,* p. 8, NCDAH; "CSR of M. C. Butler," staff papers, RG 109, CSR, NA; Ezra J. Warner, *Generals in Gray,* p. 78; Lynwood Holland, *Pierce Young,* p.

94; Waring, *Diary*, Sept. 23 and Oct. 4 and 10, 1864, SHC; Sommers, op. cit., v. III, pp. 653–55.

17. Waring, *Diary*, pp. 117, 121, 131, 136, SHC; *OR*, v. XLII, pt. 1, p. 947, and pt. 2, pp. 1,011, 1,106; Brooks, *Butler*, pp. 195–96; RG 109, entry 15, No. 3-P-24, NA; R. L. T. Beale, *9th Virginia Cavalry*, p. 146; "Returns of Staff-F-I/9th Virginia Cavalry, S-O, 1864," RG 109, ch. 1, entry 18, NA; J. W. Biddle to his wife, Sept. 25, 1864, Biddle Papers, DU; Pressley Persons, letters of Sept. 13 and Oct. 4, 1864, Persons Papers, DU; Julius Summers to his wife, Sept. 28, 1864, Summers Papers, DU; John W. Gordon, *Diary*, Sept. 13 and 29 and Oct. 3, 1864, SHC; William McGregor, *Report*, Dec. 7, 1864, Edwin L. Halsey Papers, SHC.

18. *OR*, v. XLII, pt. 1, pp. 619, 634, and pt. 2, pp. 1,106–7; New York *Herald*, Oct. 3, 1864; Preston, op. cit., p. 227; Bushnell, *History*, p. 311, Palmer Coll., WRHS; Waring, *Diary*, pp. 135–36, SHC; RG 391, CC, v. XXII, bk. 34, pp. 94–95, NA; Rappalyea, *Diary*, Sept. 29, 1864, NJHS; "Return of I/1st Massachusetts Cavalry, S-O, 1864," RG 94, M594, NA.

19. *OR*, v. XLII, pt. 1, pp. 94, 619, 634, and pt. 2, pp. 944, 1,043, 1,106–8, 1,139; Richmond *Whig*, Oct. 1, 1864; Edward F. Tobie, *1st Maine Cavalry*, p. 358; Clark, *Diary*, Sept. 29, 1864, NYPL; Bushnell, *History*, p. 311, Palmer Coll., WRHS; Brooks, *Butler*, pp. 190, 194–95, 299.

20. *OR*, v. XLII, pt. 1, p. 947, and pt. 2, pp. 1,107–8; RG 77, entry 161, box 244, No. 35-4-18-1, NA; Waring, *Diary*, Sept. 29–30, 1864, SHC; John Saussy to Bob Saussy, Oct. 23, 1864, Joachim Saussy Papers, DU; "Return of F/20th Georgia Cavalry Battalion, S-O, 1864," RG 109, ch. 1, entry 18, NA; RG 391, CC, v. XXII, bk. 34, pp. 92–93, NA; Brooks, *Butler*, pp. 195–96; Charleston *Courier*, Oct. 15, 1864; Edward C. Anderson, Jr., to his mother, Oct. 9, 1864, Wayne-Stites-Anderson Coll., Georgia Historical Society.

21. *OR*, v. XLII, pt. 1, pp. 87, 92, 94, 435, 619, 947, and pt. 2, pp. 1,069, 1,074, 1,094, 1,106–8, 1,140–41, and pt. 3, p. 361; New York *Herald*, Oct. 3, 1864; RG 109, entry 12, 1864 file, No. T1263, NA; RG 77, *Maps*, Nos. G149, G443-II-16, and G153-2, NA; Waring, *Diary*, Sept. 29, 1864, SHC; Charleston *Courier*, Oct. 15, 1864; Brooks, *Butler*, p. 196; Tobie, op. cit., pp. 358–60; Petersburg *Daily Express*, Sept. 30, 1864; Sommers, op. cit., v. III, pp. 661–63.

22. *OR*, v. XL, pt. 1, pp. 747–48, and v. XLII, pt. 1, pp. 87–94, 619, 947, and pt. 2, pp. 1,094, 1,108; Waring, *Diary*, Sept. 29 and Oct. 10, 1864, SHC; Brooks, *Butler*, p. 196, and *Stories of the Confederacy*, p. 269; Charleston *Courier*, Oct. 15, 1864; Lyman, *Diary*, Sept. 29, 1864, MSHS; New York *Herald*, Oct. 3, 1864; Tobie, op. cit., pp. 358–60; S. H. Merrill, *1st Maine Cavalry*, p. 286; Agassiz, op. cit., p. 233; "Returns of A-D/4th Pennsylvania Cavalry, S-O, 1864," RG 94, M594, NA; RG 391, CC, v. XXXII, bk. 75, p. 45, NA.

23. *OR*, v. XLII, pt. 2, pp. 1,094, 1,108; New York *Herald*, Oct. 2, 1864; E. J. Allen et al., *Maltese Cross*, p. 320; Charles W. Reed, letter of Oct. 5, 1864, Reed Papers, Princeton.

24. Gordon, *Diary*, Sept. 29, 1864, SHC; *OR*, v. XLII, pt. 1, pp. 87,

90, 94, 947, and pt. 2, pp. 1,094, 1,108; Dowdey, op. cit., p. 507; McGregor, *Report,* Dec. 7, 1864, Halsey Papers, SHC; Clark, *NC,* v. I, p. 436, and v. II, p. 103, and v. III, p. 627; "Returns of H/1st and A-D/3rd North Carolina Cavalry, S-O, 1864," RG 109, ch. 1, entry 18, NA; Petersburg *Daily Express,* Sept. 30, 1864; RG 391, CC, v. XIX, bk. 28, p. 116, NA; Tobie, op. cit., pp. 358–60; Waring, *Diary,* Sept. 29, 1864, SHC; Charleston *Courier,* Oct. 15, 1864; Merrill, op. cit., p. 287; Allen et al., op. cit., p. 320; Sommers, op. cit., v. III, pp. 666–68.

25. Gordon, *Diary,* Sept. 29, 1864, SHC; *OR,* v. XLII, pt. 1, pp. 94, 142–43, 619–20, 634, 947, and pt. 2, pp. 1,107–8, 1,124; New York *Herald,* Oct. 3, 1864; Waring, *Diary,* Sept. 29, 1864, SHC; Charleston *Courier,* Oct. 12, 1864; Charleston *Mercury,* Oct. 12, 1864; RG 391, CC, v. XXII, bk. 34, pp. 92–95, NA; RG 109, entry 199, misc. roll 49 and box 282, NA; Sommers, op. cit., v. III, pp. 668–69.

26. *OR,* v. XLII, pt. 1, pp. 84, 89, 92, 94, 619, 634–35, and pt. 2, pp. 1,093, 1,106–9, 1,139–40; RG 94, entry 12, 1864 file, Nos. B1379 and M1763, NA; Bushnell, *History,* p. 312, Palmer Coll., WRHS; RG 391, CC, v. XXII, bk. 34, pp. 94–95, NA; *AG-Mass-1864,* p. 938; "Return of Staff/1st Massachusetts Cavalry, S-O, 1864," RG 94, M594, NA; Preston, op. cit., p. 227; Clark, *Diary,* Sept. 29–30, 1864, NYPL; Sommers, op. cit., v. III, pp. 669–70.

CHAPTER VIII

1. Sale, *Diary,* Sept. 29–30, 1864, VSL; A. L. P. Vairen, *Diary,* Sept. 29–30, 1864, MDAH; Butler to Finklemeier, Sept. 30, 1864, RG 391, 2AC, misc. box 5, NA; *OR,* v. XLII, pt. 1, pp. 65–66, 210, and pt. 2, pp. 1,065, 1,074, 1,095–96, 1,103, 1,123, 1,305, 1,309; Cavaness, *Diary,* Sept. 29, 1864, TXU; Mullen, *Diary,* Sept. 29, 1864, CM; "Returns of H/48th North Carolina, A/2nd Mississippi, H/26th Mississippi, B-D-F/42nd Mississippi, F/1st Confederate Battalion, and Staff-B-C-E-F/2nd Maryland Battalion, S-O, 1864," RG 109, ch. 1, entry 18, NA; Willie Pegram to Mary Pegram, Oct. 5, 1864, PJM Coll., VHS; R. S. Webb to his sister, Oct. 3, 1864, Webb-Moore Papers, SHC; Sam Brooke to his sister, Oct. 4, 1864, John Binckley Papers, LC; Clark, *NC,* v. III, p. 249; W. W. Goldsborough, *Maryland Line,* p. 139; Sommers, op. cit., v. III, pp. 695–98.

2. William Mosely to his parents, Sept. 30, 1864, Mosely Papers, microfilm, GDAH; *OR,* v. XLII, pt. 2, p. 1,118, and pt. 3, p. 52.

3. *OR,* v. XLII, pt. 2, p. 1,143, and pt. 3, p. 38; RG 109, ch. 6, v. CCCLXII, p. 442, and v. CCCLXIV, p. 501, and v. DCXLII, pp. 89–90, NA; "Return of C/1st Confederate Engineers, S-O, 1864," RG 109, ch. 1, entry 18, NA; John Ramsay to Maggie, Oct. 5, 1864, Ramsay Papers, SHC; *ORN,* v. X, pp. 796–97.

4. Sommers, op. cit., v. III, p. 701.

5. *OR,* v. XLII, pt. 2, p. 1,302.

6. Ibid., pp. 845, 890, 893, 1,243–44, 1,267, 1,309, and pt. 1, pp.

858–60, 904, and pt. 3, pp. 228, 274, 1,193, 1,339–43, and v. XL, pt. 1, pp. 755–60, 783; D. E. Henderson, *Sketch of Confederate and Federal Lines,* EPA Coll., SHC; E. P. Alexander to his father, Sept. 22, 1864, Alexander-Hillhouse Papers, SHC; Richardson, *Sketch of Rives's Salient,* Andrew and George Hero Papers, Louisiana State University; J. W. Shank to J. B. Smith, Sept. 21, 1864, Shank Papers, GDAH; "Returns of C/11th Georgia Light Artillery Battalion, A/12th Virginia Light Artillery Battalion, and Price's Virginia Battery, S-O, 1864, and histories of the Washington Artillery of Louisiana, 1865," RG 109, ch. 1, entry 18, NA; Washington Artillery File, Confederate Coll., TU; James Coit, "Letter," *SHSP,* v. X, pp. 124–28; John Clopton to his family, Sept. 22 and Oct. 28, 1864, Clopton Papers, DU; James Albright, *Diary,* Nov. 4, 1864, SHC; Hatton, *Memoirs,* pp. 647, 674, LC; W. N. Pendleton to Moseley, Sept. 20, 1864, and D. D. Pendleton to W. N. Pendleton, Oct. 2, 1864, WNP Coll., SHC; "Inspection Report of Walker's Brigade, Sept. 20, 1864, and Return of Moseley's Brigade, Sept. 10, 1864," RG 109, entries 15 and 65, respectively, NA; W. N. Pendleton, *Ms. Orderbook,* p. 101, CM; Louis Manarin, *North Carolina Troops,* v. I, pp. 51, 113, 125, 567.

7. *OR,* v. XLII, pt. 1, pp. 892–903; "Inspection Report of Beauregard's Department, Sept. 20, 1864," RG 109, ch. 2, entry 65, box 13, NA; RG 109, entry 15, No. P-33, NA; Fleming, *Diary,* Sept. 24–25, 1864, Floyd County UDC Coll., GDAH; E. P. Alexander to his father, Sept. 22, 1864, Alexander-Hillhouse Papers, SHC; Charles Baughman to his parents, Sept. 23 and Nov. 1, 1864, Baughman Papers, CM; Beauregard, *Letterbook,* v. XXXIII, p. -2, LC; D. D. Pendleton to W. N. Pendleton, Oct. 2, 1864, WNP Coll., SHC; "Return of G/1st Confederate Engineers, S-O, 1864," RG 109, ch. 1, entry 18, NA.

8. The commander of the 3rd Virginia Reserve Battalion will be called "Fletcher Archer" to differentiate him from Heth's senior brigadier, who will simply be called "Archer." Fletcher Archer's battalion should not be confused with George Chrisman's unit of the same name in Ewell's department. Sale, *Diary,* Oct. 2–3, 1864, VSL; *OR,* v. XLII, pt. 2, pp. 1,048–49, 1,306; James Verdery to Blanche, Nov. 7, 1864, Eugene and James Verdery Papers, DU; RG 109, entry 15, No. 27-P-33, NA; Douglas Southall Freeman, *A Calendar of Confederate Papers,* p. 273.

9. J. H. Lane, "Lane's Brigade," *SHSP,* v. IX, p. 356; *OR,* v. XLII, pt. 2, p. 1,207; Clark, *NC,* v. II, p. 58; RG 109, entry 15, No. 7-P-24, NA.

10. *OR,* v. XLII, pt. 2, pp. 1,270–78.

11. The Georgian will be called "Joel Griffin" to distinguish him from the Northern division commander, who will simply be termed "Griffin." James Dearing to Thomas L. Rosser, Nov. 24, 1864, Rosser Papers, UV; R. E. Lee to Zebulon Vance, Sept. 20, 1864, Lee Papers, DU; Dennis Ferebee to Zebulon Vance, Sept. 10, 1864, Vance Papers, NCDAH; *OR,* v. XLII, pt. 1, p. 947; Sommers, op. cit., v. III, pp. 653–54.

12. W. D. Alexander, *Diary,* Sept. 30, 1864, SHC; Caldwell, op. cit., p. 182; Dunlop, op. cit., p. 209.

13. David Lane, *A Soldier's Diary,* p. 209; Stephen Rogers to his par-

ents, Oct. 3, 1864, Rogers Papers, ISHL; Perry, *Diary,* Sept. 29, 1864, WHS; Pope, *Diary,* Sept. 29, 1864, CWTI Coll., MHRC; DeTrobriand, *Diary,* Sept. 29, 1864, WP.

14. *OR,* v. XLII, pt. 1, pp. 897–98, and pt. 2, pp. 1,070, 1,100–1, 1,127, 1,129; RG 391, 6AC, v. XC, bk. 199, p. 67, NA; DeTrobriand, *Diary,* Sept. 29, 1864, WP; Sale, *Diary,* Sept. 29–30, 1864, VSL; Butler to Finklemeier, Sept. 30, 1864, RG 391, 2AC, misc. box 5, NA; Cavaness, *Diary,* Sept. 29, 1864, TXU; Frederick E. Lockley to his wife, Sept. 30, 1864, Lockley Papers, HHL; Cox, *Diary,* Sept. 30, 1864, UV; A. C. Jones, *Diary,* Sept. 29, 1864, TU; Eldridge, *Diary,* Sept. 29, 1864, CNHS; Sommers, op. cit., v. III, p. 727.

15. *OR,* v. XLII, pt. 1, p. 210, and pt. 2, pp. 1,094, 1,097–1,103, 1,108, 1,111, 1,126–27; Hancock to Humphreys, 8:00–8:16 A.M., Sept. 30, 1864, RG 94, entry 731, box 57, NA; Lyman, *Diary,* Sept. 29, 1864, MSHS; A. A. Humphreys to his wife, Oct. 28, 1864, personal corre-spondence, v. XXXIII, AAH Coll., HSP; Sommers, op. cit., v. III, pp. 728–30.

16. Humphreys' instructions of 12:15 A.M. to Hancock contained the added provision that "where camps are exposed to the view of the enemy they will be struck at daybreak." *OR,* v. XLII, pt. 1, pp. 67, 139, 545, 570, 585, 587, 599–605, and pt. 2, pp. 999, 1,021, 1,041, 1,043, 1,075, 1,094, 1,102–5, 1,126, 1,130, 1,139, and pt. 3, pp. 20, 22; Humphreys to Hancock and Warren, 12:15 A.M., Sept. 30, 1864, RG 94, entry 731, boxes 51 and 63, and entry 730, box 3, NA; Driver to Glenny, Sept. 29, 1864, RG 391, 2AC, box 12, NA; Pope, *Diary,* Sept. 29, 1864, CWTI Coll., MHRC; George Arnold, *Diary,* Sept. 30, 1864, MH; Wainwright, *Diary,* Sept. 25–Oct. 1, 1864, HHL; DeTrobriand, *Diary,* Sept. 29, 1864, WP; Benjamin Partridge, Dec. 28, 1866, 16th Michigan Coll., MH; John S. McNaught, *Diary,* Sept. 29–30, 1864, DU; Henry Gawthorp, letter of Oct. 6, 1864, Gawthorp Papers, HSD; RG 391, 5AC, v. XXV, bk. 186, pp. 113, 138, NA; John Robertson, *Michigan in the War,* p. 184; Perry, *Diary,* Sept. 29, 1864, WHS; Charles Wainwright, *Report,* Nov. 5, 1864, box 11, HJH Papers, LC; Wainwright, Circular, Sept. 28, 1864, RG 18, B/1st Pennsyl-vania Light Artillery Papers, Pennsylvania History Commission; *AG-Mass-1864,* p. 1,065; Baker, op. cit., pp. 145–46, 239; Charles W. Reed, *Diary,* Sept. 29–30, 1864, and letter to his mother, Sept. 28–Oct. 1, 1864, Reed Papers, LC; RG 391, 9AC, v. LXVI, bk. 232, Sept. 26, 1864, NA; "Monthly and Trimonthly Returns of the V and IX Corps, Sept. 30 and Oct. 31, 1864," RG 94, entry 65, 5AC and 9AC, respectively, NA; RG 391, 5AC, v. XI, bk. 39, pp. 100–3, and v. XXXIX, bk. 205, Sept. 30, 1864, and v. LIV, bk. 260, Sept. 30, 1864, NA; RG 393, AP, v. LXXXVI, bk. 240, pp. 112–13, NA; John Hartranft to Sallie, Oct. 5, 1864, Hartranft Papers, Gettysburg College; statistics on Meade's striking and garrison forces pre-sented in this chapter are discussed in Sommers, op. cit., v. III, pp. 732–41.

17. Lieutenant George Dresser, Wainwright's inspector, served as act-ing Chief-of-Artillery of Crawford's seven batteries. *OR,* v. XLII, pt. 1, pp. 65, 78–79, 344, 558, 600–5, and pt. 2, pp. 844–45, 1,014, 1,016, 1,046–47,

1,075, 1,104–5, 1,127–28, 1,131, 1,134–35, 1,139, and pt. 3, pp. 24, 61, 81, 148; Nathan Appleton et al., *5th Massachusetts Battery,* pp. 918–22; Alfred Roe, *39th Massachusetts,* pp. 258–59; John Vautier, *88th Pennsylvania,* p. 202; Bates, *Pennsylvania Volunteers,* v. III, p. 864; RG 391, 5AC, v. XI, bk. 39, p. 369, NA; *AG-Mass-1864,* pp. 851–52; McKnight, *Diary,* Sept. 30, 1864, HSP; Charles W. Reed to his mother, Sept. 28–Oct. 1, 1864, and *Diary,* Sept. 30, 1864, Reed Papers, LC; Charles W. Reed, letter of Oct. 5, 1864, Princeton University; William Osborne, *29th Massachusetts,* pp. 321–22; RG 391, 9AC, v. LXIV, bk. 228, p. 32, and box 6, Parke to Hartranft, Sept. 28, 1864, NA; T. H. Parker, *51st Pennsylvania,* p. 509; Wainwright, *Diary,* Sept. 25–Oct. 9, 1864, HHL; Robert Tilney, *My Life,* p. 21; Meade to Williams, 10:45–11:10 A.M., Sept. 30, 1864, RG 94, entry 731, box 51, NA; Sommers, op. cit., v. III, pp. 734–35; see also the returns cited in the preceding footnote.

18. *OR,* v. XL, pt. 1, pp. 655–74, and v. XLII, pt. 1, pp. 42, 44, 48, and pt. 2, pp. 895, 991–96, 1,004, 1,014–20, 1,037–41, 1,070, 1,127, 1,129; RG 391, 2AC, Miles to Bingham, Sept. 25, 1864, letter box 1, and Bingham to Miles, Sept. 25, 1864, First Division box 4, and Hunt to Hazard, Sept. 28, 1864, box 21, and v. XX, bk. 83, pp. 327, 332, and v. I, bk. 8, pp. 433–34, and v. LXIX, bk. 344, p. 31, and bk. 348, p. 201, and v. LXVIII, bk. 347, pp. 35–36, NA; Smyth to Wilson, Sept. 25, 1864, RG 94, entry 731, box 57, NA; Hunt, *Journal,* p. 129, HJH Papers, LC; RG 94, entry 113, 1st Connecticut Heavy Artillery, *Order Book,* p. 148, NA; Hatfield and Taylor, op. cit., p. 90; RG 391, 6AC, v. XC, bk. 201, pp. 133, 142–44, NA; "Trimonthly and monthly returns of II Corps; Artillery Brigade, VI Corps; Shaffer's brigade, Army of the Potomac; and Abbot's command, Army of the James, Sept. 30 and Nov. 3, 1864," RG 94, entry 65, 2AC and 6AC, and entry 62, AP and DVNC, respectively, NA; Sommers, op. cit., v. III, pp. 737–38.

19. "Monthly and Trimonthly Returns of the Army of the Potomac and of Shaffer's, Patrick's, and Benham's brigades, Sept. 30, 1864," RG 94, entry 62, AP, NA; "Returns of 4th U. S., Oct. 3, and 5th U. S. Cavalry, Nov. 8, 1864," RG 94, entry 66, NA; "Returns of 15th New York Engineers, Oct. 5, and 10th USCT, Oct. 11, 1864," RG 94, entry 57, NA; *OR,* v. XLII, pt. 2, pp. 999, 1,136, and pt. 3, pp. 10, 236–37; Porter, op. cit., pp. 31–34; RG 391, CC, v. XXVI, bk. 51, pp. 84–85, NA; Sommers, op. cit., v. III, pp. 738–40.

20. *OR,* v. XLII, pt. 2, pp. 1,046–47, 1,069–70, 1,120, 1,126, 1,130.

21. Ibid., pp. 964, 990, 1,000, 1,020, 1,103, and pt. 1, p. 472, and pt. 3, p. 18, and v. XXXIX, pt. 2, p. 438; "Return of Staff/198th Pennsylvania, S-O, 1864," RG 94, M594, NA; RG 108, entry 1, v. XXI, p. 418, NA; Evan Woodward, *198th Pennsylvania,* pp. 1–4; Sickel to Davis, Sept. 23, 1864, RG 393, DVNC, telegram box 12, NA.

22. The Hampshireman will be called "Simon Griffin" when there is any danger of confusing him with Charles or Joel Griffin. RG 391, 9AC, v. XVIII, bk. 34, p. 126, and v. XXXIV, bk. 89, p. 235, and v. XXXVIII, bk. 98, p. 23, NA; Willcox to Parke, Sept. 29, 1864, RG 94, entry 731, box 51,

NA; *OR*, v. XLII, pt. 1, p. 75, and pt. 2, pp. 1,137–38, 1,143; Wainwright, *Diary*, Sept. 30, 1864, HHL.

23. *OR*, v. XLII, pt. 1, pp. 227, 547–48; Sumner Carruth et al., *35th Massachusetts*, pp. 283–84, 290–93; *AG-Mass-1865*, p. 479; O. C. Bosbyshell, *48th Pennsylvania*, p. 181; Francis Wister, *12th U.S.*, p. 15.

24. Augustus Meyers, *Ten Years*, p. 336; *OR*, v. XLII, pt. 2, pp. 1,069, 1,073, 1,103; Perry, *Diary*, Sept. 30, 1864, WHS.

25. *OR*, v. XLII, pt. 1, pp. 435–36, 545–46, and pt. 2, pp. 1,069, 1,076–77, 1,102–5, 1,118, 1,130–32, 1,137–40; Grant to Meade, 8:10–8:15 A.M., Sept. 30, 1864, Grant Papers, HHL; Humphreys to Parke, 9:00–9:09 A.M., Sept. 30, 1864, and Williams, order of Sept. 28, 1864, RG 94, entry 731, boxes 63 and 66, respectively, NA; Sommers, op. cit., v. III, pp. 745–47.

CHAPTER IX

1. Perry, *Diary*, Sept. 30, 1864, WHS; Locke to Griffin, received 7:20 A.M., Sept. 30, 1864, RG 94, entry 730, box 3, NA; Robertson, op. cit., pp. 184, 369; Z. C. Monks to Sarah, Oct. 3, 1864, Monks-Rohrer Papers, EU; Charles LaMotte to Annie, Oct. 4, 1864, LaMotte Papers, DPAC; Detroit *Advertiser and Tribune*, Oct. 20, 1864; "Returns of Staff/8th Maryland and A/8th Michigan, S-O, 1864," RG 94, M594, NA; *118th Pennsylvania*, p. 513; *OR*, v. XLII, pt. 1, pp. 75, 477–78, 558, 562, 565, 578, 587, 599, 603, and pt. 2, pp. 1,043, 1,069, 1,103, 1,125, 1,140–41, and v. LI, pt. 1, p. 257; Allen et al., op. cit., p. 320; "Return of the V Corps, Sept. 1864," RG 94, entry 65, 5AC, NA; RG 391, 5AC, v. XXVII, bk. 73, No. 52, and v. XV, bk. 56, p. 121, NA; Wainwright, *Diary*, Sept. 30, 1864, HHL; William Strong, *121st Pennsylvania*, p. 85; RG 391, 9AC, v. XVI, bk. 18, Sept. 30, 1864, NA; Pope, *Diary*, Sept. 30, 1864, CWTI Coll., MHRC; Stephen Rogers to his parents, Oct. 3, 1864, Rogers Papers, ISHL; Rutland *Weekly Herald*, Oct. 13, 1864; Daniel Heald, *Diary*, Sept. 30, 1864, HHL; "Return of the 11th New Hampshire, Oct. 1864," New Hampshire Archives and Records Management Commission; Arnold, *Diary*, Sept. 30, 1864, MH; Byron Mac Cutcheon, *Report*, Nov. 4, 1864, 20th Michigan Papers, MH; RG 94, entry 729, box 93, Nos. 222a–b, NA; Sommers, op. cit., v. III, pp. 766–69.

2. *OR*, v. XLII, pt. 1, pp. 436, 511, 645, and pt. 2, pp. 843, 865, 942, 972, 1,001, 1,043, 1,104, 1,131, and pt. 3, pp. 19–20; *V Corps Letterbooks*, v. XIX, endpaper, and G. K. Warren to his wife, Oct. 1, 1864, GKW Coll., NYSL; Mays to Maitland, Sept. 27, 1864, RG 393, AP, container 38-30-6-4016, NA; *ANJ*, v. II, p. 98; New York *Herald*, Oct. 3, 1864; *118th Pennsylvania*, pp. 513–14; Wainwright, *Diary*, Sept. 30, 1864, HHL; Allen et al., op. cit., p. 320; Eugene Nash, *44th New York*, p. 209; Robertson, op. cit., pp. 184, 369; Z. C. Monks to Sarah, Oct. 3, 1864, Monks-Rohrer Papers, EU; Detroit *Advertiser and Tribune*, Oct. 20, 1864; Amos Judson, *83rd Pennsylvania*, p. 108; Ellis Spear, *1865*, p. 1, box 8,

JLC Coll., LC; RG 391, 5AC, v. XI, bk. 39, pp. 100–3, and box 4, Griffin to Locke, Oct. 14, 1864, NA; Rufus Jacklin, "Third Brigade," *MOLLUS-Mich,* v. II, p. 48; Grant, op. cit., v. II, p. 445.

3. Agassiz, op. cit., p. 234; *OR,* v. XLII, pt. 2, pp. 1,103, 1,118–19, 1,122–26, 1,131–33, 1,137–40; RG 393, AP, v. VI, bk. 6, pp. 507–10, NA; RG 391, 5AC, v. V, pt. 3, Babcock to Humphreys, received 11:00 A.M., Sept. 30, 1864, and pt. 4, Humphreys to Warren, 8:45 and 11:30 A.M., "Oct. 1" (sic), 1864, NA; Williams to Humphreys, 9:30 A.M.–3:25 P.M., Sept. 30, 1864, RG 94, entry 730, box 3, NA; Humphreys to Warren, 8:45 A.M., Sept. 30, 1864, RG 94, entry 731, box 51, NA; John R. Mitchell, *Diary,* Sept. 30, 1864, MHRC; Sommers, op. cit., v. III, pp. 771–73.

4. Detroit *Advertiser and Tribune,* Oct. 20, 1864; James Dearing to Thomas L. Rosser, Nov. 20, 1864, Rosser Papers, UV; Wainwright, *Diary,* Sept. 30, 1864, HHL; *118th Pennsylvania,* pp. 513–14; Allen et al., op. cit., p. 320; Robertson, op. cit., pp. 184, 369; Judson, op. cit., p. 108; *OR,* v. XLII, pt. 1, p. 586.

5. Wilkinson's farm just west of Peebles's should not be confused with E. Wilkinson's, where the Squirrel Level Road enters the Vaughan Road. Though some Union sources say that only half Graham's guns on Peebles's farm were in Fort Archer, more credible Northern accounts put all four pieces in the redoubt. *ORA,* pl. LXXVII, no. 2; *OR,* v. XLII, pt. 1, pp. 76, 435–36, 575, 599, 948, and pt. 2, pp. 1,011, 1,065, 1,132, and pt. 3, pp. 41–43; *V Corps Letterbooks,* v. XIX, endpaper, GKW Coll., NYSL; "History of L/2nd Mississippi," s. L, v. II, MDAH; R. S. Webb to Jennie, Sept. 27, 1864, Webb-Moore Papers, SHC; Charles J. Mills to his mother, Oct. 3, 1864, Coco mss.; Judson, op. cit., pp. 108–9; "History of A/2nd Mississippi, March 21, 1865, and returns of B/2nd Mississippi and C/8th Georgia Cavalry, S-O, 1864," RG 109, ch. 1, entry 18, NA; Wainwright, *Diary,* Sept. 30, 1864, HHL; Allen et al., op. cit., pp. 320–21; *118th Pennsylvania,* p. 514; Nash, op. cit., pp. 210–11; Petersburg *Daily Express,* Oct. 1 and 3, 1864; Yeary, op. cit., p. 133; Manarin, op. cit., v. II, p. 658; Clark, *NC,* v. III, p. 249; Fayetteville *Observer,* Nov. 17, 1864; Richmond *Dispatch,* Sept. 6, 1864; Tobie, op. cit., p. 318; RG 109, entry 15, No. 18-P-24, and entry 199, misc. rolls, boxes 6, 261–62, 282, NA; Goldsborough, op. cit., p. 139; Robertson, op. cit., pp. 184, 369; Detroit *Advertiser and Tribune,* Oct. 6 and 20, 1864; Henry James, *Memories,* pp. 98–99; Theodore Gerrish, *Army Life,* pp. 215–16; Agassiz, op. cit., p. 235; Spear, *1865,* p. 2, box 8, JLC Coll., LC; Sommers, op. cit., v. III, pp. 774–75, 777.

6. Allen et al., op. cit., p. 320; Nash, op. cit., pp. 209–10; Woodward, op. cit., p. 14; Sanderson-Talmage Letters, Petersburg National Battlefield Park; RG 391, 5AC, v. I, bk. 2, p. 153, and v. III, bk. 7, No. T59, NA; *OR,* v. XLII, pt. 1, pp. 436, 512–13, and pt. 2, p. 1,131; W. P. Hopkins, *7th Rhode Island,* p. 214; Agassiz, op. cit., p. 235; Theodore Lyman to Frank Palfrey, Nov. 11, 1864, Lyman Papers, 20th Massachusetts Coll., BU; Wainwright, *Diary,* Sept. 30, 1864, HHL; Wainwright, *Report,* Nov. 5, 1864, box 11, HJH Papers, LC; Judson, op. cit., p. 108; *118th Pennsylvania,* p. 514; Francis Parker, *32nd Massachusetts,* p. 238.

7. Theodore Lyman to his wife, Oct. 1, 1864, Lyman Papers, MSHS; *OR*, v. XLII, pt. 1, pp. 477–78, 545–46, 574, 578, 581, 586, and pt. 2, pp. 1,131, 1,133, 1,137; "Return of C/11th U.S., S-O, 1864," RG 94, entry 53, NA; Cutcheon, op. cit., p. 155; Hopkins, op. cit., p. 215; Jones, *Diary,* Sept. 30, 1864, and Pope, *Diary,* Sept. 30, 1864, CWTI Coll., MHRC.

8. Robertson, op. cit., pp. 184, 369–70; Allen et al., op. cit., pp. 320–21; Judson, op. cit., p. 108; Spear, *1865,* pp. 1–2, box 8, JLC Coll., LC; *118th Pennsylvania,* p. 514; RG 391, 5AC, v. XXVII, bk. 73, No. 52, NA; Gerrish, op. cit., p. 215; Nash, op. cit., pp. 209–10; Woodward, op. cit., p. 14; Henry Charles, *Memoirs,* p. 21, Ronald Boyer Coll., MHRC; *ANJ,* v. II, p. 98; Charles H. Salter to Isabella Duffield, Oct. 5, 1864, Divie B. Duffield Papers, Charles Burton Coll., DPL; Z. C. Monks to Sarah, Oct. 3, 1864, Monks-Rohrer Papers, EU; Lewiston *Evening Journal,* Oct. 19, 1864; Sommers, op. cit., v. III, pp. 780–82.

9. Detroit *Advertiser and Tribune,* Oct. 20, 1864; Charles, *Memoirs,* p. 21, Boyer Coll., MHRC.

10. Robertson, op. cit., p. 184.

11. Ibid., p. 370; Jacklin, loc. cit., v. II, p. 48; Detroit *Advertiser and Tribune,* Oct. 6, 1864; Charles Salter to Isabella Duffield, Oct. 5, 1864, Duffield Papers, Burton Coll., DPL; Nash, op. cit., p. 210.

12. Z. C. Monks to Sarah, Oct. 9, 1864, Monks-Rohrer Papers, EU.

13. Ibid., and Oct. 3, 1864, EU; Allen et al., op. cit., pp. 320–21; Judson, op. cit., p. 108; *118th Pennsylvania,* pp. 514–18; Charles Salter to Isabella Duffield, Oct. 5, 1864, Duffield Papers, Burton Coll., DPL; Detroit *Advertiser and Tribune,* Oct. 6 and 20, 1864; Spear, *1865,* p. 2, box 8, JLC Coll., LC; Woodward, op. cit., pp. 14–15; Robertson, op. cit., pp. 184, 369–70; *V Corps Letterbooks,* v. XIX, endpaper, GKW Coll., NYSL; Agassiz, op. cit., p. 235; Carruth et al., op. cit., p. 296; Nash, op. cit., p. 210; Gerrish, op. cit., pp. 215–16; Wainwright, *Diary,* Sept. 30, 1864, HHL; Jacklin, loc. cit., v. II, p. 48; James, op. cit., pp. 98–99; F. Parker, op. cit., pp. 234, 236, 238; William Powell, *V Corps,* p. 730; Benjamin Partridge, Dec. 28, 1866, 16th Michigan Coll., MH; *Roll of Officers and Men of Graham's Battery,* p. 3, CM; Edward Wells, *Hampton and His Cavalry in '64,* p. 319; William Sanderson to his mother, Oct. 6, 1864, Sanderson-Talmage Papers, Petersburg National Battlefield Park; *OR,* v. XXXVI, pt. 1, p. 545, and v. XLII, pt. 2, pp. 1,131–35, 1,205, and v. LI, pt. 1, p. 1,194; New York *Tribune,* Oct. 3, 1864; RG 391, 5AC, v. XI, bk. 39, p. 368, NA; RG 109, entry 199, misc. rolls, box 6, and camp rolls, boxes 261–62 and 282, NA; Charles, *Memoirs,* p. 21, Boyer Coll., MHRC; Yeary, op. cit., p. 133; Heth, *Report,* Dec. 7, 1864, CM; Sommers, op. cit., v. III, p. 787.

14. Carruth et al., op. cit., p. 296; Pope, *Diary,* Sept. 30, 1864, CWTI Coll., MHRC; *OR,* v. XLII, pt. 1, pp. 546, 558, 562–65, 570, 574, 578, 581, 586–87, 599, 601–5, and pt. 2, p. 1,132; Ephraim Myers, *True Story,* pp. 34–35; Hopkins, op. cit., p. 215; Rutland *Weekly Herald,* Oct. 13, 1864; Wainwright, *Diary,* Sept. 30, 1864, HHL; RG 391, 9AC, v. LXVI, bk. 232, Sept. 30, 1864, NA; RG 94, entry 729, box 93, No. 222a, NA; Robertson, op. cit., p. 184; Sommers, op. cit., v. III, pp. 803–8.

15. *OR*, v. XLII, pt. 1, pp. 558, 563, 565, 570, 578, 587, 897–98, and pt. 2, pp. 1,118, 1,132, 1,134, and pt. 3, p. 52; Myers, op. cit., pp. 34–35; Robertson, op. cit., pp. 184, 370; Detroit *Advertiser and Tribune,* Oct. 20, 1864; Charles Salter to Isabella Duffield, Oct. 5, 1864, Duffield Papers, Burton Coll., DPL; Clarke to Locke, 1:55 P.M., Sept. 30, 1864, *V Corps Letterbooks,* v. XIX, GKW Coll., NYSL; Judson, op. cit., p. 109; Nash, op. cit., p. 210; Gerrish, op. cit., p. 216; *118th Pennsylvania,* p. 517; F. Parker, op. cit., p. 236; Charles, *Memoirs,* p. 21, Boyer Coll., MHRC; "Returns of H/4th North Carolina Cavalry, Apr.–Sept. 1864, and F/1st Confederate Battalion, S-O, 1864," RG 109, ch. 1, entry 18, NA; James K. Wilkerson to his mother, Oct. 5, 1864, Wilkerson Papers, DU; Mullen, *Diary,* Sept. 30, 1864, CM; Sale, *Diary,* Sept. 30–Oct. 3, 1864, VSL; Wilcox, *Report,* pp. 62–63, LHQ Coll., VHS; Heth, *Report,* Dec. 7, 1864, Heth Papers, CM; Charles LaMotte to Annie, Oct. 4, 1864, LaMotte Papers, DPAC; Sommers, op. cit., v. III, pp. 805–7, 902–3.

16. Gerrish, op. cit., p. 216; *118th Pennsylvania,* p. 517; Nash, op. cit., p. 210; Wainwright, *Diary,* Sept. 30, 1864, HHL; James, op. cit., pp. 98–99; F. Parker, op. cit., pp. 236–38; Detroit *Advertiser and Tribune,* Oct. 6, 1864; William Sanderson to his mother, Oct. 6, 1864, Sanderson-Talmage Papers, Petersburg National Battlefield Park; Z. C. Monks to Sarah, Oct. 3, 1864, Monks-Rohrer Papers, EU; Charles, *Memoirs,* p. 21, Boyer Coll., MHRC.

17. *OR*, v. XLII, pt. 1, pp. 31, 476–78, 545–46, 578, 581, 587, and pt. 2, pp. 1,120, 1,131–32, 1,135, and pt. 3, pp. 19–20; RG 391, 5AC, v. XVII, bk. 69, p. 450, NA; "Returns of Staff-E-F-H/4th Maryland, Staff/8th Maryland, 5th New York, and F/121st Pennsylvania, and of B-F/11th U.S. and D-F/14th U.S., S-O, 1864," RG 94, M594 and entry 53, respectively, NA; Strong, op. cit., p. 85; Powell, op. cit., p. 731; Charles LaMotte to Annie, Oct. 4, 1864, LaMotte Papers, DPAC; Henry Gawthorp, letter of Oct. 6, 1864, Gawthorp Papers, HSD; Eyre, *Diary,* Sept. 30, 1864, Casebier mss.; Charles Camper et al., *1st Maryland,* p. 176; William Sanderson to his mother, Oct. 6, 1864, Sanderson-Talmage Papers, Petersburg National Battlefield Park; Wainwright, *Diary,* Sept. 30, 1864, HHL; G. K. Warren to his wife, Oct. 1, 1864, GKW Coll., NYSL; Sommers, op. cit., v. III, pp. 807–11, 822–23.

18. *OR*, v. XLII, pt. 1, pp. 84, 87, 89–90, 92, 94, 558, 620, 634–35, 947–48, and pt. 2, pp. 1,107, 1,133, 1,136, 1,139–41; Agassiz, op. cit., p. 234; Waring, *Diary,* Sept. 30, 1864, SHC; RG 391, CC, v. XXII, bk. 34, pp. 94–95, NA; "Return of F/20th Georgia Cavalry Battalion, S-O, 1864," RG 109, ch. 1, entry 18, NA; "Returns of Staff/1st Massachusetts Cavalry and Staff/10th New York Cavalry, S-O, 1864," RG 94, M594, NA; RG 94, entry 12, 1864 file, No. B1379, NA; Rappalyea, *Diary,* Sept. 30, 1864, NJHS; Bushnell, *History,* pp. 312–13, Palmer Coll., WRHS; RG 94, entry 160, v. XI, p. 731, NA; RG 393, AP, v. VI, bk. 6, p. 517, NA; Clark, *Diary,* Sept. 30, 1864, NYPL; Sommers, op. cit., v. III, pp. 812–15.

19. The 39th New York of the Consolidated Brigade and the 28th

Massachusetts of the First Brigade were among Miles's five reserve regiments that initially remained near the front rather than go to Shand's. *OR,* v. XLII, pt. 1, p. 167, and pt. 2, pp. 1,036, 1,119, 1,122, 1,126–30, 1,140, and pt. 3, pp. 10–11, 14, 39–40, 56, 73; RG 393, AP, v. VI, bk. 6, p. 520, and v. LV, bk. 119, p. 169, and v. XLIX, bk. 104, No. A9, and box 7, Mathews to Clapp, Sept. 30, 1864, and container 38-30-6-4035, Bull to Majtheny, Oct. 4, 1864, NA; James Snook, *Diary,* Sept. 30, 1864, MDHS; "Returns of B-E-G-M/50th New York Engineers, Staff/5th Michigan, Staff/28th Massachusetts, and 14th Massachusetts Battery, S-O, 1864," RG 94, M594, NA; RG 391, 2AC, box 1, Miles to Bingham, Sept. 25, 1864, and box 7, John Pulford, *Report,* Oct. 7, 1864, and v. I, bk. 8, pp. 433–34, and box 8, Collis to Hancock, 4:00 P.M., Oct. 1, 1864, and v. IX, bk. 29, Patrick to Hancock, Sept. 30, 1864, and v. XX, bk. 83, p. 341, and v. XL, bk. 198, No. 172, NA; William Rawle Brooke et al., *3rd Pennsylvania Cavalry,* pp. 458–59; George Gordon Meade, *Letters and Telegrams Received,* v. VIII, pp. 3–4, GGM Coll., HSP; Hunt, *Journal,* p. 130, HJH Papers, LC; Detroit *Advertiser and Tribune,* Oct. 20, 1864; Faulkner, *Diary,* Sept. 30, 1864, HHL; Gilbert Frederick, *57th New York,* p. 269; Ezra Simons, *125th New York,* p. 251; Sommers, op. cit., v. III, pp. 815–20.

20. *OR,* v. XLII, pt. 2, pp. 1,125, 1,128, 1,131, 1,134–36, 1,138–39; Eldridge, *Diary,* Sept. 30, 1864, CNHS; John Irvin, *Diary,* Sept. 30, 1864, HSP; Edmund L. Dana, *Diary,* Sept. 30–Oct. 4, 1864, WHGS; Robert McAllister to his wife, Oct. 7, 1864, McAllister Papers, Palmer Coll., WRHS; RG 391, 2AC, v. LIII, bk. 256, p. 147, and v. IX, bk. 29, Patrick to Hancock, Sept. 30, 1864, NA; "Return of Staff/210th Pennsylvania, S-O, 1864," RG 94, M594, NA; George Meade, *George Gordon Meade,* v. II, pp. 231–32; RG 393, AP, v. VI, bk. 6, pp. 510–12, and box 1, Leslie to Patrick, Sept. 30, 1864, and container 38-30-6-4035, Dallas to Williams, Sept. 30, 1864, NA; RG 94, entry 731, box 51, Sharpe to Williams, received 10:25 A.M., and Williams to Meade, 10:45–10:50 A.M., and Williams to Sharpe, 10:40–11:00 A.M. and 11:10–11:15 A.M., and Meade to Williams, 11:00 A.M. and 1:15–1:30 P.M., and Williams to Pitkin, 1:30–1:40 P.M., Sept. 30, 1864, and box 63, Pitkin to Williams, Sept. 30, 1864, NA; Sommers, op. cit., v. III, pp. 820–22.

21. *OR,* v. XLII, pt. 1, pp. 546, 558, 562–63, 581, 587, and pt. 2, pp. 1,119–20, 1,131–34; Lyman, *Diary,* Sept. 30, 1864, MSHS; Meade to Williams and Hancock, 2:30 P.M., Sept. 30, 1864, RG 94, entry 731, box 63, NA; Agassiz, op. cit., pp. 235–36; Theodore Lyman to Frank Palfrey, Nov. 11, 1864, Lyman Papers, 20th Massachusetts Coll., BU; RG 391, 9AC, v. XVI, bk. 18, Sept. 30, 1864, NA; "Return of Staff/11th New Hampshire, S-O, 1864," New Hampshire Archives and Records Management Commission; "Return of A/8th Michigan, S-O, 1864," RG 94, M594, NA; Rutland *Weekly Herald,* Oct. 13, 1864; Allen et al., op. cit., p. 321; Charles J. Mills to his mother, Oct. 3, 1864; Coco mss.; Burrage, op. cit., p. 259; Carruth et al., op. cit., p. 297; Hopkins, op. cit., pp. 215–16; Sommers, op. cit., v. III, pp. 822–26.

22. *OR,* v. XLII, pt. 2, pp. 1,117–20, 1,123–24, 1,133–34, 1,140, 1,142–43; RG 108, entry 11, box 85, No. P408, NA; Grant to Meade, 3:00 and 3:15 P.M., Sept. 30, 1864, Grant Papers, HHL; Sommers, op. cit., v. III, pp. 824–25.

CHAPTER X

1. *OR,* v. XLII, pt. 1, pp. 87, 546, 552, 558, 565, 570, 574, 578–79, 582, 586–87, 599–605, and pt. 2, pp. 1,140–41; Pope, *Diary,* Sept. 30, 1864, CWTI Coll., MHRC; Hopkins, op. cit., p. 215; Cutcheon, op. cit., p. 155.

2. By the time of the Civil War the pronunciation of the doctor's name had been Virginiacized from "Bwa-so" to "Boy-saw." *OR,* v. XLII, pt. 1, p. 436; *ORA,* pl. C, no. 2; Caldwell, op. cit., pp. 182–83; Wilcox, *Report,* p. 63, LHQ Coll., VHS.

3. *OR,* v. XLII, pt. 1, pp. 553, 558, 565, 570–74, 578–83, 586–87, 599–605; Heth, *Report,* Dec. 7, 1864, Heth Papers, CM; Leander Cogswell, *11th New Hampshire,* p. 499; Lyman Jackman, *6th New Hampshire,* p. 335; Burrage, op. cit., p. 260; Carruth et al., op. cit., p. 297; Hopkins, op. cit., pp. 215–16; Jones, *Diary,* Sept. 30, 1864, CWTI Coll., MHRC; G. H. Allen, *4th Rhode Island,* p. 304; H. V. Hicks, "At Peebles' and Pegram's Farms," *NT,* May 11, 1911; Frank Merrill, "Poplar Spring Church," *NT,* Oct. 4, 1894; Pope, *Diary,* Sept. 30, 1864, CWTI Coll., MHRC; M. Gyla McDowell, *The Roundheads' Own Story,* ch. XVII, p. 23, McDowell Coll., PSU.

4. Wainwright, *Diary,* Sept. 30, 1864, HHL.

5. Lyman, *Diary,* Sept. 30, 1864, MSHS.

6. Ibid.; *OR,* v. XLII, pt. 1, pp. 546, 558, 579, 581, 587, and pt. 2, pp. 1,120–21; Wainwright, *Diary,* Sept. 30, 1864, HHL; Pope, *Diary,* Sept. 30, 1864, CWTI Coll., MHRC; Wilcox, *Report,* pp. 62–65, LHQ Coll., VHS; Cogswell, op. cit., p. 499; Agassiz, op. cit., p. 236; Lyman to Frank Palfrey, Nov. 4, 1864, Lyman Papers, 20th Massachusetts Coll., BU; Charles LaMotte to Annie, Oct. 4, 1864, LaMotte Papers, DPAC; Strong, op. cit., p. 85; "Returns of A/8th Michigan and F/45th and K/56th and F/121st Pennsylvania, S-O, 1864," RG 94, M594, NA; *AG-Mass-1864,* p. 1,065; Charles Reed to his mother, Sept. 28–Oct. 1, 1864, Reed Papers, LC; Wainwright, *Report,* Nov. 5, 1864, box 11, HJH Papers, LC; RG 391, 9AC, v. XVI, bk. 18, Sept. 30, 1864, NA; Detroit *Advertiser and Tribune,* Oct. 6, 1864; Burrage, op. cit., pp. 259–60; Stephen Rogers to his parents, Oct. 3, 1864, Rogers Papers, ISHL; Sommers, op. cit., v. III, pp. 853–55.

7. The two guns that did not accompany the Third Cavalry Division to the works remained at the bivouac on the plank road. Waring, *Diary,* p. 121, SHC; *OR,* v. XLII, pt. 1, pp. 565, 570, 859, 876, 947, and pt. 2, pp. 1,120, 1,134; McGregor, *Report,* Dec. 7, 1864, Halsey Papers, SHC; Gordon, *Diary,* Sept. 29–30, 1864, SHC; Beale, op. cit., p. 146; Clark, *NC,* v.

III, p. 627; Wilcox, *Report,* p. 62, LHQ Coll., VHS; Heth, *Report,* Dec. 7, 1864, Heth Papers, CM; Lane, *Glimpses,* v. XVIII, pp. 411–12; W. D. Alexander, *Diary,* Sept. 30, 1864, SHC; Caldwell, op. cit., p. 182; Harris, op. cit., pp. 56–57; RG 111, entry 13, v. XLIV, p. 170, NA; Mullen, *Diary,* Sept. 30, 1864, CM; Cavaness, *Diary,* Sept. 30, 1864, TXU; J. K. Wilkerson to his mother, Oct. 5, 1864, Wilkerson Papers, DU; "Returns of H/48th North Carolina, F/1st Confederate Battalion, B-C/2nd and H/26th and D/42nd Mississippi, and C/11th Georgia Light Artillery Battalion, S-O, 1864," RG 109, ch. 1, entry 18, NA; W. J. Pegram to Mary Pegram, Oct. 5, 1864, PJM Coll., VHS; J. W. Shank to his sister, Oct. 21, 1864, Joseph Smith Papers, DU; J. A. Shank to J. B. Smith, Oct. 9, 1864, Shank Papers, GDAH; Sommers, op. cit., v. III, pp. 855–58.

8. The varying figures for Hampton are caused by uncertainty over whether or not "Rooney" Lee's dismounted men served with his horsemen in this sector. Lane, *Glimpses,* v. XVIII, p. 412, and *Lane's Brigade,* v. IX, pp. 354–55, respectively; Folder 82, James H. Lane Papers, AU; Wilcox, *Report,* pp. 62–64, 68, LHQ Coll., VHS; Caldwell, op. cit., pp. 182–83; Dunlop, op. cit., p. 210; J. H. Lane, "Lane's Corps of Sharpshooters," *SHSP,* v. XXVIII, p. 4; *OR,* v. XLII, pt. 1, pp. 587, 852, 941, 947, and pt. 3, p. 1,130; Harris, op. cit., p. 57; Heth, *Report,* Dec. 7, 1864, Heth Papers, CM; C. M. Wilcox, "Jones's Farm," Transactions of the Southern Historical Society, *Southern Magazine,* v. IX, no. 4, p. 68; Clark, *NC,* v. II, p. 669; H. A. Brown, "Colonel W. M. Barbour," *CV,* v. VII, p. 30; C. M. Wilcox, *Autobiography,* pp. 100–3, and letter to sister, Oct. 18, 1864, and *Notes on Richmond Campaign of 1864–1865,* p. 29, C. M. Wilcox Papers, LC; "CSR of Robert M. Mayo, 47th Virginia," RG 109, CSR, NA; C. A. Porter Hopkins, "The James J. Archer Letters, Part II," *Maryland Historical Magazine,* v. LVI, p. 380; Petersburg *Daily Express,* Oct. 1, 1864; Hicks, loc. cit., May 11, 1911; Sommers, op. cit., v. III, pp. 858–62.

9. Wilcox, *Report,* p. 63, LHQ Coll., VHS; *OR,* v. XLII, pt. 1, pp. 546, 565, 574, 579, 581–84, 587–88; RG 94, entry 160, v. VIII, pp. 823–25, NA; Jackman, op. cit., p. 335, 339–40; Myers, op. cit., p. 35; Rutland *Weekly Herald,* Oct. 13, 1864; William F. Draper, *Recollections,* p. 172; Carruth et al., op. cit., p. 297; Agassiz, op. cit., p. 236; RG 391, 9AC, v. LIV, bk. 194, p. 158, and v. LXVIII, bk. 102, Oct. 1–3, 1864, NA; "Monthly Return of Second Brigade, Second Division, IX Corps, and Trimonthly Return of IX Corps, Sept. 30, 1864," RG 94, entry 65, 9AC, NA; Burrage, op. cit., pp. 260–61; Albert, op. cit., p. 333; Pope, *Diary,* Sept. 30, 1864, CWTI Coll., MHRC; Hicks, loc. cit., May 11, 1911; Sommers, op. cit., v. III, pp. 862–65.

10. "Return of Staff/11th New Hampshire, Oct. 1864," New Hampshire Archives and Records Management Commission.

11. E. A. Lord, *9th New Hampshire,* p. 524; Caldwell, op. cit., p. 183.

12. Wooten covered Lane's right during the drive across Jones's field. Jackman, op. cit., pp. 336, 342–43; Lord, op. cit., pp. 524–27; Caldwell, op. cit., p. 183; Dunlop, op. cit., pp. 211–12; Wilcox, *Report,* p. 63, LHQ Coll.,

VHS; Lane, *Lane's Brigade,* v. IX, pp. 355–56; "Return of Staff/11th New Hampshire, Oct. 1864," New Hampshire Archives and Records Management Commission; *OR,* v. XLII, pt. 1, pp. 546, 579, 581–82, 587–88; Cogswell, op. cit., p. 499; Folder 82, Lane Papers, AU; Lane, *Glimpses,* v. XVIII, p. 412; Harris, op. cit., p. 57; Heth, *Report,* Dec. 7, 1864, Heth Papers, CM; Rutland *Weekly Herald,* Oct. 13, 1864; J. H. Lane, "28th North Carolina," *SHSP,* v. XXIV, p. 337; Lewiston *Evening Journal,* Oct. 15, 1864; *AG-Maine-1864/65,* v. I, p. 296; *AG-Vt-Revised Roster,* p. 573; Lyman, *Diary,* Sept. 30, 1864, MSHS; Richmond *Enquirer,* Oct. 4, 1864; Allen, op. cit., p. 309; Hicks, loc. cit., May 11, 1911; Merrill, loc. cit., Oct. 4, 1894; Sommers, op. cit., v. III, pp. 865–68.

13. Stephen Rogers to his parents, Oct. 3, 1864, Rogers Papers, ISHL.

14. William Lamont to his sister, Oct. 2, 1864, Lamont Papers, WHS.

15. Agassiz, op. cit., p. 237.

16. *OR,* v. XLII, pt. 1, p. 565.

17. *Ibid.,* p. 584; Pope, *Diary,* Sept. 30, 1864, CWTI Coll., MHRC.

18. Burrage, op. cit., p. 262.

19. During the drive to Boisseau's, the 37th North Carolina apparently served with Lane's main body, not with Cowan. Ibid., pp. 261–63; *OR,* v. XLII, pt. 1, pp. 141–42, 553–54, 565–66, 570–73, 582–84, 948; Caldwell, op. cit., pp. 183–84; Lane, *Lane's Brigade,* v. IX, pp. 355–56; Folder 82, Lane Papers, AU; Wilcox, *Report,* pp. 64–65, LHQ Coll., VHS; Wilcox, loc. cit., v. IX, No. 4, p. 68; Wilcox, *Autobiography,* p. 103, Wilcox Papers, LC; Clark, *NC,* v. I, p. 600, and v. II, p. 103, and v. III, p. 627; Carruth et al., op. cit., pp. 290–92, 297–300; Stephen Rogers to his parents, Oct. 3, 1864, Rogers Papers, ISHL; Henry Heisler to his sister, Oct. 1, 1864, Heisler Papers, LC; Joseph Gould, *48th Pennsylvania,* p. 274; Bosbyshell, op. cit., pp. 181–82; C. F. Walcott, *21st Massachusetts,* pp. 357–58; Draper, op. cit., p. 173; Eugene A. Barrett, "John F. Hartranft," *Pennsylvania History,* v. XXXII, p. 182; Cutcheon, op. cit., p. 156; DeLand to Robertson, Aug. 14, 1881, and Murdock to Robertson, Sept. 5, 1881, 1st Michigan Sharpshooters Coll., MH; Detroit *Advertiser and Tribune,* Oct. 7, 13, 15, 26, 1864; Gordon, *Diary,* Sept. 30, 1864, SHC; "Returns of H/1st and A/3rd North Carolina Cavalry, S-O, 1864," RG 109, ch. 1, entry 18, NA; Foard, op. cit., p. 6, NCDAH; Richmond *Whig,* Oct. 5, 1864; Robertson, op. cit., p. 547; Pope, *Diary,* Sept. 30, 1864, CWTI Coll., MHRC; *AG-Mass-1865,* pp. 340, 479–80; Right General Guide, "A Fatal Gap," *NT,* Nov. 29, 1894; S. Bullock, "Col. W. C. Raulston," *NT,* Jan. 15, 1891; Hezekiah Bradds, "60th Ohio," *NT,* April 8, 1926; Sommers, op. cit., v. III, pp. 868–76.

20. Wilcox, *Report,* pp. 64–65, LHQ Coll., VHS; *OR,* v. XLII, pt. 1, pp. 141–42, 565, 579, 581–82, 585, 852, 870, 947–48, and pt. 3, pp. 479–80; Albert, op. cit., pp. 63–64, 164–66, 297, 333; Myers, op. cit., p. 35; Clark, *NC,* v. I, p. 600, and v. III, p. 627; Heth, *Report,* Dec. 7, 1864, Heth Papers, CM; Bates, *Pennsylvania Volunteers,* v. I, p. 1,070; Foard, op. cit., p. 6, NCDAH; Beale, op. cit., p. 146; McGregor, *Report,* Dec. 7, 1864, Halsey Papers, SHC; *AG-Mass-1864,* p. 913; RG 94, entry 12, No. S1946,

NA; RG 391, 9AC, v. LIV, bk. 194, p. 159, and v. LXVIII, bk. 102, Oct. 1, 1864, NA; Burrage, op. cit., p. 261; Lane, *Glimpses,* v. XVIII, p. 412; Boston *Daily Courier,* Oct. 11, 1864; RG 109, entry 15, No. 17-P-31, NA; *History of 9th N. H. Vols.,* p. 16, 9th New Hampshire Coll., NHHS; Frederick Cushman, *58th Massachusetts,* p. 18; Jerome Loving, ed., *Civil War Letters of George Washington Whitman,* pp. 132–33; Sommers, op. cit., v. III, pp. 876–80.

21. Caldwell, op. cit., p. 184.

22. *OR,* v. XLII, pt. 1, p. 553.

23. Hopkins, op. cit., p. 216.

24. Ibid., pp. 216–17; Caldwell, op. cit., pp. 184–85; Folder 82, Lane Papers, AU; Lane, *Lane's Brigade,* v. IX, pp. 355–56; Wilcox, *Report,* pp. 64–67, LHQ Coll., VHS; *OR,* v. XLII, pt. 1, pp. 553, 558–59, 563, 574, 579, 586, 599–605; Joseph Carter, "Poplar Spring Church," *NT,* March 22, 1894; S. W. Pierce, *38th Wisconsin,* p. 51; E. B. Quiner, *Military History of Wisconsin,* pp. 841, 849; Howard Aston, *13th Ohio Cavalry,* p. 23; Cuffel, op. cit., p. 215; A. S. Twitchell, *7th Maine Battery,* p. 31; Jacob Roemer, *Reminiscences,* pp. 252–53, 309; "CSR of Alonzo Garretson, Thomas Heasley, and John J. Johnston, 34th New York Battery," RG 94, entry 519, NA; "Return of the IX Corps, Oct. 1, 1864," RG 94, entry 65, 9AC, NA; RG 391, 9AC, v. LII, bk. 226, p. 87, and v. LXI, bk. 190, pp. 28, 36, and v. LXVI, bk. 232, Sept. 30, 1864, NA; R. C. Eden, *37th Wisconsin,* p. 35; *AG-Vt-Revised Roster,* p. 573; Jones, *Diary,* Sept. 30, 1864, CWTI Coll., MHRC; Sommers, op. cit., v. III, pp. 895–98.

25. Burrage, op. cit., p. 262.

26. Ibid.; RG 94, entry 160, v. VIII, p. 825, and v. IX, p. 252, NA; *OR,* v. XLII, pt. 1, pp. 553–54, 558, 562–63, 566, 571, 573–74, 579, 582, 586, 588, and pt. 3, pp. 479–80; Murdock to Robertson, Sept. 5, 1881, 1st Michigan Sharpshooters Coll., MH; Robertson, op. cit., p. 547; Cutcheon, op. cit., p. 157; Eden, op. cit., p. 35; Quiner, op. cit., p. 841; Hopkins, op. cit., p. 217; Caldwell, op. cit., p. 184; Allen, op. cit., p. 309; Charles J. Mills to his mother, Oct. 3 and 5–6, 1864, Coco mss.; Stephen Rogers to his parents, Oct. 3, 1864, Rogers Papers, ISHL; Carruth et. al., op. cit., pp. 299–300; Cogswell, op. cit., p. 499ff; Lewiston *Evening Journal,* Oct. 15, 1864; Carter, loc. cit., March 22, 1894; Sommers, op. cit., v. III, pp. 898–99.

27. Manuel Eyre, *Diary,* Oct. 7, 1864, Casebier mss.

28. The 1st Maryland replaced the 16th Michigan on the skirmish line. The 4th Maryland went on outpost duty so far east as not to engage Mahone. Ibid.; Judson, op. cit., p. 109; Robertson, op. cit., pp. 184, 369; Nash, op. cit., p. 210; Charles Salter to Isabella Duffield, Oct. 5, 1864, Duffield Papers, Burton Coll., DPL; Charles LaMotte to Annie, Oct. 4, 1864, LaMotte Papers, DPAC; "Returns of E/4th and Staff/8th Maryland, B-D/5th New York, K/56th and F/121st Pennsylvania, B-F/11th and A-C/12th and B/14th and A-B-D-G-H/17th U.S., S-O, 1864," RG 94, M594 and entry 53, respectively, NA; *OR,* v. XLII, pt. 1, p. 66, and pt. 2, pp. 1,132–35; Strong, op. cit., p. 85; Henry Gawthorp, letter of Oct. 6,

1864, Gawthorp Papers, HSD; Camper et al., op. cit., p. 176; RG 94, entry 160, v. XI, p. 344, and entry 729, box 93, No. 146, NA; Heth, *Report,* Dec. 7, 1864, Heth Papers, CM; RG 109, entry 199, box 282, NA; "Return of H/4th North Carolina Cavalry, Apr.–Sept. 1864," RG 109, ch. 1, entry 18, NA; Sommers, op. cit., v. III, pp. 899–903.

29. Detroit *Advertiser and Tribune,* Oct. 20, 1864; Charles Salter to Isabella Duffield, Oct. 5, 1864, Duffield Papers, Burton Coll., DPL; Judson, op. cit., p. 109; Nash, op. cit., pp. 210–11; Robertson, op. cit., pp. 184, 370; Wainwright, *Diary,* Sept. 30, 1864, HHL; Agassiz, op. cit., pp. 236–37; *118th Pennsylvania,* pp. 516–19; Allen et al., op. cit., pp. 321–23, 745; *OR,* v. XLII, pt. 1, pp. 139, 599–605, 941–42, and pt. 2, pp. 1,121, 1,133, and v. LI, pt. 1, p. 1,194; Powell, op. cit., p. 731; Gerrish, op. cit., pp. 216–17; *AG-Maine-1864/65,* v. I, p. 469; "Map Room, F48F, G819, green box," Berks County Historical Society; *Fifth Reunion of 155th Pennsylvania,* p. 42; Lyman, *Diary,* Sept. 30, 1864, MSHS; Z. C. Monks to Sarah, Oct. 18, 1864, Monks-Rohrer Papers, EU; Twitchell, op. cit., p. 31; James, op. cit., p. 100; Goldsborough, op. cit., p. 140; *V Corps Letterbooks,* v. XIX, endpaper, GKW Coll., NYSL; Charles, op. cit., p. 21, Boyer Coll., MHRC; Sommers, op. cit., v. III, pp. 903–7, 914–15.

30. Wainwright, *Diary,* Sept. 30, 1864, HHL; Wainwright, *Report,* Nov. 5, 1864, box 11, HJH Papers, LC; Augustus Buell, "Mink's Battery," *NT,* June 6, 1895; *OR,* v. XLII, pt. 1, pp. 66–67, 140, 573, 579, 582, 599–605; RG 391, 9AC, v. LVI, bk. 232, Sept. 30, 1864, NA; Agassiz, op. cit., pp. 236–37; J. Albert Monroe, "Reminiscences," *RISSHS,* s. 2, v. III, No. 11, pp. 68–69; Strong, op. cit., p. 85; "Return of A/8th U.S., S-O, 1864," RG 94, entry 53, NA; Sommers, op. cit., v. III, pp. 906–10.

31. "Annual Reunion of Pegram Battalion Association," *SHSP,* v. XIV, p. 17; cf. Wilcox, *Report,* p. 64, LHQ Coll., VHS.

32. Henry Heisler to his sister, Oct. 4, 1864, Heisler Papers, LC.

33. Hugh Torrence, *War Between the States,* Lowen Shuford Coll., NCDAH; R. S. Webb to his mother, Oct. 6, 1864, Webb-Moore Papers, SHC; Caldwell, op. cit., pp. 184–85; "Return of D/3rd Maryland, S-O, 1864," RG 94, M594, NA; Carter, loc. cit., March 22, 1894; *OR,* v. XLII, pt. 1, pp. 553, 558, 563, 566, 571–74, 586, 588, 603; McDowell, op. cit., ch. XVII, pp. 20–21, McDowell Coll., PSU; Eden, op. cit., p. 35; Quiner, op. cit., p. 841; Allen, op. cit., p. 309; Pierce, op. cit., p. 51; Hopkins, op. cit., p. 217; Jones, *Diary,* Sept. 30, 1864, CWTI Coll., MHRC; RG 94, entry 160, v. VIII, p. 825, NA; Stephen Rogers to his parents, Oct. 3, 1864, Rogers Papers, ISHL; *118th Pennsylvania,* p. 520; Dunlop, op. cit., p. 213; Wilcox, *Report,* p. 64, LHQ Coll., VHS; Folder 82, Lane Papers, AU; Lane, *Lane's Brigade,* v. IX, p. 356; Sommers, op. cit., v. III, pp. 910–12.

34. Foard, op. cit., pp. 6–7, NCDAH; McGregor, *Report,* Dec. 7, 1864, Halsey Papers, SHC.

35. *OR,* v. XLII, pt. 1, p. 941.

36. Charles Salter to Isabella Duffield, Oct. 5, 1864, Duffield Papers, Burton Coll., DPL.

37. *118th Pennsylvania,* p. 519.

38. Ibid., p. 520; John Pullen, *20th Maine*, p. 227.

39. Gerrish, op. cit., p. 217; Wainwright, *Diary*, Sept. 30, 1864, HHL.

40. The poor performance of the Lindsay rifle in the field, Warren later snorted, showed "the more than worthlessness of the arm sent for trial, and I beg to be relieved from having to make such experiments again." The government heeded such complaints. It withdrew the guns sent for testing and purchased no new ones. Wilcox, *Report*, p. 64, LHQ Coll., VHS; *OR*, v. XLII, pt. 1, pp. 66–67, 941–42, and pt. 2, pp. 1,121, 1,133; Goldsborough, op. cit., p. 140; "Returns of Staff-F/2nd Maryland Battalion, S-O, 1864," RG 109, ch. 1, entry 18, NA; *118th Pennsylvania*, pp. 518–21; Powell, op. cit., pp. 731–32; Pullen, op. cit., p. 227; Judson, op. cit., p. 109; Allen et al., op. cit., pp. 321–23; Gerrish, op. cit., pp. 216–17; Nash, op. cit., p. 211; Detroit *Advertiser and Tribune*, Oct. 6, 1864; Wainwright, *Diary*, Sept. 30, 1864, HHL; "Return of Third Brigade, First Division, V Corps, Sept. 30, 1864," RG 94, entry 65, 5AC, NA; Robertson, op. cit., p. 184; Charles Salter to Isabella Duffield, Oct. 5, 1864, Duffield Papers, Burton Coll., DPL; Claude Fuller, *The Rifled Musket*, pp. 234–36; Francis A. Lord, *Civil War Collector's Encyclopedia*, pp. 244–45; RG 391, 2AC, v. V, bk. 3, p. 398, and 5AC, v. III, bk. 7, No. W174, and v. IV, bk. 13, pp. 184–85, 226, and v. XIII, bk. 53, p. 105, and box 4, Bowers to Meade, Sept. 5, 1864, NA; Strong, op. cit., p. 85; "Returns of K/56th and the 121st Pennsylvania, S-O, 1864," RG 94, M594, NA; Wainwright, *Report*, Nov. 5, 1864, box 11, HJH Papers, LC; Sam Brooke to his sister, Oct. 4, 1864, Binckley Papers, LC; Buell, loc. cit., June 6, 1895; David Allen, "More About Mink," *NT*, July 11, 1895; Sommers, op. cit., v. III, pp. 913–18.

41. Wainwright, *Diary*, Sept. 30, 1864, HHL; Wainwright, *Report*, Nov. 5, 1864, box 11, HJH Papers, LC; Wilcox, *Report*, p. 64, LHQ Coll., VHS; Allen et al., op. cit., p. 323.

42. Heth, *Report*, Dec. 7, 1864, Heth Papers, CM.

CHAPTER XI

1. *OR*, v. XLII, pt. 1, pp. 59, 139–43, 546–47, 620; Wainwright, *Diary*, Sept. 30, 1864, HHL; Winthrop to LaMotte, Nov. 8, 1864, RG 94, entry 729, box 93, No. 146, NA; RG 391, 5AC, v. XXXIX, bk. 206, Oct. 1, 1864, NA; Roemer, op. cit., pp. 310–16; Eckert to Smith, Sept. 30, 1864, RG 393, AP, container 38-30-6-4016, NA; Goldsborough, op. cit., pp. 141–42, and "Grant's Change of Base," *SHSP*, v. XXIX, p. 289; Sommers, op. cit., pp. 918, 943–44, 972, 1,345–56.

2. Whether Wilcox's Division encamped right at Jones's house or inside the log works just north of it is not clear. More certain is that his men who escorted prisoners to Petersburg turned them over to provost troops there and then returned to the field. Whether or not the 5th Alabama Battalion left the trenches that night to resume such guard duty is not known, but the arrival of the captives likely explains why E/1st Virginia Battalion rejoined its parent unit (the army's provost troops) on Saturday. No matter who

guarded the prisoners, the Unionists suffered. Plundered by their captors right on the battlefield, then made to march through the storm to Petersburg and wade the Battersea Canal to enter a prison pen along the Appomattox, they spent a miserable night, lashed in body by the elements and in spirit by the consciousness of their inglorious defeat. Clark, *NC,* v. I, p. 600, and v. III, p. 627; Caldwell, op. cit., p. 185; Wainwright, *Diary,* Sept. 30, 1864, HHL; Ransom Sargent, *Diary,* Sept. 30, 1864, NYPL; Heth, *Report,* Dec. 7, 1864, Heth Papers, CM; Dunlop, op. cit., p. 212; Wilcox, *Report,* p. 64, LHQ Coll., VHS; Wilcox, loc. cit., v. I, p. 69; Folder 82, Lane Papers, AU; Lane, *Lane's Brigade,* v. IX, p. 356; W. D. Alexander, *Diary,* Sept. 30, 1864, SHC; Albert, op. cit., pp. 324–25, 333, 336; "Return of E/1st Virginia Battalion, S-O, 1864," RG 109, ch. 1, entry 18, NA; *OR,* v. XLII, pt. 1, p. 948; Byrd Willis, *Diary,* Sept. 30, 1864, VSL; McGregor, *Report,* Dec. 7, 1864, Halsey Papers, SHC; Gordon, *Diary,* Sept. 30, 1864, SHC; Henry B. McClellan to Ellen Fontaine, Oct. 6, 1864, VHS; Sommers, op. cit., v. IV, pp. 943–46, 949.

3. Wilcox, *Notes,* copy 1, p. 30, Wilcox Papers, LC; Heth, *Report,* Dec. 7, 1864, Heth Papers, CM; *OR,* v. XLII, pt. 1, pp. 859, 898, 941, 948, and pt. 2, p. 1,121; Wilcox, *Report,* pp. 65–67, LHQ Coll., VHS; J. K. Wilkerson to his mother, Oct. 5, 1864, Wilkerson Papers, DU; "Returns of B-C/2nd and H/26th and B/42nd Mississippi and A-C-E-F/2nd Maryland Battalion, S-O, 1864, and H/4th North Carolina Cavalry, Apr.–Sept. 1864," RG 109, ch. 1, entry 18, NA; Goldsborough, op. cit., pp. 139–42; Cavaness, *Diary,* Sept. 30, 1864, TXU; Mullen, *Diary,* Sept. 30–Oct. 1, 1864, CM; R. S. Webb to his sister, Oct. 3, 1864, Webb-Moore Papers, SHC; James A. Bryan, *Diary,* Oct. 1, 1864, Bryan Family Papers, SHC; RG 109, entry 15, No. 16-P-24, NA; W. J. Pegram to Mary, Oct. 5, 1864, PJM Coll., VHS; Battleflag of Crenshaw's Battery, Warren County (Virginia) Historical Society; Lane, *Glimpses,* v. XVIII, p. 412; Sommers, op. cit., v. IV, pp. 946–50.

4. Wainwright, *Diary,* Sept. 30, 1864, HHL; *OR,* v. XLII, pt. 1, pp. 66–67, and pt. 2, pp. 1,121, 1,135; Wainwright, *Report,* Nov. 5, 1864, box 11, HJH Papers, LC; Sommers, op. cit., v. IV, p. 950.

5. *OR,* v. XLII, pt. 2, p. 1,121.

6. This message evidently reached Birchett's at 10:35 P.M. Ibid.; Grant to Meade, 10:35 P.M., Sept. 30, 1864, RG 94, entry 731, box 63, NA.

7. It is not clear whether Williams also forwarded to City Point either Hancock's report of 5:30 P.M. that he could detect no weakening in Johnson's line or miscellaneous intelligence reports throughout the day of stragglers and wagons heading north through Chesterfield toward Richmond. Wainwright, *Diary,* Sept. 30, 1864, HHL; *OR,* v. XLII, pt. 2, pp. 1,120–22, 1,145; RG 94, entry 731, box 51, Scott to Caldwell, 10:00 A.M., and Meade to Williams, 9:30 P.M., Sept. 30, 1864, and box 63, Holman to Fisher, 10:00 A.M., and Grant to Meade, 10:35 P.M., Sept. 30, 1864, NA; RG 111, entry 13, v. XLIV, p. 171, NA; Sommers, op. cit., v. IV, pp. 950–52.

8. Meade left Globe Tavern shortly after 9:30 P.M. Lyman, *Diary,* Sept. 30, 1864, MSHS; Wainwright, *Diary,* Sept. 30, 1864, HHL; Agassiz, op. cit., pp. 231, 237; *OR,* v. XLII, pt. 2, pp. 1,120–22, 1,128–29, 1,133,

1,138, 1,143–45, and pt. 3, pp. 4–5, 17, 25–26, 31–32; RG 393, AP, v. VI, bk. 6, p. 517, NA; Andrew A. Humphreys to his wife, Oct. 1, 1864, AAH Coll., HSP; RG 391, 5AC, v. V, pt. 3, Butler to Grant, 11:30 P.M., Sept. 30, 1864, and pt. 4, Grant to Meade, 3:00 A.M., Oct. 1, 1864, NA; RG 94, entry 731, box 51, Meade to Williams, 9:30 P.M., and Grant to Meade, received 10:00 P.M., Sept. 30, 1864, and box 57, Humphreys to Hancock, 11:50 P.M., Sept. 30, 1864, NA; Sommers, op. cit., v. IV, pp. 952–53.

9. *OR,* v. XLII, pt. 1, p. 898, and pt. 2, pp. 1,128–29, 1,306–7, and pt. 3, pp. 11–12, 14, 17, 39–40; Russell, *Diary,* Oct. 1, 1864, DU; Charles Baughman to his father, Oct. 1, 1864, Baughman Papers, CM; Sale, *Diary,* Sept. 30, 1864, VSL; Lobrano, *Diary,* Sept. 30, 1864, TU; Eldridge, *Diary,* Sept. 30, 1864, CNHS; Hunt, *Journal,* p. 130, HJH Papers, LC; RG 391, 6AC, v. XC, bk. 199, p. 54, NA; *AG-Vt-1864/65,* p. 48; RG 391, CC, v. XXVI, bk. 51, pp. 84–95, NA; RG 393, AP, container 38-30-6-4015, Robison to Smith, Oct. 5, 1864, NA; RG 94, entry 731, box 51, Morgan to Miles, and Pierce to Mitchell, Sept. 30, 1864, and box 57, Humphreys to Hancock, 12:04 A.M., Oct. 1, 1864, NA; Sommers, op. cit., v. IV, pp. 953–56.

10. Before leaving Pegram's, soldiers of the 16th Michigan prowled among the litter of battle to pick up rifles more serviceable than their now discredited Lindsay guns. Lyman, *Diary,* Sept. 30, 1864, MSHS; Wainwright, *Diary,* Sept. 30, 1864, HHL; *OR,* v. XLII, pt. 1, pp. 59, 66–67, 139, 143, 554, 558, 562, 566, 571–75, 588, and pt. 2, pp. 1,132, 1,137, and pt. 3, p. 25; Wilcox, *Report,* p. 64, LHQ Coll., VHS; Robertson, op. cit., p. 184; *118th Pennsylvania,* pp. 520–21; Jones, *Diary,* Sept. 30, 1864, CWTI Coll., MHRC; Pierce, op. cit., pp. 51, 59; Jackman, op. cit., p. 337; Lord, op. cit., p. 525; Lewiston *Evening Journal,* Oct. 15, 1864; Nash, op. cit., p. 211; Judson, op. cit., p. 109; Allen et al., op. cit., p. 323; *AG-Vt-Revised Roster,* p. 573; Strong, op. cit., p. 85; "Returns of K/56th and F/121st Pennsylvania, S-O, 1864," RG 94, M594, NA; Sommers, op. cit., v. IV, pp. 956–57.

11. RG 391, 5AC, v. XVII, bk. 69, p. 450, NA.

12. Before going on picket, the 12th U.S. held Otis' line between the fort and the 14th, while the 10th was in reserve. Once the two Regular regiments went on outpost duty, the 12th relieved the 1st Maryland. Even so, Graham continued providing his own pickets for the rightmost sector, likely a composite detail, not an organic regiment. Ibid.; *OR,* v. XLII, pt. 1, pp. 61–62, 478, 481, 553–54, 558, 561–63, 566, 571–75, 579, 588, 599–605, and pt. 2, pp. 1,132–33, 1,135, 1,137; Jones, *Diary,* Oct. 1, 1864, CWTI Coll., MHRC; Wainwright, *Diary,* Oct. 1 and 5, 1864, HHL; Wainwright, *Report,* Nov. 5, 1864, box 11, HJH Papers, LC; RG 391, 9AC, v. LXVI, bk. 232, Sept. 30, 1864, NA; "Returns of the Third Brigade, First Division, 5th Corps, Sept. 30, 1864," RG 94, entry 65, 5AC, NA; *118th Pennsylvania,* p. 525; Judson, op. cit., p. 109; Robertson, op. cit., p. 184; Woodward, op. cit., p. 15; Bates, *Pennsylvania Volunteers,* v. V, p. 79; Allen et al., op. cit., p. 323; Charles, *Memoirs,* pp. 21–22, Boyer Coll., MHRC; Camper et al., op. cit., pp. 176–77; Eyre, *Diary,* Oct. 7, 1864, Casebier mss.; "Returns of

C/11th and B-D-E-F/14th and A/17th U.S., and of the 5th New York, S-O, 1864," RG 94, entry 53 and M594, respectively, NA; Henry Gawthorp, letter of Oct. 6, 1864, Gawthorp Papers, HSD; Mary Brainard, *146th New York,* p. 245; Charles LaMotte to Annie, Oct. 4, 1864, LaMotte Papers, DPAC; Sommers, op. cit., v. IV, pp. 957–60.

13. The 143rd Pennsylvania held the left of Bragg's main line. The 15th New York Battery may have been on that regiment's sector. *OR,* v. XLII, pt. 1, p. 67, and pt. 2, pp. 1,132, 1,135, and pt. 3, p. 24; Irvin, *Diary,* Oct. 1, 1864, HSP; O. B. Curtis, *24th Michigan,* p. 276; Wainwright, *Diary,* Oct. 1, 1864, HHL; Perry, *Diary,* Oct. 1, 1864, WHS; Edmund L. Dana to friend, "Sept." 5, 1864, and *Diary,* Oct. 1, 1864, Dana Papers, WHGS; Sommers, op. cit., v. IV, pp. 960–61.

14. Whether or not the 2/38th actually reported to Crawford during its brief stay in his sector is not clear. Even more in doubt is the identity of the two New York companies that remained at City Point. Although one provost officer there indicated that they were part of a New York regiment just being organized, at least one of them is thought to have been a large detachment of recruits for the 1st New York Light Artillery, just arrived from Elmira via Baltimore. Sending those men to the war zone was a mistake; by October 10 they were in Washington, assigned to Battery K. The other company may have comparably been a makeshift grouping of recruits, not an organic company at all. Other, less likely possibilities include A/188th New York, K/189th New York, Bevines' New York Company (soon to become A/80th New York), or the vanguard of the 186th New York, although no evidence has been found that any of those units arrived that early. *OR,* v. XLII, pt. 1, p. 558, and pt. 2, pp. 1,121, 1,125, 1,135–36, and pt. 3, p. 22; Pierce, op. cit., pp. 58–59; RG 393, AP, v. VI, bk. 6, pp. 502–3, 514–17, and v. LV, bk. 119, p. 225, and box 1, Leslie to Patrick, Sept. 30, 1864, and container 38-30-6-4035, Dallas to Williams, Oct. 5, 1864, and box 3, morning report of Benham's command, Oct. 5–6, 1864, NA; RG 94, entry 731, box 51, Williams to Sharpe, 10:20–11:20 P.M., Sept. 29, 1864, and Williams to Meade, 3:45–4:44 P.M. and 6:15–6:40 P.M., and Meade to Williams, 5:13–6:10 P.M., and Williams to Ingalls, 6:10–6:30 P.M., and Ingalls to Williams, ca. 9:00 P.M., and Pierce to Mitchell and to Parke, Sept. 30, 1864, and box 63, Sharpe to Williams, received 10:10 P.M., Sept. 29, 1864, NA; Perry, *Diary,* Oct. 1, 1864, WHS; Clarence Johnson, letters of Sept. 28–29 and Oct. 5 and 10, 1864, Johnson Papers, CWTI Coll., MHRC; Sommers, op. cit., v. IV, pp. 961–63.

15. Bradds, loc. cit., Apr. 8, 1926; A. Wentz, "Closing Days," *NT,* Feb. 11, 1904; W. H. Sanderson to Mr. Talmage, March 8, 1911, Sanderson-Talmage Papers, Petersburg National Battlefield Park; Charles LaMotte to Annie, Oct. 4, 1864, LaMotte Papers, DPAC; Wainwright, *Diary,* Sept. 30, 1864, HHL; *118th Pennsylvania,* pp. 523–24; *OR,* v. XLII, pt. 1, p. 584, and pt. 3, pp. 12, 16, 26; Henry Gawthorp, letter of Oct. 6, 1864, Gawthorp Papers, HSD; Eyre, *Diary,* Oct. 7, 1864, Casebier mss.; Cushman, op. cit., pp. 18–19; S. B. Hinckley, "58th Mass.," *NT,* May 20, 1915; Pope, *Diary,* Sept. 30–Oct. 1, 1864, CWTI Coll., MHRC; *AG-Mass-1865,*

p. 480; William Lamont to his sister, Oct. 2, 1864, WHS; Sommers, op. cit., v. IV, pp. 963–64.

16. Considerable discrepancy exists in estimates of Northern strength. Subtracting Friday's casualties from the estimated strength that morning should leave 17,384 men in the field. Of these, 6,751 should belong to Willcox and Potter. Yet their returns, Saturday morning, list only 5,150 effectives. Some of the 1,600 unaccounted for may have been stragglers, others men present for duty not considered effective. *OR*, v. XLII, pt. 2, pp. 1,132, 1,138, and pt. 3, pp. 17–19, 25; RG 391, 9AC, v. XVI, bk. 80, Bertolette to Youngman, Oct. 1, 1864, and v. LXIX, bk. 163, Oct. 1, 1864, and v. LXVIII, bk. 102, Oct. 1–3, 1864, NA; Wainwright, *Diary*, Sept. 30, 1864, HHL; *AG-Maine-1864/65*, v. I, p. 293; *History*, p. 119, 9th New Hampshire Coll., NHHS; Rutland *Weekly Herald*, Oct. 13, 1864; Windsor *Vermont Journal*, Oct. 15, 1864; RG 94, entry 12, 1864 file, No. S1946, and entry 731, box 57, Humphreys to Warren, 12:15–12:20 A.M., Oct. 1, 1864, and box 63, Humphreys to Parke, 11:50 P.M., Sept. 30–5:00 A.M., Oct. 1, 1864, NA; Sommers, op. cit., v. IV, pp. 964–65.

17. Just where Dunovant's peregrinations took him prior to his fight with Davies near dark is not known. *OR*, v. XLII, pt. 1, pp. 84, 87, 89, 90, 92, 94, 96, 620, 635, 947–48, and pt. 2, pp. 1,121, 1,140–41; Waring, *Diary*, Sept. 30 and Oct. 4, 1864, SHC; Eckert to Smith, Sept. 30, 1864, RG 393, AP, container 38-30-6-4016, NA; Rappalyea, *Diary*, Sept. 30, 1864, NJHS; "Return of Staff/10th New York Cavalry, S-O, 1864," RG 94, M594, NA; RG 94, entry 12, 1864 file, No. B1379, NA; Preston, op. cit., p. 228; "Return of F/20th Georgia Cavalry Battalion, S-O, 1864," RG 109, ch. 1, entry 18, NA; RG 109, entry 15, Nos. 3- and 4- and 5-P-24, NA; Gilbert J. Wright to his wife, Oct. 6, 1864, Wright Papers, VHS; Brooks, *Butler*, pp. 196, 325, 344–46; Charleston *Mercury*, Oct. 29, 1864; Clark, *Diary*, Sept. 30, 1864, NYPL; Orrin Ellis, *Diary*, Sept. 30, 1864, CWTI Coll., MHRC; Sommers, op. cit., v. IV, pp. 965–69.

18. Brooks, *Butler*, p. 325.

19. Ibid., pp. 326, 345; Preston, op. cit., p. 229; *OR*, v. XLII, pt. 1, p. 635.

20. Preston, op. cit., pp. 228–29; Robert VanFossen, "Davis' Farm," *48th Reunion of 6th Ohio Cavalry*, pp. 42–43; New York *Herald*, Oct. 5, 1864; RG 94, entry 160, v. XI, p. 731, and entry 12, 1864 file, No. B1379, NA; *OR*, v. XLII, pt. 1, pp. 84, 143, 620, 635, and pt. 2, pp. 1,140–41, and pt. 3, p. 27; Rappalyea, *Diary*, Sept. 30, 1864, NJHS; Brooks, *Butler*, pp. 196, 325–27, 338, 344–47, 361; Bushnell, *History*, pp. 312–13, Palmer Coll., WRHS; RG 391, CC, v. XXII, bk. 34, pp. 94–95, NA; Adelia Dunovant, "John Dunovant," *CV*, v. XVI, p. 184; Eckert to Smith, Sept. 30, 1864, RG 393, AP, container 38-30-6-4016, NA; Henry Pyne, *Ride to War* (1961 ed.), p. 247; Sommers, op. cit., v. IV, pp. 969–73.

21. RG 94, entry 12, 1864 file, No. B1379, NA; *OR*, v. XLII, pt. 1, pp. 89–90, 92, 94, 96, 619–20, and pt. 2, pp. 1,141–42, and pt. 3, p. 27; Merrill, op. cit., p. 287; Sommers, op. cit., v. IV, pp. 973–74.

CHAPTER XII

1. Lane's regiments deployed in the same relative order as on Friday. McGowan's deployment is uncertain. Also unknown is whether Joel Griffin took position next to Davis' left or Barringer's right. *OR*, v. XLII, pt. 1, pp. 478, 942, 948, and pt. 3, pp. 9, 21–22; Mullen, *Diary*, Oct. 1, 1864, CM; "Return of H/4th North Carolina Cavalry, Apr.–Sept. 1864," RG 109, ch. 1, entry 18, NA; RG 109, entry 199, box 282, NA; Goldsborough, op. cit., pp. 140–41; Heth, *Report*, Dec. 7, 1864, Heth Papers, CM; Caldwell, op. cit., p. 185; Wilcox, *Report*, pp. 65–67, LHQ Coll., VHS; Harris, op. cit., p. 57; Folder 82, Lane Papers, AU; Lane, *Lane's Brigade*, v. IX, p. 356; Wilcox, loc. cit., v. IX, No. 4, p. 69; Willis, *Diary*, Oct. 1, 1864, VSL; Gordon, *Diary*, Oct. 1, 1864, SHC; McGregor, *Report*, Dec. 7, 1864, Halsey Papers, SHC; Carruth et al., op. cit., p. 300; Pope, *Diary*, Oct. 1, 1864, CWTI Coll., MHRC; Sommers, op. cit., v. IV, pp. 987–90.

2. Curtin posted the trustworthy 7th Rhode Island right behind the unreliable 35th with orders to be on guard against the danger that the Massachusetts men might flee again if attacked. *OR*, v. XLII, pt. 1, pp. 554, 558, 563, 566, 571–75, 599–605, and pt. 3, pp. 9, 18–21, 25–26; RG 391, 9AC, v. LXVI, bk. 232, Oct. 1, 1864, NA; Jones, *Diary*, Oct. 2, 1864, CWTI Coll., MHRC; Sommers, op. cit., v. IV, pp. 990–91.

3. Battery D is thought to have joined Ayres at this time rather than during the main attack at 9:00 A.M. "Returns of A-F/12th and Staff-A/1/17th U.S., S-O and Oct., 1864," RG 94, entries 53 and 66, respectively, NA; J. K. Wilkerson to his father, Oct. 6, 1864, Wilkerson Papers, DU; *OR*, v. XLII, pt. 1, pp. 61–62, 140, 478, 481, 566, 859, 942, and pt. 3, pp. 18, 21; Goldsborough, op. cit., p. 141; R. S. Webb to his mother, Oct. 6, 1864, Webb-Moore Papers, SHC; Cavaness, *Diary*, Oct. 1, 1864, TXU; Clark, *NC*, v. II, p. 448; Jesse Frank to his mother, Oct. 5, 1864, Frank Papers, DU; Mullen, *Diary*, Oct. 1, 1864, CM; "Returns of B/46th and H/48th North Carolina, S-O, 1864," RG 109, ch. 1, entry 18, NA; H. M. Wagstaff, ed., "Graham," *Sprunt Studies*, v. XX, p. 193; RG 391, 5AC, v. XVII, bk. 69, p. 450, NA; Charles LaMotte to his mother and Annie, Oct. 3 and 4, 1864, LaMotte Papers, DPAC; Wilcox, *Report*, p. 67, LHQ Coll., VHS; Rochester *Daily Union & Advertiser*, Oct. 15, 1864; Lane, *Glimpses*, v. XVIII, p. 413; Heth, *Report*, Dec. 7, 1864, Heth Papers, CM; Wainwright, *Report*, Nov. 5, 1864, box 11, HJH Papers, LC; Wainwright, *Diary*, Oct. 1, 1864, HHL; RG 94, entry 160, v. VII, p. 344, NA; Sommers, op. cit., v. IV, pp. 991–94.

4. The 142nd Pennsylvania, serving just right of the 121st, evidently was among the units that fled precipitously, since it lost no prisoners. Despite the 121st's heavy losses, its flag escaped capture, but just barely. Fort Archer, in contrast, was hardly in such danger of imminent capture. Wooten's claim that the redoubt was virtually within his grasp and would have fallen, had not Brander's fire caused him to pull back, is not convincing. Wilcox, *Report*, p. 67, LHQ Coll., VHS; Bryan, *Diary*, Oct. 1, 1864, Bryan

Family Papers, SHC; Folder 82, Lane Papers, AU; Lane, *Glimpses,* v. XVIII, p. 412, and *Lane's Brigade,* v. IX, p. 356, and *Sharpshooters,* v. XXVIII, p. 4; Willie Pegram to Mary, Oct. 5, 1864, PJM Coll., VHS; Dunlop, op. cit., p. 213; *OR,* v. XLII, pt. 1, pp. 59, 67, 75, 139–42, 546–47, 554, 566, 588–89, and pt. 3, pp. 18, 25, 479–80; Pierce, op. cit., p. 59; Strong, op. cit., pp. 85–86; Lord, op. cit., p. 528; Wilcox, loc. cit., v. IX, No. 4, p. 70; Caldwell, op. cit., p. 185; N. Ingraham Hasell, "Incident," *CV,* v. XX, p. 159; RG 391, 5AC, v. XII, bk. 44, p. 42, NA; Lewiston *Evening Journal,* Oct. 15, 1864; RG 391, 9AC, v. LIV, bk. 194, p. 159, NA; Philadelphia *Evening Bulletin,* Oct. 6, 1864; Clark, *NC,* v. II, p. 669; *AG-Vt-Revised Roster,* p. 573; Sommers, op. cit., v. IV, pp. 994–96.

5. Monroe's six guns fired forty-four rounds. The other eighteen pieces covering the northwestern front did not go into action. *OR,* v. XLII, pt. 1, pp. 67, 554, 566, 599–605, and pt. 3, p. 18; RG 391, 9AC, v. LXVI, bk. 232, Oct. 1, 1864, NA; Wainwright, *Report,* Nov. 5, 1864, box 11, HJH Papers, LC; Pope, *Diary,* Oct. 1, 1864, CWTI Coll., MHRC; Lane, *Lane's Brigade,* v. IX, p. 356; Wilcox, *Autobiography,* p. 105, Wilcox Papers, LC; Sommers, op. cit., v. IV, pp. 996–97.

6. Humphreys did not receive this message until 11:00 A.M. *OR,* v. XLII, pt. 3, pp. 27–28; Meade, *Letters Received,* v. VII, pp. 17–18, GGM Coll., HSP.

7. *OR,* v. XLII, pt. 1, pp. 84, 89–90, 92, 94, 96–97, 620, 635, and pt. 3, pp. 25, 27–28, 46; VanFossen, loc. cit., p. 43; RG 94, entry 12, 1864 file, No. B1563, NA; Gordon, *Diary,* Oct. 1, 1864, SHC; Pyne, op. cit., pp. 245–48; Waring, *Diary,* Sept. 30–Oct. 1, 1864, SHC; E. C. Anderson, Jr., to his mother, Oct. 9, 1864, Wayne-Stites-Anderson Papers, Georgia Historical Society; Gilbert Wright to his wife, Oct. 6, 1864, Wright Papers, VHS; "Return of F/20th Georgia Cavalry Battalion, S-O, 1864," RG 109, ch. 1, entry 18, NA; Merrill, op. cit., p. 287; Clark, *Diary,* Oct. 1, 1864, NYPL; Tobie, op. cit., p. 689; Brooks, op. cit., pp. 327, 331, 334; Sommers, op. cit., v. IV, pp. 997, 1,069.

8. Charles LaMotte to his mother and Annie, Oct. 3 and 4, 1864, LaMotte Papers, DPAC.

9. R. S. Webb to his sister and mother, Oct. 3 and 6, 1864, Webb-Moore Papers, SHC.

10. RG 109, entry 12, 1864 file, No. V462, NA.

11. J. K. Wilkerson to his father, Oct. 6, 1864, Wilkerson Papers, DU.

12. Pegram, in the thick of the fray as usual, was slightly wounded in the leg but did not leave the field. Ibid.; Heth, *Report,* Dec. 7, 1864, Heth Papers, CM; Fayetteville *Observer,* Nov. 17, 1864; Warren to Humphreys, 8:00 A.M., Oct. 1, 1864, *Letterbooks,* v. XIX, GKW Coll., NYSL; Meade, *Letters Received,* v. VII, p. 16, GGM Coll., HSP; *OR,* v. XLII, pt. 1, pp. 56, 478, 566, 942, and pt. 3, pp. 5, 18, 21, 25; George Merryweather, letter of Nov. 9, 1864, Merryweather Papers, CHHS; Wainwright, *Report,* Nov. 5, 1864, box 11, HJH Papers, LC; Wainwright, *Diary,* Oct. 1, 1864, HHL; *ANJ,* v. II, p. 98; Wilcox, *Report,* p. 67, LHQ Coll., VHS; Wilcox, *Autobiography,* p. 105, Wilcox Papers, LC; R. S. Webb to his sister and mother,

Oct. 3 and 6, 1864, Webb-Moore Papers, SHC; Hopkins, op. cit., p. 217; "CSR of Arthur Grimshaw, 4th Delaware," RG 94, entry 519, NA; Charles LaMotte to his mother and Annie, Oct. 3 and 4, 1864, LaMotte Papers, DPAC; Eyre, *Diary,* Oct. 7, 1864, Casebier mss.; RG 109, entry 12, 1864 file, No. V462, NA; Goldsborough, op. cit., p. 141; Cavaness, *Diary,* Oct. 1, 1864, TXU; RG 391, 5AC, v. XVII, bk. 69, p. 450, NA; G. W. Beale to his mother, Oct. 10, 1864, Beale Family Papers, UV; "Returns of Staff/2nd Maryland Battalion and B/46th and H/48th North Carolina, S-O, 1864," RG 109, ch. 1, entry 18, NA; Richmond *Dispatch,* Oct. 10, 1864; Richmond *Enquirer,* Oct. 14 and 19, 1864; Sam Brooke to his sister, Oct. 4, 1864, Binckley Papers, LC; John Johnson, *University Sketches,* p. 673; Hotchkiss, op. cit., v. III, p. 973; Richmond *Sentinel,* Oct. 15, 1864; "Return of B/14th U.S., S-O, 1864," RG 94, entry 53, NA; RG 109, entry 199, boxes 261–62, 282, NA; Mullen, *Diary,* Oct. 1, 1864, CM; Willie Pegram to Mary, Oct. 5, 1864, PJM Coll., VHS; Jesse Frank to his mother, Oct. 5, 1864, Frank Papers, DU; Clark, *NC,* v. II, p. 448; Sommers, op. cit., v. IV, pp. 997–1,003.

13. *OR,* v. XLII, pt. 1, pp. 61, 478, 481, and pt. 3, pp. 9, 18, 22; RG 391, 5AC, v. XI, bk. 39, p. 361, NA; Camper et al., op. cit., p. 177; Charles LaMotte to Annie, Oct. 4, 1864, LaMotte Papers, DPAC; "Return of H/48th North Carolina, S-O, 1864," RG 109, ch. 1, entry 18, NA; Sommers, op. cit., v. IV, pp. 1,002–4.

14. Of Ayres's estimated 124 casualties, approximately 80 per cent occurred in the First Brigade. Two thirds of its loss, in turn, was suffered by the four regiments on the skirmish line. *OR,* v. XLII, pt. 1, pp. 61, 139–40, 481; RG 391, 5AC, v. XXXIX, bk. 206, Oct. 1–3, 1864, NA; Rochester *Daily Union & Advertiser,* Oct. 15, 1864; RG 391, 9AC, v. LIV, bk. 194, p. 159, NA; Camper et al., op. cit., p. 177; Sommers, op. cit., pp. 1,004, 1,345–56.

15. Preston, op. cit., pp. 228–30; Pyne, op. cit., pp. 247–48; *OR,* v. XLII, pt. 1, pp. 84, 85, 635–36, and pt. 3, p. 28; RG 94, entry 12, 1864 file, No. B1563, NA; Sommers, op. cit., v. IV, p. 1,070.

16. RG 77, entry 161, box 136, bk. 13-4-51-13, No. 8, NA; Sommers, op. cit., pp. 1,070–71, 1,392–98.

17. Brooks, op. cit., p. 327.

18. Beaumont's men evidently brought up the First Brigade's rear. Whether they arrived in time to go into reserve before it attacked is not clear. Ibid., pp. 197, 327–30; Preston, op. cit., p. 231; VanFossen, loc. cit., p. 43; Pyne, op. cit., p. 248; *OR,* v. XLII, pt. 1, pp. 89, 90, 92, 620, 635, and pt. 3, pp. 28–29; Merrill, op. cit., p. 287; Gregg, letter of Jan. 17, 1865, RG 94, entry 731, box 73, NA; Dunovant, loc. cit., v. XVI, p. 184; Sommers, op. cit., v. IV, pp. 1,071–72.

19. Preston, op. cit., p. 231.

20. RG 94, entry 12, 1864 file, No. B1563, NA.

21. Brooks, op. cit., p. 330.

22. At least one squadron of the 6th Ohio Cavalry secured the 10th's northern flank west of the swamp. The other ten companies may have been

there, too. If not, they probably served with the 1st on the right bank. Ibid.; Preston, op. cit., p. 231; *OR*, v. XLII, pt. 1, pp. 97, 620, 635, 948; Bushnell, *History*, p. 313, Palmer Coll., WRHS; RG 94, entry 160, v. XI, pp. 733–35, and entry 12, 1864 file, No. B1563, NA; Pyne, op. cit., pp. 248–49; Dunovant, loc. cit., v. XVI, p. 184; McGregor, *Report*, Dec. 7, 1864, Halsey Papers, SHC; New York *Herald*, Oct. 5, 1864; Gregg to Dyer, Nov. 8, 1864, RG 391, CC, v. XXI, bk. 31, NA; Sommers, op. cit., v. IV, pp. 1,071–74.

23. *OR*, v. XLII, pt. 1, pp. 89, 90, 92, 94, 620, and pt. 2, p. 1,108, and pt. 3, pp. 28–29; Waring, *Diary*, Sept. 30–Oct. 1, 1864, SHC; Ellis, *Diary*, Oct. 1, 1864, CWTI Coll., MHRC; Sommers, op. cit., v. IV, pp. 1,074–75.

24. *OR*, v. XLII, pt. 3, p. 28.

25. In late afternoon, Gregg's headquarters were one-quarter mile west of Wyatt's house. Ibid., pp. 26–29, and pt. 1, p. 620; Youngman to Gregg, Oct. 1, 1864, RG 393, AP, container 38-30-6-4010, NA; RG 391, 9AC, v. XVIII, bk. 34, p. 131, NA; Lyman to his wife, Oct. 5, 1864, and *Diary*, Oct. 1, 1864, Lyman Papers, MSHS; Pyne, op. cit., p. 248; Sommers, op. cit., v. IV, pp. 1,075–76; Paine, *Diary*, Oct. 1, 1864, dePeyster Papers, ISHL.

26. What time the 9th and the 13th left the Third Cavalry Division to reinforce Butler is not clear. A soldier of the 9th says he left the trenches, preparatory to moving, at 11:00 A.M. The Cavalry Corps Chief-of-Staff, however, implies that Hampton did not even propose the move until several hours later. *OR*, v. XLII, pt. 1, pp. 84–85, 97, 620, 948; H. B. McClellan to Ellen Fontaine, Oct. 6, 1864, VHS; Willis, *Diary*, Oct. 1, 1864, VSL; Beale, op. cit., p. 146; Brooks, op. cit., pp. 197, 330–31; Dunovant, loc. cit., v. XVI, pp. 183–84; Preston, op. cit., pp. 228, 231; Bushnell, *History*, p. 313, Palmer Coll., WRHS; RG 94, entry 160, v. XI, p. 735, NA; Sommers, op. cit., v. IV, pp. 1,076–78.

27. The orderly's version, in Brooks, op. cit., p. 331, is accepted because, as he put it, the encounter "(being the first time I had ever heard generals discussing a movement on a battlefield) deeply impressed me." Butler's own milder version, doubtless mellowed for the old soldiers to whom he recounted it, is reprinted in Dunovant, loc. cit., v. XVI, pp. 183–84.

28. Beaumont's boast that one of his sergeants shot Dunovant brought the enlisted man the Medal of Honor. Historical perspective, however, raises grave doubts about the claim, which appears as yet another fabrication of the major, made up to glorify himself. Equally farfetched is the statement by a trooper of the 7th Georgia Cavalry that Butler, Young, Dunovant, and Fontaine were all drunk that afternoon. His line of "reasoning" follows: "Dr. Fontaine, the Medical Director of the Cav. Corps, who was killed, was also intoxicated, for had he been sober and attending to his duties, he would have been entirely out of all danger." Brooks, op. cit., pp. 197, 331–37; Dunovant, loc. cit., v. XVI, pp. 183–84; H. B. McClellan to Ellen Fontaine, Oct. 6, 1864, VHS; Preston, op. cit., pp. 229–31; *OR*, v. XLII, pt. 1, pp. 635–36, and pt. 3, p. 1,133; RG 94, entry 12, 1864 file, No. B1563, NA; Wells, op. cit., pp. 321–22; Wade Hampton to Mary Fisher Hampton, Oct.

5, 1864, Hampton Papers, SCL; Waring, *Diary,* Oct. 2, 1864, SHC; Bob Saussy to Rad, Oct. 23, 1864, Saussy Papers, DU; Sommers, op. cit., v. IV, pp. 1,078–81.

29. Brooks, op. cit., p. 197.

30. Ibid., p. 332.

31. Which part of Butler's sector Farley held remains unclear. Ibid., pp. 197, 332–36, 548; RG 94, entry 12, 1864 file, No. B1563, NA; Mullen, *Diary,* Oct. 1, 1864, CM; Preston, op. cit., pp. 228–31; Pyne, op. cit., p. 249; Rappalyea, *Diary,* Oct. 1, 1864, NJHS; *OR,* v. XLII, pt. 1, pp. 620, 948, and pt. 3, pp. 7, 26, 29; Willis, *Diary,* Oct. 1, 1864, VSL; "CSR of Hugh Aiken, 6th South Carolina Cavalry," RG 109, CSR, NA; RG 109, ch. 1, v. LXV, No. A1077, and v. CLXII, p. 40, and entry 15, No. 5-P-24, NA; Gordon, *Diary,* Oct. 2, 1864, SHC; Clark, *NC,* v. I, p. 436, and v. III, p. 627; RG 391, CC, v. XXII, bk. 34, pp. 94–95, NA; "Returns of H/4th North Carolina Cavalry, Apr.–Sept., 1864, and H/1st North Carolina Cavalry and C/8th Georgia Cavalry, S-O, 1864," RG 109, ch. 1, entry 18, NA; Foard, op. cit., p. 6, NCDAH; Richmond *Enquirer,* Oct. 7, 1864; New York *Herald,* Oct. 5, 1864; Sommers, op. cit., v. IV, pp. 1,081–84.

32. Willis, *Diary,* Oct. 1, 1864, VSL.

33. Ibid.

34. A wartime Richmond newspaper and postwar accounts by the colonel of the 9th and by Gregg's Chief-of-Staff indicate that the Federals captured two companies of Virginians, fifty to sixty strong, during this battle. The capture probably occurred during the counterattack if it took place at all. Wartime reports by Gregg's medical officer and provost marshal do not note this sizable seizure but assert that only three prisoners were taken all day, two of whom may have been captured near Hawks's, not McDowell's. Ibid.; RG 94, entry 12, 1864 file, No. B1563, and entry 160, v. XI, pp. 735–37, NA; Preston, op. cit., pp. 229–31; *OR,* v. XLII, pt. 1, pp. 620, 635–36, and pt. 3, p. 29; Brooks, op. cit., pp. 333–34; Pyne, op. cit., pp. 248–49; Merrill, op. cit., p. 287; New York *Herald,* Oct. 5, 1864; RG 391, CC, v. XXI, bk. 31, Gregg to Dyer, Nov. 8, 1864, and v. XXII, bk. 34, pp. 94–95, and v. XXXII, bk. 75, pp. 45–47, NA; Lyman Tremain, *Frederick Lyman Tremain,* p. 77; G. W. Beale to his mother, Oct. 10, 1864, Beale Family Papers, UV; Richmond *Sentinel,* Oct. 3, 1864; Beale, op. cit., p. 146; Rea, op. cit., p. 100; Sommers, op. cit., v. IV, pp. 1,084–87.

35. *OR,* v. XLII, pt. 1, p. 636.

36. Brooks, op. cit., p. 437.

37. Hampton Thomas, "Reminiscences," *The United Service,* s. 2, v. I, p. 20.

38. The 9th Virginia Cavalry was recalled on account of the reported threat to Young's rear. Whether that regiment was actually sent to help meet that danger is not clear, though. Ibid.; E. C. Anderson, Jr., to his mother, Oct. 9, 1864, Wayne-Stites-Anderson Papers, Georgia Historical Society; *OR,* v. XLII, pt. 1, pp. 636, 948; Pyne, op. cit., pp. 248–49; Brooks, op. cit., p. 437; Waring, *Diary,* Oct. 2, 1864, SHC; Holland, op. cit., p. 93; Preston, op. cit., p. 231; Willis, *Diary,* Oct. 1, 1864, VSL; Sommers, op. cit., v. IV, pp. 1,087–89.

39. Brooks, op. cit., pp. 197, 334–35; Willis, *Diary,* Oct. 1, 1864, VSL; *OR,* v. XLII, pt. 1, pp. 85, 620, 948; Preston, op. cit., pp. 230–31; Pyne, op. cit., p. 248; RG 94, entry 12, 1864 file, No. B1563, and entry 160, v. XI, pp. 735–37, NA; Sommers, op. cit., v. IV, p. 1,089.

40. Among the Northern casualties was Gregg's Chief-of-Staff, Captain Henry C. Weir, severely wounded. *OR,* v. XLII, pt. 1, pp. 97, 142, 620, 635–36, and pt. 3, p. 64; Pyne, op. cit., p. 249; New York *Herald,* Oct. 5, 1864; Tobie, op. cit., p. 689; Rea, op. cit., p. 100; Charleston *Courier,* Oct. 12, 1864; Charleston *Mercury,* Oct. 12 and Nov. 5, 1864; *Roll of Graham's Battery,* CM; Willis, *Diary,* Oct. 1, 1864, VSL; Dick Beale to his mother, Oct. 2, 1864, Beale Family Papers, UV; Beale, op. cit., p. 146; Richmond *Examiner,* Oct. 7, 1864; Preston, op. cit., pp. 229–30; RG 94, entry 12, 1864 file, No. B1563, and entry 160, v. XI, pp. 735–37, NA; Sommers, op. cit., v. IV, pp. 1,089–90.

41. *OR,* v. XLII, pt. 3, p. 13.

CHAPTER XIII

1. Richardson's fall reportedly left his battery without commissioned officers, so a successor had to be found elsewhere. Wainwright selected and promptly sent forward the experienced and capable Lieutenant James Hazelton, at the time the senior subordinate of Battery C-E/1st New York Light Artillery back in Fort Wadsworth. Dunlop, op. cit., p. 214; Wilcox, *Report,* p. 67, LHQ Coll., VHS; Caldwell, op. cit., p. 185; Lane, *Lane's Brigade,* v. IX, p. 356; Folder 82, Lane Papers, AU; Wilcox, *Autobiography,* pp. 105–6, Wilcox Papers, LC; *OR,* v. XLII, pt. 1, p. 478, and pt. 3, p. 21; R. S. Webb to his mother, Oct. 6, 1864, Webb-Moore Papers, SHC; Wainwright, *Diary,* Oct. 1, 1864, HHL; Wainwright, *Report,* Nov. 5, 1864, box 11, HJH Papers, LC; "Return of Artillery Brigade, 5th Corps, Sept. 30, 1864," RG 94, entry 65, 5AC, NA; Charles LaMotte to Annie, Oct. 4, 1864, LaMotte Papers, DPAC; Mullen, *Diary,* Oct. 1, 1864, CM; J. K. Wilkerson to his mother, Oct. 5, 1864, Wilkerson Papers, DU; Vairen, *Diary,* Oct. 2, 1864, MDAH; "Return of Staff/2nd Maryland Battalion, S-O, 1864," RG 109, ch. 1, entry 18, NA; Heth, *Report,* Dec. 7, 1864, Heth Papers, CM; Sommers, op. cit., v. IV, pp. 1,023–24.

2. *OR,* v. XLII, pt. 1, pp. 211, 571, 898, and pt. 3, pp. 6, 21, 23; Willis, *Diary,* Oct. 1, 1864, VSL; Caldwell, op. cit., p. 185; Harris, op. cit., p. 57; Bryan, *Diary,* Oct. 1, 1864, Bryan Family Papers, SHC; Lane, *Lane's Brigade,* v. IX, p. 356; Wilcox, *Report,* p. 67, LHQ Coll., VHS; Russell, *Diary,* Oct. 3, 1864, DU; Jacob Smith, letter of Oct. 11, 1864, Hutchinson Family Papers, VHS; W. J. Mosely to his parents, Oct. 2 and 5, 1864, Mosely Papers, microfilm, GDAH; Sale, *Diary,* Oct. 1–2, 1864, VSL; R. C. Mabry to his wife, Oct. 11, 1864, Mabry Papers, NCDAH; RG 108, entry 11, box 85, No. P435, NA; "Return of E/11th Alabama, S-O, 1864," RG 109, ch. 1, entry 18, NA; Sommers, op. cit., v. IX, pp. 1,024–25.

3. The 10th Georgia Battalion was among Gibson's units to skirmish with Crawford that day. The general continued directing resistance to these

probes from Globe Tavern, but his senior subordinate moved his headquarters to Aiken's sometime that afternoon. "Return of E/11th Alabama, S-O, 1864," RG 109, ch. 1, entry 18, NA; Richmond *Sentinel,* Oct. 29, 1864; W. J. Mosely to his parents, Oct. 5, 1864, Mosely Papers, microfilm, GDAH; *OR,* v. XLII, pt. 2, p. 1,122, and pt. 3, pp. 21–24; Charles Reed to his mother, Sept. 28–Oct. 1, 1864, Reed Papers, LC; Wainwright, *Diary,* Oct. 1, 1864, HHL; Hunt, *Journal,* p. 131, HJH Papers, LC; RG 393, AP, v. VI, bk. 6, pp. 521–24, NA; A. P. Smith, *76th New York,* p. 311; Eldridge, *Diary,* Oct. 1, 1864, CNHS; Hicks to Stearns and Russell, Oct. 1, 1864, RG 391, 9AC, boxes 6 and 7, respectively, NA; Sommers, op. cit., v. IV, pp. 1,025–28.

4. Wainwright's claim that Ayres retook Fort Cherry that afternoon appears unfounded and presumably refers to what happened on Sunday. *OR,* v. XLII, pt. 1, pp. 67, 478, 481, 566, 571, and pt. 3, pp. 18–26; Bates, *Pennsylvania Volunteers,* v. IV, p. 491, and v. V, p. 79; Wilcox, *Autobiography,* pp. 105–6, Wilcox Papers, LC; Meyers, op. cit., pp. 336–37; Wainwright, *Diary,* Oct. 1 and 5, 1864, HHL; Wainwright, *Report,* Nov. 5, 1864, box 11, HJH Papers, LC; RG 391, 5AC, v. XVII, bk. 69, pp. 450–51, NA; RG 94, entry 160, v. VII, p. 344, and entry 12, 1864 file, Nos. E546 and S1946, NA; Charles LaMotte to his mother and sister, Oct. 3 and 4, 1864, respectively, LaMotte Papers, DPAC; Henry Gawthorp, letter of Oct. 6, 1864, Gawthorp Papers, HSD; Eyre, *Diary,* Oct. 7, 1864, Casebier mss.; Philip Cheek, *Sauk County Riflemen,* p. 138; Thomas Chamberlin, *150th Pennsylvania,* p. 280; Edmund L. Dana to friend, "Sept." 5, 1864, and *Diary,* Oct. 1, 1864, Dana Papers, WHGS; Irvin, *Diary,* Oct. 2, 1864, HSP; McNaught, *Diary,* Sept. 30, 1864, DU; McKnight, *Diary,* Oct. 1, 1864, HSP; *AG-Mass-1864,* p. 913 and *-1865,* p. 480; Pope, *Diary,* Oct. 1, 1864, and Jones, *Diary,* Oct. 1, 1864, CWTI Coll., MHRC; Hinckley, loc. cit., May 20, 1915; Pierce, op. cit., p. 59; Joseph J. Bartlett to Joseph Howland, Oct. 21, 1864, Howland Papers, NYHS; New York *Herald,* Oct. 4, 1864; "Return of Third Brigade, First Division, 5th Corps, Oct. 31, 1864," RG 94, entry 65, 5AC, NA; Sommers, op. cit., v. IV, pp. 1,028–32.

5. Lacking a current report from Gates, except for the 43 men of VanRaden's battery, Benham had to use the last available return, which showed the colonel with 660 men. That outdated report of September 19, in fact, underrated the New Yorker's strength as of October 1 by 810 men. *OR,* v. XLII, pt. 1, p. 213, and pt. 3, pp. 4, 10; RG 393, AP, v. VI, bk. 6, pp. 524–28, and v. XXV, bk. 26, pp. 388–89, and v. LIII, bk. 121, p. 208, and v. LV, bk. 119, pp. 173–75, NA; "Return of Staff/127th USCT, S-O, 1864," RG 94, M594, NA; Sparks, op. cit., p. 426; Gates to Benham, Oct. 1, 1864, RG 94, entry 731, box 48, NA; Sommers, op. cit., v. IV, pp. 1,032–33.

6. Edie to Ashbrook and Warren, Oct. 1, 1864, RG 391, 5AC, v. V, pt. 4, NA; Meyers, op. cit., pp. 336–37; Henry Gawthorp, letter of Oct. 6, 1864, Gawthorp Papers, HSD; *OR,* v. XLII, pt. 1, p. 571, and pt. 3, pp. 21–22; Bradds, loc. cit., Apr. 8, 1926; Wentz, loc. cit., Feb. 11, 1904; Pope, *Diary,* Oct. 1, 1864, CWTI Coll., MHRC; Allen, op. cit., p. 309; Sommers, op. cit., v. IV, pp. 1,029, 1,033.

7. *OR,* v. XLII, pt. 3, pp. 18–19.

8. Ibid., p. 4.

9. Joseph J. Bartlett to Joseph Howland, Oct. 21, 1864, Howland Papers, NYHS.

10. Rood, *Memoirs,* p. 170, UCSB.

11. *OR,* v. XLII, pt. 3, p. 4.

12. Ibid., p. 5.

13. Ibid.

14. Whether or not Warren had received the attack orders of 10:00 A.M. when he wrote at 11:30 is not clear. Even if he had not, his suggestion was clearly contrary to Meade's directives ever since midnight. Ibid., p. 19.

15. Grant and Meade received further confirmation of enemy strength around Petersburg from Williams' message of 11:45 A.M. that escaped slaves reported that Hoke had left the town and that on Friday the military hospitals had been transferred to Chesterfield County. Although the Union generals did not grasp the full significance of the breakup of the hospitals, they did regard the report as sustaining their view, as opposed to Butler's, of how many Graycoats had left the Cockade City. Ibid., pp. 4–5, 8–9, 11, 18–21, 23, 25–26, 28, and pt. 1, p. 366; RG 393, AP, v. VI, bk. 6, p. 525, and container 38-30-6-4010, Youngman to Gregg, Oct. 1, 1864, NA; Meade to Grant, 10:30 A.M., Oct. 1, 1864, Meade, *Letters Sent,* v. VIII, GGM Coll., HSP; RG 108, entry 11, box 85, No. P429, NA; RG 391, 9AC, v. XVIII, bk. 34, p. 131, and Parke to Crawford, 2:00 P.M., Oct. 1, 1864, NA; Sommers, op. cit., v. IV, pp. 1,034–36.

16. *OR,* v. XLII, pt. 3, pp. 18, 22, 25–26; Lyman to his wife, Oct. 1, 1864, and *Diary,* Oct. 1, 1864, Lyman Papers, MSHS; Sommers, op. cit., v. IV, pp. 1,036–37.

17. This message reached Birchett's at 1:40 A.M. *OR,* v. XLII, pt. 3, p. 11; Hancock to Humphreys, received 1:40 A.M., Oct. 1, 1864, RG 94, entry 731, box 57, NA.

18. At 9:10 A.M., Hancock reiterated his message of 8:00 A.M. that the Third Division was in reserve. These dispatches reached Birchett's at 8:25 and 10:12. Also in reserve then were Lynch's eight hundred men. That force presumably included the two regiments sent to Shand's during the cavalry scare on Friday afternoon. The colonel's reserve, however, did not include either the 28th Massachusetts, which now entered the fortifications at last, or the little 26th Michigan, which continued guarding Cedar Level Station, where the Military Railroad left the City Point Railroad. *OR,* v. XLII, pt. 1, pp. 44–45, 52, 78–79, 344, 371, 377, 385, 387, 393, 401–4, and pt. 2, pp. 1,127–30, and pt. 3, pp. 11–16, 23, 57, 81, 83, 104; Hancock to Humphreys, received 1:40 A.M., Oct. 1, 1864, RG 94, entry 731, box 57, NA; William Child, *5th New Hampshire,* p. 284; Faulkner, *Diary,* Oct. 1, 1864, HHL; RG 393, AP, v. VI, bk. 6, p. 504, NA; "Return of Staff/28th Massachusetts and Staff/10th New York, S-O, 1864," RG 94, M594, NA; "Morning Reports of G/26th Michigan, A/61st New York, B/53rd and I/69th and H/106th and E/148th Pennsylvania, Oct. 1, 1864," RG 94, entry 115, NA; John Gibbon, *Personal Recollections,* p. 271; Detroit *Advertiser and Tribune,* Oct. 20, 1864; DeTrobriand, *Diary,* Oct. 1, 1864, WP;

Gustave Magnitzky, *Diary*, Oct. 11, 1864, 20th Massachusetts Coll., BU; RG 391, 2AC, box 21, Morgan to Hazard, 1:00 A.M., Oct. 1, 1864, and v. XX, bk. 83, pp. 340–47, and box 14, Embler to Murphy, Oct. 5, 1864, and Murphy to Embler, Oct. 6, 1864, and v. XXIII, bk. 76, pp. 288–91, and v. XL, bk. 168, No. 178, and v. I, bk. 8, pp. 433–34, and v. XLVII, bk. 229, Gilder to Welch and to Rugg and to Curtis and to Jenkins, and Egan to Embler, Oct. 1, 1864, and box 15, Gilder, order of Oct. 3, 1864, and box 18, Mott to Bingham, 7:15 A.M., Oct. 1, 1864, and misc. box 7, Pulford to TenEyck, Oct. 7, 1864, NA; Sommers, op. cit., v. IV, pp. 1,037–42.

19. *OR*, v. XLII, pt. 3, p. 8.

20. The indication that Humphreys' order of 9:30 did not reach Hancock until 10:45 is dubious, since the corps commander was familiar with its contents by 10:30. Among the units on the first train to Globe Tavern was the 110th Pennsylvania. Ibid., pp. 8, 11–13, 16, 18, 23, 26, and pt. 2, pp. 798, 899, and pt. 1, pp. 193, 344, 366, 377, 393, 401–4, and v. LI, pt. 1, p. 277; Humphreys to Hancock, received 10:45 A.M., Oct. 1, 1864, Hancock Papers, Harvard; Edwin Houghton, *17th Maine*, p. 237; James C. Hamilton, *History of 110th Pennsylvania*, p. 346, MOLLUS-War Library; RG 94, Entry 12, 1864 file, No. H1341, NA; Lyman, *Diary*, Oct. 1, 1864, MSHS; RG 391, 2AC, v. LIX, bk. 297, pp. 30–31, NA; RG 391, 9AC, v. XVIII, bk. 34, p. 131, and Parke to Crawford, 2:00 P.M., Oct. 1, 1864, NA; Regis DeTrobriand, *Four Years*, p. 651; DeTrobriand, *Diary*, Oct. 1, 1864, WP; Sommers, op. cit., v. IV, pp. 1,042–45.

21. Robison to Smith, Oct. 5, 1864, RG 393, AP, container 38-30-6-4015, NA.

22. *OR*, v. XLII, pt. 3, p. 14; Hunt to Hazard, 3:30–4:45 P.M., Oct. 1, 1864, RG 391, 2AC, misc. box 4, NA.

23. Sometime Saturday, Hazard strengthened Lynch by returning to him big Company D/4th New York Heavy Artillery to serve as infantry. To replace D in working the six mortars of the Artillery Brigade, the colonel provided little Company C of that regiment. *OR*, v. XLII, pt. 3, pp. 11, 14–15, 38–40; RG 391, 2AC, v. XIV, bk. 17, p. 473, and v. XXIII, bk. 76, pp. 286–87, and box 18, Collis to Hancock, 4:00 P.M., Oct. 1, 1864, and v. XLVII, bk. 229, Egan to Embler, Oct. 1, 1864, NA; Magnitzky, *Diary*, Oct. 11, 1864, 20th Massachusetts Coll., BU; RG 393, AP, v. VI, bk. 6, p. 525, NA; Hazard to Hunt, Oct. 1, 1864, box 10, HJH Papers, LC; Isaac Fox, *Diary*, Oct. 2, 1864, HSP; Sparks, op. cit., p. 426; Snook, *Diary*, Oct. 1, 1864, MDHS; Sommers, op. cit., v. IV, pp. 1,045–46, 1,130.

24. *OR*, v. XLII, pt. 1, pp. 344, 366, 371, 381, 393, 403, 405, 546, and pt. 3, pp. 5–7, 26; Lyman, *Diary*, Oct. 1, 1864, MSHS; DeTrobriand, *Diary*, Oct. 1, 1864, WP; RG 391, 2AC, v. LIX, bk. 297, pp. 30–31, NA; Sommers, op. cit., v. IV, pp. 1,046–48.

25. Seventy of Mott's original 300 outposts remained on the II Corps's picket line. The others who were relieved to head west overtook him about 8:00 P.M.—but whether on October 1 or 2 is not clear. "Monthly and trimonthly returns of the 2nd and 5th Corps, Sept. 30, 1864," RG 94, entry 65, 2AC and 5AC, NA; *OR*, v. XLII, pt. 1, p. 558, and pt. 3, pp. 13,

16, 17, 20, 33, 36; Hancock to Mott, received 1:00 P.M. (?), Oct. 2, 1864, RG 391, 2AC, box 20, NA; Sommers, op. cit., v. IV, pp. 1,047–48, 1,123–26; James Goodwin to his sister, Oct. 5, 1864, Goodwin Papers, Civil War Misc. Coll., MHRC.

26. At 7:00 P.M., Meade informed Grant of "Tige" Anderson's supposed presence. The Illinoisan forwarded this intelligence to Butler fifteen minutes later. *OR*, v. XLII, pt. 3, pp. 7, 19, 26–27, 31; Lyman, *Diary*, Oct. 1, 1864, MSHS; Sommers, op. cit., v. IV, p. 1,126.

27. *OR*, v. XLII, pt. 3, pp. 19–20; G. K. Warren to his wife, Oct. 1, 1864, GKW Coll., NYSL; Sommers, op. cit., v. IV, pp. 1,126–27.

28. *OR*, v. XLII, pt. 3, p. 6.

29. Ibid., pp. 6–7, 24–25; Cowdrey to Sergeant and Jenney, Oct. 1, 1864, RG 391, 5AC, v. XXVI, bk. 87, NA; Sommers, op. cit., v. IV, pp. 1,127–28.

30. Prior to when Meade fixed the cavalry's role, Parke had notified Gregg that the infantry would advance at 7:00 A.M. and that the troopers should either fight at McDowell's or return to Route 673 to join the main advance. The corps commander let the cavalry general choose either option and asked simply to be kept informed. Humphreys to Batchelder, 7:10 P.M., Oct. 1, 1864, RG 393, AP, v. VI, bk. 6, NA; Lyman, *Diary*, Oct. 1, 1864, MSHS; *OR*, v. XLII, pt. 3, pp. 6–7, 29–30, 47; Houghton, op. cit., p. 237; Sommers, op. cit., v. IV, pp. 1,128–31.

31. *OR*, v. XLII, pt. 3, p. 7; Lyman to his wife, Oct. 5, 1864, and *Diary*, Oct. 1, 1864, Lyman Papers, MSHS; A. A. Humphreys to his wife, Oct. 2, 1864, personal correspondence, v. XXXIII, AAH Coll., HSP; Sommers, op. cit., v. IV, p. 1,129.

32. "Returns of A-E-F/48th Mississippi, S-O, 1864," RG 109, ch. 1, entry 18, NA; RG 109, entry 15, No. 13-P-24, NA; Lobrano, *Diary*, Oct. 2, 1864, TU; Jones, *Diary*, Oct. 2, 1864, TU; RG 108, entry 11, box 85, No. P435, NA; *OR*, v. XLII, pt. 3, pp. 37, 46–47; Eldridge, *Diary*, Oct. 2, 1864, CNHS; RG 391, 2AC, box 18, Smyth to Embler, 5:30 A.M., Oct. 2, 1864, and v. XVI, bk. 33, p. 118, NA; Sommers, op. cit., v. IV, pp. 1,129–30.

33. RG 109, ch. 6, v. CCCLXIV, p. 501, NA.

34. The light infantry that remained at Fort Cherry included part of the 2nd Mississippi and presumably the sharpshooter battalion of Davis' Brigade. Farther southwest, Joel Griffin is believed to have remained in the works to Barringer's left. Ibid., pp. 220, 496, 501, and v. CCCLXII, p. 442, and v. DL, Sept. 21–Oct. 31, 1864, and v. DLIV, pp. 18–19, and v. DCXLII, pp. 89–90, NA; Brooks, op. cit., pp. 197, 335; *OR*, v. XLII, pt. 1, pp. 95, 948, and pt. 3, pp. 29, 37–39, 44; Willis, *Diary*, Oct. 1–2, 1864, VSL; McGregor, *Report*, Dec. 7, 1864, Halsey Papers, SHC; Vairen, *Diary*, Oct. 2, 1864, MDAH; "Returns of Staff-A-E-F/2nd Maryland Battalion, F/1st Confederate Battalion, D/2nd Mississippi, K/7th North Carolina, and C/8th Georgia Cavalry, S-O, 1864, and of A/8th Georgia Cavalry, Aug.–Dec. 1864, and of H/4th North Carolina Cavalry, Apr.–Sept. 1864, and history of A/2nd Mississippi, Mar. 21, 1865," RG 109, ch. 1, entry 18, NA; Richmond *Whig*, Oct. 20, 1864; Heth, *Report*, Dec. 7, 1864, Heth

Papers, CM; Bryan, *Diary*, Oct. 1, 1864, Bryan Family Papers, SHC; Mullen, *Diary*, Oct. 1, 1864, CM; J. K. Wilkerson to his mother, Oct. 5, 1864, Wilkerson Papers, DU; Goldsborough, op. cit., pp. 140–41; Folder 82, Lane Papers, AU; Lane, *Lane's Brigade*, v. IX, p. 357, and *28th North Carolina*, v. XXIV, p. 337; Clark, *NC*, v. I, p. 385, and v. II, pp. 575–76; Wilcox, *Report*, pp. 67–68, LHQ Coll., VHS; T. J. Linebarger to Ann, Oct. 3, 1864, A. L. Snuggs Coll., SHC; W. D. Alexander, *Diary*, Oct. 2–3, 1864, SHC; Caldwell, op. cit., pp. 185–87; Harris, op. cit., p. 57; Gordon, *Diary*, Oct. 2–3, 1864, SHC; RG 108, entry 11, box 85, No. P435, NA; RG 391, 2AC, v. XVI, bk. 33, pp. 118, 258, NA; Sale, *Diary*, Oct 2, 1864, VSL; RG 111, entry 13, v. XLIV, p. 172, NA; Preston, op. cit., p. 231; Sommers, op. cit., v. IV, pp. 1,117–22, 1,128–29.

35. *OR*, v. XLII, pt. 1, pp. 897–98; RG 109, entry 15, No. 13-P-24, NA; Sommers, op. cit., v. IV, pp. 1,122–23.

36. The reference to the "comforts" of Fort Sedgwick was made by an officer of the 1st Maine Heavy Artillery of the First Brigade. Charles House, "1st Maine Heavy Artillery," *Maine Bugle*, c. IV, pp. 137–38; Hamilton, *110th Pennsylvania*, p. 347, MOLLUS-War Library; DeTrobriand, *Diary*, Oct. 1, 1864, WP; DeTrobriand, op. cit., p. 651; RG 391, 9AC, box 6, Youngman to Willcox, Oct. 1, 1864, and v. XVI, bk. 80, Youngman to Potter, Oct. 1, 1864, and Mills to Willcox, 1:30 A.M., Oct. 2, 1864, NA; Jones, *Diary*, Oct. 2, 1864, and Pope, *Diary*, Oct. 2, 1864, CWTI Coll., MHRC; Stephen Rogers to his parents, Oct. 3, 1864, Rogers Papers, ISHL; Mullen, *Diary*, Oct. 1, 1864, CM; Dana, *Diary*, Oct. 1, 1864, WHGS; Sommers, op. cit., v. IV, p. 1,131.

CHAPTER XIV

1. Agassiz, op. cit., p. 238; *ANJ*, v. II, p. 113; Charles Baughman, letter of Oct. 1–3, 1864, Baughman Papers, CM; Waring, *Diary*, Oct. 1, 1864, SHC; Wainwright, *Diary*, Oct. 5, 1864, HHL; Sargent, *Diary*, Oct. 2, 1864, NYPL; Green, *Diary*, Oct. 2, 1864, WHS; *OR*, v. XLII, pt. 3, p. 41.

2. *OR*, v. XLII, pt. 1, pp. 344, 366, 393, 402, 546–47, 600, 603, and pt. 3, pp. 25, 40–45; RG 391, 2AC, v. LII, bk. 254, p. 282, NA; Youngman to Willcox and Potter, Oct. 1, 1864, RG 391, 9AC, v. XVI, bk. 18, NA; Sommers, op. cit., v. IV, pp. 1,131–32.

3. According to an attacking Unionist, only about thirty to forty Butternuts garrisoned Fort MacRae. *OR*, v. XLII, pt. 1, pp. 138, 344, 366, 371, 377, 381, 385, 393–94, 401, 403–5, 435, and pt. 3, p. 44; Houghton, op. cit., p. 237; A. Judson Gibbs et al., *93rd New York*, p. 83; William Stryker, *New Jersey Officers and Men*, v. I, p. 267; RG 391, 2AC, v. LIX, bk. 297, p. 31, NA; House, loc. cit., c. IV, p. 138; RG 94, entry 12, 1864 file, Nos. B1549 and H1341, NA; DeTrobriand, *Diary*, Oct. 2, 1864, WP; Gordon, *Diary*, Oct. 2, 1864, SHC; Thomas Marbaker, *11th New Jersey*, p. 224; Robert McAllister to Ellen, Oct. 3, 1864, McAllister Papers, Palmer Coll., WRHS; RG 109, entry 15, No. 39-P-24, NA; Sommers, op. cit., v. IV, pp. 1,132–35.

4. Bangor *Daily Whig and Courier*, Oct. 10, 1864; DeTrobriand, op. cit., p. 652.

5. It is not certain that the 6th–8th New Jersey contributed a company to McAllister's skirmish line. Even more in doubt is the composition of De-Trobriand's voltigeur force; the 1st Maine Heavy Artillery may have supplied his skirmishers at this time. These Yankees definitely encountered enemy resistance at C. Smith's. The Southerners may have been the refugees from Fort MacRae, fresh troops from Barringer's main body, or the 4th North Carolina Cavalry and/or 8th Georgia Cavalry of Joel Griffin's brigade. The latter two regiments definitely skirmished with some advancing Federals that morning, either Mott or Parke's main body. Green, *Diary*, Oct. 2, 1864, WHS; Robert McAllister to Ellen, Oct. 2 and 3, 1864, McAllister Papers, Palmer Coll., WRHS; Bangor *Daily Whig and Courier*, Oct. 10, 1864; *OR*, v. XLII, pt. 1, pp. 344, 366, 371, 377, 381–82, 385, 393, 401, 403–5, 559; Robert Lamberton, *Diary*, Oct. 2, 1864, WRHS; RG 391, 2AC, v. LIX, bk. 297, p. 31, NA; DeTrobriand, op. cit., p. 652; De-Trobriand, *Diary*, Oct. 2, 1864, WP; House, loc. cit., c. IV, p. 138; Jacob Lyons, *Diary*, Oct. 2, 1864, SHC; Hamilton, *110th Pennsylvania*, p. 347, MOLLUS-War Library; "Returns of A/8th Georgia Cavalry, Aug.–Dec., 1864, and C/8th Georgia Cavalry, S-O, 1864, and H/4th North Carolina Cavalry, Apr.–Sept., 1864," RG 109, ch. 1, entry 18, NA; RG 94, entry 12, 1864 file, No. H1341, NA; Sommers, op. cit., v. IV, pp. 1,135–38.

6. Mott's division, too, contained many raw recruits, but no evidence has been found that he left them on Peebles's. DeTrobriand may thus have referred to the 2/38th Wisconsin when he wrote:

We have received in the army a number of recruits and conscripts lacking even knowledge of how to load a gun. What is to be done with these men?! . . . during our engagement with the enemy I saw a detachment dressed and armed brand new; they were ordered to remain behind, and their greatest joy was to obey. What's the use of such reinforcements except to furnish arms and uniforms to the enemy if one puts them in line of battle?! The best thing to do is to put them in the dustpan or in the pocket.

DeTrobriand, *Diary*, Oct. 3, 1864, WP; Robert McAllister to Ellen, Oct. 3, 1864, McAllister Papers, Palmer Coll., WRHS; *OR*, v. XLII, pt. 1, p. 558.

7. Potter's brigades presumably deployed in double lines, too. Whether or not the 7th Rhode Island remained behind the 35th Massachusetts, as on Saturday, is not known. Mills to Willcox, 1:30 A.M., Oct. 2, 1864, RG 391, 9AC, v. XVI, bk. 18, NA; Stephen Rogers to his parents, Oct. 3, 1864, Rogers Papers, ISHL; *OR*, v. XLII, pt. 1, pp. 554, 558–59, 562–63, 566, 571, 575, 600–5, and pt. 3, pp. 36, 43–45; Arnold, *Diary*, Oct. 2, 1864, MH; Jones, *Diary*, Oct. 2–3, 1864, and Pope, *Diary*, Oct. 2, 1864, CWTI Coll., MHRC; McDowell, op. cit., ch. XVII, p. 23, McDowell Coll., PSU; William Lamont to his sister, Oct. 2, 1864, Lamont Papers, WHS; Sommers, op. cit., v. IV, pp. 1, 138–40; see also note 5 supra.

8. The claim that the 9th Massachusetts Battery left the field force for

Fort Dushane on Sunday is groundless. That company had remained in the fort throughout the battle. Henry Gawthorp, letter of Oct. 6, 1864, Gawthorp Papers, HSD; McNaught, *Diary,* Oct. "1" [2], 1864, DU; *OR,* v. XLII, pt. 1, p. 58, and pt. 3, pp. 36, 41–44, 59; Charles LaMotte to Annie, Oct. 4, 1864, LaMotte Papers, DPAC; Chamberlin, op. cit., pp. 280–81; Cheek, op. cit., p. 138; Curtis, op. cit., p. 276; Irvin, *Diary,* Oct. 2, 1864, HSP; Dana, *Diary,* Oct. 2, 1864, WHGS; New York *Herald,* Oct. 5, 1864; Wainwright, *Report,* Nov. 5, 1864, box 11, HJH Papers, LC; Wainwright, *Diary,* Oct. 1–5, 1864, HHL; Allen et al., op. cit., p. 323; RG 391, 9AC, v. XVIII, bk. 34, p. 132, NA; *AG-Mass-1864,* p. 1,065; Sommers, op. cit., v. IV, pp. 1,140–42.

9. The platoon of A/50th New York Engineers that had long served at City Point stayed there and did not accompany the pontoons to Jones's. The battalion of that regiment originally at Birchett's started west at 10:00 A.M. Harwood left there two hours later. Lyman, *Diary,* Oct. 2, 1864, MSHS; *OR,* v. XLII, pt. 1, p. 167, and pt. 3, pp. 37–40, 46–47, 73, 92; Hunt to Hazard, 8:00 A.M., Oct. 2, 1864, RG 391, 2AC, box 21, NA; RG 393, AP, v. VI, bk. 6, pp. 536–38, 557–58, NA; Fox, *Diary,* Oct. 2, 1864, HSP; Hunt, *Journal,* p. 130, HJH Papers, LC; "Return of F-M/50th New York Engineers, S-O, 1864," RG 94, M594, NA; Gilbert Thompson, "Engineer Battalion," *Occasional Papers, Engineer School,* v. XLIV, p. 88; Snook, *Diary,* Oct. 2, 1864, MDHS; RG 108, entry 11, box 85, No. P435, NA; RG 111, entry 13, v. XLIV, p. 172, NA; Folwell, *Diary,* Sept. 29–30, 1864, MNHS; Sommers, op. cit., v. IV, pp. 1,142–44.

10. *OR,* v. XLII, pt. 3, p. 36.

11. Ibid.

12. Ibid.

13. Ibid., pp. 5, 36, 44, 48–50; Lyman, *Diary,* Oct. 2, 1864, MSHS; Agassiz, op. cit., p. 237; Sommers, op. cit., v. IV, p. 1,144.

14. *OR,* v. XLII, pt. 3, pp. 39, 41; Sommers, op. cit., v. IV, p. 1,175.

15. *OR,* v. XLII, pt. 3, p. 41; Warren to Ayres, Oct. 2, 1864, RG 391, 5AC, v. V, pt. 4, NA.

16. Charles LaMotte to Annie, Oct. 4, 1864, LaMotte Papers, DPAC.

17. The 14th U.S. set some of W. W. Davis' buildings ablaze that morning, reportedly at 4:00 A.M. These or other structures fired later were still burning by the forenoon. The Davis house itself, however, was not razed on October 2, Grindlay's implicit report to the contrary notwithstanding. Ibid.; *OR,* v. XLII, pt. 1, pp. 56, 478, and pt. 3, pp. 41–44, 133; Henry Gawthorp, letter of Oct. 6, 1864, Gawthorp Papers, HSD; Meyers, op. cit., p. 337; New York *Herald,* Oct. 5, 1864; Eyre, *Diary,* Oct. 7, 1864, Casebier mss.; Richmond *Whig,* Oct. 4 and 20, 1864; RG 109, entry 199, misc. rolls, boxes 5–6, NA; R. E. McBride, *In the Ranks,* p. 120; "CSR of Neri Kinsey and William Overdorf, 190th Pennsylvania," RG 94, entry 519, NA; New York *Times,* Oct. 13, 1864; Vincent, *Diary,* Oct. 2, 1864, VHS; Sommers, op. cit., v. IV, pp. 1,176–78.

18. *OR,* v. XLII, pt. 1, pp. 377, 393, 405, 554, 566, and pt. 3, pp. 43–44; DeTrobriand, op. cit., p. 652; Sommers, op. cit., v. IV, p. 1,178.

19. J. K. Wilkerson to his mother, Oct. 5, 1864, Wilkerson Papers, DU.

20. Heth's claim to have sent MacRae to the Harman Road only as general precaution, not in reaction to Mott's advance, is implausible. More uncertain is Barringer's role in holding the works against the Third Division. His 1st and 2nd regiments were apparently too far right in the works to be able to engage. Whether or not the 3rd and the 5th were within firing range of the Harman Road is not known. Ibid.; *OR*, v. XLII, pt. 1, pp. 344, 366, 371, 393, 404, 554, 859, and pt. 3, pp. 36, 43–44, 86–87, 91–92, 96, 120, 1,341–42; "Returns of Staff-A-E-F/2nd Maryland Battalion, C/8th Georgia Cavalry, and H/1st and A-C-I/3rd North Carolina Cavalry, S-O, 1864, and A/8th Georgia Cavalry, Aug.–Dec. 1864, and H/4th North Carolina Cavalry, Apr.–Sept. 1864," RG 109, ch. 1, entry 18, NA; Goldsborough, op. cit., pp. 141–43; Heth, *Report*, Dec. 7, 1864, Heth Papers, CM; Hopkins, loc. cit., v. LVI, p. 381; Bryan, *Diary*, Oct. 8, 1864, Bryan Family Papers, SHC; RG 109, entry 199, misc. rolls, box 6, NA; Gordon, *Diary*, Oct. 2, 1864, SHC; RG 391, 2AC, v. LIX, bk. 297, p. 31, NA; DeTrobriand, op. cit., p. 652; DeTrobriand, *Diary*, Oct. 2, 1864, WP; Mullen, *Diary*, Oct. 1–2, 1864, CM; William J. Pegram to Mary, Oct. 5, 1864, PJM Coll., VHS; Jesse Frank to his mother, Oct. 5, 1864, Frank Papers, DU; Lamberton, *Diary*, Oct. 2, 1864, WRHS; RG 94, entry 12, 1864 file, No. H1341, NA; Charles Young and Thomas Ellett, "Crenshaw Battery," *SHSP*, v. XXXI, p. 284; Agassiz, op. cit., p. 238; A. A. Humphreys to his wife, Oct. 2, 1864, personal correspondence, v. XXXIII, AAH Coll., HSP; Sommers, op. cit., v. IV, pp. 1,178–83.

21. The 1st Maine Heavies definitely served on DeTrobriand's front line at this time, whether or not they had skirmished for him during the move from Fort MacRae. The 110th was on his main line, too, and it was exposed in the open field, lacking the cover of the edge of the wood. *OR*, v. XLII, pt. 1, pp. 138, 344, 366, 377, 385, 393–94, 401, 405; DeTrobriand, op. cit., p. 652; DeTrobriand, *Diary*, Oct. 2, 1864, WP; RG 391, 2AC, v. LIX, bk. 297, p. 31, NA; "Return of A/17th Maine, S-O, 1864," RG 94, M594, NA; Lyons, *Diary*, Oct. 2, 1864, SHC; Bangor *Daily Whig and Courier*, Oct. 10, 1864; Isaiah Simpson, "1st Maine Heavy Artillery," *NT*, Sept. 15, 1927; House, loc. cit., c. IV, p. 138; Hamilton, *110th Pennsylvania*, pp. 347–48, MOLLUS-War Library; RG 94, entry 12, 1864 file, No. H1341, NA; Marbaker, op. cit., p. 224; Cornelius VanSantvoord, *120th New York*, pp. 152–53; Sommers, op. cit., v. IV, p. 1,183.

22. As the IX Corps reoccupied Pegram's farm, two companies of the 7th Rhode Island were detailed to bury the many corpses still lying there from the two previous days' fighting. *OR*, v. XLII, pt. 1, pp. 371, 554, 559, 566, 571, 580, 583, 588, and pt. 3, pp. 41, 45–46; Burrage, op. cit., p. 266; Jones, *Diary*, Oct. 2, 1864, and Pope, *Diary*, Oct. 2, 1864, CWTI Coll., MHRC; Sommers, op. cit., v. IV, pp. 1,183–84.

23. Daniels' regiment helped the batteries entrench. *OR*, v. XLII, pt. 1, pp. 547, 600, 603, 859; Burrage, op. cit., p. 266; Stephen Rogers to his parents, Oct. 3, 1864, Rogers Papers, ISHL; Carruth et al., op. cit., pp.

302–3; Pope, *Diary,* Oct. 2, 1864, and Jones, *Diary,* Oct. 2, 1864, CWTI Coll., MHRC; Allen et al., op. cit., p. 323; Woodward, op. cit., p. 15; RG 94, entry 729, box 93, No. 222b, NA; Wainwright, *Report,* Nov. 5, 1864, box 11, HJH Papers, LC; Wainwright, *Diary,* Oct. 1–5, 1864, HHL; Sommers, op. cit., v. IV, pp. 1,184–85.

24. A. A. Humphreys to his wife, Oct. 2, 1864, personal correspondence, v. XXXIII, AAH Coll., HSP.

25. Meade, op. cit., v. II, p. 231.

26. Agassiz, op. cit., p. 238.

27. Graham's battery evidently fired the nearly fatal shot. Neither Meade nor Humphreys bear out a newsman's allegation that Warren, too, was in the gathering when the shell struck. Ibid., pp. 237–38; *OR,* v. XLII, pt. 1, pp. 344–45, and pt. 3, pp. 37–39, 44, 1,341–42; New York *Times,* Oct. 5, 1864; Lyman, *Diary,* Oct. 2, 1864, MSHS; Pope, *Diary,* Oct. 2, 1864, CWTI Coll., MHRC; RG 111, entry 13, v. XLIV, p. 173, NA; Allen, loc. cit., July 11, 1895; Sommers, op. cit., v. IV, pp. 1,185–86.

28. Whether Grimshaw still led the Third Brigade at this time is not known. Sometime Sunday, he was relieved of command for some reason not now apparent. Whatever the cause, it proved to be a "misapprehension," and Ayres issued orders shortly before midnight for him to resume command. During the colonel's temporary absence, his brigade presumably devolved on his senior subordinate, Lieutenant Colonel Joseph B. Pattee of the 190th Pennsylvania. "CSR of Arthur Grimshaw, 4th Delaware," RG 94, entry 519, NA; "Return of Third Brigade, Second Division, 5th Corps, Oct. 6, 1864," RG 94, entry 65, 5AC, NA; *OR,* v. XLII, pt. 1, p. 478, and pt. 3, pp. 41–43, 86; RG 111, entry 13, v. XLIV, p. 173, NA; "Return of Price's Virginia Battery, S-O, 1864," RG 109, ch. 1, entry 18, NA; Henry Gawthorp, letter of Oct. 6, 1864, Gawthorp Papers, HSD; William Sanderson to Mr. Talmage, March 8, 1911, Sanderson-Talmage Papers, Petersburg National Battlefield Park; "Returns of Staff/190th Pennsylvania, and of Staff-B-C-F/1st Battalion/11th U.S. and A-C-D-E-F-G/1st Battalion/14th U.S., S-O, 1864," RG 94, M594 and entry 53, respectively, NA; Charles LaMotte to Annie, Oct. 4, 1864, LaMotte Papers, DPAC; Brainard, op. cit., p. 246; McNaught, *Diary,* Oct. 2, 1864, DU; Chamberlin, op. cit., p. 281; Curtis, op. cit., p. 276; Dana, *Diary,* Oct. 2, 1864, WHGS; Sommers, op. cit., v. IV, pp. 1,186–88.

29. For some reason, Lane stretched slightly rightward at 1:00 P.M. RG 111, entry 13, v. XLIV, p. 173, NA; T. James Linebarger, *Diary,* Oct. 2, 1864, Snuggs Coll., SHC; Bryan, *Diary,* Oct. 2, 1864, Bryan Family Papers, SHC; W. D. Alexander, *Diary,* Oct. 2, 1864, SHC; Sommers, op. cit., v. IV, pp. 1,203–4.

30. It is not clear whether Stokes or Colonel B. Huger Rutledge of the 4th South Carolina Cavalry led Dunovant's Brigade on Sunday. More certain is the fact that Waring did not command his own battalion all day. Sometime after bolstering his pickets, he personally was sent back to camp by Young to bring up stragglers. *OR,* v. XLII, pt. 1, pp. 85, 89, 90, 92, 94, 96, and pt. 3, pp. 47, 64; Rappalyea, *Diary,* Oct. 2, 1864, NJHS; Benjamin

Crowninshield, *1st Massachusetts Cavalry*, p. 243; Preston, op. cit., p. 231; Bushnell, *History*, p. 314, Palmer Coll., WRHS; Maitland to regimental commanders, 4:00 A.M., Oct. 2, 1864, RG 391, CC, v. XLV, bk. 67, NA; "Return of Staff/2nd Pennsylvania Cavalry, Oct., 1864," RG 94, M594, NA; RG 94, entry 12, 1864 file, No. B1563, NA; Clark, *Diary*, Oct. 1–2, 1864, NYPL; Willis, *Diary*, Oct. 2, 1864, VSL; Brooks, op. cit., p. 336; Waring, *Diary*, Oct. 2, 1864, SHC; McGregor, *Report*, Dec. 7, 1864, Halsey Papers, SHC; Thaxter to Gregg, Oct. 2, 1864, RG 94, entry 731, box 70, NA; RG 391, 2AC, v. LIX, bk. 297, p. 31, NA; DeTrobriand, *Diary*, Oct. 2, 1864, WP; Sommers, op. cit., v. IV, pp. 1,188–91.

31. *OR*, v. XLII, pt. 1, pp. 344–45, 554, 575, and pt. 3, p. 45; Sommers, op. cit., v. IV, pp. 1,191–92.

32. These words are Mott's paraphrase of Parke's order. *OR*, v. XLII, pt. 1, pp. 344–45.

33. Whether Willcox's other two brigades shifted left when Harriman did is not clear. Ibid., pp. 344–45, 366–67, 371, 377, 382, 385, 393–94, 401, 559; Lamberton, *Diary*, Oct. 2, 1864, WRHS; Robert Carter, *Four Brothers in Blue*, p. 490; Alfred Roe and Charles Nutt, *1st Massachusetts Heavy Artillery*, p. 192; Gibbs et al., op. cit., p. 83; William J. Pegram to Mary Pegram, Oct. 5, 1864, PJM Coll., VHS; Richmond *Enquirer*, Oct. 7, 1864; R. S. Webb to his sister, Oct. 3, 1864, Webb-Moore Papers, SHC; Jesse Frank to his mother, Oct. 5, 1864, Frank Papers, DU; "CSR of George Zinn, 84th Pennsylvania," RG 94, entry 519, NA; Robert McAllister to Ellen, Oct. 3, 1864, McAllister Papers, Palmer Coll., WRHS; RG 391, 2AC, v. LIX, bk. 297, p. 31, NA; DeTrobriand, *Diary*, Oct. 2, 1864, WP; "Return of A/17th Maine, S-O, 1864," RG 94, M594, NA; Heth, *Report*, Dec. 7, 1864, Heth Papers, CM; Sommers, op. cit., v. IV, pp. 1,192–96.

34. Whether Joel Griffin, too, was far enough right to fire on McLaughlen is not known. *OR*, v. XLII, pt. 1, pp. 554, 575; Heth, *Report*, Dec. 7, 1864, Heth Papers, CM; R. S. Webb to his sister, Oct. 3, 1864, Webb-Moore Papers, SHC; J. K. Wilkerson to his mother, Oct. 5, 1864, Wilkerson Papers, DU; "Returns of D-E-F/2nd and H/26th Mississippi and B-H/46th North Carolina, S-O, 1864," RG 109, ch. 1, entry 18, NA; "Histories of F-H-K/11th Mississippi, Apr. 26, 1861–Jan. 1, 1865," military records, s. L, v. XII, MDAH; Lewis Warlick to Cornelia McGimsey, Oct. 6, 1864, McGimsey Papers, SHC; Cavaness, *Diary*, Oct. 2, 1864, TXU; Mullen, *Diary*, Oct. 2, 1864, CM; Sommers, op. cit., v. IV, pp. 1,196–98.

35. Hancock's most significant move on Sunday, far from a demonstration, was just a routine shifting of troops. He transferred the 28th Massachusetts of Lynch's brigade back north to garrison Battery No. 4 and begin transforming it into a fort. "Return of Staff/28th Massachusetts, S-O, 1864," RG 94, M594, NA.

36. Sale, *Diary*, Oct. 2, 1864, VSL; Charles Baughman, letter of Oct. 1–3, 1864, Baughman Papers, CM; Waring, *Diary*, Oct. 2, 1864, SHC; Wilfred McDonald, *Diary*, Oct. 2, 1864, Crimmins Coll., TXU; *OR*, v. XLII, pt. 1, pp. 211, 898, and pt. 2, pp. 1,306, 1,311, and pt. 3, pp. 37,

1,130; Cox, *Diary,* Oct. 2, 1864, UV; RG 111, entry 13, v. XLIV, p. 173, NA; Chambers, *Diary,* Oct. 2, 1864, NCDAH; Jacob Smith, letter of Oct. 4, 1864, Hutchinson Papers, VHS; Russell, *Diary,* Oct. 2–3, 1864, DU; Coleman, *Diary,* Oct. 2, 1864, CMC-Ib, EU; W. J. Mosely to his parents, Sept. 30, 1864, microfilm, GDAH; "Returns of A-B-D/10th Georgia Battalion, S-O, 1864," RG 109, ch. 1, entry 18, NA; Sommers, op. cit., v. IV, pp. 1,205–7.

37. Besides Pierce's brigade, Mott had some local reserves, at least the 11th New Jersey. Rivers, the 5th–7th, and the 120th manned McAllister's works. Whether the 6th–8th was in the trenches, too, or in local reserve is not clear. *OR,* v. XLII, pt. 1, pp. 58, 167, 173, 345, 367, 371, 377, 382, 394, 401, 403–5, 436, 478, 554, 559, 562, 566, 571, 575, 580, 583, and pt. 3, pp. 38–39, 45–46, 50, 54, 59–64, 73, 86–87, 141; Charles Weygant, *124th New York,* p. 378; DeTrobriand, *Diary,* Oct. 2, 1864, WP; Hamilton, *110th Pennsylvania,* p. 348, MOLLUS-War Library; "Returns of 50th New York Engineers and A/8th Michigan, S-O, 1864," RG 94, M594, NA; L. E. Walker, *Map of Union Lines West of the Weldon Railroad,* Jan. 16, 1865, LC maps; Willcox to Mills, Oct. 3, 1864, RG 391, 9AC, v. XVI, bk. 80, NA; Pierce, op. cit., pp. 59–60; Pope, *Diary,* Oct. 2–3, 1864, CWTI Coll., MHRC; Hinckley, loc. cit., May 20, 1915; Woodward, op. cit., p. 15; Allen et al., op. cit., p. 323; Snook, *Diary,* Oct. 2, 1864, MDHS; Agassiz, op. cit., pp. 237–38; Wainwright, *Diary,* Oct. 5, 1864, HHL; Sparks, op. cit., p. 426; Thompson, loc. cit., v. XLIV, p. 88; William Folwell to Kätchur, Oct. 3, 1864, William Folwell Papers, MNHS; Sommers, op. cit., v. IV, pp. 1,143, 1,185, 1,198–1,203.

38. Gregg definitely conferred with Meade prior to 8:30 P.M. Whether the cavalryman came to Peebles's more than once that day is not clear. *OR,* v. XLII, pt. 1, pp. 87, 89, 90, 92, 94, 96, 620, 636, and pt. 3, pp. 46–47; Rappalyea, *Diary,* Oct. 2, 1864, NJHS; RG 94, entry 12, 1864 file, No. B1563, NA; Preston, op. cit., pp. 231–32; "Returns of Staff/1st Massachusetts Cavalry and Staff/2nd Pennsylvania Cavalry, S-O, 1864," RG 94, M594, NA; Clark, *Diary,* Oct. 1–2, 1864, NYPL; Sommers, op. cit., v. IV, p. 1,203.

39. *OR,* v. XLII, pt. 3, pp. 5, 39.

40. Fletcher Archer served at Battery No. 45 by October 3. He presumably moved there the preceding evening to help replace the Light Division—if, indeed, he had not already gone there during one of the previous pullouts earlier in the battle. Cox, *Diary,* Oct. 2, 1864, UV; Russell, *Diary,* Oct. 3, 1864, DU; Beauregard, *Letterbook,* v. XXXIII, p. -1, LC; *OR,* v. XLII, pt. 3, pp. 68, 86–87, 92, 96, 120, 158, 1,130; Sale, *Diary,* Oct. 3, 1864, VSL; "Returns of A/8th Georgia Cavalry, Aug.–Dec. 1864, and H/6th Virginia, S-O, 1864," RG 109, ch. 1, entry 18, NA; Coleman, *Diary,* Oct. 2, 1864, CMC-Ib, EU; Fletcher H. Archer to his wife, Oct. 3, 1864, Archer Papers, Petersburg Siege Museum; Joseph Stapp, letter of Oct. 5, 1864, Joseph Stapp Papers, VHS; Alfred Scales to his wife, Oct. 7, 1864, Scales Papers, East Carolina University; Bryan, *Diary,* Oct. 2, 1864, Bryan Family Papers, SHC; T. J. Linebarger to Ann, Oct. 3, 1864, and *Diary,* Oct.

2, 1864, Snuggs Coll., SHC; W. D. Alexander, *Diary*, Oct. 3, 1864, SHC; Harris, op. cit., pp. 57–58; Caldwell, op. cit., p. 187; Latrobe, *Diary*, Oct. 3, 1864, VHS; J. H. Pegram to his brother and sisters, Oct. 6, 1864, CMC, DU; Sommers, op. cit., v. IV, pp. 1,207–9.

41. Gordon, *Diary*, Oct. 2–3, 1864, SHC; Brooks, op. cit., pp. 196–97; Willis, *Diary*, Oct. 2, 1864, VSL; Waring, *Diary*, Oct. 2–4, 1864, SHC; Sommers, op. cit., v. IV, pp. 1,209–10.

42. *OR,* v. XLII, pt. 1, p. 898, and pt. 3, p. 1,133; Lee, *Telegram Book,* p. 404, LHQ Coll., VHS; Sommers, op. cit., v. IV, p. 1,210.

43. *OR,* v. XLII, pt. 1, pp. 139–42, 367, 547, 899; RG 391, 9AC, v. XVIII, bk. 34, p. 135, and v. XVI, bk. 80, Willcox to Youngman, Oct. 7, 1864, NA; RG 391, 2AC, v. LII, bk. 254, p. 284, NA; RG 391, 5AC, v. XXXIX, bk. 206, Oct. 3, 1864, and v. XII, bk. 44, p. 42, NA; RG 94, entry 729, box 93, No. 146, NA; Richmond *Enquirer,* Oct. 7, 1864; R. S. Webb to his sister, Oct. 3, 1864, Webb-Moore Papers, SHC; RG 109, entry 199, misc. rolls, box 26, NA; Willis, *Diary,* Oct. 2, 1864, VSL; Richmond *Whig,* Oct. 4, 1864; Sommers, op. cit., v. IV, pp. 1,210–11.

44. *OR,* v. XLII, pt. 1, pp. 138–43, 897–99; Sommers, op. cit., v. IV, p. 1,211, and v. V, pp. 1,345–56.

CHAPTER XV

1. Operations during the Fifth Offensive after October 2 are only outlined in this volume. They are covered more fully in other writings by the author, including op. cit., v. V, pp. 1,212–37 and "The Battle No One Wanted," *Civil War Times Illustrated,* v. XIV, No. 5, pp. 10–18, Aug. 1975.

2. See also Sommers, op. cit., v. V, pp. 1,238–95a.

3. Meade's 6,000 horsemen and Butler's 2,650 actually exceeded Hampton's 6,900, Gary's 865, and an estimated 235 at Richmond and Dunn's Hill. However, over 1,100 mounted and 400 dismounted Bluecoats were scattered in detachments and did not take the field. The Second Cavalry Division, too, left 550 pickets covering the flanks and rear. Gregg's and Kautz's mobile forces totaled only 6,550, compared to 7,900 Graycoats. This disparity was even more pronounced below Petersburg: 4,350 to 6,900.

4. The author suggests the following as a promising first-strike strategy. Ord would lead Stannard, Heckman, and Duncan up the Varina Road to storm Fort Harrison. Birney would either follow the XVIII Corps into the entrenched camp to exploit the breakthrough or else would take a more westerly route along the lower Kingsland Road and the Osborne Turnpike to attack Fort Maury frontally. Meantime, Warren would lead Griffin, Ayres, Draper, Holman, and four V Corps batteries from Deep Bottom against New Market Heights. Once the right wing took them and headed west on the New Market Road, Gregg would pass around the infantry with Smith and Kautz and raid toward Richmond along more northerly routes. While this massive onslaught was closing in on the capital, Meade would remain on the vigilant

defensive on the Southside. Hancock, Ferrero, Crawford, and seven of Wainwright's and two of Monroe's batteries would hold the works, and Davies would patrol the rear. Willcox, Potter, and the other four IX Corps batteries would be in mobile reserve near Jones's to meet any Confederate attack or to exploit any withdrawal from Petersburg. This plan, though, is purely hypothetical, devised by this author. There is no evidence that Grant considered such a move. For criticism of the approach he did take, see *OR*, v. XLII, pt. 3, pp. 19–20, and William Swinton, *Army of the Potomac*, pp. 550–53. The role of the "entrenched camp" strategy is discussed in Chapter VIII.

5. To permit these additional troops to take the field immediately, Miles, Gibbon, and Ferrero could have initially extended leftward to hold the positions they occupied by Saturday morning. The 210th and, if necessary, the 200th Pennsylvania could also have come forward on September 29 to bolster the sector just right of Fort Wadsworth. Then Bragg and Pierce could have accompanied the strike force on Friday morning, and De-Trobriand and McAllister, after remaining in reserve near Hancock's Station all day, could have gone to the front that night or early the next morning. In such a case, Ferrero could have taken charge of the garrison west of the II Corps; Crawford could have commanded his two brigades in the field; and Pierce could have reported to either him or Potter until rejoining Mott on October 1.

6. Samuel Roberts to Cecil Clay, Jan. 31, 1884, Clay Papers, HSP; Agassiz, op. cit., p. 235.

7. J. F. C. Fuller's claim that storming Fort Harrison was a great vindication of the offensive school of tactics ignores the extreme vulnerability of that redoubt. Fuller is attempting to pass off his pet theories of tank tactics for the twentieth century in the guise of Civil War history. *The Generalship of Ulysses S. Grant*, pp. 305, 370–71.

8. Walter Taylor to Bettie, Oct. 6, 1864, Taylor Papers, VSL.

9. Terry's discomfort with responsibility on October 13, which was probably similar to his feelings a fortnight earlier, is described in Joseph R. Hawley to his wife, Oct. 18, 1864, Hawley Papers, LC.

10. The I Corps commander's relative lack of contribution on September 29 is inferred from lack of mention of him in available sources. Such a deduction is, admittedly, risky, yet it is made because those sources do recount the services of the other senior officers, Ewell, Gregg, and later Field.

11. See supra, pp. 385–88.

12. Sommers, op. cit., v. V, pp. 1,320–60.

13. Ewell's claim that the loss of Fort Harrison was inconsequential is a self-serving attempt to cover up his failure to hold it initially, not a reflection of Lee's attitude toward its fall. E. P. Alexander to his wife, Oct. 3, 1864, EPA Coll., SHC; *OR*, v. XLII, pt. 3, p. 1,133; U. S. Grant to J. Russell Jones, Oct. 4, 1864, U. S. Grant Papers, CHHS; Ewell, *Letterbook*, pp. 18–19, DU.

APPENDIX A

1. This table is based on returns for the end of September 1864, now filed in RG 94, entries 62 and 65, NA. See also *OR*, v. XLII, pt. 1, pp. 133–43.

2. The 16th remained behind on the Jerusalem Plank Road.

3. Only Shaffer's own Company F remained with him throughout the battle. The 14th left him on Friday to join Hazard; the next day two of its guns went to Fort Bross. The 2nd was with Benham, and the other two batteries served under Harn. On Saturday, though, one Vermont section went to Prince George Court House; it returned the next day. Harn's command, in turn, reported to Hazard.

4. Of the engineers, most of the 15th and one platoon of A/50th plus the 50th's recruits served at City Point. Spaulding's main body, though, operated in the field with the Army of the Potomac, and C/15th had charge of the bridge at Deep Bottom. Their absence was more than offset by the following units stationed at City Point, either under Benham's command or at least in his potential defense force: the 2nd Maine Battery of Shaffer's brigade, the 200th and 205th Pennsylvania of Potter's brigade, the 22nd Massachusetts of Gregory's brigade, the 10th USCT of Duncan's brigade, the 5th U. S. Cavalry and the 4th U.S. of Grant's headquarters, the cavalry remount camp of Gregg's division, and B/3rd Pennsylvania Cavalry, A-B-C-E/68th Pennsylvania, and the 80th New York of Patrick's brigade. The 127th USCT, 185th New York, 210th Pennsylvania, and 2/38th Wisconsin also spent a little time at the point before going to the front.

5. Gates led that portion of the brigade, listed in the preceding note, at City Point. The remaining outfits were commanded by Collis at Prince George Court House, except for the Massachusetts squadron, which continued as Meade's escort.

6. Officially by Sunday, unofficially the two preceding days, Hancock was responsible for Collis', Brainerd's, and Robison's troops on the rear line as well as the II Corps. Within his own corps, most regiments and battalions preserved their independence. However, the 5th and 7th New Jersey were paired, as were the 6th and 8th New Jersey. The 2nd Delaware and 72nd New York, each only one company strong, were moreover attached to the 1st Delaware and 120th New York, respectively. All those II Corps outfits, save for the Delawareans, belonged to Mott's division. Except for the 5th Michigan, which remained in and around Battery No. 37, that division was attached to the IX Corps, October 1–5.

7. On October 1, Lynch sent C/4th to Hazard to relieve D/4th as the mortar crew. Company D then rejoined its regiment. Besides his own fourteen batteries, the major also had charge of Harn's demibrigade and all of Shaffer's outfits except for the 2nd and F/15th. Brooker's six batteries of the 1st Connecticut Heavy Artillery—A, E, I, K, L, and M—served on the II Corps's front, too.

8. Except for the 22nd Massachusetts at City Point, the First and Second divisions, Hofmann's brigade (attached to Ayres), and six batteries (B-D-H-L/1st New York Light Artillery, the 15th New York Battery, and B/1st Pennsylvania Light Artillery) took the field on September 30. Wainwright led those batteries that day but went back to Globe Tavern with the latter three of them that night. He stayed there for the rest of the battle, even though the two New York companies accompanied Bragg to Flowers' on Saturday. By then, Fitzhugh had charge of the three batteries remaining around Peebles's. Other changes of command came on October 1, when Grindlay succeeded the wounded Otis and when Bartlett superseded Spear, who had taken over from the injured Gwyn on Friday afternoon. On Sunday, Grimshaw was briefly relieved of command, only to be restored to duty the next morning. In his temporary absence, Pattee presumably led the brigade.

9. Crawford commanded the garrison west of the II Corps: his own First and Second brigades, Ferrero's reinforced division, first five and then eight of Wainwright's batteries, plus the 210th and the 185th. The latter were two new regiments that just came forward from City Point on Friday and Saturday, respectively. They were apparently not assigned to brigades until October 3. Even when Bragg moved to Flowers', he remained under Crawford. So did Baxter's three detachments: the 16th, 97th, and 107th under McCoy in Fort Wadsworth, the 39th, 11th, 88th, 90th, and 104th under Coulter in Fort Dushane, and the 94th in Fort Davison. Hofmann, however, was detached with Ayres. The 2/38th Wisconsin, en route to join the IX Corps, bivouacked in Crawford's sector on Friday night but probably was not assigned to him.

10. Parke led most of his First and Second divisions and four batteries into the field. However, the 29th Massachusetts and the 11th Massachusetts Battery in Fort Howard and the 79th New York, the 51st Pennsylvania, and the 27th New York Battery in Fort Alexander Hays remained in the works with Ferrero. After midday on Friday, that division commander, in turn, reported to Crawford. The Negroes' absence from the field force was more than offset on October 1–5 by the presence with the IX Corps of Mott's entire division except for Pulford. The 2/38th Wisconsin also arrived on Saturday to join its sister battalion.

11. On September 28, K/1st New York Engineers, the 89th New York, the 1st and 37th USCT, and Holman's headquarters left this brigade to rejoin the XVIII Corps. The 2nd New Hampshire did the same thing three days later. Also on Saturday, Marston's illness compelled him to relinquish command, presumably to Patterson, although the latter officer did not formally take charge until Monday.

12. This detail was detached to garrison Fort Converse.

13. Only half of this regiment served with the Army of the James: B at Broadway Landing, part of C at Dutch Gap, and the rest of C, D, F, G, and H on Bermuda Hundred. The other six batteries were stationed on Hancock's sector.

14. The eight companies of this regiment serving with the Army of the James were attached to the XVIII Corps during the Battle of Chaffin's Bluff.

15. Besides this company, C/15th New York Engineers of Benham's brigade served in Butler's department, in charge of the pontoons at Deep Bottom.

16. The 1st Maryland Cavalry rejoined Plaisted on the night of September 28–29. The next morning the 203rd was left to hold Deep Bottom. The previous garrison there, Paine's division, was attached to the X Corps until returning to the XVIII Corps in midmorning on Friday. During his service with the X Corps and on until Friday night, his mounted squadron, E-H/4th Massachusetts Cavalry, operated with the First Battalion and F Company of that regiment at Birney's headquarters. On rejoining the XVIII Corps, the squadron reported to Weitzel's headquarters.

17. On Thursday night, Daggett relinquished his brigade to Barney for the rest of the battle. Also that evening, Pennypacker may have briefly turned over operational control of his brigade to Price, but the colonel soon resumed it if, indeed, he ever gave it up. Whoever led the Second Brigade, it was temporarily attached to the XVIII Corps that night and early Friday morning. The following day, Plaisted's brigade was attached to the Second Division during Terry's absence on the Darbytown Road.

18. Jackson's whole brigade accompanied its corps from Petersburg, but most of it remained on Jones's Neck. On Thursday, only C/3rd, D/4th, and M/1st crossed the James, and just the last unit saw any action. The next day, the 4th and D/1st came to the front, and E/1st moved to the Peninsula. The 1st and E/3rd did not go to the Northside until Sunday, and the 5th not until Monday. The service of the Requa gun section of the 16th has not been documented.

19. After Ord was wounded on Thursday morning, he turned over the corps to Heckman. Weitzel took charge of it that night. The following evening, Companies E-H/4th left Rand for duty at corps headquarters. On October 1, part of the 11th Connecticut was transferred there, too.

20. Each brigade left a unit on Bermuda Hundred, September 29: C/13th from the First, the 5th Maryland from the Second, and the 40th Massachusetts from the Third. The 5th came to Henrico County on Saturday but apparently to serve in White's temporary brigade rather than to rejoin the Second Brigade. The 2nd and 12th New Hampshire, too, likely joined White, not Moffitt, that day. The major changes in the First Division, though, were not regiments but senior officers. The division itself was led by Stannard until Friday afternoon, then by first Cullen and then Jourdan. Raulston succeeded Stevens the preceding morning. Burnham's death shortly thereafter created a gap that Donohoe, Cullen, probably Moffitt, and Cullen again eventually filled. Cullen and Moffitt also led the Third Brigade after Roberts was incapacitated on Thursday morning, and Brown and perhaps Reichard had charge of it the following afternoon. By the end of the battle, Jourdan led the division, and Raulston, Cullen, and likely Moffitt headed its three brigades. Sommers, op. cit., v. V, pp. 1,388–91.

21. While Heckman commanded the corps, his division presumably passed to Fairchild. The latter's supposed promotion, in turn, likely caused either Anderson or Guion to take over the Third Brigade. If the major did so, his death soon thereafter caused a vacancy that probably either Lewis or

Guion filled. The lieutenant colonel, in any case, definitely took over the First Brigade when Jourdan was promoted on Friday. Throughout, Ripley remained in charge of the Second Brigade. Some evidence suggests that the 12th New Hampshire reinforced him on October 1, but it more likely served under White. The equivalent of a company of Ripley's own regiment meantime remained on Bermuda Hundred.

22. This division was attached to the X Corps until midmorning on September 30. The preceding morning, Ames succeeded the wounded Duncan. Boernstein took over the Third Brigade late Friday, when Ames replaced the ill Draper in charge of the Second Brigade. The colonel of the 6th evidently oversaw both brigades for the remainder of the battle. Under all these officers, the Third Brigade contained only two regiments; the 10th remained at City Point all the while.

23. When the 5th, 2nd, and 12th reinforced the Northside on Saturday, they may have rejoined Cullen, Moffitt, and either Ripley or Moffitt, respectively. More likely, though, they formed a temporary brigade under White, which existed as a separate unit until October 7.

24. The 17th and one section of M served at Deep Bottom. One section of the 7th was at Dutch Gap. The rest of the 7th and of M plus E/3rd, L/4th, and A/5th garrisoned Bermuda Hundred. The other six batteries accompanied the XVIII Corps into the field.

25. The following units were also in or attached to Potter's brigade during the battle: his own 12th New Hampshire, a detail of the 9th Vermont from the Second Division, and C/13th New Hampshire, the 5th Maryland, and the 40th Massachusetts from the First Division. On October 1, the 5th, 12th, and a battalion of the 11th were sent to the Northside. Just prior to the battle, moreover, the 200th and 205th, both under Mathews, took charge of Benham's principal outpost at Old Court House. Two other new companies, H-I/206th, were detached on provost duty at Bermuda Hundred Landing.

26. This table is based on documents in RG 109, entries 15 and 65, NA. See also *OR*, v. XLII, pt. 2, pp. 1,213–22, 1,244–45, 1,266–68, 1,306–11, and pt. 3, pp, 1,186–93, 1,197, 1,354.

27. Within Chew's battalion, Hart's, McGregor's, and Graham's batteries were often attached to the First and Third divisions and Dearing's Brigade, respectively. Another common grouping was to pair the 4th and 20th battalions of the Georgia Brigade with the Phillips and Jeff Davis legions, respectively. That brigade itself may have been grouped with Griffin's brigade into a demidivision for Young, at least on Thursday. Waring, in any case, led Young's Brigade that day. Another change of command was caused by Dunovant's death on October 1. Stokes immediately succeeded him, but Rutledge may have taken over as early as Sunday.

28. Anderson's operational command on the Northside consisted of Field's and Hoke's divisions, the latter temporarily including Scales's Brigade. Most of Pickett's Division, to which Thomas' Brigade was attached, remained in Chesterfield County during the Battle of Chaffin's Bluff. However, Montague's provisional brigade, created in response to the Federal

breakthrough on September 29, did serve in Henrico County all four days of the battle. Within that brigade, his own regiment was drawn from Corse's Brigade, the 24th from Terry's, the 53rd from Steuart's, and the 56th from Hunton's. Another provisional force on Thursday was Gregg's demidivision: his own and DuBose's brigades and Elliott's and Guy's battalions. The Texan may have commanded another such demidivision around Fort Gilmer the next day, and he presumably took charge of most of the division on Saturday, when Field was detached with Bowles and Montague. Whenever Gregg exercised these higher commands, his own brigade devolved on Bass.

29. Alexander also served as acting Chief-of-Artillery of the Army of Northern Virginia during the Fifth Offensive. Of his own brigade, only three batteries actually fought under him on the Northside: F/13th, the Second Palmetto Battery, and the Nelson Battery, all under Haskell. His other forces there consisted of units already on the Peninsula—Hardaway's battalion of the II Corps and Stark's Battalion of the Department of Richmond—and of units brought from battalions at Petersburg: Marye from Pegram, Clutter from McIntosh, E/1st from Moseley, and B/38th from Read. Johnson led the two III Corps outfits; whether the two from Jones's brigade formed a comparable battalion or were attached to other battalions is not known. At a higher level, Hardaway had charge of Stark's Battalion as well as his own beginning early Friday. Alexander thus had fourteen batteries on the Peninsula. Even more of his command, though, stayed in Chesterfield: Cabell and Huger (apparently including D/1st) of the I Corps plus Poague's reinforced battalion of the III Corps and part of Smith's Battalion of Beauregard's department. Owen's battalion, however, remained east of Petersburg and passed out of Alexander's control at this time. Whether it was immediately assigned to Walker or to Jones is not clear. The other unit nominally in the I Corps, Eshelman's battalion, had long since been attached to the III Corps in place of Poague.

30. Two brigades of this corps were detached: Thomas with Pickett in Chesterfield County, and Scales with Hoke on the Peninsula. Two other forces, however, joined the corps during the Battle of Poplar Spring Church. Fletcher Archer's second-class troops of Wise's command were attached to Mahone from Thursday onward. Then briefly on Sunday, that major general led a provisional demidivision consisting of Goode's and Harris' brigades. During Mahone's absence with that force, his own division presumably devolved on Finegan. A similarly brief arrangement saw James Archer leading MacRae's Brigade as well as his own when Heth had charge of all forces on Jones's farm, Friday afternoon. The Marylander's temporary promotion caused his brigade to pass to McComb.

31. Pegram and McIntosh, respectively, sent the Marye and Clutter batteries to Chaffin's on September 29. Poague, reinforced by the Lewis Artillery of Richardson's Battalion, was also absent from the brigade, attached to Alexander's command in Chesterfield. The Washington Artillery Battalion, nominally of the I Corps, took Poague's place in the III. Walker may also have taken charge of the 13th Battalion of the I Corps during this battle. Most of these battalions reported directly to brigade headquarters, but

the two in Rives's Salient, Richardson's and Lane's, made up a demibrigade under Cutts.

32. During Beauregard's absence in the lower South, Otey continued operating his headquarters but could hardly function as a department commander. In the absence of a permanent successor, his forces were distributed among the other corps: Hoke (reinforced by Scales) and Smith to Anderson, Joel Griffin and Graham to Hampton, and Johnson, Jones, and some of Wise's units to Hill. Only Terrett seems to have remained independent. Within the troops remaining around Petersburg, Goode was briefly transferred to Mahone's provisional demidivision on Sunday afternoon. It is probable but not certain that McAfee led Ransom's Brigade during these operations.

33. Although Ker of the 44th was commandant of the post, not he but Fletcher Archer led the field force of that command that reinforced Mahone on September 29. Except for that force and Guion's, though, Wise's men did not serve near Petersburg. Walker's Brigade guarded the Danville and Southside Railroads, and Garnett's Brigade and the Holcombe Legion protected the Weldon Railroad.

34. Jones sent two companies to the Peninsula on Thursday: B/38th of Read's battalion and E/1st of Moseley's. In their place, Owen's battalion of the I Corps may have joined him.

35. Within the Tennessee brigade, the 17th and 23rd formed a pair, as did the 25th and 44th. Parts of the first two regiments and of the 63rd made up a demibrigade directly under Hughs on September 29. The rest of the brigade, cut off from him, was led by Snowden. Also on that day, Guy and Elliott were attached to Gregg's command. Two days later, the 1st Virginia Reserve Battalion was transferred to Moore's brigade.

36. Barton's Division was a provisional force formed on Thursday, Friday, or Saturday. Only when the division headquarters was set up did he turn over his City Brigade to Clark. That brigade and Owen's Cavalry consisted of individual soldiers and civilians pressed into emergency units. The rest of Kemper's forces were organic. The Local Brigade served briefly under Scruggs before Moore took charge. Even then, the junior officer likely had command of the demibrigade (at least the 2nd, 3rd, and 4th Locals) that went to Lee's main front. Moore remained near Richmond with the 5th and probably the 1st Locals and was reinforced by Strange, the cadets, and the Ambulance Company on October 1. The Marylanders, also, were only attached to his brigade. Whether or not Chrisman, too, served under him is not known. Also uncertain is whether or not the two militia regiments were brigaded under Evans.

37. The capture of Maury and Taylor on Thursday morning caused the Chaffin's Bluff Battalion to devolve on Allen. When he was soon wounded, it presumably passed briefly to Judson Jones, its only remaining captain. Hardin, however, soon arrived to take charge of it. The following day, moreover, Howard came forward to exercise more general command of the heavy artillery at the bluff. His transfer there likely made his own division pass to its senior subordinate present, Major James E. Robertson of the

20th. The relief of Atkinson the following day similarly elevated Hensley to lead the First Division. Besides these heavy guns, Lightfoot remained under Pemberton's control near the city. Stark, however, was ordered to report to Hardaway within Alexander's command, beginning September 30. By then, the Louisiana Guards were in Stark's Battalion, but whether they belonged to it when fighting erupted on Thursday morning is not clear.

38. During Mitchell's temporary absence on the morning of September 29, Rootes acted as Flag Officer. In their squadron, eight ships were combat vessels. However, the *Patrick Henry,* though formerly a gunboat, was now the Naval Academy ship. It provided details to the other vessels during the battle but was not itself prepared to engage. *ORN,* v. X, pp. 765–67.

APPENDIX B

1. This table is based on that in the *Official Records* but is altered by other sources. Gwyn is listed under his brigade rather than regiment, and Otis is added to his brigade. The Iron Brigade and the 3 batteries that Wainwright led back to Globe Tavern on Friday night are assumed to have lost no one. The 2 casualties known to have occurred in the 6th New Jersey are supposed to have been wounded after October 2. Ibid., pp. 138–43; RG 94, entry 729, box 93, No. 146, NA; Rochester *Daily Union & Advertiser,* Oct. 15, 1864; RG 391, 5AC, v. XXXIX, bk. 206, Oct. 1–3, 1864, NA; Stryker, op. cit., v. I, p. 267ff.; RG 391, 2AC, v. XII, bk. 59, Oct. 8, 1864, NA.

2. The term "Army Headquarters" here includes not only the staff but also Spaulding, Harwood, Patrick, Fisher, Shaffer, and Robison. The 16th definitely lost no one. The other forces are also presumed to have passed through the battle unscathed. Hancock and Crawford, though, did lose some men. The major general's casualties are supposed to have equaled Bushrod Johnson's and Jones's opposite him: eight a day, a total of 32. Even less is known about Crawford's loss, except that the 29th had one wounded and the 51st and 79th plus the 11th Massachusetts Battery lost no one. His overall casualties are estimated at 5 per day, or 20. *OR,* v. XLII, pt. 1, pp. 141–43, 897–99. No breakdown is possible on these surmises, so they appear only in the "corps" totals.

3. The sum of the first 3 columns is the loss of the striking force: 2,898. Of the 1,804 "missing" soldiers, only 1,663 were captured. The other 141 were presumably killed, too. Ibid., p. 870.

4. This table is based on that in the *Official Records* but is revised as other sources suggest appropriate. For Daggett, Stevens, Fairchild, and Duncan, officers wounded at brigade headquarters are here listed under those headquarters rather than under their regiments, as in *OR. OR,* v. XLII, pt. 1, pp. 133–37, 715–16, 726–27, 762, 820; Haskin, op. cit., p. 577; RG 94, entry 729, box 94, No. 301, NA; RG 393, DVNC, two-name box 5, No. W273-9, NA; RG 391, 24AC, v. XL, bk. 99, Sept. 30–Oct. 2, 1864, NA;

Daniel Baldridge to his parents, Sept. 30, 1864, Baldridge Papers, PSU; Sommers, op. cit., v. II, pp. 354–56.

5. On October 1, Barney and Bell lost two and four men wounded, respectively. Yet because these casualties' regiments are not indicated, their statistics can only be reflected in brigade and division totals, not in the breakdown by regiments. This accounts for the apparent discrepancy in totaling the regimental columns. Casualty Report of Foster's division, Sept. 29–Oct. 1, 1864, RG 391, 10AC, box 3, NA.

6. Besides his 979 casualties tabulated above, Birney is estimated to have lost 10 men on Sunday. The only breakdown on that loss, though, is that the 39th Illinois had a man captured. The other 9 casualties are simply added to the corps total, without being reflected at lower levels. "Return of Staff/39th Illinois, Oct., 1864," RG 94, M594, NA.

7. The division staff and provost guard each lost 5 men. The remaining 11 casualties occurred in the sharpshooter battalion.

8. All 25 of these losses were suffered by the divisional sharpshooter battalion.

9. The foregoing figures for the XVIII Corps total 2,321. That sum is raised by 6 to cover its supposed losses on October 2. No specifics have been found for its casualties that last day, so only in the corps total can that estimate be shown.

10. The casualty in the 12th evidently occurred before it left Potter to form part of White's brigade on Saturday.

11. Excluding Potter's 19 casualties puts the total loss of the strike force at 3,353. Of the 649 missing, only 603 fell into Butternut hands. The other 46 were, therefore, probably also killed. *OR*, v. XLII, pt. 1, pp. 870–71.

12. Of the 2,453 missing, only 2,266 were captured, so the other 187 were likely killed.

13. Readers are particularly urged to check Sommers, op. cit., v. V, pp. 1,337–44 and 1,349–56 for detailed explanations and rationales of the casualty figures used in the following table for the Graycoats.

14. Richmond *Examiner*, Oct. 8, 1864; "Returns of Staff/2nd Virginia Reserve Battalion and Staff/25th Virginia Battalion, July–Oct. 1864, and C-E-K/63rd Tennessee, S-O, 1864," RG 109, ch. 1, entry 18, NA; RG 109, entry 199, boxes 261–62, 282, NA; RG 393, DVNC, v. CXCI, bk. 466, pp. 93–107, NA; RG 391, 25AC, v. XI, bk. 17, Sept. 29–Oct. 1, 1864, NA; RG 391, 24AC, v. XXXIX, bk. 101, Sept. 29, 1864, NA; Richmond *Sentinel*, Oct. 3–4, 1864; Lindsley, op. cit., pp. 359, 408, 539–41, 592–93; Wright, loc. cit., v. XIV, p. 545; Linden Kent to his mother, Oct. 3, 1864, CM; *OR*, v. XLII, pt. 3, pp. 31–34; Trumbull, op. cit., p. 300; Sommers, op. cit., v. V, pp. 1,337–38.

15. Eight companies of the legion lost 2 killed, 7 wounded, and 5 missing on September 29. That was probably the regiment's entire loss during the battle. A claim that 6 companies of the 7th had 4 killed, 7 wounded, and 49 missing cannot be accepted. The Yankees report taking only a single prisoner from the entire regiment. "Returns of Hampton's Legion, S-O, 1864," RG 109, ch. 1, entry 18, NA; RG 393, DVNC, v. CXCI, bk. 466,

pp. 93–98, 110–12, NA; RG 391, 25AC, v. XI, bk. 17, Oct. 1, 1864, NA; RG 109, ch. 6, v. CLXXXVI, Sept. 29, 1864, NA; Columbia *Daily South Carolinian,* Oct. 1 and 12, 1864; Doyle, loc. cit., v. XXXIV, pp. 51–52; "Trimonthly returns of the Department of Richmond, Sept. 20 and Oct. 10, 1864," RG 109, entry 65, box 14, NA; "Returns of the 24th Virginia Cavalry," Confederate Army Papers, VSL; Sommers, op. cit., v. V, pp. 1,338–39.

16. Six prisoners and one wounded man in the 10th and 19th Virginia Heavy Artillery battalions almost certainly belonged to Hardin's force at Chaffin's, not to Atkinson's on the Intermediate Line. Hensley's main body had no casualties. *OR,* v. XLII, pt. 1, p. 935; Richmond *Sentinel,* Oct. 3 and 13, 1864; Richmond *Enquirer,* Dec. 1, 1864; RG 391, 24AC, v. XXXIX, bk. 101, Sept. 29, 1864, NA; RG 109, entry 199, boxes 261–62, 282, NA; Rosser Rock to his sister, Nov. 25, 1864, Rock Papers, CM; William Anderson to Peter Guerrant, Oct. 7, 1864, Guerrant Papers, VHS; H. H. Hoyer to Cecil Clay, March 26, 1888, Clay Papers, HSP; Allen, loc. cit., v. XIII, p. 418; RG 109, ch. 6, v. XIX, Oct. 1, 1864, and v. CLXXXVI, Sept. 30, 1864, NA; "Returns of Staff/10th Virginia Heavy Artillery Battalion and Green's Louisiana Battery, S-O, 1864," RG 109, ch. 1, entry 18, NA; D. E. Johnston, op. cit., p. 277; Charles Anthony to his mother, Oct. 3, 1864, Anthony Family Papers, VSL; Sommers, op. cit., v. V, pp. 1,339–40.

17. At least 1 man each of the 24th and 53rd was killed. The former regiment also lost at least 2 prisoners. Butler claims to have captured 15 other men of the brigade, but they do not appear in provost rolls. Even if they were taken, they did not come from the 56th, which suffered no missing. 56th Virginia file, I Corps data, EPA Coll., SCH; H. G. White, "G/24th Virginia," *SHSP,* v. XXXV, p. 352; "Brunswick Guard," *SHSP,* v. XXVIII, p. 13; *OR,* v. XLII, pt. 3, p. 65; RG 391, 25AC, v. XI, bk. 17, Oct. 2, 1864, NA; RG 393, DVNC, v. CXCI, bk. 466, p. 107, NA; RG 109, entry 199, boxes 261–62, 282, NA; Sommers, op. cit., v. V, pp. 1,343–44.

18. Unlike the other units, Field suffers from a plethora of contradictory brigade and regimental casualty returns. The table for him represents a synthesis of these sources in light of Union provost rolls. RG 109, entry 22, box 4, Nos. 195–204 and casualty reports of Benning's and Bratton's Brigades, May–Dec. 1864; RG 109, entry 199, boxes 261–62, 282, NA; Augusta *Chronicle and Sentinel,* Oct. 28 and 30, 1864; Charleston *Mercury,* Oct. 12, 1864; Columbia *Daily Southern Guardian,* Oct. 8, 1864; 2nd South Carolina Rifles file and Hood's Texas Brigade file, I Corps data, EPA Coll., SHC; Wylie, *Rebel Diary,* Sept. 28–Oct. 11, 1864, BU; RG 109, entry 544, v. CL, p. 115, NA; Columbus *Daily Enquirer,* Oct. 12 and Nov. 4, 1864; Morgan M. Reese, "John Bell Hood and the Texas Brigade," M.A. thesis, Southwest Texas State Teachers' College (1941), pp. 73–76; Polley, *Charming Nellie,* p. 264; *McCarty Ms.,* p. 3, TXU; "Return of Staff/5th Texas, S-O, 1864," and casualty report of 3rd Arkansas, May–Dec. 1864," RG 109, ch. 1, entry 18, NA; John Hamer, *Lowry Brothers,* Sept.

29, 1864, HJC; Galveston *News,* Nov. 22, 1864; Sommers, op. cit., v. V, pp. 1,340–42.

19. Colquitt definitely lost over 200 men. Thirteen were captured, and perhaps 60 more were killed. The balance, estimated at 149, were wounded. All 5 of his regiments took casualties. At least 4 of Hagood's outfits had losses, too; no information has been found for his 11th Regiment. For Scales and Kirkland, only fragmentary data are available. They show casualties in the 16th, 17th, and 42nd. The 17th suffered particularly heavily: all 7 prisoners and "some" killed. Clark, *NC,* v. I, p. 408, and v. III, p. 214; Hector McKethan to Thomas L. Clingman, Oct. 3, 1864, Burgwyn Coll., NCDAH; Raleigh *Daily Confederate,* Oct. 11–12, 1864; RG 109, entry 199, boxes 261–62, 282, NA; RG 109, entry 385, NA; J. D. McGeachy to his sister, Oct. 14, 1864, Buie Papers, DU; E. J. Williams to his mother, Oct. 2, 1864, SHC; Dunn, loc. cit., v. V, p. 146, GDAH; William Smith, *Diary,* Sept. 30, 1864, GDAH; RG 393, DVNC, v. CXCI, bk. 466, pp. 98–107, NA; Croom, op. cit., p. 26; RG 109, ch. 6, v. CLXXXVI, Sept. 30–Oct. 4, 1864, and v. CLXXIII, Oct. 2, 1864, NA; Richmond *Enquirer,* Oct. 11, 1864; Eisenschiml, op. cit., p. 245; Bates, *Pennsylvania Volunteers,* v. II, p. 291; Thompson, op. cit., pp. 490–92; Davie and Caleb Hampton to their uncle, Oct. 4, 1864, Caleb Hampton Papers, DU; George Moffett to Liz, Oct. 3, 1864, Moffett Papers, SCHS; Henry Greer to his mother, Oct. 3, 1864, Greer Papers, LC; Sommers, op. cit., v. V, pp. 1,342–44.

20. Probably at least 1 man of the Clutter Battery was wounded. Merrick Reid to his parents, Oct. 2, 1864, Reid Papers, SCL; RG 109, ch. 6, v. CLXXXVIII, Oct. 3, 1864, NA; Sommers, op. cit., v. V, p. 1,344.

21. At least 1 man each of the 9th Virginia and the 45th Georgia was wounded. RG 109, ch. 6, v. XX, Oct. 1, 1864, and v. CLXXXVI, Oct. 2, 1864, NA; *ORN,* v. X, pp. 753–66; Sommers, op. cit., v. V, p. 1,344.

22. A staff officer at I Corps headquarters grossly underestimated the loss on Friday at 500. McKethan alone suffered higher casualties. A newsman's claim that only 900 men fell in the entire battle is also far too low. For all its approximations, 1,700 is a reasonable estimate of Southern losses. Latrobe, *Diary,* Sept. 30, 1864, VHS; Richmond *Examiner,* Oct. 3, 1864.

23. Caldwell, op. cit., p. 185; Columbia *Daily South Carolinian,* Oct. 12, 1864; Petersburg *Daily Express,* Oct. 4, 1864; RG 109, entry 199, boxes 26–27, 261–62, 282, NA; Folders 82–83, Lane Papers, AU; *Lane's Brigade,* v. IX, p. 357; Clark, *NC,* v. I, p. 385; Raleigh *Daily Confederate,* Oct. 8, 1864; Wilcox, loc. cit., v. IX, No. 4, p. 70; Sommers, op. cit., v. V, pp. 1,349–50.

24. The 13th lost 8 men on the weekend, but its casualties on Friday, presumably equal to those the next day, are not indicated. The 27th reportedly suffered about 20 casualties. The 30 casualties at division headquarters, including 20 prisoners, cover the sharpshooters' loss at W. W. Davis' on October 2, even though Yankee provost rolls show only 6 captives at most. A postwar Confederate claim that the 2nd Mississippi lost 5 killed, 25 wounded, and 2 missing suggests that 2 of the killed and 6 of the wounded

may have been men of that regiment detailed to the sharpshooters. Louis Young to his mother, Oct. 6, 1864, Gourdin-Young Papers, CMC-Ib, EU; RG 109, entry 15, Nos. 19-P-24 and 23-P-31 and 25-P-31, NA; Fayetteville *Observer,* Nov. 17, 1864; Lewis Warlick to Cornelia McGimsey, Oct. 6, 1864, McGimsey Papers, SHC; Clark, *NC,* v. I, p. 600; "Returns of Staff/13th Alabama, F/1st Confederate Battalion, I/2nd and C-E/26th Mississippi, and B-G-K/26th and H/48th North Carolina, S-O, 1864," RG 109, ch. 1, entry 18, NA; Dr. Murchison to Dr. Albright, Oct. 2, 1864, and Henry Albright, *Diary,* Jan. 5, 1865, Albright Papers, NCDAH; RG 109, entry 199, boxes 5–6, 26, 261–62, 282, NA; *OR,* v. XLII, pt. 3, p. 9; Raleigh *Daily Confederate,* Oct. 8, 1864; R. S. Webb to his mother, Oct. 6, 1864, Webb-Moore Papers, SHC; Davis to Finney, Nov. 1, 1864, Heth Papers, CM; Richmond *Examiner,* Oct. 11, 1864; Vairen, *Diary,* Oct. 2, 1864, MDAH; Dunbar Rowland, "Military History," *Official Register of Mississippi,* pp. 436, 443, 507, 511; Thomas Burford et al., *Lamar Rifles,* pp. 15–51; W. A. Love, "Company Records," *CV,* v. XXXIII, pp. 51–52; Richmond *Dispatch,* Oct. 10, 1864; Richmond *Enquirer,* Oct. 14 and 19, 1864; Goldsborough, op. cit., pp. 140–42; Lindsley, op. cit., p. 130; RG 109, ch. 6, v. XIX, Oct. 2, 1864, NA; Sam Brooke to his sister, Oct. 4, 1864, Binckley Papers, LC; Wagstaff, loc. cit., v. XX, No. 2, p. 193; Jesse Frank to his mother, Oct. 5, 1864, Frank Papers, DU; Cavaness, *Diary,* Oct. 1, 1864, TXU; Sommers, op. cit., v. V, pp. 1,350–52.

25. Except for the Alabamians, brigade totals are only estimates. Weiseger's loss is assumed to have equaled Wallace's, and Finegan's, and Gibson's casualties are thought to have been the same as King's. Harris, by raiding Ferrero's pickets, would have endured the heaviest loss. The second-class forces likely had no casualties. Within the two brigades not broken down in the table, at least the 8th Florida and 61st Virginia suffered 1 wounded each. The 3rd and 48th Georgia and 16th, 19th, and 48th Mississippi also had men wounded. Richmond *Sentinel,* Oct. 29, 1864; *OR,* v. XLII, pt. 1, pp. 897–99, and pt. 3, p. 37; RG 109, entry 199, boxes 261–62, 282, NA; RG 109, ch. 6, v. XX, Oct. 1, 1864, and v. CLXXXVI, Oct. 4, 1864, and v. DCLXII, Oct. 1–4, 1864, NA; "Return of F/48th Mississippi, S-O, 1864," RG 109, ch. 1, entry 18, NA; RG 109, entry 15, No. 13-P-24, NA; Sommers, op. cit., v. V, pp. 1,352–53.

26. Only for the prisoners, Crenshaw, and Purcell are the figures accurate. Pegram is estimated to have lost 13 men, and the other 4 battalions two each. Willie Pegram to Mary, Oct. 5, 1864, PJM Coll., VHS; Richmond *Enquirer,* Oct. 7, 1864; Sommers, op. cit., v. V, pp. 1,355–56.

27. Young lost at least 8, probably 11, men on September 29. His total casualties for all 4 days, though, can only be estimated. His prisoners include Jones, at least 3 men of the 7th, at least 1 of the 20th, plus 5 whose unit cannot be identified. Among his other outfits to suffer killed and wounded were the 3 legions. Charleston *Mercury,* Oct. 12 and 29, 1864; Charleston *Courier,* Oct. 12, 1864; Brooks, op. cit., pp. 328, 331–32, 346; Willis, *Diary,* Oct. 2, 1864, VSL; RG 391, CC, v. XXII, bk. 34, pp. 92–95, NA; Waring, *Diary,* Sept. 29, 1864, SHC; Alexander Dun-

can, *Georgia Hussars,* p. 506; RG 109, ch. 6, v. CLXXVIII, Oct. 1, 1864, and v. CLXXXVI, Sept. 30, 1864, NA; RG 109, entry 15, No. 38-P-33, NA; Sommers, op. cit., v. V, pp. 1,353–54.

28. Although Northern provost rolls list only one trooper of the 13th, numerous other sources suggest that the regiment lost over 50 prisoners, apparently 55. Dick Beale to his mother, Oct. 2, 1864, Beale Family Papers, UV; Richmond *Examiner,* Oct. 7, 1864; RG 109, ch. 6, v. XIX, Oct. 1, 1864, and v. XX, Oct. 1, 1864, and v. LXXV, Oct. 2–3, 1864, NA; RG 391, CC, v. XXII, bk. 34, pp. 92–95, NA; *OR,* v. XLII, pt. 1, p. 620; New York *Herald,* Oct. 5, 1864; Rea, op. cit., p. 100; Beale, op. cit., p. 146; Richmond *Sentinel,* Oct. 3, 1864; Clark, *NC,* v. II, p. 103, and v. III, p. 627; Sommers, op. cit., v. V, p. 1, 354.

29. *OR,* v. XLII, pt. 2, p. 1,132; RG 109, entry 199, boxes 5–6, 261–62, 282, NA; Petersburg *Daily Express,* Oct. 1, 1864; "Return of C/8th Georgia Cavalry, S-O, 1864," RG 109, ch. 1, entry 18, NA; RG 109, ch. 6, v. CLXXXVI, Oct. 1–2, 1864, NA; Sommers, op. cit., v. V, pp. 1,354–55.

30. Five of Farley's prisoners belonged to the 7th Georgia Cavalry and the other one to Stokes's regiment. RG 391, CC, v. XXII, bk. 34, pp. 92–95, NA; Waring, *Diary,* Sept. 29, 1864, SHC; Charleston *Mercury,* Oct. 12, 1864; Sommers, op. cit., v. V, p. 1,355.

31. RG 109, entry 199, box 282, NA; Petersburg *Daily Express,* Oct. 1, 1864; Charleston *Mercury,* Nov. 5, 1864; McGregor, *Report,* Dec. 7, 1864, Halsey Papers, SHC; Sommers, op. cit., v. V, p. 1,355.

32. Jones's loss is arbitrarily assumed to equal Walker's supposed casualties, excluding Pegram's Battalion. The former's proximity to Federal lines offsets his numerical inferiority to the III Corps artillery and justifies equating their losses. Johnson's casualties show that his Virginians, on the far left and then in reserve, were virtually safe from the Bluecoats' fire, whereas his Tarheels, closest to the II Corps's works, suffered most. *OR,* v. XLII, pt. 1, pp. 897–99.

33. In this summary and the preceding tables, it is arbitrarily assumed that headquarters, engineer, provost, Signal Corps, and second-class troops suffered no casualties.

34. Of the 214 supposed prisoners, Northern provost rolls confirm only 141. Fourteen of Heth's sharpshooters, 5 of Young's men, and 54 of Lucius Davis' cannot be verified on those lists.

35. Again, Southern newspapers published casualty totals far below the actual range. The Richmond *Whig* of October 3, 1864, set it at 700. The Richmond *Sentinel* of the same date put it at 500. It really exceeded those two figures combined.

36. Of Lee's 610 missing, only 537 appear on Federal provost rolls. The balance, though, are believed to have been taken prisoner, also.

37. Only 2,266 of the 2,453 "missing" Yankees fell into Confederate hands. The other 187 were presumably killed. Just 537 of the 610 "missing" Butternuts show up on Northern prison lists, but the other 73 are thought to have been captured, too.

BIBLIOGRAPHY

LIST OF ABBREVIATIONS

AAH Coll.: Andrew Atkinson Humphreys Coll., Historical Society of Pennsylvania.

ADAH: Alabama Department of Archives and History.

AG: Annual Reports of State Adjutants General (followed by the appropriate name of state and year).

Alexander Ms.: Unabridged manuscript copy of *Military Memoirs of a Confederate,* Edward Porter Alexander Coll., Southern Historical Coll., University of North Carolina.

ANJ: The United States Army and Navy Journal and Gazette of the Regular and Volunteer Forces.

Artillery Defenses: Artillery Defenses, Department of Richmond. *Order Book,* Chicago Historical Society.

AU: Auburn University.

BFB Coll.: Benjamin F. Butler Coll., Library of Congress.

BU: Boston University.

CHHS: Chicago Historical Society.

Clark, *NC:* Walter Clark, comp. *Histories of the Several Regiments and Battalions from North Carolina in the Great War, 1861–'65.*

CM: Museum of the Confederacy, Richmond, Va.

CMC: Confederate Miscellaneous Colls., Duke University, Emory University, and the Georgia Department of Archives and History.

CNHS: Connecticut Historical Society.

CSR: Compiled Service Records, entry 519 of Record Group 94 and entry 193 of Record Group 109, National Archives.

CV: Confederate Veteran magazine.

CWR: Connecticut War Record magazine.

CWTI Coll.: *Civil War Times Illustrated* Coll., U. S. Army Military History Institute.

DPAC: Delaware Public Archives Commission.

DPL: Detroit Public Library.

DSF Coll.: Douglas Southall Freeman Colls., Library of Congress and University of Virginia.

DU: Duke University.

EPA Coll.: Edward Porter Alexander Coll., Southern Historical Coll., University of North Carolina.

EU: Emory University.

GDAH: Georgia Department of Archives and History.

GGM Coll.: George Gordon Meade Coll., Historical Society of Pennsylvania.

GKW Coll.: Gouverneur Kemble Warren Coll., New York State Library.

HHL: Henry E. Huntington Library and Art Gallery.

HJC: Hill Junior College.

HJH Papers: Henry Jackson Hunt Papers, Library of Congress.

HSD: Historical Society of Delaware.

HSP: Historical Society of Pennsylvania.

ISHL: Illinois State Historical Library.

JLC Coll.: Joshua L. Chamberlain Coll., Library of Congress.

Johnston Ms.: Nathaniel Burwell Johnston. *Battle of Fort Harrison, September 29th, 1864,* manuscript in the Charles J. Calrow folder, box 179, Douglas Southall Freeman Coll., Library of Congress.

Johnston mss.: Manuscripts formerly in the possession of the late Mr. J. Ambler Johnston, Sr., of Richmond, Va.

LC: Library of Congress.

LHQ Coll.: Lee's Headquarters Coll., Virginia Historical Society.

McCarty Ms.: Thomas McCarty. Untitled reminiscence on the Battle of Chaffin's Bluff, Thomas McCarty Papers, University of Texas.

MDAH: Mississippi Department of Archives and History.

MDHS: Maryland Historical Society.

MH: Michigan History Commission.

MHC: Michigan Historical Coll., University of Michigan.

MHRC: U. S. Army Military History Institute (formerly the U. S. Army Military History Research Collection).

MNHS: Minnesota Historical Society.

MOLLUS: Papers of the Military Order of the Loyal Legion of the United States (followed by the name of the appropriate commandery).

MSHS: Massachusetts Historical Society.

NA: National Archives. The following subheadings are used to describe material in this institution:
AP: Army of the Potomac Papers.
CC: Cavalry Corps, Army of the Potomac Papers.

DVNC: Department of Virginia and North Carolina Papers.

nAC: Army Corps Papers, where "n" represents the number of the particular corps (Thus, 2AC refers to the II Army Corps Papers).

RG: Record Group.

S-O: September-October.

NCDAH: North Carolina Department of Archives and History.

NHHS: New Hampshire Historical Society.

NJHS: New Jersey Historical Society.

NT: National Tribune.

NYHS: New-York Historical Society.

NYPL: New York (City) Public Library.

NYSL: New York State Library.

OR: War of the Rebellion: A Compilation of the Official Records of the Union and Confederate Armies (all references are to series 1 unless otherwise specified).

ORA: The Official Military Atlas of the Civil War.

ORN: Official Records of the Union and Confederate Navies in the War of the Rebellion (all references are to series 1 unless otherwise indicated).

PJM Coll.: Pegram-Johnson-McIntosh Coll., Virginia Historical Society.

PSU: Pennsylvania State University.

Ripley Ms.: Edward H. Ripley. *The Battle of Fort Harrison, or Chapin's Farm,* manuscript in the Douglas Southall Freeman Coll., University of Virginia.

RISSHS: Personal Narratives of Events in the War of the Rebellion, Being Papers Read before the Rhode Island Soldiers' and Sailors' Historical Society.

RNBP: Richmond National Battlefield Park.

SCHS: South Carolina Historical Society.

SCL: South Caroliniana Library, University of South Carolina.

SHSP: Southern Historical Society Papers.

TU: Tulane University.

TXU: University of Texas.

UCSB: University of California at Santa Barbara.

UDC Coll.: United Daughters of the Confederacy Coll., Georgia Department of Archives and History.

UM: University of Michigan.

UV: University of Virginia.

VHS: Virginia Historical Society.

VSL: Virginia State Library.

WCL: William Clements Library, University of Michigan.

WHGS: Wyoming Historical and Genealogical Society, Wilkes-Barre, Pa.

WHS: State Historical Society of Wisconsin.

WNP Coll.: William Nelson Pendleton Coll., Southern Historical Coll., University of North Carolina.

WP: U. S. Military Academy.

WRHS: Western Reserve Historical Society.

MANUSCRIPTS

ALABAMA DEPARTMENT OF ARCHIVES AND HISTORY (ADAH)

4th Alabama Infantry Regiment Coll.
  Coles, R. T. *History of the Fourth Regiment.*
  Hollis, Rufus. *Confederate Veteran.* Scottsboro, Ala.: Press of the Scottsboro Citizen, n.d.
Crenshaw, Edward. *Diary,* 1861–65.
Reed, John C. *Journal.*

AUBURN UNIVERSITY (AU)

Lane, James H. Papers, 1864.

BERKS COUNTY, PA., HISTORICAL SOCIETY

"Map Room, F4BF, G819, Green Box," newspaper clipping.

BOSTON UNIVERSITY (BU)

20th Massachusetts Infantry Regiment Coll.
  Lyman, Theodore. Correspondence.
  Magnitzky, Gustave. *Diary.*
  [Wylie, O. A.]. *Rebel Diary,* 1864–65.

UNIVERSITY OF CALIFORNIA AT SANTA BARBARA (UCSB)

Cook, E. L. Letters.
Rood, Amos D. *Something of My War Service,* 1893.

CASEBIER MSS. [Typescript in the possession of Mr. Dennis Casebier of Norco, Calif.]

Eyre, Manuel. *Diary,* May 23–Oct. 7, 1864.

CHARLESTON LIBRARY SOCIETY

Wells, Edward L. Correspondence.

CHICAGO HISTORICAL SOCIETY (CHHS)

Artillery Defenses, Department of Richmond. *Order Book.*
Grant, Ulysses S. Correspondence.
Merryweather, George. Letters.

COCO MSS. [Unpublished papers owned by Mr. Gregory Coco of Gettysburg, Pa.]

Mills, Charles J. Letters, 1864.

COHASCO, INC., 321 Broadway, New York, N.Y.

Manuscript Catalogue 9—Entry 95.

MUSEUM OF THE CONFEDERACY (CM)

Baughman, Charles C. Letters.

Harrison Coll. of Telegrams Relating to the Richmond Campaign of 1864, May–Sept.

Heth, Henry. *Reports* and Letters.

Kent, Linden. Letter, Oct. 2–3, 1864.

Lee, Robert E. Letter to John K. Mitchell, 7:45 A.M., Sept. 29, 1864.

Maps.

Mullen, Joseph. *Diary,* May 4, 1864–May 2, 1865.

Pendleton, William N. *Order Book,* June 17, 1862–Apr. 2, 1865.

Rock, Rosser. Letters.

Roll of Officers and Men of Graham's Battery of Horse Artillery, "Petersburg Artillery," 1863–64–65.

Steuart's Brigade. *Book of Letters Sent, Feb. 1863–Nov. 1864.*

CONNECTICUT HISTORICAL SOCIETY (CNHS)

Brown, Henry H. Letters and *Diary.*

Eldridge, James W. *Diary,* 1862–65.

Snow, Henry. Letters, 1861–65.

HISTORICAL SOCIETY OF DELAWARE (HSD)

Gawthorp, Henry. Letters and *Diary,* Sept. 1, 1862–Feb. 1, 1866.

DELAWARE PUBLIC ARCHIVES COMMISSION (DPAC)

LaMotte, Charles E. Letters, 1861–65.

DETROIT PUBLIC LIBRARY (DPL)

Civil War Letters to Isabella Duffield, 1864–65, Divie Bethune Duffield Papers, Charles M. Burton Historical Coll.

DUKE UNIVERSITY (DU)

Abernathy, Daniel. Letters, 1862–65.

Andrews, Charles Wesley. Letters, 1861–65.

Andrews, William B. G. Papers, 1862–70.

Biddle, Samuel Simpson. Letters, 1860–66.

Buie, Catherine. Letters, 1863–99.

Clopton, John. Letters, 1862–65.

Confederate States of America Archives. Army Miscellany, Officers' and Soldiers' Miscellaneous Letters, Aug.–Dec. 1864: J. H. Pegram, Letter, Oct. 6, 1864.

Couch, John. Papers, 1843–1940.

Danforth, John B. *Letter Press Copybook,* 1854–64.

Davis, Jasper W. Papers, 1834–68.

Ewell, Benjamin Stoddert, and Ewell, Richard Stoddert. Letters, 1862–65.

Ewell, Richard Stoddert. *Letterbook,* 1862–65.

Foote, John B. Papers, 1862–65.

Frank, Alexander. Letters, 1858–78.

Hampton, Caleb. Papers, 1864–80.

Hartman, John H. Letters, 1823–65.
Haynes, Joseph N. Papers, 1862–91.
Lee, Robert E. Letters, 1749–1939.
Maides, James F. Letters, 1862–65.
McNaught, John Smith. *Diary,* 1863–65.
Pendleton, Dudley Diggs. Letters, 1861–65.
Persons, Presley. Letters, 1864–75.
Russell, William. *Diary,* 1863–65.
Saussy, Joachim. Papers, 1854–95.
Smith, Joseph Belknap. Papers, 1802–72.
Summers, Julius A. Letters, 1861–64.
Verdery, Eugene, and Verdery, James Paul. Letters, 1864–70.
Warthen, George. Letters, 1858–93.
Wilkerson, James K. Letters, 1863–69.

EAST CAROLINA UNIVERSITY

Scales, Alfred M. Papers, 1858–1910.

EMORY UNIVERSITY (EU)

Confederate Miscellaneous Coll.
  Coleman, John A. F. *Diary* (Ib).
  Davis, Robert F. *Diary* (Ib).
  Gourdin-Young. Letters (Ic).
  Hilton, Joseph. Letters (Ib).
  Kemper, James L. Letters.
Everett, John A. Letters, 1861–65.
McFall, William. Letters, July 22, 1862–Mar. 25, 1865.
McKinney, Samuel B. Letters, 1861–64.
Monks-Rohrer. Letters.

FILSON CLUB

Fitzhugh, Lucy. *Scrapbook.*

GEORGIA DEPARTMENT OF ARCHIVES AND HISTORY (GDAH)

Confederate Miscellaneous Coll.
  Avant, Augustus. *Sandersville Volunteers.*
  Lokey, John W. *My Experiences in the War Between the States.*
  Pope, David H. Letters.
  Shank Family. Letters.
  Smith, William H. *Diary,* 1864.
Microfilm Room.
  Fleming, Donald. *Diary,* 1863–65 (Floyd County United Daughters of
    the Confederacy Coll.).
  Mosely, William J. Letters, 1855–72.
  Young, M. O. *History of the First Brigade.*
United Daughters of the Confederacy Coll.
  Bowden, John Malachi. "Reminiscences of a Confederate Soldier," v.
    VII, pp. 1–60.

Dunn, Washington L. "Diary of Captain Washington Dunn, Co. A-27 Ga. Regt.," v. V, pp. 122–61.
Graham, E. D. "Letters," v. II, pp. 302–23.

GEORGIA HISTORICAL SOCIETY

Anderson, Edward C., Jr. Letters, Wayne-Stites-Anderson Coll.

GETTYSBURG COLLEGE

Hartranft, John F. Letters.

HARVARD UNIVERSITY (THE HOUGHTON LIBRARY)

Kemper, James L. Letter, Sept. 29, 1864, Frederick M. Dearborn Coll.
Military Order of the Loyal Legion of the United States—Massachusetts Commandery Coll.
    Hancock, Winfield Scott. Dispatches, Oct. 1–Oct. 27, 1864.
    Third New Hampshire Notebook, Jan.–Oct. 1864.

HILL JUNIOR COLLEGE (HJC)

Felder, Rufus K. Letters.
Hamer, John, ed. *The Saga of the Three Lowry Brothers of Three Creeks, Arkansas.*
Hanks, O. T. *History of Captain B. F. Benton's Company, 1861–1865.*
Joskins, Joe. *A Sketch of Hood's "Texas Brigade of the Virginia Army."*
Williams, Watson D. Letters.

HENRY E. HUNTINGTON LIBRARY (HHL)

Faulkner, Robert. *Diary,* Jan. 1–Nov. 16, 1864.
Grant, Ulysses S. Letters.
Heald, Daniel. *Diaries,* 1863–65.
Lockley, Frederick E. Letters (these letters were published by John Pomfret in *The Huntington Library Quarterly . . . ,* v. XVI).
Osborn, Luther. Papers.
Raulston, John B. *History of the Eighty-first Regiment, N.Y. Vol. Infantry* [manuscript written in 1865].
Wainwright, Charles S. *Diary* (an abridged version of this source was published by Allan Nevins: *A Diary of Battle . . .*).

ILLINOIS STATE HISTORICAL LIBRARY (ISHL)

Kautz, August V. Papers, 1864–65.
dePeyster, John Watts. Papers.
    Paine, William H. *Diary,* 1864.
Pollack, Samuel. *Diary.*
Rogers, Stephen I. Papers, 1861–65.
Rowley, William R. Papers, 1864.

JOHNSTON MSS. [unpublished documents formerly in the possession of the late Mr. J. Ambler Johnston, Sr., of Richmond, Va.]

Ellzey, Mason Graham. *The Cause We Lost and the Land We Love.*
Hardaway, Robert Archelaus. Letter, June 25, 1894.

Johnston, Nathaniel Burwell. *Military Record of Nathaniel Burwell Johnston of Salem, Virginia.*

LIBRARY OF CONGRESS (LC)

Beauregard, P. G. T. *Letterbook, July–Oct. 1864*, v. XXXIII.

Binckley, John Milton. Papers, 1816–1943.

Butler, Benjamin F. Papers.

Chamberlain, Joshua L. Coll.
   [Spear, Ellis]. *1865* [sic: 1864].

Comstock, Cyrus. *Diary*, Oct. 16, 1863–Dec. 7, 1867.

Confederate States of America Coll.
   War Department. *List of Official Communications*, box 110.

Fleetwood, Christian A. *Notebook* and *Diary*.

Freeman, Douglas Southall. Coll.
   Freeman, Douglas Southall. Correspondence.
   Johnston, Nathaniel Burwell. *Battle of Fort Harrison, September 29th, 1864*, box 179, Calrow folder.

Gorgas, Josiah. *Diary*, 1857–77 (this journal was published by Frank E. Vandiver).

Grant, Ulysses S. Papers.

Greer, Henry, and Greer, Robert. Letters, Nov. 3, 1863–Apr. 27, 1865.

Hatton, John W. F. *Memoir*, 1861–65.

Hawley, Joseph R. Correspondence.

Heisler, Henry. Letters, Oct. 7, 1861–June 9, 1865.

Hunt, Henry J. Military Papers and *Journal of Operations*, Apr. 16, 1864–Mar. 23, 1865.

Kautz, August Valentine. Coll.
   Journal, 1864.
   Reminiscences of the Civil War.
   Report of the Military Services of August V. Kautz, Brevet Major General, U. S. A., from March 4th, 1861, to January 15th, 1866.
   Maps.

Patrick, Marsena R. *Diary*, 1861–65 (an abridged version of this diary was published by David Sparks: *Inside Lincoln's Army . . .*).

Porter, David Dixon. *Journals, 1860–65.*

Reed, Charles W. Letters and *Diary*.

Welles, Gideon. Correspondence and *Diary*.

Wilcox, Cadmus Marcellus. Coll.
   Fragment of Autobiography.
   Letters.
   Notes on the Richmond Campaign, 1864–65 (two different copies).

LOUISIANA STATE UNIVERSITY

Grima, Alfred. Letters.

Hero, Andrew, and Hero, George. Papers.

MARYLAND HISTORICAL SOCIETY (MDHS)

Bond-McCulloch Family. Papers.

Snook, James M. *Diary*, Jan. 1–Dec. 31, 1864.

MASSACHUSETTS HISTORICAL SOCIETY (MSHS)

Lyman, Theodore. Letters and *Diary,* 1863–65 (an abridged edition of these letters was published by George Agassiz: *Meade's Headquarters . . .*).

Robeson, Andrew. Letters, 1864–65.

Spear, John M. *Army Life in the Twenty-fourth Regiment, Massachusetts Volunteer Infantry, Dec. 1861 to Dec. 1864.* Boston, 1892.

MICHIGAN HISTORY COMMISSION (MH)

Arnold, George Benton. *Diary,* Mrs. Clayton L. Arnold Coll. of the Civil War Papers of George Benton Arnold.

Regimental Service Records.
1st Sharpshooters Regiment. Letters and Telegrams, 1861–81.
16th Infantry Regiment. History, Nov. 14, 1864.
20th Infantry Regiment. History, Nov. 4, 1864.

UNIVERSITY OF MICHIGAN (UM)

Michigan Historical Coll. (MHC)
Davis, Ferdinand. *Personal Recollections of Service in the Civil War.*
William L. Clements Library (WCL)
Marshall, Henry Grimes. Letters, 1862–65.

MILITARY ORDER OF THE LOYAL LEGION OF THE UNITED STATES—NATIONAL WAR LIBRARY

Hamilton, James C. *History of the 110th Pennsylvania Infantry Regiment.*

MINNESOTA HISTORICAL SOCIETY (MNHS)

Folwell, William Watts. Correspondence and *Diary.*

MISSISSIPPI DEPARTMENT OF ARCHIVES AND HISTORY (MDAH)

Series L, Confederate Military Records.
v. II, Second Regiment, Mississippi Volunteers, Army of Northern Virginia.
v. XII, Eleventh Regiment, Mississippi Volunteers, Army of Northern Virginia.

Vairen, A. L. P. *2nd Miss. Regiment: Old Ord's War Journal—1861, 62, 63, 64, & 65.*

MOHR MSS. [Document in the possession of Dr. James Mohr of Baltimore, Maryland]

Cormany, Samuel. *Diary,* 1864.

NATIONAL ARCHIVES (NA)

Record Group 77: Office of the Chief of Engineers.
Entries 14, 117, 120, 159, 161, 291 (21 titles).
Record Group 94: The Adjutant General's Office.
Entries 12, 14, 44, 53, 57, 62, 65, 66, 77, 112, 113, 115, 159, 160, 178, 297, 324, 352, 361, 501, 519, 534, 544, 729, 730, 731, 732.
Films M665, M594, T823.
(54 titles).

Record Group 108: Headquarters of the Army.
  Entries 1, 11, 12, 21, 30, 35, 38 (16 titles).
Record Group 109: War Department Coll. of Confederate Records.
  Chapters 1, 2, 3, 5, 6, 9.
  Entries 6, 12, 15, 18, 22, 27, 43, 65, 112, 193, 199, 385, 450.
  (75 titles).
Record Group 111: Office of the Chief Signal Officer.
  Entries 1, 12, 13 (4 titles).
Record Group 153: Office of the Judge Advocate General.
  Entry 15 (1 title).
Record Group 391: United States Army Regular Army Mobile Units,
  1821–1942.
      II Army Corps Papers (75 titles).
      V Army Corps Papers (49 titles).
      VI Army Corps Papers (3 titles).
      IX Army Corps Papers (44 titles).
      X Army Corps Papers (38 titles).
  XVIII Army Corps Papers (12 titles).
  XXIV Army Corps Papers (26 titles).
   XXV Army Corps Papers (18 titles).
  Cavalry Corps, Army of the Potomac Papers (16 titles).
Record Group 393: United States Army Continental Commands,
  1821–1920.
  Army of the Potomac Papers (46 titles).
  Department of Virginia and North Carolina Papers (58 titles).
  Department of Washington Papers (2 titles).
(The 558 titles of National Archives papers, outlined above, are specified
  in Sommers, op. cit., v. V, pp. 1,410–30.)

NEW HAMPSHIRE HISTORICAL SOCIETY (NHHS)

Duncan-Jones. Manuscripts.
Ninth New Hampshire Infantry Regiment Coll.
History of 9" N. H. Vols.

NEW HAMPSHIRE RECORDS MANAGEMENT AND ARCHIVES COMMISSION

Monthly Returns of Civil War Troops.
  11th Infantry Regiment.

NEW JERSEY HISTORICAL SOCIETY (NJHS)

Rappalyea, Lewis C. *Diary,* 1864–65.

NEW-YORK HISTORICAL SOCIETY (NYHS)

Cunningham, John L. Letters.
Howland, Joseph. Correspondence.

NEW YORK PUBLIC LIBRARY (NYPL)

Clark, Albion W. *Diary,* 1857–67.
Sargent, Ransom. *Diary,* 1864–65.

NEW YORK STATE LIBRARY (NYSL)

Warren, Gouverneur Kemble. Correspondence and *V Army Corps Letter-books*.

NORTH CAROLINA DEPARTMENT OF ARCHIVES AND HISTORY (NCDAH)

Albright, Henry Clay. Papers and *Diary*.
Brown, Henry C. Coll., 1786–1911.
Burgwyn, William H. Letters and *Diary*.
Chambers, Henry A. *Diary,* Jan. 1–Dec. 31, 1864.
Council, John W. *Diary, 1864–65.*
Foard, Fred C. *Reminiscences.*
Mabry, Robert C. Papers, 1861–64.
Shuford, Lowen. Coll.
Torrence, Hugh A. *War Between the States (Civil War).*
Vance, Zebulon. Papers, 1864–65.

PARKER MSS. [Document in the possession of Mr. E. O. Parker of Washington, D.C.]

Lyle, J. Banks. *Diary, 1864.*

HISTORICAL SOCIETY OF PENNSYLVANIA (HSP)

Clay, Curtis L. Coll.
Clay, Cecil. Miscellaneous Correspondence.
General and Special Orders, Third Brigade, First Division, XVIII Corps.
O'Mohundro, Silas B. Map, Civil War, Vicinity of Richmond, Virginia.
Fox, Isaac. *Diary, 1864.*
Gratz, Simon. Coll.
Ord, Edward O. C. Letters.
Humphreys, Andrew Atkinson. Correspondence with Mrs. Humphreys, v. XXXIII (some of these letters appear in H. H. Humphreys' book on his father).
Irvin, John. *Diary.*
Johnson, Joseph. Letter to J. Fisher Leaming, Sept. 30, 1864, enclosed in Leaming to William Meredith, Oct. 24, 1864, William Meredith Papers.
McKnight, Charles. *Diary.*
Meade, George Gordon. Coll.
Telegrams and Letters Received, Commencing June 28, 1863.
Letters and Telegrams Received, Sept. 30–Dec. 31, 1864.

PENNSYLVANIA HISTORY COMMISSION

Official Military Papers.
Adjutant General. General Correspondence.
Battery B/1st Pennsylvania Light Artillery Regiment. Papers.

PENNSYLVANIA STATE UNIVERSITY (PSU)

Baldridge Coll. of Civil War Letters.
McDowell, M. Gyla. Coll.

Dunlap, Hamilton. Letters and *Diary*.
McDowell, M. Gyla. *The Roundheads' Own Story*.

PETERSBURG NATIONAL BATTLEFIELD PARK
Sanderson-Talmage Letters on the Battle of Peebles's Farm.

PETERSBURG SIEGE MUSEUM
Archer, Fletcher H. Letters, 1864.

PRINCETON UNIVERSITY
Reed, Charles W. Papers.

RICHMOND NATIONAL BATTLEFIELD PARK (RNBP)
Calrow, Charles J. *The Battle of Chaffin's Farm*.
Taylor, Richard Cornelius. *Personal Experiences of Major Richard C. Taylor* (passages of this reminiscence are quoted in Calrow).

SOUTH CAROLINA HISTORICAL SOCIETY (SCHS)
McMichael, Peter A. *Diary*, 1861–65.
Moffett, George H. Letters and *Diary*, 1864.
Simons, Alfred D. *Diary*, May 1864–Jan. 1865.

SOUTH CAROLINIANA LIBRARY, UNIVERSITY OF SOUTH
   CAROLINA (SCL)
Coward, Asbury. *Memoirs* (this document has been published by Natalie Jenkins Bond and Osman Latrobe Coward: *The South Carolinians . . .*).
Hagood, James R. *Memoirs of the First South Carolina Regiment of Volunteer Infantry in the Confederate War for Independence, April 12, 1861, to April 10, 1865*.
Hampton, Wade. Papers (Charles Edward Cauthen has published these letters: *Family Letters of the Three Wade Hamptons . . .*).
Reid, William Moultrie. Coll.

SOUTHERN HISTORICAL COLLECTION, UNIVERSITY OF NORTH
   CAROLINA (SHC)
Albright, James. *Diary*, Apr.–Nov. 1864.
Alexander, Edward Porter. Coll.
   Correspondence.
   Data Gathered for a History of Longstreet's Corps: Regimental and Brigade Rosters, Officer Personnel, Statistics, Strength, Description of Certain Engagements, and Histories of Various Units.
   Memorandum from the 4th Alabama History.
   Maps.
   Unabridged manuscript copy of *Military Memoirs of a Confederate*.
Alexander, William D. *Diary*, May 18, 1864–Apr. 27, 1865.
Alexander-Hillhouse. Papers.
Benning, Henry L. Papers.
Brooks, N. J. *Diary*, Mar. 31–Sept. 29, 1864.
Bryan, James A. *Diary*, 1861–65, Bryan Family Papers.

Burwell, Edmund Strudwick. Papers, 1825–83.
Cocke, Harrison. Papers, 1864–76.
Gordon, John W. *Diary*.
Halsey, Edwin L. Papers.
Harllee, William C. Letters, 1863–65.
Harrison, Walter. *Record Book*.
Kennedy, Mary H. Letters, 1864–65.
Lyons, Jacob. *Diary,* 1862–65.
McGimsey, Cornelia. Letters, 1863–65.
Mercer Family. Papers, 1861–64.
Mordecai, Emma. *Diary,* May 1864–May 1865.
Pendleton, William Nelson. Coll.
Ramsay, John A. Letters, 1864.
Snuggs, Anne Linebarger. Coll.
  Linebarger, T. James. Letters and *Diary*.
Thomson, Ruffin. Letters, 1864.
Waller, George E. Letters, 1858–64.
Waring, Joseph Fred. *Diary*.
Webb-Moore. Papers.
Williams, Edmund Jones. Letters, 1861–64.
Wills, William H. Letters, 1864.

STANFORD UNIVERSITY

Bailey Family. Letters.
Newcomb, Lewis E. Letters and *Diary*.

TEXAS STATE LIBRARY

Shotwell, John J. Letters, July–Sept. 1864.

UNIVERSITY OF TEXAS (TXU)

Cavaness, I. F. *Diary of One Who Wore the Blue*.
Crimmins, Martin L. Coll.
  Crockett, Edward R. *Diary*.
  McDonald, Wilfred. *Diary*.
McCarty, Thomas. *Diary* and Untitled reminiscence on the Battle of Chaffin's Bluff.

TULANE UNIVERSITY (TU)

Bragg, Braxton. Coll.
  Endorsement Book, Mar. 15, 1864–Jan. 31, 1865.
  Letters Sent, Feb. 24, 1864–Jan. 26, 1865.
Civil War Diaries.
  Jones, A. C. *Diaries,* July 1862–Apr. 1865.
  Lobrano, Frank. *Diary,* July 10, 1864–July 25, 1865.
Civil War Papers.
  Army of Northern Virginia Papers.
  Washington Artillery Battalion Papers.
Davis, Jefferson. Coll. of Telegrams and Letters.

U. S. ARMY MILITARY HISTORY INSTITUTE (MHRC)

Boyer, Ronald. Coll.
   Charles, Henry F. *Memoirs,* 1862–65.
Civil War Miscellaneous Coll.
   Goodwin, James. Letters, 1864.
   Skinner, Theodore. Letters, 1864.
Civil War Times Illustrated Coll.
   Coleman, John K. *Diary,* 1864.
   DeGraff, Nicholas. *Memoirs,* 1862–65.
   Ellis, Orrin. *Diary,* 1862–65.
   Johnson, Clarence A. Letters, 1864–65.
   Jones, Peleg. *Diary,* 1864.
   Pope, Albert A. *Diary,* 1864.
   Scroggs, Joseph J. *Diary,* 1862–65 (part of this diary was published by
      Sig Synnestvedt in *Civil War Times Illustrated*).
Hammock, Mansel, ed. *Letters to Amanda, 1862–1865, from Sergeant
   Major Marion Hill Fitzpatrick.* Culloden, Ga., 1976.
Harrisburg Civil War Round Table Coll.
   Metzger, Henry. Letters, 1861–65.
Mensch, Andrew. *Memoirs.*
Military Order of the Loyal Legion of the United States—Massachusetts
   Commandery Coll.
      Currier, Charles A. *Recollections of Service with the Fortieth Massa-
         chusetts Infantry Volunteers,* 1862–65.
      Rand, Arnold A. *Personal Records.*
Mitchell, John R. *Diary,* 1862–65.

U. S. MILITARY ACADEMY (WP)

DeTrobriand, P. Regis. *Diary,* 1864.

VALENTINE MUSEUM

Gray Family. Papers.

VIRGINIA HISTORICAL SOCIETY (VHS)

Boyd, Robert W. "Gary as a Soldier in the Civil War, 1861–65," in
   Louella Pauline Gary, comp. *Biography of General Martin Wither-
   spoon Gary, by His Sister.*
Cooper, Samuel. Letter, Oct. 3, 1864.
Guerrant Family. Papers, 1788–1918.
Hutchinson Family. Papers, 1807–1918.
Lancaster Family. Papers, 1784–1872.
Latrobe, Osman. *Diary,* 1862–65.
Lee's Headquarters Coll.
   Anderson, Richard H. *Report of the Campaign of 1864.*
   Hampton, Wade. *Cavalry Returns,* Aug.–Dec. 1864.
   Lee, Robert E. *Telegram Book,* Mar. 18, 1862–Oct. 8, 1864.
   Wilcox, Cadmus M. *Reports,* 1863–65.
Maps.

Mason, Charles Tayloe. Papers, 1854–1906.
McClellan, Henry B. Letter, Oct. 6, 1864.
Palmore, Wesley. *Roll Book of the Powhatan Artillery, 1861–1865.*
Pegram-Johnson-McIntosh. Coll.
Report Concerning the Salem Flying Artillery of the Army of Northern Virginia, Hardaway's Battalion, Griffin's Battery.
Stapp, Joseph D. Letters, Jan. 27, 1864–Mar. 4, 1865.
Vincent, John Bell. *Diary,* May 30, 1864–Apr. 17, 1865.
Wright, Gilbert Jefferson. Letters, 1862–64.

VIRGINIA STATE LIBRARY (VSL)

Anthony Family. Letters, 1860–65.
Confederate Army Papers.
   24th Virginia Cavalry Regiment. Returns.
Confederate Soldiers. Letters, 1861–65, 1883 (No. 24238).
Hammond, Isaac. Correspondence, 1850–65.
Lucas Family. Papers, 1861, 1863–64.
Palmore, Wesley. *Roll Book of the Powhatan Artillery, 1861–1865.*
Parker, Ely S. Letter, Sept. 23, 1864.
Sale, John F. *Diary.*
Second Regiment of Virginia Reserve Forces. Paper, Oct. 1, 1864.
Sperry, Kate. *Diary,* 1864.
Taylor, Walter H. Correspondence.
Willis, Byrd C. *Diary,* Apr. 7, 1864–May 22, 1865.

UNIVERSITY OF VIRGINIA (UV)

Beale Family. Papers.
Blackford, Launcelot Minor. Letters, 1855–65.
Cox, Eugene M. *Diary.*
Dobie, David F. Letters, 1862–65.
Kent-Hunter. Letters.
Rawlings Family. Papers.
Ripley, Edward H. *The Battle of Fort Harrison, or Chapin's Farm,* Douglas Southall Freeman Coll.
Rosser, Thomas L. Papers.

WESTERN RESERVE HISTORICAL SOCIETY (WRHS)

Lamberton, Robert C. *Diary.*
Palmer, William. Coll.
   Bowles, Pinckney D. Letter, Oct. 5, 1886.
   Bushnell, Wells A. *Historical Sketch of the 6th Ohio Volunteer Cavalry.*
   McAllister, Robert. Papers (James I. Robertson published an abridged version of these letters, based on the comparable holdings of Rutgers University).

COLLEGE OF WILLIAM AND MARY

Watkins Family. Papers.

STATE HISTORICAL SOCIETY OF WISCONSIN (WHS)

Bragg, Edward S. Letters.

Green, Sullivan D. *Diaries*.

Lamont, William. Letters, 1864–65.

Merrell, Edward H. Correspondence.

Perry, James M. *Diaries, 1861–65*.

Wright, Benjamin. Correspondence.

WYOMING HISTORICAL AND GENEALOGICAL SOCIETY, Wilkes-Barre, Pa. (WHGS)

Brimble, Evan. *Diary, 1864–65*.

Dana, Edmund L. Letters and *Diary*.

YALE UNIVERSITY

Terry Family. Papers.

DISSERTATIONS AND THESES

Marino, Carl W. "General Alfred Howe Terry: Soldier from Connecticut," Ph.D. dissertation, New York University, 1968.

Reese, Morgan M. "John Bell Hood and the Texas Brigade," M.A. thesis, Southwest Texas State Teachers College, 1941.

Sommers, Richard J. "Grant's Fifth Offensive at Petersburg—A Study in Strategy, Tactics, and Generalship: The Battle of Chaffin's Bluff, the Battle of Poplar Spring Church, the First Battle of the Darbytown Road, the Second Battle of the Squirrel Level Road, the Second Battle of the Darbytown Road," Ph.D. dissertation, Rice University, 1970.

NEWSPAPERS

Augusta (Ga.) *Chronicle and Sentinel*.

Bangor *Daily Whig and Courier*.

Boston *Daily Courier*.

Boston *Evening Transcript*.

Buffalo *Morning Express*.

Charleston (S.C.) *Courier*.

Charleston (S.C.) *Mercury*.

Columbia (S.C.) *Daily South Carolinian*.

Columbia (S.C.) *Daily Southern Guardian*.

Columbus (Ga.) *Daily Enquirer*.

Connecticut War Record.

Detroit *Advertiser and Tribune*.

Fayetteville *Observer*.

Frank Leslie's Illustrated.

Galveston *News.*

Harper's Weekly.

Hartford *Daily Courant.*

Lewiston (Me.) *Evening Journal.*

Mobile *Advertiser.*

National Tribune.

New York *Herald.*

New York *Times.*

New York *Tribune.*

Petersburg *Daily Express.*

Philadelphia *Evening Bulletin.*

Philadelphia *Public Ledger.*

Pottsville (Pa.) *Miners' Journal and Pottsville General Advertiser.*

Raleigh *Daily Confederate.*

Richmond *Dispatch.*

Richmond *Enquirer.*

Richmond *Examiner.*

Richmond *Sentinel.*

Richmond *Whig.*

Rochester (N.Y.) *Daily Union & Advertiser.*

Rutland (Vt.) *Weekly Herald.*

The United States Army and Navy Journal and Gazette of the Regular and Volunteer Forces.

Windsor (Vt.) *Vermont Journal.*

ARTICLES, BOOKS, AND PAMPHLETS

OFFICIAL DOCUMENTS

Annual Report of the Adjutant-General of the Commonwealth of Massachusetts, with Reports of the Quartermaster-General, Surgeon-General, and Master of Ordnance for the Year Ending December 31, 1864. Boston: Wright & Potter, 1865.

Annual Report of the Adjutant-General of the Commonwealth of Massachusetts, for the Year Ending December 31, 1865. Boston: Wright & Potter, 1866.

Annual Report of the Adjutant-General of the State of Connecticut for the Year Ending March 31, 1865. New Haven: Carrington, Hotchkiss & Co., 1865.

Freeman, Douglas Southall. *A Calendar of Confederate Papers, with a Bibliography of Some Confederate Publications.* Richmond: Whittel & Shepperson, 1908.

The Official Military Atlas of the Civil War. New York: Arno Press— Crown Publishers, 1978.

Official Records of the Union and Confederate Navies in the War of the Rebellion. Washington, D.C.: U. S. Government Printing Office, 1894– 1922.

Report of the Adjutant and Inspector General of the State of Vermont, from Oct. 1, 1864, to Oct. 1, 1865. Montpelier: Walton Steam Printing Establishment, 1865.

Report of the Adjutant General of the State of Maine for the Years 1864 and 1865. Augusta: Stevens & Sayward, 1866.

Revised Roster of Vermont Volunteers and Lists of Vermonters Who Served in the Army and Navy of the United States During the War of the Rebellion. Montpelier: Watchman Publishing Co., 1892.

The War of the Rebellion: A Compilation of the Official Records of the Union and Confederate Armies. Washington, D.C.: U. S. Government Printing Office, 1880–1901.

AUTOBIOGRAPHIES, BIOGRAPHIES, DIARIES, LETTERS, MEMOIRS, AND PERSONAL NARRATIVES

Aaron Fletcher Stevens, August 9, 1819–May 10, 1887. n.p., n.d.

Agassiz, George R., ed. *Meade's Headquarters, 1863–1865: Letters of Col. Theodore Lyman from the Wilderness to Appomattox.* Boston: Massachusetts Historical Society, 1922.

Alexander, Edward Porter. *Military Memoirs of a Confederate.* Bloomington: Indiana University Press, 1962.

Alexander, Joseph M. "Army of the James," *National Tribune,* July 31, 1890.

Badeau, Adam. *Military History of Ulysses S. Grant, from April 1861, to April 1865.* New York: D. Appleton and Company, 1885.

Barrett, Eugene A. "The Civil War Services of John F. Hartranft," *Pennsylvania History,* v. XXXII, No. 2 (1965), pp. 166–86.

Birney, William. *General William Birney's Answer to Libels Clandestinely Circulated by James Shaw, Jr., Collector of the Port of Providence, R.I., with a Review of the Military Record of Said James Shaw, Jr., Late Colonel of the Seventh U. S. Colored Troops.* Washington, D.C.: Stanley Snodgrass, 1878.

Bond, Natalie Jenkins, and Coward, Osman Latrobe, eds. *The South Carolinians; Colonel Asbury Coward's Memoirs.* New York: Vantage Press, 1968.

Bouton, John Bell. *A Memoir of General Louis Bell, Late Col. of the Fourth N.H. Regiment, Who Fell at the Assault on Fort Fisher, January 15th, 1865.* New York: private printing, 1865.

Bratton, John. *Letters of J. Bratton to His Wife, February 1861–July 1865.* Raleigh: North Carolina Historical Records Survey, 1942.

Breckinridge, G. W. "Story of a Boy Captain," *Confederate Veteran,* v. XIII, No. 9 (1905), pp. 415–16.

Brock, Sally Putnam. *Richmond During the War; Four Years of Personal Observations.* New York: G. W. Carleton & Co., 1867.

Brown, H. A. "Col. W. H. Barbour," *Confederate Veteran,* v. VII, No. 1 (1899), p. 30.

Bullock, S. "Col. W. C. Raulston," *National Tribune,* Jan. 15, 1891.

Burr, Frank A. *A New Original, and Authentic Record of the Life and Deeds of Gen. U. S. Grant, Containing a Full History of His Early Life; His Record as a Student at the West Point Military Academy; His Gallantry in the Mexican War; His Honorable Career as a Businessman in St. Louis and Galena; His Eminent Services to His Country in Our Great Civil War; His Election to the Presidency; His Able and Patriotic Administration; His Tour around the World, with an Account of the Great Honors Shown Him by the Emperors, Kings, and Rulers of All Nations; His Lingering Sickness; Heroism in Suffering, and Pathetic Death.* Madison: J. B. Furman, 1885.

Butler, Benjamin F. *Butler's Book.* Boston: A. M. Thayer & Co., 1892.

Carter, Robert G. *Four Brothers in Blue, or Sunshine and Shadows of the War of the Rebellion: A Story of the Great Civil War from Bull Run to Appomattox.* Washington, D.C.: Gibson Brothers, 1913.

Carter, Solon A. "Fourteen Months' Service with Colored Troops," *Civil War Papers Read before the Commandery of the State of Massachusetts, Military Order of the Loyal Legion of the United States,* v. I (1900), pp. 155–82.

Cauthen, Charles Edward, ed. *Family Letters of the Three Wade Hamptons, 1782–1901.* Columbia: University of South Carolina Press, 1953.

Cockrell, Monroe, ed. *Gunner with Stonewall: Reminiscences of William Thomas Poague, Lieutenant, Captain, Major, and Lieutenant Colonel of Artillery, Army of Northern Virginia, C.S.A.; A Memoir Written for His Children in 1903.* Jackson, Tenn.: McCowat-Mercer Press, 1957.

Copp, Elbridge J. *Reminiscences of the War of the Rebellion, 1861–1865.* Nashua, N.H.: The Telegraph Publishing Company, 1911.

Daly, Louise Haskell. *Alexander Cheves Haskell, the Portrait of a Man.* Norwood, Mass.: The Plimpton Press, 1934.

Davis, Oliver W. *Life of David Bell Birney, Major General United States Volunteers.* Philadelphia: King & Baird, 1867.

Dawson, Francis W. *Reminiscences of Confederate Service, 1861–1865.* Charleston: The News and Courier Book Presses, 1882.

DeTrobriand, Philippe Regis. *Four Years with the Army of the Potomac.* Boston: Ticknor and Company, 1889.

Dollard, Robert. *Recollections of the Civil War and Going West to Grow Up with the Country.* Scotland, S.D.: Robert Dollard, 1906.

Dowdey, Clifford. *Lee.* Boston: Little, Brown and Company, 1965.

Dowdey, Clifford, and Manarin, Louis, eds. *The Wartime Papers of R. E. Lee.* Boston: Little, Brown and Company, 1961.

Doyle, W. E. "A Confederate Prisoner," *Confederate Veteran,* v. XXXIV, No. 2 (1926), pp. 51–52.

————. "A Ride with Kautz," *National Tribune,* July 6, 1899.

Draper, William F. *Recollections of a Varied Career.* Boston: Little, Brown and Company, 1909.

Dunovant, Adelia. "Gen. John Dunovant, Houston, Tex.," *Confederate Veteran,* v. XVI, No. 5 (1908), pp. 183–84.

Eisenschiml, Otto, ed. *Vermont General: The Unusual War Experiences of Edward Hastings Ripley, 1862–1865.* New York: The Devin-Adair Company, 1960.

Eyland, Seth [David Cronin]. *The Evolution of a Life.* New York: S. W. Green's Son, 1884.

Freeman, Douglas Southall. *Lee's Lieutenants: A Study in Command.* New York: Charles Scribner's Sons, 1944.

————. *R. E. Lee: A Biography.* New York: Charles Scribner's Sons, 1935.

Fuller, J. F. C. *The Generalship of Ulysses S. Grant.* Bloomington: Indiana University Press, 1958.

Gerrish, Theodore. *Army Life: A Private's Reminiscences of the Civil War.* Portland, Me.: Hoyt, Fogg & Dunham, 1882.

Gibbon, John. *Personal Recollections of the Civil War.* New York: G. P. Putnam's Sons, 1928.

Grant, Ulysses S. *Personal Memoirs of U. S. Grant.* New York: Charles L. Webster & Company, 1886.

Hagood, Johnson. *Memoirs of the War of Secession.* Columbia: The State Company, 1910.

Holland, Lynwood M. *Pierce M. B. Young: The Warwick of the South.* Athens: University of Georgia Press, 1964.

Hopkins, C. A. Porter. "The James J. Archer Letters: A Marylander in the Civil War, Part II," *Maryland Historical Magazine,* v. LVI, No. 4 (1961), pp. 352–83.

Hotchkiss, Jedediah. *Confederate Military History, v. III: Virginia.* Dayton: Morningside Press, 1975.

Howard, James McHenry. "Closing Scenes of the War About Richmond," *Southern Historical Society Papers,* v. XXXI (1903), pp. 129–45.

Humphreys, Henry H. *Andrew Atkinson Humphreys: A Biography.* Philadelphia: The John C. Winston Company, 1924.

Hunton, Eppa. *Autobiography of Eppa Hunton.* Richmond: The William Byrd Press, 1933.

Jackson, Harry F., and O'Donnell, Thomas F., eds. *Back Home in Oneida: Hermon Clarke and His Letters.* Syracuse: Syracuse University Press, 1965.

James, Henry B. *Memories of the Civil War.* New Bedford, Mass.: Franklin E. James, 1898.

Johnson, John L. *The University Memorial Sketches of the Alumni of the University of Virginia Who Fell in the Confederate War.* Baltimore: Turnbull Brothers, 1871.

Johnston, D. E. *The Story of a Confederate Boy in the Civil War.* Portland, Ore.: Glass & Prudhomme Company, 1914.

Jones, John Beauchamp. *A Rebel War Clerk's Diary at the Confederate States Capital.* Philadelphia: J. B. Lippincott Company, 1866.

Jones, J. William. *Life and Letters of Robert E. Lee, Soldier and Man.* Washington, D.C.: The Neale Publishing Company, 1906.

Kreutzer, William. *Notes and Observations Made during Four Years of Service with the Ninety Eighth N.Y. Volunteers in the War of 1861.* Philadelphia: Grant, Faires & Rodgers, 1878.

Lane, David. *A Soldier's Diary: The Story of a Volunteer, 1862–1865.* Jackson, Mich.: n.p., 1905.

Lane, James H. "Glimpses of Army Life in 1864: Extracts from Letters Written by Brigadier General J. H. Lane," *Southern Historical Society Papers,* v. XVIII (1890), pp. 406–22.

Lott, Jess B. "Two Boys of the Fifth Texas Regiment," *Confederate Veteran,* v. XIII, No. 9 (1905), pp. 416–17.

Loving, Jerome, ed. *Civil War Letters of George Washington Whitman.* Durham: Duke University Press, 1975.

Marshall, Jessie Ames, ed. *Private and Official Correspondence of Gen. Benjamin F. Butler during the Period of the Civil War.* Norwood, Mass.: The Plimpton Press, 1917.

McBride, R. E. *In the Ranks from the Wilderness to Appomattox Court House: The War as Seen and Experienced by a Private Soldier in the Army of the Potomac.* Cincinnati: Walden & Stowe, 1881.

McClendon, W. A. *Recollections of War Times by an Old Veteran under Stonewall Jackson and Lieutenant General James Longstreet; How I Got In and How I Got Out.* Montgomery: The Paragon Press, 1909.

McMurray, John. *Recollections of a Colored Troop.* Brookville, Pa.: Jefferson Democrat (?), 1913.

Meade, George. *The Life and Letters of George Gordon Meade, Major-General United States Army.* New York: Charles Scribner's Sons, 1913.

Meyers, Augustus. *Ten Years in the Ranks of the United States Army.* New York: The Stirling Press, 1914.

Mitchell, Joseph B. *The Badge of Gallantry: Recollections of Civil War Medal of Honor Winners; Letters from the Charles Kohen Collection.* New York: The Macmillan Company, 1968.

Mixson, Frank M. *Reminiscences of a Private.* Columbia: The State Company, 1910.

Monroe, John Albert. "Reminiscences of the War of the Rebellion of 1861–65," *Personal Narratives of Events in the War of the Rebellion, Being Papers Read before the Rhode Island Soldiers' and Sailors' Historical Society,* s. 2, v. III, No. 11 (1881), pp. 1–78.

Montgomery, Horace. "A Union Officer's Recollection of the Negro as a Soldier," *Pennsylvania History,* v. XXVIII, No. 2 (1961), pp. 156–86.

Moore, Edward A. *The Story of a Cannoneer Under Stonewall Jackson, in Which Is Told the Part Taken by the Rockbridge Artillery in the Army of Northern Virginia.* New York: The Neale Publishing Company, 1907.

Morgan, James D. *Recollections of a Rebel Reefer.* London: Constable and Company, 1917.

Mulholland, St. Clair. *The American Volunteer, The Most Heroic Soldier the World Has Ever Known, Letters Written to the "Public Ledger" by St. Clair A. Mulholland, formerly Colonel 116th Pa. Infantry.* Philadelphia: Town Print Company, 1909.

Myers, Ephraim E. *A True Story of a Civil War Veteran.* York, Pa.: n.p., 1910.

Nevins, Allan, ed. *A Diary of Battle: The Personal Journals of Colonel Charles S. Wainwright, 1861–1865.* New York: Harcourt, Brace & World, 1962.

Osgood, C. H. "A Sutler's Clerk," *National Tribune,* Oct. 8, 1891.

Polley, Joseph B. *A Soldier's Letters to Charming Nellie.* New York: The Neale Publishing Company, 1908.

Pomfret, John E., ed. "Letters of Fred Lockley, Union Soldier, 1864–1865," *The Huntington Library Quarterly: A Journal for the History and Interpretation of English and American Civilization,* v. XVI, No. 1 (1952), pp. 75–112.

Porter, Horace. *Campaigning with Grant.* Bloomington: Indiana University Press, 1961.

Rea, Lilian, ed. *War Record and Personal Experiences of Walter Raleigh Robbins from April 22, 1861, to August 4, 1865.* Chicago (?): n.p., 1923.

Reese, George. "What Five Confederates Did at Petersburg," *Confederate Veteran,* v. XII, No. 6 (1904), p. 286.

Robertson, James I., ed. *The Civil War Letters of General Robert McAllister.* New Brunswick, N.J.: Rutgers University Press, 1965.

Roemer, Jacob. *Reminiscences of the War of the Rebellion, 1861–1865.* Flushing, N.Y.: Estate of Jacob Roemer, 1897.

Sherman, George. "Assault on Fort Gilmer and Reminiscences of Prison Life," *Personal Narratives of Events in the War of the Rebellion, Being Papers Read before the Rhode Island Soldiers' and Sailors' Historical Society,* s. 5, v. VIII, No. 7 (1897), pp. 1–79.

Small, Abner R. "Personal Observations and Experiences in Rebel Prison, 1864, 1865," *War Papers Read before the Commandery of the State of Maine, Military Order of the Loyal Legion of the United States,* v. I (1898), pp. 295–317.

Small, Harold, ed. *The Road to Richmond: The Civil War Memoirs of Major Abner R. Small of the Sixteenth Maine Volunteers; together with the Diary Which He Kept When He Was a Prisoner of War.* Berkeley: University of California Press, 1939.

Sorrel, G. Moxley. *Recollections of a Confederate Staff Officer.* New York: The Neale Publishing Company, 1905.

Sparks, David, ed. *Inside Lincoln's Army: The Diary of Marsena Rudolph Patrick, Provost Marshal General, Army of the Potomac.* New York: Thomas Yoseloff, 1964.

Stiles, Robert. *Four Years under Marse Robert.* New York: The Neale Publishing Company, 1903.

Synnestvedt, Sig, ed. "The Earth Shook and Quivered," *Civil War Times Illustrated,* v. XI, No. 8 (Dec. 1972), pp. 30–37.

Taylor, Walter H. *General Lee: His Campaigns in Virginia, 1861–1865, with Personal Reminiscences.* Norfolk: Press of Braunworth & Company, 1906.

Thomas, Hampton. "Some Personal Reminiscences of Service in the Cavalry of the Army of the Potomac," *The United Service,* s. 2, v. I (Jan. 1889), pp. 1–26.

Tilney, Robert. *My Life in the Army: Three Years and One Half with the Fifth Army Corps, Army of the Potomac, 1862–1865.* Philadelphia: Ferris & Leach, 1912.

Timberlake, W. L. "Last Days in Front of Richmond, 1864–1865," *Confederate Veteran,* v. XX, No. 3 (1912), p. 119.

Tremain, Lyman. *Memorial of Frederick Lyman Tremain, Late Lieut. Colonel of the Tenth N.Y. cavalry, Who Was Mortally Wounded at the Battle of Hatcher's Run, Virginia, February 6th, and Died at City Point Hospital, February 8th, 1865.* Albany: VanBenthuysen's Steam Printing House, 1865.

Trumbull, Henry Clay. *The Knightly Soldier: A Biography of Major Henry Ward Camp, Tenth Connecticut Volunteers.* Boston: Noyes, Holmes & Company, 1871.

Vandiver, Frank E., ed. *The Civil War Diary of Gen. Josiah Gorgas.* Tuscaloosa: University of Alabama Press, 1947.

Wagstaff, H. M., ed. "The Jas. A. Graham Papers, 1861–1884," *The Jas. Sprunt Historical Studies,* v. XX, No. 2 (1928), pp. 87–324.

Waring, Joseph I., ed. "The Diary of William G. Hinson during the War of Secession," *The South Carolina Historical Magazine*, v. LXXV, No. 2 (April 1974), pp. 111–20.

Warner, Ezra J. *Generals in Blue: Lives of the Union Commanders.* Baton Rouge: Louisiana State University Press, 1964.

———. *Generals in Gray: Lives of the Confederate Commanders.* Baton Rouge: Louisiana State University Press, 1959.

Weigley, Russell F. "David McMurtrie Gregg—A Profile," *Civil War Times Illustrated*, v. I, No. 7 (Nov. 1962), pp. 10–13, 26–30.

Welch, Spencer G. *A Confederate Surgeon's Letters to His Wife.* New York: The Neale Publishing Company, 1911.

White, William S. "A Diary of the War, or What I Saw of It," *Contributions to the History of the Richmond Howitzer Battalion*, No. 2 (1883), pp. 89–286.

Wistar, Isaac J. *Autobiography of Isaac Jones Wistar, 1827–1905: Half A Century in War and Peace.* New York: Harper & Brothers, 1914.

Yeary, Mamie, comp. *Reminiscences of the Boys in Gray, 1861–1865.* Dallas: Smith & Lamar, 1912.

Younger, Edward, ed. *Inside the Confederate Government: The Diary of Robert Garlick Hill Kean.* New York: Oxford University Press, 1957.

CAMPAIGN AND BATTLE NARRATIVES

Allen, Cornelius Tacitus. "Fight at Chaffin's Farm, Fort Harrison," *Confederate Veteran*, v. XIII, No. 9 (1905), p. 418.

Bruce, George A. "Petersburg, June 15—Fort Harrison, September 29: A Comparison," *Papers Read before the Military Historical Society of Massachusetts*, v. XIV, No. 7 (1918), pp. 83–115.

Buel, Clarence Clough, and Johnson, Robert Underwood, eds. *Battles and Leaders of the Civil War.* New York: Thomas Yoseloff, 1956.

Camp, H. A. "Fort Harrison," *National Tribune*, June 14, 1888.

Carter, Joseph. "Poplar Spring Church," *National Tribune*, March 22, 1894.

Clay, Cecil C. "Capture of Fort Harrison," *National Tribune*, Nov. 26, 1881.

———. "Col. Clay's Account," *National Tribune*, Sept. 29, 1904.

———. "Fort Harrison," *National Tribune*, March 22, 1888.

———. "A Personal Narrative of the Capture of Fort Harrison," *War Papers, District of Columbia Commandery, Military Order of the Loyal Legion of the United States*, v. I, No. 7 (1891), pp. 1–12.

Coit, James C. "Letter to Col. F. W. McMaster, August 2, 1879," *Southern Historical Society Papers*, v. X (1882), pp. 123–30.

Field, Charles W. "The Campaign of 1864 and 1865: The Narrative of Major-General C. W. Field," *Southern Historical Society Papers*, v. XIV (1886), pp. 542–63.

Flanigan, W. A. "That Fight at Fort Gilmer," *Confederate Veteran*, v. XIII, No. 3 (1905), p. 123.

"Fort Fisher Testimony," *Report of the Joint Committee on the Conduct of the War, at the Second Session, Thirty-eighth Congress.* Washington, D.C.: U. S. Government Printing Office, 1865.

Goldsborough, W. W. "Grant's Change of Base: The Horrors of the Battle of Cold Harbor, from a Soldier's Notebook; Sights Which Filled Even Veterans with Horror—Why McClellan Failed—A Mistake That Cost Many Lives," *Southern Historical Society Papers*, v. XXIX (1901), pp. 285–91.

Granberry, J. A. H. "That Fort Gilmer Fight," *Confederate Veteran*, v. XIII, No. 9 (1905), p. 413.

Harris, Merlin C. "Fort Harrison," *National Tribune*, May 12, 1887.

Hicks, H. V. "At Peebles' and Pegram's Farms," *National Tribune*, May 11, 1911.

Humphreys, Andrew Atkinson. *The Virginia Campaign of '64 and '65: the Army of the Potomac and the Army of the James.* New York: Thomas Yoseloff, 1963.

Johnston, Charles. "Attack on Fort Gilmer, September 29th, 1864," *Southern Historical Society Papers*, v. I (1876), pp. 438–42.

Jones, A. C. "Texas and Arkansas at Fort Harrison," *Confederate Veteran*, v. XXV, No. 1 (1917), pp. 24–25.

Martin, J. H. "The Assault on Fort Gilmer," *Confederate Veteran*, v. XIII, No. 6 (1905), pp. 269–70.

May, T. J. "The Fight at Fort Gilmer," *Confederate Veteran*, v. XII, No. 12 (1904), pp. 587–88.

McCabe, W. Gordon. "Defense of Petersburg," *Southern Historical Society Papers*, v. II (1876), pp. 257–306. This article also appears as: "Address of Captain W. Gordon McCabe on the Defense of Petersburg," in J. William Jones, comp. *Army of Northern Virginia Memorial Volume.* Richmond: J. W. Randolph & English, 1880.

Merrill, Frank L. "Poplar Spring Church," *National Tribune*, Oct. 4, 1894.

Moore, James B. "The Attack of Fort Harrison," *Confederate Veteran*, v. XIII, No. 9 (1905), pp. 418–20.

Perry, Herman H. "Assault on Fort Gilmer," *Confederate Veteran*, v. XIII, No. 9 (1905), pp. 413–15.

Pickens, J. D. "Fort Harrison," *Confederate Veteran*, v. XXI, No. 10 (1913), p. 484.

Pippitt, T. Henry. "Before Richmond," *National Tribune*, Oct. 10, 1918.

Prescott, Royal B. "The Capture of Richmond," *Civil War Papers Read Before the Commandery of the State of Massachusetts, Military Order of the Loyal Legion of the United States*, v. I (1900), pp. 47–74.

"Right General Guide" [pseud.]. "A Fatal Gap," *National Tribune*, Nov. 29, 1894.

Sommers, Richard J. "The Battle No One Wanted," *Civil War Times Illustrated,* v. XIV, No. 5 (Aug. 1975), pp. 10–18.

———. "Fury at Fort Harrison," *Civil War Times Illustrated,* v. XIX, No. 6 (Oct. 1980), pp. 12–23.

Van Fossen, Robert D. "A Sketch of the Happenings at Davis' Farm, Sept. 30th and Oct. 1st, 1864," *Forty-eighth Annual Reunion of the Sixth Ohio Veteran Volunteer Cavalry Association,* 1913.

Ware, E. "Battery Harrison," *National Tribune,* Jan. 20, 1887.

Wells, Stephen F. "Forts Harrison and Gilmer," *National Tribune Scrapbook,* No. 3 (1909?), p. 32.

Wentz, A. "Closing Days of the War," *National Tribune,* Feb. 11, 1904.

Wilcox, Cadmus Marcellus. "Battle of Jones's Farm, Sept. 30, 1864," Transactions of the Southern Historical Society, printed in *The Southern Magazine,* v. IX, No. 4 (April 1875), pp. 67–71.

Winder, J. R. "Judge Martin's Report Approved," *Confederate Veteran,* v. XIII, No. 9 (1905), p. 417.

Wright, Marcus Joseph. "Bushrod Johnson's Men at Fort Harrison," *Confederate Veteran,* v. XIV, No. 12 (1906), p. 545.

UNIT HISTORIES

Albert, Allen D., ed. *History of the Forty Fifth Regiment, Pennsylvania Veteran Volunteer Infantry, 1861–1865.* Williamsport, Pa.: Grit Publishing Company, 1912.

Allen, David. "More about Mink," *National Tribune,* July 11, 1895.

Allen, E. Jay; Ewing, John; Hill, S. W.; McKenna, Charles F.; Kerr, John H.; Sias, John C.; and Porter, John T. *Under the Maltese Cross: Antietam to Appomattox: The Loyal Uprising of Western Pennsylvania, 1861–1865: Campaigns—155th Pennsylvania Regiment, Narrated by the Rank and File.* Pittsburgh: The 155th Regimental Association, 1910.

Allen, George H. *Forty-six Months in the Fourth R. I. Volunteers, in the War of 1861 to 1865, Comprising a History of Its Marches, Battles, and Camp Life, Compiled from Journals Kept While on Duty in the Field and Camp.* Providence: J. A. & R. A. Reid, 1887.

"Annual Reunion of Pegram Battalion Association in the Hall of the House of Delegates, Richmond, Va., May 21st, 1886," *Southern Historical Society Papers,* v. XIV (1886), pp. 5–34.

Appleton, Nathan; Scott, Henry; Murray, John; Chase, Thomas; and Newton, George. *History of the Fifth Massachusetts Battery: Organized October 3, 1861; Mustered Out, June 12, 1865.* Boston: Luther E. Cowles, 1902.

Aston, Howard. *History and Roster of the Fourth and Fifth Independent Battalions and Thirteenth Regiment, Ohio Cavalry Volunteers—Their Battles and Skirmishes, Roster of Dead, Etc.* Columbus: Fred J. Herr, 1902.

Aubery, James M. *The Thirty-Sixth Wisconsin Volunteer Infantry, 1st Brigade, 2d Division, 2d Army Corps, Army of the Potomac: An Authentic Record of the Regiment from Its Organization to the Muster Out; a Complete Roster of Its Officers and Men with Their Record; a Full List of Casualties in Detail, Dates, and Places; Its Itinerary from Place of Muster to Muster Out; Maps Showing Its Movements; a Copy of Every Official Paper in the War Department Pertaining to the Regiment, and Others Pertaining Indirectly to the Command; Illustrations of Events, Biography, Etc.; Statistics; with Reminiscences from the Author's Private Journal.* Milwaukee: Evening Wisconsin Company, 1900.

Baker, Levi. *History of the Ninth Mass. Battery, Recruited July, 1862; Mustered in Aug. 10, 1862; Mustered Out June 9, 1865, at the Close of the War of the Rebellion.* South Framingham, Mass.: Lakeview Press, 1888.

Bartlett, Asa W. *History of the Twelfth Regiment, New Hampshire Volunteers in the War of the Rebellion.* Concord: Ira C. Evans, 1897.

Bates, Samuel P. *History of Pennsylvania Volunteers, 1861–5.* Harrisburg: B. Singerly, 1871.

————. *Martial Deeds of Pennsylvania.* Philadelphia: T. H. Davis & Company, 1876.

Beale, Richard L. T. *History of the Ninth Virginia Cavalry in the War between the States.* Richmond: B. F. Johnson Publishing Company, 1899.

Beecher, Herbert W. *History of the First Light Battery, Connecticut Volunteers, 1861–1865; Personal Records and Reminiscences; The Story of the Battery from its Organization to the Present Time; Compiled from Official Records, Personal Interviews, Private Diaries, War Histories, and Individual Experiences.* New York: A. T. DeLaMare Printing and Publishing Company, 1901.

Bevier, R. S. *History of the First and Second Missouri Confederate Brigades, 1861–1865; and from Wakarusa to Appomattox: A Military Anagraph.* St. Louis: Bryan, Brand & Company, 1879.

Bosbyshell, Oliver Christian. *The 48th in the War, Being a Narrative of the Campaigns of the 48th Regiment, Infantry, Pennsylvania Veteran Volunteers, during the Rebellion.* Philadelphia: Avil Printing Company, 1895.

Bradds, Hezekiah. "With the 60th Ohio around Petersburg," *National Tribune,* April 8, 1926.

Brady, Robert. *The Story of One Regiment: The Eleventh Maine Infantry Volunteers in the War of the Rebellion.* New York: J. J. Little & Company, 1896.

Brainard, Mary Genevie Green. *Campaigns of the One Hundred and Forty-sixth Regiment, New York State Volunteers, Also Known as Halleck's Infantry, the Fifth Oneida, and Garrard's Tigers.* New York: G. P. Putnam's Sons, 1915.

Brooks, U. R. *Butler and His Cavalry in the War of Secession, 1861–1865.* Columbia: The State Company, 1909.

Brown, William Wells. *The Negro in the American Revolution.* Boston: Lee & Shepard, 1867.

"Brunswick Guard; A Detailed Account of Its Fine Record; Its Marches, Fights, and Roll of Members," *Southern Historical Society Papers,* v. XXVIII (1900), pp. 8–14.

Buell, Augustus. "Mink's Battery," *National Tribune,* June 6, 1895.

Burford, Thomas P.; Chilton, Thomas H.; and Price, Ben. *Lamar Rifles: A History of Company G, Eleventh Mississippi Regiment, C.S.A., with the Official Roll, Giving Each Man's Record from the Time of Enlistment to the Twenty Ninth March, Eighteen Hundred and Sixty-five; Individual and Company Sketches; Incidents of the Camp, the March, and the Battlefield, and Is Intended to Be of Especial Interest to the Friends of Members of This Company, Which Was Popularly Known as the "Lamar Rifles" Which Served in the Army of Northern Virginia from May 1861 to April 1865.* Roanoke, Va.: The Stone Publishing Company, 1902.

Burrage, Henry S. *History of the Thirty-Sixth Regiment, Massachusetts Volunteers, 1862–1865.* Boston: Rockwell and Churchill, 1884.

Caldwell, James Fitz James. *The History of a Brigade of South Carolinians, Known First as "Gregg's," and Subsequently as "McGowan's Brigade."* Philadelphia: King & Baird Printers, 1866.

Califf, Joseph. *Record of the Services of the Seventh Regiment, U. S. Colored Troops from September, 1863, to November, 1866.* Providence: E. L. Freeman & Company, 1878.

———. *To the Ex-Members and Friends of the 7th U.S.C.T.* n.p., 1878 (?).

Camper, Charles, and Kirkley, Joseph W. *Historical Record of the First Regiment, Maryland Infantry, with an Appendix Containing a Register of Officers and Enlisted Men, Biographies of Deceased Officers, Etc.* Washington, D.C.: Gibson Brothers, 1871.

Carruth, Sumner, et al. *History of the Thirty-Fifth Regiment Massachusetts Volunteers, 1862–1865, with a Roster.* Boston: Mills, Knight & Company, 1884.

Chamberlayne, Edwin H. *War History and Roll of the Richmond Fayette Artillery, 38th Virginia Battalion Artillery, Confederate States Army.* Richmond: Everett Waddey, 1883.

Chamberlin, Thomas. *History of the One Hundred and fiftieth Regiment Pennsylvania Volunteers, Second Regiment, Bucktail Brigade.* Philadelphia: F. McManus, Jr., & Company, 1905.

Chase, Philip S. *Battery F, First Regiment Rhode Island Light Artillery in the Civil War, 1861–1865.* Providence: Snow & Farnham, 1892.

Cheek, Philip. *History of the Sauk County Riflemen, Known as Company "A," Sixth Wisconsin Veteran Volunteer Infantry, 1861–1865.* Madison: Democratic Printing Company, 1909.

Child, William. *A History of the Fifth Regiment, New Hampshire Volunteers in the American Civil War, 1861–1865.* Bristol, N.H.: R. W. Musgrove, 1893.

Clark, Walter, comp. *Histories of the Several Regiments and Battalions from North Carolina in the Great War, 1861–'65.* Goldsboro, N.C.: State of North Carolina, 1901.

Cogswell, Leander. *A History of the Eleventh New Hampshire Regiment Volunteer Infantry in the Rebellion War, 1861–1865, Covering Its Entire Service with Interesting Scenes of Army Life, and Graphic Details of Battles, Skirmishes, Sieges, Marches, and Hardships in Which Its Officers and Men Participated.* Concord: Republican Press Association, 1891.

Coker, James L. *History of Company G, Ninth S. C. Regiment, Infantry, S. C. Army and of Company E, Sixth S. C. Regiment, Infantry, S. C. Army.* Charleston: Walker, Evans & Cogswell Company, 1899.

Cornish, Dudley T. *The Sable Arm: Negro Troops in the Union Army, 1861–1865.* New York: W. W. Norton & Company, 1956.

Couper, William. *One Hundred Years at V.M.I.* Richmond: Garrett and Massie, 1939.

Croffut, W. A., and Morris, John M. *The Military and Civil History of Connecticut during the War of 1861–1865, Comprising a Detailed Account of the Various Regiments and Batteries, through March, Encampment, Bivouac, and Battle; Also Instances of Distinguished Personal Gallantry and Biographical Sketches of Many Heroic Soldiers: Together with a Record of the Patriotic Action of Citizens at Home, and of Liberal Support Furnished by the State in Its Executive and Legislative Departments.* New York: Ledyard Bill, 1868.

Croom, Wendell. *The War History of Company "C," (Beauregard Volunteers), Sixth Georgia Regiment (Infantry), with a Graphic Account of Each Member.* Fort Valley, Ga.: *Advertiser,* 1879.

Crowninshield, Benjamin W. *A History of the First Regiment of Massachusetts Cavalry Volunteers.* Boston: Houghton Mifflin Company, 1891.

Cuffel, Charles A. *Durell's Battery in the Civil War (Independent Battery D, Pennsylvania Volunteer Artillery): A Narrative of the Campaigns and Battles of Berks and Bucks Counties' Artillerists in the War of the Rebellion, from the Battery's Organization, September 24, 1861, to Its Muster Out of Service, June 13, 1865.* Philadelphia: Craig, Finley & Company, 1900.

Cunningham, John L. *Three Years with the Adirondack Regiment: 118th New York Volunteer Infantry.* Norwood, Mass.: The Plimpton Press, 1920.

Curtis, O. B. *History of the Twenty Fourth Michigan of the Iron Brigade Known as the Detroit and Wayne County Regiment.* Detroit: Winn & Hammond, 1891.

Cushman, Frederick E. *History of the 58th Regt. Massachusetts Vols. from the 15th Day of September, 1863, to the Close of the Rebellion.* Washington, D.C.: Gibson Brothers, 1865.

Cutcheon, Byron Mac. *The Story of the Twentieth Michigan Infantry, July 15th, 1862, to May 30th, 1865, Embracing Official Documents on File in the Records of the State of Michigan and of the United States Referring or Relative to the Regiment.* Lansing: Robert Smith Printing Company, 1904.

Denison, Frederic. *Shot and Shell: The Third Rhode Island Heavy Artillery Regiment, in the Rebellion, 1861–1865—Camps, Forts, Batteries, Garrisons, Marches, Skirmishes, Sieges, Battles, and Victories; also the Roll of Honor and Roll of the Regiment.* Providence: J. A. & R. A. Reid, 1879.

Dennett, George M. *History of the Ninth U.S.C. Troops from Its Organization till Mustered Out, with a List of Names of All Officers and Enlisted Men Who Have Ever Belonged to the Regiment, and Remarks Attached to Each Name, Noting All Changes, Such as Promotions, Transfers, Discharges, Deaths, Etc.* Philadelphia: King & Baird, 1866.

Dickey, Luther S. *History of the Eighty-Fifth Regiment, Pennsylvania Volunteer Infantry, 1861–1865, Comprising an Authentic Narrative of Casey's Division at the Battle of Seven Pines.* New York: J. C. & W. E. Powers, 1915.

Duke, Richard T. W. "With the Confederate Reserves," *Confederate Veteran,* v. XXVI, No. 11 (1918), pp. 486–87.

Duncan, Alexander McC., comp. *Roll of Officers and Members of the Georgia Hussars and of the Cavalry Commands of Which the Hussars Are a Continuation, with a Historical Sketch Relating Facts Showing the Origin and Necessity of Rangers or Mounted Men in the Colony of Georgia from Date of Its Founding.* Savannah: *The Morning News,* 1906.

Dunlop, William S. *Lee's Sharpshooters; or, the Forefront of Battle: A Story of Southern Valor that Never Has Been Told.* Little Rock: Tunnah & Pittard, 1899.

Dusseault, John H. *Company E, Thirty-Ninth Infantry in the Civil War.* Somerville, Mass.: Somerville Journal Print, 1908.

Dyer, Frederick. *A Compendium of the War of the Rebellion.* New York: Thomas Yoseloff, 1959.

Eden, R. C. *The Sword and the Gun: A History of the 37th Wis. Volunteer Infantry from Its First Organization to Its Final Muster Out.* Madison: Atwood & Rublee, 1865.

Eldredge, Daniel. *The Third New Hampshire and All about It.* Boston: E. B. Stillings and Company, 1893.

Elliott, Charles G. "Martin's Brigade of Hoke's Division," *Southern Historical Society Papers,* v. XXIII (1895), pp. 189–98.

Embick, Milton, comp. and ed. *Military History of the Third Division, Ninth Corps, with a Record of the Division Association, Organized*

Harrisburg, March 25, 1890, and Dedication of Equestrian Statue to General John F. Hartranft, Commander Division, May 17, 1899, and the Dedication of the Monuments at Fort Stedman and Mahone on Petersburg Battlefield, May 19, 1909, with the Addresses Delivered There by President Taft and Others. Harrisburg: C. E. Aughinbaugh, 1913.

Fifth Reunion of the One Hundred and fifty-fifth Regiment Penna. Volunteers. Pittsburgh: Rawsthorne Engraving and Printing Company, 1896.

Fleetwood, Christian. *The Negro as a Soldier.* Washington, D.C.: Howard University Press, 1895.

Frederick, Gilbert. *The Story of a Regiment, Being a Record of the Military Services of the Fifty-seventh New York State Volunteer Infantry in the War of the Rebellion, 1861–1865.* Chicago: C. H. Morgan Company, 1895.

Gibbs, A. Judson; King, David A.; and Northrup, Jay H. *History of the Ninety Third Regiment, New York Volunteer Infantry, 1861–1865.* Milwaukee: Swain & Tate, 1895.

Goldsborough, W. W. *The Maryland Line in the Confederate States Army.* Baltimore: Guggenheimer, Weil & Company, 1900.

Gould, Joseph. *The Story of the Forty Eighth: A Record of the Campaigns of the Forty Eighth Regiment Pennsylvania Veteran Volunteer Infantry during the Four Eventful Years of Its Service in the War for the Preservation of the Union.* Philadelphia: Alfred M. Slocum Company, 1908.

Graves, Joseph A. *The Bedford Light Artillery, 1861–1865.* Bedford City, Va.: Bedford Democrat Press, 1903.

Hall, Henry, and Hall, James. *Cayuga in the Field: A Record of the 19th N.Y. Volunteers, All the Batteries of the 3rd New York Artillery, and 75th New York Volunteers, Comprising an Account of Their Organization, Camp Life, Marches, Battles, Losses, Toils and Triumphs, in the War for the Union, with Complete Rolls of Their Members.* Auburn, N.Y.: Truair, Smith & Company, 1873.

Harris, James S. *Historical Sketches, Seventh Regiment North Carolina Troops.* Mooresville, N.C.: Mooresville Print Company, 1893.

Harrison, Walter. *Pickett's Men: A Fragment of War History.* New York: D. Van Nostrand, 1870.

Haskin, William L. *The History of the First Regiment of Artillery from Its Organization in 1821, to January 1st, 1876, to Which Is Added a Series of Communications from Officers, Now or Formerly of the Regiment, Giving Their Personal Reminiscences of Service with It.* Portland, Me.: B. Thurston and Company, 1879.

Haynes, Martin A. *A History of the Second Regiment New Hampshire Volunteer Infantry in the War of the Rebellion.* Lakeport, N.H.: n.p., 1896.

Higgins, John W. "A Georgia Command in Active Service," *Confederate Veteran*, v. XXV, No. 1 (1917), pp. 78–79.

Hinckley, S. B. "The 58th Mass.," *National Tribune*, May 20, 1915.

History of the 118th Pennsylvania Volunteers, Corn Exchange Regiment, from Their First Engagement at Antietam to Appomattox, to Which is Added a Record of Its Organization and a Complete Roster. Philadelphia: J. L. Smith, 1905.

Hopkins, William P. *The Seventh Rhode Island Volunteers in the Civil War, 1862–1865.* Providence: Snow & Farnham, 1903.

Houghton, Edwin B. *The Campaigns of the Seventeenth Maine.* Portland, Me.: Short & Loring, 1866.

House, Charles. "First Maine Heavy Artillery in Fall of 1864," *Maine Bugle*, campaign IV, call 2 (1897), pp. 133–40.

Houston, Henry C. *The Thirty Second Maine Regiment of Infantry Volunteers: An Historical Sketch.* Portland, Me.: Southworth Brothers, 1903.

Hubbell, W. S.; Crane, A. M.; and Brown, D. D. *The Story of the Twenty First Regiment, Connecticut Volunteer Infantry during the Civil War, 1861–1865.* Middletown, Ct.: The Stewart Printing Company, 1900.

Hyde, William L. *History of the One Hundred and Twelfth Regiment New York Volunteers.* Fredonia, N.Y.: W. McKinstry & Company, 1866.

Izlar, William V. *A Sketch of the War Record of the Edisto Rifles, 1861–1865: Company "A," 1st Regiment S.C.V. Infantry, Colonel Johnson Hagood, Provisional Army of the Confederate States, 1861–1862; Company "G," 25th S.C.V. Infantry, Colonel Charles H. Simonton, Confederate States Army, 1862–1865.* Columbia: The State Company, 1914.

Jacklin, Rufus W. "The Famous Old Third Brigade," *War Papers Read before the Michigan Commandery of the Military Order of the Loyal Legion of the United States,* v. II (1898), pp. 39–50.

Jackman, Lyman. *History of the Sixth New Hampshire Regiment in the War for the Union.* Concord: Republican Press Association, 1891.

Jones, Benjamin W. *Under the Stars and Bars: A History of the Surry Light Artillery; Recollections of a Private Soldier in the War between the States.* Richmond: Everett Waddey Company, 1909.

Judson, Amos M. *History of the Eighty Third Regiment Pennsylvania Volunteers.* Erie: B. F. H. Lynn, 1865.

Lane, James H. "History of Lane's N. C. Brigade—Campaign of 1864—Anecdote about Captain G. G. Holland, 28th N. C. Troops," *Southern Historical Society Papers,* v. IX (1881), pp. 353–61.

———. "Lane's Corps of Sharpshooters: The Career of this Famous Body, with a Roster of Its Officers," *Southern Historical Society Papers,* v. XXVIII (1900), pp. 1–8.

———. "Twenty-eighth North Carolina Infantry," *Southern Historical Society Papers,* v. XXIV (1896), pp. 324–39.

Lindsley, John Berrien, ed. *The Military Annals of Tennessee, Confederate: Embracing a Review of Military Operations, with Regimental Histories and Memorial Rolls.* Nashville: J. M. Lindsley & Company, 1886.

Little, Henry W. *The Seventh Regiment, New Hampshire Volunteers in the War of the Rebellion.* Concord: Ira C. Evans, 1896.

Lord, Edward A., ed. *History of the Ninth Regiment New Hampshire Volunteers in the War of the Rebellion.* Concord: Republican Press Association, 1896.

Love, W. A. "Company Records," *Confederate Veteran,* v. XXXIII, No. 2 (1925), pp. 50–52.

Manarin, Louis, comp. *North Carolina Troops, 1861–1865.* Raleigh: The North Carolina State University Print Shop, 1966–68.

Marbaker, Thomas D. *History of the Eleventh New Jersey Volunteers from Its Organization to Appomattox, to Which Is Added Experiences of Prison Life and Sketches of Individual Members.* Trenton: MacCrellish & Quigley, 1898.

McDonald, William. *A History of the Laurel Brigade, Originally the Ashby Cavalry of the Army of Northern Virginia and Chew's Battery.* Baltimore: Sun Job Printing Office, 1907.

Merrill, Samuel H. *The Campaigns of the First Maine and First District of Columbia Cavalry.* Portland, Me.: Bailey & Noyes, 1866.

Moulder, Valentine. "The 16th N.Y.H.A.," *National Tribune,* Aug. 22, 1901.

Mowris, J. A. *A History of the One Hundred and Seventeenth Regiment, N.Y. Volunteers, (Fourth Oneida), From the Date of Its Organization, August, 1862, till That of Its Muster Out, June, 1865.* Hartford: Case, Lockwood & Company, 1866.

Nabours, W. A. "Active Service of a Texas Command," *Confederate Veteran,* v. XXIV, No. 2 (1916), pp. 69–72.

Nash, Eugene A. *A History of the Forty Fourth Regiment, New York Veteran Volunteer Infantry in the Civil War, 1861–1865.* Chicago: R. R. Donnelly & Sons Company, 1911.

Oehming, B. A. "Gen. B. R. Johnson's Tennessee Brigade," *Confederate Veteran,* v. IX, No. 12 (1901), pp. 559–60.

Osborne, William H. *The History of the Twenty Ninth Regiment of Massachusetts Volunteer Infantry in the Late War of the Rebellion.* Boston: Albert J. Wright, 1877.

Parker, Francis J. *The Story of the Thirty Second Regiment Massachusetts Infantry.* Boston: C. W. Calkins & Company, 1880.

Parker, Thomas H. *History of the 51st Regiment of P.V. and V.V. from Its Organization at Camp Curtin, Harrisburg, Pa., in 1861, to Its Being Mustered Out of the United States Service at Alexandria, Va., July 27th, 1865.* Philadelphia: King & Baird, 1869.

Pierce, S. W. *Battlefields and Camp Fires of the Thirty-Eighth: An Authentic Narrative and Record of the Organization of the Thirty-Eighth Regiment of Wis. Vol. Inf'y. and the Part Taken by It in the Late War, a Short Biographical Sketch of Each Commissioned Officer, and the Name, Age at Time of Enlistment, Nativity, Residence, and Occupation of Every Enlisted Man, with Notes of Incidents Relating to Them.* Milwaukee: Daily Wisconsin Printing House, 1866.

Polley, Joseph B. *Hood's Texas Brigade: Its Marches, Its Battles, Its Achievements.* New York: The Neale Publishing Company, 1910.

Powell, William H. *The Fifth Army Corps (Army of the Potomac): A Record of Operations during the Civil War in the United States of America, 1861–1865.* New York: G. P. Putnam's Sons, 1896.

————. *A History of the Organization and Movements of the Fourth Regiment of Infantry, United States Army, from May 30, 1796, to December 31, 1870, together with a Record of the Military Services of All Officers Who Have at Any Time Belonged to the Regiment.* Washington, D.C.: M'Gill & Witherow, 1871.

Preston, Noble D. *History of the Tenth Regiment of Cavalry, New York State Volunteers.* New York: D. Appleton and Company, 1892.

Price, George F. *Across the Continent with the Fifth Cavalry.* New York: D. Van Nostrand, 1883.

Price, Isaiah. *History of the Ninety-Seventh Regiment, Pennsylvania Volunteer Infantry, during the War of the Rebellion, 1861–65, with the Biographical Sketches of Its Field and Staff Officers and a Complete Record of Each Officer and Enlisted Man.* Philadelphia: B. & P. Printers, 1875.

Pullen, John J. *The Twentieth Maine: A Volunteer Regiment in the Civil War.* Philadelphia: J. B. Lippincott Company, 1954.

Pyne, Henry R. *Ride to War: The History of the First New Jersey Cavalry* (Earl Schenck Miers, ed.). New Brunswick: Rutgers University Press, 1961.

Quarles, Benjamin. *The Negro in the Civil War.* Boston: Little, Brown and Company, 1953.

Quiner, E. B. *The Military History of Wisconsin: A Record of the Civil and Military Patriotism of the State in the War for the Union, with a History of the Campaigns in Which Wisconsin Soldiers Have Been Conspicuous—Regimental Histories—Sketches of Distinguished Officers—the Roll of the Illustrious Dead—Movements of the Legislature and State Officers, Etc.* Chicago: Clarke & Company, 1866.

Rawle Brooke, William; Miller, William E.; McCorkell, James W.; Speese, Andrew J.; and Hunterson, John C. *History of the Third Pennsylvania Cavalry, Sixtieth Regiment Pennsylvania Volunteers in the American Civil War, 1861–1865.* Philadelphia: Franklin Printing Company, 1905.

Richardson, J. D. "The Colored Troops," *National Tribune*, Nov. 1, 1906.

Robertson, John. *Michigan in the War*. Lansing: W. S. George & Company, 1882.

Robinson, Wardwell. *History of the 184th Regiment, New York State Volunteers*. Oswego: Press of R. J. Oliphant, 1895.

Roe, Alfred; Amory, Charles B.; Cook, John C.; and Hill, George. *The Twenty-Fourth Regiment Massachusetts Volunteers, 1861–1866, "New England Guard Regiment."* Worcester: Twenty-Fourth Veteran Association, 1907.

Roe, Alfred S. *The Thirty Ninth Regiment Massachusetts Volunteers, 1862–1865*. Worcester: Thirty Ninth Regiment Veteran Association, 1914.

Roe, Alfred S., and Nutt, Charles. *History of First Regiment of Heavy Artillery, Massachusetts Volunteers, Formerly the Fourteenth Regiment of Infantry, 1861–1865*. Worcester: Commonwealth Printers, 1917.

Roper, John L.; Archibald, Henry C.; and Coles, G. W. *History of the Eleventh Pennsylvania Volunteer Cavalry together with a Complete Roster of the Regiment and Regimental Officers*. Philadelphia: Franklin Printing Company, 1902.

Rowland, Dunbar. "Military History of Mississippi, 1803–1898: Military Operations, 1803–1812; War of 1812, Creek War, Seminole War, 1836; War with Mexico, 1846–1848; Civil War, 1861–1865; Spanish–American War, 1898," *The Official and Statistical Register of the State of Mississippi* (1908), pp. 383–947.

Shaver, Lewellyn A. *A History of the Sixtieth Alabama Regiment, Gracie's Alabama Brigade*. Montgomery: Barrett & Brown, 1867.

Sherman, George. "The Negro as a Soldier," *Personal Narratives of Events in the War of the Rebellion, Being Papers Read before the Rhode Island Soldiers' and Sailors' Historical Society*, s. 7, No. 7 (1913), pp. 1–34.

Simons, Ezra D. *A Regimental History: The One Hundred and Twenty-Fifth New York State Volunteers*. New York: The Judson Printing Company, 1888.

Simpson, Harold B. *Hood's Texas Brigade: Lee's Grenadier Guard*. Waco: Texian Press, 1970.

Simpson, Isaiah. "Campaigning with the 1st Me. Hv. Art.," *National Tribune*, Sept. 15, 1927.

Smith, A. P. *History of the Seventy-Sixth Regiment New York Volunteers; What It Endured and Accomplished; Containing Descriptions of Its Twenty-Five Battles; Its Marches; Its Camp and Bivouac Scenes; with Biographical Sketches of Fifty-Three Officers, and a Complete Record of the Enlisted Men*. Cortland, N.Y.: Truair, Smith & Miles, 1866.

Stowits, George. *History of the One Hundredth Regiment of New York State Volunteers: Being A Recollection of Its Services from Its Muster*

In to Its Muster Out; Its Muster In Roll, Roll of Commissions, Recruits Furnished Through the Board of Trade of the City of Buffalo, and Short Sketches of Deceased and Surviving Officers. Buffalo: Matthews & Warren, 1870.

Strong, William. *History of the 121st Regiment, Pennsylvania Volunteers*. Philadelphia: Burk & McFetridge Company, 1893.

Stryker, William S. *Record of Officers and Men of New Jersey in the Civil War, 1861–1865*. Trenton: John L. Murphy, 1876.

Swinton, William. *Campaigns of the Army of the Potomac: A Critical History of Operations in Virginia, Maryland, and Pennsylvania, from the Commencement to the Close of the War, 1861–5*. New York: Charles B. Richardson, 1866.

Taylor, John C., and Hatfield, Samuel P. *History of the First Connecticut Artillery and of the Siege Train of the Armies Operating against Richmond, 1862–1865*. Hartford: Case, Lockwood & Brainard Company, 1893.

Thompson, Gilbert. "The Engineer Battalion in the Civil War: A Contribution to the History of the United States Engineers," *Occasional Papers, Engineer School, United States Army*, No. XLIV (1910), pp. 1–105.

Thompson, S. Millett. *Thirteenth Regiment of New Hampshire Volunteer Infantry in the War of the Rebellion, 1861–1865: A Diary Covering Three Years and a Day*. Boston: Houghton Mifflin Company, 1888.

Tobie, Edward F. *History of the First Maine Cavalry, 1861–1865*. Boston: Emery & Hughes, 1887.

Van Santvoord, Cornelius. *The One Hundred and Twentieth Regiment New York State Volunteers: A Narrative of Its Services in the War for the Union*. Rondout, N.Y.: Press of the Kingston *Freeman*, 1894.

Vautier, John D. *History of the 88th Pennsylvania Volunteers in the War for the Union*. Philadelphia: J. B. Lippincott Company, 1894.

Waite, Otis F. R. *New Hampshire in the Great Rebellion, Containing Histories of the Several New Hampshire Regiments and Biographical Notices of Many of the Prominent Actors in the Civil War of 1861–65*. Claremont, N.H.: Tracy, Chase & Company, 1870.

Walcott, Charles F. *History of the Twenty First Regiment Massachusetts Volunteers in the War for the Preservation of the Union, 1861–1865, with Statistics of the War and Rebel Prisons*. Boston: Houghton Mifflin Company, 1882.

Wallace, Lee. *A Guide to Virginia Military Organizations, 1861–1865*. Richmond: Virginia Civil War Commission, 1964.

Ward, George W. *History of the Second Pennsylvania Veteran Heavy Artillery (112th Regiment Pennsylvania Volunteers) from 1861 to 1866, Including the Provisional Second Penn'a. Heavy Artillery*. Philadelphia: George W. Ward Printer, 1904.

Wells, Edward L. *Hampton and His Cavalry in '64*. Richmond: B. F. Johnson Publishing Company, 1899.

Weygant, Charles. *History of the One Hundred and Twenty Fourth Regiment, N.Y.S.V.* Newburgh, N.Y.: Journal Printing House, 1877.

White, H. G. "Company G, Twenty Fourth Virginia Infantry: A List of Its Members and a Brief History of Them," *Southern Historical Society Papers*, v. XXXV (1907), pp. 352–56.

Williams, George W. *A History of the Negro Troops in the War of the Rebellion, 1861–1865, Preceded by a Review of the Military Services of Negroes in Ancient and Modern Times*. New York: Harper & Brothers, 1887.

Wilson, Joseph T. *The Black Phalanx: A History of the Negro Soldiers of the United States in the Wars of 1775–1812, 1861–'65*. Hartford: American Publishing Company, 1888.

Winkler, Angelina V. *The Confederate Capital and Hood's Texas Brigade*. Austin: Eugene von Borckmann, 1894.

Wise, Jennings C. *The Long Arm of Lee: A History of the Artillery of the Army of Northern Virginia*. New York: Oxford University Press, 1959.

Wister, Francis. *Recollections of the 12th U. S. Infantry & Regular Division*. Philadelphia: n.p., 1887.

Woodbury, Augustus. *Major-General Ambrose E. Burnside and the Ninth Army Corps: A Narrative of Campaigns in North Carolina, Maryland, Virginia, Ohio, Kentucky, Mississippi, and Tennessee, during the War for the Preservation of the Republic*. Providence: Sidney S. Rider & Brother, 1867.

Woodward, Evan M. *History of the One Hundred and Ninety-Eighth Pennsylvania Volunteers, Being a Complete Record of the Regiment, with Its Campaigns, Marches, and Battles; Together with the Personal Record of Every Officer and Man during His Term of Service*. Trenton: MacCrellish & Quigley, 1884.

Young, Charles P., and Ellett, Thomas. "History of the Crenshaw Battery, with Its Engagements and Roster," *Southern Historical Society Papers*, v. XXXI (1903), pp. 275–96.

MISCELLANEOUS WORKS

Boatner, Mark M. *The Civil War Dictionary*. New York: David McKay Company, 1959.

Brooks, U. R. *Stories of the Confederacy*. Columbia: The State Company, 1912.

Fuller, Claude. *The Rifled Musket*. Harrisburg: The Stackpole Company, 1958.

Hasell, N. Ingraham. "An Incident of a Sword," *Confederate Veteran*, v. XX, No. 4 (1912), p. 159.

Lord, Francis A. *Civil War Collector's Encyclopedia: Arms, Uniforms, and Equipment of the Union and Confederacy*. Harrisburg: The Stackpole Company, 1963.

Miller, Francis T., ed. *The Photographic History of the Civil War*. New York: Thomas Yoseloff, 1957.

United States Department of the Interior, National Park Service, Richmond National Battlefield Park. *Self-guide Tour of Fort Harrison*, No. OF-620229. Washington, D.C.: U. S. Government Printing Office, 1961.

PHOTOGRAPHS

Columbiana Coll., Columbia University.

Museum of the Confederacy. (CM)

Library of Congress. (LC)

National Archives. (NA)

Syms-Eaton Museum, Hampton, Va.

U. S. Army Military History Institute. (MHRC)

Virginia Historical Society. (VHS)

Virginia Military Institute.

Virginia State Library. (VSL)

ARTIFACTS

Warren County Historical Society, Front Royal, Va.
Crenshaw's Battery, battle flag.

INDEX

Page numbers in italics refer to pages in the Notes.